ELEVENTH EDITION

Human GEOGRAPHY

LANDSCAPES OF HUMAN ACTIVITIES

JEROME D. FELLMANN

University of Illinois, Urbana-Champaign

MARK D. BJELLAND

Gustavus Adolphus College

ARTHUR GETIS

San Diego State University

JUDITH GETIS

McGraw Hill

Connect
Learn
Succeed™

HUMAN GEOGRAPHY: LANDSCAPES OF HUMAN ACTIVITIES, ELEVENTH EDITION

Published by McGraw-Hill, a business unit of The McGraw-Hill Companies, Inc., 1221 Avenue of the Americas, New York, NY 10020. Copyright © 2010 by The McGraw-Hill Companies, Inc. All rights reserved. Previous editions © 2008, 2007, and 2005. No part of this publication may be reproduced or distributed in any form or by any means, or stored in a database or retrieval system, without the prior written consent of The McGraw-Hill Companies, Inc., including, but not limited to, in any network or other electronic storage or transmission, or broadcast for distance learning.

Some ancillaries, including electronic and print components, may not be available to customers outside the United States.

This book is printed on acid-free paper.

4 5 6 7 8 9 0 DOW/DOW 10 9 8 7 6 5 4 3 2

ISBN 978–0–07–352285–2
MHID 0–07–352285–6

Publisher: *Ryan Blankenship*
Executive Editor: *Margaret J. Kemp*
Director of Development: *Kristine Tibbetts*
Senior Marketing Manager: *Lisa Nicks*
Project Manager: *Joyce Watters*
Senior Production Supervisor: *Sherry L. Kane*
Design Coordinator: *Brenda A. Rolwes*
Cover Designer: *Studio Montage, St. Louis, Missouri*
(USE) Cover Image: *Getty Images*
Senior Photo Research Coordinator: *Lori Hancock*
Photo Research: *Connie Mueller*
Compositor: *S4Carlisle Publishing Services*
Typeface: *10/12 Times Roman*
Printer: *R. R. Donnelley Willard, OH*

All credits appearing on page or at the end of the book are considered to be an extension of the copyright page.

Library of Congress Cataloging-in-Publication Data

Fellmann, Jerome Donald, 1926.
  Human geography : landscapes of human activities / Jerome D. Fellmann ... [et al.]. — Eleventh ed.
    p. cm.
  Previous edition cataloged under Fellmann, Jerome D. Includes index.
  ISBN 978–0–07–352285–2 — ISBN 0–07–352285–6 (hard copy : alk. paper) 1. Human geography.
I. Fellmann, Jerome Donald, 1926- II. Fellmann, Jerome Donald, 1926- Human Geography.

GF41.H93 2010
304.2—dc22

                                                            2009020312

www.mhhe.com

Part Two

PATTERNS OF DIVERSITY AND UNITY 122

Five

LANGUAGE AND RELIGION: MOSAICS OF CULTURE 122

Six

ETHNIC GEOGRAPHY: THREADS OF DIVERSITY 164

Seven

FOLK AND POPULAR CULTURE: DIVERSITY AND UNIFORMITY 200

Part Three

DYNAMIC PATTERNS OF THE SPACE ECONOMY 233

Eight

LIVELIHOOD AND ECONOMY: PRIMARY ACTIVITIES 233

Contents   v

Part Five

HUMAN ACTIONS AND ENVIRONMENTAL IMPACTS 419

Thirteen

HUMAN IMPACTS ON NATURAL SYSTEMS 419

List of Boxes

Preface

This eleventh edition of *Human Geography* retains the organization and structure of its earlier versions. Like them, it seeks to introduce its users to the scope and excitement of geography and its relevance to their daily lives and roles as informed citizens. We recognize that for many students, human geography may be their first or only work in geography and this their first or only textbook in the discipline. For these students particularly, we seek to convey the richness and breadth of human geography and to give insight into the nature and intellectual challenges of the field of geography itself. Our goals are to be inclusive in content, current in data, and relevant in interpretations. These goals are elusive. Because of the time lapse between world events and the publication of a book, inevitably events outpace analysis. We therefore depend on a continuing partnership with classroom instructors to provide the currency of information and the interpretation of new patterns of human geographic substance that changing conditions demand.

Organization

The text can easily be read in a one-semester or one-quarter course. The emphasis on human geographic current events and interpretations builds on our initial obligation to set the stage in Chapter 1 by briefly introducing students to the scope, methods, and background basics of geography as a discipline and to the tools—especially maps—that all geographers employ. It is supplemented by Appendix A giving a more detailed treatment of map projections than is appropriate in a general introductory chapter. Both are designed to be helpful, with content supportive of, not essential to, the later chapters of the text.

The arrangement of those chapters reflects our own sense of logic and teaching experiences. The chapters are unevenly divided among five parts. Those of Part One, "Themes and Fundamentals," examine the basis of culture, culture change, and cultural regionalism, review the concepts of spatial interaction and spatial behavior, and consider population structures, patterns, and change. Parts Two through Four (Chapters 5 through 12) discuss the landscapes of cultural distinction and social organization resulting from human occupance of the earth. These include linguistic, religious, ethnic, folk, and popular differentiation of peoples and societies, and the economic, urban, and political organization of space. Chapter 13—Part Five—draws together in sharper focus selected aspects of the human impact on the natural landscape to make clear to students the relevance of the earlier-studied human geographic concepts and patterns to matters of current national and world environmental concern.

Among those concepts is the centrality of gender issues that underlie all facets of human geographic inquiry. Because they are so pervasive and significant, we felt it unwise to relegate their consideration to a single separate chapter, thus artificially isolating women and women's concerns from all the topics of human geography for which gender distinctions and interests are relevant. Instead, we have incorporated significant gender/female issues within the several chapters where those issues apply—either within the running text of the chapter or, very often, highlighted in boxed discussions.

We hope by means of these chapter clusters and sequence to convey to students the logic and integration we recognize in the broad field of human geography. We realize that our sense of organization and continuity is not necessarily that of instructors using this text and have designed each chapter to be reasonably self-contained, able to be assigned in any sequence that satisfies the arrangement preferred by the instructor.

New to This Edition

We are pleased to welcome Mark Bjelland to the author team, beginning with the eleventh edition. Dr. Bjelland brings research experience in urban and economic geography to enrich these important topics in human geography. For a complete biography, see page xvii.

Although the text's established framework of presentation has been retained in this eleventh edition, every chapter contains at least brief text additions or modifications to reflect current data, and many chapters contain new or revised illustrations, maps, and photos.

The eleventh edition contains many new and updated topics, including the following:

New Maps

Many new and updated maps have been introduced to the eleventh edition of Human Geography:

- Two new maps that use the city of New Orleans to illustrate the concepts of site and situation
- Perceptual regions of North America

- The boxed inserts that are part of each chapter expand on ideas included within the text or introduce related examples of chapter concepts and conclusions, often in gender-related contexts.

- Almost every chapter contains at least one special-purpose box labeled "Geography and Public Policy." These boxes introduce a discussion of a topic of current national or international interest and conclude with a set of questions designed to induce thought and class discussion of the topic viewed against the background of human geographic insights students have mastered.

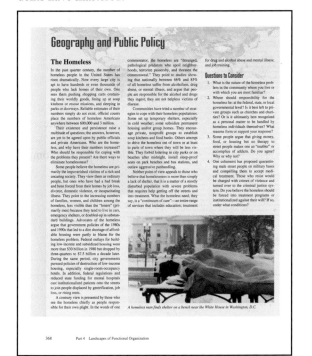

- Each chapter also includes other pedagogical aids. The "Summary" iterates the main points of the chapter and provides a bridge to the chapter that follows.

- New terms and special usages of common words and phrases are identified in boldface or italic type. The boldface terms are included in the "Key Words" list at the end of each chapter and are defined in an inclusive cross-referenced glossary at the end of the text.
- "For Review" contains questions that direct student attention to important concepts developed within the chapter.
- The "Key Concept Review" section in the end-of-chapter material summarizes the main points of the chapter and conveys additional information and explanation as integral parts of the text.

Meet the Authors

Jerome D. Fellmann

Jerome Fellmann received his B.S., M.S., and Ph.D. degrees from the University of Chicago. Except for visiting professorships at Wayne State University, the University of British Columbia, and California State University/Northridge, his professional career has been spent at the University of Illinois at Urbana-Champaign. His teaching and research interests have been concentrated in the areas of human geography in general and urban and economic geography in particular, in geographic bibliography, the geography of Russia and the CIS, and geographic education. His varied interests have been reflected in articles published in the *Annals of the Association of American Geographers, Professional Geographer, Journal of Geography,* the *Geographical Review,* and elsewhere. He is the coauthor of McGraw-Hill's *Introduction to Geography.* In addition to teaching and research, he has held administrative appointments at the University of Illinois and served as a consultant to private corporations on matters of economic and community development.

Arthur Getis

Arthur Getis received his B.S. and M.S. degrees from Pennsylvania State University and his Ph.D. from the University of Washington. He is the coauthor of several geography textbooks as well as two books dealing with map pattern analysis. He has also published widely in the areas of urban geography, spatial analysis, and geographical information systems. He is coeditor of *Journal of Geographical Systems* and for many years served on the editorial boards of *Geographical Analysis* and *Papers in Regional Science.* He has held administrative appointments at Rutgers University, the University of Illinois, and San Diego State University (SDSU) and currently holds the Birch Chair of Geographical Studies at SDSU. In 2002 he received the Association of American Geographers Distinguished Scholarship Award. Professor Getis is a member of many professional organizations and has served as an officer in, among others, the Western Regional Science Association and the University Consortium for Geographic Information Science.

Judith Getis

Judith Getis earned her B.A. and a teaching credential from the University of Michigan and her M.A. from Michigan State University. She has coauthored several geography textbooks and written the environmental handbook *You Can Make a Difference.*

In addition to numerous articles in the fields of urban geography and geography education, she has written technical reports on topics such as solar power and coal gasification. She and her husband, Arthur Getis, were among the original unit authors of the High School Geography Project, sponsored by the National Science Foundation and the Association of American Geographers. In addition, Mrs. Getis was employed by the Urban Studies Center at Rutgers University; taught at Rutgers; was a social science examiner at Educational Testing Service, Princeton, New Jersey; developed educational materials for Edcom Systems, Princeton, New Jersey; and was a professional associate in the Office of Energy Research, University of Illinois.

Mark D. Bjelland

Mark Bjelland received his B.S. and M.S. degrees in civil engineering from the University of Minnesota and University of Washington, respectively. He obtained professional engineering licensure and worked for six years as a consulting engineer in the United States and Canada on transportation systems, environmental cleanups, and major urban redevelopments. Intrigued by the geographical questions he encountered in his work, he left engineering to earn a Ph.D. in geography from the Univeristy of Minnesota. He wrote his dissertation comparing deindustrialization, environmental justice, and brownfields redevelopment in the U.S. and Canada. He has taught geography at Gustavus Adolphus College for twelve years where he chairs the geography department. He has been a visiting scholar in the Geography Department at the University of British Columbia, studied urban planning in post-reunification Germany with a Fulbright Foundation German Studies award, and was awarded a U.S.-U.K. Fulbright Scholar Award to spend a year at Cardiff University in Wales researching the redevelopment of derelict industrial land and the creation of eco-communities. He loves to take geography students into the field and in addition to local field trips to farms, small towns, and the Minneapolis-St. Paul area, he has led field courses to the Pacific Northwest, British Columbia, England, and Wales. His research interests include urban and economic geography, environmental justice, urban environmental problems, and immigration and religious diversity. His interests have been reflected in book chapters and articles published in *The Professional Geographer, Research Journal of the Water Pollution Control Federation, Urban Geography,* and elsewhere.

INTRODUCTION:
Some Background Basics

1

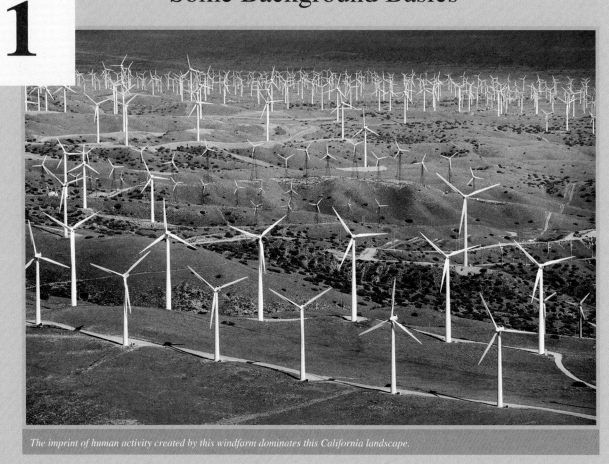

The imprint of human activity created by this windfarm dominates this California landscape.

Key Concepts

1. The nature of geography and the role of human geography, pp. 2–5.

2. Seven fundamental geographic observations and the basic concepts that underlie them, pp. 5–15.

3. The regional concept and the characteristics of regions, pp. 15–18.

4. Why geographers use maps and how maps show spatial information, pp. 18–25.

5. Other means of visualizing and analyzing spatial data: mental maps, systems, and models, pp. 25–27.

The fundamental question asked by geographers is "Does it make a difference where things are located?" If for any one item or group of objects the answer is "You bet it does!" the geographer's interest is aroused and geographic investigation is appropriate. For example, it matters a great deal that languages of a certain kind are spoken in certain places. But knowledge of the location of a specific language group is not of itself particularly significant. Geographic study of a language requires that we try to answer questions about why and how the language shows different characteristics in different locations and how the present distribution of its speakers came about. In the course of our study, we would logically discuss such concepts as migration, acculturation, the diffusion of innovation, the effect of physical barriers on communication, and the relationship of language to other aspects of culture. As geographers, we are interested in how things are interrelated in different regions and give evidence of the existence of "spatial systems."

What Is Geography?

Many people associate the word *geography* simply with knowing *where* things are: whether they be countries such as Myanmar and Uruguay, cities such as Timbuktu or Almaty, or deposits of natural resources such as petroleum or iron ore. Some people pride themselves on knowing which are the longest rivers, the tallest mountains, and the largest deserts. Such factual knowledge about the world has value, permitting us to place current events in their proper spatial setting. When we hear of an earthquake in Turkey or an assault in Timor-Leste, we at least can visualize where they occurred. Knowing *why* they occurred in those places, however, is considerably more important.

Geography is much more than place names and locations. It is the study of spatial variation, of how and why things differ from place to place on the surface of the earth. It is, further, the study of how observable spatial patterns evolved through time. Just as knowing the names and locations of organs in the human body does not equip one to perform open-heart surgery, and just as memorizing the periodic table does not enable one to formulate new medications, so knowing where things are located geographically is only the first step toward understanding why things are where they are, and what events and processes determine or change their distribution. Why is Chechnya but not Tasmania wracked by insurgency, and why do you find a concentration of French speakers in Quebec but not in other parts of Canada? Why are famines so frequent and severe in East Africa and why, among all the continents, has African food production and distribution failed to keep pace with population growth over the past half century?

In answering questions such as these, geographers focus on the interaction of people and social groups with their environment—planet Earth—and with each other; they seek to understand how and why physical and cultural spatial patterns evolved through time and continue to change. Because geographers study both the physical environment and the human use of that environment, they are sensitive to the variety of forces affecting a place and to the interactions among them. To explain why Brazilians burn a significant portion of the tropical rain forest each year, for example, geographers draw on their knowledge of the climate and soils of the Amazon Basin; population pressures, landlessness, and the need for more agricultural area in rural Brazil; the country's foreign debt status; midlatitude markets for lumber, beef, and soy beans; and economic development objectives. Understanding the environmental consequences of the burning requires knowledge of, among other things, the oxygen and carbon balance of the earth; the contribution of the fires to the greenhouse effect, acid rain, and depletion of the ozone layer; and the relationship between deforestation, soil erosion, and floods.

Geography, therefore, is about geographic space and its content. We think of and respond to places from the standpoint not only of where they are but, rather more importantly, of what they contain or what we think they contain. Reference to a place or an area usually calls up images about its physical nature or what people do there and often suggests, without conscious thought, how those physical objects and human activities are related. "Colorado," "mountains," and "skiing" might be a simple example. The content of area, that is, has both physical and cultural aspects, and geography is always concerned with understanding both (Figure 1.1).

Evolution of the Discipline

Geography, the "mother of sciences," initiated in antiquity lines of inquiry that led to the development of separate disciplines such as anthropology, demography, ecology, and economics. Geography's combination of interests was apparent even in the work of the early Greek geographers who first gave structure to the discipline. Geography's name was reputedly coined by the Greek scientist Eratosthenes over 2200 years ago from the words *geo,* "the earth," and *graphein,* "to write." From the beginning, that writing focused both on the physical structure of the earth and on the nature and activities of the people who inhabited the different lands of the known world. To Strabo (*ca.* 64 B.C.–A.D. 20) the task of geography was to "describe the several parts of the inhabited world . . . to write the assessment of the countries of the world [and] to treat the differences between countries." Even earlier, Herodotus (*ca.* 484–425 B.C.) had found it necessary to devote much of his book to the lands, peoples, economies, and customs of the various parts of the Persian Empire as necessary background to an understanding of the causes and course of the Persian wars.

Greek (and, later, Roman) geographers measured the earth, devised the global grid of parallels and meridians (marking latitudes and longitudes—see page 20), and drew upon that grid surprisingly sophisticated maps of their known world (Figure 1.2). They explored the apparent latitudinal variations in climate and

Figure 1.1 The ski development at Whistler Mountain, British Columbia, Canada, site of 2010 Winter Olympic events, clearly shows the interaction of physical environment and human activity. Climate and terrain have made specialized human use attractive and possible. Human exploitation has placed a cultural landscape on the natural environment, thereby altering it.

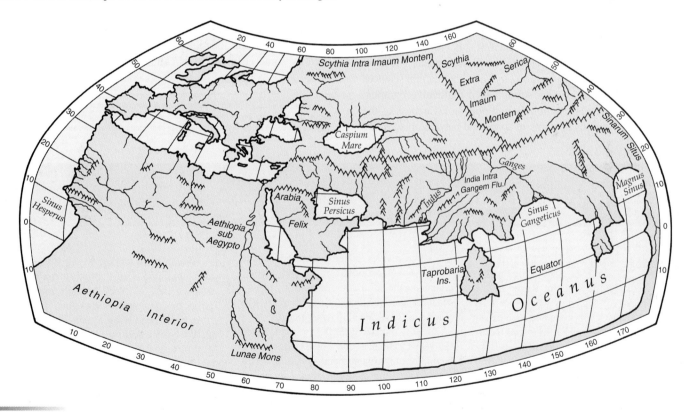

Figure 1.2 World map of the 2nd-century A.D. Greco–Egyptian geographer–astronomer Ptolemy. Ptolemy (Claudius Ptolemaeus) adopted a previously developed map grid of latitude and longitude based on the division of the circle into 360°, permitting a precise mathematical location for every recorded place. Unfortunately, errors of assumption and measurement rendered both the map and its accompanying six-volume gazetteer inaccurate. Ptolemy's map, accepted in Europe as authoritative for nearly 1500 years, was published in many variants in the 15th and 16th centuries. The version shown here summarizes the extent and content of the original. Its underestimation of the earth's size convinced Columbus a short westward voyage would carry him to Asia.

described in numerous works the familiar Mediterranean basin and the more remote, partly rumored lands of northern Europe, Asia, and equatorial Africa. Employing nearly modern concepts, they described river systems, explored causes of erosion and patterns of deposition, cited the dangers of deforestation, described areal variations in the natural landscape, and noted the consequences of environmental abuse. Against that physical backdrop, they focused their attention on what humans did in home and distant areas—how they lived; what their distinctive similarities and differences were in language, religion, and custom; and how they used, altered, and perhaps destroyed the lands they inhabited. Strabo, indeed, cautioned against the assumption that the nature and actions of humans were determined by the physical environment they inhabited. He observed that humans were the active elements in a human—environmental partnership.

These are enduring and universal interests. The ancient Chinese, for example, were as involved in geography as an explanatory viewpoint as were Westerners, though there was no exchange between them. Further, as Christian Europe entered its Middle Ages between A.D. 500 and 1400 and lost its knowledge of Greek and Roman geographical work, Muslim scholars—who retained that knowledge—undertook to describe and analyze their known world in its physical, cultural, and regional variation (see "Roger's Book").

Modern geography had its origins in the surge of scholarly inquiry that, beginning in the 17th century, gave rise to many of the traditional academic disciplines we know today. In its European rebirth, geography from the outset was recognized—as it always had been—as a broadly based integrative study. Patterns and processes of the physical landscape were early interests, as was concern with humans as part of the earth's variation from place to place. The rapid development of geology, botany, zoology, and other natural sciences by the end of the 18th century strengthened regional geographic investigation and increased scholarly and popular awareness of the intricate interconnections of items in space and between places. By that same time, accurate determination of latitude and longitude and scientific mapping of the earth made assignment of place information more reliable and comprehensive.

During the 19th century, national censuses, trade statistics, and ethnographic studies gave firmer foundation to human geographic investigation. By the end of the 19th century, geography had become a distinctive and respected discipline in universities throughout Europe and in other regions of the world where European academic examples were followed. The proliferation of professional geographers and geography programs resulted in the development of a whole series of increasingly specialized disciplinary subdivisions.

Geography and Human Geography

Geography's specialized subfields are not divisive but are interrelated. Geography in all its subdivisions is characterized by three dominating interests. The first is in the areal variation of physical and human phenomena on the surface of the earth. Geography examines relationships between human societies and the natural environments that they occupy and modify. The second is a focus on the spatial systems[1] that link physical phenomena and human activities in one area of the earth with other areas. Together, these interests lead to a third enduring theme, that of regional analysis: geography studies human—environmental—"ecological"—relationships and spatial systems in specific locational settings. This areal orientation pursued by some geographers is called *regional geography* (see also

---

[1]A "system" is simply a group of elements organized in a way that every element is to some degree directly or indirectly interdependent with every other element. For geographers, the systems of interest are those that distinguish or characterize different regions or areas of the earth.

Roger's Book

The Arab geographer Idrisi, or Edrisi (*ca.* A.D. 1099–1154), a descendant of the Prophet Mohammed, was directed by Roger II, the Christian king of Sicily in whose court he served, to collect all known geographical information and assemble it in a truly accurate representation of the world. An academy of geographers and scholars was gathered to assist Idrisi in the project. Books and maps of classical and Islamic origins were consulted, mariners and travelers interviewed, and scientific expeditions dispatched to foreign lands to observe and record. Data collection took 15 years before the final world map was fabricated on a silver disc some 200 centimeters (80 inches) in diameter and weighing over 135 kilograms (300 pounds). Lost to looters in 1160, the map is survived by "Roger's Book," containing the information amassed by Idrisi's academy and including a world map, 71 part maps, and 70 sectional itinerary maps.

Idrisi's "inhabited earth" is divided into the seven "climates" of Greek geographers, beginning at the equator and stretching northward to the limit at which, it was supposed, the earth was too cold to be inhabited. Each climate was then subdivided by perpendicular lines into 11 equal parts beginning with the west coast of Africa on the west and ending with the east coast of Asia. Each of the resulting 77 square compartments was then discussed in sequence in "Roger's Book."

Though Idrisi worked in one of the most prestigious courts of Europe, there is little evidence that his work had any impact on European geographic thought. He was strongly influenced by Ptolemy's work and misconceptions and shared the then common Muslim fear of the unknown western ocean. Yet Idrisi's clear understanding of such scientific truths as the roundness of the earth, his grasp of the scholarly writings of his Greek and Muslim predecessors, and the faithful recording of information on little-known portions of Europe, the Near East, and North Africa set his work far above the mediocre standards of contemporary Christian geography.

page 15). For some, the regions of interest may be large: Southeast Asia or Latin America, for example; others may focus on smaller areas differently defined, such as Alpine France or the United States Corn Belt.

Other geographers choose to identify particular classes of things, rather than segments of the earth's surface, for specialized study. These *systematic geographers* may focus their attention on one or a few related aspects of the physical environment or of human populations and societies. In each case, the topic selected for study is examined in its interrelationships with other spatial systems and areal patterns. *Physical geography* directs its attention to the natural environmental side of the human—environment structure. Its concerns are with landforms and their distribution, with atmospheric conditions and climatic patterns, with soils or vegetation associations, and the like. The other systematic branch of geography—and the subject of this book—is *human geography*.

Human Geography

Human geography deals with the world as it is and with the world as it might be made to be. Its emphasis is on people: where they are, what they are like, how they interact over space, and what kinds of landscapes of human use they erect on the natural landscapes they occupy. It encompasses all those interests and topics of geography that are not directly concerned with the physical environment or, like cartography, are technical in orientation. Its content provides integration for all of the social sciences, for it gives to those sciences the necessary spatial and systems viewpoint that they otherwise lack. For example, economists are generally concerned with trends and patterns over time, not space, and psychology rarely considers the interaction between space and behavior. At the same time, human geography draws on other social sciences in the analyses identified with its subfields, such as *behavioral, political, economic,* or *social geography* (Figure 1.3).

Human geography admirably serves the objectives of a liberal education. It helps us to understand the world we occupy and to appreciate the circumstances affecting peoples and countries other than our own. It clarifies the contrasts in societies and cultures and in the human landscapes they have created in different regions of the earth. Its models and explanations of how things are interrelated in particular places and regions give us a clearer understanding of the economic, social, and political systems within which we live and operate. Its analyses of those spatial systems make us more aware of the realities and prospects of our own society in an increasingly connected and competitive world. Our study of human geography, therefore, can help make us better-informed citizens, more able to understand the important issues facing our communities and our countries and better prepared to contribute to their solutions. Importantly, it can also help open the way to wonderfully rewarding and diversified careers as professional geographers (see "Careers in Geography").

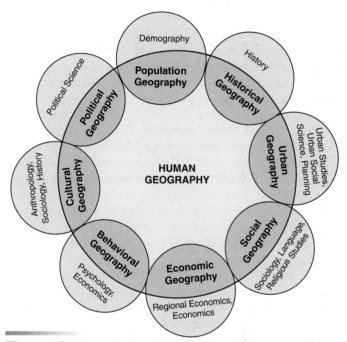

Figure 1.3 Some of the subdivisions of human geography and the allied fields to which they are related. Geography retains its ties to them and shares their insights and data reinforcing its role as an essential synthesizer of data, concepts, and models that have integrative regional and spatial implications.

background basics

Core Geographic Concepts

The topics included in human geography are diverse, but that very diversity emphasizes the reality that all geographers—whatever their particular topical or regional specialties—are united by the similar questions they ask and the common set of basic concepts they employ to consider their answers. Of either a physical or cultural phenomenon they will inquire: What is it? Where is it? How did it come to be what and where it is? Where is it in relation to other things that affect it or are affected by it? How is it changing?

How is it part of a functioning whole? How do people affect it? How does its location affect people's lives and the content of the area in which it is found? These and similar questions are rooted in geography's central concern with **space** and **place** and in the special meanings geographers attach to those terms.

For geographers, *space* implies areal extent and may be understood in both an absolute and a relative sense. *Absolute space* is objectively and physically real with measurable extent and definable boundaries. In that sense, space is fundamental to areal relationships among physical or cultural features on the earth's surface and is basic to such geographic interests as making maps, analyzing distributions, and conducting spatial analysis of locational patterns. *Relative space* is perceptual, not objective, and variable, not permanent, over time. In this relative sense, space can be seen as socially produced, reflecting activities and the interrelationships between activities. Since activities and relationships are constantly changing, relative space adjusts in size and form in response to developing socioeconomic processes and the passage of time.

For human geographers, *place* is the companion concept to *space*. In common understanding, *place* is a synonym for *location*. In human geography, however, *place* refers to the attributes and values we individually associate with a location. Our home town and neighborhood, the university we attend or the high school from which we graduated, a favorite downtown shopping area, and the like are all examples. Clearly, our *sense of place*—the attachments we have to specific locations and their complex of attributes—is unique to each of us, though we may share some aspects of our regard for a place with many others. And clearly, too, we can even have a favorable sense of place about locations we may never have personally experienced: Rome or Mecca or Jerusalem, for example, or—closer to home—Mount Rushmore or the Washington Mall.

Our individual or group sense of place and attachments can, of course, set us off from others. Our home neighborhood that we find familiar and view favorably may equally be seen as alien and, perhaps, dangerous by others. The attributes and culture of places shape the lives and outlooks of those who inhabit them in ways basic to the socioeconomic patterning of the world. The viewpoints, normative behavior, religious and cultural beliefs, and ways of life absorbed and expressed by a white, middle-class, suburban American are undoubtedly vastly different from the understandings, cultural convictions, and life expectations of, for example, a young, unemployed male resident of Baghdad or the slums of Cairo. The implicit, ingrained, place-induced differences between the two help us understand the resistance to the globalization of Western social and economic values by those of vastly different cultural backgrounds and place identification.

The sense of place is reinforced by recognized local and regional distinctiveness. It may be diminished or lost and replaced by a feeling of **placelessness** as the uniformity of brand-name fast-food outlets, national retail store chains, uniform shopping malls, repetitive highway billboards, and the like spread nationally and even internationally, reducing or eliminating the uniqueness of formerly separated locales and cultures. We'll examine some aspects of the sense of place and placelessness as we look at folk and popular cultures in Chapter 7.

Geographers use the word *spatial* as an essential modifier in framing their questions and forming their concepts. Geography, they say, is a *spatial* science. It is concerned with *spatial behavior* of people, with the *spatial relationships* that are observed between places on the earth's surface, and with the *spatial processes* that create or maintain those behaviors and relationships. The word *spatial* comes, of course, from *space,* and to geographers, it always carries the idea of the way items are distributed, the way movements occur, and the way processes operate over the whole or a part of the surface of the earth. The geographer's space, then, is earth space, the surface area occupied or available to be occupied by humans. Spatial phenomena have locations on that surface, and spatial interactions occur between places, things, and people within the earth area available to them. The need to understand those relationships, interactions, and processes helps frame the questions that geographers ask.

Additionally, those questions have their starting point in basic observations about the location and nature of places and about how places are similar to or different from one another. Such observations, though simply stated, are profoundly important to our comprehension of the world we occupy.

- Places have location, direction, and distance with respect to other places.
- A place has size; it may be large or small. Scale is important.
- A place has both physical structure and cultural content.
- The attributes of places develop and change over time.
- The elements of places interrelate with other places.
- The content of places is structured and explainable.
- Places may be generalized into regions of similarities and differences.

These are basic notions understandable to everyone. They also are the means by which geographers express fundamental observations about the earth spaces they examine and put those observations into a common framework of reference. Each of the concepts is worth further discussion, for they are not quite as simple as they at first seem.

Location, Direction, and Distance

Location, direction, and *distance* are everyday ways of assessing the space around us and identifying our position in relation to other items and places of interest. They are also essential in understanding the processes of spatial interaction that figure so importantly in the study of human geography.

Location

The location of places and objects is the starting point of all geographic study as well as all our personal movements and spatial actions in everyday life. We think of and refer to location in at least two different senses, *absolute* and *relative*.

Absolute location is the identification of place by some precise and accepted system of coordinates; it therefore is sometimes called *mathematical location*. We have several such accepted systems of pinpointing positions. One of them is the global grid of parallels and meridians (discussed later, beginning on page 18). With it the absolute location of any point on the earth can be accurately described by reference to its degrees, minutes, and seconds of *latitude* and *longitude* (Figure 1.4).

Other coordinate systems are also in use. Survey systems such as the township, range, and section description of property in much of the United States give mathematical locations on a regional level, while street address precisely defines a building according to the reference system of an individual town. For convenience or special purposes, locational grid references may be superimposed on the basic global grid. The Universal Transverse Mercator (UTM) system, for example, based on a set of 60 longitude

Careers in Geography

The study of geography is an essential part of a liberal arts education and helps students become better citizens as they come to understand local, national, and global issues.

Can it, as well, be a pathway to employment for those who wish to specialize in the discipline? The answer is "Yes," in a number of different types of jobs. One broad cluster is concerned with supporting the field itself through teaching and research. Teaching opportunities exist at all levels, from elementary to university postgraduate. Teachers with some training in geography are increasingly in demand in elementary and high schools throughout the United States, reflecting geography's inclusion as a core subject in the federally adopted *Educate America Act* (Public Law 103-227) and the national determination to create a geographically literate society. At the college level, specialized teaching and research in all branches of geography have long been established, and geographically trained scholars are prominently associated with urban, community, and environmental studies, regional science, locational economics, and other interdisciplinary programs.

Because of the breadth and diversity of the field, training in geography involves the acquisition of techniques and approaches applicable to a wide variety of jobs outside the academic world. Modern geography is both a physical and social science and fosters a wealth of technical skills. The employment possibilities it presents are as many and varied as are the agencies and enterprises dealing with the natural environment and human activities and with the acquisition and analysis of spatial data.

Many professional geographers work in government, either at the state or local level or in a variety of federal agencies and international organizations. Although many positions do not carry a geography title, physical geographers serve as water, mineral, and other natural resource analysts; weather and climate experts; soil scientists; and the like. An area of recent high demand is for environmental managers and technicians. Geographers who have specialized in environmental studies find jobs in both public and private agencies. Their work may include assessing the environmental impact of proposed development projects on such things as air and water quality and endangered species, as well as preparing the environmental impact statements required before construction can begin.

Human geographers work in many different roles in the public sector. Jobs include data acquisition and analysis in health care, transportation, population studies, economic development, and international economics. Many geography graduates find positions as planners in local and state governmental agencies concerned with housing and community development, park and recreation planning, and urban and regional planning. They map and analyze land use plans and transportation systems, monitor urban land development, make informed recommendations about the location of public facilities, and engage in basic social science research.

Most of these same specializations are also found in the private sector. Geographic training is ideal for such tasks as business planning and market analysis; factory, store, and shopping-center site selection; community and economic development programs for banks, public utilities, and railroads; and similar applications. Publishers of maps, atlases, news and travel magazines, and the like employ geographers as writers, editors, and mapmakers.

The combination of a traditional, broadly based liberal arts perspective with the technical skills required in geographic research and analysis gives geography graduates a competitive edge in the labor market. These field-based skills include familiarity with geographic information systems (GIS), cartography and computer mapping, remote sensing and photogrammetry, and competence in data analysis and problem solving. In particular, students with expertise in GIS, who are knowledgeable about data sources, hardware, and software, are finding that they have ready access to employment opportunities. The following table, based on the booklet "Careers in Geography,"* summarizes some of the professional opportunities open to students who have specialized in one (or more) of the various subfields of geography. Also, be sure to read the informative discussions under the "Careers in Geography" option on the home page of the Association of American Geographers at **www.aag.org/.** Additional links on the topic of geography careers can be found in the Online Learning Center for this text. That connection may be found at the end of this chapter.

Geographic Field of Concentration	Employment Opportunities
Geographic technology	Cartographer for federal government (agencies such as Defense Mapping Agency, U.S. Geological Survey, or Environmental Protection Agency) or private sector (e.g., Environmental Systems Research Institute, ERDAS, Intergraph, or Bentley); map librarian; GIS specialist for planners, land developers, real estate agencies, utility companies, local government; remote-sensing analyst; surveyor
Physical geography	Weather forecaster; outdoor guide; coastal zone manager; hydrologist; soil conservation/ agricultural extension agent
Environmental geography	Environmental manager; forestry technician; park ranger; hazardous waste planner
Cultural geography	Community developer; Peace Corps volunteer; map librarian
Economic geography	Site selection analyst for business and industry; market researcher; traffic/route delivery manager; real estate agent/broker/appraiser; economic development researcher
Urban and regional planning	Urban and community planner; transportation planner; housing, park, and recreation planner; health services planner
Regional geography	Area specialist for federal government; international business representative; travel agent; travel writer
Geographic education or general geography	Elementary/secondary school teacher; college professor; overseas teacher

*"Careers in Geography," by Richard G. Boehm. Washington, D.C.: National Geographic Society, 1996. Previously published by Peterson's Guides, Inc.

Figure 1.4 The latitude and longitude of Hong Kong is 22° 15′ N, 114° 10′ E (read as 22 degrees, 15 minutes north; 114 degrees, 10 minutes east). The circumference of the earth measures 360 degrees; each degree contains 60 minutes and each minute has 60 seconds of latitude or longitude. What are the coordinates of Hanoi?

Figure 1.5 The reality of *relative location* on the globe may be strikingly different from the impressions we form from flat maps. The position of Russia with respect to North America when viewed from a polar perspective emphasizes that relative location properly viewed is important to our understanding of spatial relationships and interactions between the two world areas.

zones, is widely used in geographic information system (GIS) applications and, with different notations, as a military grid reference system. Absolute location is unique to each described place, is independent of any other characteristic or observation about that place, and has obvious value in the legal description of places, in measuring the distance separating places, or in finding directions between places on the earth's surface.

When geographers—or real estate agents—remark that "location matters," their reference is usually not to absolute but to **relative location**—the position of a place in relation to that of other places or activities (Figure 1.5). Relative location expresses spatial interconnection and interdependence and may carry social (neighborhood character) and economic (assessed valuations of vacant land) implications. On an immediate and personal level, we think of the location of the school library not in terms of its street address or room number but where it is relative to our classrooms, or the cafeteria, or some other reference point. On the larger scene, relative location tells us that people, things, and places exist not in a spatial vacuum but in a world of physical and cultural characteristics that differ from place to place.

New York City, for example, may in absolute terms be described as located at (approximately) latitude 40° 43′ N and longitude 73° 58′ W. We have a better understanding of the *meaning* of its location, however, when reference is made to its spatial relationships: to the continental interior through the Hudson–Mohawk lowland corridor or to its position on the eastern seaboard of the United States. Within the city, we gain understanding of the locational significance of Central Park or the Lower East Side not solely by reference to the street addresses or city blocks they occupy, but by their spatial and functional relationships to the total land use, activity, and population patterns of New York City.

In view of these different ways of looking at location, geographers make a distinction between the *site* and the *situation* of a place.

Site, an absolute location concept, refers to the physical and cultural characteristics and attributes of the place itself. It is more than mathematical location, for it tells us something about the internal features of that place. The site of New Orleans, for example, extends from the natural levee on the Mississippi River to Lake Pontchartrain, much of which lies below sea level (Figure 1.6). **Situation,** on the other hand, refers to the external relations of a locale. It is an expression of relative location with particular reference to items of significance to the place in question. The situation of New Orleans might be described as being as close as possible to the mouth of the Mississippi River, which drains 41% of the land area of the continental United States, taking in much of the area from the Appalachian Mountains to the Rocky Mountains. Waterways on the Upper Mississippi, Missouri, Arkansas-Red-White, Ohio, and Tennessee River systems drain through the Lower Mississippi, connecting New Orleans to many of the country's important agricultural and manufacturing regions (Figure 1.7). While the flood-prone site makes it a challenging place to build a city, the incredible advantages offered by its situation have inspired generations of residents to make it their home.

Direction

Direction is a second universal spatial concept. Like location, it has more than one meaning and can be expressed in absolute or relative terms. **Absolute direction** is based on the cardinal points of north, south, east, and west. These appear uniformly and independently in all cultures, derived from the obvious "givens" of nature: the rising and setting of the sun for east and west, and the sky location of the noontime sun and of certain fixed stars for north and south.

We also commonly use **relative** or *relational* **directions.** In the United States we go "out West," "back East," or "down South"; we

Figure 1.6 The *site* of New Orleans is hardly ideal for building a city. The city was built by the French on the most suitable high ground they could find near the mouth of the Mississippi River. The site extends north from the "high ground" along the Mississippi River to former swamp and marshland near Lake Pontchartrain. Much of the city and its suburbs are located below sea level on sinking soils composed of soft sediments deposited by past river floods.

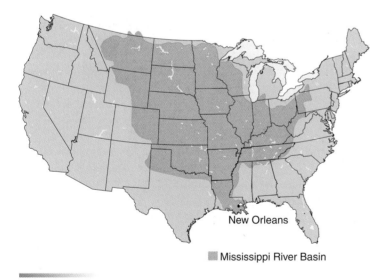

Figure 1.7 The *situation* of New Orleans is ideal for building a city. As the port at the mouth of the Mississippi River, New Orleans receives imports from Europe, Latin America, Asia, and Africa and exports grain, other food products, and petroleum from the United States. New Orleans is connected to 14,500 miles of waterways as the Mississippi River drains a basin that stretches from the Rocky Mountains to the Appalachian Mountains.

worry about conflict in the "Near East" or economic competition from the "Far Eastern countries." These directional references are culturally based and locationally variable, despite their reference to cardinal compass points. The Near and the Far East locate parts of Asia from the European perspective; they are retained in the Americas by custom and usage, even though one would normally travel westward across the

Pacific, for example, to reach the "Far East" from California, British Columbia, or Chile. For many Americans, "back East" and "out West" are reflections of the migration paths of earlier generations for whom home was in the eastern part of the country, to which they might look back. "Up North" and "down South" reflect our accepted custom of putting north at the top and south at the bottom of our maps.

Distance

Distance joins location and direction as a commonly understood term that has dual meanings for geographers. Like its two companion spatial concepts, distance may be viewed in both an absolute and a relative sense.

Absolute distance refers to the spatial separation between two points on the earth's surface measured by some accepted standard unit such as miles or kilometers for widely separated locales, feet or meters for more closely spaced points. **Relative distance** transforms those linear measurements into other units more meaningful for the space relationship in question.

To know that two competing malls are about equidistant in miles from your residence is perhaps less important in planning your shopping trip than is knowing that because of street conditions or traffic congestion one is 5 minutes and the other 15 minutes away (Figure 1.8). Most people, in fact, think of time distance

Figure 1.8 Lines of equal travel time (*isochrones:* from Greek, *isos*, equal, and *chronos*, time) mark off the different linear distances accessible within given spans of time from a starting point. The fingerlike outlines of isochrone boundaries reflect variations in road conditions, terrain, traffic congestion, and other aids or impediments to movement. On this map, the areas within 30 minutes' travel time from downtown San Diego are recorded for the year 2002. Note the effect of freeways on travel time.

rather than linear distance in their daily activities; downtown is 20 minutes by bus, the library is a 5-minute walk. In some instances, money rather than time may be the distance transformation. An urban destination might be estimated to be a $10 cab ride away, information that may affect either the decision to make the trip at all or the choice of travel mode to get there. As a college student, you already know that rooms and apartments are less expensive at a greater distance from campus.

A *psychological* transformation of linear distance is also frequent. The solitary late-night walk back to the car through an unfamiliar or dangerous neighborhood seems far longer than a daytime stroll of the same distance through familiar and friendly territory. A first-time trip to a new destination frequently seems much longer than the return trip over the same path. Distance relationships, their measurement, and their meaning for human spatial interaction are fundamental to our understanding of human geography. They are a subject of Chapter 3, and reference to them recurs throughout this book.

Size and Scale

When we say that a place may be large or small, we speak both of the nature of the place itself and of the generalizations that can be made about it. In either instance, geographers are concerned with **scale,** though we may use that term in different ways. We can, for example, study a problem—say, population or agriculture—at the local scale, the regional scale, or on a global scale. Here the reference is purely to the size of unit studied. More technically, scale tells us the mathematical relationship between the size of an area on a map and the actual size of the mapped area on the surface of the earth (see page 18). In this sense, scale is a feature of every map and essential to recognizing the areal meaning of what is shown on that map.

In both senses of the word, *scale* implies the degree of generalization represented (Figure 1.9). Geographic inquiry may be broad or narrow; it occurs at many different size scales. Climate may be an object of study, but research and generalization focused on climates of the world will differ in degree and kind from study of the microclimates of a city. Awareness of scale is very important. In geographic work, concepts, relationships, and understandings that have meaning at one scale may not be applicable at another.

For example, the study of world agricultural patterns may refer to global climatic regimes, cultural food preferences, levels of economic development, and patterns of world trade. These large-scale relationships are of little concern in the study of crop patterns within single counties of the United States, where

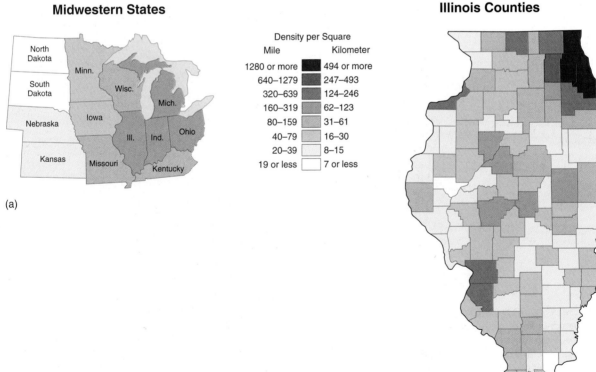

POPULATION DENSITIES

Figure 1.9 **Population density and map scale.** "Truth" depends on one's scale of inquiry. Map (*a*) reveals that the maximum year 2000 population density of Midwestern states was no more than 123 people per square kilometer (319 per sq mi). From map (*b*), however, we see that population densities in three Illinois counties exceeded 494 people per square kilometer (1280 per sq mi) in 2000. If we were to reduce our scale of inquiry even further, examining individual city blocks in Chicago, we would find densities reaching 2500 or more people per square kilometer (10,000 per sq mi). Scale matters!

topography, soil and drainage conditions, farm size, ownership, and capitalization, or even personal management preferences may be of greater explanatory significance.

Physical and Cultural Attributes

All places have physical and cultural attributes that distinguish them from other places and give them character, potential, and meaning. Geographers are concerned with identifying and analyzing the details of those attributes and, particularly, with recognizing the interrelationship between the physical and cultural components of area: the human—environmental interface.

Physical characteristics refer to such natural aspects of a locale as its climate and soil, the presence or absence of water supplies and mineral resources, its terrain features, and the like. These **natural landscape** attributes provide the setting within which human action occurs. They help shape—but do not dictate—how people live. The resource base, for example, is physically determined, though how resources are perceived and utilized is culturally conditioned.

Environmental circumstances directly affect agricultural potential and reliability; indirectly they may influence such matters as employment patterns, trade flows, population distributions, and national diets. The physical environment simultaneously presents advantages and drawbacks with which humans must deal. Thus, the danger of typhoons in central China or monsoonal floods in Bangladesh must be balanced against the agricultural bounty derived from the regions' favorable terrain, soil, and moisture conditions.

At the same time, by occupying a given place, people modify its environmental conditions. The existence of the U.S. Environmental Protection Agency (and its counterparts elsewhere) is a reminder that humans are the active and frequently harmful agents in the continuing interplay between the cultural and physical worlds (Figure 1.10). Virtually every human activity leaves its imprint on an area's soils, water, vegetation, animal life, and other resources and on the atmosphere common to all earth space. The impact of humans has been so universal and so long exerted that essentially no "natural landscape" any longer exists.

The visible expression of that human activity is the **cultural landscape.** It, too, exists at different scales and different levels of visibility. Differences in agricultural practices and land use between Mexico and southern California are evident in Figure 1.11, while the signs, structures, and people of, for instance, Los Angeles's Chinatown leave a smaller, more confined imprint within the larger cultural landscape of the metropolitan area itself.

Although the focus of this book is on the human characteristics of places, geographers are ever aware that the physical content of an area is also important in understanding the activity patterns of people and the interconnections between people and the environments they occupy and modify. Those interconnections and modifications are not static or permanent, however, but are subject to continual change. For example, marshes and wetlands, when drained, may be transformed into productive, densely settled farmland, while the threat or occurrence of eruption of a long-dormant volcano may quickly and drastically alter established patterns of farming, housing, and transportation on or near its flanks.

The Changing Attributes of Place

The physical environment surrounding us seems eternal and unchanging but, of course, it is not. In the framework of geologic time, change is both continuous and pronounced. Islands form and

Figure 1.10 Sites such as this landfill are all-too-frequent reminders of the adverse environmental impacts of humans and their waste products. Here, bulldozers compact solid waste and spread a daily cover at a "sanitary" landfill.

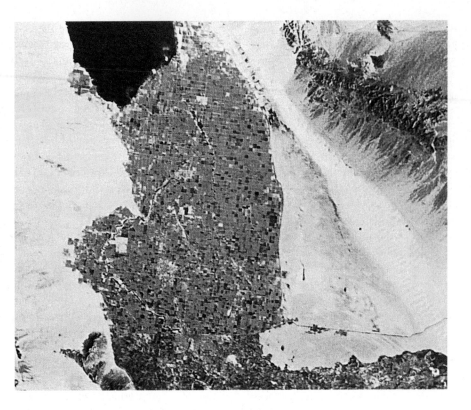

Figure 1.11 This NASA image reveals contrasting cultural landscapes along the Mexico–California border. Move your eyes from the Salton Sea (the dark patch at the top of the image) southward to the agricultural land extending to the edge of the image. Notice how the regularity of the fields and the bright colors (representing growing vegetation) give way to a marked break, where irregularly shaped fields and less prosperous agriculture are evident. Above the break is the Imperial Valley of California; below the border is Mexico.

© NASA

disappear; mountains rise and are worn low to swampy plains; vast continental glaciers form, move, and melt away, and sea levels fall and rise in response. Geologic time is long, but the forces that give shape to the land are timeless and relentless.

Even within the short period of time since the most recent retreat of continental glaciers—some 11,000 or 12,000 years ago—the environments occupied by humans have been subject to change. Glacial retreat itself marked a period of climatic alteration, extending the area habitable by humans to include vast reaches of northern Eurasia and North America formerly covered by thousands of feet of ice. With moderating climatic conditions came associated changes in vegetation and fauna. On the global scale, these were natural environmental changes; humans were as yet too few in numbers and too limited in technology to alter materially the course of physical events. On the regional scale, however, even early human societies exerted an impact on the environments they occupied. Fire was used to clear forest undergrowth, to maintain or extend grassland for grazing animals and to drive them in the hunt, and later to clear openings for rudimentary agriculture.

With the dawn of civilizations and the invention and spread of agricultural technologies, humans accelerated their management and alteration of the now no longer "natural" environment. Even the classical Greeks noted how the landscape they occupied differed—for the worse—from its former condition. With growing numbers of people and particularly with industrialization and the spread of European exploitative technologies throughout the world, the pace of change in the content of area accelerated. The built landscape—the product of human effort—increasingly replaced the natural landscape. Each new settlement or city, each agricultural assault on forests, each new mine, dam, or factory changed the content of regions and altered the temporarily established spatial interconnections between humans and the environment.

Characteristics of places today are the result of constantly changing past conditions. They are, as well, the forerunners of differing human—environmental balances yet to be struck. Geographers are concerned with places at given moments of time. But to understand fully the nature and development of places, to appreciate the significance of their relative locations, and to comprehend the interplay of their physical and cultural characteristics, geographers must view places as the present result of the past operation of distinctive physical and cultural processes (Figure 1.12).

You will recall that one of the questions geographers ask about a place or thing is "How did it come to be what and where it is?" This is an inquiry about process and about becoming. The forces and events shaping the physical and explaining the cultural environment of places today are an important focus of geography. They are, particularly in their human context, the subjects of most of the separate chapters of this book. To understand them is to appreciate more fully the changing human spatial order of our world.

(a)

(b)

Figure 1.12 **The process of change in a cultural landscape.** (*a*) Miami, Florida, in 1913 was just a small settlement on the banks of the Miami River amidst woodlands and wetlands. (*b*) By the end of the 20th century, it had grown from a few thousand inhabitants to some 350,000, with buildings, streets, and highways completely transforming its natural landscape.

Sources: (a) Historical Museum of Southern Florida; (b) South Florida Water Management District.

Interrelations between Places

The concepts of relative location and distance that we earlier introduced lead directly to a fundamental spatial reality: Places interact with other places in structured and comprehensible ways. In describing the processes and patterns of that **spatial interaction,** geographers add *accessibility* and *connectivity* to the ideas of location and distance.

Tobler's First Law of Geography tells us that in a spatial sense everything is related to everything else but that relationships are stronger when items are near one another. Our observation, therefore, is that interaction between places diminishes in intensity and frequency as distance between them increases—a statement of the idea of *distance decay,* which we explore in Chapter 3. Think about it—are you more likely to go to a fast-food outlet next door or to a nearly identical restaurant across town? Human decision making is unpredictable in many ways and decisions are frequently made for obscure reasons, but in this case you can see how you will probably frequent the nearer place more often.

Consideration of distance implies assessment of **accessibility.** How easy or difficult is it to overcome the "friction of distance"? That is, how easy or difficult is it to surmount the barrier of the time and space separation of places? Distance isolated North America from Europe until the development of ships (and aircraft) that reduced the effective distance between the continents. All parts of the ancient and medieval city were accessible by walking; they were "pedestrian cities," a status lost as cities expanded in area and population with industrialization. Accessibility between city districts could be maintained only by the development of public transit systems whose fixed lines of travel increased ease of movement between connected points and reduced it between areas not on the transit lines themselves.

Accessibility, therefore, suggests the idea of **connectivity,** a broader concept implying all the tangible and intangible ways in which places are connected: by physical telephone lines, street and road systems, pipelines and sewers; by unrestrained walking across open countryside; by radio and TV broadcasts beamed outward uniformly from a central source. Where routes are fixed and flow is channelized, *networks*—the patterns of routes connecting sets of places—determine the efficiency of movement and the connectedness of points. Demand for universal instantaneous accessibility and connectivity is common and unquestioned in today's advanced societies. Technologies and devices to achieve it proliferate, as our own lifestyles show. Cell phones, e-mail, broadband wireless Internet access, instant messaging, and more have erased time and distance barriers formerly separating and isolating individuals and groups and have reduced our dependence on physical movement and on networks fixed in the landscape. The realities of accessibility and connectivity, that is, clearly change over time (Figure 1.13).

There is, inevitably, interchange between connected places. **Spatial diffusion** is the process of dispersion of an idea or an item from a center of origin to more distant points with which it is directly or indirectly connected. The rate and extent of that diffusion are affected by the distance separating the originating center of, say, a new idea or technology and other places where it is eventually adopted. Diffusion rates are also affected by population densities, means of communication, obvious advantages of the innovation, and importance or prestige of the originating *node.* These ideas of diffusion are further explored in Chapter 2.

Geographers study the dynamics of spatial relationships. Movement, connection, and interaction are part of the social and economic processes that give character to places and regions. Geography's study of those relationships recognizes that spatial interaction is not just an awkward necessity but a fundamental

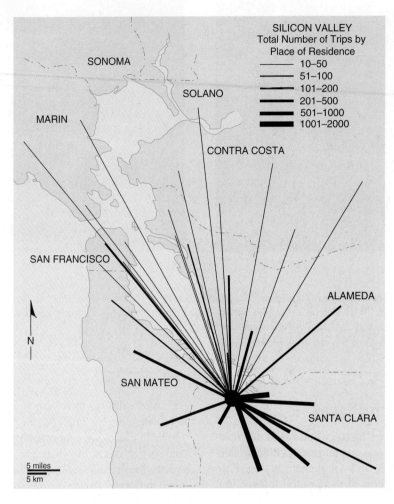

Figure 1.13 An indication of one form of spatial interaction and *connectivity* is suggested by this "desire line" map recording the volume of daily work trips within the San Francisco Bay area to the Silicon Valley employment node. The ends of the desire lines define the outer reaches of a physical interaction region defined by the network of connecting roads and routes. The region changed in size and shape over time as the network was enlarged and improved, the Valley employment base expanded, and the commuting range of workers increased. The map, of course, gives no indication of the global reach of the Valley's *accessibility* and interaction through other means of communication and interchange.

Source: Redrawn with permission from Robert Cervero, Suburban Gridlock. *© 1986 Center for Urban Policy Research, Rutgers, the State University of New Jersey.*

organizing principle of human life on earth. That recognition has become universal, repeatedly expressed in the term *globalization*. **Globalization** implies the increasing interconnection of peoples and societies in all parts of the world as the full range of social, cultural, political, economic, and environmental processes becomes international in scale and effect. Promoted by continuing advances in worldwide accessibility and connectivity, globalization encompasses other core geographic concepts of spatial interaction, accessibility, connectivity, and diffusion. More detailed implications of globalization will be touched on in later chapters of this text.

The Structured Content of Place

A starting point for geographic inquiry is how objects are distributed in area—for example, the placement of churches or supermarkets within a town. That interest distinguishes geography from other sciences, physical or social, and underlies many of the questions geographers ask: Where is a thing located? How is that location related to other items? How did the location we observe come to exist? Such questions carry the conviction that the contents of an area are comprehensibly arranged or structured. The arrangement of items on the earth's surface is called **spatial distribution** and may be analyzed by the elements common to all spatial distributions: *density, dispersion,* and *pattern.*

Density

The measure of the number or quantity of anything within a defined unit of area is its **density.** It is therefore not simply a count of items but of items in relation to the space in which they are found. When the relationship is absolute, as in population per square kilometer, for example, or dwelling units per acre, we are defining *arithmetic density* (see Figure 1.9). Sometimes it is more meaningful to relate item numbers to a specific kind of area. *Physiological density,* for example, is a measure of the number of persons per unit area of arable land. Density defined in population terms is discussed in Chapter 4.

A density figure is a statement of fact but not necessarily one useful in itself. Densities are normally employed comparatively, relative to one another. High or low density implies a comparison with a known standard, with an average, or with a different area. Ohio, with 107 persons per square kilometer (277 per sq mi) in 2000, might be thought to have a high density compared with neighboring Michigan at 68 per square kilometer (175 per sq mi), and a low one in relation to New Jersey at 438 (1134 per sq mi).

Dispersion

Dispersion (or its opposite, **concentration**) is a statement of the amount of *spread* of a phenomenon over an area. It tells us not how many or how much but how far things are spread out. If they are close together spatially, they are considered *clustered* or *agglomerated.* If they are spread out, they are *dispersed* or *scattered* (Figure 1.14).

If the entire population of a metropolitan county were all located within a confined central city, we might say the population was clustered. If, however, that same population redistributed itself, with many city residents moving to the suburbs and occupying a larger portion of the county's territory, it would become more dispersed. In both cases, the *density* of population (numbers in relation to area of the county) would be the same, but the distribution would have changed. Since dispersion deals with separation of things one from another, a distribution that might be described as *clustered* (closely spaced) at one scale of reference might equally well be considered *dispersed* (widely spread) at another scale.

Pattern

The geometric arrangement of objects in space is called **pattern.** Like dispersion, pattern refers to distribution, but that reference emphasizes design rather than spacing (Figure 1.15). The distribution of towns along a railroad or houses along a street may be seen as *linear.* A *centralized* pattern may involve items concentrated around a single node. A *random* pattern may be the best description of an unstructured irregular distribution.

The rectangular system of land survey adopted in much of the United States under the Ordinance of 1785 creates a checkerboard rural pattern of "sections" and "quarter-sections" of farmland (see Figure 6.26). As a result, in most American cities, streets display a *grid* or *rectilinear* pattern. The same is true of cities in Canada, Australia, New Zealand, and South Africa, which adopted similar geometric survey systems. The *hexagonal* pattern of service areas of farm towns is a mainstay of central place theory discussed in Chapter 11. These references to the geometry of distribution patterns help us visualize and describe the structured arrangement of items in space. They help us make informed comparisons between areas and use the patterns we discern to ask further questions about the interrelationship of things.

Place Similarity and Regions

The distinctive characteristics of places in content and structure immediately suggest two geographically important ideas. The first is that no two places on the surface of the earth can be *exactly* the same. Not only do they have different absolute locations, but—as in the features of the human face—the precise mix of physical and cultural characteristics of a place is never exactly duplicated.

Because geography is a spatial science, the inevitable uniqueness of place would seem to impose impossible problems of generalizing spatial information. That this is not the case results from the second important idea: The physical and cultural content of an area and the dynamic interconnections of people and places show patterns of spatial similarity. For example, a geographer doing fieldwork in France might find that all farmers in one area use a similar specialized technique to build fences around their fields. Often, such similarities are striking enough for us to conclude that spatial regularities exist. They permit us to recognize and define **regions**—earth areas that display significant elements of internal uniformity and external difference from surrounding territories. Places are, therefore, both unlike and like other places, creating patterns of areal differences and of coherent spatial similarity.

The problem of the historian and the geographer is similar. Each must generalize about items of study that are essentially unique. The historian creates arbitrary but meaningful and useful historical

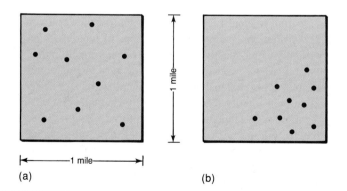

(a) (b)

Figure 1.14 Density and dispersion each tell us something different about how items are distributed in an area. *Density* is simply the number of items or observations within a defined area; it remains the same no matter how the items are distributed. The density of houses per square mile, for example, is the same in both (*a*) and (*b*). *Dispersion* is a statement about nearness or separation. The houses in (*a*) are more *dispersed* than those shown *clustered* in (*b*).

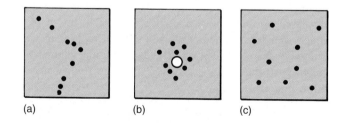

(a) (b) (c)

Figure 1.15 *Pattern* describes spatial arrangement and design. The *linear* pattern of towns in (*a*) perhaps traces the route of a road or railroad or the course of a river. The central city in (*b*) with its nearby suburbs represents a *centralized* pattern, while the dots in (*c*) are *randomly* distributed.

periods for reference and study. The "Roaring Twenties" and the "Victorian Era" are shorthand summary names for specific time spans, internally quite complex and varied but significantly distinct from what went before or followed after. The region is the geographer's equivalent of the historian's era. It is a device of areal generalization that segregates into component parts the complex reality of the earth's surface. In both the time and the space needed for generalization, attention is focused on key unifying elements or similarities of the era or area selected for study. In both the historical and geographical cases, the names assigned to those times and places serve to identify the time span or region and to convey between speaker and listener a complex set of interrelated attributes.

All of us have a general idea of the meaning of region, and all of us refer to regions in everyday speech and action. We visit "the old neighborhood" or "go downtown"; we plan to vacation or retire in the "Sunbelt"; or we speculate about the effects of weather conditions in the "Corn Belt" on next year's food prices. In each instance, we have mental images of the areas mentioned, and in each, we have engaged in an informal place classification to pass along quite complex spatial, organizational, or content ideas. We have applied the **regional concept** to bring order to the immense diversity of the earth's surface.

Regions are not "given" in nature any more than "eras" are given in the course of human events. Regions are devised; they are spatial summaries designed to bring order to the infinite diversity of the earth's surface. At their root, they are based on the recognition and mapping of *spatial distributions*—the territorial occurrence of environmental, human, or organizational features selected for study. For example, the location of Welsh speakers in Britain is a distribution that can be identified and mapped. As many spatial distributions exist as there are imaginable physical, cultural, or connectivity elements of area to examine. Since regions are mental constructs, different observers employing different criteria may bestow the same regional identity on differently bounded areal units. In each case, however, the key characteristics that are selected for study are those that contribute to the understanding of a specific topic or problem.

Types of Regions

Regions may be *formal, functional,* or *perceptual.* A **formal** or **uniform region** is one of essential uniformity in one or a limited combination of physical or cultural features. Your home state is a precisely bounded formal political region within which uniformity of law and administration is found; the "Bible Belt" suggests a region based on religious characteristics. Later in this book we will encounter formal (homogeneous) cultural regions in which standardized characteristics of language, religion, ethnicity, or economy exist. Figure 1.16a and the frontpaper foldout maps of landform regions and country units show other formal regional patterns. Whatever the basis of its definition, the formal region is the largest area over which a valid generalization of attribute uniformity may be made. Whatever is stated about one part of it holds true for its remainder.

The **functional** or **nodal region,** in contrast, may be visualized as a spatial system. Its parts are interdependent, and throughout its extent the functional region operates as a dynamic, organizational unit. A functional region has unity not in the sense of static content but in the manner of its operational connectivity. It has a *core* area in which its characterizing features are most clearly defined; they lessen in prominence toward the region's margins or *periphery.* As the degree and extent of areal control and interaction change, the boundaries of the functional region change in response. Trade areas of towns, national "spheres of influence," and the territories subordinate to the financial, administrative, wholesaling, or retailing centrality exercised by such regional capitals as Chicago, Atlanta, or Minneapolis are cases in point (Figure 1.16b).

Perceptual regions are less rigorously structured than the formal and functional regions geographers devise. They reflect feelings and images rather than objective data and because of that may be more meaningful in the lives and actions of those who recognize them than are the more abstract regions of geographers.

Ordinary people have a clear idea of spatial variation and employ the regional concept to distinguish between territorial entities. People individually and collectively agree on where they live. The *vernacular regions* they recognize have reality in their minds and are reflected in regionally based names employed in businesses, by sports teams, or in advertising slogans. The frequency of references to "Dixie" in the southeastern United States represents that kind of regional consensus and awareness. Such vernacular regions reflect the way people view space, assign their loyalties, and interpret their world. Geographer Wilbur Zelinsky created his map of the perceptual regions of North America by counting the frequency that regional terms were used in the names of businesses (Figure 1.17). At a different scale, such urban ethnic enclaves (see Chapter 6) as "Little Italy" or "Chinatown" have comparable regional identity in the minds of their inhabitants. Less clearly perceived by outsiders but unmistakable to their inhabitants are the "turfs" of urban clubs or gangs. Their boundaries are sharp, and the perceived distinctions between them are paramount in the daily lives and activities of their occupants. What perceptual regions do you have clearly in mind?

Maps

Maps are tools to identify regions and to analyze their content. The spatial distributions, patterns, and relations of interest to geographers usually cannot easily be observed or interpreted in the landscape itself. Many, such as landform or agricultural regions or major cities, are so extensive spatially that they cannot be seen or studied in their totality from one or a few vantage points. Others, such as regions of language usage or religious belief, are spatial phenomena, but are not tangible or visible. Various interactions, flows, and exchanges imparting the dynamic quality to spatial interaction may not be directly observable at all. And even if all matters of geographic interest could be seen and measured through field examination, the infinite variety of tangible and intangible content of area would make it nearly impossible to isolate for study and interpretation the few items of regional interest selected for special investigation.

Therefore, the map has become the essential and distinctive tool of geographers. Only through the map can spatial distributions and interactions of whatever nature be reduced to an observable

(a)

Figure 1.16 (*a*) This **generalized land use map of Australia** is composed of *formal regions* whose internal economic characteristics show essential uniformities, setting them off from adjacent territories of different conditions of use. (*b*) The functional (or nodal) regions shown on this map were based on linkages between large banks of major central cities and the "correspondent" banks they served in smaller towns in the 1970s, before the advent of electronic banking and bank consolidation.

Source: (b) Redrawn by permission from Annals of the Association of American Geographers, *John R. Borchert, vol. 62, p. 358, Association of American Geographers, 1972.*

(b)

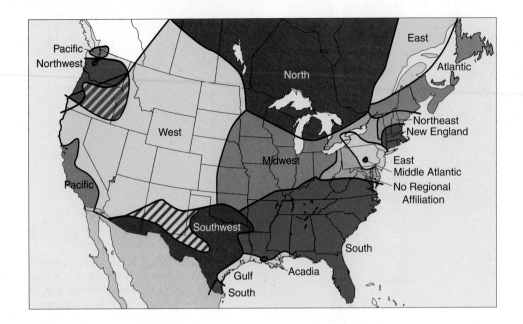

Figure 1.17 **Perceptual Regions of North America.**

Redrawn by permission from Annals of the Association of American Geographers, *Wilbur Zelinsky, "North America's Vernacular Regions, Vol. 70, No. 1, p. 14, 1980.*

scale, isolated for individual study, and combined or recombined to reveal relationships not directly measurable in the landscape itself. But maps can serve their purpose only if their users have a clear idea of their strengths, limitations, and diversity and of the conventions observed in their preparation and interpretation.

Map Scale

We have already seen that scale (page 10) is a vital element of every map. Because it is a much reduced version of the reality it summarizes, a map generalizes the data it displays. *Scale*—the relationship between size or length of a feature on the map and the same item on the earth's surface—determines the amount of that generalization. The smaller the scale of the map, the larger is the area it covers and the more generalized are the data it portrays. The larger the scale, the smaller is the depicted area and the more accurately can its content be represented (Figure 1.18). It may seem backward, but large-scale maps show small areas, and small-scale maps show large areas.

Map scale is selected according to the amount of generalization of data that is acceptable and the size of area that must be depicted. The user must consider map scale in evaluating the reliability of the spatial data that are presented. Regional boundary lines drawn on the world maps in this and other books or atlases would cover many kilometers or miles on the earth's surface. They obviously distort the reality they are meant to define, and on small-scale maps major distortion is inevitable. In fact, a general rule of thumb is that the larger the earth area depicted on a map, the greater is the distortion built into the map.

This is so because a map has to depict the curved surface of three-dimensional Earth on a two-dimensional sheet of paper. The term **projection** designates the method chosen to represent the earth's curved surface as a flat map. Since absolutely accurate representation is impossible, all projections inevitably distort. Specific projections may be selected, however, to minimize the distortion of at least one of the four main map properties—area, shape, distance, or direction.[2]

The Globe Grid

Maps are geographers' primary tools of spatial analysis. All spatial analysis starts with locations, and all locations are related to the global grid of latitude and longitude. Since these lines of reference are drawn on the spherical earth, their projection onto a map distorts their grid relationships. The extent of variance between the globe grid and a map grid helps tell us the kind and degree of distortion the map will contain.

The key reference points in the *grid system* are the North and South poles and the equator, which are given in nature, and the *prime meridian,* which is agreed on by cartographers. Because a circle contains 360°, the distance between the poles is 180° and between the equator and each pole, 90° (Figure 1.19). *Latitude* measures distance north and south of the equator (0°), and *parallels* of latitude run due east-west. *Longitude* is the angular distance east or west of the prime meridian and is depicted by north-south lines called *meridians,* which converge at the poles. The properties of the globe grid that the mapmaker tries to retain and that the map user should look for are as follows:

1. All meridians are semicircles of equal length; each is one-half the length of the equator.
2. All meridians converge at the poles and are true north–south semicircles.
3. All circles of latitude (parallels) are parallel to the equator and to each other.

[2]A more detailed discussion of map projections, including examples of their different types and purposes, may be found in Appendix A, beginning on page 453.

Figure 1.18 **The effect of scale on area and detail.** The larger the scale, the greater the number and kinds of features that can be included. Notice how individual buildings are visible in the large scale map (upper left) while the city of Boston is a mere point symbol in the smallest scale map (lower left). Scale may be reported to the map user in one (or more) of three ways. A *verbal* scale is given in words ("1 centimeter to 1 kilometer" or "1 inch to 1 mile"). A *representative fraction* (such as that placed at the left, below each of the four maps shown here) is a statement of how many linear units on the earth's surface are represented by one unit on the map. In the upper left map, for example, one map inch represents 25,000 inches on the ground. A *graphic* scale (such as that placed at the right and below each of these maps) is a line or bar marked off in map units but labeled in ground units.

4. Parallels decrease in circumference as one nears the poles.

5. Meridians and parallels intersect at right angles.

6. The scale on the surface of the globe is the same in every direction.

Only the globe grid itself retains all of these characteristics. To project it onto a surface that can be laid flat is to distort some or all of these properties and consequently to distort the reality the map attempts to portray.

How Maps Show Data

The properties of the globe grid and of various projections are the concern of the cartographer. Geographers are more interested in the depiction of spatial data and in the analysis of the patterns and interrelationships those data present. Out of the myriad items comprising the content of an area, the geographer must, first, select those that are of concern to the problem at hand and, second,

decide on how best to display them for study or demonstration. In that effort, geographers can choose among different types of maps and different systems of symbolization.

General-purpose, reference, or *location maps* make up one major class of maps familiar to everyone. Their purpose is simply to show without analysis or interpretation a variety of natural or human-made features of an area or of the world as a whole. Familiar examples are highway maps, city street maps, topographic maps (Figure 1.20), atlas maps, and the like. Until about the middle of the 18th century, the general-purpose or reference map was the dominant map form, for the primary function of the mapmaker (and the explorer who supplied the new data) was to "fill in" the world's unknown areas with reliable locational information. With the passage of time, scholars saw the possibilities to use the accumulating locational information to display and study the spatial patterns of social and physical data. The maps they made of climate, vegetation, soil, population, and other distributions introduced the thematic map, the second major class of maps.

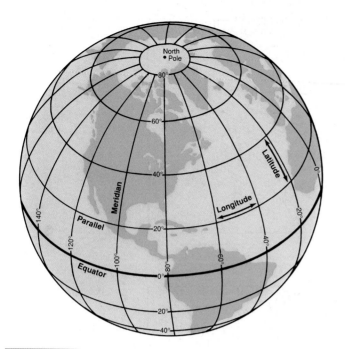

Figure 1.19 **The grid system of parallels of latitude and meridians of longitude.** Since the meridians converge at the poles, parallels become increasingly shorter away from the equator. On the globe, the 60th parallel is only one-half as long as the equator, and a degree of longitude along it measures only about 55 1/2 kilometers (about 34 1/2 miles) compared with about 111 kilometers (about 69 miles) at the equator (0°).

Figure 1.20 **A portion of the Santa Barbara, California, topographic quadrangle** of the U.S. Geological Survey 1:24,000 series. Topographic maps portray the natural landscape features of relatively small areas. Elevations and shapes of landforms, streams and other water bodies, vegetation, and coastal features are recorded, often with great accuracy. Because cultural items that people have added to the physical landscape, such as roads, railroads, buildings, political boundaries, and the like, are also frequently depicted on them, topographic maps are classed as general purpose or reference maps by the International Cartographic Association. The scale of the original map no longer applies to this photographic reduction.

Source: U.S. Geological Survey.

Thematic map is the general term applied to a map of any scale that presents a specific spatial distribution or a single category of data—that is, presents a graphic theme. The way the information is shown on such a map may vary according to the type of information to be conveyed, the level of generalization that is desired, and the symbolization selected. Thematic maps may be either *qualitative* or *quantitative*. The principal purpose of the qualitative map is to show the distribution of a particular class of information. The world location of producing oil fields, the distribution of U.S. national parks, or the pattern of areas of agricultural specialization within a state or country are examples. The interest is in where things are, and nothing is reported about—in the examples cited—barrels of oil extracted or in reserve, number of park visitors, or value or volume of crops or livestock produced.

In contrast, quantitative thematic maps show the spatial characteristic of numerical data. Usually, a single variable such as population, median income, annual wheat production, or average land value is chosen, and the map displays the variation from place to place in that feature. Important types of quantitative thematic maps include graduated circle, dot, isometric and isopleth, and choropleth maps (Figure 1.21).

Graduated circle maps use circles of different size to show the frequency of occurrence of a topic in different places; the larger the circle, the more frequent the incidence. On *dot maps,* a single or specified number of occurrences of the item studied is recorded by a single dot. The dot map serves not only to record data but to suggest their spatial pattern, distribution, and dispersion.

An *isometric map* features lines (*isolines*) that connect points registering equal values of the item mapped (*iso* means "equal"). The *isotherms* shown on the daily weather map connect points recording the same temperature at the same moment of time or the same average temperature during the day. Identical elevations above sea level may be shown by a form of isoline called a *contour line.* On *isopleth maps,* the calculation refers not to a point but to an areal statistic—for example, persons per square kilometer or average percentage of cropland in corn—and the isoline connects average values for unit areas. For emphasis, the area enclosed by isolines may be shaded to indicate approximately uniform occurrences of the thing mapped, and the isoline itself may be treated as the boundary of a uniform region.

A *choropleth map* presents average value of the data studied per preexisting areal unit—dwelling unit rents or assessed values by city block, for example, or (in the United States) population densities by individual townships within counties. Each unit area on the map is then shaded or colored to suggest the magnitude

(a) Graduated circle map

(b) Dot-distribution map

(c) Isopleth map

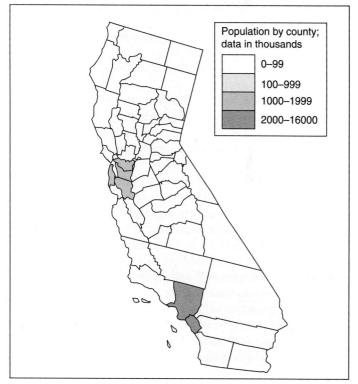

(d) Choropleth map

Figure 1.21 Types of thematic maps. Although population is the theme of each, these different California maps present their information in strikingly different ways. (*a*) In the graduated circle map, the area of the circle is approximately proportional to the absolute number of people within each county. (*b*) In a dot-distribution map where large numbers of items are involved, the value of each dot is identical and stated in the map legend. The placement of dots on this map does not indicate precise locations of people within the county, but simply their total number. (*c*) Population density is recorded by the isopleth map, while the choropleth map (*d*) may show absolute values as here or, more usually, ratio values such as population per square kilometer.

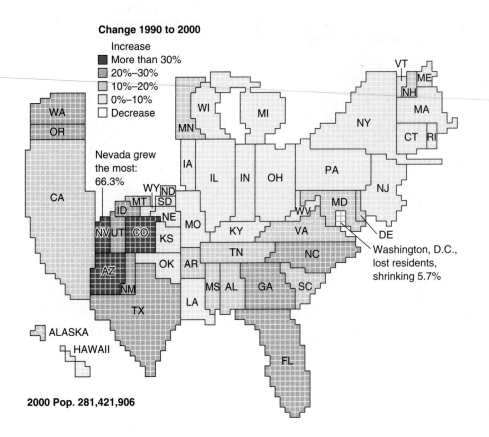

Change 1990 to 2000

Increase
- More than 30%
- 20%–30%
- 10%–20%
- 0%–10%
- Decrease

Nevada grew
the most:
66.3%

Washington, D.C.,
lost residents,
shrinking 5.7%

2000 Pop. 281,421,906

Figure 1.22 A cartogram in which each state is sized according to its number of residents in the year 2000 as reported by the U.S. Bureau of the Census. The cartogram also shows the percent change in population between 1990 and 2000.

Source: U.S. Bureau of the Census.

of the event or item found within its borders. Where the choropleth map is based on the absolute number of items within the unit area, as it is in Figure 1.21d, rather than on areal averaging (total numbers, for example, instead of numbers per square kilometer), a misleading statement about density may be conveyed.

A *statistical map* records the actual numbers or occurrences of the mapped item per established unit area or location. The actual count of each state's colleges and universities shown on an outline map of the United States or the number of traffic accidents at each street intersection within a city are examples of statistical maps. A *cartogram* uses such statistical data to transform territorial space so that the largest areal unit on the map is the one showing the greatest statistical value (Figure 1.22).

Maps communicate information but, as in all forms of communication, the message conveyed by a map reflects the intent and, perhaps, the biases of its author. Maps are persuasive because of the implied precision of their lines, scales, color and symbol placement, and information content. But maps, as communication devices, can subtly or blatantly manipulate the message they impart or contain intentionally false information (Figure 1.23). Maps, then, can distort and lie as readily as they can convey verifiable spatial data or scientifically valid analyses. The more map users are aware of those possibilities and the more understanding of map projections, symbolization, and common forms of thematic and reference mapping standards they possess, the more likely are they to reasonably question and clearly understand the messages maps communicate.

Contemporary Geospatial Technologies

The growth and advancement of three interrelated geospatial technologies—global positioning systems, remote sensing, and geographic information systems—has revolutionized geography and increased the geographer's ability to collect, analyze, and visually represent geographic data. Global positioning systems (GPS) rely upon a system of 24 orbiting satellites, earth-bound tracking stations that control the satellites, and portable receivers that determine exact geographic locations based on the signals from the satellites. Remote sensing allows the collection of vast amounts of geographic data, while geographic information systems (GIS) can integrate GPS, remote sensing, and other forms of spatial data. Google Earth and interactive mapping and navigation websites such as MapQuest are simple, everyday uses of contemporary geographic research technologies.

Remote Sensing

Remote sensing is a relatively new term, but the process it describes—detecting the nature of an object and the content of an area from a distance—is more than 150 years old. Soon after the development of the camera, photographs were being taken from balloons and kites. In the early 20th century, fixed-wing aircraft

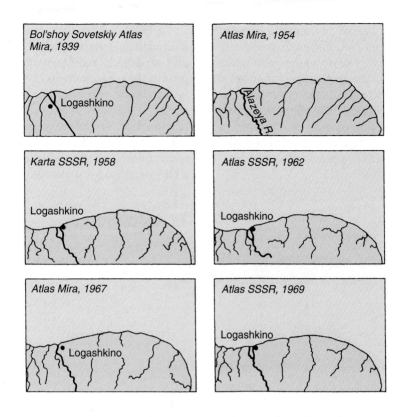

Figure 1.23 **The wandering town of Logashkino,** as traced in various Soviet atlases by Mark Monmonier. Deliberate, extensive cartographic "disinformation" and locational falsification, he reports, became a Cold War tactic of the Soviet Union. We usually use—and trust—maps to tell us exactly where things are located. On the maps shown, however, Logashkino migrates from west of the river away from the coast to east of the river on the coast, while the river itself gains and loses a distributary and, in 1954, the town itself disappears. The changing misinformation, Monmonier suggests, was intended to obscure from potential enemies the precise location of possible military targets.

Source: Mark Monmonier, How to Lie with Maps, *2nd Ed. © 1996. Reprinted by permission of the University of Chicago Press.*

provided a platform for the camera and photographer, and by the 1930s aerial photography from planned positions and routes permitted reliable data gathering for large and small area mapping purposes. Even today, high and low altitude aerial photography with returned film remains a widely used remote sensing technique. Standard photographic film detects reflected energy within the visible portion of the electromagnetic spectrum. It can be supplemented by special sensitized infrared film that has proved particularly useful for the recording of vegetation and hydrographic features and by nonphotographic imaging techniques including thermal scanning (widely used for studying various aspects of water features such as ocean currents and water pollution and, because it can be employed during nighttime hours, for military surveillance and energy budget observations) and radar mapping (also operative night and day and useful for penetrating clouds and haze).

For more than 30 years, both manned and unmanned spacecraft have supplemented the airplane as the vehicle for imaging earth features. Among the advantages of satellites are the speed of coverage and the fact that views of large regions can be obtained. In addition, they are equipped to record and report back to earth digitized information from multiple parts of the electromagnetic spectrum including some that are outside the range of human eyesight. Satellites enable us to map the invisible, including atmospheric and weather conditions, in addition to providing images with applications in agriculture and forest inventory, land use

classification, identification of geologic structures and mineral deposits, and more. The different sensors of the American Landsat satellites, first launched in 1972 (Landsat 7 was put aloft in 1999), are capable of resolving objects between 15 and 60 meters (50 and 200 ft) in size. Even sharper images are yielded by the French SPOT satellite (launched in 1986); its sensors can show objects that are larger than 10 meters (33 ft). Satellite imagery is relayed by electronic signals to receiving stations, where computers convert them into photo-like images for use in long-term scientific research and in current-condition mapping programs.

Geographic Information Systems (GIS)

Increasingly, digital computers, mapping software, and computer-based display units and printers are employed in the design and production of maps and in the development of databases used in map production. In computer-assisted cartography, the content of standard maps—locational and thematic—is digitized and stored in computers. The use of computers and printers in map production permits increases in the speed, flexibility, and accuracy of many steps in the mapmaking process but in no way reduces the obligation of the mapmaker to employ sound judgment in the design of the map or the communication of its content.

Geographic information systems (GIS) extend the use of digitized data and computer manipulation to investigate and display spatial information. A GIS is both an integrated software package for handling, processing, and analyzing geographical data and a computer database in which every item of information is tied to a precise geographic location. In the *raster approach,* that tie involves dividing the study area into a set of rectangular cells and describing the content of each cell. In the *vector approach,* the precise location of each object—point, line, or area—in a distribution is described. In either approach, a vast amount of different spatial information can be stored, accessed, compared, processed, analyzed, and displayed.

A GIS database, then, can be envisioned as a set of discrete informational overlays linked by reference to a basic locational grid of latitude and longitude (Figure 1.24). The system then permits the separate display of the spatial information contained in the database. It allows the user to overlay maps of different themes, analyze the relations revealed, and compute spatial relationships. It shows aspects of spatial associations otherwise difficult to display on conventional maps, such as flows, interactions, and three-dimensional characteristics. In short, a GIS database, as a structured set of spatial information, has

Terrain Models

Network

- Street center lines
- Drainage network

Utilities

- Sanitary sewer lines
- Water lines
- Telephone
- Gas/electric

Lots/Ownership

- Lot lines
- Property lines

Zones/Districts

- Comprehensive plan
- Municipal zoning
- Voting precincts
- School districts
- Census tracts/blocks

Base Mapping

- Road pavement
- Buildings/structures
- Fences/parking lots
- Drainage
- Wooded areas
- Spot elevation
- Contour lines
- Recreational facilities

Figure 1.24 **A model of a geographic information system.** A GIS incorporates three primary components: data storage capability, computer graphics programs, and statistical packages. In this example, the different layers of information are to be used in different combinations for city planning purposes. Different data sets, all selected for applicability to the questions asked, may be developed and used in human geography, economic geography, transportation planning, industrial location work, and similar applications.

Source: Reprinted by permission of Shaoli Huang.

become a powerful tool for automating geographical analysis and synthesis.

A GIS data set may contain the great amount of place-specific information collected and published by the U.S. Census Bureau, including population distribution, race, ethnicity, income, housing, employment, industry, farming, and so on. It may also hold environmental information downloaded from satellite imagery or taken from Geological Survey maps and other governmental and private sources. In human geography, the vast and growing array of spatial data has encouraged the use of GIS to explore models of regional economic and social structure; to examine transportation systems and urban growth patterns; and to study patterns of voting behavior, disease incidence, accessibility of public services, and a vast array of other topics. For physical geographers, the analytic and modeling capabilities of GIS are fundamental to the understanding of processes and interrelations in the natural environment.

Because of the growing importance of GIS in all manner of public and private spatial inquiries, demand in the job market is growing for those skilled in its techniques. Most university courses in GIS are taught in Geography departments, and "GIS/remote sensing" is a primary occupational specialty for which many geography undergraduate and graduate majors seek preparation.

Mental Maps

Maps that shape our understanding of distributions and locations or influence our perception of the world around us are not always drawn on paper. We carry with us *mental maps* that in some ways are more accurate in reflecting our view of spatial reality than the formal maps created by geographers or cartographers. **Mental maps** are images about an area or an environment developed by an individual on the basis of information or impressions received, interpreted, and stored. What are believed to be unnecessary details are left out, and only the important elements are incorporated. We use this information—this mental map—in organizing our daily activities: selecting our destinations and the sequence in which they will be visited, deciding on our routes of travel, recognizing where we are in relation to where we wish to be. A mental route map may also include reference points to be encountered on the chosen path of connection or on alternate lines of travel.

Such mental maps are every bit as real to their creators (and we all have them) as are the street maps or highway maps commercially available, and they are a great deal more immediate in their impact on our spatial decisions. We may choose routes or avoid neighborhoods not on objective grounds but on emotional or perceptual ones. In those choices, gender plays an important role. The mental maps of women may well contain danger zones where fear of, for example, sexual assault, harassment, or encounter with persons or conditions felt to be threatening is a determinant in routes chosen or times of journey. Whole sections of a community may be voids on our mental maps, as unknown as the interiors of Africa and South America were to Western Europeans two centuries ago. Our areas of awareness generally increase with the increasing mobility that comes with age, affluence, and education

and may be enlarged or restricted for different social groups within the city (Figure 1.25).

Systems, Maps, and Models

The content of area is interrelated and constitutes a **spatial system** that, in common with all systems, functions as a unit because its component parts are interdependent. Only rarely do individual elements of area operate in isolation, and to treat them as if they do is to lose touch with spatial reality. The systems of geographic concern are those in which the functionally important variables are spatial: location, distance, direction, density, and the other basic concepts we have reviewed. The systems that they define are not the same as regions, though spatial systems may be the basis for regional identification.

Systems have components, and the analysis of the role of components helps reveal the operation of the system as a whole. To conduct that analysis, individual system elements must be isolated for separate identification and, perhaps, manipulated to see their function within the structure of the system or subsystem. Maps and models are the devices geographers use to achieve that isolation and separate study.

Maps, as we have seen, are effective to the degree that they can segregate at an appropriate level of generalization those system elements selected for examination. By compressing, simplifying, and abstracting reality, maps record in manageable dimension the real-world conditions of interest. A model is a simplified abstraction of reality, designed to clarify relationships between its elements. Maps are a type of **model,** representing reality in an idealized form to make certain aspects more clear.

The complexities of spatial systems analysis—and the opportunities for quantitative analysis of systems made possible by computers and sophisticated statistical techniques—have led geographers to use other kinds of models in their work. Model building is the technique social scientists use to simplify complex situations, to eliminate (as does the map) unimportant details, and to isolate for special study and analysis the role of one or more interacting elements in a total system.

An interaction model discussed in Chapter 3, for instance, suggests that the amount of exchange expected between two places depends on the distance separating them and on their population size. The model indicates that the larger the places and the closer their distance, the greater is the amount of interaction. Such a model helps us to isolate the important components of the spatial system, to manipulate them separately, and to reach conclusions concerning their relative importance. When a model satisfactorily predicts the volume of intercity interaction in the majority of cases, the lack of agreement in a particular case leads to an examination of the circumstances contributing to the disparity. The quality of connecting roads, political barriers, or other variables may affect the specific places examined, and these causative elements may be isolated for further study.

Indeed, the steady pursuit of more refined and definitive analysis of human geographic questions—the "further study" that continues to add to our understanding of how people occupy and utilize the earth, interact with each other, and organize and alter

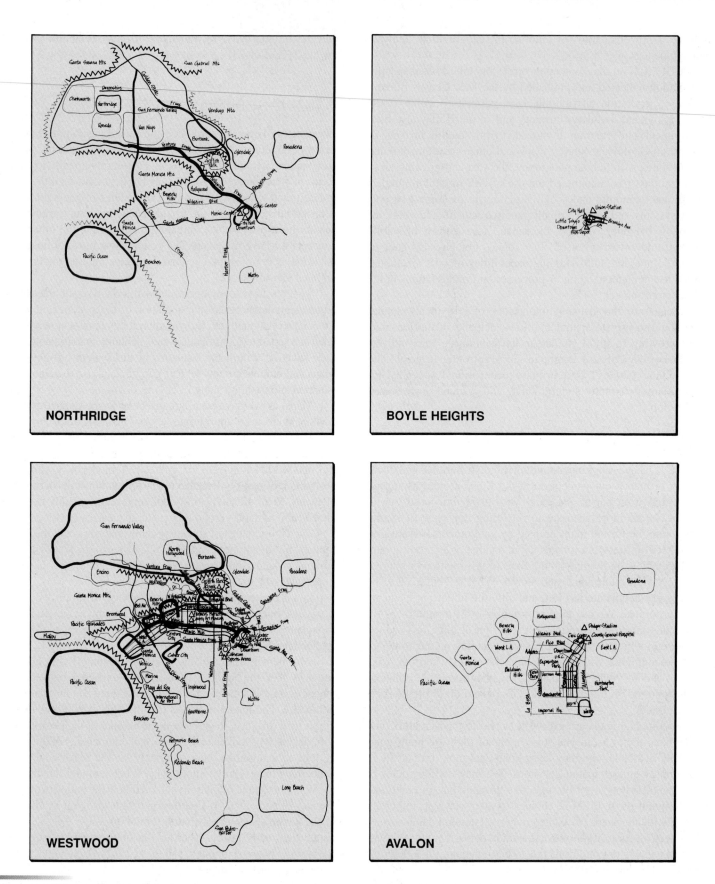

Figure 1.25 Four mental maps of Los Angeles. The upper-middle-income residents of the Northridge and Westwood communities have expansive views of the metropolis, reflecting their mobility and area of travel. Black inner city residents of the Avalon community display a more restricted view of the city because of their lower incomes, social isolation, and reliance on public transportation. Even more limited is the mental map of Hispanic residents of the Boyle Heights community, which reflects their spatial and linguistic isolation within the metropolitan area.

Source: From Department of City Planning, City of Los Angeles, The Visual Environment of Los Angeles, 1971. *Reprinted by permission.*

earth space—has led to the remarkably diversified yet coherent field of modern human geography. With the content of this introductory chapter as background to the nature, traditions, and tools of geography, we are ready to begin its exploration.

The Structure of This Book

By way of getting started, it is useful for you to know how the organization and topics of this text have been structured to help you reach the kinds of understandings we seek.

We begin in Part One (Chapters 2–4) with introductory material on cultural processes and spatial interactions among an unevenly distributed and expanding world population. Chapter 2 introduces the components and structure of culture, culture change, diffusion, and divergence. Chapter 3 presents characteristics of spatial interaction and spatial behavior that are common to all peoples and cultures. Chapter 4 examines population geography and the factors driving patterns of population movement, growth, and distribution.

While the book's first four chapters focus on geographic themes common to all peoples and cultures, Part Two (Chapters 5–7) turns to the features that distinguish societies and culture realms and create patterns of unity and diversity in the cultural landscape. While there are innumerable ways in which human populations differ, we focus on spatial patterns of three major points of contrast: language and religion (Chapter 5), and ethnicity (Chapter 6). Further, we examine the diversity of folk cultures—the material and nonmaterial aspects of daily life among groups insulated from outside influences through spatial isolation or cultural barriers (Chapter 7). Patterns of cultural diversity are in constant tension with unifying forces as the world experiences greater spatial interaction. Thus, we also examine ways in which folk cultures are undergoing erosion under the influence of globalized popular cultures.

Our focus shifts in Part Three (Chapters 8–10) to the dynamic patterns of the space economy, examining spatial patterns of food and raw material production (Chapter 8), manufacturing and services (Chapter 9), and finally measures, spatial patterns, and models of economic development (Chapter 10). Economic development is generally accompanied by more formal systems of organizing society, resources, and territory. Thus, in Part Four (Chapters 11–12), we examine systems of functional organization within systems of cities and inside of individual cities (Chapter 11) as well as systems of political control of geographic space that range from the local to the international scale (Chapter 12). Human impact on the environment is an integral part of each chapter and is the topic of Part Five, the concluding section of the book (Chapter 13). In concluding with human impacts, we return to the underlying concern of all geographic study: the relationship between human geographic patterns and processes and both the present conditions and future prospects of the physical and cultural landscapes we inhabit.

Summary

Geography is the study of the earth's surface and its physical and cultural content. Throughout its long history, geography has remained consistent in its focus on human—environmental interactions, the interrelatedness of places, and the likenesses and differences in physical and cultural content of area that exist from place to place. The collective interests of geographers are summarized by the spatial and systems analytical questions they ask. The responses to those questions are interpreted through basic concepts of space and place, location, distance, direction, content evolution, spatial interaction, and regional organization.

Geographers employ maps and models to abstract the complex reality of space and to isolate its components for separate study. Maps are imperfect renderings of the three-dimensional earth and its parts on a two-dimensional surface. In that rendering, some or all of the characteristics of the globe grid are distorted, but convenience and data manageability are gained. Spatial information may be depicted visually in a number of ways, each designed to simplify and to clarify the infinite complexity of spatial content. Geographers also use verbal and mathematical models for the same purpose, to abstract and analyze.

In their study of the earth's surface as the occupied and altered space within which humans operate, some geographers concentrate on the integration of physical and cultural phenomena in a specific earth area (regional geography). Other geographers may, instead, emphasize systematic geography through study of the earth's physical systems of spatial and human concern or, as here, devote primary attention to people. This is a text in *human geography*. Its focus is on human interactions both with the physical environments people occupy and alter and with the cultural environments they have created. We are concerned with the ways people perceive the landscapes and regions they occupy, act within and between them, make choices about them, and organize them according to the varying cultural, political, and economic interests of human societies. This is a text clearly within the social sciences, but like all geography, its background is the physical earth as the home of humans. As human geographers, our concern is with how that home has been altered by societies and cultures. Culture is the starting point, and in the next chapter we begin with an inquiry about the roots and nature of culture.

KEY WORDS

absolute direction 8	mental map 25	relative distance 9
absolute distance 9	model 25	relative location 8
absolute location 6	natural landscape 11	remote sensing 22
accessibility 13	nodal region 16	scale 10
concentration 15	pattern 15	site 8
connectivity 13	perceptual region 16	situation 8
cultural landscape 11	place 5	space 5
density 14	placelessness 6	spatial diffusion 13
dispersion 15	projection 18	spatial distribution 14
formal region 16	region 15	spatial interaction 13
functional region 16	regional concept 16	spatial system 25
geographic information system (GIS) 23	relative direction 8	uniform region 16
globalization 14		

 FOR REVIEW

1. In what two meanings and for what different purposes do we refer to *location?*

2. Describe the *site* and the *situation* of the town where you live, work, or go to school.

3. What kinds of distance transformations are suggested by the term *relative distance?* How is the concept of *psychological distance* related to relative distance?

4. What are the common elements of *spatial distribution?* What different aspects of the spatial arrangement of things do they address?

5. What are the common characteristics of *regions?* How are *formal* and *functional* regions different in concept and definition? What is a *perceptual region?*

6. List at least four properties of the globe grid. Why are globe grid

properties apt to be distorted on maps?

7. What does *prime meridian* mean? What happens to the length of a degree of longitude as one approaches the poles?

8. What different ways of displaying statistical data on maps can you name and describe?

KEY CONCEPTS REVIEW

1. **What is the nature of geography and the role of human geography?** pp. 2–5.
Geography is a *spatial* science concerned with how the content of earth areas differs from place to place. It is the study of spatial variation in the world's physical and cultural (human) features. The emphasis of human geography is on the spatial variations in characteristics of peoples and cultures, on the way humans interact over space, and the ways they utilize and alter the natural landscapes they occupy.

2. **What are the fundamental geographic observations and their underlying concepts?** pp. 5–15.
Basic geographic observations all concern the characteristics, content, and interactions of places. Their underlying concepts involve such place specifics as location, direction, distance, size, scale, physical and cultural attributes, interrelationships, and regional similarities and differences.

3. **What are the regional concept and the generalized characteristics of regions?** pp. 15–18.
The regional concept tells us that physical and cultural features of the earth's surface are rationally arranged by understandable processes. All recognized regions are characterized by location, spatial extent, defined boundaries, and position within a hierarchy of regions. Regions may be "formal" (uniform) or "functional" (nodal) in nature.

4. **Why do geographers use maps, and how do maps show spatial information?** pp. 18–25.

Maps are tools geographers use to identify and delimit regions and to analyze their content. They permit the study of areas and areal features too extensive to be completely viewed or understood on the earth's surface itself. Thematic (single category) maps may be either qualitative or quantitative. Their data may be shown in graduated circle, dot distribution, isometric, choropleth, statistical, or cartogram form.

5. **In what ways in addition to maps may spatial data be visualized or analyzed?** pp. 25–27.

Informally, we all create "mental maps" reflecting highly personalized impressions and information about the spatial arrangement of things (for example, buildings, streets, landscape features). More formally, geographers recognize the content of area as forming a spatial system to which techniques of spatial systems analysis and model building are applicable.

ROOTS AND MEANING
OF CULTURE:
Introduction

2

South African San hunter-gatherers are modern day followers of the world's oldest, most enduring livelihood system.

Key Concepts

1. Culture components and the nature of human–environmental relations, pp. 31–37.

2. Culture origins and culture hearths, pp. 37–46.

3. The structure of culture and forms of culture change, pp. 46–55.

They buried him there in the cave where they were working, less than 6 kilometers (4 miles) from the edge of the ice sheet. Outside stretched the tundra, summer feeding grounds for the mammoths whose ivory they had come so far to collect. Inside, near where they dug his grave, were stacked the tusks they had gathered and were cutting and shaping. They prepared the body carefully and dusted it with red ochre, then buried it in an elaborate grave with tundra flowers and offerings of food, a bracelet on its arm, a pendant about its throat, and 40 to 50 polished rods of ivory by its side. It rested there, in modern Wales, undisturbed for some 18,000 years until discovered early in the 19th century. The 25-year-old hunter had died far from the group's home some 650 kilometers (400 miles) away near present-day Paris, France. He had been part of a routine annual summer expedition overland from the forested south across the as-yet-unflooded English Channel to the mammoths' grazing grounds at the edge of the glacier.

As always, they were well prepared for the trip. Their boots were carefully made. Their sewn skin leggings and tunics served well for travel and work; heavier fur parkas warded off the evening chill. They carried emergency food, fire-making equipment, and braided cord that they could fashion into nets, fishing lines, ropes, or thread. They traveled by reference to sun and stars, recognizing landmarks from past journeys and occasionally consulting a crude map etched on bone.

Although the hunters returned bearing the sad news of their companion's death, they also brought the ivory to be carved and traded among the scattered peoples of Europe from the Atlantic Ocean to the Ural Mountains.

As shown by their tools and equipment, their behaviors and beliefs, these Stone Age travelers displayed highly developed and distinctive characteristics, primitive only from the vantage point of our own different technologies and customs. They represented the culmination of a long history of development of skills, of invention of tools, and of creation of lifestyles that set them apart from peoples elsewhere in Europe, Asia, and Africa who possessed still different cultural heritages.

To writers in newspapers and the popular press, "culture" means the arts (literature, painting, music, and the like). To a social scientist, **culture** is the specialized behavioral patterns, understandings, adaptations, and social systems that summarize a group of people's learned way of life. In this broader sense, culture is an ever-present part of the regional differences that are the essence of human geography. The visible and invisible evidences of culture—buildings and farming patterns, language, political organization, and ways of earning a living, for example—are all parts of the spatial diversity human geographers study. Cultural differences over time may present contrasts as great as those between the Stone Age ivory hunters and modern urban Americans. Cultural differences in area result in human landscapes with variations as subtle as the differing "feel" of urban Paris, Moscow, or New York, or as obvious as the sharp contrasts of rural Zimbabwe and the U.S. Midwest (Figure 2.1).

Because such tangible and intangible cultural differences exist and have existed in various forms for thousands of years, human geography addresses the question, Why? Why, since humankind constitutes a single species, are cultures so varied? What and where were the origins of the different culture regions we now observe? How, from whatever limited areas individual culture traits developed, were they diffused over a wider portion of the globe? How did people who had roughly similar origins come to display significant areal differences in technology, social structure, ideology, and the innumerable other expressions of human geographic diversity? In what ways and why are there distinctive cultural variations even in presumed "melting pot" societies such as the United States and Canada or in the historically homogeneous, long-established countries of Europe? How is knowledge about cultural differences important to us today? Part of the answer to these questions is to

(a)

Figure 2.1 Culture is reflected in agricultural practices and in the look of the landscape. Compare (*a*) a subsistence maize plot in Zimbabwe and (*b*) the extensive fields and mechanized farming of the U.S. Midwest.

(b)

be found in the way separate human groups developed techniques to solve regionally varied problems of securing food, clothing, and shelter and, in the process, created areally distinctive customs and ways of life.

Components of Culture

Culture is transmitted within a society to succeeding generations by imitation, instruction, and example. In short, it is learned, not biological. It has nothing to do with instinct or with genes. As members of a social group, individuals acquire integrated sets of behavioral patterns, environmental and social perceptions, and knowledge of existing technologies. Of necessity, each of us learns the culture in which we are born and reared. But we need not—indeed, cannot—learn its totality. Age, sex, status, or occupation may dictate the aspects of the cultural whole in which an individual becomes indoctrinated.

A culture, that is, despite overall generalized and identifying characteristics and even an outward appearance of uniformity, displays a social structure—a framework of roles and interrelationships of individuals and established groups. Each individual learns and is expected to adhere to the rules and conventions not only of the culture as a whole but also of those specific to the subculture to which he or she belongs. And that subgroup may have its own recognized social structure (Figure 2.2). Think back to the different subgroups and aspects of your own national culture that you became part of (and left) as you progressed from childhood through high school and on to college-age adulthood and, perhaps, to first employment.

Many different cultures, then, can coexist within a given area, each with its own influence on the thoughts and behaviors of their separate members. Subcultures are groups that can be distinguished from the wider society by their cultural patterns. Within the United States, for example, we can readily recognize a variety of subcultures within the larger "American" culture: white, black, Hispanic, Asian American, or other ethnic groups; gay and straight, urban and rural; and many others. Human geography increasingly recognizes the pluralism of cultures within regions. In addition to examining the separate content and influence of those subcultures, it attempts to record and analyze the varieties of contested cultural interactions between them, including those of political and economic nature.

Culture is a complexly interlocked web of behaviors and attitudes. Realistically, its full and diverse content cannot be appreciated, and in fact may be wholly misunderstood, if we concentrate our attention only on limited, obvious traits. Distinctive eating utensils, the use of gestures, or the ritual of religious ceremony may summarize and characterize a culture for the casual observer. These are, however, individually insignificant parts of a much more complex structure that can be appreciated only when the whole is experienced.

Out of the richness and intricacy of human life we seek to isolate for special study those more fundamental cultural variables that give structure and spatial order to societies. We begin with *culture traits,* the smallest distinctive items of culture. **Culture traits** are units of learned behavior ranging from the language spoken to the tools used or the games played. A trait may be an object (a fishhook, for example), a technique (weaving and knotting of a fishnet), a belief (in the spirits resident in water bodies), or an attitude (a conviction that fish is superior to other animal protein). Of course, the same trait—the Christian religion, perhaps, or the Spanish language—may be part of more than one culture. Traits are the most elementary expression of culture, the building blocks of the complex behavioral patterns of distinctive groups of peoples.

Figure 2.2 Both the traditional rice farmer of rural Japan and the Tokyo commuter are part of a common Japanese culture. They occupy, however, vastly different positions in its social structure.

Individual cultural traits that are functionally interrelated comprise a **culture complex.** The existence of such complexes is universal. Keeping cattle was a *culture trait* of the Masai of Kenya and Tanzania. Related traits included the measurement of personal wealth by the number of cattle owned, a diet containing milk and the blood of cattle, and disdain for labor unrelated to herding. The assemblage of these and other related traits yielded a culture complex descriptive of one aspect of Masai society (Figure 2.3). In exactly the same way, religious complexes, business behavior complexes, sports complexes, and others can easily be recognized in any society.

In the United States, for example, some environmentalists would like to wean Americans from their automobiles. However, a study of American culture reveals the difficulty in making such a change because automobiles are part of an interrelated cultural complex. Automobile brands and models speak of a person's status in U.S. society. Movies, video games, and sports often give automobiles a central role; movies such as *The Fast and the Furious* series, video games such as *Grand Theft Auto,* and NASCAR are familiar examples. Entire suburban landscapes have been built around the needs of the automobile. Even rites of passage often focus on the automobile: driver's education, passing the driver's exam, getting one's first automobile, and the practice of decorating the newlywed couple's car at the end of the wedding ceremony.

A **cultural system** is a broader generalization than a cultural complex and refers to the collection of interacting cultural traits and cultural complexes that are shared by a group within a particular territory. Multiethnic societies, perhaps further subdivided by linguistic differences, varied food preferences, and a host of other internal differentiations, may nonetheless share enough joint characteristics to be recognizably distinctive cultural systems to

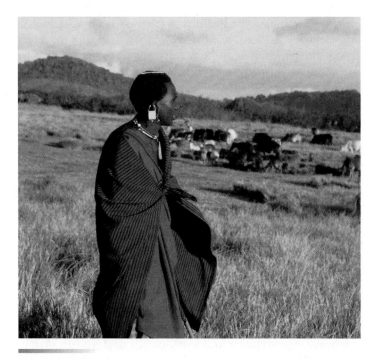

Figure 2.3 The formerly migratory Masai of Kenya are now largely sedentary, partially urbanized, and frequently owners of fenced farms. Cattle formed the traditional basis of Masai culture and were the evidence of wealth and social status.

themselves and others. Certainly, citizens of "melting pot" United States would identify themselves as *Americans,* together constituting a unique culture system on the world scene.

Culture traits, complexes, and systems have areal extent. When they are plotted on maps, the regional character of the components of culture is revealed. Although human geographers are interested in the spatial distribution of these individual elements of culture, their usual concern is with the **culture region,** a portion of the earth's surface occupied by populations sharing recognizable and distinctive cultural characteristics. Examples include the political organizations societies devise, the religions they espouse, the form of economy they pursue, and even the type of clothing they wear, eating utensils they use, or kind of housing they occupy. There are as many such conceptual culture regions as there are culture traits and complexes recognized for population groups. Their recognition will be particularly important in discussions of ethnic, folk, and popular cultures in later chapters of this book. In those later reviews as within the present chapter, we must keep in mind that within any one recognized culture region, groups united by the specific mapped characteristics may be competing and distinctive in other important cultural traits.

Finally, a set of culture regions showing related culture complexes and landscapes may be grouped to form a **culture realm.** The term recognizes a large segment of the earth's surface having an assumed fundamental uniformity in its cultural characteristics and showing a significant difference in them from adjacent realms. Culture realms are, in a sense, culture regions at the broadest scale of recognition. In fact, the scale is so broad and the diversity within the recognized realms so great that the very concept of realm may mislead more than it informs.

Indeed, the current validity of distinctive culture realms has been questioned in light of an assumed globalization of all aspects of human society and economy. The result of that globalization, it has been suggested, is a homogenization of cultures as economies are integrated and uniform consumer demands are satisfied by standardized commodities produced by international corporations.

Certainly, the increasing mobility of people, goods, and information has reduced the rigidly compartmentalized ethnicities, languages, and religions of earlier periods. Cultural flows and exchanges have increased over the recent decades and with them has come a growing worldwide intermixture of peoples and customs. Despite that growing globalism in all facets of life and economy, however, the world is far from homogenized. Although an increased sameness of commodities and experiences is encountered in distant places, even common and standardized items of everyday life—branded soft drinks, for example, or American fast-food franchises—take on unique regional meanings and roles, conditioned by the total cultural mix they enter. Those multiple regional cultural mixes are often defiantly distinctive and separatist as recurring incidents of ethnic conflict, civil war, and strident regionalism attest. Rather than leveling and removing regional contrasts, as frequently predicted, globalization continues to be countered by powerful forces of regionalism, place identity, and ethnicity.

If a global culture can be discerned, it may best be seen as a combination of multiple territorial cultures, rather than a standardized uniformity. It is those territorially different cultural mixtures that are recognized by the culture realms suggested on Figure 2.4,

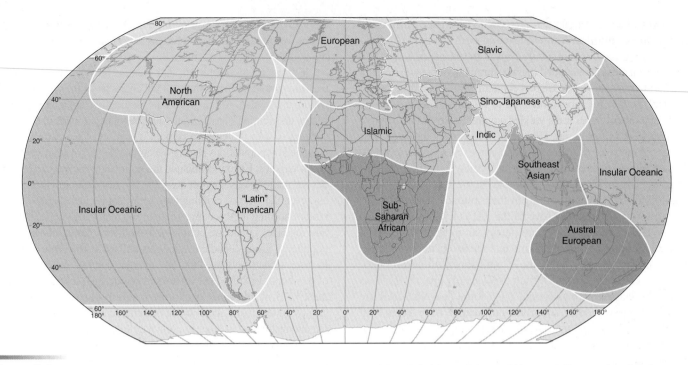

Figure 2.4 **Culture realms of the modern world.** This is just one of many possible subdivisions of the world into multifactor cultural regions.

which itself is only one of many such possible divisions. The spatial pattern and characteristics of these generalized realms will help us place the discussions and examples of human geography of later chapters in their regional context.

Interaction of People and Environment

Culture develops in a physical environment that, in its way, contributes to differences among people. In premodern subsistence societies, the acquisition of food, shelter, and clothing, all parts of culture, depends on the utilization of the natural resources at hand. The interrelations of people to the environment of a given area, their perceptions and utilization of it, and their impact on it are interwoven themes of **cultural ecology**—the study of the relationship between a culture group and the natural environment it occupies.

Cultural ecologists see evidence that subsistence pastoralists, hunter-gatherers, and gardeners adapted their productive activities—and, by extension, their social organizations and relationships—to the specific physical limitations of their different local habitats. Presumably, similar natural environmental conditions influenced the development of similar adaptive responses and cultural outcomes in separate, unconnected locales. That initial influence, of course, does not predetermine the details of the subsequent culture.

Environments as Controls

Geographers have long dismissed as intellectually limiting and demonstrably invalid the ideas of **environmental determinism,** the belief that the physical environment exclusively shapes humans,

their actions, and their thoughts. Environmental factors alone cannot account for the cultural variations that occur around the world. Levels of technology, systems of organization, and ideas about what is true and right have no obvious relationship to environmental circumstances.

The environment does place certain limitations on the human use of territory. Such limitations, however, must be seen not as absolute, enduring restrictions but as relative to technologies, cost considerations, national aspirations, and linkages with the larger world. Human choices in the use of landscapes are affected by group perception of the feasibility and desirability of their settlement and exploitation. These are not circumstances inherent in the land. Mines, factories, and cities have been created in the formerly nearly unpopulated tundra and forests of Siberia as a reflection of Russian developmental programs, not in response to recent environmental improvement.

Possibilism is the viewpoint promoted by late 19th and early 20th century French geographer Paul Vidal de la Blache that people, not environments, are the dynamic forces of cultural development. The needs, traditions, and level of technology of a culture affect how that culture assesses the possibilities of an area and shape what choices the culture makes regarding them. Each society uses natural resources in accordance with its circumstances. Changes in a group's technical abilities or objectives bring about changes in its perceptions of the usefulness of the land. Simply put, the impact of the environment appears inversely related to the level of development of a culture, while perception of environmental opportunities increases directly with growth in economic and cultural development.

Map evidence suggests the nature of some environmental limitations on use of area. The vast majority of the world's population is differentially concentrated on less than one-half of the earth's land surface, as Figure 4.21 indicates. Areas with relatively mild climates that offer a supply of fresh water, fertile soil, and abundant mineral resources are densely settled, reflecting in part the different potentials of the land under earlier technologies to support population. Even today, the polar regions, high and rugged mountains, deserts, and some hot and humid lowland areas contain very few people. If resources for feeding, clothing, or housing ourselves within an area are lacking or if we do not recognize them there, there is no inducement for people to occupy the territory.

Environments that do contain such recognized resources provide the framework within which a culture operates. Coal, oil, and natural gas have been in their present locations throughout human history, but they were rarely of use to preindustrial cultures and did not impart any understood advantage to their sites of occurrence. Not until the Industrial Revolution did coal deposits gain importance and come to influence the location of such great industrial complexes as the Midlands in England, the Ruhr in Germany, and the steel-making districts formerly so important in parts of northeastern United States. Native Americans made one use of the environment around Pittsburgh, while 19th century industrialists made quite another.

Human Impacts

People are also able to modify their environment, and this is the other half of the human–environment relationship of geographic concern. Geography, including cultural geography, examines both the reactions of people to the physical environment and their impact on that environment. By using it, we modify our environment—in part, through the material objects we place on the landscape: cities, farms, roads, and so on (Figure 2.5). The form these take is the product of the kind of culture group in which we live. The **cultural landscape,** the earth's surface as modified by human action, is the tangible physical record of a given culture. House types, transportation networks, parks and cemeteries, and the size and distribution of settlements are among the indicators of the use that humans have made of the land.

Human actions, both deliberate and inadvertent, modifying or even destroying the environment are perhaps as old as humankind itself. People have used, altered, and replaced the vegetation in wide areas of the tropics and midlatitudes. They have hunted to extinction vast herds and whole species of animals. They have, through overuse and abuse of the earth and its resources, rendered sterile and unpopulated formerly productive and attractive regions.

Fire has been called the first great tool of humans, and the impact of its early and continuing use is found on nearly every continent. Poleward of the great rain forests of equatorial South America, Africa, and South Asia lies the *tropical savanna* of extensive grassy vegetation separating scattered trees and forest groves (Figure 2.6). The trees appear to be the remnants of naturally occurring tropical dry forests, thorn forests, and scrub now largely obliterated by the use, over many millennia, of fire to remove the unwanted and unproductive trees and to clear off old grasses for more nutritious new growth. The grasses supported the immense herds of grazing animals that were the basis of hunting societies. After independence, the government of Kenya in East Africa sought to protect its national game preserves by prohibiting the periodic use of fire. It quickly found that the immense herds of gazelles, zebras, antelope, and other grazers

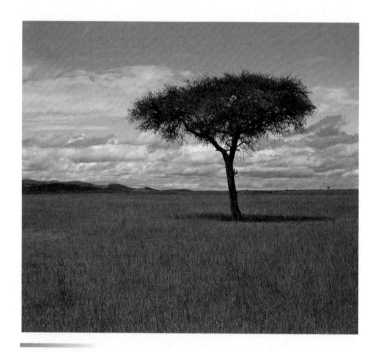

Figure 2.6 The parklike landscape of grasses and trees characteristic of the tropical savanna is seen in this view from Kenya, Africa.

Figure 2.5 The physical and cultural landscapes of Cape Town, South Africa, in juxtaposition. Advanced societies are capable of so altering the circumstances of nature that the cultural landscapes they create become the controlling environment.

(and the lions and other predators that fed on them) that tourists came to see were being replaced by less-appealing browsing species—rhinos, hippos, and elephants. With fire prohibited, the forests began to reclaim their natural habitat and the grassland fauna was replaced.

The same form of vegetation replacement occurred in midlatitudes. The grasslands of North America were greatly extended by Native Americans who burned the forest margin to extend grazing areas and to drive animals in the hunt. The control of fire in modern times has resulted in the advance of the forest once again in formerly grassy areas ("parks") of Colorado, northern Arizona, and other parts of the United States West.

Examples of adverse human impact abound. The *Pleistocene overkill*—the Stone Age loss of whole species of large animals on all inhabited continents—is often ascribed to the unrestricted hunting to extinction carried on by societies familiar with fire to drive animals and hafted (with handles) weapons to slaughter them. With the use of these,

according to one estimate, about 40% of African large-animal genera passed to extinction. The majority of large animal, reptile, and flightless bird species had disappeared from Australia around 46,000 years ago; in North America, some two-thirds of original large mammals had succumbed by 11,000 years ago under pressure from the hunters migrating to and spreading across the continent. Although some have suggested that climatic changes or pathogens carried by dogs, rats, and other camp followers were at least partially responsible, human action is the more generally accepted explanation for the abrupt faunal changes. No uncertainty exists in the record of faunal destruction by the Maoris of New Zealand or of Polynesians who had exterminated some 80% to 90% of South Pacific bird species—as many as 2000 in all—by the time Captain Cook arrived in the 18th century. Similar destruction of key marine species—Caribbean sea turtles, sea cows off the coast of Australia, sea otters near Alaska, and others elsewhere—as early as 10,000 years ago resulted in environmental damage whose effects continue to the present.

 # Chaco Canyon Desolation

It is not certain when they first came, but by A.D. 1000, the Anasazi people were building a flourishing civilization in present-day Arizona and New Mexico. They were corn farmers, thriving during the 300 years or so of the medieval warm period, beginning about A.D. 900 in the American Southwest. In the Chaco Canyon alone, they erected as many as 75 towns, all centered around pueblos, huge stone-and-adobe apartment buildings as tall as five stories and with as many as 800 rooms. These were the largest and tallest buildings of North America prior to the construction of iron-framed "cloudscrapers" in major cities at the end of the 19th century. An elaborate network of roads and irrigation canals connected and supported the pueblos. About A.D. 1200, the settlements were abruptly abandoned. The Anasazi, advanced in their skills of agriculture and communal dwelling, were—according to some scholars—forced to move on by the ecological disaster their pressures had brought to a fragile environment.

They needed forests for fuel and for the hundreds of thousands of logs used as beams and bulwarks in their dwellings. The pinyon-juniper woodland of the canyon was quickly depleted. For larger timbers needed for construction, the Anasazi first harvested stands of ponderosa pine found some 40 kilometers (25 miles) away. As early as A.D. 1030 these, too, were exhausted, and the community switched to spruce and Douglas fir from mountaintops surrounding the canyon.

When they were gone by 1200, the Anasazi fate was sealed—not only by the loss of forest but by the irreversible ecological changes deforestation and agriculture had occasioned. With forest loss came erosion that destroyed the topsoil. The surface water channels that had been built for irrigation were deepened by accelerated erosion, converting them into enlarging arroyos useless for agriculture.

The material roots of their culture destroyed, the Anasazi turned upon themselves; warfare convulsed the region and, compelling evidence suggests, cannibalism was practiced. Smaller groups sought refuge elsewhere, re-creating on reduced scale their pueblo way of life but now in nearly inaccessible, highly defensible mesa and cliff locations. The destruction they had wrought destroyed the Anasazi in turn.

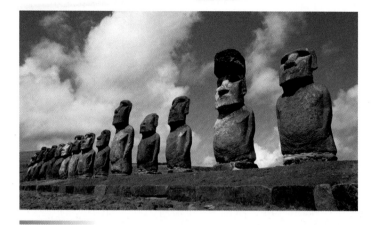

Figure 2.7 Now treeless, Easter Island once was lushly forested. The statues (some weighing up to 85 tons) dotting the island were rolled to their locations and lifted into place with logs.

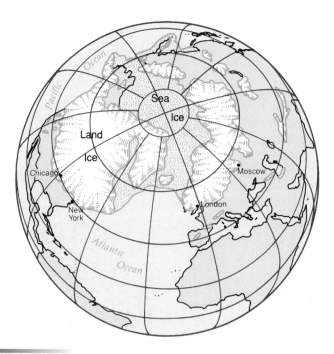

Figure 2.8 **Maximum extent of glaciation.** In their fullest development, glaciers of the most recent Ice Age covered large parts of Eurasia and North America. Even areas not covered by ice were affected as ocean levels dropped and rose and climate and vegetation regions changed with glacial advance and retreat.

Not only the destruction of animals but of the life-supporting environment itself has been a frequent consequence of human misuse of area (see "Chaco Canyon Desolation"). North Africa, the "granary of Rome" during the empire, became wasted and sterile in part because of mismanagement. Roman roads standing high above the surrounding barren wastes give testimony to the erosive power of wind and water when natural vegetation is unwisely removed and farming techniques are inappropriate. Easter Island in the South Pacific was covered lushly with palms and other trees when Polynesians settled there about A.D. 400. By the beginning of the 18th century, Easter Island had become the barren wasteland it remains today. Deforestation increased soil erosion, removed the supply of timbers needed for the vital dugout fishing canoes, and made it impossible to move the massive stone statues that were significant in the islanders' religion (Figure 2.7). With the loss of livelihood resources and the collapse of religion, warfare broke out and the population was decimated. A similar tragic sequence is occurring on Madagascar in the Indian Ocean today. Despite current romantic notions, not all early societies lived in harmony with their environment.

The more technologically advanced and complex the culture, the more apparent is its impact on the natural landscape. In sprawling urban-industrial societies, the cultural landscape has come to outweigh the natural physical environment in its impact on people's daily lives. It interposes itself between "nature" and humans, and residents of the cities of such societies—living and working in climate-controlled buildings, driving to enclosed shopping malls—can go through life with very little contact with or concern about the physical environment.

Roots of Culture

Earlier humans found the physical environment more immediate and controlling than we do today. Some 11,000 years ago, the massive glaciers—moving ice sheets of great depth—that had covered much of the land and water of the Northern Hemisphere (Figure 2.8) began to retreat. Animal, plant, and human populations

that had been spatially confined by both the ice margin and the harsh climates of middle-latitude regions began to spread, colonizing newly opened territories. The name *Paleolithic* (Old Stone Age) is used to describe the period near the end of glaciation during which small and scattered groups like the ivory hunters at this chapter's start began to develop regional variations in their ways of life and livelihood.

All were **hunter-gatherers,** preagricultural people dependent on the year-round availability of plant and animal foodstuffs they could secure with the rudimentary stone tools and weapons at their disposal. Even during the height of the Ice Age, the unglaciated sections of western, central, and northeastern Europe, which today are home to productive farms, forests and cities, were then covered with tundra vegetation, the mosses, lichens, and low shrubs typical of areas too cold to support forests. Southeastern Europe and southern Russia had forest, tundra, and Steppe (grasslands), and the Mediterranean areas, which today have shrub and scrub-oak vegetation, had forest cover (Figure 2.9). Gigantic herds of herbivores—reindeer, bison, mammoth, and horses—browsed, bred, and migrated throughout the tundra and the grasslands. An abundant animal life filled the forests.

Human migration northward into present-day Sweden, Finland, and Russia demanded a much more elaborate set of tools and provision for shelter and clothing than had previously been required. It necessitated the crossing of a number of ecological barriers and the occupation of previously avoided difficult environments. By the end of the Paleolithic period, humans had spread to all the continents but Antarctica, carrying with them their adaptive hunting-gathering cultures and social organizations. The settlement of the lands bordering the Pacific Ocean is suggested in

Figure 2.9 **Late Paleolithic environments of Europe.** During the late Paleolithic period, new food-gathering, shelter, and clothing strategies were developed to cope with harsh and changing environments, so different from those in Europe today.

Figure 2.10. As they occupied different regions, hunter-gatherers focused on a diversity of foodstuffs. Some specialized in marine or river resources, others were wholly dependent on land plants and animals. In all cases, their material culture reflected the different climate and vegetation regions they occupied, the tools they developed to exploit the resources on which they depended, and the housing and clothing solutions they differently adopted. Even today, African Bushmen have few cultural similarities with Inuit (Eskimo) hunting-fishing societies, though both culture groups are spoken of as "hunter-gatherers."

While spreading, the total population also increased. But hunting and foraging bands require considerable territory to support a relatively small number of individuals. There were contacts between groups and, apparently, even planned gatherings for trade, socializing, and selecting mates from outside the home group. Nevertheless, the bands tended to live in isolation. Estimates place the Paleolithic population of the entire island of

Great Britain, which was on the northern margin of habitation, at only some 400–500 persons living in widely separated families of 20–40 people. Total world population at about 9000 B.C. probably ranged from 5 to 10 million. Variations in the types of tools characteristic of different population groups steadily increased as people migrated and encountered new environmental problems.

Improved tool technology greatly extended the range of possibilities in the use of locally available materials. The result was more efficient and extensive exploitation of the physical environment than earlier had been possible. At the same time, regional contrasts in plant and animal life and in environmental conditions accelerated the differentiation of culture between isolated groups who under earlier, less varied conditions had shared common characteristics.

Within many environments, even harsh ones, the hunting and foraging process was not particularly demanding of either time or

Figure 2.10 **Settlement of the Americas and the Pacific basin.** Genetic studies suggest humans spread around the globe from their Old World origins beginning some 100,000 years ago. Their time of arrival in the Western Hemisphere, however, is uncertain. The older view claimed that earliest migrants to the Americas, the ancestors of modern Amerindian groups, crossed the Bering land bridge in three different waves beginning 11,500 years ago. Recent evidence suggests that those North Asian land migrants encountered (and conquered or absorbed) earlier occupants who had arrived from Europe, Polynesia, and coastal East Asia by boat traveling along frozen or open shorelines. Although genetic and linguistic research yields mixed conclusions, physical evidence considered solid by some investigators indicates that the first Asian arrivals came at least 22,000 years and more likely 30,000 or more years ago. Eastern United States artifacts that have been assigned dates of 17,000 to 30,000 years ago hint at European arrivals as early as those of coastal Asians; a South Carolina site found in 2004 has been dated at 50,000 years ago. Many researchers, however, caution that any New World population dates earlier than 18,000 years ago are questionable and that first migrants from that period probably were most closely related to prehistoric Jomon and later Ainu groups of Japan who crossed over the Bering land bridge.

energy. Recent studies of South African San people (Bushmen), for example, indicate that such bands survive well on the equivalent of a 2½-day workweek. Time was available for developing skills in working flint and bone for tools, in developing regionally distinctive art and sculpture, and in making decorative beads and shells for personal adornment and trade. By the end of the Ice Age (about 11,000 to 12,000 years ago), language, religion, long-distance trade, permanent settlements, and social stratification within groups appear to have been well developed in many European culture areas.

What was learned and created was transmitted within the cultural group. The increasing variety of adaptive strategies and technologies and the diversity of noneconomic creations in art, religion, language, and custom meant an inevitable cultural variation of humankind. That diversification began to replace the rough social uniformity among hunting and gathering people that had been based on their similar livelihood challenges, informal leadership structures, small-band kinship groups, and the like (Figure 2.11).

Seeds of Change

The retreat of the last glaciers marked the end of the Paleolithic era and the beginning of successive periods of cultural evolution leading from basic hunting and gathering economies at the outset

through the development of agriculture and animal husbandry to, ultimately, the urbanization and industrialization of modern societies and economies. Since not all cultures passed through all stages at the same time, or even at all, **cultural divergence** between human groups became evident.

Glacial recession brought new ecological conditions to which people had to adapt. The weather became warmer and forests began to appear on the open plains and tundras of Europe and northern China. In the Middle East, where much plant and animal domestication would later occur, savanna (grassland) vegetation replaced more arid landscapes. Populations grew and through hunting depleted the large herds of grazing animals already retiring northward with the retreating glacial front.

Further population growth demanded new food bases and production techniques, for the **carrying capacity**—the number of persons supportable within a given area by the technologies at their disposal—of the earth for hunter-gatherers is low. The *Mesolithic* (Middle Stone Age) period, from about 11,000 to 5000 B.C. in Europe, marked the transition from the collection of food to its production. These stages of the Stone Age—occurring during different time spans in different world areas—mark distinctive changes in tools, tasks, and social complexities of the cultures that experience the transition from "Old" to "Middle" to "New."

Figure 2.11 Hunter-gatherers practiced the most enduring lifestyle in human history, trading it for the more arduous life of farmers under the necessity to provide larger quantities of less diversified foodstuffs for a growing population. For hunter-gatherers (unlike their settled farmer rivals and successors), age and sex differences, not caste or economic status, were and are the primary basis for the division of labor and of interpersonal relations. Here a San (Bushman) hunter of Botswana, Africa, stalks his prey. Men also help collect the gathered food that constitutes 80% of the San diet.

Agricultural Origins and Spread

The population of hunter-gatherers rose slowly at the end of the glacial period. As rapid climatic fluctuation adversely affected their established plant and animal food sources, people independently in more than one world area experimented with the *domestication* of plants and animals. There is no agreement on whether the domestication of animals preceded or followed that of plants. The sequence may well have been different in different areas. What appears certain is that animal domestication—the successful breeding of species that are dependent on human beings—began during the Mesolithic, not as a conscious economic effort by humans but as outgrowths of the keeping of small or young wild animals as pets and the attraction of scavenger animals to the refuse of human settlements. The assignment of religious significance to certain animals and the docility of others to herding by hunters all strengthened the human-animal connections that ultimately led to full domestication.

Radiocarbon dates suggest the domestication of pigs in southeastern Turkey and of goats in the Near East as early as 8000–8400 B.C., of sheep in Turkey by about 7500 B.C., and of cattle and pigs in both Greece and the Near East about 7000 B.C. North Africa, India, and southeastern Asia were other Old World domestication sources, as were—less successfully—Meso-America and the Andean Uplands. Although there is evidence that the concept of animal domestication diffused from limited source regions, once its advantages were learned, numerous additional domestications were accomplished elsewhere. The widespread natural occurrence of species able to be domesticated made that certain. Cattle of different varieties, for example, were domesticated in India, north-central Eurasia, Southeast Asia, and Africa. Pigs and various domestic fowl are other examples.

The domestication of plants, like that of animals, appears to have occurred independently in more than one world region over a time span of between 10,000 and perhaps as long as 20,000 years ago. A strong case can be made that most widespread Eurasian food crops were first cultivated in the Near East beginning some 12,000 years ago and dispersed rapidly from there across the mid-latitudes of the Old World. However, clear evidence also exists that African peoples were raising crops of wheat, barley, dates, lentils, and chickpeas on the floodplains of the Nile River as early as 18,500 years ago. In other world regions, farming began more recently; the first true farmers in the Americas appeared in Mexico no more than 5000 years ago.

Familiarity with plants of desirable characteristics is universal among hunter-gatherers. In those societies, females were assigned the primary food-gathering role and thus developed the greatest familiarity with nutritive plants. Their fundamental role in initiating crop production to replace less reliable food gathering seems certain. Indeed, women's major contributions as innovators of technology—in food preparation and clothing production, for example—or as inventors of such useful and important items as baskets and other containers, baby slings, yokes for carrying burdens, and the like are unquestioned.

Agriculture itself, however, seems most likely to have been not an "invention" but the logical extension to food species of plant selection and nurturing habits developed for nonfood varieties. Plant poisons applied to hunting arrows or spread on lakes or

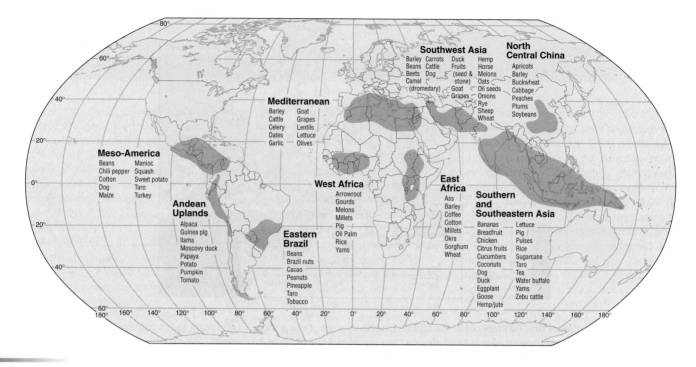

Figure 2.12 Chief centers of plant and animal domestication. The Southern and Southeastern Asia center was characterized by the domestication of plants such as taro, which are propagated by the division and replanting of existing plants (vegetative reproduction). Reproduction by the planting of seeds (e.g., maize and wheat) was more characteristic of Meso-America and Southwest Asia. The African and Andean areas developed crops reproduced by both methods. The lists of crops and livestock are selective, not exhaustive.

streams to stun fish made food gathering easier and more certain. Plant dyes and pigments were universally collected or prepared for personal adornment or article decoration. Medicinal and mood-altering plants and derivatives were known, gathered, protected, and cultivated by all early cultures. Indeed, persuasive evidence exists to suggest that early gathering and cultivation of grains was not for grinding and baking as bread but for brewing as beer, a beverage that became so important in some cultures for religious and nutritional reasons that it may well have been a first and continuing reason for sedentary agricultural activities.

Nevertheless, full-scale domestication of food plants, like that of animals, can be traced to a limited number of origin areas identified by geographer Carl Sauer and other scientists (Figure 2.12). Although there were several source regions, certain uniformities united them. In each, domestication focused on plant species selected apparently for their capability of providing large quantities of storable calories or protein. In each, there was a population already well fed and able to devote time to the selection, propagation, and improvement of plants available from a diversified vegetation. Some speculate, however, that grain domestication in the Near East may have been a forced inventive response, starting some 13,000 years ago, to food shortages reflecting abrupt increases in summertime temperatures and aridity in the Jordan Valley. That environmental stress—reducing summer food supplies and destroying habitats of wild game—favored selection and cultivation of short-season annual grains and legumes whose seeds could be stored and planted during cooler, wetter winter growing seasons.

In the tropics and humid subtropics, selected plants were apt to be those that reproduced vegetatively—from roots, tubers, or cuttings. Outside of those regions, wild plants reproducing from seeds were more common and the objects of domestication. Although there was some duplication, each of the origin areas developed crop complexes characteristic of itself alone, as Figure 2.12 summarizes. From each, there was dispersion of crop plants to other areas, slowly at first under primitive systems of population movement and communication (Figure 2.13), more rapidly and extensively with the onset of European exploration and colonization after A.D. 1500.

While adapting wild plant stock to agricultural purposes, the human cultivators, too, adapted. They assumed sedentary residence to protect the planted areas from animal, insect, and human predators. They developed labor specializations and created more formalized and expansive religious structures in which fertility and harvest rites became important elements. The regional contrasts between hunter-gatherer and sedentary agricultural societies increased. Where the two groups came in contact, farmers were the victors and hunter-gatherers the losers in competition for territorial control.

The contest continued into modern times. During the past 500 years, European expansion totally dominated the hunting and gathering cultures it encountered in large parts of the world such as North America and Australia (See "Is Geography Destiny?"). Even today, in the rain forests of central Africa, Bantu farmers put continuing pressure on hunting and gathering Pygmies, and in southern Africa, Hottentot herders and Bantu farmers constantly space differences in cultures sharing them), they must be regarded as evidence of parallel creations based on similar ecologies. From similar origins, but through separate adaptations and innovations, distinctive cultures emerged.

Diffusionism is the belief that cultural similarities occur primarily—perhaps even solely—by spatial spread (diffusion) from one or, at most, a very few common origin sites. Cultural advancement and civilizations, that is, are passed on along trade routes and through group contact rather than being the result of separate and independent creation. Although long out of favor, diffusionism has recently received renewed support from archaeological discoveries apparently documenting very long-distance transfer of ideas, technologies, and language by migrating peoples.

In any event, the common characteristics deriving from multilinear evolution and the spread of specific culture traits and complexes contained the roots of **cultural convergence.** That term describes the sharing of technologies, organizational structures, and even cultural traits and artifacts that is so evident among widely separated societies in a modern world united by instantaneous communication and efficient transportation. Convergence in those worldwide terms is, for many observers, proof of the pervasive globalization of culture.

The Structure of Culture

Understanding a culture fully is, perhaps, impossible for one who is not part of it. For analytical purposes, however, the traits and complexes of culture—its building blocks and expressions—may be grouped and examined as subsets of the whole. The anthropologist Leslie White (1900–1975) suggested that for analytical purposes, a culture could be viewed as a three-part structure composed of subsystems that he termed *ideological, technological,* and *sociological.* In a separate but similar classification, three interrelated components of culture have been identified: *mentifacts, artifacts,* and *sociofacts.* Together, according to these interpretations, the subsystems—identified by their separate components—comprise the system of culture as a whole. But they are integrated; each reacts on the others and is affected by them in turn.

The **ideological subsystem** consists of ideas, beliefs, and knowledge of a culture and of the ways in which these things are expressed in speech or other forms of communication. Mythologies and theologies, legend, literature, philosophy, and folk wisdom make up this category. Passed on from generation to generation, these abstract belief systems, or **mentifacts,** tell us what we ought to believe, what we should value, and how we ought to act. Beliefs form the basis of the socialization process. Often we know—or think we know—what the beliefs of a group are from their oral or written statements. Sometimes, however, we must depend on the actions or objectives of a group to tell us what its true ideas and values are. "Actions speak louder than words" or "Do as I say, not as I do" are commonplace recognitions of the fact that actions, values, and words do not always coincide. Two basic strands of the ideological subsystem—language and religion—are the subject of Chapter 5.

The **technological subsystem** is composed of the material objects, together with the techniques of their use, by means of which people are able to live. The objects are the tools and other instruments that enable us to feed, clothe, house, defend, transport, and amuse ourselves. We must have food, we must be protected from the elements, and we must be able to defend ourselves. Huxley termed the material objects we use to fill these basic needs **artifacts** (Figure 2.17). In Chapter 10 we

(a)

(b)

Figure 2.17 **Artifacts are an important component of culture.** (*a*) This Chinese farmer plowing with an ox uses artifacts (tools) typical of the lower technological levels of subsistence agriculture. (*b*) Cultures with advanced technological subsystems use complex machinery to harness inanimate energy for productive use.

will examine the relationship between technological subsystems and regional patterns of economic development.

The **sociological subsystem** of a culture is the sum of those expected and accepted patterns of interpersonal relations that find their outlet in economic, political, military, religious, kinship, and other associations. These **sociofacts** define the social organization of a culture. They regulate how the individual functions relative to the group—whether it be family, church, or state. There are no "givens" as far as the patterns of interaction in any of these associations are concerned, except that most cultures possess a variety of formal and informal ways of structuring behavior. Differing patterns of behavior are learned and are transmitted from one generation to the next (Figure 2.18).

Classifications are of necessity arbitrary, and these classifications of the subsystems and components of culture are no exception. The three-part categorization of culture, while helping us to appreciate its structure and complexity, can simultaneously obscure the many-sided nature of individual elements of culture. A dwelling, for example, is an artifact providing shelter for its occupants. It is, simultaneously, a sociofact reflecting the nature of the family or kinship group it is designed to house, and a mentifact summarizing a culture group's convictions about appropriate design, orientation, and building materials of dwelling units. In the same vein, clothing serves as an artifact of bodily protection appropriate to climatic conditions, available materials and techniques, or the activity in which the wearer is engaged. But garments also may be sociofacts, identifying an individual's role in the social structure of the community or culture, and mentifacts, evoking larger community value systems (Figure 2.19).

Nothing in a culture stands totally alone. Changes in the ideas that a society holds may affect the sociological and technological systems just as changes in technology force adjustments in the social system. The abrupt alteration of the ideological structure of Russia following the 1917 communist revolution from a monarchical, agrarian, capitalistic system to an industrialized, communistic society involved sudden, interrelated alteration of all facets of that country's culture system. The equally abrupt disintegration of Russian communism in the early 1990s was similarly disruptive of all its established economic, social, and administrative structures. The interlocking nature of all aspects of a culture is termed **cultural integration.**

Figure 2.18 All societies prepare their children for membership in the culture group. In each of these settings, certain values, beliefs, skills, and proper ways of acting are being transmitted to the youngsters.

(a)

Figure 2.19 (*a*) When clothing serves primarily to cover, protect, or assist in activities, it is an *artifact*. (*b*) Some garments are *sociofacts*, identifying a role or position within the social structure: the distinctive "uniforms" of the soldier, the cleric, or the beribboned ambassador immediately proclaim their respective roles in a culture's social organizations. (*c*) The sometimes mandatory burkas or chadors worn by Muslim women are *mentifacts*, indicative not specifically of the role of the wearer but of the values of the culture the wearer represents.

(b)

(c)

Culture Change

The recurring theme of cultural geography is change. No culture is, or has been, characterized by a permanently fixed set of material objects, systems of organization, or even ideologies. Admittedly, all of these may be long-enduring within a stable, isolated society at equilibrium with its resource base. Such isolation and stability have always been rare. On the whole, while cultures are essentially conservative, they are always in a state of flux. Some changes are major and pervasive. The transition from hunter-gatherer to sedentary farmer, as we have seen, affected markedly every facet of the cultures experiencing that change. Profound, too, has been the impact of the Industrial Revolution and its associated urbanization on all societies it has touched.

Not all change is so extensive as that following the introduction of agriculture or the Industrial Revolution. Many changes are so slight individually as to go almost unnoticed at their inception, though cumulatively they may substantially alter the affected culture. Think of how the culture of the United States differs today from what you know it to have been in 1940—not in essentials, perhaps, but in the innumerable electrical, electronic, and transportational devices that have been introduced and in the social, behavioral, and recreational changes they and other technological changes have wrought. Among these latter have been shifts in employment patterns to include greater participation by women in the waged workforce and associated adjustments in attitudes toward the role of women in the society at large. Such cumulative changes occur because the cultural traits of any group are not independent; they are clustered in a coherent and integrated pattern. Change on a small scale will have wide repercussions as associated traits arrive at accommodation with the adopted adjustment. Change, both major and minor, within cultures is induced by *innovation, diffusion,* and *acculturation.*

Innovation

Innovation implies changes to a culture that result from ideas created within the social group itself and adopted by the culture. The novelty may be an invented improvement in material technology, like the bow and arrow or the jet engine. It may involve the development of nonmaterial forms of social structure and interaction: feudalism, for example, or Christianity.

Many innovations are of little consequence by themselves, but sometimes the widespread adoption of seemingly inconsequential innovations may bring about large changes when viewed over a period of time. A new musical style such as hip-hop "adopted" by a few people may spread to others and bring with it changes to vernacular speech, clothing styles, dance styles, and other forms of entertainment, which, in turn, which may affect retailers' advertising campaigns and consumers' spending. Eventually, a new cultural form will be identified that may have an important impact on the thinking processes of the adopters and on those who come into contact with the adopters. Notice that a broad definition of innovation is used, but notice also that what is important is whether or not innovations are accepted and adopted.

Premodern and traditional societies characteristically are not innovative. In societies at equilibrium with their environment and with no unmet needs, change has no adaptive value and no reason to occur. Indeed, all societies have an innate resistance to change since

innovation inevitably creates tensions between the new reality and other established socioeconomic conditions. Those tensions can be solved only by adaptive changes elsewhere in the total system. The gap that may develop between, for example, a newly adopted technology and other, slower-paced social traits has been called *cultural lag.* Complaints about youthful fads or the glorification of times past are familiar examples of reluctance to accept or adjust to change.

Innovation—invention—frequently under stress, has marked the history of humankind. As we have seen, growing populations at the end of the Ice Age necessitated an expanded food base. In response, domestication of plants and animals appears to have occurred independently in more than one world area. Indeed, a most striking fact about early agriculture is the universality of its development or adoption within a very short span of human history. In 10,000 B.C., the world population of no more than 10 million was exclusively hunter-gatherers. By A.D. 1500, only 1% of the world's 350 million people still followed that way of life. The revolution in food production affected every facet of the threefold subsystems of culture of every society accepting it. All innovation has a radiating impact on the web of culture; the more basic the innovation, the more pervasive its consequences.

In most modern societies, innovative change has become common, expected, and inevitable. The rate of invention, at least as measured by the number of patents granted, has steadily increased, and the period between idea conception and product availability has been decreasing. A general axiom is that the more ideas available and the more minds able to exploit and combine them, the greater the rate of innovation. The spatial implication is that larger urban centers of advanced technologies tend to be centers of innovation. This is not just because of their size but because of the number of ideas interchanged. Indeed, ideas not only stimulate new thoughts and viewpoints but also create circumstances in which the society must develop new solutions to maintain its forward momentum (Figure 2.20).

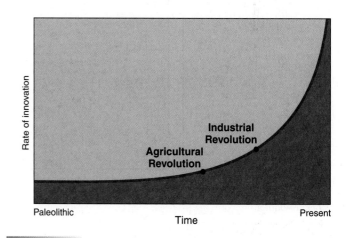

Figure 2.20 The trend of innovation through human history.
Hunter-gatherers, living in equilibrium with their environment and their resource base during the Paleolithic period had little need for innovation and no necessity for cultural change. The Agricultural Revolution accelerated the diffusion of the ideas and techniques of domestication, urbanization, and trade. With the Industrial Revolution, dramatic increases in all aspects of socioeconomic innovation began to alter cultures throughout the world.

Diffusion

Diffusion is the process by which an idea or innovation is transmitted from one individual or group to another across space. Diffusion may assume a variety of forms, each different in its impact on social groups. Basically, however, two processes are involved: (1) People move, for any of a number of reasons, to a new area and take their culture with them. For example, immigrants to the American colonies brought along crops and farming techniques, building styles, or concepts of government alien to their new home. (2) Information about an innovation (e.g., hybrid corn or compact discs) may spread throughout a society, perhaps aided by local or mass media advertising; or new adopters of an ideology or way of life—for example, a new religious creed—may be inspired or recruited by immigrant or native converts. The former is known as *relocation diffusion,* the latter as *expansion diffusion* (Figure 2.21).

Expansion diffusion involves the spread of an item or idea from one place to others. In the process, the thing diffused also remains—and is frequently intensified—in the origin area. Islam, for example, expanded from its Arabian Peninsula origin locale across much of Asia and North Africa. At the same time, it strengthened its hold over its Near Eastern birthplace by displacing pagan, Christian, and Jewish populations. When expansion diffusion affects nearly uniformly all individuals and areas outward from the source region, it is termed *contagious diffusion.* The term implies the importance of direct contact between those who developed or have adopted the innovation and those who newly encounter it, and is reminiscent of the course of infectious diseases (Figure 2.22).

If an idea has merit in the eyes of potential adopters and they themselves become adopters, the number of contacts of adopters with potential adopters will compound. Consequently, the innovation will spread slowly at first and then more and more rapidly until saturation occurs or a barrier is reached. The incidence of adoption under contagious diffusion is represented by the S-shaped curve in Figure 2.23. The rate of diffusion of a trait or idea may be influenced by *time-distance decay,* which simply tells us that the spread or acceptance of an idea is usually delayed as distance from the source of the innovation increases.

In some instances, however, geographic distance is less important in the transfer of ideas than is communication between major centers or important people. News of new clothing styles, for example, quickly spreads internationally between major cities and only later filters down irregularly to smaller towns and rural areas. The process of transferring ideas first between larger places

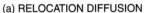

Figure 2.21 Patterns of diffusion. (*a*) In *relocation diffusion,* innovations or ideas are transported to new areas by carriers who permanently leave the home locale (see Figure 6.24). (*b*) In *expansion diffusion,* a phenomenon spreads from one place to neighboring locations, but in the process remains and is often intensified in the place of origin (see Figure 5.28).

Source: Redrawn by permission from Spatial Diffusion, *by Peter R. Gould, Resource Paper no. 4, page 4, Association of American Geographers, 1969.*

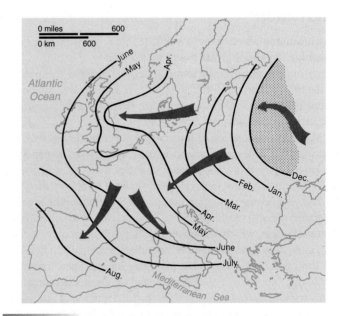

Figure 2.22 The process of *contagious diffusion* is sensitive to both time and distance, as suggested by the diffusion pathways of the European influenza pandemic of 1781. The pattern there was a wavelike radiation from a Russian nodal origin area.

Source: Based on Gerald F. Pyle and K. David Patterson, Ecology of Disease 2, *no. 3 (1984): 179.*

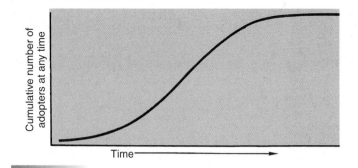

Figure 2.23 **The diffusion of innovations over time.** The number of adopters of an innovation rises at an increasing rate until the point at which about one-half of the total who ultimately decide to adopt the innovation have made the decision. At that point, the number of adopters increases at a decreasing rate.

or prominent people and only later to smaller or less important points or people is known as *hierarchical diffusion.* The Christian faith in Europe, for example, spread from Rome as the principal center to provincial capitals and thence to smaller Roman settlements in largely pagan occupied territories (see Figure 5.22). Today, new discoveries are shared among scientists at leading universities before they appear in textbooks or become general knowledge through the public press. The process works because, for many things, distance is relative to the communication network involved. Big cities or leading scientists, connected by strong information flows, are "closer" than their simple distance separation suggests.

While the diffusion of ideas may be slowed by time-distance decay, their speed of spread may be increased to the point of becoming instantaneous through the *space-time compression* made possible by modern communication. Given access to radios; telephones; worldwide transmission of television news, sports, and entertainment programs; and—perhaps most importantly—to computers and the Internet, people and areas distantly separated can immediately share in a common fund of thought and innovation. Modern communication technology, that is, has encouraged and facilitated the globalization of culture.

Stimulus diffusion is a third form of expansion diffusion. The term summarizes situations in which a fundamental idea, though not the specific trait itself, stimulates imitative behavior within a receptive population. A documented case in point involves the spread of the concept but not of a specific system of writing from European American settlers to at least one Native American culture group. Observing that white people could make marks on pieces of paper to record agreements and repeat lengthy speeches, Sequoyah, a Cherokee who could neither read nor write any language, around 1820 devised a system for writing the Cherokee language, eventually refining his initially complex pictorial system to a set of 86 syllabic signs. With time, literacy in the new system spread to others and *The Cherokee Phoenix,* a Cherokee language newspaper, was established in 1828. There was no transfer between cultures or groups of a specific technique of writing, but there was

a clear-cut case of the *idea* of writing diffusing by stimulating imitative behavior.

In **relocation diffusion,** the innovation or idea is physically carried to new areas by migrating individuals or populations that possess it (Figure 2.21a). Mentifacts or artifacts are therefore introduced into new locales by new settlers who become part of populations not themselves associated or in contact with the origin area of the innovation. The spread of religions by settlers or conquerors is a clear example of relocation diffusion, as was the diffusion of agriculture to Europe from the Middle East (Figure 2.13). Christian Europeans brought their faiths to areas of colonization or economic penetration throughout the world. At the world scale, massive relocation diffusion resulted from the European colonization and economic penetration that began in the 16th century. More localized relocation diffusion continues today as Asian refugees or foreign "guest workers" bring their cultural traits to their new areas of settlement in Europe or North America.

For either expansion or relocation diffusion, innovations in the technological or ideological subsystems may be relatively readily diffused to, and accepted by, cultures that have basic similarities and compatibilities. Continental Europe and North America, for example, could easily and quickly adopt the innovations of the Industrial Revolution diffused from England with which they shared a common economic and technological background. Industrialization was not quickly accepted in Asian and African societies of totally different cultural conditioning. On the ideological level, too, successful diffusion depends on acceptability of the innovations. The Shah of Iran's attempt at rapid westernization of traditional Iranian, Islamic culture after World War II provoked a traditionalist backlash and revolution that deposed the Shah and reestablished clerical control of the state.

The conclusion must be, therefore, that diffusion cannot be viewed solely as the outcome of knowledge dispersed. The acceptance of new traits, articles, or ways of doing or thinking by a potential receiving population depends not just on information flow to that population but also upon its entire cultural and economic structure. Innovation may be rejected not because of lack of knowledge but because the new trait violates the established cultural norms of the culture to which it is introduced. For example, cash crop specialization recommended to a peasant agricultural society may be rejected not because it is not understood, but because it unacceptably disrupts the knowledge base and culture complex devoted to assured food security in a subsistence farming economy. Similarly, less disruptive new production ideas—chemical fertilizers, deep-well irrigation, hybrid seeds, and the like—may be rejected simply because, though understood, they are not affordable. Culture is a complex organized system and culture change involves alteration of the system's established structure in ways that may be rejected even after knowledge of an innovation is received and understood.

It is not always possible, of course, to determine the precise point of origin or the routes of diffusion of innovations now widely adopted (see "Documenting Diffusion"). Nor is it always certain whether the existence of a cultural trait in two different areas is the result of diffusion or of **independent** (or *parallel*) **invention.** Cultural similarities do not necessarily prove that diffusion

The places of origin of many ideas, items, and technologies important in contemporary cultures are only dimly known or supposed, and their routes of diffusion are speculative at best. Gunpowder, printing, and spaghetti are presumed to be the products of Chinese inventiveness; the lateen sail has been traced to the Near Eastern culture world. The moldboard plow is ascribed to 6th-century Slavs of northeastern Europe. The sequence and routes of the diffusion of these innovations has not been documented.

In other cases, such documentation exists, and the process of diffusion is open to analysis. Clearly marked is the diffusion path of the custom of smoking tobacco, a practice that originated among Amerindians. Sir Walter Raleigh's Virginia colonists, returning home in 1586, introduced smoking in English court circles, and the habit very quickly spread among the general populace. England became the source region of the new custom for northern Europe; smoking was introduced to Holland by English medical students in 1590. Dutch and English together spread the habit by sea to the Baltic and Scandinavian areas and overland through Germany to Russia. The innovation continued its eastward diffusion, and within a hundred years tobacco had spread across Siberia and was, in the 1740s, reintroduced to the American continent at

Wal-Mart Diffusion to 1990

Source: Map based on data from Thomas O. Graff and Dub Ashton, "Spatial Diffusion of Wal-Mart: Contagious and Reverse Hierarchical Elements." Professional Geographer 46, no. 1 (1994): 19–29.

Alaska by Russian fur traders. A second route of diffusion for tobacco smoking can be traced from Spain, where the custom was introduced in 1558, and from which it spread more slowly through the Mediterranean area into Africa, the Near East, and Southeast Asia.

In more recent times, hybrid corn was first adopted by imaginative farmers of northern Illinois and eastern Iowa in the mid-1930s. By the late 1930s and early 1940s, the new seeds were being planted as far east as Ohio and north to Minnesota, Wisconsin, and northern Michigan. By the late 1940s, all commercial

corn-growing districts of the United States and southern Canada were cultivating hybrid corn varieties.

A similar pattern of diffusion marked the expansion of the Wal-Mart stores chain. From its origin in northwest Arkansas in 1962, the discount chain had dispersed throughout the United States by the 1990s to become the country's largest retailer in sales volume. In its expansion, Wal-Mart displayed a "reverse hierarchical" diffusion, initially spreading by being price-competitive with small town merchants before opening its first stores in larger cities and metropolitan areas (see map).

---

has occurred. The pyramids of Egypt and of the Central American Maya civilization most likely were separately conceived and are not necessarily evidence, as some have proposed, of pre-Columbian voyages from the Mediterranean to the Americas. A Neolithic monument-building culture, after all, has only a limited number of shapes from which to choose.

Historical examples of independent, parallel invention are numerous: logarithms by Napier (1614) and Burgi (1620), the calculus by Newton (1672) and Leibnitz (1675), the telephone by Elisha Gray and Alexander Graham Bell (1876) are commonly cited. It appears beyond doubt that agriculture was independently developed not only in both the New World and the Old but also in more than one culture hearth in each of the hemispheres.

Acculturation and Cultural Modification

A culture group may undergo major modifications in its own identifying traits by adopting some or all of the characteristics of another, dominant culture group. Such is the case in

acculturation—discussed at greater length in Chapter 6 (p. 164)—as immigrant populations take on the values, attitudes, customs, and speech of the receiving society, which itself undergoes change from absorption of the arriving group. A different form of contact and subsequent cultural alteration may occur in a conquered or colonized region where the subordinate or subject population is either forced to adopt the culture of the new ruling group, introduced through relocation diffusion, or does so voluntarily, overwhelmed by the superiority in numbers or the technical level of the conqueror. Tribal Europeans in areas of Roman conquest, native populations in the wake of Slavic occupation of Siberia, and Native Americans stripped of their lands following European settlement of North America experienced this kind of cultural modification or adoption.

In extreme cases, of course, small and, particularly, primitive indigenous groups brought into contact with conquering or absorbing societies may simply cease to exist as separate cultural entities. Although presumably such cultural loss has been part of all of human history, its occurrence has been noted and its pace

Figure 2.24 Baseball, an import from America, is one of the most popular sports in Japan, attracting millions of spectators annually.

quickened over the past 500 years. By one informed estimate, at least one-third of the world's inventory of human cultures has totally disappeared since A.D. 1500, along with their languages, traditions, ways of life, and, indeed, with their very identity or remembrance.

In many instances, close contact between two different groups may involve adjustments of the original cultural patterns of both rather than disappearance of either. For example, changes in Japanese political organization and philosophy were imposed by occupying Americans after World War II, and the Japanese voluntarily adopted some more frivolous aspects of American life (Figure 2.24). In turn, American society was enriched by the selective importation of Japanese cuisine, architecture, and philosophy, demonstrating the two-way nature of cultural diffusion. Where that two-way flow reflects a more equal exchange of cultural outlooks and ways of life, a process of *transculturation* has occurred. That process is observable within the United States as massive South and Central American immigration begins to intertwine formerly contrasting cultures, altering both.

Contact between Regions

All cultures are amalgams of innumerable innovations spread spatially from their points of origin and integrated into the structure of the receiving societies. It has been estimated that

no more than 10% of the cultural items of any society are traceable to innovations created by its members and that the other 90% come to the society through diffusion (see "A Homemade Culture"). Since, as we have seen, the pace of innovation is affected strongly by the mixing of ideas among alert, responsive people and is increased by exposure to a variety of cultures, the most active and innovative historical hearths of culture were those at crossroads locations and those deeply involved in distant trade and colonization. Ancient Mesopotamia and classical Greece and Rome had such locations and involvements, as did the West African culture hearth after the 5th century and, much later, England during the Industrial Revolution and the spread of its empire.

Recent changes in technology permit us to travel farther than ever before, with greater safety and speed, and to communicate without physical contact more easily and completely than was previously possible. This intensification of contact has resulted in an acceleration of innovation and in the rapid spread of goods and ideas. Several millennia ago, innovations such as smelting of metals took hundreds of years to diffuse. Today, worldwide diffusion—through Internet interest groups, for example—may be almost instantaneous.

Obstacles do exist, of course. **Diffusion barriers** are any conditions that hinder either the flow of information or the movement of people and thus retard or prevent the acceptance of an innovation. Because of the *friction of distance,* generally the farther two areas are from each other, the less likely is interaction

A Homemade Culture

Reflecting on an average morning in the life of a "100% American," Ralph Linton noted:

Our solid American citizen awakens in a bed built on a pattern which originated in the Near East but which was modified in Northern Europe before it was transmitted to America. He throws back covers made from cotton, domesticated in India, or linen, domesticated in the Near East, or wool from sheep, also domesticated in the Near East, or silk, the use of which was discovered in China. All of these materials have been spun and woven by processes invented in the Near East. . . . He takes off his pajamas, a garment invented in India, and washes with soap invented by the ancient Gauls. . . .

Returning to the bedroom, . . . he puts on garments whose form originally derived from the skin clothing of the nomads of the Asiatic steppes [and] puts on shoes made from skins tanned by a process invented in ancient Egypt and cut to a pattern derived from the classical civilizations of the Mediterranean. . . . Before going out for breakfast he glances through the window, made of glass invented in Egypt, and if it is raining puts on overshoes made of rubber discovered by the Central American Indians and takes an umbrella invented in southeastern Asia. . . .

[At breakfast] a whole new series of borrowed elements confronts him. His plate is made of a form of pottery invented in China. His knife is of steel, an alloy first made in southern India, his fork a medieval Italian invention, and his spoon a derivative of a Roman original. He begins breakfast with an orange, from the eastern Mediterranean, a cantaloupe from Persia, or perhaps a piece of African watermelon. With this he has coffee, an Abyssinian plant. . . . [H]e may have the egg of a species of bird domesticated in Indo-China, or thin strips of flesh of an animal domesticated in Eastern Asia which have been salted and smoked by a process developed in northern Europe.

When our friend has finished eating . . . he reads the news of the day, imprinted in characters invented by the ancient Semites upon a material invented in China by a process invented in Germany. As he absorbs the accounts of foreign troubles he will, if he is a good conservative citizen, thank a Hebrew deity in an Indo-European language that he is 100% American.

Source: Ralph Linton, *The Study of Man: An Introduction.* © 1936, renewed 1964, pp. 326–327. Reprinted by permission of Prentice Hall, Inc., Upper Saddle River, N.J.

to occur, an observation earlier (p. 51) summarized by the term *time-distance decay.* Distance as a factor in spatial interaction is further explored in Chapter 3. For now it is sufficient to note that distance may be an *absorbing barrier,* halting the spread of an innovation.

Interregional contact can also be hindered by the physical environment and by a lack of receptivity by a contacted culture. Oceans and rugged terrain can and have acted as physical *interrupting barriers,* delaying or deflecting the path of diffusion. Cultural obstacles that are equally impenetrable may also exist. Should reluctant adopters or nonadopters of innovations intervene between hearths and receptive cultures, the spread of an innovation can be slowed. It can also be delayed when cultural contact is overtly impeded by governments that interfere with radio reception, control the flow of foreign literature, and discourage contact between their citizens and foreign nationals.

More commonly, barriers are at least partially *permeable;* they permit passage (acceptance) of at least some innovations encountering them. The more similar two cultural areas are to each other, the greater is the likelihood of the adoption of an innovation, for diffusion is a selective process. The receiver culture may adopt some goods or ideas from the donor society and reject others. The decision to adopt is governed by the receiving group's own culture.

Political restrictions, religious taboos, and other social customs are cultural barriers to diffusion. The French Canadians, although close geographically to many Anglo-Canadian centers of diffusion such as Ottawa and Toronto, strive to be only minimally influenced by them. Both their language and culture complex govern their selective acceptance of Anglo influences, and restrictive French-only language regulations are enforced to preserve the integrity of their distinctive French culture. In a more extreme fashion, Afghan Taliban and other Mideast militant fundamentalist groups adamantly or violently reject Western socio-cultural values, seeking to preserve their religious and cultural purity through isolation from secular, non-Islamic influences. Traditional groups, perhaps controlled by firm religious conviction, may very largely reject culture traits and technologies of the larger society in whose midst they live (see Figure 7.2).

Adopting cultures do not usually accept intact items originating outside the receiving society. Diffused ideas and artifacts commonly undergo some alteration of meaning or form that makes them acceptable to a borrowing group. The process of the fusion of the old and new is called **syncretism** and is a major feature of culture change. It can be seen in alterations to religious ritual and dogma made by convert societies seeking acceptable conformity between old and new beliefs. For example, slaves brought voodoo from West Africa to the Americas where it thrived in Haiti and Louisiana. Over the years it absorbed influences from French and Spanish Catholicism, American Indian spiritual practices, and even Masonic tradition. Despite those adaptive mixings, many believers consider themselves to be Catholics and see no contradiction between Christianity and their faith in protective spirits and other tenets of voodoo. On a more familiar level, syncretism is reflected in subtle or blatant alterations of imported cuisines to make them conform to the demands of America's palate and its fast-food franchises (Figure 2.25).

Figure 2.25 Foreign foods modified for American tastes and American palates growing accustomed to dishes from all cultures together represent *syncretism* in action.

Summary

The web of culture is composed of many strands. Together, culture traits and complexes in their spatial patterns create human landscapes, define culture regions, and distinguish culture groups. Those landscapes, regions, and group characteristics change through time as human societies interact with their environment, develop for themselves new solutions to collective needs, or are altered through innovations adopted from outside the group itself. The cultural similarity of a preagricultural world composed solely of hunter-gatherers was lost as domestication of plants and animals in many world areas led to the emergence of culture hearths of wide-ranging innovation and to a cultural divergence between farmers and gatherers. Innovations spread outward from their origin points, carried by migrants through relocation diffusion or adopted by others through a variety of expansion diffusion and acculturation processes. Although diffusion barriers exist, most successful or advantageous innovations find adopters, and both cultural modification and cultural convergence

of different societies result. The details of the technological, sociological, and ideological subsystems of culture define the differences that still exist between world areas.

The ivory hunters who opened our chapter showed how varied and complex the culture of even a primitive group can be. Their artifacts of clothing, fire making, hunting, and fishing displayed diversity and ingenuity. They were part of a structured kinship system and engaged in organized production and trade. Their artistic efforts and ritual burial customs speak of a sophisticated set of abstract beliefs and philosophies. Their culture complex did not develop in isolation; it reflected at least in part their contacts with other groups, even those far distant from their Paris Basin homeland. As have culture groups always and everywhere, the hunters carried on their own pursuits and interacted with others in spatial settings. They exhibited and benefitted from structured *spatial behavior,* the topic to which we next turn our attention.

KEY WORDS

acculturation 52	culture hearth 44	innovation 49
artifact 46	culture realm 33	mentifact 46
carrying capacity 39	culture region 33	multilinear evolution 45
cultural convergence 46	culture trait 32	possibilism 34
cultural divergence 39	diffusion 50	relocation diffusion 51
cultural ecology 34	diffusion barrier 53	sociofact 47
cultural integration 47	environmental determinism 34	sociological subsystem 47
cultural landscape 35	expansion diffusion 50	syncretism 54
cultural system 33	hunter-gatherer 37	technological subsystem 46
culture 31	ideological subsystem 46	
culture complex 33	independent invention 51	

FOR REVIEW

1. What is included in the concept of *culture?* How is culture transmitted? What personal characteristics affect the aspects of culture that any single individual acquires or fully masters?

2. What do we mean by *domestication?* When and where did the domestication of plants and animals occur? What impact on culture and population numbers did plant domestication have?

3. What is a *culture hearth?* What new traits of culture characterized the early hearths? Identify and locate some of the major culture hearths that emerged at the close of the Neolithic period.

4. What do we mean by *innovation?* By *diffusion?* What different patterns of diffusion can you describe? Discuss the role played by innovation and diffusion in altering the cultural structure in which you are a participant from that experienced by your great-grandparents.

5. Differentiate between *culture traits* and *culture complexes.* Between *environmental determinism* and *possibilism.*

6. What are the components or subsystems of the three-part system of culture? What characteristics are included in each of the subsystems?

 KEY CONCEPTS REVIEW

1. **What are the components of culture and nature of culture–environment interactions?** pp. 31–37.
   Culture traits and complexes may be grouped into culture regions and realms. Differing developmental levels color human perceptions of environmental opportunities. In general, as the active agents in the relationship, humans exert adverse impacts on the natural environment.

2. **How did cultures develop and diverge** (pp. 37–39), **and where did cultural advances originate?** pp. 39–46.
   From Paleolithic hunting and gathering to Neolithic farming and then to city civilizations, different groups made differently timed cultural transitions. All early cultural advances had their origins in a few areally distinct "hearths."

3. **What are the structures of culture and forms of culture change?** pp. 46–55.
   All cultures contain ideological, technological, and sociological components that work together to create cultural integration. Cultures change through innovations they themselves invent or that diffuse from other areas and are accepted or adapted.

SPATIAL INTERACTION
AND SPATIAL BEHAVIOR

The blurred lights of traffic on the Avenue des Champs Elysees in Paris, France, typify spatial interaction in contemporary society.

Key Concepts

*E*arly *in January of 1849 we first thought of migrating to California. It was a period of National hard times . . . and we longed to go to the new El Dorado and "pick up" gold enough with which to return and pay off our debts.*

Our discontent and restlessness were enhanced by the fact that my health was not good. . . . The physician advised an entire change of climate thus to avoid the intense cold of Iowa, and recommended a sea voyage, but finally approved of our contemplated trip across the plains in a "prairie schooner."

Full of the energy and enthusiasm of youth, the prospects of so hazardous an undertaking had no terror for us, indeed, as we had been married but a few months, it appealed to us as a romantic wedding tour.[1]

So begins Catherine Haun's account of their 9-month journey from Iowa to California, just two of the quarter-million people who traveled across the continent on the Overland Trail in one of the world's great migrations. The migrants faced months of grueling struggle over badly marked routes that crossed swollen rivers, deserts, and mountains. The weather was often foul, with hailstorms, drenching rains, and burning summer temperatures. Graves along the route were a silent testimony to the lives claimed by buffalo stampedes, Indian skirmishes, cholera epidemics, and other disasters.

What inducements were so great as to make emigrants leave behind all that was familiar and risk their lives on an uncertain venture? Catherine Haun alludes to economic hard times gripping the country and to their hope for riches to be found in California. Like other migrants, the Hauns were attracted by the climate in the West, which was said to be always sunny and free of disease. Finally, like most who undertook the perilous journey West, the Hauns were young, moved by restlessness, a sense of adventure, and a perception of greater opportunities in a new land. They, like their predecessors back to the beginnings of humankind, were acting in space and across space on the basis of acquired information and anticipation of opportunity—prepared to pay the price in time, money, and hardship costs of overcoming distance.

A fundamental question in human geography is: What considerations influence how individual human beings use space and act within it? Related queries include: Are there discernible controls on human spatial behavior? How does distance affect human interaction? How do our perceptions of places influence our spatial activities? How do we overcome the consequences of distance in the exchange of commodities and information? How are movement and migration decisions (like that of the Hauns) reached? How have new technologies enabled increased spatial interaction across great distances and contributed to globalization? These are questions addressing geography's concern with understanding spatial interaction.

Spatial interaction means the movement of peoples, ideas, and commodities (goods bought and sold) within and between areas. The Hauns were engaging in spatial interaction (Figure 3.1). International trade, the movement of semitrailers on the expressways, radio broadcasts, and business or personal telephone calls are more familiar examples. Such movements and exchanges are designed to achieve effective integration between different points

Figure 3.1 A public bus negotiates a washed-out section of highway on one of the major routes connecting the capital city of Kathmandu with southern Nepal and India. Movement in Nepal is more difficult than in developed countries because of the limited road network, narrow, winding mountain roads, and frequent landslides. A ride on a public bus in Nepal can be an adventure in sharing space with people, agricultural produce, and livestock.

of human activity. Movement of whatever nature satisfies some felt need or desire. It represents the attempt to smooth out the spatially differing availability of required resources, commodities, information, or opportunities. Whatever the particular purpose of a movement, there is inevitably some manner of trade-off balancing the benefit of the interaction with the costs that are incurred in overcoming spatial separation. Because commodity movements represent simple demonstrations of the principles underlying all spatial interactions, let us turn to them first.

Bases for Interaction

Neither the world's resources nor products are uniformly distributed. Commodity flows are responses to these differences; they are links between points of supply and locales of demand. Such response may not be immediate or even direct. Matters of awareness of supplies or markets, the presence or absence of transportation connections, costs of movement, ability to pay for things wanted and needed—all and more are factors in the structure of trade. Underlying even these, however, is a set of controlling principles governing spatial interaction.

A Summarizing Model

Geographer Edward Ullman (1912–1976) speculated on the essential conditions affecting such interactions and proposed an explanatory model. He observed that spatial interaction is effectively controlled by three flow-determining factors that he called *complementarity, transferability,* and *intervening opportunity.* Although Ullman's model deals with commodity flows, it has—as we shall see—applicability to information transfers and human movements as well.

Complementarity

For two places to interact, one place must have what another place wants and can secure. That is, one place must have a supply of

[1]From Catherine Haun, "A Woman's Trip across the Plains in 1849," in Lillian Schlissel, *Women's Diaries of the Westward Journey.* (New York: Schocken Books, 1982).

an item for which there is an effective demand in the other, as evidenced by desire for the item, purchasing power to acquire it, and means to transport it. The word describing this circumstance is **complementarity.** *Effective* supply and demand are important considerations; mere differences from place to place in commodity surplus or deficit are not enough to initiate exchange. Greenland and the Amazon basin are notably unlike in their natural resources and economies, but their amount of interaction is minimal. Supply and market must come together, as they do in the flow of seasonal fruits and vegetables from California's Imperial Valley to the urban markets of the American Midwest and East or in the movement of manganese from Ukraine to the steel mills of Western Europe. The massive movement of crude and refined petroleum clearly demonstrates complementarity in international trade (Figure 3.2). More generalized patterns of complementarity underlie the exchanges of the raw materials and agricultural goods of less developed countries for the money or industrial commodities of the developed states.

Transferability

Even when complementarity exists, spatial interaction occurs only when conditions of **transferability**—acceptable costs of an exchange—are met. Spatial movement responds not just to availability and demand but to considerations of time and cost. Transferability is an expression of the mobility of a commodity and is a function of three interrelated conditions: (1) the characteristics and value of the product; (2) the distance, measured in time and money penalties, over which it must be moved; and (3) the ability of the commodity to bear the costs of movement.

If the time and money costs of traversing a distance are too great, exchange does not occur. That is, mobility is not just a physical matter but an economic one as well. If a given commodity is not affordable upon delivery to an otherwise willing buyer, it will not move in trade, and the potential buyer must seek a substitute or go without.

Transferability is not a constant condition. It differs between places, over time, depending upon what is being transferred and how it is to be moved. In the 1820s, the newly opened Erie Canal cut shipping costs from Buffalo to New York City by 90%. More recently, containerized shipping has had a similar effect on the global shipments of goods. An increasing scarcity of high-quality ores will enhance the transferability of lower-quality mine outputs by increasing their value. Low-cost bulk commodities not economically moved by air may be fully transferable by rail or water. Poorly developed and costly transportation may inhibit exchanges even at short distance between otherwise willing traders. In short, transferability expresses the changing relationships between the costs of transportation and the value of the product to be shipped.

Intervening Opportunity

Complementarity can be effective only in the absence of more attractive alternative sources of supply or demand closer at hand or cheaper. **Intervening opportunities** serve to reduce supply/demand interactions that otherwise might develop between distant complementary areas. A supply of Saharan sand is not enough to assure its flow to sand-deficient Manhattan Island because supplies of sand are more easily and cheaply available within the New York metropolitan region. For reasons of cost and convenience, a purchaser is unlikely to buy identical commodities at a distance when

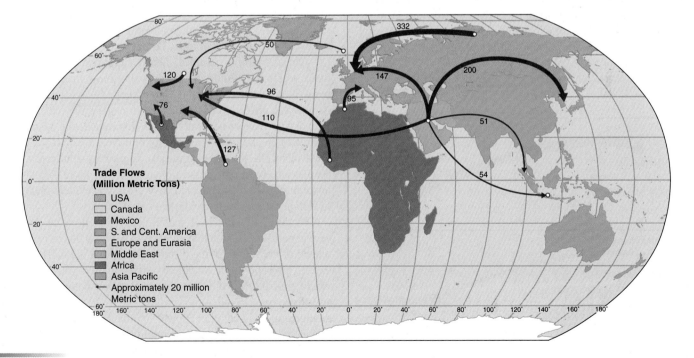

Figure 3.2 **Major international crude oil and other product exports flow, 2007.** Complementarity is so basic in initiating interaction that even relatively low-value bulk commodities such as coal, fertilizer, and grain move in trade over long distances. For many years, despite fluctuating prices, petroleum has been the most important commodity in international trade, moving long distances in response to effective supply and demand considerations.

Source: Adapted from The BP Amoco Statistical Review of World Energy, 2008.

a suitable nearby supply is available. When it is, the intervening opportunity demonstrates complementarity at a shorter distance.

Similarly, markets and destinations are sought, if possible, close at hand. Growing metropolitan demand in California reduces the importance of midwestern markets for western fruit growers. The intervening opportunities offered by Chicago or Philadelphia reduce the number of job seekers from Iowa searching for employment in New York City. People from New England are more likely to take winter vacations in Florida, which is relatively near and accessible, than in Southern California, which is not. That is, opportunities that are discerned closer at hand reduce the pull of opportunities offered by a distant destination (Figure 3.3). Patterns of spatial interaction are dynamic, reflecting the changeable structure of apparent opportunity.

Measuring Interaction

Complementarity, transferability, and intervening opportunity—the controlling conditions of commodity movement—help us understand all forms of spatial interaction, including choosing a restaurant, where to go to college, or where to buy a house, and the once-in-a-lifetime transcontinental adventure of the Hauns. The study of unique spatial interactions such as the discovery of an Inuit (Eskimo) carving in a Miami gift shop is interesting but does not establish general patterns. In this chapter we focus on general principles that govern the frequency and intensity of interaction both to validate the three preconditions of spatial exchange and to establish the probability that any given potential interaction will actually occur. Our interest is similar to that of the physical scientist investigating, for example, the response of a gas to variations in temperature and pressure. The concern there is with *all* of the gas molecules and the probability of their collective reactions; the action of any particular molecule is of little interest. Similarly, we are concerned here with the probability of aggregate, not individual, behavior.

Figure 3.3 (*a*) The volume of expected customers for a shopping mall based solely on their complementarity and distance apart, may be (*b*) reduced if a new mall opens as an intervening opportunity nearer to the customers.

That concern with aggregate behavior conceals or ignores a great deal of spatial interaction of vital importance both in the real world and in human geography. Most theoretical and observational studies of spatial interaction have focused on the standard normative spatial behavior of fully physically and economically capable Western-culture adults. That standard does not address the individual or collective spatial problems and actions of such others as children, the poor, the elderly, the handicapped, or socially disadvantaged individuals or groups, nor does it recognize the very real, though often subtle, differences between male and female spatial action responses and decisions. Our orientation to the North American culture realm means also that the aggregate spatial behavioral norms we discern there fail to recognize the many and varied sociocultural, economic, religious, legal, and similar constraints on spatial behavior operative in other culture areas of the world. Nevertheless, observational evidence suggests that the same basic influences on personal spatial behavior we recognize here have universal applicability despite their inevitable modification in different contexts.

Distance Decay

In all manner of ways, the lives and activities of people everywhere are influenced by the **friction of distance.** That phrase reminds us that distance has a retarding effect on human interaction because there are increasing penalties in time and cost associated with longer-distance, more expensive interchanges. We visit nearby friends more often than distant relatives; we go more frequently to the neighborhood convenience store cluster than to the farther regional shopping center. Telephone calls or mail deliveries between nearby towns are greater in volume than those to more distant locations. An informal study showed that college students living in dormitories near the cafeteria are more likely to use the cafeteria; students farther away do not visit the cafeteria as often.

Our common experience, clearly supported by maps and statistics tracing all kinds of flows, is that most interactions occur over short distances. That is, interchange decreases as distance increases, a reflection of the fact that transferability costs increase with distance. More generally stated, **distance decay** describes the decline of an activity or function with increasing distance from its point of origin. As the examples in Figure 3.4 demonstrate, near destinations have a disproportionate pull over more distant points in commodity movements. However, it is also evident that the rate of distance decay varies with the type of activity.

Study of all manner of spatial interconnections has led to the very general conclusion that interaction between places is inversely related to the square of the distance separating them. That is, volume of flow between two points 80 kilometers (50 miles) apart would probably be only one-quarter of that between centers at 40 kilometers (25 miles) separation. Such a rigid *inverse-square* relationship is well documented in the physical sciences. For social, cultural, and economic relations, however, it is at best a useful approximation. In human interaction, linear distance is only one aspect of transferability; cost and time are often more meaningful measures of separation.

When the friction of distance is reduced by lowered costs or increased ease of flow, the slope of the distance decay curve is flattened and more total area is effectively united than when those costs are high. When automobiles and expressways became widely available in the second half of the 20th century, U.S. cities underwent massive geographic expansion as the friction of distance was sharply reduced and large areas of rural land were brought within a reasonable commute time from the city. Figure 3.4 shows that distance decay is evident for both truck and rail shipments but that the more expensive mode (trucking) is typically used for shorter distances.

The Gravity Concept

Interaction decisions are not based on distance or distance/cost considerations alone. The large regional shopping center attracts customers from a wide radius because of the variety of shops and goods its very size promises. We go to distant big cities "to seek our fortune" rather than to the nearer small town. We are, that is, attracted by the expectation of opportunity that we associate with larger rather than smaller places. That expectation is summarized by another model of spatial interaction, the **gravity model,** also drawn from the physical sciences.

In the 1850s, Henry C. Carey (1793–1879), in his *Principles of Social Science,* observed that the physical laws of gravity and motion developed by Sir Isaac Newton (1642–1727) were applicable to the aggregate actions of humans. Newton's *law of universal gravitation* states that the attractive pull between any two objects is proportional to the product of their masses and inversely proportional to the square of the distance between them. More simply put, Newton's law tells us that big things have a stronger attraction force (greater gravitational pull) than do small objects and that things close to each other have stronger

mutual attraction than do objects at greater distance—and that the attraction decreases very rapidly with even small increases in separation.

Carey's interests were in the interaction between urban centers and in the observation that a large city is more likely to attract an individual than is a small hamlet. His first interest could be quickly satisfied by simple analogy. He assumed that the expected interaction between two places can be calculated by converting physical mass in the gravity model to population size while retaining the distance component of the Newtonian calculation (for the applicable Newton and Carey equations, see *gravity model* in the Glossary).

In social science applications of the gravity model, distance may be calculated by travel time or travel cost modifications rather than by straight line separation. Whatever the unit of measure, however, the model assures us that although spatial interaction always tends to decrease with increasing distance between places, at a given distance it tends to expand with increases in the size of the places.

Carey's second observation—that large cities have greater drawing power for individuals than do small ones—was subsequently addressed by the **law of retail gravitation,** proposed by William J. Reilly (1899–1970) in 1931. Using the population and distance inputs of the gravity model, Reilly determined the relative amount of retail trade that two cities would attract from an intermediate place in the vicinity of the *breaking point (BP).*[2] **Reilly's law** (see the Glossary for the algebraic expression) states that two cities will attract trade from intermediate locales in direct

---

[2]The breaking point between two towns is defined as the point up to which one town exerts the controlling retail trade influence and beyond which the other town dominates.

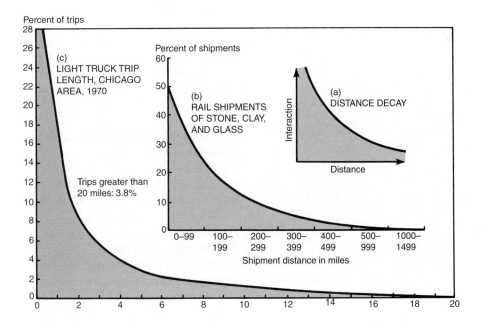

Figure 3.4 **The shape of distance decay.** The geographer W. Tobler summarized the concept of distance decay in proposing his "first law of geography: everything is related to everything else, but near things are more related than distant things." Distance decay curves vary with the type of flow. (*a*) is a generalized statement of distance decay, (*b*) summarizes United States data for a single year, and (*c*) suggests the primary use of light trucks as short haul pickup and delivery vehicles.

Source: (c) Data from Chicago Area Transportation Study, A Summary of Travel Characteristics, *1977.*

proportion to the populations of the two cities and in inverse proportion to the square of the distance of these two cities to the intermediate place.

Any farm or small-town resident located between the two cities would be inclined to shop in one or the other of them according to that resident's position relative to the calculated breaking point. Since the breaking point between cities of unequal size will lie farther from the larger of the two, its spatially greater drawing power is assured (Figure 3.5).

Later studies in location theory, city systems, trade area analysis, and other social topics all suggest that the gravity model can be used to account for a wide variety of flow patterns in human geography, including population migration, commodity flows, journeys to work or to shop, telephone call volumes, and the like. Each such flow pattern suggests that size as well as distance influences spatial interaction. Carey's observation made some 150 years ago initiated a type of analysis that in modified form is used today for a variety of practical studies that help us better understand the "friction of distance."

Interaction Potential

Spatial interaction models of distance decay and gravitational pull deal with only two places at a time. The world of reality is rather more complex. All cities, not just city pairs, within a regional system of cities have the possibility of interacting with each other. Indeed, the more specialized the goods produced in each separate center—that is, the greater their collective complementarity—the more likely it is that such multiple interactions will occur.

A **potential model,** also based on Newtonian physics, provides an estimate of the interaction opportunities available to a center in such a multicentered network. It tells us the relative position of each point in relation to all other places within a region. It does so by summing the size and distance relationships between all points of potential interaction within an area. The concept of

potential is applicable whenever the measurement of the intensity of spatial interaction is of concern—as it is in studies of marketing, land values, broadcasting, commuting patterns, and the like.

Movement Biases

Distance decay and the gravity and potential models help us understand the bases for interaction in an idealized area without natural or cultural barriers to movement or restrictions on routes followed, and in which only rational interaction decisions are made. Even under those model conditions, the pattern of spatial interaction that develops for whatever reason inevitably affects the conditions under which future interactions will occur. An initial structure of centers and connecting flows will tend to freeze into the landscape a mutually reinforcing continuation of that same pattern. The predictable flows of shoppers to existing shopping centers make those centers attractive to other merchants. New store openings increase customer flow; increased flow strengthens the developed pattern of spatial interaction. And increased road traffic calls for the highway improvement that encourages additional traffic volume.

Such an aggregate regularity of flow is called a **movement bias.** We have already noted a *distance bias* favoring short movements over long ones. There is also *direction bias,* in which of all possible directions of movement, actual flows are restricted to only one or a few. Direction bias is simply a statement that from a given origin, flows are not random (Figure 3.6); rather, certain places have a greater attraction than do others. The movement patterns from an isolated farmstead are likely oriented to a favored shopping town. On a larger scale, in North America or Siberia, long-distance freight movements are directionally biased in favor of east-west flows. Direction bias reflects not just the orientation but also the intensity of flow. Movements from a single point—from Novosibirsk in Siberia, for example, or from Winnipeg, Canada, or Kansas City in the United States—may occur in all directions; they are in reality more intense along the east-west axis.

Such directional biases are in part a reflection of *network bias,* a shorthand way of saying that the presence or absence of connecting channels strongly affects the likelihood that spatial interaction will occur. A set of routes and the set of places that they connect are collectively called a **network.** Flows cannot occur between all points if not all points are linked. In Figure 3.6a, the interchange between *A* and *X,* though not necessarily impossible, is unlikely because the routeway between them is indirect and circuitous. In information flows, a worker on the assembly line is less likely to know of company production plans than is a secretary in the executive offices; these two workers are tied into quite different information networks.

A recognition of movement biases helps to refine the coarser generalizations of spatial interaction based solely on complementarity, transferability, and intervening opportunity. Other modifying statements have been developed, but each further refinement moves us away from aggregate behavior toward less predictable individual movements and responses. The spatial interaction questions we ask and the degree of refinement of the answers we require determine the modifications we must introduce into the models we employ.

Figure 3.5 The *law of retail gravitation* provides a quick determination of the trade boundary (or breaking point) between two cities. In the diagram, cities 1 and 2 are 201 kilometers (125 mi) apart. Reilly's law tells us that the breaking point between them lies 81.6 kilometers (50.7 mi) distant from City 1. A potential customer located at *M,* midway (100.5 km or 62.5 mi) between the cities, would lie well within the trade zone of City 2. A series of such calculations would define the "trade area" of any single city.

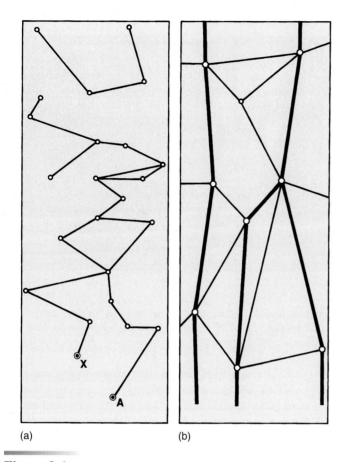

(a)   (b)

Figure 3.6 Direction bias. (*a*) When direction bias is absent, movements tend to be almost random, occurring in all possible directions, but less likely between points, such as *A* and *X,* not directly connected. (*b*) Direction bias indicating predominantly north-south movements, likely as a result of transportation routes and/or major destinations being aligned north to south.

Human Spatial Behavior

Humans are not commodities and individually do not necessarily respond predictably to the impersonal dictates of spatial interaction constraints. Yet, to survive, people must be mobile and collectively do react to distance, time, and cost considerations of movement in space and to the implications of complementarity, transferability, and intervening opportunity. Indeed, an exciting line of geographic inquiry involves how individuals make spatial behavioral decisions and how those separate decisions may be summarized by models and generalizations to explain collective actions.

Mobility is the general term applied to all types of human territorial movement. Two aspects of that mobility behavior concern us. The first is the daily or temporary use of space—the journeys to stores, to work, or to school, or for longer periods on vacation or college students' relocation between home and school dormitory. These types of mobility are often designated as *circulation* and have no suggestion of relocation of residence (Figure 3.7). The second type of mobility is the longer-term commitment related to decisions to permanently leave the home territory and find residence in a new location. This second form of spatial behavior is termed *migration.*

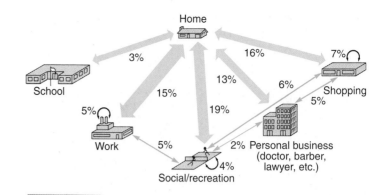

Figure 3.7 Seven County Minneapolis–St. Paul Metropolitan Area travel patterns. The numbers are the percentage of all urban trips taken on a typical weekday. In recent decades the relative importance of work and school trips has decreased while other types of trips have risen in importance.

Source: Data from Metropolitan Council: The 2000 Travel Behavior Inventory.

Both aspects imply a time dimension. Humans' spatial actions are not instantaneous. They operate over time, frequently imparting a rhythm to individual and group activity patterns and imposing choices among time-consuming behaviors. Elements of both aspects of human spatial behavior are also embodied in how individuals perceive space and act within it and how they respond to information affecting their space-behavioral decisions. The nature of those perceptions and responses affect us all in our daily movements. The more permanent movement embodied in migration involves additional and less common decisions and behaviors, as we shall see later in this chapter.

Individual Activity Space

One of the realities of life is that groups and countries draw boundaries around themselves and divide space into territories that are, if necessary, defended. Some see the concept of **territoriality**—the emotional attachment to and the defense of home ground—as a root explanation of much of human action and response. It is true that some individual and collective activity appears to be governed by territorial defense responses: the conflict between street groups in claiming and protecting their "turf" (and their fear for their lives when venturing beyond it) and the sometimes violent rejection by ethnic urban neighborhoods of any different advancing population group it considers threatening. On a more individualized basis, each of us claims as **personal space** the zone of privacy and separation from others our culture or our physical circumstances require or permit. Anglo Americans demand greater face-to-face separation in conversations than do Latin Americans. Personal space on a crowded beach or in a department store is acceptably more limited than it is in our homes or when we are studying in a library (Figure 3.8).

For most of us, our personal sense of territoriality is a tempered one. We regard our homes and property as defensible private domains but open them to innocent visitors, known and unknown, or to those on private or official business. Nor do we confine our activities so exclusively within controlled home territories as street-gang members do within theirs. Rather, we have a more or

(a)

(b)

Figure 3.8 Our demanded *personal space* is not necessarily uniform in shape or constant in size. We tolerate strangers closer to our sides than directly in front of us; we accept more crowding in an elevator than in a store. (*a*) We accept the press of the crowd on a popular beach—as do these students on spring break in the Florida Keys (*b*), but tend to distance ourselves from others in a public square.

less extended home range, an **activity space** or area within which we move freely on our rounds of regular activity, sharing that space with others who are also about their daily affairs. Figure 3.9 suggests probable activity spaces for a suburban family of five for a day. Note that the activity space is different and for the mapped day rather limited for each individual, even though two members of the family use automobiles. If one week's activity were shown, more paths would be added to the map, and in a year's time, one or more long trips would probably have to be noted.

The types of trips that individuals make and thus the extent of their activity space depend on at least three interrelated variables: their stage in life course (age); the means of mobility at their command; and the demands or opportunities implicit in their daily activities. The first variable, *stage in life,* refers to membership in specific age groups. School-age children usually travel short distances to lower schools and longer distances to upper-level schools. After-school activities tend to be limited to walking or to bicycle trips to nearby locations. Greater mobility is characteristic of high-school students. Adults responsible for household duties make shopping trips and trips related to child care as well as journeys away from home for social, cultural, or recreational purposes. Wage-earning adults usually travel farther from home than other family members. Elderly people may, through infirmity or interests, have less extensive activity spaces.

The second variable that affects the extent of activity space is *mobility,* or the ability to travel. An informal consideration of the cost and effort required to overcome the friction of distance is implicit. Where incomes are high, automobiles are available, and the cost of fuel is reckoned minor in the family budget, mobility may be great and individual activity space large. In societies or neighborhoods where cars are not a standard means of conveyance, the daily non-emergency activity space may be limited to walking, bicycling, or taking infrequent trips on public transportation. Wealthy suburbanites are far more mobile than are residents of inner-city slums, a circumstance that affects ability to learn

about, seek, or retain work and to have access to medical care, educational facilities, and social services.

A third factor limiting activity space is the individual assessment of the existence of possible activities or *opportunities.* In subsistence economies where the needs of daily life are satisfied at home, the impetus for journeys away from home is minimal. If there are no stores, schools, factories, or even roads, expectations and opportunities are limited. Not only are activities spatially restricted, but **awareness space**—knowledge of opportunity locations beyond normal activity space—is minimal, distorted, or absent. In low-income neighborhoods of modern cities in any country, poverty and isolation limit the inducements, opportunities, destinations, and necessity of travel (Figure 1.25). Opportunities plus mobility conditioned by life stage bear heavily on the amount of spatial interaction in which individuals engage.

The Tyranny of Time

The daily activities of humans—eating, sleeping, traveling between home and destination, working or attending classes—all consume time as well as involve space. An individual's spatial reach is restricted because one cannot be in two different places at the same moment or engage simultaneously in activities that are spatially separate. Further, since there is a finite amount of time within a day and each of us is biologically bound to a daily rhythm of day and night, sleeping and eating, time tyrannically limits the spatial choices we can make and the activity space we can command.

Our daily space-time constraints—our *time-geography*—may be represented by a **space-time prism,** the volume of space and length of time within which our activities must be confined. Its size and shape are determined by our mobility; its boundaries define what we can or cannot accomplish spatially or temporally (Figure 3.10). If our circumstances demand that we walk to work or school (Figure 3.10b), the sides of our prism are steep and the space available for our activities is narrow. We cannot use time spent in transit for other activities,

Figure 3.9 Activity space for each member of one author's family of five for a typical weekday. Routes of regular movement and areas recurrently visited help to foster a sense of territoriality and to affect one's perceptions of space.

and the area reasonably accessible to the pedestrian is limited. The space-time prism for the driver (Figure 3.10c) has angled sides and the individual's spatial range is wide. The dimensions of the prism determine what spatially defined activities are possible, for no activity can exceed the bounds of the prism (see "Space, Time, and Women"). Since most activities have their own time constraints, the choices of things you can do and the places you can do them are strictly limited. Defined class hours, travel time from residence to campus, and dining hall location and opening and closing hours, for example, may be the constraints on your *space-time path* (Figure 3.11). If you also need part-time work, your choice of jobs is restricted by their respective locations and work

hours, for the job, too, must fit within your daily space-time prism. Parenting responsibilities, particularly for single parents, place major constraints on the spatial range of individuals. In households where one partner (typically the woman) bears greater responsibilities for childcare and household chores, their job choices may be limited by their narrow time-geographic constraints and they may be forced to accept lower pay and/or a less prestigious job.

Figure 3.10 The space-time prism. An individual's daily prism has both geographical limits and totally surrounding space-time walls. The *time* (vertical axis) involved in movement affects the space that is accessible, along with the time and space available for other than travel purposes. (*a*) When collecting firewood for household use may take an entire day, as it does in some deforested developing countries, no time or space is left for other activities, and the gatherer's space-time prism may be represented by a straight line. (*b*) Walking to and from work or school and spending the required number of hours there leave little time to broaden one's area of activity. (*c*) The automobile permits an extension of the geographical boundaries of the driver's space-time prism; the range of activity possibilities and locations is expanded for the highly mobile.

Space, Time, and Women

From a time-geographic perspective, it is apparent that many of the limitations women face in their choices of employment or other activities outside the home reflect the restrictions that women's time budgets and travel paths place on their individual daily activities.

Consider the case* of the unmarried working woman with one or more pre-school-age children. The location and operating hours of available child-care facilities may have more of an influence on her choice of job than do her labor skills or the relative merits of alternative employment opportunities. For example, the woman may not be able to leave her home base before a given hour because the only available full-day, child-care service is not open earlier. She must return at the specified child pickup time and arrive home to prepare food at a reasonable (for the child) dinner time. Her travel mode and speed determine the outer limits of her daily space-time prism.

Suppose both of two solid job offers have the same working hours and fall within her possible activity space. She cannot accept the preferred, better paying job because drop-off time at the child-care center would make her late for work, and work hours would make her miss the center's closing time. On the other hand, although the other job is acceptable from a child-care standpoint, it leaves no time (or store options) for shopping or errands except during the lunch break. Job choice and shopping opportunities are thus determined not by the woman's labor skills or awareness of store price comparisons but by her time-geographic constraints. Other women in other job skill, parenthood, locational, or mobility circumstances experience different but comparable space-path restrictions.

Mobility is a key to activity mix, time-budget, and activity space configurations. Again, research indicates that women are frequently disadvantaged. Because of their multiple work, child-care, and home maintenance tasks, women on average make more—though shorter—trips than men, leaving less time for alternate activities.

The lower income level of many single women with or without children limits their ability to own cars and leads them to use public transit disproportionately to their numbers—to the detriment of both their money and time-space budgets. They are, it has been observed, "transportation deprived and transit dependent."

Geographer Mei-Po Kwan used GIS and travel diaries to create three-dimensional diagrams of the time-geography patterns of a sample of men and women who all had driver's licenses and access to automobiles. Despite their relative affluence, Kwan found that women experience more time-geographic constraints than men because of their responsibilities for child-care or school drop-off. Women with other adults in the household to share domestic responsibilities experienced fewer constraints and the women with the most time-geographic constraints were more likely to have to accept part-time work.

*Suggested by Risa Palm and Allan Pred, *A Time-Geographic Perspective on Problems of Inequality for Women.* Institute of Urban and Regional Development, Working Paper no. 236. University of California, Berkeley, 1974.

Source: Mei-Po Kwan, 1999. "Gender, the Home-Work Link, and Space-Time Patterns of Non-Employment Activities, Economic Geography, *75, no. 4 (1999): 370–394.*

Figure 3.11 School day space-time path for a hypothetical college student.

Distance and Human Interaction

People make many more short-distance trips than long ones, a statement in human behavioral terms of the concept of *distance decay.* If we drew a boundary line around our activity space, it would be evident that trips to the boundary are taken much less often than short-distance trips around the home. The tendency is for the frequency of trips to fall off very rapidly beyond an individual's **critical distance**—the distance beyond which cost, effort, and means strongly influence our willingness to travel. Figure 3.12 illustrates the point with regard to journeys from the homesite.

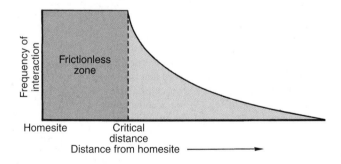

Figure 3.12 **Critical distance.** This general diagram indicates how most people observe distance. For each activity, there is a distance beyond which the intensity of contact declines. This is called the *critical distance.* The distance up to the critical distance is identified as a *frictionless zone,* in which time or distance considerations do not effectively figure in the trip decision.

Regular movements defining our individual activity space are undertaken for different purposes and are differently influenced by time and distance considerations. The kinds of activities individuals engage in can be classified according to type of trip: journeys to work, to school, to shop, for recreation, and so on. People in nearly all parts of the world make these same types of journeys, though the spatially variable requirements of culture, economy, and personal circumstance dictate their frequency, duration, and significance to an individual (Figure 3.13). A small child, for example, will make many trips up and down the block but is inhibited by parental admonitions from crossing the street. Different but equally effective distance constraints control adult behavior.

The journey to work plays a decisive role in defining the activity space of most adults. Formerly restricted by walking distance or by the routes and schedules of mass transit systems, the critical distances of work trips have steadily increased in European and Anglo American cities as the private automobile figures more importantly in the movement of workers (Figure 3.14). Daily or weekly shopping may be within the critical distance of an individual, and little thought may be given to the cost or the effort involved. That same individual, however, may relegate shopping for special goods to infrequent trips and carefully consider their cost and effort. The majority of our social contacts tend to be at short distance within our own neighborhoods or with friends who live relatively close at hand; longer social trips to visit relatives are less frequent. In all such trips, however, the distance decay function is clearly at work (Figure 3.15).

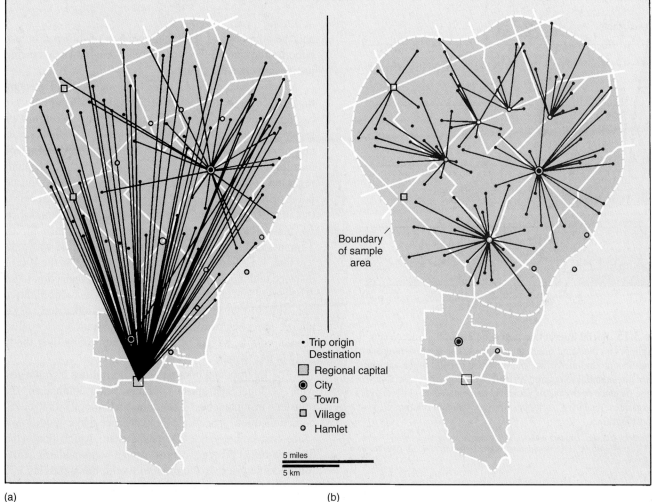

(a)　　　　　　　　　　　　　　　(b)

Figure 3.13 **Travel patterns for purchases of clothing and yard goods** of (*a*) rural cash-economy Canadians and (*b*) Canadians of the Old Order Mennonite sect. These strikingly different travel behaviors mapped many years ago in central Canada demonstrate the great differences that may exist in the action spaces of different culture groups occupying the same territory. At that time, "modern" rural Canadians, owning cars and wishing to take advantage of the variety of goods offered in the more distant regional capital, were willing and able to travel longer distances than were neighboring people of a traditionalist culture who had different mobility and whose different demands in clothing and other consumer goods were, by preference or necessity, satisfied in nearby small settlements. Unpublished studies suggest that similar contrasts in mobility and purchase travel patterns currently exist between buggy-using Old Order Amish (see Figure 7.2) and their car-driving neighbors.

Source: Robert A. Murdie, "Cultural Differences in Consumer Travel," Economic Geography *41, no. 3 (Worcester, Mass.: Clark University, 1965). Redrawn by permission.*

Figure 3.14 **The frequency distribution of work and nonwork trip lengths in minutes in the seven-county Minneapolis–St. Paul Metropolitan Area.** Studies in various metropolitan areas support the conclusions documented by this graph: work trips are usually longer than other recurring journeys. In the United States in the early 1990s, the average work trip covered 17.1 kilometers (10.6 mi), and half of all trips to work took under 22 minutes; for suburbanites commuting to the central business district, the journey to work involved between 30 and 45 minutes. By 2000, increasing sprawl had lengthened average commuting distances and, because of growing traffic congestion, had increased the average work trip commuting time to 25 minutes; many workers had commutes of more than 45 minutes.

Source: Metropolitan Council: The 2000 Travel Behavior Inventory.

and the area beyond. The accumulation of information about the opportunities and rewards of spatial interaction helps increase and justify movement decisions.

For information flows, however, space has a different meaning than it does for the movement of commodities. Communication, for example, does not necessarily imply the time-consuming physical relocations of freight transportation (though in the case of letters and print media it usually does). Indeed, in modern telecommunications, the process of information flow may be instantaneous regardless of distance. The result is space-time convergence to the point of the obliteration of space. A Bell System report tells us that in 1920, putting through a transcontinental telephone call took 14 minutes and eight operators and cost more than $15.00 for a 3-minute call. By 1940, the call completion time was reduced to less than 1½ minutes, and the cost fell to $4.00. In the 1960s, direct distance dialing allowed a transcontinental connection in less than 30 seconds, and electronic switching has now reduced the completion time to that involved in dialing a number and answering a phone. The price of long-distance conversation essentially disappeared with the advent of voice communication over the Internet early in this century.

The Internet and communication satellites have made worldwide personal and mass communication immediate and data transfers instantaneous. The same technologies that have led to communication space-time convergence have tended toward a space-cost convergence. Domestic mail, which once charged a distance-based postage, is now carried nationwide or across town for the same price. In the modern world, transferability is no longer a consideration in information flows.

A speculative view of the future suggests that as distance ceases to be a determinant of the cost or speed of communication, the spatial structure of economic and social decision making may be fundamentally altered. Determinations about where people live and work, the role of cities and other existing command centers, flows of domestic and international trade, constraints on human mobility, and even the concepts and impacts of national boundaries may fundamentally change with new and unanticipated consequences for patterns of spatial interaction.

Figure 3.15 **Social interaction as a function of distance.** Visits with neighbors on the same street are frequent; they are less common with neighbors around the corner and diminish quickly to the vanishing point after a residential relocation. Friends exert a greater spatial pull, though the distance decay factor is clearly evident. Visits with relatives offer the greatest incentive for longer distance (though relatively infrequent) journeys.

Source: Frederick P. Stutz, "Distance and Network Effects on Urban Social Travel Fields," Economic Geography 49, no. 2 (Worcester, Mass.: Clark University, 1973), p. 139. Redrawn by permission.

Spatial Interaction and the Accumulation of Information

Critical distances, even for the same activity, are different for each person. The variables of life stage, mobility, and opportunity, together with an individual's interests and demands, help define how often and how far a person will travel. On the basis of these variables, we can make inferences about the amount of information a person is likely to acquire about his or her activity space

Information Flows

Spatially significant information flows are of two types: individual (person-to-person) exchanges and mass (source-to-area) communication. A further subdivision into formal and informal interchange recognizes, in the former, the need for an interposed channel (radio, press, postal service, or telephone, for example) to convey messages. Informal communication requires no such institutionalized message carrier.

Short-range informal *individual communication* is as old as humankind itself. Contacts and exchanges between individuals and within small groups tend to increase as the complexity of social organization increases, as the size and importance of the population center grow, and as the range of interests and associations of the communicating person expands. Each individual develops a **personal communication field,** the informational counterpart of that person's activity space. Its size and shape are defined by the individual's contacts in work, recreation, shopping, school, or other regular activities. Those activities, as we have seen, are functions of the age, sex, education, employment, income, and so on of each person. An idealized personal communication field is suggested in Figure 3.16.

Each interpersonal exchange constitutes a link in the individual's personal communication field. Each person, in turn, is a node in the communication field of those with whom he or she makes or maintains contact. The total number of such separate informal networks equals the total count of people alive. Despite the number of those networks, all people, in theory, are interconnected by multiple shared nodes (Figure 3.17). One debated experiment suggested that through such interconnections no person in the United States is more than six links removed from any other person, no matter where located or how unlikely the association.

Mass communication is the formal, structured transmission of information in essentially a one-way flow between single points of origin and broad areas of reception. There are few transmitters and many receivers. The mass media are by nature "space filling." From single origin points, they address their messages by print, radio, or television to potential receivers within a defined area. The number and location of disseminating points, therefore, are related to their spatial coverage characteristics, to the minimum size of area and population necessary for their support, and to the capability of the potential audiences to receive their message. The coverage area is determined both by the nature of the medium and by the corporate intent of the agency.

There are no inherent spatial restrictions on the dissemination of printed materials, though of course limitations and restrictions may be imposed by obscenity laws, religious prohibitions (throughout the Islamic world and parts of the Catholic world), restrictions in some countries on certain forms of political speech, and the like. And not everyone has access to bookstores or libraries or funds to buy printed material, and not everyone can read. Unlike the distance limitations on the transmission of AM or FM radio waves, however, these restrictions are independent of the area over which printed material could be physically distributed and made available.

In the United States, much book and national magazine publishing has localized in metropolitan New York City, as have the services supplying news and features for sale to the print media located there and elsewhere in the country. Paris, Buenos Aires, Moscow, London—indeed, the major metropolises and/or capital cities of other countries—show the same spatial concentration. Regional journals emanate from regional capitals, and major metropolitan newspapers, though serving primarily their home markets, are distributed over (or produce special editions for distribution within) tributary areas whose size and shape depend on the intensity of competition from other metropolises. A spatial information hierarchy has thus emerged.

Hierarchies are also reflected in the market-size requirements for different levels of media offerings. National and international organizations are required to expedite information flows (and, perhaps, to control their content), but market demand is heavily weighted in favor of regional and local coverage. In the electronic media, the result has been national networks with local affiliates acting as the gatekeepers of network offerings and adding to them locally originating programs and news content. A similar market subdivision is represented by the regional editions of national newspapers and magazines.

The technological ability to fill space with messages from different mass media is unavailing if receiving audiences do not exist. In illiterate societies, publications cannot inform or influence. Unless the appropriate receivers are widely available, television and radio broadcasts are a waste of resources. Perhaps no invention in history has done more to weld isolated individuals and purely person-to-person communicators into national societies exposed to centralized information flows than has the low-cost transistor radio. Its battery-powered transportability converts the remotest village and the most isolated individual into a receiving node of entertainment, information, and political messages. The direct

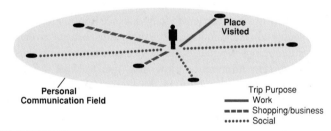

Figure 3.16 **A personal communication field** is determined by individual spatial patterns of communication related to work, shopping, business trips, social visits, and so on.

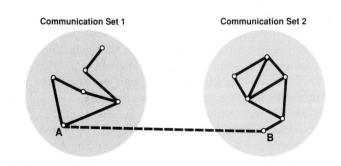

Figure 3.17 Separate population sets (groups) are interconnected by the links between individuals. If link A–B exists, everyone in the two sets is linked.

satellite broadcast of television programs to community antennae or communal sets brings that mass medium to remote areas of Arctic Canada, India, Indonesia, and other world areas able to invest in the technology but as yet unserved by ground stations.

Information and Perception

Human spatial interaction, as we have seen, is conditioned by a number of factors. Complementarity, transferability, and intervening opportunities help pattern the movement of commodities and peoples. Flows between points and over area are influenced by distance decay and partially explained by gravity and potential models. Individuals in their daily affairs operate in activity spaces that are partly determined by stage in life, mobility, and a variety of socioeconomic characteristics. In every instance of spatial interaction, however, decisions are based on information about opportunity or feasibility of movement, exchange, or want satisfaction.

More precisely, actions and decisions are based on **place perception**—the awareness we have, as individuals, of home and distant places and the beliefs we hold about them. Place perception involves our feelings and understandings, reasoned or irrational, about the natural and cultural characteristics of an area and about its opportunity structure. Whether our view accords with that of others or truly reflects the "real" world seen in abstract descriptive terms is not the major concern. Our perceptions are the important thing, for the decisions people make about the use of their lives or about their actions in space are based not necessarily on reality but on their assumptions and impressions of reality.

Perception of Environment

Psychologists and geographers are interested in determining how we arrive at our perceptions of place and environment both within and beyond our normal activity space. The images we form firsthand of our home territory have been in part reviewed in the discussion of mental maps in Chapter 1. The perceptions we have of more distant places are less directly derived (Figure 3.18). In technologically advanced societies, television and radio, magazines and newspapers, books and lectures, travel brochures and hearsay all combine to help us develop a mental picture of unfamiliar places and of the interaction opportunities they may contain. Again, however, the most effectively transmitted information seems to come from word-of-mouth reports. These may be in the form of letters or visits from relatives, friends, and associates who supply information that helps us develop lines of attachment to relatively unknown areas.

There are, of course, barriers to the flow of information, including that of distance decay. Our knowledge of close places is greater than our knowledge of distant points; our contacts with nearby persons theoretically yield more information than we receive from afar. Yet in crowded areas with maximum interaction potential, people commonly set psychological barriers around

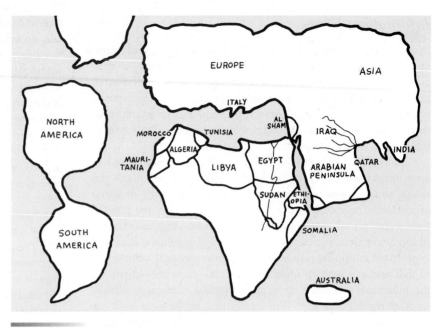

Figure 3.18 A Palestinian student's view of the world. The map was drawn by a Palestinian high-school student from Gaza. The map reflects the instruction and classroom impressions the student has received. The Gaza curriculum conforms to the Egyptian national standards and thus is influenced by the importance of the Nile River and pan-Arabism. Al Sham is the old, but still used, name for the area including Syria, Lebanon, and Palestine. The map might be quite different in emphasis if the Gaza school curriculum were designed by Palestinians or if it had been drawn by an Israeli student.

themselves so that only a limited number of those possible interactions and information exchanges actually occur. We raise barriers against information overload and to preserve a sense of privacy that permits the filtering out of information that does not directly affect us. There are obvious barriers to long-distance information flows as well, such as time and money costs, mountains, oceans, rivers, and differing religions, languages, ideologies, and political systems.

Barriers to information flow give rise to what we earlier (p. 70) called *direction bias*. In the present usage, this implies a tendency to have greater knowledge of places in some directions than in others. Not having friends or relatives in one part of a country may represent a barrier to individuals, so interest in and knowledge of the area beyond the "unknown" region are low. In the United States, both northerners and southerners tend to be less well informed about each other's areas than about the western part of the country. Traditional communication lines in the United States follow an east-west rather than a north-south direction, the result of early migration patterns, business connections, and the pattern of the development of major cities. In Russia, directional bias favors a north-south information flow within the European part of the country and less familiarity with areas far to the east. Within Siberia, however, east-west flows dominate.

When information about a place is sketchy, blurred pictures develop. These influence the impression—the perception—we have of places and cannot be discounted. Many important decisions are made on the basis of incomplete information or biased reports, such as decisions to visit or not, to migrate or not, to hate or not, even to make war or not. Awareness of places is usually accompanied by opinions about them, but there is no necessary relationship between the depth of knowledge and the perceptions held. In general, the more familiar we are with a locale, the more sound the factual basis of our mental image of it will be. But individuals form firm impressions of places totally unknown to them personally, and these may color interaction decisions.

One way to determine how individuals envisage home or distant places is to ask them what they think of different locales. For instance, they may be asked to rate places according to desirability—perhaps residential desirability—or to make a list of the 10 best and the 10 worst cities in their country of residence. Certain regularities appear in such inquiries. Figure 3.19 presents some residential desirability data elicited from college students in three provinces of Canada. These and comparable mental maps derived from studies conducted by researchers in many countries suggest that near places are preferred to far places unless much information is available about the far places. Places of similar culture are favored, as are places with high standards of living. Individuals tend to be indifferent to unfamiliar places and areas and to dislike those that have competing interests (such as distasteful political and military activities or conflicting economic concerns) or a physical environment perceived to be unpleasant.

On the other hand, places perceived to have superior climates or landscape amenities are rated highly in mental map studies and favored in tourism and migration decisions. Holiday tours to Spain, the south of France, and the Mediterranean islands are heavily booked by the British seeking to escape their damp, cloudy climate. A U.S. Census Bureau study indicates that "climate" is, after work and family proximity, the most often reported reason for interstate moves by adults of all ages. International studies reveal a similar migration motivation based not only on climate but also on concepts of natural beauty and amenities.

Perception of Natural Hazards

Less certain is the negative impact on spatial interaction or relocation decisions of assessments of *natural hazards*. Natural hazards are elements, processes, or events in the environment that can cause

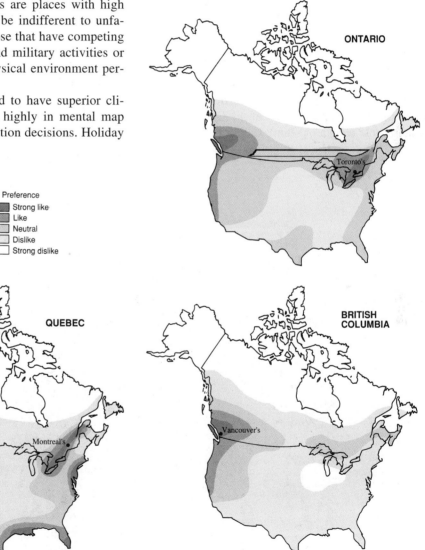

Figure 3.19 Residential preferences of Canadians. These maps show the residential preference of a sampled group of Canadians from the Provinces of British Columbia, Ontario, and Quebec, respectively. Note that each group of respondents prefers its own area, but all like the Canadian and U.S. west coasts.

Source: Herbert A. Whitney, "Preferred Locations in North America: Canadians, Clues, and Conjectures," Journal of Geography *83, no. 5, p. 222. (Indiana, Pa.: National Council for Geographic Education, 1984). Redrawn by permission.*

harm to humans. While the term implies that these hazards are "natural," human adaptation and location decisions play a major role in determining how disastrous the results are.

Mental images of home areas do not generally include as an overriding concern an acknowledgment of potential natural dangers. The cyclone that struck the delta area of Bangladesh on November 12, 1970, left at least 500,000 people dead, yet after the disaster the movement of people into the area swelled population above precyclone levels—a resettlement repeated after other, more recent cyclones. The July 28, 1976, earthquake in the Tangshan area of China devastated a major urban industrial complex, with casualties estimated at about a quarter-million, and between 50,000 and 100,000 city dwellers and villagers reportedly perished during and after the January, 2001, quake in Gujarat state of western India. In both cases, rebuilding began almost immediately, as it usually does following earthquake damage (Figure 3.20) or after the devastation of earthquake-induced tsunamis like the December, 2004, inundation of the Indonesian, Thai, and Indian coasts. The human response to even such major and exceptional natural hazards is duplicated by a general tendency to discount dangers from more common hazard occurrences. Johnstown, Pennsylvania, has suffered recurrent floods, and yet its residents rebuild; violent storms like Hurricane Katrina recurrently strike the Gulf and East coasts of the United States (Figure 3.21), and people remain or return. Californians may be concerned about Kansas tornadoes if contemplating a move there but be unconcerned about earthquake dangers at home.

Why do people choose to settle in areas of high-consequence hazards in spite of the potential threat to their lives and property? Why do hundreds of thousands of people live along the San Andreas Fault in California, build houses in Pacific coastal areas known to experience severe erosion during storms, return to flood-prone river valleys in Europe or Asia, or avalanche-threatened Andean valleys? What is it that makes the risk worth taking? Ignorance of natural hazard danger is not necessarily a consideration. People in seismically active regions of the United States and Europe, at least, do believe that damaging earthquakes are a possibility in their districts but, research indicates, are reluctant to do anything about the risk. Similar awareness and reticence accompanies other low-incidence/high-consequence natural dangers. Less than one-tenth of 1% of respondents to a federal survey gave "natural disaster" as the reason for their interstate residential move.

There are many reasons why natural hazard risk does not deter settlement or adversely affect space-behavioral decisions. Of importance, of course, is the persistent belief that the likelihood of an earthquake or a flood or other natural calamity is sufficiently remote so that it is not reasonable or pressing to modify behavior because of it. People are influenced by their innate optimism and the predictive uncertainty about timing or severity of

Figure 3.20 Destruction from the San Francisco earthquake and fire. The first shock struck San Francisco early on the morning of April 18, 1906, damaging the city's water system. Fire broke out and raged for three days. It was finally stopped by dynamiting buildings in its path. When it was over, some 700 people were dead or missing, and 25,000 buildings had been destroyed. Locally, the event is usually referred to as the Great Fire of 1906, suggesting a denial of the natural hazard in favor of assigning blame to correctable human error. Post-destruction reconstruction began at once. Rebuilding following earthquake damage is the general rule.

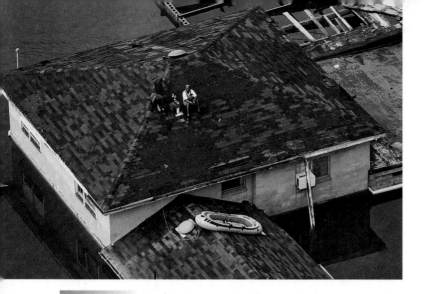

Figure 3.21 People waiting to be rescued from a New Orleans rooftop following Hurricane Katrina's assault in late August, 2005. More than 1600 died, hundreds of thousands were left homeless, and tens of billions of dollars of damage were incurred from the storm, which was immediately followed by government and private efforts at recovery and rebuilding.

Table 3.1	
Common Responses to the Uncertainty of Natural Hazards	
Eliminate the Hazard	
Deny or Denigrate Its Existence	**Deny or Denigrate Its Recurrence**
"We have no floods here, only high water."	"Lightning never strikes twice in the same place."
"It can't happen here."	"It's a freak of nature."
Eliminate the Uncertainty	
Make It Determinate and Knowable	**Transfer Uncertainty to a Higher Power**
"Seven years of great plenty. . . . After them seven years of famine."	"It's in the hands of God."
"Floods come every five years."	"The government is taking care of it."

Source: Burton and Kates, "The Perception of Natural Hazards in Resource Management," 3 *Natural Resources Journal* 435 (1964). Used by permission of the University of New Mexico School of Law, Albuquerque, N.M.

a calamitous event and by their past experiences in high-hazard areas. If they have not suffered much damage in the past, they may be optimistic about the future. If, on the other hand, past damage has been great, they may think that the probability of repetition in the future is low (Table 3.1).

Perception of place as attractive or desirable may be quite divorced from any understanding of its hazard potential. Attachment to locale or region may be an expression of emotion and economic or cultural attraction, not just a rational assessment of risk. The culture hearths of antiquity discussed in Chapter 2 and shown on Figure 2.15 were for the most part sited in flood-prone river valleys; their enduring attraction was undiminished by that potential danger. The home area, whatever disadvantages an outside observer may discern, exerts a force not easily dismissed or ignored.

Indeed, high-hazard areas are often sought out because they possess desirable topography or scenic views, as do, for instance, coastal areas subject to storm damage. Once people have purchased property in a known hazard area, they may be unable to sell it for a reasonable price even if they so desire. They think that they have no choice but to remain and protect their investment. The cultural hazard—loss of livelihood and investment—appears more serious than whatever natural hazards there may be.

Carried further, it has been observed that spatial adjustment to perceived natural hazards is a luxury not affordable to impoverished people in general or to the urban and rural poor of Third World countries in particular. Forced by population growth and economic necessity to exert ever-greater pressures upon fragile environments or to occupy at higher densities hazardous hillside and floodplain slums, their margin of safety in the face of both chronic and low-probability hazards is minimal to nonexistent (Figure 3.22).

Migration

When continental glaciers began their retreat some 11,000 years ago, the activity space and awareness space of Stone Age humans were limited. As a result of pressures of numbers, need for food, changes in climate, and other inducements, those spaces were collectively enlarged to encompass the world. **Migration**—the permanent or planned long-term relocation of residential place and activity space—has been one of the enduring themes of human history. It has contributed to the evolution of separate cultures, to the diffusion of those cultures and their components by interchange and communication, and to the frequently complex mix of peoples and cultures found in different areas of the world. Indeed, it has been a major force in shaping the world as it is today.

Massive movements of people within countries, across national borders, and between continents have emerged as a pressing concern of recent decades. They affect national economic structures, determine population density and distribution patterns, alter traditional ethnic, linguistic, and religious mixtures, and inflame national debates and international tensions. Because migration patterns and conflicts touch so many aspects of social and economic relations and have become so important a part of current human geographic realities, their specific impact is a significant aspect of several of our topical concerns. Portions of the story of migration have been touched on already in Chapter 2; other elements of it are part of later discussions of population (Chapter 4), ethnicity (Chapter 6), economic development (Chapter 10), urbanization

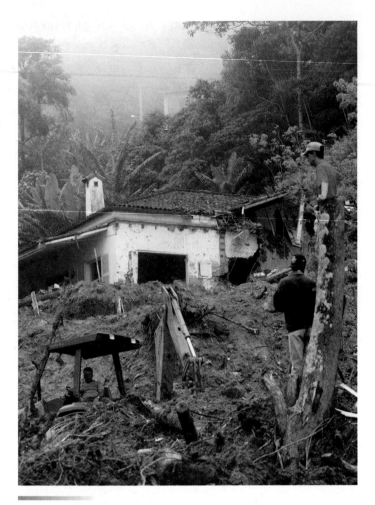

Figure 3.22 Many of the poor of Rio de Janeiro, Brazil, occupy steep hillside locations above the reach of sewer, water, and power lines that hold the more affluent at lower elevations. Frequent heavy rains cause mudflows from the saturated hillsides that wipe away the shacks and shelters that insecurely cling to them, and deposit the homes and hopes of the poor in richer neighborhoods below.

(Chapter 11), and international political relations (Chapter 12). Because voluntary migration is a near-universal expression of spatial assessment and interaction, reviewing its behavioral basis now will give us common ground for understanding its impacts in other contexts later.

Migration embodies all the principles of spatial interaction and space relations we have already discussed. Complementarity, transferability, and intervening opportunities and barriers all play a role. Space information and perception are important, as are the sociocultural and economic characteristics of the migrants and the distance relationships between their original and prospective locations of settlement. In less abstract terms, mass and individual migration decisions may express real-life responses to poverty, rapid population growth, environmental deterioration, or international and civil conflict or war. In its current troubling dimensions, migration may be as much a strategy for survival as an unforced but reasoned response to economic and social opportunity.

Naturally, the length of a specific move and its degree of disruption of established activity space patterns raise distinctions important in the study of migration. A change of residence from the central city to the suburbs certainly changes both residence and activity space of schoolchildren and of adults in many of their nonworking activities, but the working adults may still retain the city—indeed, the same place of employment there—as an action space. On the other hand, the immigration from Europe to the United States and the massive farm-to-city movements of rural Americans late in the 19th and early in the 20th centuries clearly meant a total change of all aspects of behavioral patterns.

Principal Migration Patterns

Migration flows can be discussed at different scales, from massive intercontinental torrents to individual decisions to move to a new house or apartment within the same metropolitan area. At each level, although the underlying controls on spatial behavior remain constant, the immediate motivating factors influencing the spatial interaction are different, with differing impacts on population patterns and cultural landscapes.

At the broadest scale, *intercontinental* movements range from the earliest peopling of the habitable world to the most recent flight of Asian or African refugees to countries of Europe or the Western Hemisphere. The population structure of the United States, Canada, Australia and New Zealand, Argentina, Brazil, and other South American countries—as Chapter 4 suggests—is a reflection and result of massive intercontinental flows of immigrants that began as a trickle during the 16th and 17th centuries and reached a flood during the 19th and early 20th (Figure 4.20). Later in the 20th century, World War II (1939–1945) and its immediate aftermath involved more than 25 million permanent population relocations, all of them international but not all intercontinental.

Intracontinental and *interregional* migrations involve movements between countries and within countries, most commonly in response to individual and group assessments of improved economic prospects, but often reflecting flight from difficult or dangerous environmental, military, economic, or political conditions. The millions of refugees leaving their homelands following the dissolution of Eastern European communist states, including the former USSR and Yugoslavia, exemplify that kind of flight. Between 1980 and 2005, Europe received some 23 million newcomers, often refugees, who joined the 15 million labor migrants ("guest workers") already in West European countries by the early 1990s (Figure 3.23). North America has its counterparts in the hundreds of thousands of immigrants coming (many illegally) to the United States each year from Mexico, Central America, and the Caribbean region.

The Hauns, whose westward trek opened this chapter, were part of a massive 19th-century regional shift of Americans that continues today (Figure 3.24). Russia experienced a similar, though eastward, flow of people in the 20th century. In 2007, nearly 200 million people—roughly 1 of every 33 then alive—lived outside the country of their birth, and migration had become a world social, economic, and political issue of first priority.

In the 20th century, nearly all countries experienced a great movement of peoples from agricultural areas to the cities, continuing a pattern of *rural-to-urban* migration that first became prominent during the 18th- and 19th-century Industrial

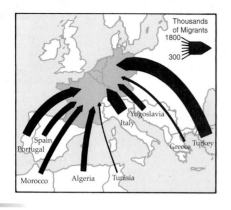

Figure 3.23 International "guest worker" flows to Western Europe. Labor shortages in expanding Western European economies beginning in the 1960s offered job opportunities to workers immigrating under labor contract from Eastern and Southern Europe and North Africa. Economic stagnation and domestic unemployment halted foreign worker contracting in Germany, France, Belgium, Netherlands, and Switzerland in the later 1980s and 1990s, but continuing immigration raised the share of foreign workers in the labor force to 20% in Switzerland, 10% in Austria, and 9.5% in Germany by 2000.

Source: Data from Gunther Glebe and John O'Loughlin, eds., "Foreign Minorities in Continental European Cities," Erdkundliches Wissen *84 (Wiesbaden, Germany: Franz Steiner Verlag, 1987).*

induces help force migration to cities. As a result, while the rate of urban growth is decreasing in the more developed countries, urbanization in the developing world continues apace, as will be discussed more fully in Chapter 11.

Types of Migration

Migrations may be forced or voluntary or, in many instances, reluctant relocations imposed on the migrants by circumstances.

In *forced migrations,* the relocation decision is made solely by people other than the migrants themselves (Figure 3.25). An estimated 10 to 12 million Africans were forcibly transferred as slaves to the Western Hemisphere from the late 16th to early 19th centuries. Half or more were destined for the Caribbean and most of the remainder for Central and South America, though nearly a million arrived in the United States. Australia owed its earliest European settlement to convicts transported after the 1780s to the British penal colony established in southeastern Australia (New South Wales). More recent involuntary migrants include millions of Soviet citizens forcibly relocated from countryside to cities and from the western areas to labor camps in Siberia and the Russian Far East beginning in the late 1920s. During the 1980s and 90s, many refugee destination countries in Africa, Europe, and Asia expelled immigrants or encouraged or forced the repatriation of foreign nationals within their borders.

Less than fully voluntary migration—*reluctant relocation*—of some 8 million Indonesians has taken place under an aggressive governmental campaign begun in 1969 to move people from densely settled Java (roughly 775 per square kilometer or 2000 people per square mile) to other islands and territories of

Revolution in advanced economies and now is even more massive than international migrant flows. Rapid increases in impoverished rural populations of developing countries put increasing and unsustainable pressures on land, fuel, and water in the countryside. Landlessness and hunger as well as the loss of social cohesion that growing competition for declining resources

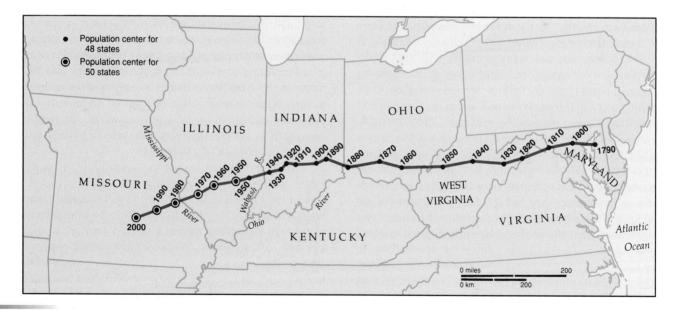

Figure 3.24 Westward shift of population, 1790–2000. More than 200 years of western migration and population growth are recorded by the changing U.S. center of population. (The "center of population" is that point at which a rigid map of the United States would balance, reflecting the identical weights of all residents in their location on the census date.) The westward movement was rapid for the first 100 years of census history and slowed between 1890 and 1950. Some of the post-1950 acceleration reflects population growth in the "Sunbelt." However, the two different locations for the population center in 1950 and the symbol change indicate the geographic pull on the center of population exerted by the admission of Alaska and Hawaii to statehood.

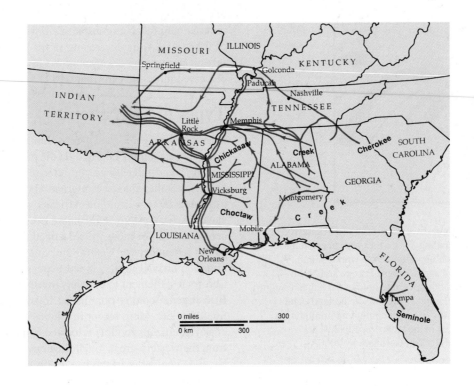

Figure 3.25 Forced migrations: The Five Civilized Tribes. Between 1825 and 1840, some 100,000 southeastern Amerindians were removed from their homelands and transferred by the Army across the Mississippi River to "Indian Territory" in present-day Oklahoma. By far, the largest number were members of the Five Civilized Tribes of the South: Cherokees, Choctaws, Chickasaws, Creeks, and Seminoles. Settled, Christianized, literate small-farmers, their forced eviction and arduous journey—particularly along what the Cherokees named their "Trail of Tears" in the harsh winter of 1837–1838—resulted in much suffering and death.

the country in what has been called the "biggest colonization program in history." International refugees from war and political turmoil or repression numbered nearly 13.5 million in 2005 according to the United Nations.

In recent decades, the vast majority of new international migrants has been absorbed by the developed countries. But there has also been an increasing flight from developing countries to other developing regions, and many countries with the largest refugee populations are among the world's poorest. Sub-Saharan Africa alone houses over 3 million refugees (Figure 3.26). Between 2003 and 2007, Iran, Syria, and Jordan became home to millions of Iraqis fleeing persecution, terrorism, and war. Additionally, at the end of 2005, the Internal Displacement Monitoring Centre estimated that there were 25.3 million people in some 40 countries worldwide who were "refugees" in their own countries as a result of conflicts or human rights violations; in a search for security or sustenance, they had left their home area but not crossed an international boundary. The total did not include those additional millions internally displaced by environmental disasters such as the 2004 southeast Asian tsunami or the 2005 U.S. Hurricane Katrina.

The great majority of migratory movements, however, are *voluntary* (volitional), representing individual response to the factors influencing all spatial interaction decisions. At root, migrations take place because the migrants believe that their opportunities and life circumstances will be better at their destination than they are at their present location.

Poverty is the great motivator. Some 30% of the world's population—nearly 2 billion persons—have less than $1.00 per day income. Many additionally are victims of drought, floods, other natural catastrophes, or wars and terrorism. Poverty in developing countries is greatest in the countryside; rural areas are home to around 750 million of the world's poorest people. Of these, some 20 to 30 million move each year to towns and cities, many as "environmental refugees" abandoning land so eroded or exhausted it can no longer support them. In the cities, they join the 40% or more of the labor force that is unemployed or underemployed in their home country and seek legal or illegal entry into more promising economies of the developed world. All, rural or urban, respond to the same basic forces—the push of poverty and the pull of perceived or hoped-for opportunity.

Those motivating forces are controlling in much of the international flow of illegal migrants whose economic condition in their homelands, they feel, is so intolerable that to seek employment they risk their lives in flight by unsafe boat and raft or through forbidding natural boundary barriers as *involuntary* but unforced migrants. Without immigration papers or legal status, subject to arrest and deportation or worse, illegals able to find work and income satisfy some of their migration objectives by sending money home to ensure their families' survival. Immigrants from poor countries, the World Bank estimated, sent more than 260 billion traceable dollars home in 2006; money sent through informal channels increased that total by as much as 50%. The traceable remittance amount alone in 2005 was

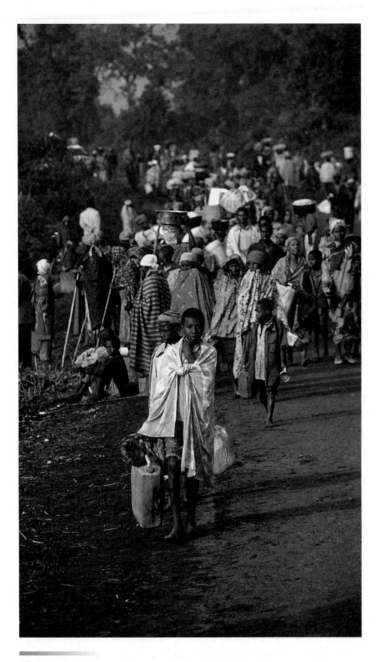

Figure 3.26 Rwandan refugees near the border of Rwanda and Tanzania. More than 1 million Rwandans fled into neighboring Zaire (now, the Democratic Republic of the Congo), Tanzania, Uganda, and Burundi in 1994 to escape an interethnic civil war in their home country and the genocide that killed at least 750,000 people. Early in the 21st century, more than 14 million Africans remained uprooted (that is, internally displaced and refugees combined). Fleeing war, repression, and famine, millions of people in developing nations have become reluctant migrants from their homelands.

on a par with the total of foreign direct investment in developing countries and twice the value of foreign aid. The estimated 17 million Latin American immigrants (again, not all illegal) in the United States sent an estimated $45 billion a year in legal and illegal remittances to their home countries in 2006 ($19 billion to Mexico alone). For some Latin American countries, those remittances account for about 20% of the money circulating in their economies.

Controls on Migration

Economic considerations crystallize most migration decisions, though nomads fleeing the famine and spreading deserts of the Sahel obviously are impelled by different economic imperatives than is the executive considering a job transfer to Montreal or the resident of Appalachia seeking factory employment in the city. Among the aging, affluent populations of highly developed countries, retirement amenities figure importantly in perceptions of residential attractiveness of areas. Educational opportunities, changes in life cycle, and environmental attractions or repulsions are but a few other possible migration motivations.

Migration theorists attribute international economic migrations to a series of often overlapping mechanisms. Differentials in wages and job opportunities between home and destination countries are perhaps the major driving force in such individual migration decisions. Those differentials are in part rooted in a built-in demand for workers at the bottom of the labor hierarchy in more prosperous developed countries whose own workers disdain low-income, menial jobs. Migrants are available to fill those jobs, some argue, because advanced economies make industrial investment in developing or colonial economies to take advantage of lower labor costs there. New factories inevitably disturb existing peasant economies, employ primarily short-term female workers, and leave a residue of unemployed males available and prone to migrate in search of opportunity. If successful, international economic migrants, male or female, help diversify sources of family income through their remittances from abroad, a form of household security that in itself helps motivate some international economic migration.

Negative home conditions that impel the decision to migrate are called **push factors.** They might include loss of job, lack of professional opportunity, overcrowding or slum clearance, or a variety of other influences including poverty, war, and famine. The presumed positive attractions of the migration destination are known as **pull factors.** They include all the attractive attributes perceived to exist at the new location—safety and food, perhaps, or job opportunities, better climate, lower taxes, quality schools, more room, and so forth. Very often migration is a result of both perceived push and pull factors. It is *perception* of the areal pattern of opportunities and want satisfaction that is important here, whether or not perceptions are supported by objective reality. In China, for example, a "floating" population of more than 100 million surplus workers has flooded into cities from the countryside, seeking urban employment that exists primarily in their anticipation.

The concept of *place utility* helps us to understand the decision-making process that potential voluntary migrants undergo. **Place utility** is the measure of an individual's satisfaction with a given residential location. The decision to migrate is a reflection of the appraisal—the perception—by the prospective migrant of the current homesite as opposed to other sites of which something is known or hoped for. In the evaluation of comparative place utility, the decision maker considers not only perceived value of the present location, but also expected place utility of potential destinations.

Those evaluations are matched with the individual's *aspiration level,* that is, the level of accomplishment or ambition that the person sees for herself or himself. Aspirations tend to be adjusted to what one considers attainable. If one finds present circumstances satisfactory, then **spatial search** behavior—the process by which locational alternatives are evaluated—is not initiated. If, on the other hand, dissatisfaction with the home location is felt, then a utility is assigned to each of the possible migration locations. The utility is based on past or expected future rewards at various sites. Because new places are unfamiliar to the searcher, the information received about them acts as a substitute for the personal experience of the homesite. Decision makers can do no more than sample information about place alternatives and, of course, there may be errors in both information and interpretation. Ultimately, they depend on their image—perhaps a mental map—of the place being considered and on the motivations that impel them to consider long distance migration or even local area relocation of residence. In the latter instance, of course, the spatial search usually involves actual site visits in evaluating the potential move (Figure 3.27).

One goal of the potential migrant is to avoid physically dangerous or economically unprofitable outcomes in the final migration decision. Place utility evaluation, therefore, requires assessments not only of hoped-for pull factors of new sites but also of the potentially negative economic and social reception the migrant might experience at those sites. An example of that observation can be seen in the case of the large numbers of young Mexicans and Central Americans who have migrated both legally and illegally to the United States (Figure 3.28). Faced with poverty and overpopulation at home, they regard the place utility in Mexico as minimal. With a willingness to work, they learn from friends and relatives of job opportunities north of the border and, hoping for success or even wealth, quickly place high utility on relocation to the United States. Many know that dangerous risks are involved in entering the country illegally, but even legal immigrants face legal restrictions or rejections that are advocated or designed to reduce the pull attractions of the United States (see "Broken Borders").

Another migrant goal is to reduce uncertainty. That objective may be achieved either through a series of transitional relocation stages or when the migrant follows the example of known predecessors. **Step migration** involves the place transition from, for example, rural to central city residence through a series of less extreme locational changes—from farm to small town to suburb and, finally, to the major central city itself. **Chain migration** assures that the mover is part of an established migrant flow from a common origin to a prepared destination. An advance group of migrants, having established itself in a new home area, is followed by second and subsequent migrations originating in the same home district and frequently united by kinship or friendship ties. Public and private services for legal migrants and informal service networks for undocumented or illegal migrants become established and contribute to the continuation or expansion of the chain migration flow. Ethnic and foreign-born enclaves in major cities and rural areas in a number of countries are the immediate result, as we shall see more fully in Chapter 6.

Sometimes the chain migration is specific to occupational groups. For example, nearly all newspaper vendors in New Delhi, in the north of India, come from one small district in Tamil Nadu, in the south of India. Most construction workers in New Delhi come either from Orissa, in the east of India, or Rajasthan, in the northwest. The diamond trade of Mumbai, India, is dominated by a network of about 250 related families who come from a small town several hundred miles to the north.

Certainly, not all immigrants stay permanently at their first destination. Of the some 80 million newcomers to the United States between 1900 and 1980, some 10 million returned to their homelands or moved to another country. Estimates for Canada indicate that perhaps 40 of each 100 immigrants eventually leave, and about 25% of newcomers to Australia also depart permanently. A corollary of all out-migration flows is, therefore, **counter** (or **return**) **migration,** the likelihood that as many as 25% of all migrants will return to their place of origin.

Within the United States, return migration—defined as moving back to one's state of birth—makes up about 20% of all domestic moves. That figure varies dramatically between states. More than

Figure 3.27 An example of a residential spatial search. The dots represent the house vacancies in the price range of a sample family. Note (1) the relationship of the new house location to the workplaces of the married couple; (2) the relationship of the old house location to the chosen new home site; and (3) the limited total area of the spatial search. This example from the San Fernando Valley area of Los Angeles is typical of intraurban moves.

Source: Redrawn by permission from J. O. Huff, Annals of the Association of American Geographers, *Vol. 76, pp. 217–221. Association of American Geographers, 1986. Reprinted by permission of Blackwell Publishing Ltd.*

(a)

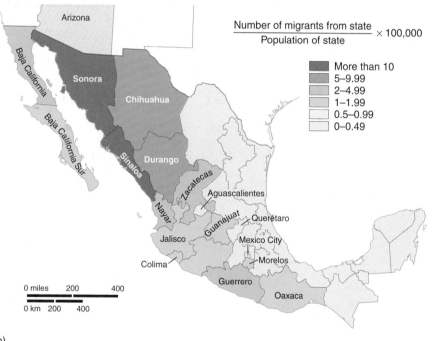

Arizona

Baja California

Baja California Sur

Sonora

Chihuahua

Sinaloa

Durango

Zacatecas

Aguascalientes

Nayar

Guanajuat

Querétaro

Jalisco

Mexico City

Colima

Morelos

Guerrero

Oaxaca

Number of migrants from state / Population of state × 100,000

More than 10
5–9.99
2–4.99
1–1.99
0.5–0.99
0–0.49

0 miles   200   400
0 km   200   400

(b)

Figure 3.28 (*a*) Undocumented (illegal) Mexican immigrants running from the Border Patrol. (*b*) **Undocumented migration rate to Arizona.** The Arizona region and nearby Mexican states have long-standing ties that reach back to the early 1800s. In many respects the international border cuts through a cultural region. Note that distance decay is evident in the likelihood a person will migrate to the United States. Over half of the migrants come from three nearby Mexican states: Sonora, Sinaloa, and Chihuahua.

Source: (b) Redrawn from John Harner, "Continuity Amidst Change," The Professional Geographer 47, No. 4, Figure 2, p. 403. Association of American Geographers, 1995. Reprinted by permission of Blackwell Publishing Ltd.

Geography and Public Policy

Broken Borders

Migrants can enter a country legally—with passport, visa, working permit, or other authorization—or illegally. Some aliens enter a country legally but on a temporary basis (as a student or tourist, for example), but then remain after their official departure date. Others arrive claiming the right of political asylum but actually seeking economic opportunity. The Department of Homeland Security estimates that between one-fourth and one-third of the illegal residents in the United States entered the country legally but then overstayed their visas.

Although it is impossible to determine the precise number of people residing illegally in the United States, a number that changes daily, most authorities estimate there are anywhere from 10 to 12 million. About 55% have come from Mexico, another 20 to 25% from other Latin American countries and the Caribbean, 13% from Asia, and the remainder from Canada, Europe, and Africa. The rising tide of emotion against unauthorized immigrants is directed mainly against those from Latin America, most of whom are unskilled workers.

Once they are in the United States, Latin American immigrants find work in agricultural fields, animal slaughtering and meat packing facilities, construction, hotels, and restaurants. Many work in private residences as maids, nannies, and gardeners. While most undocumented workers initially enter California, Arizona, Texas, or Florida, and many remain in those states, they go where they find jobs. Many blend into the large migrant communities not just of Los Angeles, El Paso, and Houston, for example, but also those of Chicago and New York City. Iowa and North Carolina have some of the fastest growing populations of illegal immigrants. The demand for their labor is great enough that nearly all of the males have higher labor force participation rates than native-born men (92% versus 83%).

Concern over the growing number of illegal aliens has been reflected in a number of actions in recent years.

- Security fears since the September 11, 2001, assaults on the World Trade Center and Pentagon have led to more stringent visa applicant background checks, greater restrictions on admitting refugees and asylum seekers, stricter enforcement of Immigration and Naturalization Service (INS) rules on alien residency reports and visa time restrictions, and stricter border controls.

- Greater efforts are being made to deter illegal crossings along the 3380-kilometer (2100-mi) U.S.-Mexico border. To supplement the 120 kilometers (75 mi) of steel fences near a few U.S. cities, the Bush administration in 2007 proposed 1125 kilometers (700 mi) of new fencing, and Congress approved money for a small portion of it. The administration also increased the number of Border Patrol agents, who use automotive vehicles, helicopters, unmanned aircraft known as *drones,* night-vision cameras, and hidden electronic sensors for surveillance. In parts of Arizona and California, self-appointed Minutemen—groups of volunteer militia—patrol the border "to protect our country from a 40-year long invasion across our southern border with Mexico," as one vigilante put it.

- Because the burden of coping with illegal immigration falls mostly on state and local governments, four states (Florida, Texas, Arizona, and California) have sued the federal government—so far unsuccessfully—to win reimbursement for the costs of illegal immigration.

- Concerned that large numbers of unauthorized immigrants impose a financial burden on taxpayers, congest schools and public health clinics, and result in the reduction of services to legal residents, voters in California approved Proposition 187, which barred illegal immigrants and their families from public schools, social services, and non-emergency health care. The courts struck down Proposition 187, declaring most of the provisions to be unconstitutional, and the measure was never implemented.

- In Arizona, a new law targeting employers of undocumented workers took effect on

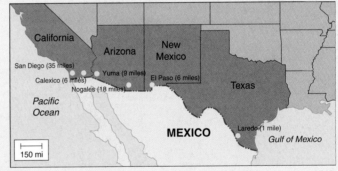

Existing miles of steel fences near U.S. cities along the Mexico border, 2007.

a third of recent in-migrants to West Virginia, for example, were returnees—as were over 25% of those moving to Pennsylvania, Alabama, Iowa, and a few other states. Such widely different states as New Hampshire, Maryland, California, Florida, Wyoming, and Alaska were among the several that found returnees were fewer than 10% of their in-migrants. Interviews suggest that states deemed attractive draw new migrants in large numbers, while those with high proportions of returnees in the migrant stream are not perceived as desirable destinations by other than former residents.

Once established, origin and destination pairs of places tend to persist. Areas that dominate a locale's in- and out-migration patterns make up the *migration fields* of the place in question. As we would expect, areas near the point of origin comprise the largest part of the migration field, though larger cities more distantly located may also be prominent as the ultimate destination of hierarchical step migration (Figure 3.29). As Figure 3.30 shows, some migration fields reveal a distinctly *channelized* pattern of flow. The channels link areas that are in

January 1, 2008. Employers are required to check the status of each worker with the federal government. A company found to have knowingly hired an illegal resident has its business license suspended for ten days for the first offense. A second offense results in the permanent revocation of the business license. Other states are considering similar legislation.

Millions of illegal residents managed to legalize themselves by taking advantage of government amnesties offered between 1984 and 2000. In his State of the Union address in 2005, President Bush called for a temporary-worker program that would legalize the presence of millions of undocumented workers. "We should not be content with laws that punish hard-working people who want only to provide for their families . . . It is time for an immigration policy that permits temporary guest-workers to fill jobs that Americans will not take," he declared. Congressional efforts to pass a comprehensive immigration reform bill failed in 2007, however. It called for more border security, a guest worker program, and a path to citizenship for those already here.

Questions to Consider

1. It is estimated that some 800,000 unauthorized immigrants enter the United States each year, and most find gainful employment, yet the country issues only 5,000 visas a year for unskilled foreigners seeking year-round work. Should the United States increase the number of visas available?

2. Making illegal crossings more difficult in California has not diminished the number of migrants making the journey north; it has simply pushed *coyotes,* the people who lead migrants across the border, into Arizona. Some people believe resourceful migrants will always find a way to get across the border. As one observer noted, "It's like putting rocks in a river—the water just goes around it." Do you think there is any way to seal the entire United Stats/Mexico border, or will immigration continue as long as the income gap between the United States and Latin America remains great? Could the United States reduce immigration pressures by improving the Mexican economy?

3. Why is anti-immigrant sentiment directed chiefly against unauthorized immigrants from Latin America? Will such feelings eventually fade, as did earlier ones about the immigration of Irish Catholics, Chinese, Eastern Europeans and other groups?

4. With regard to President Bush's proposal for a temporary-worker program, the libertarian Cato Institute argues that when there is no immigration barrier, *circular migration* occurs, with migrant workers entering and leaving almost at will. It cites Puerto Rico as an example; many who move to the mainland stay for just a few years, and out-migration from the island is very low. A temporary-worker program, on the other hand, encourages migrants to move north with their entire families, and those who are already in the United States stay for good, because border crossings become more expensive and dangerous. If you were a member of Congress, would you be in favor of creating a guest worker program? Why or why not?

5. It is often said that illegal aliens perform jobs Americans won't take. Why do you think the immigrants are willing to work for low wages, often under poor working conditions? Would Americans take the jobs if they were paid, say, $20 per hour and offered health care and other benefits?

6. What would happen if all states followed Arizona's lead in passing and enforcing laws targeting employers of undocumented workers? One in ten or eleven workers in Arizona is undocumented, and opponents of the legislation contend that the state has put its economy in jeopardy. The workers tend to be reliable, they fill necessary jobs, spend their wages in the communities in which they live and work, and most pay taxes because employers in the construction, hotel, restaurant, and other industries withhold taxes from paychecks.

7. Should illegal residents already here be given the opportunity to get worker permits and the possibility of eventual citizenship if they have no criminal record, pay a fine, and demonstrate that they are gainfully employed and have paid taxes?

8. Do you believe the federal government has an obligation to fully or partially reimburse state and local governments for the costs of education, medical care, incarceration, and other legal services for unauthorized immigrants? Why or why not?

9. Should the United States require citizens to have a national identification card and to present it to officials upon demand? If so, would all people who look like they may have been born abroad feel it necessary to carry proof of citizenship at all times?

some way tied to one another by past migrations, by economic trade considerations, or some other affinity. The flow along them is greater than otherwise would be the case but does not necessarily involve individuals with personal or family ties. The former streams of southern blacks and whites to northern cities, of Scandinavians to Minnesota and Wisconsin, and of U.S. retirees to Florida and Arizona or their European counterparts to Spain, Portugal, or the Mediterranean coast are all examples of **channelized migration.**

Voluntary migration is responsive to other controls that influence all forms of spatial interaction. Push-pull factors may be equated with *complementarity;* costs (emotional and financial) of a residence relocation are expressions of *transferability.* Other things being equal, large cities exert a stronger migrant pull than do small towns, a reflection of the impact of the *gravity model.* The *distance decay* effect has often been noted in migration studies. Movers seek to minimize the *friction of distance.* In selecting between two potential destinations of equal merit, a migrant tends

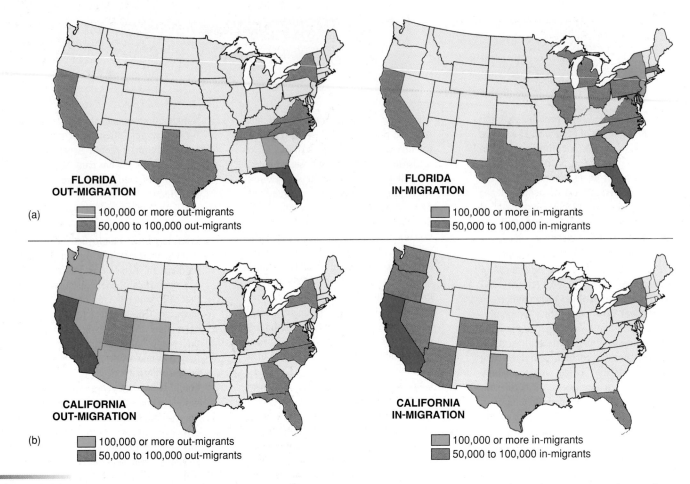

Figure 3.29 **The migration fields of Florida and California in 1995–2000.** (*a*) For Florida, nearby Georgia receives most out-migrants, but in-migrants originate in large numbers from the northeastern United States. (*b*) For California, the nearby western states receive large numbers of out-migrants, and there are fewer in-migrants from those states.

Source: United States Census Bureau.

to choose the nearer as involving less effort and expense. And since information about distant areas is less complete and satisfying than awareness of nearer localities, short moves are favored over long ones. Research indicates that determined migrants with specific destinations in mind are unlikely to be deterred by distance considerations. However, groups for whom push factors are more determining than specific destination pulls are likely to limit their migration distance in response to encountered apparent opportunities. For them, *intervening opportunities* affect locational decisions. The concept of *hierarchical migration* also helps explain some movement decisions. The observed tendency is for individuals in domestic relocations to move up the level in the urban hierarchy, from small places to larger ones. Often, levels are skipped on the way up; only in periods of general economic decline is there considerable movement down the hierarchy. Since suburbs of large cities are considered part of the metropolitan area, the movement from a town to a suburb is considered a move up the hierarchy.

Observations such as these were summarized in the 1870s and 1880s as a series of "laws of migration" by E. G. Ravenstein (1834–1913). Among those that remain relevant are the following:

1. Most migrants go only a short distance.
2. Longer-distance migration favors big city destinations.
3. Most migration proceeds step-by-step.
4. Most migration is rural to urban.
5. Each migration flow produces a counterflow.
6. Most migrants are adults; families are less likely to make international moves.
7. Most international migrants are young males.

The latter two "laws" introduce the role of personal attributes (and attitudes) of migrants: their age, sex, education, and economic status. Migrants do not represent a cross section of the populace from which they come. Selectivity of movers is evident, and the selection shows some regional differences. In most societies, young adults are the most mobile (Figure 3.31). In the United States, mobility peaks among those in their twenties, especially the later twenties, and tends to decline thereafter. Among West African cross-border migrants, a World Bank study reveals, the age group 15–39 predominated.

Ravenstein's conclusion that young adult males are dominant in economically pushed international movement is less valid today than when first proposed. In reality, women and girls now comprise 40% to 60% of all international migrants worldwide (see "Gender and Migration"). It is true that legal and illegal migrants

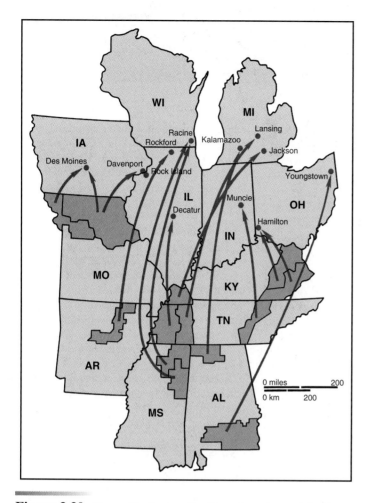

Figure 3.30 **Channelized migration flows** from the rural South to Midwestern cities of medium size in the late 20th century. Distance is not necessarily the determinant of flow direction. Perhaps through family and friendship links, the rural southern areas were tied to particular Midwestern destinations.

Source: Redrawn by permission from Proceedings of the Association of American Geographers, *C. C. Roseman, Vol. 3, p. 142. Copyright © Association of American Geographers. Reprinted by permission of Blackwell Publishers.*

Figure 3.31 **Percentage of 2004 population over 5 years of age with a different residence than in 2003.** Young adults figure most prominently in both short- and long-distance moves in the United States, an age-related pattern of mobility that has remained constant over time. For the sample year shown, 28% of people in their 20s moved whereas fewer than 5% of those 65 and older did so. Short distance moves predominate; 58% of the 39 million total U.S. movers between March, 2003 and March, 2004, relocated within the same county and another 20% moved to another county in the same state. Some two-thirds of intracounty (mobility) moves in that year were made for housing-related reasons; long distance moves (migration) were made for work-related (31%) and family (25%) reasons.

Source: U.S. Bureau of the Census.

to the United States from Mexico and Central America are primarily young men, as were first generation "guest workers" in European cities. But population projections for West European countries suggest that women will shortly make up the largest part of their foreign-born population, and in one-third of the countries of sub-Saharan Africa, including Burkina Faso, Swaziland, and Togo, the female share of foreign-born populations was as large as the male. Further, among rural to urban migrants in Latin America since the 1960s, women have been in the majority.

Female migrants are motivated primarily by economic pushes and pulls. Surveys of women migrants in southeast Asia and Latin America indicate that 50% to 70% moved in search of employment and commonly first moved while in their teens. The proportion of young, single women is particularly high in rural-to-urban migration flows, reflecting their limited opportunities in increasingly overcrowded agricultural areas. To the push and pull factors normally associated with migration decisions are sometimes added family pressures that encourage young women with few

employment opportunities to migrate as part of a household's survival strategy. In Latin America, the Philippines, and parts of Asia, emigration of young girls from large, landless families is more common than from smaller families or those with land rights. Their remittances of foreign earnings help maintain their parents and siblings at home.

An eighth internationally relevant observation may be added to those cited in Ravenstein's list: On average, emigrants tend to be relatively well-educated. A British government study reveals three-quarters of Africa's emigrants have higher (beyond high-school) education, as do about half of Asia's and South America's. Of the more than 1 million Asian Indians living in the United States, more than three-quarters of those of working age have at least a bachelor's degree. The loss to home countries can be draining; about 30% of all highly educated West African Ghanaians and Sierra Leoneans live abroad. Outward migration of the educated affects developed countries as well as poorer developing states. Between 1997 and 2002, it is claimed, between 15% and 40% of each year's Canadian colleges' graduating class emigrated to the United States, while in Europe, for one example, half the mid-1990s' graduating physics classes of Bucharest University left the country.

For modern Americans, the decisions to migrate are more ordinary but individually just as compelling. They appear to involve (1) changes in life course (e.g., getting married, having

Gender is involved in migration at every level. In a household or family, women and men are likely to play different roles regarding decisions or responsibilities for activities such as child care. These differences, and the inequalities that underlie them, help determine who decides whether the household moves, which household members migrate, and the destination for the move. Outside the household, societal norms about women's mobility and independence often restrict their ability to migrate.

The economies of sending and receiving areas play a role as well. If jobs are available for women in the receiving area, women have an incentive to migrate, and families are more likely to encourage the migration of women as necessary and beneficial. Thousands of women from East and Southeast Asia have migrated to the oil-rich countries of the Middle East, for example, to take service jobs.

The impact of migration is also likely to be different for women and men. Moving to a new economic or social setting can affect the regular relationships and processes that occur within a household or family. In some cases, women might remain subordinate to the men in their families. A study of Greek-Cypriot immigrant women in London and of Turkish immigrant women in the Netherlands found that although these women were working for wages in their new societies, these new economic roles did not affect their subordinate standing in the family in any fundamental way.

In other situations, however, migration can give women more power in the family. In former Zaire [now the Democratic Republic of the Congo], women in rural areas moved to towns to take advantage of job opportunities there, and gain independence from men in the process.

One of the keys to understanding the role of gender in migration is to disentangle household decision-making processes. Many researchers see migration as a family decision or strategy, but some members will benefit more than others from those decisions.

For many years, men predominated in the migration streams flowing from Mexico to the United States. Women played an important role in this migration stream, even when they remained in Mexico. Mexican women influenced the migration decisions of other family members; they married migrants to gain the benefits from and opportunity for migration; and they resisted or accepted the new roles in their families that migration created.

In the 1980s, Mexican women began to migrate to the United States in increasing numbers. Economic crises in Mexico and an increase in the number of jobs available for women in the United States, especially in factories, domestic service, and service industries, have changed the backdrop of individual migration decisions. Now, women often initiate family moves or resettlement efforts.

Mexican women have begun to build their own migration networks, which are key to successful migration and resettlement in the United States. Networks provide migrants with information about jobs and places to live and have enabled many Mexican women to make independent decisions about migrating.

In immigrant communities in the United States, women are often the vital links to social institution services and to other immigrants. Thus, women have been instrumental in the way that Mexican immigrants have settled and become integrated into new communities.

Source: From "Gender, Power, and Population Change" by Nancy E. Riley in *Population Bulletin*, Vol. 52, No. 1, May 1997, pp. 32–33. Reprinted by permission of Population Reference Bureau.

children, getting a divorce); (2) changes in the career course (getting a first job or a promotion, receiving a career transfer, seeking work in a new location, retiring); (3) changes of residence associated with individual personality (Figure 3.32). Work-related relocations are most important in U.S. long-distance (intercounty) migrations, and in both intra- and interstate relocations, more migrants move down the urban hierarchy—that is, from larger to smaller centers—than vice versa. Some observers suggest that pattern of deconcentration reflects modern transportation and communication technologies, more and younger retirees, and the attractions of amenity-rich smaller places. Some people, of course, simply seem to move often for no discernible reason, whereas others, *stayers,* settle into a community permanently. For other developed countries, a different set of summary migration factors may be present.

Childhood	Adolescence	Young Adulthood	Middle Age	Young-Old	Older-Old
Family Homes			Homes		
		College Students			
				Snowbirds	
		Getting Started			
		Apartment Living			
Repeated Stays		Commuting Couples			
with Relatives				RV Full-Timers	
		Itinerant Workers			
		Long-Distance Commuters			
Divorced, Geographically				Repeated Visits with Children	
Separated Parents		Temporary Job Assignments			

Figure 3.32 **Examples of multiple residences by stage in life.** Each horizontal line represents a period of time in a possible new residence.

Source: From K. McHugh, T. Hogan, and S. Happel, "Multiple Residence and Cyclical Migration." The Professional Geographer 47, no. 3, Figure 1, p. 253. Association of American Geographers, 1995. Reprinted by permission of Blackwell Publishing Ltd.

Globalization

We have seen how the cost of communication affects the degree of spatial interaction. Since the 1980s, the Internet and relatively low transportation costs have made it increasingly easy to buy goods from abroad and to travel throughout the world. There has been simultaneously a strong international movement to reduce barriers to trade and to foreign investment and ownership. For example, the creation of the European Union has dismantled restrictive national borders there, and its monetary unit, the *euro,* makes possible financial transactions in a single currency over a massive multinational common market.

Integration and interdependence characterize globalization and affect economic, political, and cultural patterns across the world. The unification of Eastern and Western Europe or the creation of regional trade alliances such as NAFTA in North America or Mercosur in South America is as much a function of the revolution in communication and computer technology as it is of the will of political or financial leaders. Low-cost high-speed computers, communication satellites, fiber-optic networks, and the Internet are the main technologies of the revolution, with robotics, microelectronics, electronic mail, cell phones, and more making their contributions.

The fact that a consumer in Italy can order a book from Amazon.com or clothes from Lands' End, obtain news from CNN, or make an investment through the London Stock Exchange while talking on a cell phone to a colleague in Tokyo is revolutionary and proof that globalization brings about greater world integration and spatial interaction (Figure 3.33). The Web browsers and calculators built into even basic mobile phone handsets enable large numbers of people to be fully integrated into the global community. The cell phone's capacity for immediate voice, instant message, and Internet data transfer has made it an agent of universal globalization in the early 21st century.

International banking is a financial case in point with instantaneous movements across borders of billions of dollars in response to changing foreign exchange values and investment opportunities. Split-second changes in all the interconnected markets are certain. Within minutes of the September 11, 2001, attacks on the World Trade Center, stock markets everywhere went down as investors sensed that the international marketplace was in danger of losing stability. Internationalization of finance is also demonstrated by the immense sums in foreign investments held by citizens of all countries. American ownership of foreign stocks and bonds directly or through mutual funds and pension plans, for example, tie citizens of this country to the economic institutions of distant areas; at the same time, people outside the United States have significant holdings in U.S. companies and in U.S. treasury bonds. The U.S. subprime lending crisis and housing price bubble collapse of 2008 led to financial crises and an economic slowdown around the globe.

Transnational corporations (TNCs), discussed more fully in Chapter 9, are important forces driving the globalization of the world economy. With headquarters in one country and subsidiary companies, factories, warehouses, laboratories, and so on in several others, the some 65,000 transnational corporations

Figure 3.33 The old and the new: a traditional gondolier in Venice, Italy, conducting business on a cellular phone.

control several hundred thousand affiliates worldwide and sell their multitude of products on the international market. TNCs, by some estimates controlling about one-third of the world's productive assets, exploit the large differential in wage rates around the world to keep production costs low, not only decentralizing manufacturing and other business activities internationally but also diffusing the infrastructure and technology of modern business and industry to formerly underdeveloped regions, integrating them more fully and competitively into the global economy.

The internationalization of popular culture is more apparent to most of the world's people than is the less visible globalization of commerce and industry. In widely different culture realms, teenagers wear Yankee baseball caps, Gap shirts, Levis, and Reeboks; eat at McDonald's; drink coffee at Starbucks; and listen to pop music on their iPod. The culture they embrace is largely Western in origin and chiefly American. U.S. movies, television shows, video games, software, music, food, and fashion are marketed worldwide. They influence the beliefs, tastes, and aspirations of people in virtually every country, though their effect is most pronounced on young people. Like the globalization of finance, industry, and commerce, this internationalization of popular culture is further evidence of the transformative nature and impact of modern spatial behavior and interaction.

Summary

Spatial interaction is the dynamic evidence of a world marked by large differences between places and of the interdependence between geographic locations. The term refers to the movement of goods, information, people, ideas—indeed, of every facet of economy and society—between one place and another. It includes the daily spatial activities of individuals and the collective patterns of their short- and long-distance behavior in space. The principles and constraints that unite, define, and control spatial behavior in this sense constitute an essential organizing focus for the study of human geographic patterns of the earth.

We have seen that whatever the type of spatial behavior or flow, a limited number of recurring mechanisms of guidance and control are encountered. Three underlying bases for spatial interaction are *complementarity*, which encourages flows between areas by balancing supply with demand or satisfying need with opportunity; *transferability*, which affects movement decisions by introducing cost, effort, and time considerations; and *intervening opportunities*, which suggests that costs of overcoming distance may be reduced by finding closer alternate points where needs can be satisfied. The flows of commodities, ideas, or people governed by these interaction factors are interdependent and additive. Flows of commodities establish and reinforce traffic patterns, for example, and also channelize the movement of information and people.

Those flows and interactions may further be understood by the application of uniform models to all forms of spatial interaction from interregional commodity exchanges to an individual's daily pattern of movement. Distance decay tells us of the inevitable decline of interaction with increasing distance. The gravity model suggests that major centers of activity can exert interaction pulls that partly compensate for distance decay. Recognition of movement biases explains why spatial interaction in the objective world may deviate from that proposed by abstract models.

Humans in their individual and collective short- and long-distance movements are responsive to these impersonal spatial controls. Their spatial behaviors are also influenced by their separate circumstances. Each has an activity and awareness space reflective of individual socioeconomic and life-cycle conditions. Each differs in mobility. Each has unique wants and needs and perceptions of their satisfaction. Human response to distance decay is expressed in a controlling critical distance beyond which the frequency of interaction quickly declines. That decline is partly conditioned by unfamiliarity with distant points outside normal activity space. Perceptions of home and distant territory therefore color interaction flows and space evaluations. In turn, those perceptions, well or poorly based, underlie travel and migration decisions, part of the continuing spatial diffusion and interaction of people. It is to people and their patterns of distribution and regional growth and change that we turn our attention in the following chapter.

KEY WORDS

activity space 64
awareness space 64
chain migration 78
channelized migration 81
complementarity 59
counter migration 78
critical distance 66
distance decay 60
friction of distance 60
gravity model 61
intervening opportunity 59

law of retail gravitation 61
migration 73
mobility 63
movement bias 62
network 62
personal communication field 69
personal space 63
place perception 70
place utility 77
potential model 62
pull factor 77

push factor 77
Reilly's law 61
return migration 78
space-time prism 64
spatial interaction 58
spatial search 78
step migration 78
territoriality 63
transferability 59

FOR REVIEW

1. What is meant by *spatial interaction?* What are the three fundamental conditions governing all forms of spatial interaction? What is the distinctive impact or importance of each of the conditions?

2. What variations in *distance decay* curves might you expect if you were to plot shipments of ready-mixed concrete, potato chips, and computer parts? What do these respective curves tell us about transferability?

3. What is *activity space?* What factors affect the areal extent of an individual's activity space?

4. On a piece of paper, and following the model of Figure 3.11, plot your *space-time path* for your movements

on a typical class day. What alterations in your established movement habits might be necessary (or become possible) if (a) Instead of walking, you rode a bike? (b) Instead of biking, you drove a car? (c) Instead of driving, you had to use the bus or go by bike or afoot?

5. What does the thought that transportation and communication are *space-adjusting* imply? In what ways has technology affected the "space adjustment" in commodity flows? In information flows?

6. Recall the places you have visited in the past week. In your movements, were the rules of *distance decay* and *critical distance* operative? What variables affect *your* critical distances?

7. What considerations appear to influence the decision to migrate? How do perceptions of *place utility* induce or inhibit migration?

8. What is a *migration field?* Some migration fields show a *channelized* flow of people. Select a particular channelized migration flow (such as the movement of Scandinavians to Michigan, Wisconsin, and Minnesota, or people from the Great Plains to California, or southern blacks to the North) and speculate why a channelized flow developed.

KEY CONCEPTS REVIEW

1. **What are the three bases for all spatial interaction?** pp. 58–60.
   Spatial interaction reflects areal differences and is controlled by three "flow-determining" factors. *Complementarity* implies a local supply of an item for which effective demand exists elsewhere. *Transferability* expresses the costs of movement from source of supply to locale of demand. An *intervening opportunity* serves to reduce flows of goods between two points by presenting nearer or cheaper sources.

2. **How is the likelihood of spatial interaction probability measured?** pp. 60–62.
   The probability of aggregate spatial movements and interactions may be assessed by the application of established models. *Distance decay* reports the decline of interaction with increase in separation; the *gravity model* tells us that distance decay can in part be overcome by the enhanced attraction of larger centers of activity; and *movement bias* helps explain interaction flows contrary to model predictions.

3. **What are the forms, attributes, and controls of human spatial behavior?** pp. 63–67.
   While humans react to distance, time, and cost considerations of spatial movement, their spatial behavior is also affected by separate conditions of activity and awareness space, of individual economic and life-cycle circumstances, by degree of mobility, and by unique perceptions of wants and needs.

4. **What roles do information and perception play in human spatial actions?** pp. 68–73.
   Humans base decisions about the opportunity or feasibility of spatial movements, exchanges, or want satisfactions on *place perceptions*. These condition the feelings we have about physical and cultural characteristics of areas, the opportunities they possess, and their degree of attractiveness. Those perceptions may not be based on reality or supported by balanced information. Distant places are less known than nearby ones, for example, and real natural hazards of areas may be mentally minimized through familiarity or rationalization.

5. **What kinds of migration movements can be recognized and what influences their occurrence?** pp. 73–85.
   Migration means the permanent relocation of residence and activity space. It is subject to all the principles of spatial interaction and behavior and represents both a survival strategy for threatened people and a reasoned response to perceptions of opportunity. Migration has been enduring throughout human history and occurs at separate scales from intercontinental to regional, and includes flights of refugees and relocations of retirees. Negative home conditions (push factors) coupled with perceived positive destination attractions (pull factors) are important, as are age and sex of migrants and the spatial search they conduct. Step and chain migration and return migratory flows all affect patterns and volume of flows.

POPULATION:
World Patterns, Regional Trends

4

The Djemaa el Fna open air market in the old quarter of Marrakesh, Morocco, is among the liveliest of markets in North Africa.

Key Concepts

1. Data and measures used by population geographers: the meaning and purpose of population cohorts, rates, and other measurements, pp. 89–102.

2. What we are told by the demographic transition model and the demographic equation, pp. 102–109.

3. World population distributions, densities, and urban components, pp. 110–115.

4. Population projections, controls, and prospects: estimating the future, pp. 115–119.

"Zero, possibly even negative [population] growth" was the 1972 slogan proposed by the prime minister of Singapore, an island country in Southeast Asia. *His nation's population, which stood at 1 million at the end of World War II (1945), had doubled by the mid-1960s. To avoid the overpopulation he foresaw, the government decreed "Boy or girl, two is enough" and refused maternity leaves and access to health insurance for third or subsequent births. Abortion and sterilization were legalized, and children born fourth or later in a family were to be discriminated against in school admissions policy. In response, by the mid-1980s birth rates had fallen to below the level necessary to replace the population, and abortions were terminating more than one-third of all pregnancies.*

"At least two. Better three. Four if you can afford it" was the national slogan proposed by that same prime minister in 1986, reflecting fears that the stringencies of the earlier campaign had gone too far. From concern that overpopulation would doom the country to perpetual Third World poverty, Prime Minister Lee Kuan Yew was moved to worry that population limitation would deprive it of the growth potential and national strength implicit in a youthful, educated workforce adequate to replace and support the present aging population. His 1990 national budget provided for sizable long-term tax rebates for second children born to mothers under 28. Not certain that financial inducements alone would suffice to increase population, the Singapore government annually renewed its offer to take 100,000 Hong Kong Chinese who might choose to leave when China took over that territory in 1997.

The policy reversal in Singapore reflects an inflexible population reality: the structure of the present controls the content of the future. The size, characteristics, growth trends, and migrations of today's populations help shape the well-being of peoples yet unborn but whose numbers and distributions are now being determined. The numbers, age, and sex distribution of people; patterns and trends in their fertility and mortality; and their density of settlement and rate of growth all affect and are affected by the social, political, and economic organization of a society. Through population data, we begin to understand how the people in a given area live, how they may interact with one another, how they use the land, what pressure on resources exists, and what the future may bring.

Population geography provides the background tools and understandings of those interests. It focuses on the number, composition, and distribution of human beings in relation to variations in the conditions of earth space. It differs from **demography,** the statistical study of human population, in its concern with *spatial* analysis—the relationship of numbers to area. Regional circumstances of resource base, type of economic development, level of living, food supply, and conditions of health and well-being are basic to geography's population concerns. They are, as well, fundamental expressions of the human–environmental relationships that are the substance of all human geographic inquiry.

Population Growth

Sometime before July 2007, a human birth raised Earth's population to about 6.6 billion people. In mid-1995, the count was 5.6 billion. That is, over the 12 years between those dates, the world population grew on average by more than 80 million people annually, or some 220,000 per day. The average, however, conceals the reality that annual increases have been declining over the years. During the early 1990s, the U.S. Census Bureau and the United Nations Population Division regularly reported yearly growth at 85 to 90 million; by the early 21st century that increase had dropped to 76 or 77 million annually. Even with the slower pace of estimated increase, the United Nations in 2006 still projected that the world would likely contain about 9.2 billion inhabitants in 2050. Even then, it would continue to add a few million persons annually and grow to perhaps 9.4 or 9.5 billion by the year 2100.

However, impressed by dramatic birth rate reductions reported by 2008 for many developing and populous countries—India, importantly—many demographers lowered their estimates to predict end-of-century world totals peaking at between 8 and 9 billion, followed by numerical decline, not stability or slow increase. All do agree, however, that essentially all of any future growth will occur in countries now considered "developing," (Figure 4.1), with especially rapid growth in the 50 least-developed states. The world's ten most populous countries are mostly found in the developing regions of the world and that trend will become even more pronounced by 2050 (Table 4.1). We will return to these projections and to the difficulties and disagreements inherent in making them later in this chapter.

Just what is implied by numbers in the millions and billions? With what can we compare the 2008 population of Estonia in Europe (about 1.3 million) or of China (about 1.3 billion)? Unless we have some grasp of their scale and meaning, our understanding of the data and data manipulations of the population geographer can at best be superficial. It is difficult to appreciate a number as

Table 4.1

World's Most Populous Countries, 2008 and 2050

2008		2050	
Country	Population (millions)	Country	Population (millions)
China	1,325	India	1,755
India	1,149	China	1,437
United States	305	United States	438
Indonesia	240	Indonesia	343
Brazil	195	Pakistan	295
Pakistan	173	Nigeria	282
Nigeria	148	Brazil	260
Bangladesh	147	Bangladesh	215
Russia	142	Congo, Dem. Rep.	189
Japan	128	Philippines	150

Source: Population Reference Bureau, 2008.

(a)

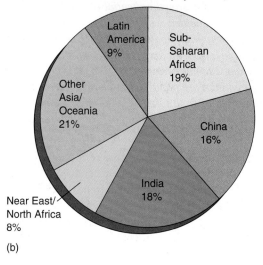

(b)

Figure 4.1 **World population numbers and projections.** (*a*) After two centuries of slow growth, world population began explosive expansion after World War II (1939–1945). United Nations demographers project a global population of 9.2 billion in 2050. Declining growth rates in much of the developing world have lowered earlier year 2100 estimates of global population from 10 billion to no more than 9.4 to 9.5 billion; some demographers argue for further reducing it to between 8 and 9 billion. Numbers in more developed regions at the middle of the century will be the same or lower than at its start, thanks to population stability or decline below early-2000 levels in 51 countries and areas. However, higher fertility rates and immigration are projected to increase the U.S. population by more than 50% between 2000 and 2050, and large-volume immigration into Europe could alter its population decline projections. In contrast, the populations of the less-developed regions may increase by more than 60% between 2000 and 2050. (*b*) Although only a little more than 80% of world population was found in regions considered "less developed" in 2000, more than 9 out of 10 of a larger total will be located there in 2050.

Sources: (a) Estimates from Population Reference Bureau and United Nations Population Fund; (b) Based on United Nations and U.S. Bureau of the Census data and projections.

vast as 1 million or 1 billion, and the great distinction between them. Some examples offered by the Population Reference Bureau may help in visualizing their immensity and implications.

- A 2.5-centimeter (1-inch) stack of U.S. paper currency contains 233 bills. If you had a *million* dollars in thousand-dollar bills, the stack would be 11 centimeters (4.3 inches) high. If you had a *billion* dollars in thousand-dollar bills, your pile of money would reach 109 meters (358 feet)—about the length of a football field.

- You had lived a *million* seconds when you were 11.6 days old. You won't be a *billion* seconds old until you are 31.7 years of age.

The implications of the present numbers and the potential increases in population are of vital current social, political, and ecological concern. Population numbers were much smaller some 12,000 years ago when continental glaciers began their retreat, people spread to formerly unoccupied portions of the globe, and human experimentation with food sources initiated the Agricultural Revolution. The 5 or 10 million people who then constituted all of humanity obviously had considerable potential to expand their numbers. In retrospect, we see that the natural resource base of the earth had a population-supporting capacity far in excess of the pressures exerted on it by early hunting and gathering groups.

Some observers maintain that despite present numbers or even those we can reasonably anticipate for the future, the adaptive and exploitive ingenuity of humans is in no danger of being taxed. Others, however, frightened by the resource demands of a growing world population that had already expanded four-fold—from 1.6 billion to 6.1 billion—in the century from 1900 to 2000, compare Earth to a self-contained spaceship and declare with chilling conviction that a finite vessel cannot bear an ever-increasing number of passengers. They point to recurring problems of malnutrition and starvation (though these are realistically more a matter of failures of distribution than of inability to produce enough foodstuffs worldwide). They cite dangerous conditions of air and water pollution, the loss of forest and farmland, the apparent nearing exhaustion of many minerals and fossil fuels, and other evidences of strains on world resources as foretelling the discernible outer limits of population growth.

On a worldwide basis, populations grow only one way: The number of births in a given period exceeds the number of deaths. Ignoring for the moment regional population changes resulting from migration, we can conclude that observed and projected increases in population must result from the failure of natural controls to limit the number of births or to increase the number of deaths, or from the success of human ingenuity in circumventing such controls when they exist. In contrast, current estimates of slowing population growth and eventual stability or decline in world totals clearly indicate that humans by their individual and collective decisions may effectively limit growth and control global population numbers. The implications of these observations will become clearer after we define some terms important in the study of world population and explore their significance.

Some Population Definitions

Demographers employ a wide range of measures of population composition and trends, though all their calculations start with a count of events: of individuals in the population, of births, deaths, marriages, and so on. To those basic counts, demographers bring refinements that make the figures more meaningful and useful in population analysis. Among them are *rates* and *cohort* measures.

Rates simply record the frequency of occurrence of an event during a given time frame for a designated population—for example, the marriage rate as the number of marriages performed per 1000 population in the United States last year. **Cohort** measures refer data to a population group unified by a specified common characteristic—the age cohort of 1–5 years, perhaps, or the college class of 2011 (Figure 4.2). Basic numbers and rates useful in the analysis of world population and population trends have been reprinted with the permission of the Population Reference Bureau as Appendix B to this book. Examination of them will help illustrate the discussion that follows.

Birth Rates

The **crude birth rate (CBR),** often referred to simply as the *birth rate,* is the annual number of live births per 1000 population. It is "crude" because it relates births to total population without regard to the age or sex composition of that population. A country with a population of 2 million and with 40,000 births a year would have a crude birth rate of 20 per 1000.

$$\frac{40,000}{2,000,000} = \frac{20}{1000} = 20 \text{ per thousand}$$

The birth rate of a country is, of course, strongly influenced by the age and sex structure of its population, by the customs and family size expectations of its inhabitants, and by its adopted population policies. Because these conditions vary widely, recorded national birth rates vary—in the early 21st century, from a high of 45 to 50 or more in some West African states to lows of 9 or 10 per

Figure 4.2 Whatever their differences may be by race, sex, or ethnicity, these babies will forever be clustered demographically into a single *birth cohort.*

1000 in 20 or more European countries. Although birth rates of 30 or above per 1000 are considered *high,* almost one-fifth of the world's people (down from one-half in 1990) live in countries with rates that are that high or higher (Figure 4.3). In these countries—found chiefly in Africa, western and southern Asia, and Latin America—the population is predominantly agricultural and rural, and a high proportion of the female population is young. In many of them, birth rates may be significantly higher than official records indicate. Available data suggest that every year around 50 million births go unregistered and therefore uncounted.

Birth rates of less than 18 per 1000 are reckoned *low* and are characteristic of industrialized, urbanized countries. All European countries including Russia, as well as Anglo America, Japan, Australia, and New Zealand, have low rates as, importantly, do an increasing number of developing states. Some of these, such as China (see "China's Way—and Others"), have adopted effective family planning programs. In others, changed cultural norms have reduced desired family size. *Transitional* birth rates (between 18 and 30 per 1000) characterize some, mainly smaller, developing and newly industrializing countries, though giant India entered that group in 1994.

As the recent population histories of Singapore and China indicate, birth rates are subject to change. The decline to current low birth rates of European countries and of some of the areas that they colonized is usually ascribed to industrialization, urbanization, and, in recent years, maturing populations. While restrictive family planning policies in China rapidly reduced the birth rate from over 33 per 1000 in 1970 to 18 per 1000 in 1986, industrializing Japan experienced a comparable 15-point decline in the decade 1948–1958 with little governmental intervention. Indeed, the stage of economic development appears closely related to variations in birth rates among countries, although rigorous testing of this relationship proves it to be imperfect (Figure 4.3). As a group, the more developed states of the world showed a crude birth rate

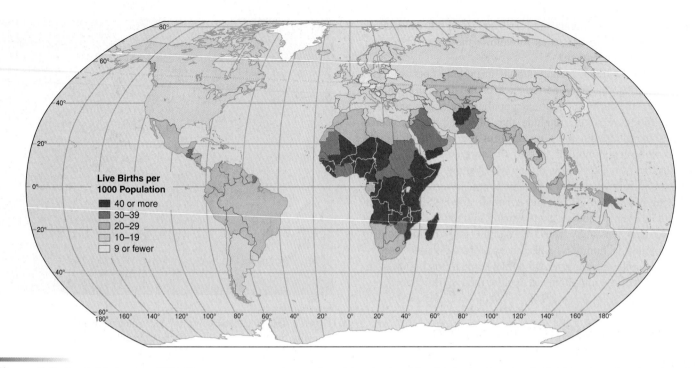

Figure 4.3 **Crude birth rates, 2007.** The map suggests a degree of precision that is misleading in the absence of reliable, universal registration of births. The pattern shown serves, however, as a generally useful summary of comparative reproduction patterns if class divisions are not taken too literally. Reported or estimated population data vary annually, so this and other population maps may not agree in all details with the figures recorded in Appendix B.

Source: Data from Population Reference Bureau, 2008.

of 11 per 1000 in the early years of the 21st century; less developed countries (excluding China) registered about 27 per 1000 (down from 35 in 1990).

Religious and political beliefs can also affect birth rates. The convictions of many Roman Catholics and Muslims that their religion forbids the use of artificial birth control techniques often lead to high birth rates among believers. However, dominantly Catholic Italy has nearly the world's lowest birth rate, and Islam itself does not prohibit contraception. Similarly, some European governments—concerned about birth rates too low to sustain present population levels—subsidize births in an attempt to raise those rates. Regional variations in projected percentage contributions to world population growth are summarized in Figure 4.4.

Fertility Rates

Crude birth rates may display such regional variability because of differences in age and sex composition or disparities in births among the reproductive-age, rather than total, population. The rate is "crude" because its denominator contains persons who have no chance at all of giving birth—males, young girls, and old women. The **total fertility rate (TFR)** is a more refined and thus more satisfactory statement than the crude birth rate for showing the rate and probability of reproduction among fertile females, the only segment of population who is bearing children.

The TFR (Figure 4.5) tells us the average number of children that would be born to each woman if, during her childbearing years, she bore children at the current year's rate for women that age. Thus, a TFR of 3 means that the average woman in a

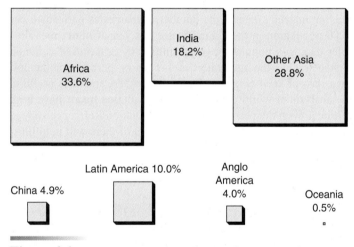

Figure 4.4 **Projected percentage contributions to world population growth by region 2000–2050.** Birth rate changes recorded by different-sized regional populations with differing age structures are altering the world pattern of population increase. Africa, containing 13% of world population in 2000, will probably account for more than one-third of total world increase between 2000 and 2050. Between 1965 and 1975, China's contribution to world growth was 2.5 times that of Africa; between 2000 and 2050, Africa's numerical growth will be more than 8 times that of China. India, which reached the 1 billion level in 2000, is projected to grow by more than 50% over the first half of the 21st century and have by far the world's largest population. In contrast to the growth within the world regions shown, Europe's population is expected to decrease by 90 million over the same half-century period, according to UN projections.

Sources: Projections based on World Bank and United Nations figures.

An ever larger population is "a good thing," Chairman Mao announced in 1965 when China's birth rate was 37 per 1000 and population totaled 540 million. At Mao's death in 1976, numbers reached 852 million, though the birth rate then had dropped to 25. During the 1970s, when it became evident that population growth was consuming more than half of the annual increase in the country's gross domestic product, China introduced a well-publicized campaign advocating the "two-child family" and providing services, including abortions, supporting that program. In response, China's birth rate dropped to 19.5 per 1000 by the late 1970s.

"One couple, one child" became the slogan of a new and more vigorous population control drive launched in 1979, backed by both incentives and penalties to assure its success in China's tightly controlled society. Late marriages were encouraged; free contraceptives, cash awards, abortions, and sterilizations were provided to families limited to a single child. Penalties, including steep fines, were levied for second births. At the campaign's height in 1983, the government ordered the sterilization of either husband or wife for couples with more than one child. Infanticide—particularly the exposure or murder of female babies—was a reported means both of conforming to a one-child limit and of increasing the chances that the one child would be male.

By 1986, China's officially reported crude birth rate had fallen to 18 per 1000, far below the 37 per 1000 then registered among the rest of the world's less developed countries. The one-child policy was relaxed in 1984 to permit two-child limits in rural areas where 63% of Chinese population still resides, but in 2002 it was partially reinstated as nationwide law following documentation of extensive underreporting of rural births. In contrast, newly prosperous urbanites have voluntarily reduced their fertility to well below replacement levels, with childless couples increasingly common.

Nationally, past and current population controls have been so successful that by 2000 China's population was 300 million less than it otherwise would have been. By 2001, indeed, serious concerns were being expressed by demographers and government officials that population decrease, not increase, is the problem next to be confronted. Projections suggest that by 2042, because of lowered fertility rates, China's population numbers will actually start falling. The country is already beginning to face a pressing social problem: a declining proportion of working-age persons and an absence of an adequate welfare network to care for a rapidly growing number of senior citizens.

Concerned with their own increasing numbers, many developing countries have introduced their own less extreme programs of family planning, stressing access to contraception and sterilization. International agencies have encouraged these programs, buoyed by such presumed success as the 21% fall in fertility rates in Bangladesh from 1970 to 1990 as the proportion of married women of reproductive age using contraceptives rose from 3% to 40% under intensive family planning encouragement and frequent adviser visits. The costs per birth averted, however, were reckoned at more than the country's $160 per capita gross domestic product.

Research suggests that fertility falls because women decide they want smaller families, not because they have unmet needs for contraceptive advice and devices. Nineteenth-century northern Europeans without the aid of science had lower fertility rates than their counterparts today in middle-income countries. With some convincing evidence, improved women's education has been proposed as a surer way to reduce births than either encouraged contraception or China's coercive efforts. Studies from individual countries indicate that 1 year of female schooling can reduce the fertility rate by between 5% and 10%. Yet the fertility rate of uneducated Thai women is only two-thirds that of Ugandan women with secondary education. Obviously, the demand for children is not absolutely related to educational levels.

FIRMLY IMPLEMENT THE BASIC NATIONAL POLICY OF FAMILY PLANNING!

population would be expected to have 3 births in her lifetime. The fertility rate minimizes the effects of fluctuation in the population structure and summarizes the demonstrated and expected reproductive behavior of women. It is thus a more useful and more reliable figure for regional comparative and predictive purposes than the crude birth rate.

Although a TFR of 2.0 would seem sufficient exactly to replace present population (one baby to replace each parent), in reality replacement levels are reached only with TFRs of 2.1 to 2.3 or more. The fractions over 2.0 are required to compensate for infant and childhood mortalities, childless women, and unexpected deaths in the general population. The concept of *replacement level*

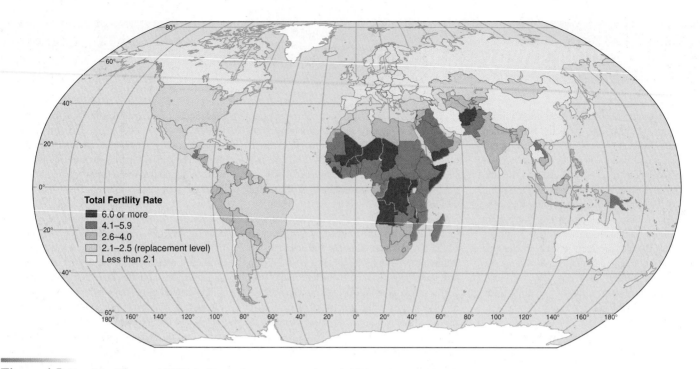

Figure 4.5 **Total fertility rate (TFR)** indicates the average number of children that would be born to each woman if, during her childbearing years, she bore children at the same rate as women of those ages actually did in a given year. Since the TFR is age-adjusted, two countries with identical birth rates may have quite different fertility rates and therefore different prospects for growth. Depending on mortality conditions, a TFR of 2.1 to 2.5 children per woman is considered the "replacement level," at which a population will eventually stop growing.

Source: Data from Population Reference Bureau, 2007.

fertility is useful here. It marks the level of fertility at which each successive generation of women produces exactly enough children to ensure that the same number of women survive to have offspring themselves. In general, then, the higher the level of mortality in a population, the higher the replacement level of fertility will be. For Mozambique early in the 21st century, for example, the replacement level fertility was 3.4 children per woman.

On a worldwide basis, the TFR in 2008 was 2.7; 20 years earlier it was 3.6. The more developed countries recorded a 1.6 TFR in 2007, down from a near-replacement 2.0 in 1987. That decrease has been dwarfed in amount and significance by the rapid changes in reproductive behavior in much of the developing world. Since 1960, the average TFR in the less developed world has fallen by half from the traditional 6.0 or more to 2.8 in 2008. That dramatic decline reflects the fact that women and men in developing countries are marrying later and having fewer children, following the pattern earlier set in the developed world. There has been, as well, a great increase in family planning and contraceptive use. By 2001, according to a UN world fertility report, 92% of all national governments supported family planning and distributed contraceptives, either directly or indirectly.

The recent fertility declines in developing states have been more rapid and widespread than anyone expected. The TFRs for so many of them have dropped so dramatically since the early 1960s (Figure 4.6), that earlier widely believed world population projections anticipating 10.5 billion or more at the end of this century are now generally discounted and rejected. Indeed, worldwide in 2007, 82 countries and territories containing nearly 50% of global population had fertility rates of 2.1 or less, with more poised to join

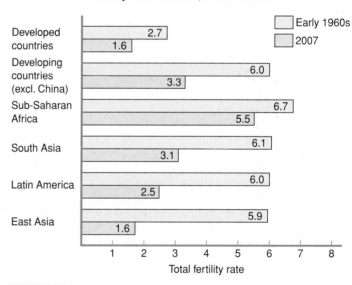

Figure 4.6 **Differential fertility rate declines.** Fertility has declined most rapidly in Latin America and Asia and much more slowly in sub-Saharan Africa. In more than 20 developing countries, the 2007 fertility rate was below the replacement level, as it was for developed countries as a group. Europe was far below with a 2007 TFR of 1.5; the United States, however, with a TFR of 2.1 is just at the replacement point of 2.1.

Sources: Population Reference Bureau and United Nations Population Fund.

their ranks. China's decrease from a TFR of 5.9 births per woman in the period 1960–1965 to (officially) about 1.8 in 2000 (an estimated 1.6 in 2008) and comparable drops in TFRs of Bangladesh,

A Population Implosion?

For much of the last half of the 20th century, demographers and economists focused on a "population explosion" and its implied threat of a world with too many people and too few resources of food and minerals to sustain them. By the end of that century, those fears for some observers were being replaced by a new prediction of a world with too few rather than too many people.

That possibility was suggested by two related trends. The first became apparent by 1970 when it was noted that the total fertility rates (TFRs) of 19 countries, almost all of them in Europe, had fallen below the **replacement level**—the level of fertility at which populations replace themselves—of 2.1. Simultaneously, Europe's population pyramid began to become noticeably distorted, with a smaller proportion of young and a growing share of middle-aged and retirement-age inhabitants. The decrease in native working-age cohorts had already, by 1970, encouraged the influx of non-European "guest workers" whose labor was needed to maintain economic growth and to sustain the generous security provisions guaranteed to what was becoming the oldest population of any continent.

Many countries of Western and Eastern Europe sought to reverse their birth rate declines by adopting pronatalist policies. The communist states of the East rewarded pregnancies and births with generous family allowances, free medical and hospital care, extended maternity leaves, and child care. France, Italy, the Scandinavian countries, and others gave similar bonuses or awards for first, second, and later births. Despite those inducements, however, reproduction rates continued to fall. By 2003, every one of the 43 European countries and territories had fertility rates below replacement levels in widespread response to a host of cultural influences and personal lifestyle decisions. Those decisions were influenced by increased educational levels of women with longer years of schooling and deferred marriage ages, opportunities for women to experience challenging professional or employment careers, the increasing cost of rearing multiple children, and the attractiveness of enjoying without restrictive family obligations the increasing number of recreational opportunities that growing prosperity afforded. The effect on national growth prospects has been striking. For example, the populations of Spain and Italy are projected to shrink by a quarter between 2000 and 2050 (and that of Ukraine by 43% between 2005 and 2050). Europe as a whole is forecast to shrink by 70 million people by mid-century. "In demographic terms," France's prime minister remarked, "Europe is vanishing."

Europe's experience soon was echoed in other societies of advanced economic development on all continents. By 1995, Canada, Australia, New Zealand, Japan, Taiwan, South Korea, Singapore, and other older and newly industrializing countries (NICs) registered fertility rates below the replacement level. As they have for Europe, simple projections foretold their aging and declining population. Japan's numbers, for example, began to decline in 2006 when 21% of its population was age 65 or older; Taiwan forecasts negative growth by 2035.

The second trend indicating to many that world population numbers should stabilize and even decline during the lifetimes of today's college cohort is a simple extension of the first: TFRs are being reduced to or below the replacement levels in countries at all stages of economic development in all parts of the world. While only 18% of total world population in 1975 lived in countries with a fertility rate below replacement level, nearly 45% did so by the end of the century. By 2015, demographers estimate, half the world's countries and about two-thirds of its population will show TFRs below 2.1 children per woman. Exceptions to the trend are and still will be found in Africa, especially sub-Saharan Africa, and in some areas of South, Central, and West Asia; but even in those regions, fertility rates have been decreasing in recent years. "Powerful globalizing forces [are] at work pushing toward fertility reduction everywhere," was an observation of the French National Institute of Demographic Studies.

That conclusion is plausibly supported by assumptions of the United Nations' 2006 forecast of a decline of long-term fertility rates of most less developed states to an average of 1.9. The same UN assessment envisions that those countries will reach those below-replacement fertilities before 2050. Should these assumptions prove valid, global depopulation could commence by or before mid-century. Between 2040 and 2050, one projection indicates, world population would fall by about 85 million (roughly the amount of its annual growth during much of the 1990s) and shrink further by about 25% with each successive generation.

If the UN scenario is realized in whole or in part, a much different worldwide demographic and economic future is promised than that prophesied so recently by "population explosion" forecasts. Declining rather than increasing pressure on world food and mineral resources would be in our future along with shrinking rather than expanding world, regional, and national economies. Even the achievement of **zero population growth (ZPG),** a condition for individual countries when births plus immigration equal deaths plus emigration, has social and economic consequences not always perceived by its advocates. These inevitably include an increasing proportion of older citizens, fewer young people, a rise in the median age of the population, and a growing old-age dependency ratio with ever-increasing pension and social services costs borne by a shrinking labor force.

Brazil, Mozambique, and other states demonstrate that fertility reflects cultural values, not biological imperatives. If those values now favor fewer children than formerly, population projections based on earlier, higher TFR rates must be adjusted.

In fact, demographers have long assumed that recently observed developing country—and therefore global—fertility rate declines to the replacement level would continue and in the long run lead to stable population numbers. However, nothing in logic or history requires population stability at any level. Indeed, rather than assume, as in the past, a fertility decline to a constant continuing rate of 2.1, the 2004 revision of the United Nations' world population projections predicts a long-term world fertility rate of 2.05—*below* the replacement rate. Should the UN's assessment of global fertility prove correct, world population would not just stop growing as past UN projections envisioned; it would inevitably decline (see "A Population Implosion?"). Of course, should cultural values change to again favor children, growth would resume. Different TFR estimates imply conflicting population projections and vastly different regional and world population concerns.

Individual country projections based on current fertility rates, it should be noted, may not accurately anticipate population levels even in the near future. As we saw in Chapter 3, massive international population movements are occurring in response to political instabilities and, particularly, to differentials in perceived economic opportunities. Resulting migration flows may cause otherwise declining national populations to stabilize or even grow. For example, the European Union in recent years has had a negative rate of natural increase, yet since 2000 has experienced essentially a constant population solely because of immigrant influx from Eastern Europe, Asia, and Africa.

World regional and national fertility rates reported in Appendix B and other sources are summaries that conceal significant variations between population groups. The Caribbean region, for example, showed a total fertility rate of 2.6 in 2006, but the TFRs of individual states ranged from a low of 1.5 in Cuba to a high of 4.7 in Haiti. The United States 2006 national average fertility rate of 2.0 did not reveal that the TFR for Hispanics was about 2.8, about 2.1 for African Americans, or only 1.8 for non-Hispanic whites.

Death Rates

The **crude death rate (CDR),** also called the **mortality rate,** is calculated in the same way as the crude birth rate: the annual number of events per 1000 population. In the past, a valid generalization was that the death rate, like the birth rate, varied with national levels of development. Characteristically, highest rates (over 20 per 1000) were found in the less developed countries of Africa, Asia, and Latin America; lowest rates (less than 10) were associated with developed states of Europe and Anglo America. That correlation became decreasingly valid as dramatic reductions in death rates occurred in developing countries in the years following World War II. Infant mortality rates and life expectancies improved as antibiotics, vaccinations, and pesticides to treat diseases and control disease carriers were made available in almost all parts of the world and as increased attention was paid to funding improvements in urban and rural sanitary facilities and safe water supplies.

Distinctions between more developed and less developed countries in mortality (Figure 4.7), indeed, have been so reduced that by 1994 death rates for less developed countries as a group actually dropped below those for the more developed states and have remained lower since. Notably, that reduction did not extend to maternal mortality rates (see "The Risks of Motherhood"). Like crude birth rates, death rates are meaningful for comparative purposes only when we study identically structured populations. Countries with a high proportion of elderly people, such as Denmark and Sweden, would be expected to have higher death rates than those with a high proportion of young people, such as Iceland, assuming equality in other national conditions affecting health and longevity. The pronounced youthfulness of populations in developing countries, as much as improvements in sanitary and health conditions, is an important factor in the recently reduced mortality rates of those areas.

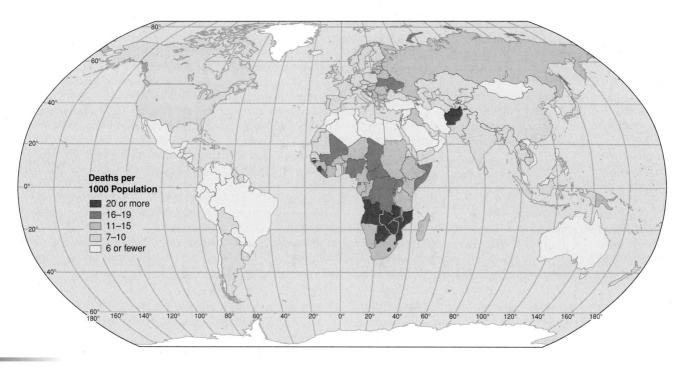

Figure 4.7 **Crude death rates** show less worldwide variability than do the birth rates displayed in Figure 4.3. The widespread availability of at least minimal health protection measures and a generally youthful population in the developing countries yield death rates frequently lower than those recorded in "old age" Europe.

Source: Data from Population Reference Bureau, 2007.

The Risks of Motherhood

The worldwide leveling of crude death rates does not apply to pregnancy-related deaths. In fact, the maternal mortality ratio—maternal deaths per 100,000 live births—is the single greatest health disparity between developed and developing countries. According to the World Health Organization, approximately 530,000 women die each year from causes related to pregnancy and childbirth; 99% of them live in less developed states where, as a group, the maternal mortality ratio is some 30 times greater than in the more developed countries. Pregnancy complications, childbirth, and abortions are the leading slayers of women of reproductive age throughout the developing world, though the incidence of maternal mortality is by no means uniform, as the chart indicates. According to 2000 data, in Africa the risk is 1 death in 20 pregnancies compared with 1 in 160 in Latin America and the Caribbean, and 1 in 7700 in Europe. Country-level differences are even more striking: in Angola, for example, the lifetime risk is 1 death out of every 7 pregnancies compared to 1 in almost 30,000 in Sweden.

The developing countries as a group in 2000 had a maternal mortality ratio of 440, and 10% of all deaths were due to perinatal and maternal causes; least developed states registered a ratio of 890. In 2000, Asia and Africa recorded almost the same number of maternal deaths (48% and 47% of the world total, respectively), but sub-Saharan African women, burdened with 45% of world maternal mortality, were at greatest statistical risk. There, maternal death ratios in 2000 reached above 1600 in Angola, Malawi, and Niger and to more than 2000 in Sierra Leone; 1 in 16 women in sub-Saharan Africa dies of maternal causes. In contrast, the maternal mortality ratio in developed countries as a group (including Russia and eastern Europe) is 20, and in some—Ireland, Austria, and Sweden, for example—it is as low as 2 to 5 (it was 6 in Canada and 17 in the United States in 2000).

The vast majority of maternal deaths in the developing world are preventable. Most result from causes rooted in the social, cultural, and economic barriers confronting females in their home environment throughout their lifetimes: malnutrition, anemia, lack of access to timely basic maternal health care, physical immaturity due to stunted growth, and unavailability of adequate prenatal care or trained medical assistance at birth. Part of the problem is that women are considered expendable in societies in which their status is low, although the correlation between women's status and maternal mortality is not exact. In those cultures, little attention is given to women's health or their nutrition, and pregnancy, although a major cause of death, is simply considered a normal condition warranting no special consideration or management. To alter that perception and increase awareness of the affordable measures available to reduce maternal mortality worldwide, 1998 was designated "The Year of Safe Motherhood" by a United Nations inter-agency group.

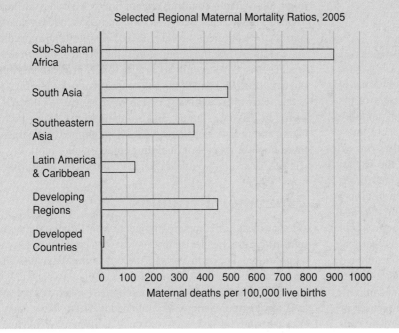

Selected Regional Maternal Mortality Ratios, 2005

Source: Graph data from Maternal Mortality in 2005, *Geneva, Switzerland: WHO Press, 2007.*

To overcome that lack of comparability, death rates can be calculated for specific age groups. The *infant mortality rate,* for example, is the ratio of deaths of infants aged 1 year or under per 1000 live births:

$$\frac{\text{deaths age 1 year or less}}{1000 \text{ live births}}$$

Infant mortality rates are significant because it is at these ages that the greatest declines in mortality have occurred, largely as a result of the increased availability of health services. The drop in infant mortality accounts for a large part of the decline in the general death rate in the last few decades, for mortality during the first year of life is usually greater than in any other year.

Two centuries ago, it was not uncommon for 200–300 infants per 1000 to die in their first year. Even today, despite significant declines in those rates over the last 70 years in many countries (Figure 4.8), striking world regional and national variations remain. For all of Africa, infant mortality rates are near 85 per 1000, and individual African states (for example, Angola, Liberia, Niger, and Sierra Leone) showed rates above 150 early in this century. Nor are rates uniform within single countries. The former Soviet Union reported a national infant mortality rate of 23 (1991), but it registered above 110 in parts of its Central Asian region. In contrast, infant

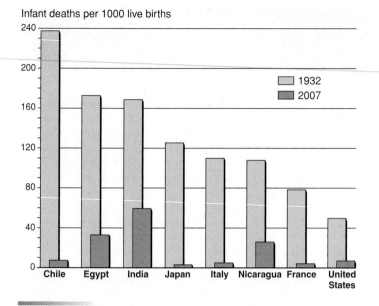

Infant deaths per 1000 live births

Figure 4.8 **Infant mortality rates for selected countries.**
Dramatic declines in the rate have occurred in all countries, a result
of international programs of health care delivery aimed at infants and
children in developing states. Nevertheless, the decreases have been
proportionately greatest in the urbanized, industrialized countries, where
sanitation, safe water, and quality health care are widely available.

Sources: Data from U.S. Bureau of the Census and Population Reference Bureau.

mortality rates in more developed countries are more uniformly in
the 2–7 range. Infant mortality rates are not solely a matter of the
economic status of a country. For example, the U.S. infant mortality
rate exceeds that of Canada, South Korea, Japan, Singapore, most
Northern and Western European countries, and even Cuba.

Modern medicine and sanitation have increased life expectancy and altered age-old relationships between birth and death
rates. In the early 1950s, only five countries, all in northern Europe,
had life expectancies at birth of over 70 years. In the first decade
of the 21st century, some 75 countries outside of Europe and North
America—though none in sub-Saharan Africa—were on that list.
The availability and employment of modern methods of health and
sanitation have varied regionally, and the least developed countries
have least benefited from them. In such underdeveloped and impoverished areas as much of sub-Saharan Africa, the chief causes of
death other than HIV/AIDS are those no longer of immediate concern in more developed lands: diseases such as malaria, intestinal
infections, typhoid, cholera, and especially among infants and children, malnutrition and dehydration from diarrhea.

HIV/AIDS is the tragic and, among developing regions particularly, widespread exception to observed global improvements in life
expectancies and reductions in adult death rates and infant and childhood mortalities. AIDS has become the fourth most common cause of
death worldwide and is forecast to surpass the Black Death of the 14th
century—which caused an estimated 25 million deaths in Europe and
13 million in China—as history's worst-ever epidemic. According to a
report by UNAIDS, AIDS is expected to kill 68 million people between
2000 and 2020 in the 45 most affected countries; about 55 million of
those deaths will occur in sub-Saharan Africa. The United Nations
estimated nearly 40 million people were HIV positive in 2006. Some

90% of those infected live in developing countries, and 65% reside
in sub-Saharan Africa, where women account for 60% of all cases.
In that hardest-hit region, as much as one-fourth of the adult population in some countries is HIV positive, and average life expectancy has
been cut drastically. In South Africa, the life expectancy of a baby born
in the early 21st century should have been 66 years; AIDS has cut that
down to 47. In Botswana, it is 34 years instead of 70; in Zimbabwe the
decline has been to 37 years from 69. Overall, AIDS has killed some
17 million Africans since the 1950s when HIV (originally a disease
of monkeys) appears to have established itself in Africa as a virulent
human epidemic strain. Along with the deep cuts in sub-Saharan life
expectancies, total population by 2015 is now projected to be 60 million less than it would have been in the absence of the disease.

Economically, AIDS will cut an estimated 8% off national
incomes in the worst-hit sub-Saharan countries by 2010. Southern
Africa's economies are based on farming, and women do much of
the farming as well as run households. Because AIDS kills more
women than men, sub-Saharan food insecurity is rising and food
shortages result because many young adults are too feeble to farm.
Malnutrition, starvation, and susceptibility to other diseases are
thus AIDS costs added to impersonal national income reductions.

Nonetheless, because of their high fertility rates, populations
in all sub-Saharan countries except South Africa are still expected
to grow significantly between 2000 and 2050, adding nearly 1 billion to the continent's total. Indeed, despite high mortality rates
due to HIV/AIDS, the population of the world's 48 least developed
countries as a group will, according to UN projections, almost triple between 2000 and 2050, the consequence of their high fertility
levels. However, warnings of the rapid spread of the AIDS epidemic in Russia, Ukraine, and South and East Asia—particularly
China and India—raise new global demographic concerns even as
more hopeful reports of declining infection and mortality rates in
some African and Southeast Asian countries are appearing.

Population Pyramids

Another means of comparing populations is through the **population
pyramid,** a graphic device that represents a population's age and sex
composition. The term *pyramid* describes the diagram's shape for
many countries in the 1800s, when the display was created: a broad
base of younger age groups and a progressive narrowing toward the
apex as older populations were thinned by death. Now many different shapes are formed, each reflecting a different population history
(Figure 4.9), and some suggest "population profile" is a more appropriate label. By grouping several generations of people, the pyramids
or profiles highlight the impact of "baby booms," population-reducing
wars, birth rate reductions, and external migrations.

A rapidly growing country such as Uganda has most people in
the lowest age cohorts; the percentage in older age groups declines
successively, yielding a pyramid with markedly sloping sides.
Typically, female life expectancy is reduced in older cohorts of
less developed countries, so that for Uganda, the proportion of
females in older age groups is lower than in, for example, Sweden.
Female life expectancy and mortality rates may also be affected by
cultural rather than economic developmental causes (see "Millions
of Women Are Missing"). In Sweden, a wealthy country with a
very slow rate of growth, the population is nearly equally divided

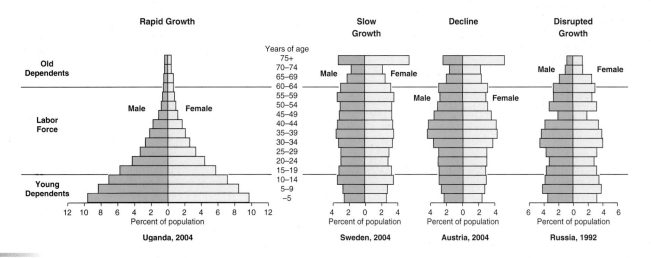

Figure 4.9 **Four patterns of population structure.** These diagrams show that population "pyramids" assume many shapes. The age distribution of national populations reflects the past, records the present, and foretells the future. In countries such as Uganda, social costs related to the young are important and economic expansion is vital to provide employment for new entrants in the labor force. Their 2004 pyramids suggest Sweden will only slowly grow by 6% between 2025 and 2050 and Austria will decline by 2.5% over the same period. For comparison, the United States was in 2004 projected to increase by 20% over that quarter century. Austria's negative growth means a future with fewer workers to support a growing demand for social services for the elderly. The 1992 pyramid for Russia reported the sharp decline in births during World War II as a "pinching" of the 45–49 cohort, and showed in the large deficits of men above age 65 the heavy male mortality of both World Wars and late-Soviet period sharp reductions in Russian male longevity.

Sources: The 2004 pyramids for Uganda, Sweden, and Austria: U.S. Bureau of the Census, International Data Bases; and for Russia; Carl Haub, "Population Change in the Former Soviet Republics." Population Bulletin 49, No. 4 (1994).

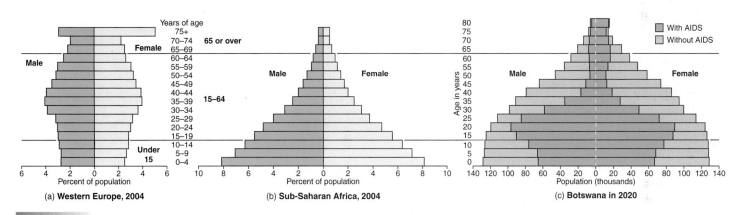

Figure 4.10 **Summary population pyramids.** The 2004 pyramids for (*a*) Western Europe and (*b*) sub-Saharan Africa show the sharp contrasts in the age structure of older developed regions with their characteristic lowered birth and total fertility rates and that of the much more youthful developing sub-Saharan states. Even in 2004, about 44% of the sub-Saharan population was below age 15. That percentage, however, was smaller than it had been just 5 years earlier and hinted at more dramatic declines possible in years to come. Part of the projected decline will come as a result of economic development and changing family size decisions, but for some countries (*c*) and perhaps for the region as a whole, tremendous pyramid distortions will result from the demographic impact of AIDS. By 2020, the otherwise expected "normal" pyramid of Botswana may well be distorted into a "population chimney" in which there would be more adults in their 60s and 70s than adults in their 40s and 50s.

Sources: (a) and (b) U.S. Bureau of the Census, International Data Base; (c) U.S. Bureau of the Census, World Population Profile 2000.

among the age groups, giving a "pyramid" with almost vertical sides. Among older cohorts, as Austria shows, there may be an imbalance between men and women because of the greater life expectancy of the latter. The impacts of war, as Russia's 1992 pyramid vividly demonstrated, were evident in that country's depleted age cohorts and male-female disparities. The sharp contrasts between the composite pyramids of sub-Saharan Africa and Western Europe summarize the differing population concerns of the developing and developed regions of the world; the projection for Botswana suggests the degree to which accepted pyramid shapes can quickly change (Figure 4.10).

The population profile provides a quickly visualized demographic picture of immediate practical and predictive value. For example, the percentage of a country's population in each age group strongly influences demand for goods and services within that national economy. A country with a high proportion of young has a high demand for educational facilities and certain types of health delivery services. In addition, of course, a large portion of the population is too young to be employed (Figures 4.10 and 4.11). On the other hand, a population with a high percentage of elderly people also requires medical goods and services specific to that age group, and these people must be supported by a smaller

Millions of Women Are Missing

Worldwide, according to one UN estimate, between 113 million and 200 million women are demographically missing, victims of nothing more than their sex. Their absence is the result of girl fetus abortion and female infanticide in countries where boys are favored; deprivation of food and medical attention disproportionately given to brothers, fathers, husbands and sons; "honor killings" in Muslim communities, dowry deaths in India, and other forms of domestic violence. If the UN estimate is correct, between 1.5 and 3 million women and girls are lost to gender-based discrimination and violence each year in a regionally variable pattern. The majority of that loss appears due to birth disparities.

In China, India, Pakistan, New Guinea, and many other developing countries, a traditional preference for boys has meant neglect and death for girls, millions of whom are killed at birth, deprived of adequate food, or denied the medical attention provided to sons, favored as old-age and wealth-gathering insurance for parents. In both China and India, ultrasound and amniocentesis tests are employed, often against government directives, to determine the sex of a fetus so that it can be aborted if it is a female.

The evidence for the missing women starts with one fact: About 106 males are conceived and born for every 100 females. Normally, girls are hardier and more resistant to disease than boys, and in populations where the sexes are treated equally in matters of nutrition and health care, there are about 105 to 106 females for every 100 males. However, the 2001 census of India found just 93.2 females for every 100 males, while in China, according to the latest census, nearly 10% of all girls of the 1990s birth cohorts are "missing," and there were 120 boys under age 5 for every 100 girls. China's 2000 census recorded a national average disparity in births of 117 boys for every 100 girls—a deepening imbalance from the 1990 census ratio of 111 newborn boys to 100 newborn girls. Even higher 2000 differentials were registered in Hainan and Guangdong provinces in southeastern China with newborn ratios of between 130 and 140 males to 100 females.

Ratio deviations are most striking for second and subsequent births. In China, South Korea, Taiwan, and Hong Kong, for example, the most recent figures for first-child sex ratios are near normal, but rise to 121 boys per 100 girls for a second Chinese child and to 185 per 100 for a third Korean child. On that evidence, the problem of missing females is getting worse. Conservative calculations suggest there are more than 60 million females missing in China alone, almost 5% of the national population and more than are unaccounted for in any other country.

The problem is seen elsewhere. The UN Population Fund reports that countries such as Bahrain, Oman, Qatar, Saudi Arabia, and United Arab Emirates have male-to-female ratios ranging between 116:100 and 186:100. In much of South and West Asia and North Africa, there are only some 94 females for every 100 males, a shortfall of about 12% of normal (Western) expectations. A 2000 United Nations report on South Asia suggests the "100 million" world total of missing females is a gross understatement. It declares that abortions of female fetuses along with infanticide and the food favoritism shown boys have meant that 79 million lost females are attributable to discrimination in South Asia, including some 40 million in India alone.

But not all poor countries show the same disparities. In sub-Saharan Africa, where poverty and disease are perhaps more prevalent than on any other continent, but where there is no tradition of deadly violence against women, there are 102 females for every 100 males, and in Latin America and the Caribbean, there are equal numbers of males and females. Cultural norms and practices, not poverty or underdevelopment, seem to determine the fate and swell the numbers of the world's millions of missing women.

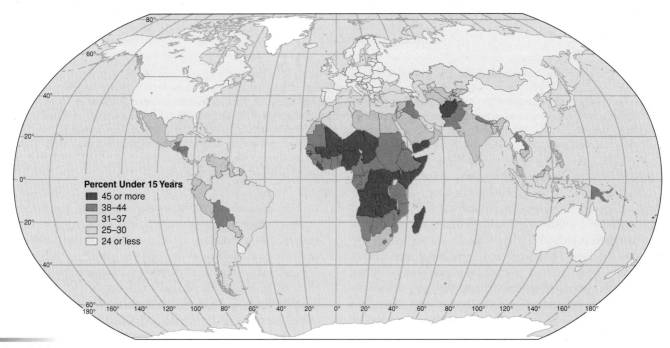

Figure 4.11 **Percentage of population under 15 years of age.** A high proportion of a country's population under 15 increases the dependency ratio of that state and promises future population growth as the youthful cohorts enter childbearing years.

Source: Data from Population Reference Bureau, 2008.

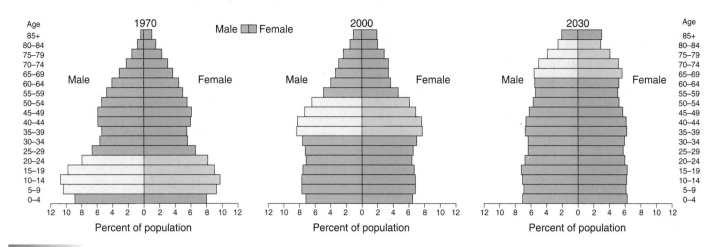

Figure 4.12 **The progression of the "boomers"**—the baby boom cohort born between 1946 and 1964—through the U.S. population pyramid has been associated with changing American lifestyles and expenditure patterns. In 1970, national priorities focused on childhood and young adult interests and the needs, education, and support of younger age groups. At the turn of the 21st century, boomers formed the largest share of the working-age adult population, and their wants and spending patterns shaped the national culture and economy. By 2030, the pyramid foretells, their desires and support needs—now for retirement facilities and old-age care—will again be central concerns.

Source: Redrawn from Christine L. Himes, "Elderly Americans," Population Bulletin 56, no. 4 (December 2001), Fig. 1.

proportion of workers. As the profile of a national population changes, differing demands are placed on a country's social and economic systems (Figure 4.12). The **dependency ratio** is a simple measure of the number of economic dependents, old or young, that each 100 people in the productive years (usually, 15–64) must support. Population pyramids give quick visual evidence of that ratio.

They also foretell future problems resulting from present population policies or practices. The strict family-size rules and widespread preferences for sons in China, for example, skews the pyramid in favor of males. On current evidence, about 1 million excess males a year will enter an imbalanced marriage market in China beginning about 2010. Even now, the Chinese population pyramid shows never-married men ages 20–44 outnumber their female counterparts by nearly 2 to 1. The 40 million bachelors China is likely to have in 2020, unconnected to society by wives and children, may pose threats to social order and, perhaps, national stability not foreseen or planned when family control programs were put in place, but clearly suggested when made evident by population pyramid distortions.

Natural Increase and Doubling Times

Knowledge of a country's sex and age distributions also enables demographers to forecast its future population levels, though the reliability of projections decreases with increasing length of forecast (Figure 4.13). Thus, a country with a high proportion of young people will experience a high rate of natural increase unless there is a very high mortality rate among infants and juveniles or fertility and birth rates change materially. The **rate of natural increase** of a population is derived by subtracting the crude death rate from the crude birth rate. *Natural* means that increases or decreases due to migration are not included. If a country had a birth rate of 22 per 1000 and a death rate of 12 per 1000 for a given year, the rate of natural increase would be 10 per 1000. This rate is usually expressed as a percentage, that is, as a rate per 100 rather than per 1000. In the example given, the annual increase would be 1%.

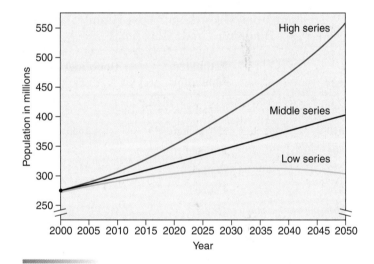

Figure 4.13 **Possible population futures for the United States.** As these population projections to 2050 illustrate, expected future numbers vary greatly because the fertility, birth and death rate, and immigration flow assumptions they are based on are different. Depending on those assumptions, 2000 Census Bureau projections of U.S. population in 2050 ranged from 313.5 million (low series) to 552.7 million (high series). The middle series estimate of 403.6 million is the one most often cited. The folly of basing planning decisions on very long range projections is made clear by the Bureau's extension of its trends for a full century. By 2100, it calculates, U.S. population could range from a low series 282.7 million to a high series 1.18 billion.

Source: U.S. Bureau of the Census.

The rate of increase can be related to the time it takes for a population to double if the present growth rate remains constant—that is, the **doubling time.** Table 4.2 shows that it would take 70 years for a population with a rate of increase of 1% (approximately the rate of growth of Thailand or Argentina at the turn of the century) to double. A 2% rate of increase—recorded in 2008 by Egypt, Ecuador,

Table 4.2

Doubling Time in Years at Different Rates of Increase

Annual Percentage Increase	Doubling Time (Years)
0.5	140
1.0	70
2.0	35
3.0	24
4.0	18
5.0	14
10.0	7

Table 4.3

Population Growth and Approximate Doubling Times Since A.D. 1

Year	Estimated Population	Doubling Time (Years)
1	250 million	
1650	500 million	1650
1804	1 billion	154
1927	2 billion	123
1974	4 billion	47
World population may reach:		
2030	8 billion	56[a]

[a]The final estimate of doubling time reflects assumptions of decreasing and stabilizing fertility rates. No current projections contemplate a further doubling to 16 billion people.
Source: United Nations.

Here, then, lies the answer to the question posed earlier. Even small annual additions accumulate to large total increments because we are dealing with geometric or exponential (1, 2, 4, 8) rather than arithmetic (1, 2, 3, 4) growth. The ever-increasing world base population has reached such a size that each additional doubling results in an astronomical increase in the total. A simple mental exercise suggests the inevitable consequences of such doubling, or **J-curve,** growth. Take a very large sheet of the thinnest paper you can find and fold it in half. Fold it in half again. After seven or eight folds, the sheet will have become as thick as a book—too thick for further folding by hand. If you could make 20 folds, the stack would be nearly as high as a football field is long. From then on, the results of further doubling are astounding. At 40 folds, the stack would be well on the way to the moon, and at 70 it would reach twice as far as the distance to the nearest star. Rounding the bend on the J-curve, which Figure 4.15 suggests world population did around 1900, fostered after 1950, dire predictions of inevitable unsupportable pressures on the planet's population support capabilities.

By 2000, however, it became apparent that few developed countries, particularly in Europe, were likely in the foreseeable future or ever to double their population size if their growth were projected—as usually done—solely on current rates of natural increase. But individual country growth is also dependent on patterns of immigration and emigration and of changes in life expectancy. That is, a country's "natural" population growth based solely on births and deaths may yield significantly lower population projections and longer doubling times than does that same country's "overall" growth taking migration into account. The contrast may be striking. The United States in the early years of this century had a 0.6% rate of natural increase and a doubling time of 117 years; it had, however, an *overall* growth rate of 1.2% with a doubling time of 58 years.

With immigration largely absent, declining fertility rates in most of the developing world, and the incidence of AIDS in sub-Saharan Africa and parts of populous Asia, doubt is cast on the utility or applicability of long-term doubling time projections even for present high growth rate countries. Although the United Nations estimates that the population of the 50 least developed countries will possibly almost triple between 2000 and 2050, we should understand that doubling time assumptions are inherently misleading and population increases are limited.

The Demographic Transition

The theoretical consequence of exponential population growth cannot be realized. Some form of braking mechanism must necessarily operate to control totally unregulated population growth. If voluntary population limitation is not undertaken, involuntary controls of an unpleasant nature may be set in motion.

One attempt to summarize an observed voluntary relationship between population growth and economic development is the **demographic transition** model. It traces the changing levels of human fertility and mortality presumably associated with industrialization and urbanization. Over time, the model assumes, high birth and death rates will gradually be replaced by low rates (Figure 4.16). The *first stage* of that replacement process—and of

Libya and Micronesia—means that the population would double in only 35 years. (Population doubling time can be roughly estimated by applying the Rule of 72, which simply involves dividing 72 by the growth rate.) How could adding only 20 people per 1000 cause a population to grow so quickly? The principle is the same as that used to compound interest in a bank.

Until recently, for the world as a whole, the rates of increase have risen over the span of human history. Therefore, the doubling time has decreased (Table 4.3). Growth rates vary regionally, and in countries with high rates of increase (Figure 4.14), the doubling time is less than the 60 years projected for the world as a whole at 2008 growth rates. Should world fertility rates decline (as they have in recent years), theoretical population doubling time would correspondingly increase, as it has since 1990.

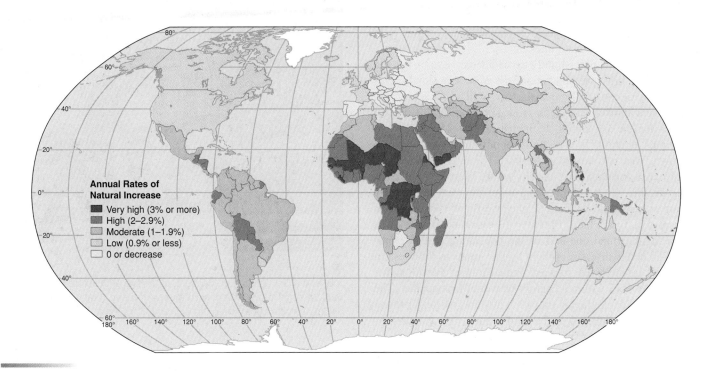

Figure 4.14 **Annual rates of natural increase.** The world's 2008 rate of natural increase (1.2%) would mean a doubling of population in 60 years. Since many demographers now anticipate world population will stabilize at around 9.5 billion (in about A.D. 2100) and perhaps actually decline after that, the "doubling" implication and time frame of current rates of natural increase reflect mathematical, not realistic, projections. Many individual continents and countries, of course, deviate widely from the global average rate of growth and have vastly different potential doubling times. Africa as a whole has the highest rates of increase, followed by Central America and Western Asia. Europe as a whole (including Russia) had negative growth early in the 21st century, with some individual countries showing increases so small that their doubling times would be measured in millennia.

Source: Data from Population Reference Bureau, 2008.

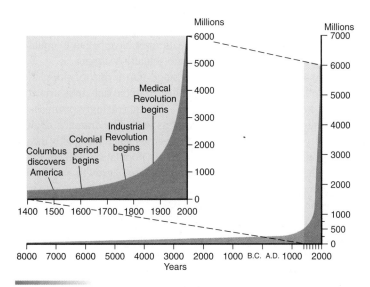

Figure 4.15 **World population growth 8000 B.C. to A.D. 2000.** Notice that the bend in the J-curve begins in about the mid-1700s when industrialization started to provide new means to support the population growth made possible by revolutionary changes in agriculture and food supply. Improvements in medical science, sanitation, and nutrition reduced death rates near the opening of the 20th century in the industrializing countries.

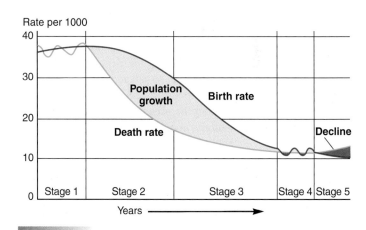

Figure 4.16 **Stages in the demographic transition.** During the first stage, birth and death rates are both high, and population grows slowly. When the death rate drops and the birth rate remains high, there is a rapid increase in numbers. During the third stage, birth rates decline, and population growth is less rapid. The fourth stage is marked by low birth and death rates and, consequently, by a low rate of natural increase or even by decrease if death rates should exceed those of births. The negative growth rates of many European countries and the falling birth rates in other regions suggest that a fifth stage, one of population decline, is regionally—and ultimately worldwide—a logical extension of the transition model.

the demographic transition model—is characterized by high birth and high but fluctuating death rates.

As long as births only slightly exceed deaths, even when the rates of both are high, the population will grow only slowly. This was the case for most of human history until about A.D. 1750. Demographers think that it took from approximately A.D. 1 to A.D. 1500 for the population to increase from 250 million to 500 million, a doubling time of a millennium and a half.

Growth was not steady, of course. There were periods of regional expansion that were usually offset by sometimes catastrophic decline. Wars, famine, and other disasters took heavy tolls. For example, the bubonic plague (the Black Death), which swept across Europe in the 14th century, is estimated to have killed between one-third and one-half of the population of that continent, and epidemic diseases brought by Europeans to the Western Hemisphere are believed to have reduced New World native populations by 95% within a century or two of first contact. The first stage of the demographic transition model is no longer found in any country. By the end of the 20th century, few countries—even in poorer regions of sub-Saharan Africa—had death rates as high as 20 per 1000. However, in several African states birth rates approached or were above 50 per 1000.

The Western Experience

The demographic transition model was developed to explain the population history of Western Europe, parts of which began to experience declining death rates through the conversion of epidemic diseases to endemic forms even before the Industrial Revolution that began about 1750. The *second stage* of the transition model, however, is usually associated with the modernizing consequences of the industrialization of Europe. Its effects—declining death rates accompanied by continuing high birth rates—were gradually dispersed worldwide even without universal conversion to an industrial economy.

Rapidly rising population during the second demographic stage results from dramatic increases in life expectancy. That, in turn, reflects falling death rates due to advances in medical and sanitation practices, improved foodstuff storage and distribution, a rising per capita income, and the urbanization that provides the environment in which sanitary, medical, and food distributional improvements are concentrated (Figure 4.17). Birth rates do not fall as soon as death rates; ingrained cultural patterns change more slowly than technologies. In many agrarian societies, large families are considered advantageous. Children contribute to the family by starting to work at an early age and by supporting their parents in old age.

Many countries in southern Asia and Latin America display the characteristics of this second stage in the population model. Pakistan, with a birth rate of 31 and a death rate of 8, and Guatemala, with respective rates of 34 and 6 (2007 estimates), are typical. The annual rates of increase of such countries are near 30 per 1000, and their populations will double in about 25 to 30 years. Such rates, of course, do not mean that the full impact of the Industrial Revolution has been worldwide; they do mean that the underdeveloped societies have been beneficiaries of the life preservation techniques associated with it.

Figure 4.17 Liverpool, England, in the late 19th century. A modernizing Europe experienced improved living conditions and declining death rates during that century of progress.

The *third stage* follows when birth rates decline as people begin to control family size. The advantages of having many children in an agrarian society are not so evident in urbanized, industrialized cultures. In fact, such cultures may view children as economic liabilities rather than assets. When the birth rate falls and the death rate remains low, the population size begins to level off. Many countries are now registering the low death rates and transitional birth rates of the third stage.

The classic demographic transition model ends with a *fourth* and final stage characterized by very low birth and death rates. This stage yields at best only very slight percentage increases in population and doubling times stretch to a thousand years or more. A significant and irreversible aging of the world's population is a direct and profound consequence of the worldwide transition from high to low levels of fertility and mortality associated with this fourth stage of the model (see p. 118). In a few countries, death rates have begun to equal or exceed birth rates and populations are actually declining.

This extension of the fourth stage into a *fifth* of population decrease has so far been largely confined to the rich, industrialized world—notably Europe and Japan—but increasingly promises to affect much of the rest of the world as well. The dramatic decline in fertility recorded in almost all countries since the 1980s means that by 2010 a majority of the world's population will reside in areas where the only significant population growth will result from demographic momentum (see p. 117), not from second-stage expansion.

The original transition model was devised to describe the experience of northwest European countries as they went from rural-agrarian societies to urban-industrial ones. It may not fully reflect the prospects of all developing countries. In Europe, church and municipal records, some dating from the 16th century, show that people tended to marry late or not at all. In England before the Industrial Revolution, as many as half of all women in the 15–50 age cohort were unmarried. Infant mortality was high, life expectancy low. With the coming of industrialization in the 18th and 19th centuries, immediate factory wages instead of long apprenticeship programs permitted earlier marriage and more children.

Since improvements in sanitation and health came only slowly, death rates remained high. Around 1800, 25% of Swedish infants died before their first birthday. Population growth rates remained below 1% per year in France throughout the 19th century.

Beginning about 1860, first death rates and then birth rates began their significant, though gradual, decline. This "mortality revolution" came first, as an *epidemiologic transition* echoed the demographic transition with which it is associated. Many formerly fatal epidemic diseases—already locally in decline a century earlier—became endemic, that is, essentially continual within a population, and mortality patterns showed a shift from communicable to noncommunicable diseases. As people developed partial immunities, mortalities associated with them declined. Improvements in animal husbandry, crop rotation and other agricultural practices, and new foodstuffs (the potato was an early example) from overseas colonies raised the level of health of the European population in general.

At the same time, sewage systems and sanitary water supplies became common in larger cities, and general levels of hygiene improved everywhere (Figure 4.18). Deaths due to infectious, parasitic, and respiratory diseases and to malnutrition declined, while those related to chronic illnesses associated with a maturing and aging population increased. Western Europe passed from a first stage "Age of Pestilence and Famine" to a presumed ultimate "Age of Degenerative and Human-Origin Diseases." However, recent increases in drug- and antibiotic-resistant diseases, pesticide resistance of disease-carrying insects, and such new scourges of both the less developed and more developed countries as AIDS (acquired immune deficiency syndrome) cast doubt on the finality of that "ultimate" stage (see "Our Delicate State of Health"). Nevertheless, even the resurgence of old and emergence of new scourges such as malaria, tuberculosis, and AIDS (which together caused an estimated 160 million deaths between 1945 and 2006) are unlikely to have decisive demographic consequences on the global scale.

In Europe, the striking reduction in death rates was echoed by similar declines in birth rates as societies began to alter their traditional concepts of ideal family size. In cities, child labor laws and mandatory schooling meant that children no longer were important contributors to family economies. As "poor-relief" legislation and other forms of public welfare substituted for family support structures, the insurance value of children declined. Family consumption patterns altered as the Industrial Revolution made more widely available goods that served consumption desires, not just basic living needs. Children hindered rather than aided the achievement of the age's promise of social mobility and lifestyle improvement. Perhaps most important, and by some measures preceding and independent of the implications of the Industrial Revolution, were changes in the status of women and in their spreading conviction that control over childbearing was within their power and to their benefit.

A Divided World Converging

The demographic transition model described the presumed inevitable course of population events from the high birth and death rates of premodern (underdeveloped) societies to the low and stable rates of advanced (developed) countries. The model failed to anticipate, however, that the population history of Europe was apparently not relevant to all developing countries of the middle and late 20th century. Many developing societies remained in the second stage of the model, unable to realize the economic gains and social changes necessary to progress to the third stage of falling birth rates.

Figure 4.18 Pure piped water replacing individual or neighborhood wells, and sewers and waste treatment plants instead of privies, became increasingly common in urban Europe and North America during the 19th century. Their modern successors, such as the Las Vegas, Nevada, treatment plant shown here, helped complete the *epidemiologic transition* in developed countries.

Death rates have plummeted, and the benefits of modern medicines, antibiotics, and sanitary practices have enhanced both the quality and expectancy of life in the developed and much of the developing world. Far from being won, however, the struggle against infectious and parasitic diseases is growing in intensity and is, perhaps, unwinnable. More than a half century after the discovery of antibiotics, the diseases they were to eradicate are on the rise, and both old and new disease-causing microorganisms are emerging and spreading all over the world. Infectious and parasitic diseases kill between 17 and 20 million people each year; they officially account for one-quarter to one-third of global mortality and, because of poor diagnosis, certainly are responsible for far more. And their global incidence is rising.

The five leading infectious killers are acute respiratory infections such as pneumonia, diarrheal diseases, tuberculosis, malaria, and measles. In addition, AIDS was killing 3 million or more persons yearly early in this century, far more than measles or malaria. The incidence of infection, of course, is much greater than the occurrence of deaths. Nearly 30% of the world's people, for example, are infected with the bacterium that causes tuberculosis, but only 2 to 3 million are killed by the disease each year. More than 500 million people are infected with such tropical diseases as malaria, sleeping sickness, schistosomiasis, and river blindness, with perhaps 3 million annual deaths. Newer

pathogens are constantly appearing, such as those causing Lassa fever, Rift Valley fever, Ebola fever, hantavirus pulmonary syndrome, West Nile encephalitis, hepatitis C, and severe acute respiratory syndrome (SARS), incapacitating and endangering far more than they kill. In fact, at least 30 previously unknown infectious diseases have appeared since the mid-1970s.

The 1918–1919 Spanish Flu pandemic demonstrates how diseases can diffuse globally with devastating effect. Striking as World War I was drawing to an end, the epidemic's spread was likely aided by massive troop movements as it diffused along shipping routes. The influenza virus struck down the young and healthy and killed an estimated 20 to 40 million people. The spread and virulence of infectious diseases are linked to the dramatic changes so rapidly occurring in the earth's physical and social environments. Climate warming permits temperature-restricted pathogens to invade new areas and claim new victims. Deforestation, water contamination, wetland drainage, and other human-induced alterations to the physical environment disturb ecosystems and simultaneously disrupt the natural system of controls that keep infectious diseases in check.

Rapid population growth and explosive urbanization, increasing global tourism, population-dislocating wars and migrations, and expanding world trade all increase interpersonal disease-transmitting contacts and the

mobility and range of disease-causing microbes, including those brought from previously isolated areas by newly opened road systems and air routes. Add in poorly planned or executed public health programs, inadequate investment in sanitary infrastructures, and inefficient distribution of medical personnel and facilities, and the causative role of humans in many of the current disease epidemics is clearly visible.

In response, a worldwide Program for Monitoring Emerging Diseases (ProMED) was established in 1993 and developed a global on-line infectious disease network linking health workers and scientists in more than 100 countries to battle what has been called a growing "epidemic of epidemics." The most effective weapons in that battle are already known. They include improved health education; disease prevention and surveillance; research on disease vectors and incidence areas (including GIS and other mapping of habitats conducive to specific diseases); careful monitoring of drug therapy; mosquito control programs; provision of clean water supplies; and distribution of such simple and cheap remedies and preventatives as childhood immunizations, oral rehydration therapy, and vitamin A supplementation. All, however, require expanded investment and attention to those spreading infectious diseases—many with newly developed antibiotic-resistant strains—so recently thought to be no longer of concern.

The introduction of Western technologies of medicine and public health, including antibiotics, insecticides, sanitation, immunization, infant and child health care, and eradication of smallpox, quickly and dramatically increased life expectancies in developing countries. Such imported technologies and treatments accomplished in a few years what it took Europe 50 to 100 years to experience. Sri Lanka, for example, sprayed extensively with DDT to combat malaria; life expectancy jumped from 44 years in 1946 to 60 only 8 years later. With similar public health programs, India also experienced a steady reduction in its death rate after 1947. Simultaneously, with international sponsorship, food aid cut the death toll of developing states during drought and other disasters. The dramatic decline in mortality that had emerged only gradually throughout the European world occurred with startling speed in developing countries after 1950.

Corresponding reductions in birth rates did not immediately follow, and world population totals soared: from 2.5 billion in 1950 to 3 billion by 1960 and 5 billion by the middle 1980s. Alarms about the "population explosion" and its predicted devastating impact on

global food and mineral resources were frequent and strident. In demographic terms, the world was viewed by many as permanently divided between developed regions that had made the demographic transition to stable population numbers and the underdeveloped, endlessly expanding ones that had not.

Birth rate levels, of course, unlike life expectancy improvements, depend less on supplied technology and assistance than they do on social acceptance of the idea of fewer children and smaller families (Figure 4.19). That acceptance began to grow broadly but unevenly worldwide even as regional and world population growth seemed uncontrollable. In 1984, only 18% of world population lived in countries with fertility rates at or below replacement levels (that is, countries that had achieved the demographic transition). By 2000, however, 44% lived in such countries, and early in the 21st century it is increasingly difficult to distinguish between developed and developing societies on the basis of their fertility rates. Those rates in many separate Indian states (Kerala and Tamil Nadu, for example) and in such countries as Sri Lanka, Thailand,

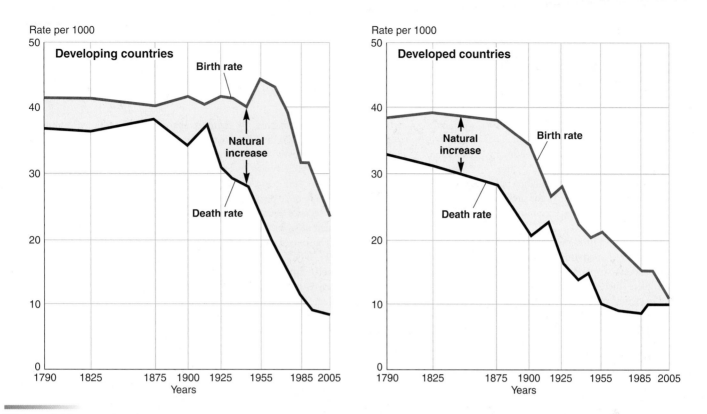

Figure 4.19 World birth and death rates to 2005. The "population explosion" after World War II (1939–1945) reflected the effects of drastically reduced death rates in developing countries without simultaneous and compensating reductions in births. By the end of the 20th century, however, three interrelated trends had appeared in many developing world countries: (1) fertility had overall dropped further and faster than had been earlier predicted; (2) contraceptive acceptance and use had increased markedly; and (3) age at marriage was rising. In consequence, the demographic transition had been compressed from a century to a generation in some developing states. In others, fertility decline began to slacken in the mid-1970s, but continued to reflect the average number of children—four or more—still desired in many societies.

Source: Revised and redrawn from Elaine M. Murphy, World Population: Toward the Next Century, *revised ed. (Washington, D.C.: Population Reference Bureau, 1989).*

South Korea, and China are below those of the United States and some European countries. Significant decreases to near the replacement level have also occurred in the space of a single generation in many other Asian and Latin American states with high recent rates of economic growth. Increasingly, it appears, low fertility is becoming a feature of both rich and poor, developed and developing states.

Despite this substantial merging of fertility rates, many observers point not to a convergence of world demographic trends but to a continuing and growing demographic divide. On one side of the divide, they remind us, are high-growth countries that accounted for just 8% of world population in 2005 but were then projected to triple in size and increase their global population share to 20% by 2050. On the other side of the divide are the mainly wealthy states whose low birth rates guarantee future population decline and rapid aging. Nearly all of the high-growth countries are included on the United Nation's list of least-developed countries. Most of them are in sub-Saharan Africa and all suffer from low per capita income, illiteracy, low living levels, and inadequate health facilities and care.

The established patterns of both high and low fertility regions tend to be self-reinforcing. Low growth permits the expansion of personal income and the accumulation of capital that enhance the quality and security of life and make large families less attractive or essential. In contrast, in high birth rate regions, population growth consumes in social services and assistance the investment capital that

might promote economic expansion. Increasing populations place ever greater demands on limited soil, forest, water, grassland, and cropland resources. As the environmental base deteriorates, productivity declines and population-supporting capacities are so diminished as to make difficult or impossible the economic progress on which the demographic transition depends (see "The Cairo Plan"). The vastly different future prospects for personal and national prosperity and well-being between the high-growth countries and the rest of the world, it is claimed, make the demographic divide a matter of continuing concern to the entire world community and render the presumed convergence of the divided world largely illusory.

The Demographic Equation

Births and deaths among a region's population—natural increases or decreases—tell only part of the story of population change. Migration involves the long-distance movement of people from one residential location to another. When that relocation occurs across political boundaries, it affects the population structure of both the origin and destination jurisdictions. The **demographic equation** summarizes the contribution made to regional population change over time by the combination of *natural change* (difference between births and deaths) and *net migration* (difference

Geography and Public Policy

The Cairo Plan

After a sometimes rancorous 9-day meeting in Cairo in September, 1994, the United Nations International Conference on Population and Development endorsed a strategy for stabilizing the world's population at 7.27 billion by no later than 2015. The 20-year program of action accepted by 179 signatory countries sought to avoid the environmental consequences of excessive population growth. Its proposals were therefore linked to discussions and decisions of the UN Conference on Environment and Development held in Rio de Janeiro in June 1992.

The Cairo plan abandoned several decades of top-down governmental programs that promoted "population control" (a phrase avoided by the conference) based on targets and quotas and, instead, embraced for the first time policies giving women greater control over their lives, greater economic equality and opportunity, and a greater voice in reproduction decisions. It recognized that limiting population growth depends on programs that lead women to want fewer children and make them partners in economic development. In that recognition, the Conference accepted the documented link between increased educational access and economic opportunity for women and falling birth rates and smaller families. Earlier population conferences—1974 in Bucharest and 1984 in Mexico City—did not fully address these issues of equality, opportunity, education, and political rights; their adopted goals failed to achieve hoped-for changes in birth rates in large part because women in many traditional societies had no power to enforce contraception and feared their other alternative, sterilization.

The earlier conferences carefully avoided or specifically excluded abortion as an acceptable family planning method. It was the more open discussion of abortion in Cairo that elicited much of the spirited debate that registered religious objections by the Vatican and many Muslim and Latin American states to the inclusion of legal abortion as part of health care, and to language suggesting approval of sexual relations outside of marriage. Although the final text of the conference declaration did not promote any universal right to abortion and excluded it as a means of family planning, some delegations still registered reservations to its wording on both sex and abortion. At conference close, however, the Vatican endorsed the declaration's underlying principles, including the family as "the basic unit of society" and the need to stimulate economic growth, and to promote "gender equality, equity, and the empowerment of women."

A special United Nations "Cairo + 5" session in 1999 recommended some adjustments in the earlier agreements. It urged emphasis on measures ensuring safe and accessible abortion in countries where it is legal, called for school children at all levels to be instructed in sexual and reproductive health issues, and told governments to provide special family planning and health services for sexually active adolescents, with particular stress on reducing their vulnerability to AIDS.

In 2004, the UN reported on conclusions reached after a series of regional conferences that assessed progress toward reaching Cairo and Cairo + 5 goals. The consensus was that much remained to be done to broaden programs for the poorest population groups, to invest in rural development and urban planning, to strengthen laws ending discrimination against women, and to encourage donor countries to fully meet their agreed-on contributions to the program (in 2002, those contributions were only half the promised total). Nevertheless, positive Cairo plan results were also seen in declining fertility rates in many of the world's most populous developing countries. Some demographers and many women's health organizations pointedly claim that those declines have little to do with government planning policies. Rather, they assert, current lower and falling fertility rates are the expected result of women assuming greater control over their economic and reproductive lives. The director of the UN Population Division noted: "A woman in a village making a decision to have one or two or at most three children is a small decision in itself. But . . . compounded by millions and millions . . . of women in India and Brazil and Egypt, it has global consequences."

That women are making those decisions, population specialists have observed, reflects important cultural factors emerging since Cairo. Satellite television brings contraceptive information to even remote villages and shows programs of small, apparently happy families that viewers think of emulating. Increasing urbanization reduces some traditional family controls on women and makes contraceptives easier to find, and declining infant mortality makes mothers more confident their babies will survive. Perhaps most important, population experts assert, is the dramatic increase in most developing states in female school attendance and corresponding reductions in the illiteracy rates of girls and young women who will themselves soon be making fertility decisions.

Questions to Consider

1. Do you think it is appropriate or useful for international bodies to promote policies affecting such purely personal or national concerns as reproduction and family planning? Why or why not?

2. Do you think that current international concerns over population growth, development, and the environment are sufficiently valid and pressing to risk the loss of long-enduring cultural norms and religious practices in many of the world's traditional societies? Why or why not?

3. The Cairo plan called for sizeable monetary pledges from developed countries to support enhanced population planning in the developing world. For the most part, those pledges have not been honored. Do you think the financial obligations assigned to donor countries are justified in light of the many other international needs and domestic concerns faced by their governments? Why or why not?

4. Many environmentalists see the world as a finite system unable to support ever-increasing populations; to exceed its limits would cause frightful environmental damage and global misery. Many economists counter that free markets will keep supplies of needed commodities in line with growing demand and that science will, as necessary, supply technological fixes in the form of substitutes or expansion of production. In light of such diametrically opposed views of population growth consequences, is it appropriate or wise to base international programs solely on one of them? Why or why not?

between in-migration and out-migration).[1] On a global scale, of course, all population change is accounted for by natural change. The impact of migration on the demographic equation increases as the population size of the areal unit studied decreases.

Population Relocation

In the past, emigration proved an important device for relieving the pressures of rapid population growth in at least some European countries (Figure 4.20). For example, in one 90-year span, 45% of the natural increase in the population of the British Isles emigrated, and between 1846 and 1935 some 60 million Europeans of all nationalities left that continent. Despite recent massive movements of economic and political refugees across Asian, African, and Latin American boundaries, emigration today provides no comparable relief valve for developing countries. Total population numbers are too great to be much affected by migrations of even millions of people. In only a few countries—Afghanistan, Cuba, El Salvador, and Haiti, for example—have as many as 10% of the population emigrated in recent decades.

Immigration Impacts

Where cross-border movements are massive enough, migration may have a pronounced impact on the demographic equation and result in significant changes in the population structures of both

---

[1]See the Glossary definition for the calculation of the equation.

the origin and destination regions. Past European and African migrations, for example, not only altered but substantially created the population structures of new, sparsely inhabited lands of colonization in the Western Hemisphere and Australasia. In some decades of the late 18th and early 19th centuries, 30% to more than 40% of population increase in the United States was accounted for by immigration. Similarly, eastward-moving Slavs colonized underpopulated Siberia and overwhelmed native peoples.

Migrants are rarely a representative cross section of the population group they leave, and they add an unbalanced age and sex component to the group they join. A recurrent research observation is that emigrant groups are heavily skewed in favor of young singles. Whether males or females dominate the outflow varies with circumstances. Although males traditionally far exceeded females in international flow, in recent years females have accounted for between 40% and 60% of all transborder migrants.

At the least, then, the receiving country will have its population structure altered by an outside increase in its younger age and, probably, unmarried cohorts. The results are both immediate in a modified population pyramid, and potential in future impact on reproduction rates and excess of births over deaths. The origin area will have lost a portion of its young, active members of childbearing years. It perhaps will have suffered distortion in its young adult sex ratios, and it certainly will have recorded a statistical aging of its population. The destination society will likely experience increases in births associated with the youthful newcomers and, in general, have its average age reduced.

Figure 4.20 Principal migrations of recent centuries. The arrows suggest the major free and forced international population movements since about 1700. The shaded areas on the map are regions whose present population is more than 50% descended from the immigrants of recent centuries. More recently there have been significant population movements into the United Kingdom, France, Belgium, and the Netherlands from their former colonies and from less prosperous countries within the European Union.

Source: Shaded zones after Daniel Noin, Géographie de la Population *(Paris: Masson, 1979), p. 85.*

World Population Distribution

The millions and billions of people of our discussion are not uniformly distributed over the earth. The most striking feature of the world population distribution map (Figure 4.21) is the very unevenness of the pattern. Some land areas are nearly uninhabited, others are sparsely settled, and still others contain dense agglomerations of people. Until about 2007, rural folk—unevenly concentrated—always outnumbered urban people. After 2007, however, urbanites will remain dominant with a constantly growing proportion of them residents of very large cities of 1 million or more.

Earth regions of apparently very similar physical makeup show quite different population numbers and densities, perhaps the result of differently timed settlement or of settlement by different cultural groups. Northern and Western Europe, for example, inhabited thousands of years before North America, contain as many people as the United States on 70% less land; the present heterogeneous population of the Western Hemisphere is vastly more dense than was that of earlier Native Americans.

We can draw certain generalizing conclusions from the uneven, but far from irrational, distribution of population shown in Figure 4.21. First, almost 90% of all people live north of the equator and two-thirds of the total dwell in the midlatitudes between 20° and 60° North (Figure 4.22). Second, a large majority of the world's inhabitants occupy only a small part of its land surface. More than half the people live on about 5% of the land, two-thirds on 10%, and almost nine-tenths on less than 20%. Third, people congregate in lowland areas; their numbers decrease sharply with increases in elevation. Temperature, length of growing season, slope and erosion problems, even oxygen reductions at very high altitudes, all appear to limit the habitability of higher elevations. One estimate is that between 50% and 60% of all people live below 200 meters (650 ft), a zone containing less than 30% of total land area. Nearly 80% reside below 500 meters (1650 ft).

Fourth, although low-lying areas are preferred settlement locations, not all such areas are equally favored. Continental margins have attracted the densest settlement. By United Nations estimates, some 3 billion people—nearly 50% the world's population—live within 200 kilometers (125 mi) of a coastline, most of them on alluvial lowlands and river valleys. By 2025, that figure is likely to double. On average, density in coastal areas is about 80 persons per square kilometer (over 200 per square mile), twice the world's average population density. Latitude, aridity, and elevation, however, limit the attractiveness of many seafront locations. Low temperatures and infertile soils of the extensive Arctic coastal lowlands of the Northern Hemisphere have restricted settlement there. Mountainous or desert coasts are sparsely occupied at any latitude, and some tropical lowlands and river valleys that are marshy, forested, and disease-infested are also unevenly settled.

Within the sections of the world generally conducive to settlement, four areas contain great clusters of population: East Asia, South Asia, Europe, and northeastern United States/southeastern Canada. The *East Asia* zone, which includes Japan, China, Taiwan, and South Korea, is the largest cluster in both area and numbers. The four countries forming it contain nearly 25% of all people on earth; China alone accounts for one in five of the world's inhabitants. The *South Asia* cluster is composed primarily of countries associated with the Indian subcontinent—Bangladesh, India, Pakistan, and the island state of Sri Lanka—though some might add to it the Southeast Asian countries of Cambodia, Myanmar, and Thailand. The four core countries contain another one-fifth, 22%, of the world's inhabitants. The South and the East Asian concentrations are thus home to nearly one-half the world's people.

Europe—southern, western, and eastern through Ukraine and much of European Russia—is the third extensive world population concentration, with another 12% of its inhabitants. Much smaller in extent and total numbers is the cluster in *northeastern United*

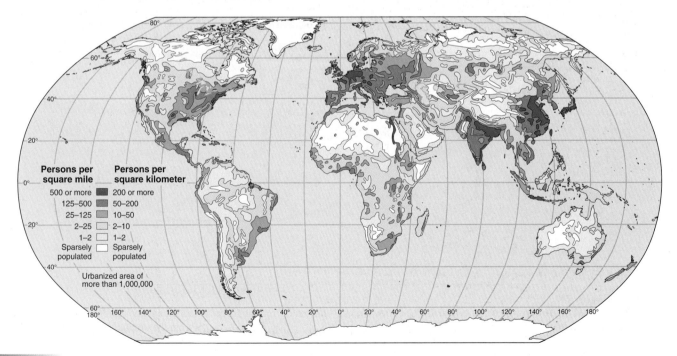

Figure 4.21 World population density.

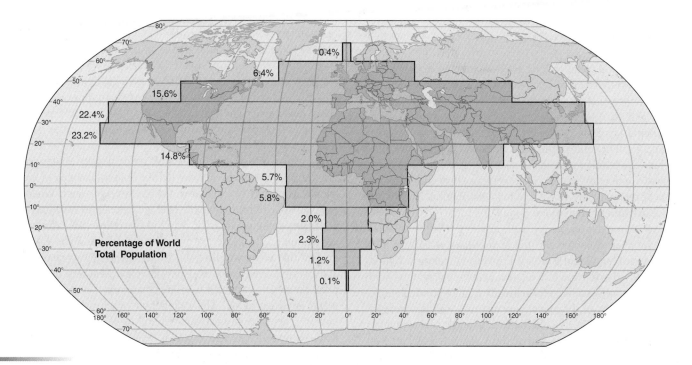

Figure 4.22 **The population dominance of the Northern Hemisphere** is strikingly evident from this bar chart. Only one out of nine people lives south of the equator—not because the Southern Hemisphere is underpopulated, but because it is mainly water.

States/southeastern Canada. Other smaller but pronounced concentrations are found around the globe: on the island of Java in Indonesia, along the Nile River in Egypt, and in discontinuous pockets in Africa and Latin America.

The term **ecumene** is applied to permanently inhabited areas of the earth's surface. The ancient Greeks used the word, derived from their verb "to inhabit," to describe their known world between what they believed to be the unpopulated, searing southern equatorial lands and the permanently frozen northern polar reaches of the earth. Clearly, natural conditions are less restrictive than Greek geographers believed. Both ancient and modern technologies have rendered habitable areas that natural conditions make forbidding. Irrigation, terracing, diking, and draining are among the methods devised to extend the ecumene locally (Figure 4.23).

At the world scale, the ancient observation of habitability appears remarkably astute. The **nonecumene,** or *anecumene,* the uninhabited or very sparsely occupied zone, does include the permanent ice caps of the Far North and Antarctica and large segments of the tundra and coniferous forest of northern Asia and North America. But the nonecumene is not continuous, as the ancients supposed. It is discontinuously encountered in all portions of the globe and includes parts of the tropical rain forests of equatorial zones, midlatitude deserts of both the Northern and Southern Hemispheres, and high mountain areas.

Even parts of these unoccupied or sparsely occupied districts have localized dense settlement nodes or zones based on irrigation agriculture, mining and industrial activities, and the like. Perhaps the most striking case of settlement in an environment elsewhere considered part of the nonecumene world is that of the dense population in the Andes Mountains of South America and the plateau of Mexico. Here Native Americans found temperate conditions away from the dry coast regions and the hot, wet Amazon basin.

Figure 4.23 Terracing of hillsides is one device to extend a naturally limited productive area. The technique is effectively used here on the island of Bali, Indonesia.

The fertile high basins have served a large population for more than a thousand years.

Even with these locally important exceptions, the nonecumene portion of the earth is extensive. Some 35% to 40% of all the world's land surface is inhospitable and without significant settlement. This is, admittedly, a smaller proportion of the earth than would have qualified as uninhabitable in ancient times or even during the 19th century. Since the end of the Ice Age some 11,000 to 12,000 years ago, humans have steadily expanded their areas of settlement.

Population Density

Margins of habitation could only be extended, of course, as humans learned to support themselves from the resources of new settlement areas. The numbers that could be sustained in old or new habitation zones were and are related to the resource potential of those areas and the cultural levels and technologies possessed by the occupying populations. The term **population density** expresses the relationship between number of inhabitants and the area they occupy.

Density figures are useful, if sometimes misleading, representations of regional variations of human distribution. The **crude density,** or **arithmetic density,** of population is the most common and least satisfying expression of that variation. It is the calculation of the number of people per unit area of land, usually within the boundaries of a political entity. It is an easily reckoned figure. All that is required is information on total population and total land area, both commonly available for national or other political units. The figure can, however, be misleading and may obscure more of reality than it reveals. The calculation is an average, and a country may contain extensive regions that are only sparsely populated or largely undevelopable (Figure 4.24) along with intensively settled and developed districts. A national average density figure reveals nothing about either class of territory. In general, the larger the political unit for which crude or arithmetic population density is calculated, the less useful is the figure.

Various modifications may be made to refine density as a meaningful abstraction of distribution. Its descriptive precision is improved if the area in question can be subdivided into comparable regions or units. Thus it is more revealing to know that in 2005, New Jersey had a density of 454 and Wyoming of 2 persons per square kilometer (1175 and 5.2 per sq mi) of land area than to know only that the figure for the conterminous United States

(48 states) was 38.5 per square kilometer (99.6 per sq mi). If Hawaii and large, sparsely populated Alaska are added, the U.S. density figure drops to 32.4 per square kilometer (83.8 per sq mi). The calculation may also be modified to provide density distinctions between classes of population—rural versus urban, for example. Rural densities in the United States rarely exceed 115 per square kilometer (300 per sq mi), while portions of major cities can have many thousands of people in equivalent space.

Another revealing refinement of crude density relates population not simply to total national territory but to that area of a country that is or may be cultivated, that is, to *arable* land. When total population is divided by arable land area alone, the resulting figure is the **physiological density,** which is, in a sense, an expression of population pressure exerted on agricultural land. Table 4.4 makes evident that countries differ in physiological density and that the contrasts between crude and physiological densities of countries point up actual settlement pressures that are not revealed by arithmetic densities alone. The calculation of physiological density, however, depends on uncertain definitions of arable and cultivated land, assumes that all arable land is equally productive and comparably used, and includes only one part of a country's resource base.

Agricultural density is still another useful variant. It simply excludes city populations from the physiological density calculation and reports the number of rural residents per unit of agriculturally productive land. It is, therefore, an estimate of the pressure of people on the rural areas of a country.

Overpopulation

It is an easy and common step from concepts of population density to assumptions about overpopulation or overcrowding. It is wise to remember that **overpopulation** is a value judgment reflecting

Figure 4.24 **Tundra vegetation and landscape in the Alaska National Wildlife Refuge.** While this area may contain underground petroleum deposits, it is part of the *nonecumene*—sparsely populated portions of the earth's surface.

Table 4.4

Comparative Densities for Selected Countries

Country	Crude (Arithmetic) Density		Physiological Density[a]		Agricultural Density[b]	
	sq mi	km²	sq mi	km²	sq mi	km²
Argentina	36	14	384	149	44	17
Australia	7	3	100	38	10	4
Bangladesh	2648	1023	4169	1610	3195	1233
Canada	8	3	176	68	36	14
China	360	139	2713	1048	1869	721
Egypt	194	75	6436	2485	3407	1316
India	906	350	1672	646	1225	473
Iran	114	44	1270	490	434	168
Japan	876	338	7321	2827	1562	603
Nigeria	414	160	1274	492	736	284
United Kingdom	652	252	2709	1046	280	108
United States	83	32	417	161	96	37

[a]Total population divided by area of arable land.
[b]Rural population divided by area of arable land.
Rounding may produce apparent conversion discrepancies.

Sources: World Bank, *World Development Indicators;* and Population Reference Bureau, *World Population Data Sheet, 2008.*

an observation or conviction that an environment or territory is unable adequately to support its present population. (A related but opposite concept of *underpopulation* refers to the circumstance of too few people to sufficiently develop the resources of a country or region to improve the level of living of its inhabitants.)

Overpopulation is not the necessary and inevitable consequence of high density of population. Tiny Monaco, a principality in southern Europe about half the size of New York's Central Park, has a crude density of nearly 17,000 people per square kilometer (44,000 per sq mi). Mongolia, a sizable state of 1,565,000 square kilometers (604,000 sq mi) between China and Siberian Russia, has 1.6 persons per square kilometer (4.1 per sq mi); Iran, only slightly larger, has 42 per square kilometer (110 per sq mi). Macao, a former island possession of Portugal off the coast of China, has some 24,000 persons per square kilometer (62,000 per sq mi); the Falkland Islands off the Atlantic coast of Argentina count at most 1 person for every 5 square kilometers (2 sq mi) of territory. No conclusions about conditions of life, levels of income, adequacy of food, or prospects for prosperity can be drawn from these density comparisons.

Overcrowding is a reflection not of numbers per unit area but of the **carrying capacity** of land given the prevailing technology. A region devoted to energy-intensive commercial agriculture that makes heavy use of irrigation, fertilizers, and biocides can support more people at a higher level of living than one engaged in the slash-and-burn agriculture described in Chapter 8. An industrial society that takes advantage of resources such as coal and iron ore and has access to imported food will not feel population pressure at the same density levels as a country with rudimentary technology.

Since carrying capacity is related to the level of economic development, maps such as Figure 4.21, displaying present patterns of population distribution and density, do not suggest a correlation with conditions of life. Many industrialized, urbanized countries have lower densities and higher levels of living than do less developed ones. Densities in the United States, where there is a great deal of unused and unsettled land, are considerably lower than those in Bangladesh, where essentially all land is arable and which, with (in 2008) some 1023 people per square kilometer (2648 per sq mi), is the most densely populated non-island state in the world. At the same time, many African countries have low population densities and low levels of living, whereas Japan combines both high densities and wealth.

Overpopulation can be equated with levels of living or conditions of life that reflect a continuing imbalance between numbers of people and carrying capacity of the land. One measure of that imbalance might be the unavailability of food supplies sufficient in caloric content to meet individual daily energy requirements or so balanced as to satisfy normal nutritional needs. Unfortunately, dietary insufficiencies—with long-term adverse implications for life expectancy, physical vigor, and mental development—are most likely to be encountered in the developing countries, where much of the population is in the younger age cohorts (Figure 4.11).

If those developing countries simultaneously have rapidly increasing population numbers dependent on domestically produced foodstuffs, the prospects must be for continuing undernourishment and overpopulation. Much of sub-Saharan Africa finds itself in this circumstance. Its per capita food production decreased during the 1990s, with continuing decline predicted over the following quarter century as the population-food gap widens (Figure 4.25). The countries of North Africa are similarly strained. Egypt already must import well over half the food it consumes. Africa is not alone. The international Food and Agriculture Organization (FAO) estimates that early in the 21st century, at least 65 separate countries with over 30% of the population of the developing world were unable to adequately feed their inhabitants from their own national territories at the low level of agricultural technology and inputs employed. Even rapidly industrializing China, an exporter of grain until 1994, now in most years is a net grain importer.

In the contemporary world, insufficiency of domestic agricultural production to meet national caloric requirements cannot be considered a measure of overcrowding or poverty. Only a few countries are agriculturally self-sufficient. Japan, a leader among the advanced states, is the world's biggest food importer and supplies from its own production only 40% of the calories its population consumes. Its physiological density is high, as Table 4.4 indicates, but it obviously does not rely on an arable land resource for its present development. Largely lacking in either agricultural or industrial resources, it nonetheless ranks well on all indicators of national well-being and prosperity. For countries such as Japan, South Korea, Malaysia, and Taiwan—all of which currently import more than 70% of the grain they consume—a sudden cessation of the international trade that permits the exchange of industrial products for imported food and raw materials would be disastrous. Domestic food production could not maintain the dietary levels now enjoyed by their populations and they, more starkly than many underdeveloped countries, would be "overpopulated."

Urbanization

Pressures on the land resource of countries are increased not just by their growing populations but by the reduction of arable land caused by such growth. More and more of world population increase must be accommodated not in rural areas, but in cities that hold the promise of jobs and access to health, welfare, and other public services. As a result, the *urbanization* (transformation from rural to urban status according to individual state's definition of "urban") of population in developing countries is increasing dramatically. Since the 1950s, cities have grown faster than rural areas in nearly all developing states. Indeed, because of the now rapid flow of migrants from countrysides to cities, population growth in the rural areas of the developing world has essentially stopped. Although Latin America, for example, has experienced substantial overall population increase, the size of its rural population is actually declining, according to definitions of "urban" applied in most of its countries.

On UN projections, essentially all world population increase between 2000 and 2030 will be in urban areas and almost entirely within the developing regions and countries, continuing a pattern established by 1950 (Figure 4.26). In those areas collectively, cities are growing by more than 3% a year, and the poorest regions are experiencing the fastest growth. By 2020, the UN anticipates, a majority of the population of less developed countries will live in urban areas. In East, West, and Central Africa, for example, cities are expanding

Urban and rural population growth, 1950–2030

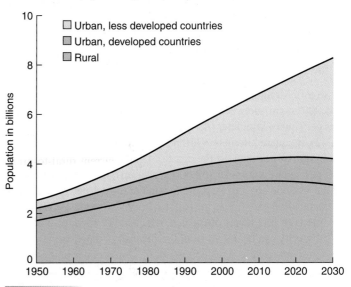

Figure 4.25 **Carrying capacity and potentials in sub-Saharan Africa.** The map assumes that (1) all cultivated land is used for growing food; (2) food imports are insignificant; (3) agriculture is conducted by low-technology methods. Projections indicate that the continent will be able to feed only 40% of its population from its own production by 2025.

Sources: World Bank; United Nations Development Programme; Food and Agriculture Organization (FAO); and Bread for the World Institute.

Figure 4.26 **Past and projected urban and rural population growth.** According to UN projections, some 65% of the world's total population may be urbanized by 2030. No universal definition of "urban" exists; the Population Reference Bureau, however, notes that "typically, the population living in towns of 2000 or more . . . is classified as 'urban.'"

Source: Redrawn from Population Bulletin, *Vol. 53, No. 1, Figure 3, page 12 (Population Reference Bureau, 1998).*

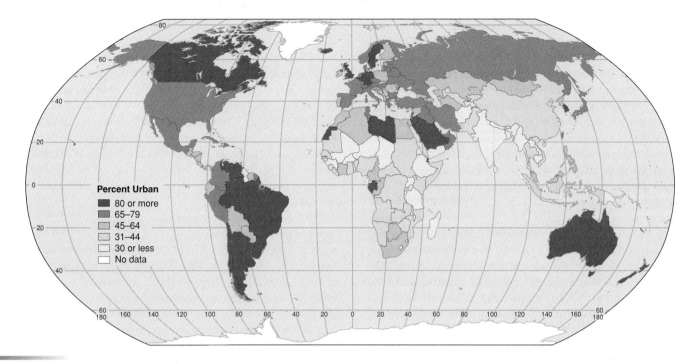

Figure 4.27 **Percentage of national population classified as urban, 2007.** Urbanization has been particularly rapid in the developing continents. In 1950, only 17% of Asians and 15% of Africans were urban; by 2007, nearly 40% of Africans and more than 40% of Asians were city dwellers, and collectively the less developed areas contained 72% of the world's city population.

Source: Data from Population Reference Bureau.

by 5% a year, a pace that can double their population every 14 years. Global urban population, just 750 million in 1950, grew to 3.3 billion by 2008 and is projected to rise to 5.1 billion by 2030. The uneven results of past urbanization are summarized in Figure 4.27.

The sheer growth of those cities in people and territory has increased pressures on arable land and adjusted upward both arithmetic and physiological densities. Urbanization consumes millions of hectares of cropland each year. In Egypt, for example, urban expansion and new development between 1965 and 1985 took out of production as much fertile soil as the massive Aswan dam on the Nile River made newly available through irrigation with the water it impounds. And during much of the 1990s, China lost close to 1 million hectares of farmland each year to urbanization, road construction, and industrialization. The pace of such loss continued into the new century for the current rural-to-urban population shift in China represents the largest mass migration in world history. By themselves, some of these developing world cities, often surrounded by concentrations of people living in uncontrolled settlements, slums, and shantytowns, are among the most densely populated areas in the world. They face massive problems in trying to provide housing, jobs, education, and adequate health and social services for their residents. These and other matters of urban geography are the topics of Chapter 11.

Population Data and Projections

Population geographers, demographers, planners, governmental officials, and a host of others rely on detailed population data to make their assessments of present national and world population patterns and to estimate future conditions. Birth rates and death rates, rates of fertility and of natural increase, age and sex composition of the population, and other items are all necessary ingredients for their work.

Population Data

The data that students of population employ come primarily from the United Nations Statistical Office, the World Bank, the Population Reference Bureau, and ultimately, from national censuses and sample surveys. Unfortunately, the data as reported may on occasion be more misleading than informative. For much of the developing world, a national census is a massive undertaking. Isolation and poor transportation, insufficiency of funds and trained census personnel, high rates of illiteracy limiting the type of questions that can be asked, and populations suspicious of government data collectors serve to restrict the frequency, coverage, and accuracy of population reports.

However derived, detailed data are published by the major reporting agencies for all national units even when those figures are poorly based on fact or are essentially fictitious. For years, data on the total population, birth and death rates, and other vital statistics for Somalia were regularly reported and annually revised. The fact was, however, that Somalia had never had a census and had no system whatsoever for recording births. Seemingly precise data were regularly reported as well for Ethiopia. When that country had its first-ever census in 1985, at least one data source had to drop its estimate of the country's birth rate by 15% and increase its figure for Ethiopia's total population by more than 20%. And a disputed 1991 census of Nigeria officially reported a population of

88.5 million, still the largest in Africa but far below the then generally accepted and widely cited estimates of between 105 and 115 million Nigerians. The 2006 census in Nigeria was surrounded by protests, boycotts, and fraud charges despite leaving out questions about religious and ethnic identity that were controversial in a country with over 250 ethnic groups and a population nearly evenly divided between Muslims and Christians.

Fortunately, census coverage on a world basis is improving. Almost every country has now had at least one census of its population (though 15 worldwide did not conduct one between 1990 and 2006), and most have been subjected to periodic sample surveys (Figure 4.28). However, only about 10% of the developing world's population live in countries with anything approaching complete systems for registering births and deaths. Estimates are that 40% or less of live births in Indonesia, Pakistan, India, or the Philippines are officially recorded; sub-Saharan Africa has the highest percentage of unregistered births (71%), according to UNICEF. Apparently, deaths are even less completely reported than births throughout Asia. And whatever the deficiencies of Asian states, African statistics are still less complete and reliable. It is, of course, on just these basic birth and death data that projections about population growth and composition are founded.

Population Projections

For all their inadequacies and imprecisions, current data reported for country units form the basis of **population projections,** estimates of future population size, age, and sex composition based on current data. Projections are not forecasts, and demographers are not the social science equivalent of meteorologists. Weather forecasters work with a myriad of accurate observations applied against a known, tested model of the atmosphere. The demographer, in contrast, works with sparse, imprecise, out-of-date, and missing

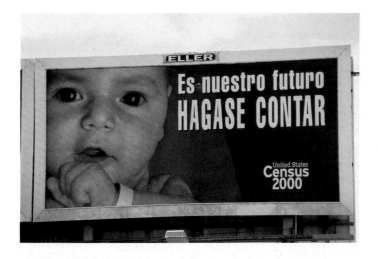

Figure 4.28 To encourage complete participation in the 2000 census, the U.S. government created this billboard and other advertisements aimed at Hispanic residents.

data applied to human actions that will be unpredictably responsive to stimuli not yet evident.

Population projections, therefore, are based on assumptions for the future applied to current data that are, themselves, frequently suspect. Since projections are not predictions, they can never be wrong. They are simply the inevitable result of calculations about fertility, mortality, and migration rates applied to each age cohort of a population now living, and the making of birth rate, survival, and migration assumptions about cohorts yet unborn. Of course, the perfectly valid *projections* of future population size and structure resulting from those calculations may be dead wrong as *predictions*.

Because those projections are invariably treated as scientific expectations by a public that ignores their underlying qualifying assumptions, agencies such as the UN that estimate the population of, say, Africa in the year 2025, do so by not one but by three or more projections: high, medium, and low, for example. For areas as large as Africa, a medium projection is assumed to benefit from compensating errors and statistically predictable behaviors of very large populations. For individual African countries and smaller populations, the medium projection may be much less satisfying. The usual tendency in projections is to assume that something like current conditions will be applicable in the future. Obviously, the more distant the future, the less likely is that assumption to remain true. The resulting observation should be that the further into the future the population structure of small areas is projected, the greater is the implicit and inevitable error (see Figure 4.13).

Population Controls

All population projections include an assumption that at some point in time population growth will cease and plateau at the replacement level. Without that assumption, future numbers become unthinkably large. For the world at unchecked present growth rates, there would be 1 trillion people three centuries from now, 4 trillion four centuries in the future, and so on. Although there is reasonable debate about whether the world is now overpopulated and about what either its optimum or maximum sustainable population should be, totals in the trillions are beyond any reasonable expectation.

Population pressures do not come from the amount of space humans occupy. It has been calculated, for example, that the entire human race could easily be accommodated within the boundaries of the state of Delaware. The problems stem from the food, energy, and other resources necessary to support the population and from the impact on the environment of the increasing demands and the technologies required to meet them. Rates of growth currently prevailing in many countries make it nearly impossible for them to achieve the kind of social and economic development they would like.

Clearly, at some point population will have to stop increasing as fast as it has been. That is, either the self-induced limitations on expansion implicit in the demographic transition will be adopted or an equilibrium between population and resources will be established in more dramatic fashion. Recognition of this eventuality is not new. "[P]estilence, and famine, and wars, and earthquakes have to be regarded as a remedy for nations, as the means of pruning the luxuriance of the human race," was the opinion of the theologian Tertullian during the 2nd century A.D.

Thomas Robert **Malthus** (1766–1834), an English economist and demographer, put the problem succinctly in a treatise published in 1798: All biological populations have a potential for increase that exceeds the actual rate of increase, and the resources for the support of increase are limited. In later publications, Malthus amplified his thesis by noting the following:

1. Population is inevitably limited by the means of subsistence.
2. Populations invariably increase with increase in the means of subsistence unless prevented by powerful checks.
3. The checks that inhibit the reproductive capacity of populations and keep it in balance with means of subsistence are either "private" (moral restraint, celibacy, and chastity) or "destructive" (war, poverty, pestilence, and famine).

The deadly consequences of Malthus's dictum that unchecked population increases geometrically while food production can increase only arithmetically[2] have been reported throughout human history, as they are today. Starvation, the ultimate expression of resource depletion, is no stranger to the past or present. By conservative estimate, some 100 people worldwide will starve to death during the 2 minutes it takes you to read this page; half will be children under 5. They will, of course, be more than replaced numerically by new births during the same 2 minutes. Losses are nearly always recouped. All battlefield deaths, perhaps 70 million, in all of humankind's wars over the past 300 years equal less than a 1-year replacement period at present rates of natural increase.

Yet, inevitably—following the logic of Malthus, the apparent evidence of history, and our observations of animal populations—equilibrium must be achieved between numbers and support resources. When overpopulation of any species occurs, a population

dieback is inevitable. The madly ascending leg of the J-curve is bent to the horizontal, and the J-curve is converted to an S-curve. It has happened before in human history, as Figure 4.29 summarizes. The top of the **S-curve** represents a population size consistent with and supportable by the exploitable resource base. When the population is equivalent to the carrying capacity of the occupied area, it is said to have reached a **homeostatic plateau.**

In animals, overcrowding and environmental stress apparently release an automatic physiological suppressant of fertility. Although famine and chronic malnutrition may reduce fertility in humans, population limitation usually must be either forced or self-imposed. The demographic transition to low birth rates matching reduced death rates is cited as evidence that Malthus's first assumption was wrong: Human populations do not inevitably grow geometrically. Fertility behavior, it was observed, is conditioned by social determinants, not solely by biological or resource imperatives.

Although Malthus's ideas were discarded as deficient by the end of the 19th century in light of the European population experience, the concerns he expressed were revived during the 1950s. Observations of population growth in underdeveloped countries and the strain that growth placed on their resources inspired the viewpoint that improvements in living standards could be achieved only by raising investment per worker. Rapid population growth was seen as a serious diversion of scarce resources away from capital investment and into unending social welfare programs. In order to lift living standards, the existing national efforts to lower mortality rates had to be balanced by governmental programs to reduce birth rates. **Neo-Malthusianism,** as this viewpoint became known, has been the underpinning of national and international programs of population limitation primarily through birth control and family planning (Figure 4.30).

Figure 4.29 The steadily higher *homeostatic plateaus* (states of equilibrium) achieved by humans are evidence of their ability to increase the carrying capacity of the land through technological advance. Each new plateau represents the conversion of the J-curve into an S-curve. "Medical revolution" implies the range of modern sanitary and public health technologies and disease preventative and curative advances that materially reduced morbidity and mortality rates.

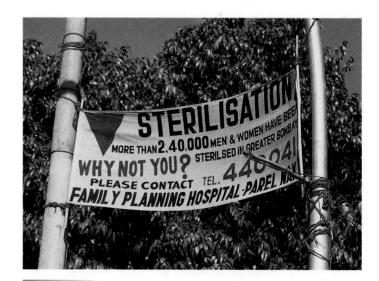

Figure 4.30 A Mumbai, India, sign promoting the government's continuing program to reduce the country's high fertility rate. Female sterilization is the world's most popular form of birth prevention, and in India, Brazil, and China a reported one-third or more of all married women have been sterilized. The comparable worldwide married male sterilization rate, in contrast, is 4%.

[2]"Within a hundred years or so, the population can increase from fivefold to twentyfold, while the means of subsistence . . . can increase only from three to five times," was the observation of Hung Liangchi of China, a spatially distant early 19th-century contemporary of Malthus.

Neo-Malthusianism has had a mixed reception. Asian countries, led by China and India, have in general—though with differing successes—adopted family planning programs and policies. In some instances, success has been declared complete. Singapore established its Population and Family Planning Board in 1965, when its fertility rate was 4.9 lifetime births per woman. By 1986, that rate had declined to 1.7, well below the 2.1 replacement level for developed countries, and the board was abolished as no longer necessary. Caribbean and South American countries, even the poorest and most agrarian, have also experienced declining fertility rates, though often these reductions have been achieved despite pronatalist views of governments influenced by the Roman Catholic Church.

Africa and the Middle East have generally been less responsive to the neo-Malthusian arguments because of ingrained cultural convictions among people, if not in all governmental circles, that large families—six or seven children—are desirable. Although total fertility rates have begun to decline in most sub-Saharan African states, they still remain nearly everywhere far above replacement levels. Islamic fundamentalism opposed to birth restrictions also is a cultural factor in the Near East and North Africa. However, the Muslim theocracy of Iran has endorsed a range of contraceptive procedures and developed one of the world's more aggressive family planning programs.

Other barriers to fertility control exist. When first proposed by Western states, neo-Malthusian arguments that family planning was necessary for development were rejected by many less developed countries. Reflecting both nationalistic and Marxist concepts, they maintained that remnant colonial-era social, economic, and class structures, rather than population increase, hindered development. Some government leaders think there is a correlation between population size and power and pursue pronatalist policies, as did Mao's China during the 1950s and early 1960s. And a number of American economists called *cornucopians* expressed the view, beginning in the 1980s, that population growth is a stimulus, not a deterrent, to development and that human minds and skills are the world's ultimate resource base. Since the time of Malthus, they observe, world population has grown from 900 million to over 6.7 billion (2008) without the predicted dire consequences—proof that Malthus failed to recognize the importance of technology in raising the carrying capacity of the earth. Still higher population numbers, they suggest, are sustainable, perhaps even with improved standards of living for all.

A third view, modifying cornucopian optimism, admits that products of human ingenuity such as the Green Revolution (see p. 245) increases in food production have managed to keep pace with rapid population growth since 1970. But its advocates argue that scientific and technical ingenuity to enhance food production do not automatically appear; both complacency and inadequate research support have hindered continuing progress in recent years. And even if further advances are made, they observe, not all countries or regions have the social and political will or capacity to take advantage of them. Those that do not, third-view advocates warn, will fail to keep pace with the needs of their populace and will sink into varying degrees of poverty and environmental decay, creating national and regional—though not necessarily global—crises.

Population Prospects

Regardless of population philosophies, theories, or cultural norms, the fact remains that many or most developing countries are showing significantly declining population growth rates. Global fertility and birth rates are falling to an extent not anticipated by pessimistic Malthusians and at a pace that suggests a peaking of world population numbers sooner—and at lower totals—than previously projected (see "A Population Implosion?" p. 95). In all world regions, steady and continuous fertility declines have been recorded over the past years, reducing fertility from global 5.0-children-per-woman levels in the early 1950s to 2.6 per woman by 2008.

Momentum

Reducing fertility levels even to the replacement level of about 2.1 births per woman does not mean an immediate end to population growth. Because of the age composition of many societies, numbers of births will continue to grow even as fertility rates per woman decline. The reason is to be found in **population** (or **demographic**) **momentum,** and the key to that is the age structure of a country's population.

When a high proportion of the population is young, the product of past high fertility rates, larger and larger numbers enter the childbearing age each year; that is the case for major parts of the world early in the 21st century. The populations of developing countries are far younger than those of the established industrially developed regions (see Figure 4.11), with 30% (in Asia and Latin America) to over 40% (in Africa) below the age of 15. The consequences of the fertility of these young people are yet to be realized. A population with a greater number of young people tends to grow rapidly regardless of the level of childbearing. The results will continue to be felt until the now-youthful groups mature and work their way through the population pyramid.

Inevitably, while this is happening, even the most stringent national policies limiting growth cannot stop it entirely. A country with a large present population base will experience large numerical increases despite declining birth rates. Indeed, the higher fertility was to begin with and the sharper its drop to low levels, the greater will be the role of momentum even after rates drop below replacement. A simple comparison of South Korea and the United Kingdom may serve to demonstrate the point. The two countries had (in 2002) the same level of fertility, with women averaging about 1.6 children each. Between that year and 2025, the larger population of the U.K. (without considering immigration or the births associated with newcomers) was projected to decline by 2 million persons while the smaller, more youthful South Korea was expected to continue growing, adding 2 million people.

The realities of population momentum (Figure 4.31) have, for some demographers, cast serious doubt on the UN's 2006 projection of a world population reaching a maximum of about 9.7 billion in 2075. Instead, they note, a large share of currrent world population is concentrated in the 15–40 age span where birth rates are high. Even if everyone everywhere adopted a policy of only 2 children per couple, it would take (because of momentum)

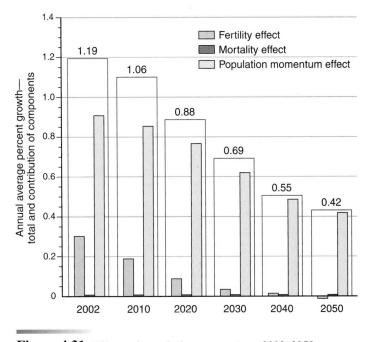

The components of yearly world population growth: 2002–2050

Legend:
- Fertility effect
- Mortality effect
- Population momentum effect

Figure 4.31 Effects of population momentum, 2002–2050.
Population momentum represents the lingering effects of past high fertility. Worldwide declines in total fertility rates will not immediately be reflected by equivalent declines in the growth of population. Because of past high fertility, the numbers of women in their childbearing years are increasing both absolutely and relative to the rest of the population. As a result, population momentum will account for a growing share of projected world population increase.

Source: U.S. Bureau of the Census, 2004.

approximately 70 years before world population would stabilize at about 12 billion, far above the UN projection.

Aging

Eventually, of course, young populations grow older, and even the youthful developing countries are beginning to face the consequences of that reality. The problems of a rapidly aging population that already confront the industrialized economies are now being realized in the developing world as well. Before 2000, young people always outnumbered the elderly; since the start of this century, old people will continue to outnumber the young. Globally, there will be more than 1 billion persons 60 years of age and older by 2025 and 2 billion by 2050, when the world will contain more people aged 60 and above than children under the age of 15. That momentous reversal in relative proportions of young and old already occurred in 1998 in the more developed regions.

The progression toward older populations is considered irreversible, the result of the now-global demographic transition from high to low levels of fertility and mortality. The youthful majorities of the past are unlikely to occur again, for globally, the population of older persons early in the century was growing by 2% per year—much faster than the population as a whole—and between 2025 to 2030, the 60+ growth rate will reach 2.8% per year. By 2050, the UN projects, one out of five persons worldwide will be 60 years old or older.

About 80% of the mid-century elderly folk will live in the less developed world, for the growth rate of older people is three times as high in developing countries as in the developed ones. In the developing world, older persons are projected to make up 20% of the population by 2050 in contrast to the 8% over age 60 there in 2000. Since the pace of aging is much faster in the developing countries, they will have less time than the developed world did to adjust to the consequences of that aging. And those consequences will be experienced at lower levels of personal and national income and economic strength.

In both rich and poor states, the working-age populations will face increasing burdens and obligations. The potential support ratio, or PSR (the number of persons aged 15–64 years per one citizen aged 65 or older), has steadily fallen. Between 1950 and 2000, it dropped from 12 to 9 workers for each older person; by mid-century, the PSR is projected to drop to 4. The implications for social security schemes and social support obligations are obvious and made more serious because the older population itself is aging. By the middle of the century, one-fifth of older persons will be 80 years or older and on average require more support expenditures for health and long-term care than do younger seniors. The consequences of population aging appear most intractable for the world's poorest developing states that generally lack health, income, housing, and social service support systems adequate to the needs of their older citizens. To the social and economic implications of their present population momentum, therefore, developing countries must add the aging consequences of past patterns and rates of growth (Figure 4.32).

Figure 4.32 These senior residents of a Moroccan nursing home are part of the rapidly aging population of many developing countries. Worldwide, the over-60 cohort will number some 22% of total population by 2050 and be larger than the number of children less than 15 years of age. But by 2020, a third of Singapore citizens will be 55 or older, and China will have as large a share of its population over 60—about one in four—as will Europe. Already, the numbers of old people in the world's poorer countries are beginning to dwarf those in the rich world. At the start of the 21st century, there were nearly twice as many persons over 60 in developing countries as in the advanced ones, but most are without the old age assistance and welfare programs that developed countries have put in place.

Summary

Birth, death, fertility, and growth rates are important in understanding the numbers, composition, distribution, and spatial trends of population. Recent "explosive" increases in human numbers and the prospects of continuing population expansion may be traced to sharp reductions in death rates, increases in longevity, and the impact of demographic momentum on a youthful population largely concentrated in the developing world. Control of population numbers historically was accomplished through a demographic transition first experienced in European societies that adjusted their fertility rates downward as death rates fell and life expectancies increased. The introduction of advanced technologies of preventive and curative medicine, pesticides, and famine relief have reduced mortality rates in developing countries without, until recently, always a compensating reduction in birth rates. Recent fertility declines in many developing regions suggest the demographic transition is no longer limited to the advanced industrial countries and promise world population stability earlier and at lower numbers than envisioned just a few years ago.

Even with the advent of more widespread fertility declines, the 6 billion human beings present at the end of the 20th century will still likely grow to perhaps 9.2 billion by the middle of the 21st. That growth will largely reflect increases unavoidable because of the size and youth of populations in developing countries. Eventually, a new balance between population numbers and carrying capacity of the world will be reached, as it has always been following past periods of rapid population increase.

People are unevenly distributed over the earth. The ecumene, or permanently inhabited portion of the globe, is discontinuous and marked by pronounced differences in population concentrations and numbers. East Asia, South Asia, Europe, and northeastern United States/southeastern Canada represent the world's greatest population clusters, though smaller areas of great density are found in other regions and continents. Since growth rates are highest and population doubling times generally shorter in world regions outside these four present main concentrations, new patterns of population localization and dominance are taking form.

A respected geographer once commented that "population is the point of reference from which all other elements [of geography] are observed." Certainly, population geography is the essential starting point of the human component of the human–environment concerns of geography. But human populations are not merely collections of numerical units; nor are they to be understood solely through statistical analysis. Societies are distinguished not just by the abstract data of their numbers, rates, and trends, but by experiences, beliefs, understandings, and aspirations that collectively constitute that human spatial and behavioral variable called *culture*. It is to that fundamental human diversity that we next turn our attention.

KEY WORDS

agricultural density 112	doubling time 101	population (demographic) momentum 118
arithmetic density 112	ecumene 111	population density 112
carrying capacity 113	homeostatic plateau 117	population geography 89
cohort 91	J-curve 102	population projection 116
crude birth rate (CBR) 91	Malthus 117	population pyramid 98
crude death rate (CDR) 96	mortality rate 96	rate of natural increase 101
crude density 112	natural increase 101	rates 91
demographic equation 107	neo-Malthusianism 117	replacement level 95
demographic transition 102	nonecumene 111	S-curve 117
demography 89	overpopulation 112	total fertility rate (TFR) 92
dependency ratio 101	physiological density 112	zero population growth (ZPG) 95

FOR REVIEW

1. How do the *crude birth rate* and the *fertility rate* differ? Which measure is the more accurate statement of the amount of reproduction occurring in a population?

2. How is the *crude death rate* calculated? What factors account for the worldwide decline in death rates since 1945?

3. How is a *population pyramid* constructed? What shape of "pyramid" reflects the structure of a rapidly growing country? Of a population with a slow rate of growth? What can we tell about future population numbers from those shapes?

4. What variations do we discern in the spatial pattern of the *rate of natural increase* and, consequently, of population growth? What rate of natural increase would double population in 35 years?

5. How are population numbers projected from present conditions? Are projections the same as predictions? If not, in what ways do they differ?

6. Describe the stages in the *demographic transition*. Where has the final stage of the transition been achieved? Why do some analysts doubt the applicability of the demographic transition to all parts of the world?

7. Contrast *crude population density, physiological density,* and *agricultural density.* For what differing purposes might each be useful? How is *carrying capacity* related to the concept of density?

8. What was Malthus's underlying assumption concerning the relationship between population growth and food supply? In what ways do the arguments of *neo-Malthusians* differ from the original doctrine? What governmental policies are implicit in *neo-Malthusianism?*

9. Why is *population momentum* a matter of interest in population projections? In which world areas are the implications of demographic momentum most serious in calculating population growth, stability, or decline?

KEY CONCEPTS REVIEW

1. **What are some basic terms and measures used by population geographers?** pp. 89–102.
A *cohort* is a population group, usually an age group, treated as a unit. *Rates* record the frequency of occurrence of an event over a given unit of time. Rates are used to trace a wide range of population features and trends: births, deaths, fertility, infant or maternal mortality, natural increase, and others. Those rates tell us both the present circumstances and likely prospects for national, country group, or world population structures. Population pyramids give visual evidence of the current age and sex cohort structure of countries or country groupings.

2. **What are meant and measured by the demographic transition model and the demographic equation?** pp. 102–109.
The *demographic transition* model traces the presumed relationship between population growth and economic development. In Western countries, the transition model historically displayed four stages: (a) high birth and death rates; (b) high birth and declining death rates; (c) declining births and reduced growth rates; and (d) low birth and death rates.

A fifth stage of population decline is observed for some aging societies. The transition model has been observed to be not fully applicable to all developing states. The *demographic equation* attempts to incorporate cross-border population migration into projections of national population trends.

3. **What descriptive generalizations can be made about world population distributions and densities?** pp. 110–115.
World population is primarily concentrated north of the equator, in lower (below 200 meters) elevations, along continental margins. Major world population clusters include *East Asia* with 25% of the total, *South Asia* with over 20%, *Europe* and *northeastern United States/southeastern Canada* with significant but lesser shares of world population. Other smaller but pronounced concentrations are found discontinuously on all continents. Within the permanently inhabited areas—the "ecumene"—population densities vary greatly. Highest densities are found in cities; almost one-half of the world's people are urban residents now and the vast majority of world population growth over the first quarter of the 21st century will occur in cities of the developing world.

4. **What are population projections, and how are they affected by various controls on population growth?** pp. 115–119.
Population projections are merely calculations of the future size, age, and sex composition of regional, national, or world populations; they are based on current data and manipulated by varying assumptions about the future. As simple calculations, projections cannot be wrong. They may, however, totally misrepresent what actually will occur because of faulty current data or erroneous assumptions used in their calculation. They may also be invalid because of unanticipated self-imposed or external brakes on population growth, such as changing family size desires or limits on areal carrying capacity that slow or halt current growth trends. Even with such growth limitations, however, population prospects are always influenced greatly by *demographic momentum,* the inevitable growth in numbers promised by the high proportion of younger cohorts yet to enter childbearing years in the developing world, and by the consequences of global population aging.

Part Two

PATTERNS OF DIVERSITY AND UNITY

LANGUAGE AND RELIGION:
Mosaics of Culture

5

Ethiopia's 1600-year-old Coptic Christian Meskel Festival marks the finding of the true cross on which Christ was crucified.

Key Concepts

Language

The classification, spread, and distribution of the world's languages; the nature of language change, pp. 124–131.

Language standards and variants, from dialects to official tongues, pp. 131–139.

Language as cultural identity and landscape relic, pp. 139–143.

Religion

The cultural significance and role of religion, pp. 143–144.

How world religions are classified and distributed, pp. 144–147.

The origins, nature, and diffusions of principal world religions, pp. 147–161.

*W*hen God saw [humans become arrogant], he thought of something to bring confusion to their heads: he gave the people a very heavy sleep. They slept for a very, very long time. They slept for so long that they forgot the language they had used to speak. When they eventually woke up from their sleep, each man went his own way, speaking his own tongue. None of them could understand the language of the other any more. That is how people dispersed all over the world. Each man would walk his way and speak his own language and another would go his way and speak in his own language. . . .

God has forbidden me to speak Arabic. I asked God, "Why don't I speak Arabic?" and He said, "If you speak Arabic, you will turn into a bad man." I said, "There is something good in Arabic!" And He said, "No, there is nothing good in it! . . ."

Here, I slaughter a bull and I call [the Muslim] to share my meat. I say, "Let us share our meat." But he refuses the meat I slaughter because he says it is not slaughtered in a Muslim way. If he cannot accept the way I slaughter my meat, how can we be relatives? Why does he despise our food? So, let us eat our meat alone. . . . Why, they insult us, they combine contempt for our black skin with pride in their religion. As for us, we have our own ancestors and our own spirits; the spirits of the Rek, the spirits of the Twic, we have not combined our spirits with their spirits. The spirit of the black man is different. Our spirit has not combined with theirs.[1]

While Chapters 2–4 focused on concepts of culture, spatial behavior, and population geography that can be applied to each

---

[1]The words of Chief Makuei Bilkuei of the Dinka, a Nilotic people of the southern Sudan. His comments are directed at the attempts to unite into a single people the Arabic Muslims of the north of the Republic of the Sudan with his and other black, Luo-speaking animist and Christian people of the country's southern areas. Recorded by Francis Mading Deng, *Africans of Two Worlds: The Dinka in Afro-Arab Sudan.* Copyright © 1978 Yale University Press, New Haven, CT. Reprinted by permission of the author.

of the world's diverse cultures, in Chapters 5–7 we turn to the distinguishing characteristics of cultures and cultural landscapes. We begin with two prominent threads in the tapestry of cultural diversity—language and culture. Language and religion are basic components of cultures, the learned ways of life of different human communities. They help identify who and what we are and clearly place us within larger communities of persons with similar characteristics. At the same time, as the words of Chief Makuei suggest, they separate and divide peoples of different tongues and faiths. In the terminology introduced in Chapter 2, language and religion are *mentifacts,* components of the *ideological subsystem* of culture that help shape the belief system of a society and transmit it to succeeding generations. Both within and between cultures, language and religion are fundamental strands in the complex web of culture, serving to shape and to distinguish people and groups.

They are ever-changing strands, for languages and religions in their present-day structure and spatial patterns are simply the temporary latest phase in a continuing progression of culture change. Languages evolve in place, responding to the dynamics of human thought, experience, and expression and to the exchanges and borrowings ever more common in a closely integrated world. They disperse in space, carried by streams of migrants, colonizers, and conquerors. They may be rigorously defended and preserved as essential elements of cultural identity, or abandoned in the search for acceptance into a new society. To trace their diffusions, adoptions, and disappearances is to understand part of the evolving course of historical cultural geography. Religions, too, are dynamic, sweeping across national, linguistic, and cultural boundaries by conversion, conviction, and conquest. Their broad spatial patterns—distinctive culture regions in their own right— are also fundamental in defining the culture realms outlined in Figure 2.4, while at a different scale religious differences may contribute to the cultural diversity and richness within the countries of the world (Figure 5.1).

The Geography of Language

Forever changing and evolving, language in spoken or written form makes possible the cooperative efforts, the group understandings, and shared behavior patterns that distinguish culture groups. Language is the most important medium by which culture is transmitted. It is what enables parents to teach their children what the world they live in is like and what they must do to become functioning members of society. Some argue that the language of a society structures the perceptions of its speakers. By the words that it contains and the concepts that it can formulate, language is said to determine the attitudes, the understandings, and the responses of the society to which it belongs.

If that conclusion be true, one aspect of cultural heterogeneity may be easily understood. The more than 6 billion people on earth speak many thousands of different languages. Knowing that more than 1500 languages and language variants are spoken in sub-Saharan Africa (though 85% of Africans speak one or more variants of 15 core languages) gives us a clearer appreciation of the political and social divisions in that continent. Europe alone has some 225 languages and dialects (Figure 5.2). Language is a hallmark of cultural diversity, an often fiercely defended symbol of cultural identity helping to distinguish the world's diverse social groups.

Figure 5.1 **Advertised evidence of religious diversity in the United States.** The sign details only a few Christian congregations. In reality, the United States has become the most religiously diverse country in the world, with essentially all of the world's faiths represented within its borders.

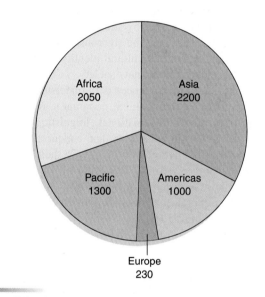

Figure 5.2 **World distribution of living languages, 2006.** Of the perhaps 6800 languages still spoken today, one-third are found in Asia, 30% in Africa, 19% in the Pacific area, 15% in the Americas, and 3% in Europe. Linguists' estimates of the number of languages ever spoken on Earth range from 31,000 to as many as 300,000 or more. Assuming the lower estimate or even one considerably smaller, dead languages far outnumber the living. One or two additional tongues, most spoken in the forests of Papua New Guinea or in Indonesia, are lost each week.

Source: Estimates based on Ethnologue *and other sources.*

Classification of Languages

On a clear, dark night, the unaided eye can distinguish between 4000 and 6000 stars, a number comparable to some estimates of the probable total number of the world's languages. In reality, no precise figure is possible, for even today in Africa, Latin America, New Guinea, and elsewhere, linguists are still in the

| HOUSE | RICE | TREE |

Figure 5.3 All literate Chinese, no matter which of the many languages of China they speak, recognize the same ideographs for house, rice, and tree.

process of identifying and classifying the tongues spoken by isolated peoples. Even when they are well known, languages cannot always be easily or unmistakably recognized as distinctly separate entities.

In the broadest sense, language is any systematic method of communicating ideas, attitudes, or intent through the use of mutually understood signs, sounds, or gestures. For our geographic purposes, we may define **language** as an organized system of spoken words by which people communicate with each other with mutual comprehension. But such a definition fails to recognize the gradations among and between languages or to grasp the varying degrees of mutual comprehension between two or more of them. The language commonly called "Chinese," for example, is more properly seen as a group of distinct but related languages—Mandarin, Cantonese, Hakka, and others—that are as different from each other as are such comparably related European languages as Spanish, Italian, French, and Romanian. "Chinese" has uniformity only in the fact that all of the varied Chinese languages are written alike. No matter how it is pronounced, the same symbol for 'house' or for 'rice,' for example, is recognized by all literate speakers of any Chinese language variant (Figure 5.3). Again, the language known as "Arabic" represents a number of related but distinct tongues, so Arabic spoken in Morocco differs from Palestinian Arabic roughly as Portuguese differs from Italian.

Languages differ greatly in their relative importance, if "importance" can be taken to mean the number of people using them. More than half of the world's inhabitants are native speakers of just eight of its thousands of tongues, and at least half regularly use or have competence in just four of them. That restricted language dominance reflects the reality that the world's linguistic diversity is rapidly shrinking. Of the at most 7000 tongues still remaining, between 20% and 50% are no longer being learned by children and are effectively dead. One estimate anticipates that no more than 600 of the world's current living languages will still be in existence in A.D. 2100. Table 5.1 lists those languages currently spoken as a native or second tongue by 65 million or more people, a list that includes nearly 90% of the world's population. At the other end of the scale are a number of rapidly declining languages whose speakers number in the hundreds or, at most, the few thousands.

The diversity of languages is simplified when we recognize among them related *families*. A **language family** is a group of languages descended from a single, earlier tongue. By varying estimates,

Table 5.1

Languages Spoken by 60 million or More People, 2006

Language	Millions of Speakers (Primary and Secondary)	Approximate % of World Population
Mandarin[a] (China)	1,100	17
English	1,000	16
Hindi/Urdu[b] (India, Pakistan)	750	12
Spanish	450	7
Russian/Belorussian	270	4
Arabic[c]	260	4
Bengali (Bangladesh/India)	250	4
Malay/Indonesian	205	3
Portuguese	195	3
Japanese	132	2
French	125	2
German	121	2
Thai/Lao	90	1
Punjabi	85	1
Wu (China)	85	1
Javanese	80	1
Turkish/Azeri/Turkmen (Turkey, Azerbaijan/Turkmenistan)	80	1
Korean (Korea, China, Japan)	78	1
Marathi (India)	77	1
Vietnamese	75	1
Telugu (India)	75	1
Tamil (India, Sri Lanka)	74	1
Yue (Cantonese) (China)	70	1
Italian	68	1
Ukrainian	65	1

[a]The official dialect of Mandarin is spoken by perhaps 650 million; as many as 1500 other dialects, many mutually incomprehensible, are also designated as "Mandarin."

[b]Hindi and Urdu are basically the same language: Hindustani. Written in the Devangari script, it is called *Hindi,* the official language of India; in the Arabic script, it is called *Urdu,* the official language of Pakistan.

[c]The figure given includes speakers of the many often mutually unintelligible versions of colloquial Arabic. Classical or literary Arabic, the language of the Koran, is uniform and standardized but restricted to formal usage as a spoken tongue. Because of its religious association, Arabic is a second language for many inhabitants of Muslim countries with other native tongues.

Sources: Based on data from *Ethnologue: Languages of the World,* 15th ed.; *Linguisphere 2000;* and other sources.

from at least 30 to perhaps 100 such families of languages are found worldwide. The families, in turn, may be subdivided into subfamilies, branches, or groups of more closely related tongues. Some 2000 years ago, Latin was the common language spoken throughout the Roman Empire. The fall of the empire in the 5th century A.D. broke the unity of Europe, and regional variants of Latin began to develop in isolation. In the course of the next several centuries, these Latin derivatives, changing and developing as all languages do, emerged as the individual *Romance* languages— Italian, Spanish, French, Portuguese, and Romanian—of modern Europe and of the world colonized by their speakers. Catalan, Sardinian, Provençal, and a few other spatially restricted tongues are also part of the Romance language group.

Family relationship between languages can be recognized through similarities in their vocabulary and grammar. By tracing regularities of sound changes in different languages back

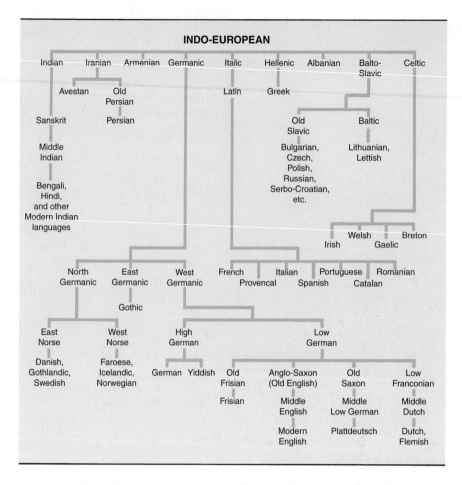

Figure 5.4 **The Indo-European linguistic family tree.** Euskara (Basque), Estonian, Finnish, Hungarian, Maltese, and Lappish are the only European languages *not* in the Indo-European family. (See also Figure 5.8.)

through time, linguists are able to reconstruct earlier forms of words and, eventually, determine a word's original form before it underwent alteration and divergence. Such a reconstructed earlier form is said to belong to a **protolanguage.** In the case of the Romance languages, of course, the well-known ancestral tongue was Latin, which needs no such reconstruction. Its root relationship to the Romance languages is suggested by modern variants of *panis,* the Latin word for "bread": *pane* (Italian), *pain* (French), *pan* (Spanish), *pão* (Portuguese), *pâine* (Romanian). In other language families similar word relationships are less confidently traced to their protolanguage roots. For example, the *Germanic* languages, including English, German, Dutch, and the Scandinavian tongues, are related descendants of a less well-known proto-Germanic language spoken by peoples who lived in southern Scandinavia and along the North Sea and Baltic coasts from the Netherlands to western Poland. The classification of languages by origin and historical relationship is called a *genetic classification.*

Further tracing of language roots tells us that the Romance and the Germanic languages are individual branches of an even more extensive family of related languages derived from *proto-Indo-European,* or simply *Indo-European.* Of the principal recognized language clusters of the world, the Indo-European family is the largest, embracing most of the languages of Europe and a large part of Asia, and the introduced—not the native—languages of the Americas (Figure 5.4). All told, languages in the Indo-European family are spoken by about half the world's peoples.

By recognizing similar words in most Indo-European tongues, linguists deduce that the Indo-European people—originally hunters and fishers but later becoming pastoralists and learning to grow crops—developed somewhere in eastern Europe or the Ukrainian steppes about 5000 years ago (though some conclude that central Turkey was the more likely site of origin and that the ancestral tongue existed 8700 to 10,000 or more years ago). By at least 2500 B.C., their society apparently fragmented; they left the homeland, carrying segments of the parent culture in different directions. Some migrated into Greece, others settled in Italy, still others crossed central and western Europe, ultimately reaching the British Isles. Another group headed into the Russian forest lands, and still another branch crossed Iran and Afghanistan, eventually to reach India. Wherever this remarkable people settled, they appear to have dominated local populations and imposed their language on them. For example, the word for sheep is *avis* in Lithuanian, *ovis* in Latin, *avis* in Sanskrit (the language of ancient India), and *hawi* in the tongue used in Homer's Troy. Modern English retains its version in "ewe." All, linguists infer, derive from an ancestral word *owis* in Indo-European. Similar relationships and histories can be traced for other protolanguages.

World Pattern of Languages

The present world distribution of major language families (Figure 5.5) records not only the migrations and conquests of our linguistic ancestors but also the continuing dynamic pattern of human movements, settlements, and colonizations of more recent centuries. Indo-European languages have been carried far beyond their Eurasian homelands from the 16th century onwards by western European colonizers in the Americas, Africa, Asia, and Australasia. In the process of linguistic imposition and adoption, innumerable indigenous languages and language groups in areas of colonization have been modified or totally lost. Most of the estimated 1000 to 2000 *Amerindian* tongues of the Western Hemisphere disappeared in the face of European conquest and settlement (Figure 5.6).

The Slavic expansion eastward across Siberia beginning in the 16th century obliterated most of the *Paleo-Asiatic* languages there. Similar loss occurred in Eskimo and Aleut language areas. Large linguistically distinctive areas comprise the northern reaches of both Asia and America (see Figure 5.5). Their sparse populations are losing the mapped languages as the indigenous people adopt the tongues of the majority cultures of which they have been forcibly made a part. In the Southern Hemisphere, the several hundred original *Australian* languages also loom large spatially on the map but have at most 50,000 speakers, exclusively Australian aborigines. Numerically and effectively, English dominates that continent.

Examples of linguistic conquest by non-Europeans also abound. In Southeast Asia, formerly extensive areas identified with different members of the *Austro-Asiatic* language family have been reduced through conquest and absorption by *Sino-Tibetan* (Chinese, Thai, Burmese, and Lao, principally) expansion. Arabic—originally a minor *Afro-Asiatic* language of the Arabian Peninsula—was dispersed by the explosive spread of Islam through much of North Africa and southwestern Asia, where it largely replaced a host of other locally variant tongues and became the official or the dominant language of more than 20 countries and over 250 million people. The more than 300 Bantu languages found south of the "Bantu line" in sub-Saharan Africa are variants of a proto-Bantu carried by an expanding, culturally advanced population that displaced more primitive predecessors (Figure 5.7).

Language Spread

Language spread as a geographical event represents the increase or relocation through time in the area over which a language is spoken. The Bantu of Africa or the English-speaking settlers of North America displaced preexisting populations and replaced as well the languages previously spoken in the areas of penetration. Therefore, we find one explanation of the spread of language

families to new areas of occurrence in massive population relocations such as those accompanying the colonization of the Americas or of Australia. That is, languages may spread because their speakers occupy new territories.

Latin, however, replaced earlier Celtic languages in western Europe not by force of numbers—Roman legionnaires, administrators, and settlers never represented a majority population—but by the gradual abandonment of their former languages by native populations brought under the influence and control of the Roman Empire and, later, of the Western Christian church. Adoption rather than eviction of language was the rule followed in perhaps the majority of historical and contemporary instances of language spread. Knowledge and use of the language of a dominating culture may be seen as a necessity when that language is the medium of commerce, law, civilization, and personal prestige. It was on that basis, not through numerical superiority, that Indo-European tongues were dispersed throughout Europe and to distant India, Iran, and Armenia. Likewise, Arabic became widespread in western Asia and North Africa not through massive population relocations but through conquest, religious conversion, and dominating culture. That is, languages may spread because they acquire new speakers.

Either form of language spread—dispersion of speakers or acquisition of speakers—represents one of the *spatial diffusion* processes introduced in Chapter 2. Massive population relocation in which culture is transported to and made dominant in a new territory is a specialized example of *relocation diffusion*. When the advantages of a new language are discerned and it is adopted by native speakers of another tongue, a form of *expansion diffusion* has occurred along with partial or total *acculturation* of the adopting population. Usually, those who are in or aspire to positions of importance are the first to adopt the new language of control and prestige. Later, through schooling, daily contact, and business or social necessity, other, lower social strata of society may gradually be absorbed into the expanding pool of language adopters.

Such *hierarchical diffusion* of an official or prestigious language has occurred in many societies. In India during the 19th century, the English established an administrative and judicial system that put a very high premium on their language as the sole medium of education, administration, trade, and commerce. Proficiency in it was the hallmark of the cultured and educated person (as knowledge of Sanskrit and Persian had been in earlier periods under other conquerors of India). English, French, Dutch, Portuguese, and other languages introduced during the acquisition of empire retain a position of prestige and even status as the official language in multilingual societies, even after independence has been achieved by former colonial territories. In Uganda and other former British possessions in Africa, a stranger may be addressed in English by one who wishes to display his or her education and social status, though standard Swahili, a second language for many different culture groups, may be chosen if certainty of communication is more important than pride.

As a diffusion process, language spread may be impeded by barriers or promoted by their absence. Cultural barriers may retard or prevent language adoption. Speakers of Greek resisted centuries of Turkish rule of their homeland, and the language remained a focus of cultural identity under foreign domination.

Figure 5.5 World language families.

Language families are groups of individual tongues that had a common but remote ancestor. By suggesting that the area assigned to a language or language family uses that tongue exclusively, the map pattern conceals important linguistic detail. Many countries and regions have local languages spoken in territories too small to be recorded at this scale. The map also fails to report that the population in many regions is fluent in more than one language or that a second language serves as the necessary vehicle of commerce, education, or government. Nor is important information given about the number of speakers of different languages; the fact that there are more speakers of English in India or Africa than in Australia is not even hinted at by a map at this scale.

Note that some linguistic boundaries match political boundaries and others do not.

Language Families

1 Indo-European
   a. Romance b. Germanic c. Slavic
   d. Baltic e. Celtic f. Albanian g. Greek
   h. Armenian k. Indo-Iranian
2 Uralic-Altaic
3 Sino-Tibetan
4 Japanese-Korean
5 Dravidian
6 Afro-Asiatic
7 Niger-Congo
8 Sudanic
9 Saharan
10 Khoisan
11 Paleo-Asiatic
12 Austro-Asiatic
13 Malayo-Polynesian
14 Australian
15 Amerindian
   Other
   16. Eskimo-Aleut 17. Papuan 18. Caucasian
   19. Basque 20. Vietnamese
16 Unpopulated

Breton, Catalan, Gaelic, and other localized languages of Europe remain symbols of ethnic separateness from surrounding dominant national cultures and controls.

Physical barriers to language spread have also left their mark (see Figure 5.5). Migrants or invaders follow paths of least topographic resistance and disperse most widely where access is easiest. Once past the barrier of the Pamirs and the Hindu Kush mountains, Indo-European tongues spread rapidly through the Indus and Ganges river lowlands of the Indian subcontinent but made no headway in the mountainous northern and eastern border zones. The Pyrenees Mountains serve as a linguistic barrier separating France and Spain. They also house the Basques who speak the only language—*Euskara* in their tongue—in southwestern Europe that survives from pre-Indo-European times (Figure 5.8). Similarly, the Caucasus Mountains between the

Black and Caspian seas separate the Slavic speakers to the north and the areas of *Ural-Altaic* languages to the south. At the same time, in their rugged topography they contain an extraordinary mixture of languages, many unique to single valleys or villages, lumped together spatially if not by origin into a separate *Caucasian* language family.

Language Change

Migration, segregation, and isolation give rise to separate, mutually unintelligible languages because the society speaking the parent protolanguage no longer remains unitary. Comparable changes occur normally and naturally within a single language in word meaning, pronunciation, vocabulary, and *syntax* (the way

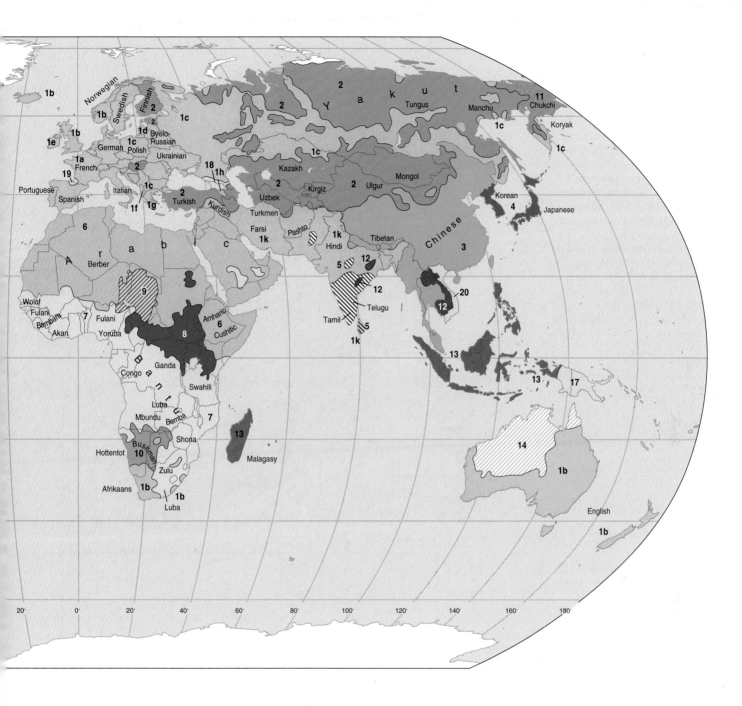

words are put together in phrases and sentences). Because they are gradual, minor, and made part of group use and understanding, such changes tend to go unremarked. Yet, cumulatively, they can result in language change so great that in the course of centuries an essentially new language has been created. The English of 17th-century Shakespearean writings or the King James Bible (1611) sounds stilted to our ears. Few of us can easily read Chaucer's 14th-century *Canterbury Tales,* and 8th-century *Beowulf* is practically unintelligible.

Change may be gradual and cumulative, with each generation deviating in small degree from the speech patterns and vocabulary of its parents, or it may be massive and abrupt. English gained about 10,000 new words from the Norman conquerors of the 11th century. In some 70 years (1558–1625) of literary and linguistic creativity during the reigns of Elizabeth I and James I, an estimated 12,000 words—based on borrowings from Latin, Greek, and other languages—were introduced.

Discovery and colonization of new lands and continents in the 16th and 17th centuries greatly and necessarily expanded English as new foods, vegetation, animals, and artifacts were encountered and adopted along with their existing aboriginal American, Australian, or African names. The Indian languages of the Americas alone brought more than 200 relatively common daily words to English, 80 or more from the North American native tongues and the rest from Caribbean, Central, and South American. More than two thousand more specialized or localized words were also added. *Moose, raccoon, skunk, maize, squash, succotash, igloo, toboggan, hurricane, blizzard, hickory, pecan,* and a host of other names were taken directly into English; others were adopted second hand from Spanish variants of South American native words: *cigar, potato, chocolate, tomato, tobacco, hammock.* More

Figure 5.6 Amerindian language families of North America. As many as 300 different North American and more than 70 Meso-American tongues were spoken at the time of first European contact. The map summarizes the traditional view that these were grouped into 9 or 10 language families in North America, as many as 5 in Meso-America, and another 10 or so in South America. More recent research, however, suggests close genetic relationships between Native American tongues, clustering them into just 3 families: Eskimo-Aleut in the extreme north and Greenland; Na-Dené in Canada and the U.S. Southwest, and Amerind elsewhere in the hemisphere. Because each family has closer affinities with Asian language groups than with one another, it is suggested that each corresponds to a separate wave of Asian migration to the Americas: the first giving rise to the Amerind family, the second to the Na-Dené, and the last to the Eskimo-Aleut. Many Amerindian tongues have become extinct; others are still known only to very small groups of mostly elderly speakers.

Source: Data from various sources, including C. F. and F. M. Voegelin, Map of North American Indian Languages *(Seattle: University of Washington Press, 1986).*

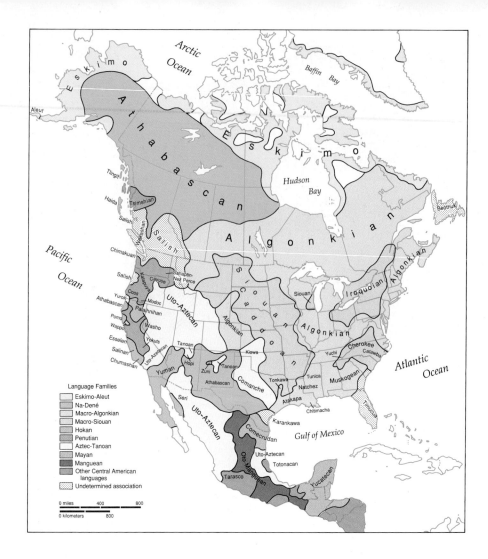

Figure 5.7 Bantu advance, Khoisan retreat in Africa. Linguistic evidence suggests that proto-*Bantu* speakers originated in the region of the Cameroon-Nigeria border, spread eastward across the southern Sudan, then turned southward to Central Africa. From there they dispersed slowly eastward, westward, and against slight resistance, southward. The earlier *Khoisan*-speaking occupants of sub-Saharan Africa were no match against the advancing metal-using Bantu agriculturalists. Pygmies, adopting a Bantu tongue, retreated deep into the forests; Bushmen and Hottentots retained their distinctive Khoisan "click" language but were forced out of forests and grasslands into the dry steppes and deserts of the southwest.

Figure 5.8 In their mountainous homeland, the Basques have maintained a linguistic uniqueness despite more than 2000 years of encirclement by dominant lowland speakers of Latin or Romance languages. This sign—thanking travelers for their visit and wishing them a good trip home—gives its message in both Spanish and the Basque language, Euskara.

recently, and within a short span of years, new scientific and technological developments have enriched and expanded the vocabularies not only of English but of all languages spoken by modern societies by adding many words of Greek and Latin derivation.

The Story of English

English itself is a product of change, an offspring of proto-Germanic (see Figure 5.4) descending through the dialects brought to England in the 5th and 6th centuries by conquering Danish and North German Frisians, Jutes, Angles, and Saxons. Earlier Celtic-speaking inhabitants found refuge in the north and west of Britain and in the rugged uplands of what are now Scotland and Wales. Each of the transplanted tongues established its own area of dominance, but the West Saxon dialect of southern England emerged in the 9th and 10th centuries as Standard Old English on the strength of its literary richness.

It lost its supremacy after the Norman Conquest of 1066, as the center of learning and culture shifted northeastward from Winchester to London, and French rather than English became the language of the nobility and the government. When the tie between France and England was severed after the loss of Normandy (1204), French fell into disfavor and English again became the dominant tongue, although now as the French-enriched Middle English used by Geoffrey Chaucer and mandated as the official language of the law courts by the Statute of Pleading (1362). During the 15th and 16th centuries, English as spoken in London emerged as the basic form of Early Modern English.

During the 18th century, attempts to standardize and codify the rules of English were unsuccessful. But the *Dictionary* of Samuel Johnson (published 1755)—based on cultured language of

contemporary London and the examples of major authors—helped establish norms of proper form and usage. A worldwide diffusion of the language resulted as English colonists carried it as settlers to the Western Hemisphere and Australasia; through merchants, conquest, or territorial claim, it established footholds in Africa and Asia. In that spatial diffusion, English was further enriched by its contacts with other languages. By becoming the accepted language of commerce and science, it contributed, in turn, to the common vocabularies of other tongues (see "Language Exchange").

Within some 400 years, English has developed from a localized language of 7 million islanders off the European coast to a truly international language with some 400 million native speakers, perhaps the same number who use it as a second language, and another 750 million who have reasonable competence in English as a foreign language. With over one billion speakers worldwide, English also serves as an official language of some 60 countries (Figure 5.9), far exceeding in that role French (32), Arabic (25), or Spanish (21), the other leading current international languages. At the end of the 20th century, over 78% of Internet Web pages used English (Japanese was second with 2.5%). No other language in history has assumed so important a role on the world scene.

Standard and Variant Languages

People who speak a common language such as English are members of a **speech community,** but membership does not necessarily imply linguistic uniformity. A speech community usually possesses both a **standard language**—comprising the accepted community norms of syntax, vocabulary, and pronunciation—and a number of more or less distinctive *dialects* reflecting the ordinary speech of areal, social, professional, or other subdivisions of the general population.

Standard Language

A dialect may become the standard language through identity with the speech of the most prestigious, highest-ranking, and most powerful members of the larger speech community. A rich literary tradition may help establish its primacy, and its adoption as the accepted written and spoken norm in administration, economic life, and education will solidify its position, minimizing linguistic variation and working toward the elimination of deviant, nonstandard forms. The dialect that emerges as the basis of a country's standard language is often the one identified with its capital or center of power at the time of national development. Standard French is based on the dialect of the Paris region, a variant that assumed dominance in the latter half of the 12th century and was made the only official language in 1539. Castilian Spanish became the standard after 1492 with the Castile-led reconquest of Spain from the Moors and the export of the dialect to the Americas during the 16th century. Its present form, however, is a modified version associated not with Castile but with Madrid, the modern capital of Spain. Standard Russian is identified with the speech patterns of the former capital, St. Petersburg, and Moscow, the current capital. Modern Standard Chinese is based on the Mandarin dialect of Beijing. In England, *Received Pronunciation*—"Oxford English," the speech

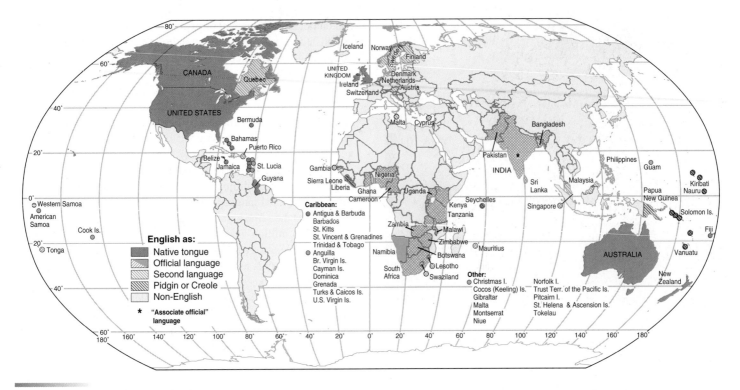

Figure 5.9 International English. In worldwide diffusion and acceptance, English has no past or present rivals. Along with French, it is one of the two working languages of the United Nations and the effective common language of the workers and committees of European Union institutions; some two-thirds of all scientific papers are published in it, making it the first language of scientific discourse, and it is the accepted language of international air traffic control. English is the sole or joint official language of more nations and territories, some too small to be shown here, than any other tongue. It also serves as the effective unofficial language of administration in other multilingual countries with different formal official languages. "English as a second language" is indicated for countries with near-universal or mandatory English instruction in public schools. Not evident on this map is the full extent of English penetration of Continental Europe, where more than 80% of secondary school students (and 92% of those of European Union states) study it as a second language.

Language Exchange

English has a happily eclectic vocabulary. Its foundations are Anglo-Saxon (*was, that, eat, cow*) reinforced by Norse (*sky, get, bath, husband, skill*); its superstructure is Norman-French (*soldier, Parliament, prayer, beef*). The Norman aristocracy used their words for the food, but the Saxon serfs kept theirs for the animals. The language's decor comes from Renaissance and Enlightenment Europe: 16th-century France yielded *etiquette, naive, reprimand,* and *police.*

Italy provided *umbrella, duet, bandit,* and *dilettante;* Holland gave *cruise, yacht, trigger, landscape,* and *decoy.* Its elaborations come from Latin and Greek: *misanthrope, meditate,* and *parenthesis* all first appeared

during the 1560s. In the 20th century, English adopted *penicillin* from Latin, *polystyrene* from Greek, and *sociology* and *television* from both. And English's ornaments come from all round the world: *slogan* and *spree* from Gaelic, *hammock* and *hurricane* from Caribbean languages, *caviar* and *kiosk* from Turkish, *dinghy* and *dungarees* from Hindi, *caravan* and *candy* from Persian, *mattress* and *masquerade* from Arabic.

Redressing the balance of trade, English is sharply stepping up its linguistic exports. Not just the necessary *imotokali* (motor car) and *izingilazi* (glasses) to Zulu; or *motokaa* and *shillingi* (shilling) to Swahili; but also *der Bestseller, der Kommunikations*

Manager, das Teeshirt and *der Babysitter* to German; and, to Italian, *la pop art, il popcorn* and *la spray.* In some Spanish-speaking countries you might wear *un sueter* to *el beisbol,* or witness *un nocaut* at *el boxeo.* And in Russia, *biznesmen* prepare a *press rilis* on the *lep-top kompyuter* and print it by *lazerny printer.* Indeed, a sort of global English word list can be drawn up: *airport, passport, hotel, telephone; bar, soda, cigarette; sport, golf, tennis; stop, OK,* and increasingly, *weekend, jeans, know-how, sex-appeal,* and *no problem.*

Excerpted by permission from *The Economist*, London, December 20, 1986, p. 131.

of educated people of London and Southeastern England and used by the British Broadcasting System—was until recently the accepted standard though it is now being modified, or replaced by a dialect called "Estuary English," which refers to the region around the lower River Thames in southeastern England.

Other forces than the political may affect language standardization. In its spoken form, Standard German is based on norms established and accepted in the theater, the universities, public speeches, and radio and television. The Classical or Literary Arabic of the Koran became the established norm from the Indian to the Atlantic Ocean. Standard Italian was derived from the Florentine dialect of the 13th and 14th centuries, which became widespread as the language of literature and economy.

In many societies, the official or unofficial standard language is not the dialect of home or daily life, and populations in effect have two languages. One is their regional dialect they employ with friends, at home, and in local community contacts; the other is the standard language used in more formal situations. In some cases, the contrast is great; regional variants of Arabic may be mutually unintelligible. Most Italians encounter Standard Italian for the first time in primary school. In India, the several totally distinct official regional languages are used in writing and taught in school but have no direct relationship to local speech; citizens must be bilingual to communicate with government officials who know only the regional language but not the local dialect.

Dialects

Just as no two individuals talk exactly the same, all but the smallest and most closely knit speech communities display recognizable speech variants called **dialects.** Vocabulary, pronunciation, rhythm, and the speed at which the language is spoken may set groups of speakers apart from one another and, to a trained observer, clearly mark the origin of the speaker. In George Bernard Shaw's play *Pygmalion,* on which the musical *My Fair Lady* was based, Henry Higgins—a professor of phonetics—is able to identify the London neighborhood of origin of a flower girl by listening to her vocabulary and accent. In many instances, such variants are totally acceptable modifications of the standard language; in others, they mark the speaker as a social, cultural, or regional "outsider" or "inferior." Professor Higgins makes a lady out of the uneducated flower girl simply by teaching her upper-class pronunciation.

Shaw's play tells us dialects may coexist in space. Cockney and cultured English share the streets of London; black English and Standard American are heard in the same school yards throughout the United States. In many societies, **social dialects** denote social class and educational level. Speakers of higher socioeconomic status or educational achievement are most likely to follow the norms of their standard language; less-educated or lower-status persons or groups consciously distinguishing themselves from the mainstream culture are more likely to use the **vernacular**— nonstandard language or dialect native to the locale or adopted by the social group. In some instances, however, as in Germany and German-Switzerland, local dialects are preserved and prized as badges of regional identity.

Different dialects may be part of the speech patterns of the same person. Professionals discussing, for example, medical, legal, financial, or scientific matters with their peers employ vocabularies and formal modes of address and sentence structure that are quickly changed to informal colloquial speech when the conversation shifts to sports, vacations, or personal anecdotes. Even gender may be the basis for linguistic differences added to other determinants of social dialects.

More commonly, we think of dialects in spatial terms. Speech is a geographic variable; each locale is apt to have its own, perhaps slight, language differences from neighboring places. Such differences in pronunciation, vocabulary, word meanings, and other language characteristics tend to accumulate with distance from a given starting point. When they are mapped, they help define the **linguistic geography**—the study of the character and spatial pattern of dialects and languages—of a generalized speech community.

Every dialect feature has a territorial extent. The outer limit of its occurrence is a boundary line called an **isogloss** (the term *isophone* is used if the areal variant is marked by difference in sound rather than word choice), as shown in Figure 5.10. Each isogloss is a distinct entity, but taken together isoglosses give clear map evidence of dialect regions that in their turn may reflect topographic barriers and corridors, long-established political borders, or past migration flows and diffusions of word choice and pronunciation.

Geographic or **regional dialects** may be recognized at different scales. On the world scene, for example, British, American, Indian, and Australian English are all acknowledged distinctive dialects of the same evolving language (see "World Englishes"). Regionally, in Britain alone, one can recognize Southern British English, Northern British English, and Scottish English, each containing several more localized variants. Japanese has three recognized dialect groups; and China's Han ethnic group—making up more than 90% of the population of a country whose official language is Standard Mandarin—speak as many as 1500 dialects, many almost entirely mutually incomprehensible.

Indeed, all long-established speech communities show their own structure of geographic dialects whose number and diversity tend to increase in areas longest settled and most fragmented and isolated. For example, the local speech of Newfoundland— isolated off the Atlantic coast of mainland Canada—retains much of the 17th-century flavor of the four West Counties of England from which the overwhelming majority of its settlers came. Yet the isolation and lack of cultural mixing of the islanders have not led to a general Newfoundland "dialect"; settlement was coastal and in the form of isolated villages in each of the many bays and indentations. There developed from that isolation and the passage of time nearly as many dialects as there are bay settlements, with each dialect separately differing from Standard English in accent, vocabulary, sounds, and syntax. Isolation has led to comparable linguistic variation among the 47,000 inhabitants of the 18 Faeroe Islands between Iceland and Scotland; their Faeroese tongue has 10 dialects.

Dialects in America

Mainland North America had a more diversified colonization than did Newfoundland, and its more mobile settlers mixed and carried linguistic influences away from the coast into the continental

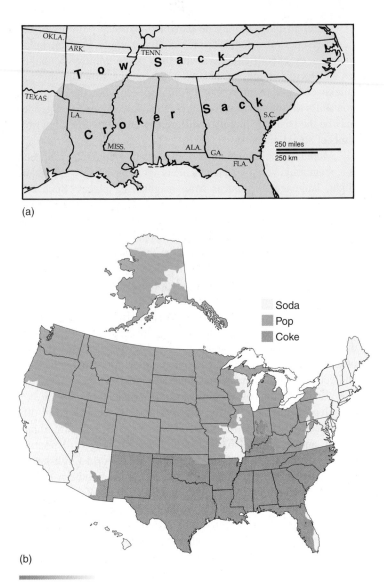

(a)

(b)

Figure 5.10 (a) **Dialect boundaries.** Descriptive words or terms for common items are frequently employed indicators of dialect difference. The limit of their areas of use is marked by an isogloss, such as that shown here for now-obsolete terms describing a coarse sack. Usually such boundary lines appear in clusters, or *bundles;* together, they help define the frontier of the dialect under study. (b) The generic term for a soft drink varies regionally across the United States from soda to pop to coke. Maps such as this visually record variations over space in word usage or accent or pronunciation. Despite the presumed influence of national radio and television programs in promoting a "general" or "standard" American word usage, regional variations persist.

Source: (a) Adapted from Gordon R. Wood, Vocabulary Change: A Study of Variation in Regional Words in Eight of the Southern States *(Carbondale: Southern Illinois University Press, 1971), Map 81, p. 357. Used by permission of the publisher; (b) Adopted and generalized from* Web Atlas of Oklahoma.*"*

interior. Nonetheless, as early as the 18th century, three distinctive dialect regions had emerged along the Atlantic coast of the United States (Figure 5.11) and are evident in the linguistic geography of North America to the present day.

With the extension of settlement after the Revolutionary War, each of the dialect regions expanded inland. Speakers of the Northern dialect moved along the Erie Canal and the Great Lakes. Midland speakers from Pennsylvania traveled down the Ohio River, and the related Upland Southern dialect moved through the mountain gaps into Kentucky and Tennessee. The Coastal Southern dialect was less mobile, held to the east by plantation prosperity and the long resistance to displacement exerted by the Cherokees and the other Civilized Tribes (Figure 5.12).

Once across the Appalachian barrier, the diffusion paths of the Northern dialect were fragmented and blocked by the time they reached the Upper Mississippi. Upland Southern speakers spread out rapidly: northward into the old Northwest Territory, west into Arkansas and Missouri, and south into the Gulf Coast states. But the Civil War and its aftermath halted further major westward movements of the southern dialects. The Midland dialect, apparently so restricted along the eastern seaboard, became, almost by default, the basic form for much of the interior and West of the United States. It was altered and enriched there by contact with the Northern and Southern dialects, by additions from Native American languages, by contact with Spanish culture in the Southwest, and by contributions from the great non-English immigrations of the late 19th and early 20th centuries. Naturally, dialect subregions are found in the West, but their boundary lines—so clear in the eastern interior—become less distinct from the Plains States to the Pacific.

The immigrant contributions of the last centuries are still continuing and growing. In areas with strong infusions of recently arrived Hispanic, Asian, and other immigrant groups, language mixing tends to accelerate language change as more and different non-English words enter the general vocabulary of all Americans. In many cases, those infusions create or perpetuate pockets of linguistically unassimilated peoples whose urban neighborhoods in shops, signage, and common speech bear little resemblance to the majority Anglo communities of the larger metropolitan area. Even as immigrant groups learn and adopt English, there is an inevitable retention of familiar words and phrases and, for many, the unstructured intermixture of old and new tongues into such hybrids as "Spanglish" among Latin and Central American immigrants, for example, or "Runglish" among the thousands of Russian immigrants of the Brighton Beach district of New York City.

Local dialects and accents do not display predictable patterns of consistency or change. In ethnically and regionally complex United States, for example, mixed conclusions concerning local speech patterns have been drawn by researchers examining the linguistic results of an increasingly transient population, immigration from other countries and cultures, and the pervasive and presumed leveling effects of the mass media. The distinct evidence of increasing contrasts between the speech patterns and accents of Chicago, New York, Birmingham, St. Louis, and other cities is countered by reports of decreasing local dialect pronunciations in such centers as Dallas and Atlanta that have experienced major influxes of Northerners. And other studies find that some regional accents are fading in small towns and rural areas, presumably because mass media standardization is more influential than local

Non-native speakers of English far outnumber those for whom English is the first language. Most of the more than 1.5 billion people who speak and understand at least some English as a second language live in Asia; they are appropriating the language and remaking it in regionally distinctive fashions to suit their own cultures, linguistic backgrounds, and needs.

It is inevitable that widely spoken languages separated by distance, isolation, and cultural differences will fragment into dialects that, in turn, evolve into new languages. Latin splintered into French, Spanish, Italian, and other Romance languages; the many national variants of spoken Arabic are effectively different tongues. English is similarly experiencing that sort of regional differentiation, shaped by the variant needs and inputs of its far-flung community of speakers, and following the same path to mutual unintelligibility. Although Standard English may be one of or the sole official language of their countries of birth, millions of people around the world claiming proficiency in English or English as their national language cannot understand each other. Even teachers of English from India, Malaysia, Nigeria, or the Philippines, for example, may not be able to communicate in their supposedly common tongue—and find cockney English of London utterly alien.

The splintering of spoken English is a fact of linguistic life and its offspring—called "World Englishes" by linguists—defy frequent attempts by different governments to remove localisms and encourage adherence to international standards. Singlish (Singapore English) and Taglish (a mixture of English and Tagalog, the dominant language of the Philippines) are commonly cited examples of the multiplying World Englishes, but equally distinctive regional variants have emerged in India, Malaysia, Hong Kong, Nigeria, the Caribbean, and elsewhere. One linguist suggests that beyond an "inner circle" of states where English is the first and native language—for example, Canada, Australia, United States—lies an "outer circle" where English is a second language (Bangladesh, Ghana, India, Kenya, Pakistan, Zambia, and many others) and where the regionally distinctive World Englishes are most obviously developing. Even farther out is an "expanding circle" of such states as China, Egypt, Korea, Nepal, Saudi Arabia, and others where English is a foreign language and distinctive local variants in common usage have not yet developed.

Each of the emerging varieties of English is, of course, "correct," for each represents a coherent and consistent vehicle for communication with mutual comprehension between its speakers. Each also represents a growing national cultural confidence and pride in the particular characteristics of the local varieties of English, and each regional variant is strengthened by local teachers who do not themselves have a good command of the standard language. Conceivably, these factors may mean that English will fragment into scores or hundreds of mutually unintelligible tongues. But equally conceivably, the worldwide influence of globalized business contacts, the Internet, worldwide American radio and television broadcasts, near-mandatory use of English in scientific publication, and the like will mean a future English more homogeneous and, perhaps, more influenced and standardized by American usage.

Most likely, observers of World Englishes suggest, both divergence and convergence will take place. While use of English as the major language of communication worldwide is a fact in international politics, business, education, and the media, increasingly, speakers of English learn two "dialects"—one of their own community and culture and one in the international context. While the constant modern world electronic and literary interaction between the variant regional Englishes make it likely that the common language will remain universally intelligible, it also seems probable that mutually incomprehensible forms of English will become entrenched as the language is taught, learned, and used in world areas far removed from contact with first-language speakers and with vibrant local economies and cultures independent of the Standard English community. "Our only revenge," said a French official, deploring the declining role of French within the European Union, "is that the English language is being killed by all these foreigners speaking it so badly."

---

dialect reinforcement as areal populations decline and physical and social mobility increase.

Pidgins and Creoles

Language is rarely a total barrier in communication between peoples, even those whose native tongues are mutually incomprehensible. Bilingualism or multilingualism may permit skilled linguists to communicate in a jointly understood third language, but long-term contact between less able populations may require the creation of new language—a pidgin—learned by both parties. In the past 400 years, more than 100 new languages have been created out of the mixings of peoples and cultures throughout the world.

A **pidgin** is an amalgam of languages, usually a simplified form of one, such as English or French, with borrowings from another, perhaps non-European local language. In its original form, a pidgin is not the mother tongue of any of its speakers; it is a second language for everyone who uses it, a language generally restricted to such specific functions as commerce, administration, or work supervision. For example, such is the variety of languages spoken among the some 270 ethnic groups of the Democratic Republic of the Congo that a special tongue called Lingala, a hybrid of Congolese dialects and French, was created to permit, among other things, issuance of orders to army recruits drawn from all parts of the country.

Pidgins are initially characterized by a highly simplified grammatical structure and a sharply reduced vocabulary,

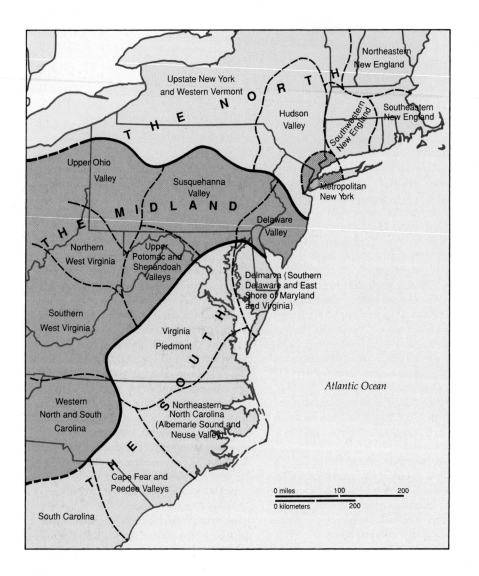

Figure 5.11 **Dialect areas of the eastern United States.** The Northern dialect and its subdivisions are found in New England and adjacent Canada (the international boundary has little effect on dialect borders in Anglo America), extending southward to a secondary dialect area centered on New York City. Midland speech is found along the Atlantic Coast only from central New Jersey southward to central Delaware, but spreads much more extensively across the interior of the United States and Canada. The Southern dialect dominates the East Coast from Chesapeake Bay south.

Source: Redrawn by permission from Hans Kurath, A Word Geography of the Eastern United States *(Ann Arbor: University of Michigan Press, 1949).*

adequate to express basic ideas but not complex concepts. For example, fanagalo, a pidgin created earlier in South Africa's gold mines to allow spoken communication between workers of different tribes and nationalities and between workers and Afrikaner bosses, is being largely abandoned. Since the mid-1990s, workers have increasingly been schooled in basic English as fanagalo—which lacks the vocabulary to describe how to operate new, automated mining machinery and programmable winches with their multiple sensors and warnings in English—became decreasingly useful. In South America, when the Portuguese arrived five centuries ago, difficulties of communication with conquered native peoples speaking more than 700 languages led Jesuit priests to concoct a mixture of Indian, Portuguese, and African words they called "lingua geral," or the "general language," and impose it on their colonial subjects. As a living language, lingua geral gradually died out in most of Brazil but has been retained and adopted as an element of their cultural identity by some isolated Indian groups that have lost their own original mother tongue. If a pidgin becomes the

first language of a group of speakers—who may have lost their former native tongue through disuse—a **creole** has evolved. In their development, creoles invariably acquire a more complex grammatical structure and enhanced vocabulary.

Creole languages have proved useful integrative tools in linguistically diverse areas; several have become symbols of nationhood. Swahili, a pidgin formed from a number of Bantu dialects with major vocabulary additions from Arabic, originated in the coastal areas of East Africa and spread inland first by Arab ivory and slave caravans and later by trade during the period of English and German colonial rules. When Kenya and Tanzania gained independence, they made Swahili the national language of administration and education. Other examples of creolization are Afrikaans (a pidginized form of 17th-century Dutch used in the Republic of South Africa); Haitian Creole (the language of Haiti, derived from the pidginized French used in the slave trade); and Bazaar Malay (a pidginized form of the Malay language, a version of which is the official national language of Indonesia).

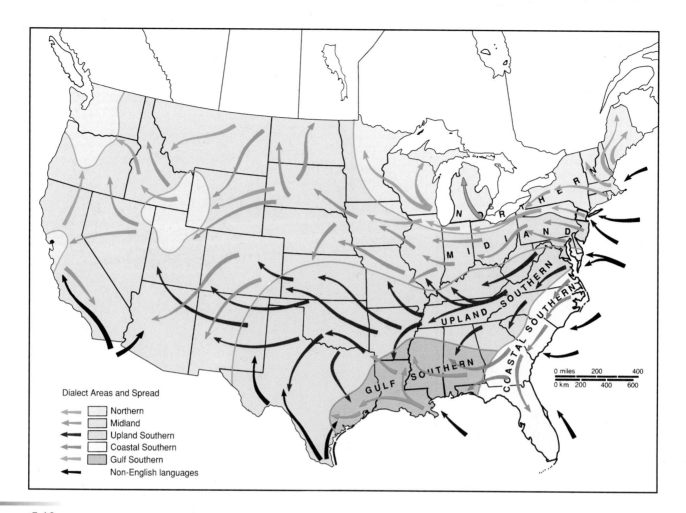

Figure 5.12 Speech regions and dialect diffusion in the United States. This generalized map is most accurate for the eastern seaboard and the easternmost diffusion pathways where most detailed linguistic study has been concentrated. West of the Mississippi River, the Midland dialect becomes dominant, though altered through modifications reflecting intermingling of peoples and speech patterns. Northern speech characteristics are still clearly evident in the San Francisco Bay area, brought there in the middle of the 19th century by migrants coming by sea around Cape Horn. Northerners were also prominent among the travelers of the Oregon Trail and the California Gold Rush.

Sources: Based on Raven I. McDavid, Jr. "The Dialects of American English," in W. Nelson Francis, The Structure of American English *(New York: Ronald Press, 1958); "Regional Dialects in the United States,"* Webster's New World Dictionary, *2nd College Edition (New York: Simon and Schuster, 1980); and Gordon R. Wood,* Vocabulary Change *(Carbondale: Southern Illinois University Press, 1971), Map 83, p. 358.*

Lingua Franca

A **lingua franca** is an established language used habitually for communication by people whose native tongues are mutually incomprehensible. For them it is a *second language,* one learned in addition to the native tongue. Lingua franca, literally "Frankish tongue," was named from the dialect of France adopted as their common tongue by the Crusaders assaulting the Muslims of the Holy Land. Later, it endured as a language of trade and travel in the eastern Mediterranean, useful as a single tongue shared in a linguistically diverse region.

Between 300 B.C. and A.D. 500, the Mediterranean world was unified by Common Greek. Later, Latin became a lingua franca, the language of empire and, until replaced by the vernacular European tongues, of the Church, government, scholarship, and the law. Outside the European sphere, Aramaic served the role from the 5th century B.C. to the 4th century A.D. in the Near East and Egypt; Arabic followed Muslim conquest as the unifying language of that

international religion after the 7th century. Mandarin Chinese and Hindi in India both formerly and today have a lingua franca role in their linguistically diverse countries. The immense linguistic diversity of Africa has made regional lingua francas there necessary and inevitable (Figure 5.13), and in a polyglot world, English increasingly serves everywhere as the global lingua franca.

Official Languages

Governments may designate a single tongue as a country's **official language,** the required language of instruction in the schools and universities, government business, the courts, and other official and semiofficial public and private activities. In societies in which two or more languages are in common use **(multilingualism),** such an official language may serve as the approved national lingua franca, guaranteeing communication among all citizens of differing native tongues. In many immigrant societies, such as the United States, only one of the many spoken languages may have

Figure 5.13 Lingua francas of Africa.
The importance and extent of competing lingua francas in sub-Saharan Africa change over time, reflecting the spread of populations and the relative economic or political stature of speakers of different languages. In many areas, an individual may employ different lingua francas, depending on activity: dealing with officials, trading in the marketplace, conversing with strangers. Among the elite in all areas, the preferred lingua franca is apt to be a European language. When a European tongue is an official language (Figure 5.14) or the language of school instruction, its use as a lingua franca is more widespread. Throughout northern Africa, Arabic is the usual lingua franca for all purposes.

Source: Adapted from Bernd Heine, Status and Use of African Lingua Francas *(Munich, Germany: Weltforum Verlag; and New York: Humanities Press, 1970).*

Figure 5.14 **Europe in Africa through official languages.** Both the linguistic complexity of sub-Saharan Africa and the colonial histories of its present political units are implicit in the designation of a European language as the sole or joint "official" language of the different countries.

implicit or official government sanction (see "An Official U.S. Language?").

Nearly every country in linguistically complex sub-Saharan Africa has selected a European language—usually that of their former colonial governors—as an official language (Figure 5.14), only rarely designating a native language or creole as an alternate official tongue. Indeed, less than 10% of the population of sub-Saharan Africa live in countries with any indigenous African tongue given official status. Nigeria has some 350 clearly different languages and is dominated by three of them: Hausa, Yoruba, and Ibo. For no Nigerian is English a native tongue, yet throughout the country English is the sole language of instruction and the sole official language. Effectively, all Nigerians must learn a foreign language before they can enter the mainstream of national life. Most Pacific Ocean countries, including the Philippines (with between 80 and 110 Malayo-Polynesian languages) and Papua New Guinea (with over 850 distinct Papuan tongues), have a European language as at least one of their official tongues.

Increasingly, the "purity" of official European languages has been threatened by the popular and widespread inclusion of English words and phrases in everyday speech, press, and television. So common has such adoption become, in fact, that some nearly new language variants are now recognized: *franglais* in

France and *Denglish* in Germany are the best-known examples. Both have spurred resistance movements from officially sanctioned language monitors of, respectively, the French Academy and the Institute for the German Language. Poland, Spain, and Latvia are among other European states seeking to preserve the purity of their official languages from contamination by English or other foreign borrowings. Japan's Council on the Japanese Language is doing the same.

In some countries, multilingualism has official recognition through designation of more than a single state language. Canada and Finland, for example, have two official languages (*bilingualism*), reflecting rough equality in numbers or influence of separate linguistic populations comprising a single country. In a few multilingual countries, more than two official languages have been designated. Bolivia and Belgium have three official tongues and Singapore has four. South Africa's constitution designates 11 official languages, and India gives official status to 18 languages at the regional, though not at the national, level.

Multilingualism may reflect significant cultural and spatial divisions within a country. In Canada, the Official Languages Act of 1969 accorded French and English equal status as official languages of the Parliament and of government throughout the nation (Figure 5.15). French-speakers are concentrated in the Province of Quebec, however, and constitute a culturally distinct population sharply divergent from the English-speaking majority of other parts of Canada (Figure 5.16). Within sections of Canada, even greater linguistic diversity is recognized; the legislature of the Northwest Territories, for example, has eight official languages—six native, plus English and French.

Few countries remain purely *monolingual,* with only a single language of communication for all purposes among all citizens, though most are officially so. Past and recent movements of peoples as colonists, refugees, or migrants have assured that most of the world's countries contain linguistically mixed populations.

Maintenance of native languages among such populations is not assured, of course. Where numbers are small or pressures for integration into an economically and socially dominant culture are strong, immigrant and aboriginal (native) linguistic minorities tend to adopt the majority or official language for all purposes. On the other hand, isolation and relatively large numbers of speakers may serve to preserve native tongues. In Canada, for example, aboriginal languages with large populations of speakers—Cree, Ojibwe, and Inuktitut—are well maintained in their areas of concentration (respectively, northern Quebec, the northern prairies, and Nunavut). In contrast, much smaller language groups in southern and coastal British Columbia have a much lower ratio of retention among native speakers.

Language, Territoriality, and Cultural Identity

The designation of more than one official language does not always satisfy the ambitions of linguistically distinct groups for recognition and autonomy. Language is an inseparable part of group identity and a defining characteristic of ethnic and cultural distinction. The view that cultural heritage is rooted in language is well-established and found throughout the world, as is the feeling that losing linguistic identity is the worst and final evidence of discrimination and subjugation. Language has often been the focus of separatist movements, especially of spatially distinct linguistic groups outside the economic heartlands of the strongly centralized countries to which they are attached.

In Europe, France, Spain, Britain—and Yugoslavia and the Soviet Union before their dismemberment—experienced such language "revolts" and acknowledged, sometimes belatedly, the local concerns they express. After 1970 France dropped its ban on teaching regional tongues and Spain relaxed its earlier total rejection of Basque and Catalan as regional languages, recognizing Catalan as a co-official language in its home region in northeastern Spain. In Britain, parliamentary debates concerning greater regional autonomy in the United Kingdom have resulted in bilingual road and informational signs in Wales, a publicly supported Welsh-language television channel, and compulsory teaching of Welsh in all schools in Wales.

In fact, throughout Europe in the 1980s and 1990s, nonofficial native regional languages have increasingly not only been tolerated but encouraged—in Western Europe, particularly, as a buffer against the loss of regional institutions and traditions threatened by a multinational "superstate" under the European Union. The Council of Europe, a 41-nation organization promoting democracy and human rights, has adopted a charter pledging encouragement of

Figure 5.15 French/English Bilingual Stop sign in Ottawa, Ontario. While "stop" is considered an acceptable French word by the Quebec Board of the French language, a variety of bilingual combinations can be observed on stop signs in Canada including some featuring French or English alongside an indigenous language.

Geography and Public Policy

An Official U.S. Language?

Within recent years in Lowell, Massachusetts, public school courses have been offered in Spanish, Khmer, Lao, Portuguese, and Vietnamese, and all messages from schools to parents have been translated into five languages. Polyglot New York City has given bilingual programs in Spanish, Chinese, Haitian Creole, Russian, Korean, Vietnamese, French, Greek, Arabic, and Bengali. In most states, it is possible to get a high-school-equivalency diploma without knowing English because tests are offered in French and Spanish. In at least 39 states, driving tests have been available in foreign languages; California has provided 30 varieties, New York 23, and Michigan 20, including Arabic and Finnish. And as required by the 1965 federal Voting Rights Act, multilingual ballots are provided in some 300 electoral jurisdictions in 30 states.

These, and innumerable other evidences of governmentally sanctioned linguistic diversity, may come as a surprise to those many Americans who assume that English is the official language of the United States. It isn't; nowhere does the Constitution provide for an official language, and no federal law specifies one. The country was built by a great diversity of cultural and linguistic immigrants who nonetheless shared an eagerness to enter mainstream American life. At the start of the 21st century, a reported 18% of all U.S. residents spoke a language other than English in the home. In California public schools, 1 out of 3 students uses a non-English tongue within the family. In Washington, D.C. schools, students speak 127 languages and dialects, a linguistic diversity duplicated in other major city school systems.

Nationwide bilingual teaching began as an offshoot of the civil rights movement in the 1960s, was encouraged by a Supreme Court opinion authored by Justice William O. Douglas, and has been actively promoted by the U.S. Department of Education under the Bilingual Education Act of 1974 as an obligation of local school boards. Its purpose has been to teach subject matter to minority-language children in the language in which they think while introducing them to English, with the hope of achieving English proficiency in 2 or 3 years. Disappointment with the results achieved led to a successful 1998 California anti-bilingual education initiative,

Proposition 227, to abolish the program. Similar rejection elsewhere—Arizona in 2000 and Massachusetts in 2003, for example—has followed California's lead.

Opponents of the implications of governmentally encouraged multilingual education, bilingual ballots, and ethnic separatism argue that a common language is the unifying glue of the United States and all countries; without that glue, they fear, the process of "Americanization" and *acculturation*—the adoption by immigrants of the values, attitudes, ways of behavior, and speech of the receiving society—will be undermined. Convinced that early immersion and quick proficiency in English is the only sure way for minority newcomers to gain necessary access to jobs, higher education, and full integration into the economic and social life of the country, proponents of "English only" use in public education, voting, and state and local governmental agencies, successfully passed Official English laws or constitutional amendments in 27 states from the late 1980s to 2002.

Although the amendments were supported by sizable majorities of the voting population, resistance to them—and to their political and cultural implications—has been in every instance strong and persistent. Ethnic groups, particularly Hispanics, who are the largest of the linguistic groups affected, charged that they were evidence of blatant Anglo-centric racism, discriminatory and repressive in all regards. Some educators argued persuasively that all evidence proved that while immigrant children eventually acquire English proficiency in any event, they do so with less harm to their self-esteem and subject matter acquisition when initially taught in their own language. Business people with strong minority labor and customer ties and political leaders—often themselves members of ethnic communities or with sizable minority constituencies—argued against "discriminatory" language restrictions.

And historians noted that it had all been unsuccessfully tried before. The anti-Chinese Workingmen's Party in 1870s California led the fight for English-only laws in that state. The influx of immigrants from central and southeastern Europe at the turn of the century led Congress to make oral English a requirement for naturalization, and anti-German sentiment during and after World War I led some states to ban any use of German. The Supreme

Court struck down those laws in 1923, ruling that the "protection of the Constitution extends to all, to those who speak other languages as well as to those born with English on their tongue." Following suit, some of the recent state language amendments have also been voided by state or federal courts. In ruling its state's English-only law unconstitutional, Arizona's Supreme Court in 1998 noted it "chills First Amendment rights."

To counter those judicial restraints and the possibility of an eventual multilingual, multicultural United States in which English and, likely, Spanish would have co-equal status and recognition, U.S. English—an organization dedicated to the belief that "English is, and ever must remain, the only official language of the people of the United States"—actively supports the proposed U.S. Constitutional amendment first introduced in Congress by former Senator S. I. Hayakawa in 1981, and resubmitted by him and others in subsequent years. The proposed amendment would simply establish English as the official national language but would impose no duty on people to learn English and would not infringe on any right to use other languages. Whether or not these modern attempts to designate an official U.S. language eventually succeed, they represent a divisive subject of public debate affecting all sectors of American society.

Questions to Consider

1. Do you think multiple languages and ethnic separatism represent a threat to U.S. cultural unity that can be avoided only by viewing English as a necessary unifying force? Or do you think making English the official language might divide its citizens and damage its legacy of tolerance and diversity? Why or why not?

2. Do you feel that immigrant children would learn English faster if bilingual classes were reduced and immersion in English was more complete? Or do you think that a slower pace of English acquisition is acceptable if subject matter comprehension and cultural self-esteem are enhanced? Why or why not?

3. Do you think Official English laws serve to inflame prejudice against immigrants or to provide all newcomers with a common standard of admission to the country's political and cultural mainstream?

Figure 5.16 Bilingualism and diversity in Canada. The map shows areas of Canada that have a minimum of 5000 inhabitants and include a minority population identified with an official language.

Source: Commissioner of Official Languages, Government of Canada.

the use of indigenous languages in schools, the media, and public life. The language charter acknowledges that cultural diversity is part of Europe's wealth and heritage and that its retention strengthens, not weakens, the separate states of the continent and the larger European culture realm as a whole. In North America, the designation of French as the official language of the Canadian province of Quebec reinforces and sustains the distinctive cultural and territorial identity so important to the *Québecois*. Quebec's language laws enforce a French appearance to the landscape as they require that billboards and commercial signs give priority to the French language.

Many other world regions have continuing linguistically based conflict. Language has long been a divisive issue in South Asia, for example, leading to wars in Pakistan and Sri Lanka and periodic demands for secession from India by southern states such as Tamil Nadu, where the Dravidian Tamil language is defended as an ancient tongue as worthy of respect as the Indo-European official language, Hindi. In Russia and several other successor states of the former USSR (which housed some 200 languages and dialects), linguistic diversity forms part of the justification for local separatist movements, as it did in the division of Czechoslovakia into Czech- and Slovak-speaking successor states and in the violent dismemberment of former Yugoslavia.

Even more than in its role in ethnic identity and separatism, language embodies the culture complex of a people, reflecting environment and gender distinctions. Arabic has 80 words related to camels, an animal on which a regional culture relied for food, transport, and labor, and Japanese contains more than 20 words for various types of rice. Russian is rich in terms for ice and snow, indicative of the prevailing climate of its linguistic cradle; Hawaiians reportedly have 108 words for sweet potato, 65 for fishing nets, and 47 for bananas. The 15,000 tributaries and subtributaries of the Amazon River have obliged the Brazilians to enrich Portuguese with words that go beyond "river." Among them are *paraná* (a stream that leaves and reenters the same river), *igarapé* (an offshoot that runs until it dries up), and *furo* (a waterway that connects two rivers).

Most—perhaps all—cultures display subtle or pronounced differences in ways males and females use language. Most have to do with vocabulary and with grammatical forms peculiar to individual cultures. For example, among the Caribs of the Caribbean, the Zulu of Africa, and elsewhere, men have words that women through custom or taboo are not permitted to use, and the women have words and phrases that the men never use "or they would be laughed to scorn," an informant reports. Evidence from English and many other unrelated tongues indicates that as a rule female speakers use forms considered to be "better" or "more correct" than do males of the same social class. The greater and more inflexible the difference in the social roles of men and women in a particular culture, the greater and more rigid are the observed linguistic differences between the sexes.

Language on the Landscape: Toponymy

Toponyms—place names—are language on the land, the record of past inhabitants whose namings endure, perhaps corrupted and disguised, as reminders of their existence and their passing. **Toponymy** is the study of place names, a special interest of linguistic geography. It is also a revealing tool of historical cultural geography, for place names become a part of the cultural landscape that remains long after the name givers have passed from the scene.

In England, for example, place names ending in *chester* (as in Winchester and Manchester) evolved from the Latin *castra,* meaning "camp." Common Anglo-Saxon suffixes for tribal and family settlements were *ing* (people or family) and *ham* (hamlet or, perhaps, meadow) as in Birmingham or Gillingham. Norse and Danish settlers contributed place names ending in *thwaite* ("meadow") and others denoting such landscape features as *fell* (an uncultivated hill) and *beck* (a small brook). The Celts, present in Europe for more than 1000 years before Roman times, left their tribal names in corrupted form on territories and settlements taken over by their successors. The Arabs, sweeping out from Arabia across North Africa and into Iberia, left their imprint in place names to mark their conquest and control. *Cairo* means "victorious," *Sudan* is "the land of the blacks," and *Sahara* is "wasteland" or "wilderness." In Spain, a corrupted version of the Arabic *wadi,* "watercourse," is found in *Guadalajara* and *Guadalquivir.*

In the New World, not one people but many placed names on landscape features and new settlements. In doing so they remembered their homes and homelands, honored their monarchs and heroes, borrowed and mispronounced from rivals, followed fads, recalled the Bible, and adopted and distorted Amerindian names. Homelands were recalled in New England, New France, or New Holland; settlers' hometown memories brought Boston, New Bern, New Rochelle, and Cardiff from England, Switzerland, France, and Wales. Monarchs were remembered in Virginia for the Virgin Queen Elizabeth, Carolina for one English king, Georgia for another, and Louisiana for a king of France. Washington, D.C.; Jackson, Mississippi and Michigan; Austin, Texas; and Lincoln, Illinois memorialized heroes and leaders. Names given by the Dutch in New York were often distorted by the English; Breukelyn, Vlissingen, and Haarlem became Brooklyn, Flushing, and Harlem. French names underwent similar twisting or translation, and Spanish names were adopted, altered, or, later, put into such bilingual combinations as Hermosa Beach. Amerindian tribal names— the Yenrish, Maha, Kansa—were modified, first by French and later by English speakers—to Erie, Omaha, and Kansas. A faddish "Classical Revival" after the Revolution gave us Troy, Athens, Rome, Sparta, and other ancient town names and later spread them across the country. Bethlehem, Ephrata, Nazareth, and Salem came from the Bible. Names adopted were transported as settlement moved westward across the United States (Figure 5.17).

Place names, whatever their language of origin, frequently consist of two parts: *generic* (classifying) and *specific* (modifying or particular). *Big River* in English is found as *Rio Grande* in Spanish, *Mississippi* in Algonquin, and *Ta Ho* in Chinese. The *order* of generic and specific, however, may alter between languages and give a clue to the group originally bestowing the place name. In English, the specific usually comes first: *Hudson River, Bunker Hill, Long Island.* When, in the United States, we find *River Rouge* or *Isle Royale,* we also find evidence of French settlement—the French reverse the naming order. Some generic names can be used to trace the migration paths across the United States of the three Eastern dialect groups (see Figure 5.11). Northern dialect settlers tended to carry with them their habit of naming a community and calling its later neighbors by the same name modified by direction—Lansing and East Lansing, for example. *Brook* is found in the New England settlement area, *run* is from the Midland dialect, *bayou* and *branch* are from the Southern area.

European colonists and their descendants gave place names to a physical landscape already adequately named by indigenous peoples. Those names were sometimes adopted, but often shortened, altered, or—certainly—mispronounced. The vast territory that local Amerindians called "Mesconsing," meaning "the long river," was recorded by Lewis and Clark as "Quisconsing," later to be further distorted into "Wisconsin." *Milwaukee*

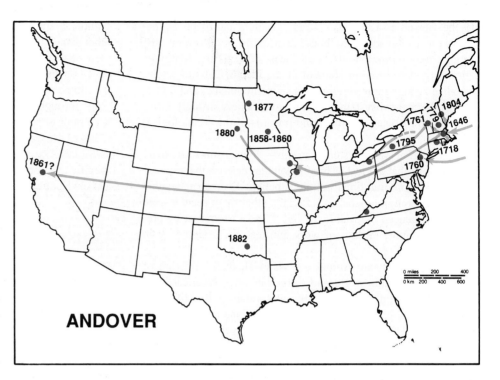

Figure 5.17 Migrant Andover. Place names in a new land tend to be transportable, carried to new locales by migrating town founders. They are a reminder of the cultural origins and diffusion paths of settlers. Andover, a town name from England, was brought to New England in 1646 and later carried westward.

Source: Reprinted with kind permission of the American Name Society.

and *Winnipeg, Potomac* and *Niagara, Adirondack, Chesapeake, Shenandoah,* and *Yukon;* the names of 27 of the 50 United States; and the present identity of thousands of North American places and features, large and small, had their origin in Native American languages.

In the Northwest Territories of Canada, Indian and Inuit (Eskimo) place names are returning. The town of Frobisher Bay has reverted to its Eskimo name *Iqaluit* ("place of the fish"); Resolute Bay becomes *Kaujuitok* ("place where the sun never rises") in Inuktitut, the lingua franca of the Canadian Eskimos; the Jean Marie River returns to *Tthedzehk'edeli* ("river that flows over clay"), its earlier Slavey name. These and other official name changes reflect the decision of the territory's Executive Council that community preference will be the standard for all place names, no matter how entrenched European versions might be.

It was a decision that recognized the im Print Style portance of language as a powerful unifying thread in the culture complex of peoples. In India, for example, the changing of various long-accepted municipal place names—*Mumbai* instead of Bombay, *Chennai* but not Madras, or *Thiruvananthapuram* replacing Trivandrum—demonstrates both post-colonial pride and growing Hindu nationalism. Language may serve as a fundamental evidence of ethnicity and be the fiercely defended symbol of the history and individuality of a distinctive social group. Hispanic Americans demand the right of instruction in their own language, and Basques wage civil war to achieve a linguistically based separatism. Indian states were adjusted to coincide with language boundaries, and the Polish National Catholic Church was created in America, not Poland, to preserve Polish language and culture in an alien environment.

Religion and Culture

Unlike language, which is an attribute of all people, religion varies in its cultural role—dominating among some societies, unimportant or denied totally in others. All societies have *value systems*—common beliefs, understandings, expectations, and controls—that unite their members and set them off from other, different culture groups. Such a value system is termed a **religion** when it involves systems of formal or informal worship and faith in the sacred and divine. In a more inclusive sense, religion

Patterns of Religion

Religion, like language, is a symbol of group identity and a cultural rallying point. Religious enmity forced the partition of the Indian subcontinent between Muslims and Hindus after the departure of the British in 1947. French Catholics and French Huguenots (Protestants) freely slaughtered each other in the name of religion in the 16th century. English Roman Catholics were hounded from their country after the establishment of the Anglican Church. Religion has continued to be a root cause of many local and regional conflicts throughout the world during the 20th and into the 21st century, as Chief Makuei's words opening this chapter suggest, including confrontations among Catholic and Protestant Christian groups in Northern Ireland; Muslim sects in Lebanon, Iran, Iraq, and Algeria; Muslims and Jews in Palestine; Christians and Muslims in the Philippines and Lebanon; and Buddhists and Hindus in Sri Lanka. More peacefully, in the name of their beliefs, American Amish, Hutterite, Shaker, and other religious communities have isolated themselves from the secular world and pursued their own ways of life.

may be viewed as a unified system of beliefs and practices that join all those who adhere to them into a single moral community. Religion may intimately affect all facets of a culture. Religious belief is by definition an element of the ideological subsystem; formalized and organized religion is an institutional expression of the sociological subsystem. And religious beliefs strongly influence attitudes toward the tools and rewards of the technological subsystem.

Nonreligious value systems can exist—humanism or Marxism, for example—that are just as binding on the societies that espouse them as are more traditional religious beliefs. Even societies that largely reject religion—that are officially atheistic or secular—are strongly influenced by traditional values and customs set by predecessor religions, in days of work and rest, for example, or in legal principles.

Since religions are formalized views about the relation of the individual to this world and to the hereafter, each carries a distinct conception of the meaning and value of this life, and most contain strictures about what must be done to achieve salvation. These beliefs become interwoven with the traditions of a culture. For Muslims, the observance of the *sharia* (law) is a necessary part of *Islam,* submission to Allah (see Figure 5.26). In classical Judaism, the keeping of the *Torah,* the Law of Moses, involved ritual and moral rules of holy living. For Hindus, the *dharma,* or teaching, includes the complex laws enunciated in the ancient book of Manu. Ethics of conduct and human relations rather than religious rituals are central to the Confucian tradition of China, while the Sikh *khalsa,* or holy community, is defined by various rules of observance, such as prohibiting the cutting of one's hair.

Economic patterns may be intertwined with past or present religious beliefs. Traditional restrictions on food and drink may affect the kinds of animals that are raised or avoided, the crops that are grown, and the importance of those crops in the daily diet. Occupational assignment in the Hindu caste system is in part religiously supported. In many countries, there is a state religion—that is, religious and political structures are intertwined. Buddhism, for example, has been the state religion in Myanmar, Laos, and Thailand. By their official names, the Islamic Republic of Pakistan and the Islamic Republic of Iran proclaim their identity of religion and government. Despite Indonesia's overwhelming Muslim majority, that country sought and formerly found domestic harmony by recognizing five official religions and a state ideology— *pancasila*— whose first tenet is belief in one god.

The landscape imprint of religions may be both obvious and subtle. The structures of religious worship—temples, churches, mosques, stupas, or cathedrals—landscape symbols such as shrines or statues, and such associated land uses as monasteries may give an immediately evident and regionally distinctive cultural character to an area. "Landscapes of death" may also be visible regional variables, for different religions and cultures dispose of their dead in different manners. Cemeteries are significant and reserved land uses among Christians, Jews, and Muslims who typically bury their deceased with headstones or other markers and monuments to mark graves. Egyptian pyramids or elaborate mausoleums like the Taj Mahal are more grandiose structures of entombment and remembrance. On the other hand, Hindus and Buddhists have traditionally cremated their dead and scattered their ashes, leaving no landscape evidence or imprint.

Some religions may make a subtle cultural stamp on the landscape through recognition of sacred places and spaces not otherwise built or marked. Grottos, lakes, single trees or groves, such rivers as the Ganges or Jordan, or special mountains or hills, such as Mount Ararat or Mount Fuji, are examples that are unique to specific religions and express the reciprocal influences of religion and environment.

Classification of Religion

Religions are cultural innovations. They may be unique to a single culture group, closely related to the faiths professed in nearby areas, or derived from or identical to belief systems spatially far removed. Although interconnections and derivations among religions can frequently be discerned—as Christianity and Islam can trace descent from Judaism—family groupings are not as useful to us in classifying religions as they were in studying languages. A distinction between **monotheism,** belief in a single deity, and **polytheism,** belief in many gods, is frequent, but not particularly spatially relevant. Simple territorial categories have been offered recognizing origin areas of religions: Western versus Eastern, for example, or African, Far Eastern, or Indian. With proper detail such distinctions may inform us where particular religions had their roots but do not reveal their courses of development, paths of diffusion, or current distributions.

Our geographic interest in the classification of religions is different from that of, say, theologians or historians. We are not so concerned with the beliefs themselves or with their birthplaces (though both help us understand their cultural implications and areal arrangements). We are more interested in religions' patterns and processes of diffusion once they have developed, with the spatial distributions they have achieved, and with the impact of the practices and beliefs of different religious systems on the landscape. To satisfy at least some of those interests, geographers have found it useful to categorize religions as *universalizing, ethnic,* or *tribal (traditional).*

Christianity, Islam, and Buddhism are the major world **universalizing religions,** faiths that claim applicability to all humans and proselytize; that is, they seek to transmit their beliefs through missionary work and conversion. Membership in universalizing religions is open to anyone who chooses to make some sort of symbolic commitment, such as baptism in Christianity. No one is excluded because of nationality, ethnicity, or previous religious belief.

Ethnic religions have strong territorial and cultural group identification. One usually becomes a member of an ethnic religion by birth or by adoption of a complex lifestyle and cultural identity, not by simple declaration of faith. These religions do not usually proselytize, and their members form distinctive closed communities identified with a particular ethnic group or political unit. An ethnic religion—for example, Judaism, Indian Hinduism, or Japanese Shinto—is an integral element of a specific culture; to be part of the religion is to be immersed in the totality of the culture.

Tribal, or traditional religions, are special forms of ethnic religions distinguished by their small size, their unique identity with localized culture groups not yet fully absorbed into modern society, and their close ties to nature. **Animism** is the name given to their belief that life exists in all objects, from rocks and trees to lakes and mountains, or that such inanimate objects are the abode of the dead, of spirits, and of gods. **Shamanism** is a form of tribal religion that involves community acceptance of a *shaman,* a religious leader, healer, and worker of magic who, through special powers, can intercede with and interpret the spirit world.

Patterns and Flows

The nature of the different classes of religions is reflected in their distributions over the world (Figure 5.18) and in their number of adherents. Universalizing religions tend to be expansionary, carrying their message to new peoples and areas. Ethnic religions, unless their adherents are dispersed, tend to be regionally confined or to expand only slowly and over long periods. Tribal religions tend to contract spatially as their adherents are incorporated increasingly into modern society and converted by proselytizing faiths.

As we expect in human geography, the map records only the latest stage of a constantly changing cultural reality. While established religious institutions tend to be conservative and resistant to change, religion as a culture trait is dynamic. Personal and collective beliefs may alter in response to developing individual and societal needs and challenges. Religions may be imposed by conquest, adopted by conversion, or defended and preserved in the face of surrounding hostility or indifference.

The World Pattern

Figure 5.18 (at this scale) cannot present a full picture of current religious affiliation or regionalization. Few societies are homogeneous, and most modern ones contain a variety of different faiths or, at least, variants of the dominant professed religion. Some of those variants in many religions are intolerant or antagonistic toward other faiths or toward those sects and members of their own faith deemed insufficiently committed or orthodox (see "Militant Fundamentalism").

Frequently, members of a particular religion show areal concentration within a country. Thus, in urban Northern Ireland, Protestants and Catholics reside in separate areas whose boundaries are clearly understood. The "Green Line" in Beirut, Lebanon, marked a guarded border between the Christian East

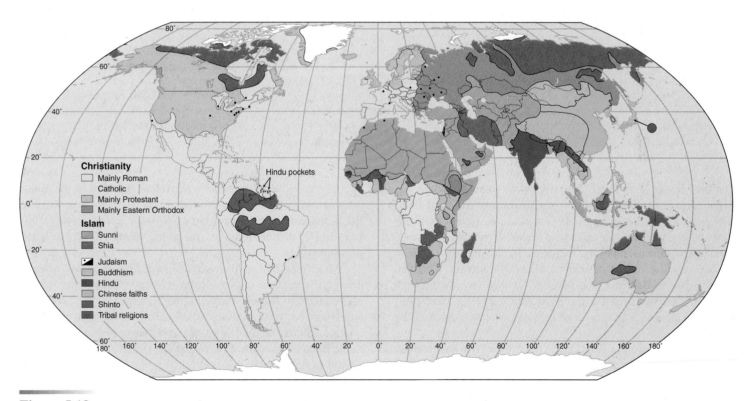

Christianity
- Mainly Roman Catholic
- Mainly Protestant
- Mainly Eastern Orthodox

Islam
- Sunni
- Shia

- Judaism
- Buddhism
- Hindu
- Chinese faiths
- Shinto
- Tribal religions

Hindu pockets

Figure 5.18 Principal world religions. The assignment of individual countries to a single religion category conceals a growing intermixture of faiths in European and other western countries that have experienced recent major immigration flows. In some instances, those influxes are altering the effective, if not the numerical, religious balance. In nominally Christian, Catholic France, for example, low church-going rates suggest that now more Muslims than practicing Catholics reside there and, considering birth rate differentials, that someday Islam may be the country's predominant religion as measured by the number of practicing adherents. Secularism—rejection of religious belief—is common in many countries but is not indicated on this map.

The term *fundamentalism* entered the social science vocabulary in the late 20th century to describe any religious orthodoxy that is revivalist and ultraconservative in nature. Originally it designated an American Christian movement named after a set of volumes—*The Fundamentals: A Testimony of the Truth*—published between 1910 and 1915 and embracing both absolute religious orthodoxy and a commitment to inject its beliefs into the political and social arenas. More recently, fundamentalism has become a generic description for all religious movements that seek to regain and publicly institutionalize traditional social and cultural values that are usually rooted in the teachings of a sacred text or written dogma.

Springing from rejection of the secularist tendencies of modernity, fundamentalism is now found in every dominant religion wherever a western-style society has developed, including Christianity, Islam, Hinduism, Judaism, Sikhism, Buddhism, Confucianism, and Zoroastrianism. Fundamentalism is therefore a reaction to the modern world; it represents an effort to draw upon a "golden age" religious tradition in order to cope with and counteract an already changing society that is denounced as trying to erase the true faith and traditional religious values. The near-universality of fundamentalist movements is seen by some as another expression of a widespead rebellion against the presumed evils of secular globalization.

Fundamentalists always place a high priority on doctrinal conformity and its necessity to achieve salvation. Further, they are convinced of the morally superior and unarguable correctness of their beliefs and the necessity of the unquestioned acceptance of those beliefs by the general society. Since the truth is knowable and indisputable, fundamentalists hold, there is no need to discuss it or argue it in open forum. To some observers, therefore, fundamentalism is by its nature undemocratic and states controlled by fundamentalist regimes combining politics and religion, of necessity, stifle debate and punish dissent. In the modern world, that rigidity seems most apparent in Islam where, it is claimed, "all Muslims believe in the absolute inerrancy of the Quran . . ." (*The Islamic Herald,* April, 1995) and several countries—for example, the Islamic Republic of Iran and the Islamic Republic of Pakistan—proclaim by official name their administrative commitment to religious control.

In most of the modern world, however, such commitment is not overt or official, and fundamentalists often believe that they and their religious convictions are under mortal threat. They view modern secular society—with its assumption of equality of competing voices and values—as trying to eradicate the true faith and religious verities. Initially, therefore, every fundamentalist movement begins as an intrareligious struggle directed against its own co-religionists and countrymen in response to a felt assault by the liberal or secular society they inhabit. At first, the group may blame its own weakness and irresolution for the oppression they feel and the general social decay they perceive. To restore society to its idealized standards, the aroused group may exhort its followers to ardent prayer, ascetic practices, and physical or military training.

If it is unable peacefully to impose its beliefs on others, the fundamentalist group—seeing itself as the savior of society—may justify other more extreme actions against perceived oppressors. Initial protests and nonviolent actions may escalate to attacks on corrupt public figures thwarting their vision and to outright domestic guerrilla warfare. That escalation is advanced and gains willing supporters when inflexible fundamentalism is combined with the unending poverty and political impotence felt in many—particularly Middle Eastern—societies today. When an external culture or power—commonly a demonized United States—is seen as the unquestioned source of the pollution and exploitation frustrating their social vision, some fundamentalists have been able to justify any extreme action and personal sacrifice for their cause. In their struggle it appears an easy progression from domestic dispute and disruption to international terrorism.

and the Muslim West sides of the city, while within the country as a whole regional concentrations of adherents of different faiths and sects are clearly recognized (Figure 5.19). Religious diversity within countries may reflect the degree of toleration a majority culture affords minority religions. In dominantly (55% to 88% depending on the definition) Muslim Indonesia, Christian Bataks, Hindu Balinese, and Muslim Javanese for many years lived in peaceful coexistence. By contrast, the fundamentalist Islamic regime in Iran has persecuted and executed those of the Baha'i faith.

Data on religious affiliation are not precise. Most nations do not have religious censuses, and different religious groups differently and inconsistently report their membership. When communism was supreme in the former Soviet Union and Eastern European countries, official atheism dissuaded many from openly professing or practicing any religion; in nominally Christian Europe and North America, many who claim to be believers are not active church members and others renounce religion altogether. Table 5.2 presents a reasonable ranking of the major religions of the world by estimated number of adherents. The list is not exhaustive; the *World Christian Encyclopedia* tabulates 10,000 distinct religions, including nearly 12,000 Christian denominations.

More than half of the world's population probably adheres to one of the major universalizing religions: Christianity, Islam, or Buddhism. Of these three, Figure 5.18 indicates, Christianity and Islam are most widespread; Buddhism is largely an Asian religion. Hinduism, the largest ethnic faith, is essentially confined to the Indian subcontinent, showing the spatial restriction characteristic of most ethnic and traditional religions even when found outside of their homeland area. Small Hindu emigrant communities in Africa, southeast Asia, England, or the United States, for example, tend to remain isolated even in densely crowded urban areas. Although it is not localized, Judaism is also included among the ethnic religions because of its identification with a particular people and cultural tradition.

Figure 5.19 **Religious regions of Lebanon.** Religious territoriality and rivalry contributed to a prolonged period of conflict and animosity in this troubled country.

Table 5.2

Major Religions Ranked by Estimated Number of Adherents

Religion	Number of Adherents (millions)
Christianity	2,100
Islam	1,500
Secular/Nonreligious/ Agnostic/Atheist	1,100
Hinduism	900
Chinese traditional religions	394
Buddhism	376
Tribal/animist religions	300
African traditional religions	100
Sikhism	23
Judaism	15
Baha'ism	7
Jainism	4
Shinto	4
Cao Dai	4
Zoroastrianism	2.6
Tenrikyo	2
Neo-Paganism	1
Unitarian-Universalism	.8
Rastafarianism	.6
Scientology	.5

Source: *Adherents.com.*

Extensive areas of the world are peopled by those who practice tribal or traditional religions, often in concert with the universalizing religions to which they have been outwardly converted. Tribal religions are found principally among peoples who have not yet been fully absorbed into modern cultures and economies or who are on the margins of more populous and advanced societies. Although the areas assigned to tribal religions in Figure 5.18 are significant, the number of adherents is small and declining.

The Principal Religions

Each of the major religions has its own unique mix of cultural values and expressions, each has had its own pattern of innovation and spatial diffusion (Figure 5.20), and each has had its own impact on the cultural landscape. Together they contribute importantly to the worldwide pattern of human diversity.

Judaism

We begin our review of world faiths with **Judaism,** whose belief in a single God laid the foundation for both Christianity and Islam. Unlike its universalizing offspring, Judaism is closely identified with a single ethnic group and with a complex and restrictive set of beliefs and laws. It emerged some 3000 to 4000

years ago in the Near East, one of the ancient culture hearth regions (see Figure 2.15). Early Near Eastern civilizations, including those of Sumeria, Babylonia, and Assyria, developed writing, codified laws, and formalized polytheistic religions featuring rituals of sacrifice and celebrations of the cycle of seasons.

Judaism was different. The Israelites' conviction that they were a chosen people, bound with God through a covenant of mutual loyalty and guided by complex formal rules of behavior, set them apart from other peoples of the Near East. Theirs became a distinctively *ethnic* religion, the determining factors of which are descent from Israel (the patriarch Jacob), the Torah (law and scripture), and the traditions of the culture and the faith. Early military success gave the Jews a sense of territorial and political identity to supplement their religious self-awareness. Later conquest by nonbelievers led to their dispersion (*diaspora*) to much of the Mediterranean world and farther east into Asia by A.D. 500 (Figure 5.21).

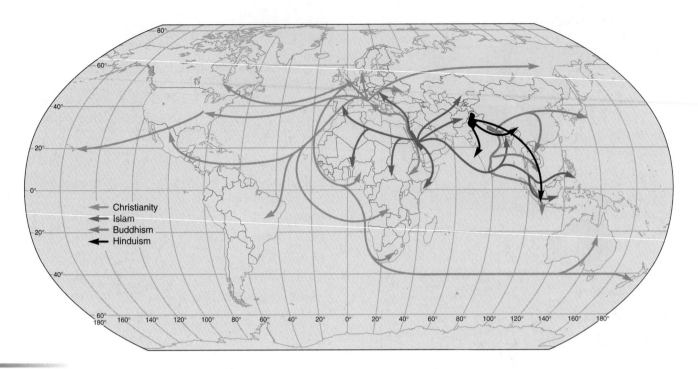

Figure 5.20 **Innovation areas and diffusion routes of major world religions.** The monotheistic (single deity) faiths of Judaism, Christianity, and Islam arose in southwestern Asia, the first two in Palestine in the eastern Mediterranean region and the last in western Arabia near the Red Sea. Hinduism and Buddhism originated within a confined hearth region in the northern part of the Indian subcontinent. Their rates, extent, and directions of diffusions are suggested here and detailed on later maps.

Alternately tolerated and persecuted in Christian Europe, occasionally expelled from countries, and usually, as outsiders of different faith and custom, spatially isolated in special residential quarters (ghettos), Jews retained their faith even though two separate branches of Judaism developed in Europe during the Middle Ages. The Sephardim were originally based in the Iberian Peninsula and expelled from there in the late 15th century; with ties to North African and Babylonian Jews, they retained their native Judeo-Spanish language (Ladino) and culture. Between the 13th and 16th centuries, the Ashkenazim, seeking refuge from intolerable persecution in western and central Europe, settled in Poland, Lithuania, and Russia (Figure 5.21). It was from eastern Europe that many of the Jewish immigrants to the United States came during the later 19th and early 20th centuries, though German-speaking areas of central Europe were also important source regions.

The Ashkenazim constitute perhaps 80% of all Jews in the world and differ from the Sephardim in cultural traditions (for example, their widespread use of Yiddish until the 20th century) and liturgy. Both groups are present in roughly equal numbers in Israel. The mass destruction of Jews in Europe before and during World War II—the Holocaust—drastically reduced their representation among that continent's total population.

The establishment of the state of Israel in 1948 was a fulfillment of the goal of *Zionism,* the belief in the need to create an autonomous Jewish state in Palestine. It demonstrated a determination that Jews not lose their identity by absorption into alien cultures and societies. The new state represented a reversal of the preceding 2000-year history of dispersal and relocation

diffusion. Israel became largely a country of immigrants, an ancient homeland again identified with a distinctive people and an ethnic religion.

Judaism's imprint on the cultural landscape has been subtle and unobtrusive. The Jewish community reserves space for the practice of communal burial; the spread of the cultivated citron in the Mediterranean area during Roman times has been traced to Jewish ritual needs; and the religious use of grape wine assured the cultivation of the vine in their areas of settlement. The synagogue as place of worship has tended to be less elaborate than its Christian counterpart. The essential for religious service is a community of at least 10 adult males, not a specific structure.

Christianity

Christianity had its origin in the life and teachings of Jesus, a Jewish preacher of the 1st century of the modern era, whom his followers believed was the messiah promised by God. The new covenant he preached was not a rejection of traditional Judaism but a promise of salvation to all humankind rather than to just a chosen people.

Christianity's mission was conversion, and missionary work was critical to its diffusion. As a universal religion of salvation and hope, it spread quickly among the underclasses of both the eastern and western parts of the Roman Empire, carried to major cities and ports along the excellent system of Roman roads and sea lanes (Figure 5.22). *Expansion diffusion* followed the establishment of missions and colonies of converts in locations distant

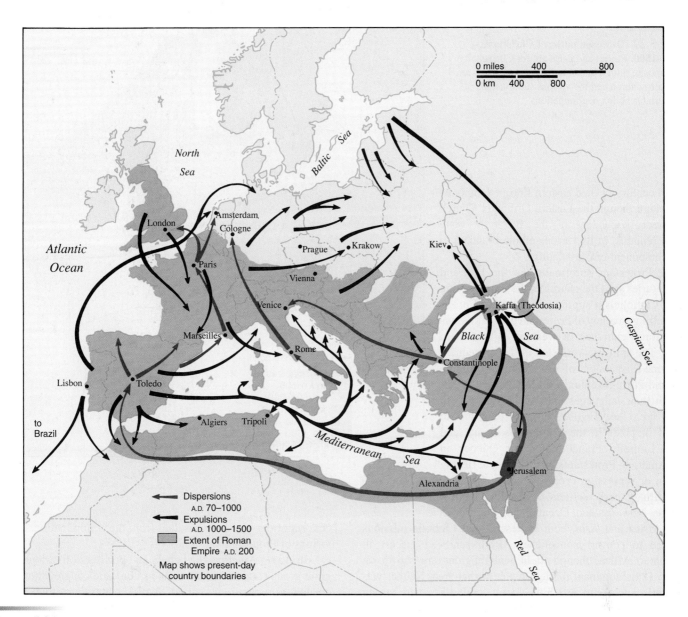

Figure 5.21 Jewish dispersions, A.D. 70–1500. A revolt against Roman rule in A.D. 66 was followed by the destruction of the Jewish Temple 4 years later and an imperial decision to Romanize the city of Jerusalem. Judaism spread from the hearth region by *relocation diffusion,* carried by its adherents dispersing from their homeland to Europe, Africa, and eventually in great numbers to the Western Hemisphere. Although Jews established themselves and their religion in new lands, they did not lose their sense of cultural identity and did not seek to attract converts to their faith.

from the hearth region. Important among them were the urban areas that became administrative seats of the new religion. For the Western Church, Rome was the principal center for dispersal, through *hierarchical diffusion,* to provincial capitals and smaller Roman settlements of Europe. From those nodes and from monasteries established in pagan rural areas, *contagious diffusion* disseminated Christianity throughout the continent. The acceptance of Christianity as the state religion of the empire by the Emperor Constantine in A.D. 313 was also an expression of hierarchical diffusion of great importance in establishing the faith throughout the full extent of the Roman world. Finally, and much later, *relocation diffusion,* missionary efforts, and in Spanish colonial areas, forced conversion of Native Americans brought the faith to the New World with European settlers (see Figure 5.18).

The dissolution of the Roman Empire into a western and an eastern half after the fall of Rome also divided Christianity. The Western Church, based in Rome, was one of the very few stabilizing and civilizing forces uniting western Europe during the Dark Ages. Its bishops became the civil as well as ecclesiastical authorities over vast areas devoid of other effective government. Parish churches were the focus of rural and urban life, and the cathedrals replaced Roman monuments and temples as the symbols of the social order (Figure 5.23). Everywhere, the Roman Catholic Church and its ecclesiastical hierarchy were dominant.

Secular imperial control endured in the eastern empire, whose capital was Constantinople. Thriving under its protection, the Eastern Church expanded into the Balkans, eastern Europe, Russia, and the Near East. The fall of the eastern empire to the Turks in

Figure 5.22 **Diffusion paths of Christianity,** A.D. 100–1500. Routes and dates are for Christianity as a composite faith. No distinction is made between the Western church and the various subdivisions of the Eastern Orthodox denominations.

Northern limit of Islam ca. A.D. 1050

← Diffusion direction

Area Christianized:
- to A.D. 600
- A.D. 600–800
- A.D. 800–1100
- A.D. 1100–1300
- A.D. 1300–1500

Map shows present-day country boundaries.

the 15th century opened eastern Europe temporarily to Islam, though the Eastern Orthodox Church (the direct descendant of the Byzantine state church) remains, in its various ethnic branches, a major component of Christianity.

The Protestant Reformation of the 15th and 16th centuries split the church in the west, leaving Roman Catholicism supreme in southern Europe but installing a variety of Protestant denominations and national churches in western and northern Europe. The split was reflected in the subsequent worldwide dispersion of Christianity. Catholic Spain and Portugal colonized Latin America, taking both their languages and the Roman church to that area (see Figure 5.20), as they did to colonial outposts in the Philippines, India, and Africa. Catholic France colonized Quebec in North America. Protestants, many of them fleeing Catholic or repressive Protestant state churches, were primary early settlers of Anglo America, Australia, New Zealand, Oceania, and South Africa.

In Africa and Asia, both Protestant and Catholic missions attempted to convert nonbelievers. Both achieved success in sub-Saharan Africa, though traditional religions are shown on Figure 5.18 as dominant through much of that area. Neither was particularly successful in China, Japan, or India, where strong ethnic religious cultural systems were barriers largely impermeable to the diffusion of the Christian faith. Although accounting for nearly one-third of the world's population and territorially the most extensive belief system, Christianity is no longer numerically important in or near its original hearth. Nor is it any longer dominated by Northern Hemisphere adherents. In 1900, 80% of all Christians lived in Europe and North America; in 2000, two-thirds of an estimated 2.1 billion total lived elsewhere—in South America, Africa, and Asia.

Regions and Landscapes of Christianity

All of the principal world religions have experienced theological, doctrinal, or political divisions; frequently these have spatial expression. In Christianity, the early split between the Western and Eastern Churches was initially unrelated to dogma but nonetheless resulted in a territorial separation still evident on the world map. The later subdivision of the Western Church into Roman Catholic and Protestant branches gave a more intricate spatial patterning in western Europe that can only be generally suggested at the scale of Figure 5.18. Still more intermixed are the areal segregations and

concentrations that have resulted from the denominational subdivisions of Protestantism.

In Anglo America, the beliefs and practices of various immigrant groups and the innovations of domestic congregations have created a particularly varied spatial patterning (Figure 5.24), though intermingling rather than rigid territorial division is characteristic of the North American, particularly United States, scene (see Figure 5.1). While 85% of Canadian Christians belong to one of three denominations (Roman Catholic, Anglican, or United Church of Canada), it takes at least 20 denominations to account for 85% of religious adherents in America. Nevertheless, for the United States, one observer has suggested a pattern of "religious regions" of the country (Figure 5.25) that, he believes, reflects a larger cultural regionalization of the United States.

Strongly French-, Irish-, and Portuguese-Catholic New England, the Hispanic-Catholic Southwest, and the French-Catholic vicinity of New Orleans (evident on Figure 5.25) are commonly recognized regional subdivisions of the United States. Each has a cultural identity that includes, but is not limited to, its dominant religion. The western area of Mormon (more properly, Church of Jesus Christ of Latter-day Saints, or LDS) cultural and religious dominance is prominent and purely American. The Baptist presence in the South and that of the Lutherans in the Upper Midwest (see Figure 5.24a) help determine the boundaries of other distinctive composite regions. The zone of cultural mixing across the center of the country from the Middle Atlantic states

Figure 5.23 The building of Notre Dame Cathedral of Paris, France, begun in 1163, took more than 100 years to complete. Perhaps the best known of the French Gothic churches, it was part of the great period of cathedral construction in Western Europe during the late 12th and the 13th centuries. Between 1170 and 1270, some 80 cathedrals were constructed in France alone. The cathedrals were located in the center of major cities; their plazas were the sites of markets, public meetings, morality plays, and religious ceremonies. They were the focus of public and private life and the symbol not only of the faith but of the pride and prosperity of the towns and regions that erected them.

to the western LDS region—so evident in the linguistic geography of the United States (see Figure 5.12)—is again apparent on the map of religious affiliation. No single church or denomination dominates, a characteristic as well of the Far Western zone.

Indeed, in no large section of the United States is there a denominational dominance to equal the overwhelming (over 88%) Roman Catholic presence in Quebec suggested, on Figure 5.24b, by the absence of any "second rank" religious affiliation. The "leading" position of the United Church of Canada in the Canadian West or of the Anglican Church in the Atlantic region of Newfoundland is much less commanding. Much of interior Canada shows a degree of cultural mixing and religious diversity only hinted at by Figure 5.24b, where only the largest church memberships are noted.

The mark of Christianity on the cultural landscape has been prominent and enduring. In pre-Reformation Catholic Europe, the parish church formed the center of life for small neighborhoods of every town, and the village church was the centerpiece of every rural community. In York, England, with a population of 11,000 in the 14th century, there were 45 parish churches, one for each 250 inhabitants. In addition, the central cathedral served simultaneously as a glorification of God, a symbol of piety, and the focus of religious and secular life. The Spanish Laws of the Indies (1573) perpetuated that landscape dominance in the New World, decreeing that all Spanish American settlements should have a church or cathedral on a central plaza (Figure 5.26a).

While in Europe and Latin America a single dominant central church was the rule, North American Protestantism placed less importance on the church edifice as a monument and urban symbol. The structures of the principal denominations of colonial New England were, as a rule, clustered at the village center (Figure 5.26b), and that centrality remained a characteristic of small-town America to the present. In earlier periods, too, they

were often adjoined by a cemetery, for Christians—in common with Muslims and Jews—practice burial in areas reserved for the dead. In Christian countries in particular, the cemetery—whether connected to the church, separate from it, or unrelated to a specific denomination—has traditionally been a significant land use within urban areas. Frequently, the separate cemetery, originally on the outskirts of the community, becomes with urban expansion a more central land use and often one that distorts or blocks the growth of the city.

Islam

Islam—the word means "submission" (to the will of God)—springs from the same Judaic roots as Christianity and embodies many of the same beliefs: There is only one God, who may be revealed to humans through prophets; Adam was the first human; Abraham was one of his descendants. Mohammed is revered as the prophet of *Allah* (God), succeeding and completing the work of earlier prophets of Judaism and Christianity, including Moses, David, and Jesus. The Koran, the word of Allah revealed to Mohammed, contains not only rules of worship and details of doctrine but also instructions on the conduct of human affairs. For fundamentalists, it thus becomes the unquestioned guide to matters both religious and secular. Observance of the "five pillars" (Figure 5.26) and surrender to the will of Allah unites the faithful into a brotherhood that has no concern with race, color, or caste.

That law of brotherhood served to unify an Arab world sorely divided by tribes, social ranks, and multiple local deities. Mohammed was a resident of Mecca but fled in A.D. 622 to Medina, where the Prophet proclaimed a constitution and announced the universal mission of the Islamic community. That flight—*Hegira*—marks the starting point of the Islamic (lunar) calendar. By the time of Mohammed's death in 11 A.H. (anno—the

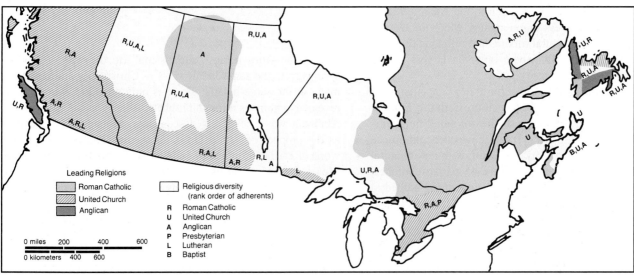

Distribution of Major Christian Groups

- Baptist
- Catholic
- Latter Day Saints (Mormon)
- Lutheran
- Methodist / Mixed Protestant
- No dominant group
- **S** 15% or more of state's adults claim "no religion"

(a)

Leading Religions

- Roman Catholic
- United Church
- Anglican
- Religious diversity (rank order of adherents)

R	Roman Catholic
U	United Church
A	Anglican
P	Presbyterian
L	Lutheran
B	Baptist

0 miles 200 400 600

0 kilometers 400 600

(b)

Figure 5.24 (*a*) **Religious affiliation in the conterminous United States.** The greatly generalized areas of religious dominance shown conceal the reality of immense diversity of church affiliations throughout the United States. "Major" simply means that the indicated category had a higher percentage response than any other affiliation; in practically no case was that as much as 50%. A sizable number of Americans claim to have "no religion." Secularism (marked by **S** on the map) is particularly prominent in the Western states, in the industrial Midwest, and in the Northeast. (*b*) **Religious affiliation in Canada.** The richness of Canadian religious diversity is obscured by the numerical dominance of a small number of leading Christian denominations.

Sources: (a) Based on data or maps from: the 2001 "American Religious Identity Survey" by the Graduate School at City University of New York: religious denomination maps prepared by Ingolf Vogeler of the University of Wisconsin, EauClaire, based on data compiled by the Roper Center for Public Research; and Churches and Church Membership in the United States (Atlanta, Georgia: Glenmary Research Center, 1992). (b) Based on Statistics Canada, Population: Religion (Ottawa, 1984); and The National Atlas of Canada.

(a)

(b)

Figure 5.25 **In Christian societies, the church assumes a prominent central position in the cultural landscape.** (*a*) By royal decree, Spanish planned settlements in the New World were to focus on cathedral and plaza centered within a gridiron street system. On average, 1 vara equals about 84 centimeters (33 inches). (*b*) Individually less imposing than the central cathedral of Catholic areas, the several Protestant churches common in small and large Anglo American towns collectively constitute an important land use, frequently seeking or claiming space in the center of the community. The distinctive New England spired church became a model for Protestant edifices elsewhere in the United States and a symbol of religion in national life.

Figure 5.26 **Worshipers gathered durin** *hajj,* **the annual pilgrimage to Mecca.** The black structure is the Ka'ba, the symbol of God's oneness and of the unity of God and humans. Many rules concerning daily life are given in the Koran, the holy book of the Muslims. All Muslims are expected to observe the five pillars of the faith: (1) repeated saying of the basic creed; (2) prayers five times daily, facing Mecca; (3) a month of daytime fasting (Ramadan); (4) almsgiving; and, (5) if possible, a pilgrimage to Mecca. Two of the five pillars of Islam are explicitly geographical: prayer facing Mecca and pilgrimage to Mecca. To pray facing Mecca, the direction known as Qiblah, has traditionally required Muslim scholars to calculate a great circle route. Thus, for example, most North American Muslims pray facing northeast.

Figure 5.27 **Spread and extent of Islam.** Islam predominates in over 35 countries along a band across northern Africa to Central Asia, and the northern part of the Indian subcontinent. Still farther east, Indonesia has the largest Muslim population of any country. Islam's greatest development is in Asia, where it is second only to Hinduism, and in Africa, where some observers suggest it may be the leading faith. Current Islamic expansion is particularly rapid in the Southern Hemisphere.

year of—Hegira, or A.D. 632), all of Arabia had joined Islam. The new religion swept quickly by *expansion diffusion* outward from that source region over most of Central Asia and, at the expense of Hinduism, into northern India (Figure 5.27).

The advance westward was particularly rapid and inclusive in North Africa. In western Europe, 700 years of Muslim rule in much of Spain were ended by Christian reconquest in 1492. In eastern Europe, conversions made under an expansionary Ottoman Empire are reflected in Muslim components in Bosnia and Kosovo regions of former Yugoslavia, in Bulgaria, and in the 70% Muslim population of Albania. Later, by *relocation diffusion,* Islam was dispersed into Indonesia, southern Africa, and the Western Hemisphere. Muslims now form the majority population in 39 countries.

Asia has the largest absolute number and Africa the highest proportion of Muslims among its population—more than 42%. Islam, with an estimated 1.3 billion adherents worldwide, has been a prominent element in recent and current political affairs. Sectarian hatreds fueled the 1980–1988 war between Iran and Iraq; Afghan *mujahedeen*—"holy warriors"—found inspiration in their faith to resist Soviet occupation of their country, and Chechens drew strength from Islam in resisting the Russian assaults on their Caucasian homeland during the 1990s and after. Islamic fundamentalism led to the 1979 overthrow of Iran's shah. Muslim separatism is a recurring theme in Philippine affairs, and militant groups seek establishment of religiously rather than secularly based governments in several Muslim states. Extremist Muslim militants carried out the September 11, 2001, World Trade Center attack and other acts of terrorism.

Islam initially united a series of separate tribes and groups, but disagreements over the succession of leadership after the Prophet led to a division between two groups, Sunnis and Shi'ites. Sunnis, the majority (80% to 85% of Muslims) recognize the first four *caliphs* (originally, "successor" and later the title of the religious and civil head of the Muslim state) as Mohammed's rightful successors. The Shi'ites reject the legitimacy of the first three and believe that Muslim leadership rightly belonged to the fourth caliph, the Prophet's son-in-law, Ali, and his descendants. At the start of the 21st century, Sunnis constitute the majority of Muslims in all countries except Iran, Iraq, Bahrain, and perhaps Yemen.

The mosque—place of worship, community club house, meeting hall, and school—is the focal point of Islamic communal life and the primary imprint of the religion on the cultural landscape. Its principal purpose is to accommodate the Friday communal service mandatory for all male Muslims. It is the congregation rather than the structure that is important. Small or poor communities are as well served by a bare whitewashed room as are larger cities by architecturally splendid mosques with domes and minarets. The earliest mosques were modeled on or converted from Christian churches. With time, however, Muslim architects united Roman, Byzantine, and Indian design elements to produce the distinctive mosque architecture found throughout the world of Islam. With its perfectly proportioned, frequently gilded or tiled domes, its graceful, soaring towers

Figure 5.28 The common architectural features of the mosque make it an unmistakable landscape evidence of the presence of Islam in any local culture. The Blue Mosque in Istanbul, Turkey, would not be out of place architecturally in Muslim Malaysia or Indonesia.

and minarets (from which the faithful are called to prayer), and its delicately wrought parapets and cupolas, the carefully tended mosque is frequently the most elaborate and imposing structure of the town (Figure 5.28).

Hinduism

Hinduism is the world's oldest major religion. Though it has no datable founding event or initial prophet, some evidence traces its origin back 4000 or more years. Hinduism is not just a religion but an intricate web of religious, philosophical, social, economic, and artistic elements comprising a distinctive Indian civilization. Its estimated 850 million to 1 billion adherents are largely confined to India, where it claims 80% of the population.

Hinduism derives its name from its cradle area in the valley of the Indus River. From that district of present-day Pakistan, it spread by *contagious diffusion* eastward down the Ganges River and southward throughout the subcontinent and adjacent regions by amalgamating, absorbing, and eventually supplanting earlier native religions and customs (see Figure 5.20). Its practice eventually spread throughout southeastern Asia, into Indonesia, Malaysia, Cambodia, Thailand, Laos, and Vietnam, as well as into neighboring Myanmar (Burma) and Sri Lanka. The largest Hindu temple complex is in Cambodia, not India, and Bali remains a Hindu pocket in dominantly Islamic Indonesia. Hinduism's more recent growing presence in western Europe and North America reflects a *relocation diffusion* of its adherents.

No common creed, single doctrine, or central ecclesiastical organization defines the Hindu. A Hindu is one born into a caste, a member of a complex social and economic—as well as religious—community. Hinduism accepts and incorporates all forms of belief; adherents may believe in one god or many or none. It emphasizes the divinity of the soul and is based on the concepts of reincarnation and passage from one state of existence to another in an unending cycle of birth and death in which all living things are

caught. One's position in this life is determined by one's *karma,* or deeds and conduct in previous lives. Upon that conduct depends the condition and the being—plant, animal, or human—into which a soul, after a stay in heaven or hell, is reborn. All creatures are ranked, with humans at the top of the ladder. But humans themselves are ranked, and the social caste into which an individual is born is an indication of that person's spiritual status. The goal of existence is to move up the hierarchy, eventually to be liberated from the cycle of rebirth and redeath and to achieve salvation and eternal peace through union with the *Brahman,* the universal soul.

The **caste** (meaning "birth") structure of society is an expression of the eternal transmigration of souls. For the Hindu, the primary aim of this life is to conform to prescribed social and ritual duties and to the rules of conduct for the assigned caste and profession. Those requirements comprise that individual's *dharma*—law and duties. To violate them upsets the balance of society and nature and yields undesirable consequences. To observe them improves the chance of promotion at the next rebirth. Traditionally, each craft or profession is the property of a particular caste: brahmins (scholar-priests), kshatriyas (warrior-landowners), vaishyas (businessmen, farmers, herdsmen), sudras (servants and laborers). Dalits, *untouchables* for whom the most menial and distasteful tasks were reserved, and backwoods tribes—together accounting for around one-fifth of India's population—stand outside the caste system. Caste rules define who you can mingle with, where you can live, what you may wear, eat, and drink, and how you can earn your livelihood. Conversion of Dalits out of Hinduism to Buddhism, Islam, Christianity, or Sikkhism has been seen as a way to escape the prejudice and discrimination of the caste system. As a secular democracy, religious freedom and protection against caste-based discrimination are written into the Indian constitution. However, well-publicized mass conversions to Buddhism and Christianity in the past decade have provoked a strong response from Hindu fundamentalists who have successfully fought for legal restrictions on conversions in some Indian states.

The practice of Hinduism is rich with rites and ceremonies, festivals and feasts, processions and ritual gatherings of literally millions of celebrants. It involves careful observance of food and marriage rules and the performance of duties within the framework of the caste system. Pilgrimages to holy rivers and sacred places are thought to secure deliverance from sin or pollution and to preserve religious worth (Figure 5.29). In what is perhaps the largest periodic gathering of humans in the world, millions of Hindus of all castes, classes, and sects gather about once in 12 years for ritual washing away of sins in the Ganges River near Allahabad. Worship in the temples and shrines that are found in every village and the leaving of offerings to secure merit from the gods are required. The doctrine of *ahimsa*—also fundamental in Buddhism—instructs Hindus to refrain from harming any living being.

Temples and shrines are everywhere; their construction brings merit to their owners—the villages or individuals who paid for them. Temples must be erected on a site that is beautiful and auspicious, in the neighborhood of water since the gods will not come to other locations. Within them, innumerable icons of gods in various forms are enshrined, the objects of veneration, gifts, and daily care. All temples have a circular spire as a reminder that the sky is the real dwelling place of the god who temporarily resides within the temple (Figure 5.30). The temples, shrines, daily rituals and

(a)

Figure 5.34 **New Religious Landscapes of the United Kingdom.** (*a*) A vacant, boarded-up church in Cardiff, Wales most recently used for a home and garden store. (*b*) The London Central Mosque and Islamic Cultural Centre in Regents Park. The main hall holds 5,000 worshipers.

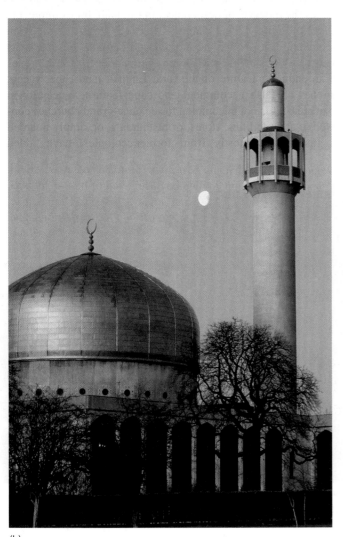

(b)

mosques, temples, and new storefront churches to the landscape (Figure 5.34).

One striking aspect of the U.S. religious landscape is the great number of different churches, synagogues, mosques, temples, and related structures (Figure 5.35). In addition to the formal structures of the more established groups, innumerable storefront places of worship—mainly associated with poorer neighborhoods, changing immigrant ethnic communities, and splinter Protestant sects—have become part of the American scene. Compared with more secularized Europe, the religious diversity and vitality of America is remarkable. Some scholars attribute this vitality to the lack of an established state religion and to the successive waves of immigrants, most of whom are religious and have found that creating a religious congregation of their own is a way to be American while preserving their ethnic identity. Another important feature on the American religious landscape is the megachurch, defined as a congregation that draws more than 2,000 attendees in a typical weekend. Megachurches are often located in suburban areas and feature massive parking lots and architecture more typical of convention centers, arenas, movie theaters, or shopping malls (not surprisingly since many meet in converted buildings once used for those purposes). Also, distinctively, though not exclusively, American is the proliferation of religious and denominational signage (see Figure 5.1) on city buildings, storefronts, or highway billboards.

5. In what ways do *isoglosses* and the study of *linguistic geography* help us understand other human geographic patterns?

6. Cite examples that indicate the significance of religion as a cultural dominant in the internal and foreign relations of nations.

7. How does the classification of religions as *universalizing, ethnic,* or *tribal* help us to understand their patterns of distribution and spatial diffusion?

8. What connection, if any, do you see between language, religion, and intergroup rivalry and violence in the contemporary world?

 ## KEY CONCEPTS REVIEW

Language

1. **How are the world's languages classified and distributed?** pp. 123–131.
The some 6000 languages spoken today may be grouped within a limited number of language families that trace their origins to common protolanguages. The present distribution of tongues reflects the current stage of continuing past and recent dispersion of their speakers and their adoption by new users. Languages change through isolation, migration, and the passage of time.

2. **What are standard languages and what kinds of variants from them can be observed?** pp. 131–139.
All speakers of a given language are members of its speech community, but not all use the language uniformly. The standard language is that form of speech that has received official sanction or acceptance as the "proper" form of grammar and pronunciation. Dialects, regional and social, represent nonstandard or vernacular variants of the common tongue. A pidgin is a created, composite, simple language designed to promote exchange between speakers of different tongues. When evolved into a complex native

language of a people, the pidgin has become a creole. Governments may designate one or more official state languages (including, perhaps, a creole such as Swahili).

3. **How does language serve as a cultural identifier and landscape artifact?** pp. 139–143.
Language is a mentifact, a part of the ideological subsystem of culture. It is, therefore, inseparable from group identity and self-awareness. Language may also be divisive, creating rifts within multilingual societies when linguistic minorities seek recognition or separatism. Toponyms (place names) record the order past and present occupants have tried to place on areas they inhabit or transit. Toponymy in tracing that record becomes a valuable tool of historical cultural geography.

Religion

4. **What is the cultural role of religion?** pp. 143–144.
Like language, religion is a basic identifying component of culture, a mentifact that serves as a cultural rallying point. Frequently, religious beliefs and adherence divide and alienate different groups within and among societies. Past and present

belief systems of a culture may influence its legal norms, dietary customs, economic patterns, and landscape imprints.

5. **How are religions classified and distributed?** pp. 144–147.
As variable cultural innovations, religions do not lend themselves to easy clustering or classification. Distinctions among universalizing, ethnic, and traditional religions have some geographic significance, but geographers are more interested in religions' spatial patterns and diffusion processes and landscape impacts than in their theologies. Those patterns reflect their origin areas, the migrations and conquests achieved by their past adherents, and the converts they have attracted in home and distant areas.

6. **What are the principal world religions and how are they distinguished in patterns of innovation, diffusion, and landscape imprint?** pp. 147–161.
The text briefly traces those differing origins, spreads, and cultural landscape impacts of Judaism, Christianity, Islam, Hinduism, Buddhism, and certain East Asian ethnic religions.

ETHNIC GEOGRAPHY:
Threads of Diversity

6

This Native American girl in traditional costume dances in a pow wow at Port Huron, Michigan.

Key Concepts

1. Ethnicity, ethnic diversity, and the changing immigration streams to multiethnic Anglo America, pp. 165–171.

2. Acculturation and the persistence of ethnic clusters and identities in Anglo America and elsewhere, pp. 171–184.

3. Anglo American and world urban ethnic diversity and patterns of segregation, pp. 184–191.

4. The landscape impacts and residues of ethnic diversity, pp. 191–197.

*W*e must not forget that these men and women who file through the narrow gates at Ellis Island, hopeful, confused, with bundles of misconceptions as heavy as the great sacks upon their backs—we must not forget that these simple, rough-handed people are the ancestors of our descendants, the fathers and mothers of our children.

So it has been from the beginning. For a century a swelling human stream has poured across the ocean, fleeing from poverty in Europe to a chance in America. Englishman, Welshman, Scotchman, Irishman; German, Swede, Norwegian, Dane; Jew, Italian, Bohemian, Serb; Syrian, Hungarian, Pole, Greek—one race after another has knocked at our doors, been given admittance, has married us and begot our children. We could not have told by looking at them whether they were to be good or bad progenitors, for racially the cabin is not above the steerage, and dirt, like poverty and ignorance, is but skin-deep. A few hours, and the stain of travel has left the immigrant's cheek; a few years, and he loses the odor of alien soils; a generation or two, and these outlanders are irrevocably our race, our nation, our stock.[1]

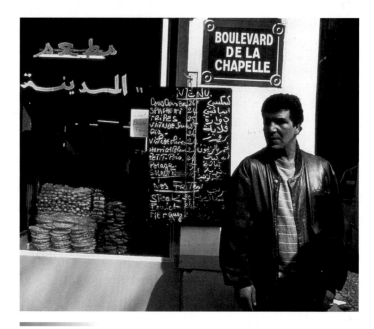

Figure 6.1 "Guest workers"—frequently called by their German name, *Gastarbeiter*—have substantially altered the ethnic mix in formerly unicultural cities of Western Europe. The restaurant shown here is in an Algerian neighborhood of Paris, France. On average, foreigners comprise nearly 10% of Western Europe's labor force. They form the majority of the workforce in many Middle Eastern countries; between 60% and 90% of the workers of the Persian Gulf countries of Bahrain, Kuwait, Oman, Qatar, Saudi Arabia, and the United Arab Emirates are foreigners.

The United States is a cultural composite—as increasingly are most of the countries of the world. North America's peoples include aborigine and immigrant, native born and new arrival. Had this chapter's introductory passage been written in the 21st century rather than early in the 20th, the list of foreign origins would have been lengthened to include many Latin American, African, and Asian countries as well as the European sources formerly most common.

The majority of the world's societies, even those outwardly seemingly most homogeneous, house distinctive **ethnic groups,** populations that feel themselves bound together by a common origin and set off from other groups by ties of culture, race, religion, language, or nationality. Ethnic diversity is a near-universal part of human geographic patterns; the current some 200 or so independent countries are home to at least 5000 ethnic groups. The factors driving globalization such as the growth of transnational corporations, relaxed border restrictions, low cost travel, and high-speed global communications are all encouraging greater movement and ethnic mixing. European Union states house increasing numbers of workers from other European Union states as well as African and Asian immigrants and guest workers, effectively making them multiethnic societies. Refugees and job-seekers are found in alien lands throughout both hemispheres (Figure 6.1). Cross-border movements and resettlements in Southeast Asia and Africa are well-reported current events. European colonialism created pluralistic societies in tropical lands through introduction of both ruling elites and, frequently, nonindigenous laboring groups. Polyethnic Russia, Afghanistan, China, India, and most African countries have native—rather than immigrant—populations more characterized by racial and cultural diversity than by uniformity. Tricultural Belgium has a nearly split personality in matters political and social. The idea of an ethnically pure nation-state is largely irrelevant.

Like linguistic and religious differences within societies, such population interminglings are masked by the "culture realms" shown in Figure 2.4 but are, at a larger scale, important threads in the cultural-geographic web of our complex world. The multiple movements, diffusions, migrations, and mixings of peoples of different origins making up that world are the subject of **ethnic geography.** Its concerns are those of spatial distributions and interactions of ethnic groups, of the cultural characteristics and influences underlying them, and of how the built environment reflects the imprint of various ethnic groups.

Culture, we saw in Chapter 2, is the composite of traits making up the way of life of a human group—collective beliefs, symbols, values, forms of behavior, and complexes of such nonmaterial and material traits as social customs, language, religion, food habits, tools, structures, and the like. Culture is learned; it characterizes the group and distinguishes it from all other groups that have collectively created and transmitted to its children still other "ways of life." *Ethnicity,* in contrast, is simply the summary term of identification assigned to a large group of people recognized as sharing the traits of a distinctive common culture. It is always based on a firm understanding by members of a group that they are in some fundamental ways different from others who do not share their distinguishing characteristics or cultural heritage.

Ethnicity is, at root, a spatial concept. Ethnic groups are associated with clearly recognized territories—either larger homeland districts or smaller rural or urban enclaves—in which they are primary or exclusive occupants and upon which they have placed distinctive cultural marks. Since territory and ethnicity are inseparable concepts, ethnicity becomes an important concern in the cultural patterning of space and clearly an item of human geographic interest. Further, since ethnicity is often identified with language or religious practices setting a minority group off from a surrounding

[1]From Walter E. Weyl, "The New Americans," *Harper's Magazine* 129 (1914): 615. Copyright 1914 Harper's Magazine Foundation, New York, NY.

majority culture, consideration of ethnicity flows logically from the discussions of language and religion in Chapter 5.

Our examination of ethnic patterns will concentrate on Anglo America (the United States and Canada). Originally, this region was occupied by a multitude of distinctive Native American peoples, each with their own territory, culture, and language. Over time, these populations were overwhelmed and displaced by a wide spectrum of Old World ethnic groups. Although Anglo America lacks the homelands that gave territorial identity to immigrant ethnics in their countries of origin, it has provided a case study of how distinctive culture groups partition space and place their claims and imprints on it. It shows, as well, the durability of ethnic distinction even under conditions and national myths that emphasize intermixing and homogenization of population as the accepted norm. Examples drawn from other countries and environments will serve to highlight ways in which American-based generalizations may be applied more broadly or in which the North American experience reflects a larger world scene.

Ethnic Diversity and Separatism

Each year on a weekend in May, New York City celebrates its ethnic diversity and vitality by closing off to all but pedestrian traffic a 1-mile stretch of street to conduct the Ninth Avenue International Food Festival. Along the reserved route from 37th to 57th streets, a million or more New Yorkers come together to sample the foods, view the crafts, and hear the music of the great number of the world's ethnic groups represented among the citizens of the city. As a resident of the largest U.S. metropolis, each of the merchants and artists contributing one of the several hundred separate storefront, stall, or card-table displays of the festival becomes a member of the Anglo American culture realm. Each, however, preserves a distinctive small-group identity within that larger collective "realm" (Figure 6.2).

The threads of diversity exhibited in the festival are expressions of **ethnicity,** a term derived from the Greek word *ethnos,* meaning a "people" or "nation." Intuitively we recognize that the literal translation is incomplete. Ethnic groups are composed of individuals who share some prominent cultural traits or characteristics, some evident physical or social identifications setting them apart both from the majority population and from other distinctive minorities among whom they may live.

Race and ethnicity are frequently equated with each other, but are actually very different concepts. Race is an outdated categorization of humans based on outward physical characteristics such as skin color, hair texture, or eye color or shape (see "The Matter of Race"). In reality, humans are all one species and biologists have rejected race as a meaningful way to describe human variation. While race does not exist in a scientific, biological sense, it does persist as an idea and basis for group identity, and racism—prejudice and discrimination based on racial categories—is very much alive. The U.S. Census Bureau asked respondents to classify themselves into one of five racial categories for the 2000 census and fifteen categories for the 2010 census. In 2000, they began allowing people to identify as multiracial (Table 6.1). No single trait denotes ethnicity. Group recognition may be based on language, religion, national origin, unique customs, or—improperly—an

Figure 6.2 The annual Ninth Avenue International Fair in New York City became one of the largest of its kind. Similar festivals celebrating America's ethnic diversity are found in cities and small towns across the country.

ill-defined concept of race. Common unifying bonds of ethnicity are a shared ancestry and cultural heritage, distinctive traditions, territorial identification, and sense of community. The principal ethnic groups of the United States and Canada are shown in Table 6.2 and Table 6.4, respectively.

Ethnocentrism is the term describing a tendency to evaluate other cultures against the standards of one's own. It implies the feeling that one's own ethnic group is superior. Ethnocentrism can divide multiethnic societies by establishing rivalries and provoking social and spatial discord and isolation. It can, as well, be a sustaining and identifying emotion, giving familiar values and support to the individual in strange and complex surroundings. The ethnic group maintains familiar cultural institutions and shares traditional food and music. More often than not, it provides the friends, spouses, business opportunities, and political identification of ethnic group members.

Territorial isolation is a strong and supporting trait of ethnic separatism and assists individual groups to retain their identification. In Europe, Asia, and Africa, ethnicity and territorial identity are inseparable. Ethnic minorities are first and foremost associated with *homelands.* This is true of the Welsh, Bretons, and Basques of Western Europe (Figure 12.20); the Slovenes, Croatians, or Bosnians of Eastern Europe (Figure 6.6a); the non-Slavic "nationalities" of Russia; and the immense number of ethnic communities of South and Southeast Asia. These minorities have specific spatial identity even though they may not have political independence.

Table 6.1

U.S. Resident Population by Race and Hispanic Origin: July 1, 2007

	Number (millions)	Percent of U.S. Population
Total Population	**301.6**	**100.0**
One race option[a]	296.8	98.4
White	241.2	80.2
Black or African American	38.8	12.9
Asian	13.4	4.4
American Indian and Alaskan Native	2.9	1.0
Native Hawaiian and other Pacific Islander	0.5	0.2
Two or more races	4.9	1.6
Hispanic or Latino (of any race)	45.5	15.1

Note: Race as reported reflects the self-identification of respondents.

[a]A single race was claimed in 2000 for over half the children of interracial couples.

Source: U.S. Bureau of the Census.

Table 6.2

Leading U.S. Ancestries Reported, Census 2000

Ancestry	Number (millions)	Percentage of Total Population
German	42.8	15.2
Irish	30.5	10.8
African American	24.9	8.8
English	24.5	8.7
Mexican	18.4	6.5
Italian	15.6	5.6
Polish	9.0	3.2
French	8.3	3.0
American Indian	7.9	2.8
Scottish	4.9	1.7
Dutch	4.5	1.6
Norwegian	4.5	1.6
Scotch-Irish	4.3	1.5
Swedish	4.0	1.4

Note: More than 20 million persons indicated "United States" or "American" as their ancestry. The tabulation is based on self-identification of respondents, not on objective criteria. Many persons reported multiple ancestries and were tabulated by the Census Bureau under each claim.

Source: Census 2000 special tabulation.

Where ethnic groups are intermixed and territorial boundaries imprecise—former Yugoslavia (Figure 6.6a) is an example—or where a single state contains disparate, rival populations—the case of many African and Asian (Figure 6.6b) countries—conflict among groups can be serious if peaceful relations or central governmental control break down. "Ethnic cleansing," a polite term with grisly implications, has become a past or present justification and objective for civil conflict in parts of the former Soviet Union and Eastern Europe and in several African and southeast Asian countries. The Holocaust slaughter of millions of Jews before and during World War II in Western and Eastern Europe was an extreme case of ethnic extermination, but comparable murderous assaults on racial or cultural target populations by conquering or controlling groups are as old as human history. Such "cleansing" involves, through mass genocide, the violent elimination of a target ethnic group from a particular geographic or political area to achieve racial or cultural homogeneity and expanded settlement area by the perpetrating state or ethnic group. Its outcome is not only an alteration of the ethnic composition of regions and states, but of the ethnic mix in, usually, adjacent areas and countries to which assaulted and displaced populations have fled as refugees.

Few true homelands exist within the North American cultural mix. However, the "Chinatowns" and "Little Italys" as created enclaves within North American cities have provided both the spatial refuge and the support systems essential to new arrivals in an alien culture realm. Asian and West Indian immigrants in London and other English cities and foreign *guest workers*—originally migrant and temporary laborers, usually male—that reside in Continental European communities assume similar spatial separation. While serving a support function, this segregation is as much the consequence of the housing market and of public and private restriction as it is simply of self-selection. In Southeast Asia, with the exception of Thailand, Chinese communities remain aloof from the majority culture not as a transitional phase to incorporation with it but as a permanent chosen isolation.

By retaining what is familiar of the old in a new land, ethnic enclaves have reduced cultural shock and have paved the way for the gradual process of adaptation that prepares both individuals and groups to operate effectively in the new, larger **host society**—the established, dominant group. The traditional ideal of the United States "melting pot," in which ethnic identity and division would be lost and full amalgamation of all minorities into a blended, composite majority culture would occur, was the expectation voiced in the chapter-opening quotation. For many even long-resident ethnic groups, however, that ideal has not become a reality.

Recent decades have seen a resurgence of cultural pluralism and an increasing demand for ethnic autonomy not only in North America but also in multiethnic societies around the world (see "Nations of Immigrants,"). At least, recognition is sought for ethnicity as a justifiable basis for special treatment in the allocation of political power, the structure of the educational system, the toleration or encouragement of minority linguistic rights, and other evidences of group self-awareness and promotion. In some multiethnic societies, second- and third-generation descendants of

Human populations may be differentiated from one another on any number of bases: gender, nationality, stage of economic development, and so on. One common form of differentiation is based on recognizable inherent physical characteristics, or *race*.

While humans are all one species that can freely interbreed and produce fertile offspring, there is obvious variation in our physical characteristics. The spread of human beings over the earth and their occupation of different environments was accompanied by the development of variations in visible characteristics such as skin pigmentation, hair and eye color, and hair texture, as well as internal differences such as blood composition or lactose intolerance. Physical differentiation among human groups is old and can reasonably be dated to the Paleolithic (100,000 to about 11,000 years ago) spread and isolation of population groups.

Geographic patterns of distinct combinations of physical traits emerged due to causative forces of evolutionary **natural selection** or **adaptation,** and **genetic drift.** Natural selection favors the transmission of characteristics that enable humans to adapt to a particular environmental feature, such as climate. Studies have suggested some plausible relationship between, for example, solar radiation and skin color, and between temperature and body size. Dark skin indicates the presence of melanin, which protects against the penetration of damaging ultraviolet rays from the sun. Conversely, the production of vitamin D in the body, which is necessary to good health, is linked to the penetration of ultraviolet rays. In high latitudes where winter days are short and the sun is low in the sky, light skin confers an adaptive advantage by allowing the production of vitamin D. Genetic drift refers to a heritable trait that appears by chance in a group and is accentuated by inbreeding. If two populations are too spatially separated for much interaction to occur (*isolation*), a trait may develop in one but not in the other. Unlike natural selection, genetic drift differentiates populations in nonadaptive ways. Natural selection and genetic drift promote differentiation. Countering them is **gene flow** via interbreeding, which acts to homogenize neighboring populations. Opportunities for interbreeding, always part of the spread and intermingling of human populations, have accelerated with the growing mobility and migrations of people in the past few centuries.

Racial categorization is a scientifically outdated way of making sense of human variation. A **race** is usually understood to be a population subset whose members have in common some hereditary biological characteristics that set them apart physically from other human groups. Focusing on visible physical characteristics, anthropologists in the 18th and 19th century created a variety of racial classification schemes, most of which derived from geographical variations of populations. Some anthropological studies at that time attempted to link physical traits with mental ability in order to construct racial hierarchies that were used to justify slavery, imperialism, immigration restrictions, anti-miscegenation laws, and eugenics. Contemporary biology has rejected racial categorization as a meaningful description of human variation. Skin color does not correspond to genetic closeness between "race" groups. Further, pure races do not exist and DNA-based evidence shows that there is more variation within the so-called racial groups than there is between the groups.

Living in a society where racial categorization has been widespread, we may be tempted to group humans racially and attribute intellectual ability, athletic prowess or negative characteristics to particular racial groups. This is problematic for many reasons, the most important being that geneticists have rejected race as a scientific concept—there is only race, the human race. Second, intellectual ability as measured on standardized tests is mostly a function of socioeconomic status. Finally, the athletic abilities displayed by top athletes are the property of particular individuals, not a group trait, and like intellectual ability are strongly influenced by social factors.

Nor does race have meaningful application to any human characteristics that are culturally acquired. That is, race is *not* equivalent to ethnicity or nationality and has no bearing on differences in religion or language. There is no "Irish" or "Hispanic" race, for example. Such groupings are based on culture, not genes. Culture summarizes the way of life of a group of people, and members of the group may adopt it irrespective of their individual genetic heritage, or race. Nevertheless, despite the fact that the older view of race as a biological category has been thoroughly discredited, race and ethnicity remain as defining and divisive realities in American society. Both are deeply rooted in individual and group consciousness, and both are strongly ingrained in the country's social and institutional life. While biological notions of race have little meaning, the society itself is extremely "racialized."

immigrants, now seeking "roots" and identity, embrace the ethnicity that their forebears sought to deny.

Immigration Streams

The ethnic diversity found on the Anglo American scene today is the product of continuous flows of immigrants—some 80 million of them by the early 21st century—representing, at different periods, movements to this continent of members of nearly all of the cultures and races of the world (Figure 6.3). For the United States, that movement took the form of three distinct immigrant waves, all of which, of course, followed much earlier Amerindian arrivals.

The first wave, lasting from pioneer settlement to about 1870, was made up of two different groups. One comprised white arrivals from western and northern Europe, with Britain and Germany best represented. Together with the Scots and Scotch-Irish, they established a majority society controlled by Protestant Anglo-Saxons and allied groups. The Europeans dominated numerically the second group of first-wave immigrants, Africans brought involuntarily to the New World, who made up nearly 20% of U.S. population in 1790. The mass immigration that occurred beginning after the middle of the 19th century began to reduce both the northwest European dominance of American society and the percentage of blacks within the growing total population.

Geography and Public Policy

Nations of Immigrants

Americans, steeped in the country's "melting pot" myth and heritage, are inclined to forget that many other countries are also "nations of immigrants" and that their numbers are dramatically increasing. In the United States, Canada, Australia, and New Zealand, early European colonists and, later, immigrants from other continents overwhelmed indigenous populations. In each, immigration has continued, contributing not only to national ethnic mixes but maintaining or enlarging the proportion of the population that is foreign born. In Australia, as one example, that proportion now equals 25%; for Canada it is some 18%.

In Latin America, foreign population domination of native peoples was and is less complete and uniform than in Anglo America. While in nearly all South and Central American states, European and other nonnative ethnic groups dominate the social and economic hierarchy, in a few they constitute only a minority of the total population. In Bolivia, for example, the vast majority (71%) of pride themselves on their Native American descent, and Amerindian comprise between 25% and 55% of the populations of Bolivia, Guatemala, Peru, and Ecuador. Mestizo (mixed European and Amerindian ancestry) populations are the majority in many Latin American countries. But nonnative, largely European, ethnics make up essentially all—over 94%—of the population of Argentina, Costa Rica, and southern Chile.

The original homelands of those immigrant groups are themselves increasingly becoming multiethnic, and several European countries are now home to as many or more of the foreign-born proportionately than is the United States. Some 20% of Switzerland's population, 13% of France's, 10% of Sweden's, and over 9% of Germany's are of foreign birth, compared with America's 11%. Many came as immigrants and refugees fleeing unrest or poverty in post-communist Eastern Europe. Many are "guest workers" and their families who were earlier recruited in Turkey and North Africa; or they are immigrants from former colonial or overseas territories in Asia, Africa, and the Caribbean. More than 7% of Germany's inhabitants come from outside the European Union, as do over 3% of Holland's and Belgium's.

The trend of ethnic mixing is certain to continue and accelerate. Cross-border movements of migrants and refugees in Africa, Asia, the Americas, as well as Europe are continuing common occurrences, reflecting growing incidences of ethnic strife, civil wars, famines, and economic hardships. But of even greater long-term influence are the growing disparities in population numbers and economic wealth between the older developed states and the developing world. The population of the world's poorer countries is growing twice as fast as Europe's of the late 19th century, when that continent fed the massive immigration streams across the Atlantic. The current rich world, whose population is projected to stabilize well below 1.5 billion, will increasingly be a magnet for those from poorer countries where numbers will rise from some 4 billion to more than 6.5 billion by A.D. 2025 and to nearly 8 billion in a half-century. The economic and population pressures building in the developing world ensure greater international and intercontinental migration and a rapid expansion in the numbers of "nations of immigrants."

Many of those developed host countries are beginning to resist that flow. Although the Universal Declaration of Human Rights declares individuals are to be free to move within or to leave their own countries, no right of admittance to any other country is conceded. Political asylum is often—but not necessarily—granted; refugees or migrants seeking economic opportunity or fleeing civil strife or starvation have no claims for acceptance. Increasingly, they are being turned away. The Interior Minister of France advocates "zero immigration"; Germany's government closed its doors in 1993 by increasing border controls and changing its constitutional right to asylum; Britain in 1994 tightened immigration rules even for foreign students and casual workers. And all European Union countries—which have no common EU policies on illegal immigration—have measures for turning back refugees who come via another EU country. In 1995, the EU's members materially narrowed the definition of who may qualify for asylum. Additional individual and collective restrictions have been enforced during the later 1990s and into the 21st century.

Nor is Europe alone. Hong Kong ejects Vietnamese refugees; Congo orders Rwandans to return to their own country; India tries to stem the influx of Bangladeshis; the United States rejects "economic refugees" from Haiti. Algerians are increasingly resented in France as their numbers and cultural presence increase. Turks feel the enmity of a small but violent group of Germans, and East Indians and Africans find growing resistance among the Dutch. In many countries, policies of exclusion or restriction appear motivated by unacceptable influxes of specific racial, ethnic, or national groups.

Questions to Consider

1. Do you think all people everywhere should have a universal right of admittance to a country of choice equivalent to their declared right to depart their homelands? Why or why not?

2. Do you think it appropriate that destination states make a distinction between political and economic refugees? Why or why not?

3. Do you think it legitimate for countries to establish immigration quotas based on national origin or to classify certain potential immigrants as unacceptable or undesirable on the grounds that their national, racial, or religious origins are incompatible with the culture of the prospective host country? Why or why not?

That second immigrant wave, from 1870 to 1914, was heavily weighted in favor of eastern and southern Europeans, who comprised more than 50% of new arrivals by the end of the 19th century. The second period ended with congressional adoption of a quota system regulating both the numbers of individuals who would be accepted and the countries from which they could come. That system, plus a world depression and World War II (1939–1945), greatly slowed immigration until a third-wave migration, rivaling the massive influx of the late 19th and early 20th centuries was launched with the Immigration and Nationality Act of 1965.

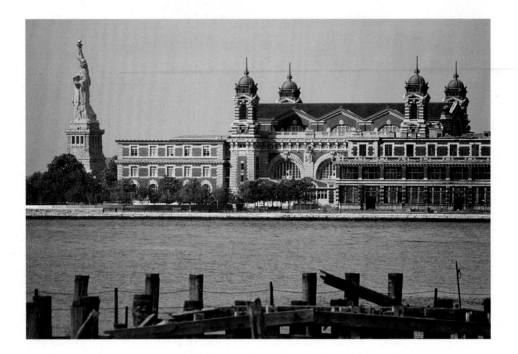

Figure 6.3 Although it was not opened until 1892, New York harbor's Ellis Island—the country's first federal immigration facility—quickly became the symbol of all the migrant streams to the United States. By the time it was closed in late 1954, it had processed 17 million immigrants. Today their descendants number over 100 million Americans. A major renovation project was launched in 1984 to restore Ellis Island as a national monument.

At that time the old national quota system of immigrant regulation was replaced by one more liberal in its acceptance of newcomers from Latin America, Asia, and Africa. Since then, some 28 million legal immigrants have entered the United States, in addition to an estimated (2006) 12 million illegal ones (though one careful study suggests illegals may number up to 20 million). Quickly, Hispanics, particularly Mexicans, dominated the inflow and became the largest segment of new arrivals. The changing source areas of the newcomers are traced in Table 6.3 and Figure 6.4.

Canada experienced three quite different immigration streams. Until 1760, most settlers came from France. After that date, the pattern abruptly altered as a flood of United Kingdom (English, Irish, and Scottish) immigrants arrived. Many came by way of the United States, fleeing, as Loyalists, to Canada during and after the American Revolutionary War. Others came directly from overseas. Another pronounced shift in arrival pattern occurred during the 20th century as the bulk of new immigrants began originating in Continental Europe and, more recently, in other continents. By 2001, 18% of all Canadians had been born outside of the country, and immigration accounted for more than one-half of Canada's population growth between 1996 and 2001. The ten leading ethnicities in 2001 (of more than 200 different ethnic origins reported) are listed in Table 6.4.

The United States' cultural diversity has increased as its immigration source regions have changed from the original European areas to Latin America and Asia, and both the number of visible and vocal ethnic communities and the number of regions housing significant minority populations have multiplied. Simultaneously, the proportion of foreign-born residents has increased in the U.S. population mix. In 1920, at the end of the period of the most active

Table 6.3

Immigrants to the United States: Major Flows by Origin

Ethnic Groups	Time Period	Numbers in Millions (approximate)
Blacks	1650s–1800	1
Irish	1840s and 1850s	1.75
Germans	1840s–1880s	4
Scandinavians	1870s–1900s	1.5
Poles	1880s–1920s	1.25
East European Jews	1880s–1920s	2.5
Austro-Hungarians	1880s–1920s	4
Italians	1880s–1920s	4.75
Mexicans	1950s–Present	13
Cubans	1960s–Present	1.4
Asians	1960s–Present	9

European immigration, more than 13% of the American population had been born in another country. That percentage declined each decade until a low of 4.8% foreign born was reported in 1970. So great was the inflow after 1970, however, that by 2005 some 36.8 million people—12.4% of the population—had been born abroad. In the early years of the current century, half of the

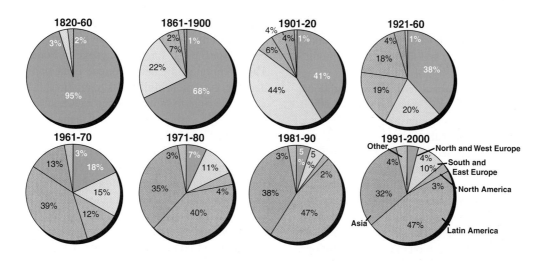

Figure 6.4 **Legal immigrants admitted to the United States by region of origin, 1820–2000.** The diagrams clearly reflect the dramatic change in geographic origins of immigrants. After 1965, immigration restrictions based on national origin were shifted to priorities based on family reunification and needed skills and professions. Those priorities underwent Congressional reconsideration in 1995 and 1996. What is not shown is the dramatic increase in the *total* numbers of entrants to the United States in the 1980s and 1990s, years that witnessed the highest legal and illegal immigrant and refugee volumes in the nation's history.

Sources: Data from Leon F. Bouvier and Robert W. Gardner, "Immigration to the United States: The Unfinished Story," Population Bulletin 41, *no. 4 (Washington, D.C.: Population Reference Bureau, 1986); and Immigration and Naturalization Service.*

Table 6.4

Canadian Population Ranked by Claimed Ethnic Origin, 2001

Rank	Ethnic Group
1	Canadian
2	English
3	French
4	Scottish
5	Irish
6	German
7	Italian
8	Chinese
9	Ukrainian
10	North American Indian

Source: Statistics Canada.

total population growth of the country was accounted for by legal and illegal immigration. Illegal immigration alone appears to have totaled more than 6 million during the 1990s, with more than 700,000 to 800,000 undocumented arrivals entering per year—more than the 600,000 or so legal entrants. One consequence of increased national security measures after the World Trade Center assaults in 2001, in fact, has been a diminished influx of legal immigrants, with illegal entrants far surpassing those legally admitted; by 2006, illegal immigrants accounted for roughly 30% of the entire U.S. foreign-born population.

Individual cities and counties showed very high concentrations of the foreign born at the end of the century. New York City,

for example, received one million immigrants in the 1990s and, by 2000, 40% of its population had been born abroad. Similar proportionate immigration flows and foreign-born ratios were recorded for Dade County (Miami) Florida; the Silicon Valley, California, counties of San Mateo and Santa Clara; and others. Monterey Park, California, has a population that is 60% Asian, the vast majority recent Chinese immigrants. During the early years of the 21st century, however, a pronounced trend has occurred away from the largest immigrant states—California, Florida, Illinois, New Jersey, New York, and Texas—toward new destinations in formerly unfavored states such as Alabama, Georgia, Iowa, Tennessee, and North Carolina.

As had been the case during the 19th century, growing influxes from new immigrant source regions and, particularly, the unstemmed flood of illegal entrants prompted movements to halt the flow and to preserve the ethnic status quo (see "Broken Borders," Chapter 3, p. 80). In 2005 and 2006, Congressional debate focused on different immigration control proposals, including building a 700-mile wall (authorized in 2006) on the border between Mexico and the United States, increasing efforts to enforce existing immigration controls, initiating expanded guest worker programs, and granting legal status to some unauthorized entrants and easing their path to citizenship.

Acculturation and Assimilation

In the United States, at least, the sheer volume of multiple immigration streams makes the concept of "minority" suspect when no single "majority" ethnic group exists (see Table 6.2). Indeed, high rates of immigration and declining birth rates among white Americans have placed the country on the verge of becoming a state with no racial—as well as no ethnic—majority. No later than 2050, current trends promise, America will be truly multiracial, with no group constituting more than 50% of the total population. Even now, American society is a composite of unity and diversity with immigrants being both shaped by and shaping the larger community they joined.

Amalgamation theory is the formal term for the traditional "melting pot" concept of the merging of many immigrant ethnic heritages into a composite American mainstream. Popular and accepted in the late 19th and early 20th centuries, amalgamation theory has more recently been rejected by many as unrealistic in light of current widespread social and cultural tensions. Recent experience in western European countries and Anglo America—destination areas of multiple immigration flows—indicates that strongly retained and defended ethnic identities are increasingly the rule and that a militant multiculturalism rather than voluntary amalgamation is a more realistic description of current conditions. Such cultural separatism is buttressed by the current ease—through radio, telephone, Internet, television, and rapid transportation—of communication and identification with the homeland societies of immigrants who no longer are essentially divorced from their past to make new lives in an alien land. The old "melting pot" concept of America has largely dissolved, replaced with a greater emphasis on preserving the diverse cultural heritages of the country's many ethnic components.

Nonetheless, as we shall see, all immigrant groups after the first found a controlling host group culture in place, with accustomed patterns of behavior and response and a dominant language of the workplace and government. The customs and practices familiar and expected among those already in place had to be learned by newcomers if they were to be accepted. The process of **acculturation** is that of the adoption by the immigrants of the values, attitudes, ways of behavior, and speech of the receiving society. In the process, the ethnic group loses much of its separate cultural identity as it accepts over time the culture of the larger host community. It may, however, resist total absorption into the host society and proudly retain identifying features of its distinctive ethnic heritage: adherence to a national church, celebration of traditional national or religious holidays with parades or festivals, and the like. To the extent that those ethnic retentions and identifications are long lasting and characteristic of multiple ethnic groups, the presumed ideal of the "melting pot" is unattained and a "salad bowl" ethnic mixture is the result. Although acculturation most usually involves a minority group adopting the patterns of the dominant population, the process can be reciprocal. That is, the dominant group may also adopt at least some patterns and practices typical of new minority groups and become a "lumpy stew" in which the immigrant groups maintain their identity while both taking on the flavor of the host society and adding new flavor to the broader societal mix. Ethnic restaurants and broadened fruit and vegetable choices in both ethnic shops and mainstream supermarkets are familiar evidences of those immigrant impacts—as is the emergence of salsa as perhaps the most popular condiment today.

Acculturation is a slow process for many immigrant individuals and groups, and the parent tongue may of choice or necessity be retained as an ethnically identifying feature even after fashions of dress, food, and customary behavior have been substantially altered in the new environment. In 2004, nearly 20% of Americans above the age of 5 spoke a language other than English in the home; for 60% of them, that language was Spanish. In the light of recent immigration trends, we can assume that the number of people speaking a foreign language at home will only increase. The retention of the native tongue is encouraged rather than hindered by American civil rights regulations that give to new immigrants the right to bilingual education and (in some cases) special assistance in voting in their own language (see "An Official U.S. Language?", p. 140).

The language barrier that has made it difficult for foreign-born groups, past and present, to gain quick entrance to the labor force has encouraged their high rate of initiation of or entry into small businesses. The consequence has been a continuing stimulus to the American economy and, through the creation of family-held neighborhood enterprises, the maintenance of the ethnic character of immigrant communities (Figure 6.5). The result has also been the gradual integration of the new arrivals into the economic and cultural mainstream of American society.

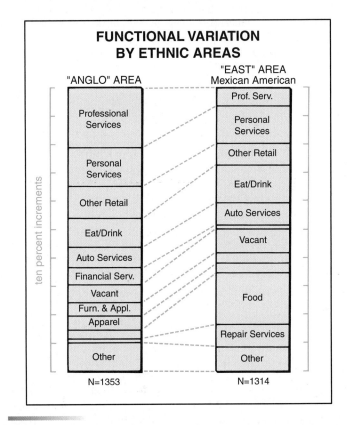

Figure 6.5 Variations in business establishments in Anglo and Mexican American neighborhoods of Los Angeles in the late 1960s. Although the total populations of the two areas were comparable, the Mexican American community had over three times more food stores because of the dominance of corner grocery stores over supermarkets. Bakeries (*tortillerías*) were a frequent expression of ethnic dietary habits. Neighborhood businesses conducted in Spanish and related to the needs of the community were the rule. Anglo neighborhoods, because of greater affluence, had larger numbers of professional services (doctors, lawyers) available. More recent studies of Asian, Latin American, and African immigrant business districts have observed a similar distribution of business types that differ from established older majority neighborhoods.

Source: Redrawn by permission from Annals of the Association of American Geographers, *Keith D. Harries, Vol. 61, p. 739, Association of American Geographers, 1971.*

When that integration is complete, **assimilation** has occurred. Full assimilation may be seen as a two-part process. **Behavioral** (or **cultural**) **assimilation** is the rough equivalent of acculturation; it implies integration into a common cultural life through shared experience, language, intermarriage, and sense of history. **Structural assimilation** refers to the fusion of immigrant ethnics with the groups, social systems, and occupations of the host society and the adoption of common attitudes and values. Structural assimilation is a two-way street. Not only does it require immigrant groups to absorb majority cultural values and practices, but it also demands that the majority society give full and unrestricted acceptance to members of the minority group and allow them to rise to positions of authority and power. The extent of structural assimilation is frequently measured by the degree of residential segregation that sets off the minority group from the larger general community. Employment segregation and intermarriage rates are also indicative. For most of the "old" (pre-1921 European) immigrants and their descendants, both forms of assimilation are complete. Most indicative of at least individual if not total group full structural assimilation is election or appointment to high public office and business leadership positions. For most of the "new" (post-1960s) immigrants, acculturation is proceeding or has already occurred, but for many of them and for racial minorities as well, structural assimilation has been elusive.

Assimilation does not necessarily mean that ethnic consciousness or awareness of racial and cultural differences is lost. *Competition theory,* in fact, suggests that as ethnic minorities begin to achieve success and enter into mainstream social and economic life, awareness of ethnic differences may be heightened. Frequently, ethnic identity may be most clearly experienced and expressed by those who can most successfully assimilate but who choose to promote group awareness and ethnic mobilization movements. That promotion, the theory holds, is a reflection of pressures of American urban life and the realities of increased competition. Those pressures transform formerly isolated groups into recognized, self-assertive ethnic minorities pursuing goals and interests dependent on their position within the larger society.

While in the United States it is usually assumed that acculturation and assimilation are self-evidently advantageous, Canada established multiculturalism in the 1970s as the national policy designed to reduce tensions between ethnic and language groups and to recognize that each thriving culture is an important part of the country's priceless personal resources. Since 1988, multiculturalism has been formalized by an act of the Canadian parliament and supervised by a separate government ministry. An example of its practical application can be seen in the way Toronto, Canada's largest and the world's most multicultural city with 46% of its residents (2006) foreign-born, routinely sends out property tax notices in six languages—English, French, Chinese, Italian, Greek, and Portuguese. Nevertheless, Canada—which takes in more immigrants per capita than any other industrialized country—began in 1995 to reduce the number of newcomers it was prepared to admit.

Both Canada and the United States seek to incorporate their varied immigrant minorities into composite national societies. In other countries, quite different attitudes and circumstances may prevail when indigenous—not immigrant—minorities feel their cultures and territories threatened. The Sinhalese comprise 75% of

Sri Lanka's population, but the minority Tamils have waged years of guerrilla warfare to defend what they see as majority threats to their culture, rights, and property. In India, Kashmiri nationalists fight to separate their largely Muslim valley from the Hindu majority society. Expanding ethnic minorities made up nearly 8.5% of China's 2000 population total. Some, including Tibetans, Mongols, and Uighurs, face assimilation largely because of massive migrations of ethnic Chinese into their traditional homelands. And in many multiethnic African countries, single-party governments seek to impose a sense of national unity on populations whose primary and nearly unshakable loyalties are rooted in their tribes and regions and not the state that is composed of many tribes (see Figure 12.5). Across the world, conflicts between ethnic groups within states have proliferated in recent years. Armenia, Azerbaijan, Burma, Burundi, Ethiopia, Indonesia, Iraq, Russia, Rwanda, and the former Yugoslavia are others in a long list of countries where ethnic tensions have erupted into civil conflict.

Basques and Catalans of Spain and Corsicans, Bretons, and Normans of France have only recently seen their respective central governments relax strict prohibitions on teaching or using the languages that identified those ethnic groups. On the other hand, in Bulgaria, ethnic Turks, who unofficially comprise 10% of the total population, at least temporarily officially ceased to exist in 1984 when the government obliged Turkish speakers and Muslims to replace their Turkish and Islamic names with Bulgarian and Christian ones. The government also banned their language and strictly limited practice of their religion. The intent was to impose an assimilation not sought by the minority.

Elsewhere, ethnic minorities—including immigrant minorities—have grown into majority groups, posing the question of who will assimilate whom. Ethnic Fijians sought to resolve that issue by staging a coup to retain political power when the majority immigrant ethnic Indians came to power by election in 1987 and another in 2000 after the election of an ethnic-Indian prime minister. As these and innumerable other examples from all continents demonstrate, Anglo American experiences and expectations have limited application to other societies differently constituted and motivated.

Areal Expressions of Ethnicity

Throughout much of the world, the close association of territoriality and ethnicity is well recognized, accepted, and often politically disruptive. Indigenous ethnic groups have developed over time in specific locations and, through ties of kinship, language, culture, religion, and shared history, have established themselves in their own and others' eyes as distinctive peoples with defined homeland areas. The boundaries of most countries of the world encompass a number of racial or ethnic minorities, whose demands for special territorial recognition have increased rather than diminished with advances in economic development, education, and self-awareness (Figure 6.6).

The dissolution of the Soviet Union in 1991, for example, not only set free the 14 ethnically based union republics that formerly had been dominated by Russia and Russians, but also opened the way for many smaller ethnic groups—the Chechens

(a)   (b)

Figure 6.6   (*a*) **Ethnicity in former Yugoslavia.** Yugoslavia was formed after World War I (1914–1918) from a patchwork of Balkan states and territories, including the former kingdoms of Serbia and Montenegro, Bosnia-Herzegovina, Croatia-Slavonia, and Dalmatia. The authoritarian central government, created in 1945 and led by Josep Broz Tito, tried to forge a new Yugoslav ethnic identity but failed when in 1991 Serb minorities voted for regional independence. In response, Serb guerillas backed by the Serb-dominated Yugoslav military engaged in a policy of territorial seizure and "ethnic cleansing" to secure areas claimed as traditional Serb "homelands." Religious differences between Eastern Orthodox, Roman Catholic, and Muslim adherents compound the conflicts rooted in nationality. (*b*) **Afghanistan** houses Pathan, Tajik, Uzbek, and Hazara ethnic groups speaking Pashto, Dari Persian, Uzbek, and several minor languages, and split between majority Sunni and minority Shia Moslem believers. Ethnic and local warlord rivalries and regional guerilla resistance to the NATO-supported central government contribute to national instability.

of the northern Caucasus, for example—to seek recognition and greater local control from the majority populations, including Russians, within whose territory their homelands lay. In Asia, the Indian subcontinent was subdivided to create separate countries with primarily religious-territorial affiliations, and the country of India itself has adjusted the boundaries of its constituent states to accommodate linguistic-ethnic realities. Other continents and countries show a similar acceptance of the importance of ethnic territoriality in their administrative structure (see "The Rising Tide of Nationalism").

With the exceptions of some—largely Canadian—Native American groups and of French Canadians, there is not the coincidence in Anglo America between territorial claim and ethnic-racial distinctiveness so characteristic elsewhere in the world (Figure 6.7). The general absence of such claims is the result of the immigrant nature of American society. Even the Native American "homeland" reservations in the United States are dispersed, non-contiguous, and in large part artificial impositions.[2] The spatial pattern of ethnicity that has developed is therefore more intricate and shifting than in many other pluralistic societies. It is not based on absolute ethnic dominance but on interplay between a majority culture and, usually, several competing minority groups. It shows the enduring consequences of early settlement and the changing structure of a fluid, responsive, freely mobile North American society.

---

[2]In Canada, a basic tenet of Aboriginal policy since 1993 has been the recognition of the inherent right of self-government under Section 35 of the Canadian Constitution. The new territory of Nunavut, the central and eastern portion of the earlier Northwest Territories, is based largely on Inuit land claims and came into existence as a self-governing district in 1999.

Charter Cultures

Although, with the Canadian French and Native American exceptions noted, no single ethnic minority homeland area exists in present-day Anglo America, a number of separate social and ethnic groups are of sufficient size and regional concentration to have put their impress on particular areas. Part of that imprint results from what the geographer Wilbur Zelinsky termed the "doctrine of **first effective settlement.**" That principle holds that

> Whenever an empty territory undergoes settlement, or an earlier population is dislodged by invaders, the specific characteristics of the first group able to effect a viable, self-perpetuating society are of crucial significance for the later social and cultural geography of the area, no matter how tiny the initial band of settlers may have been.[3]

On the North American stage, the English and their affiliates, although few in number, were the first effective entrants in the eastern United States and shared with the French that role in eastern Canada. Although the French were ousted from parts of Seaboard Canada, they retained their cultural and territorial dominance in Quebec Province, where today their political power and ethnocentricity foster among some the determination to achieve separate nationhood. In the United States, British immigrants (English, Welsh, Scottish, and Scotch-Irish) constituted the main portion of the new settlers in eastern Colonial America and retained their significance in the immigrant stream until after 1870.

---

[3]*The Cultural Geography of the United States.* Rev. ed. (Englewood Cliffs, N.J.: Prentice-Hall, 1992), p. 13.

The Rising Tide of Nationalism

The end of the 20th and start of the 21st centuries are witness to spreading ethnic self-assertion and demands for national independence and cultural purification of homeland territories. To some, these demands and the conflicts they frequently engender are the expected consequences of the decline of strong central governments and imperial controls. It has happened before. The collapse of the Roman and the Holy Roman Empires were followed by the emergence of the nation-states of medieval and Renaissance Europe. The fall of Germany and the Austro-Hungarian Empire after World War I saw the creation of new ethnically based countries in Eastern Europe. The brief decline of post-czarist Russia permitted freedom for Finland, and for 20 years for Estonia, Latvia, and Lithuania. The disintegration of British, French, and Dutch colonial control after World War II resulted in new state formation in Africa, South and East Asia, and Oceania.

Few empires have collapsed as rapidly and completely as did that of the Soviet Union and its Eastern European satellites in the late 1980s and early 1990s. In the subsequent loss of strong central authority, the ethnic nationalisms that communist governments had for so long tried to suppress asserted themselves in independence movements. At one scale, the Commonwealth of Independent States and the republics of Estonia, Latvia, Lithuania, and Georgia emerged from the former Soviet Union. At a lesser territorial scale, ethnic animosities and assertions led to bloodshed in the Caucasian republics of the former USSR, in former Yugoslavia (see Figure 6.6a), in Moldova, and elsewhere, while Czechs and Slovaks agreed to peacefully go their separate ways at the start of 1993.

Democracies, too, at least before legal protections for minorities are firmly in place, risk disintegration or division along ethnic, tribal, or religious lines. African states with their multiple ethnic loyalties (see Figure 12.5) have frequently used those divisions to justify restricting political freedoms and continuing one-party rule. However, past and present ethnically inspired civil wars and regional revolts in Somalia, Ethiopia, Nigeria, Uganda, Liberia, Angola, Rwanda, Burundi, and elsewhere show the fragility of the political structure on that continent.

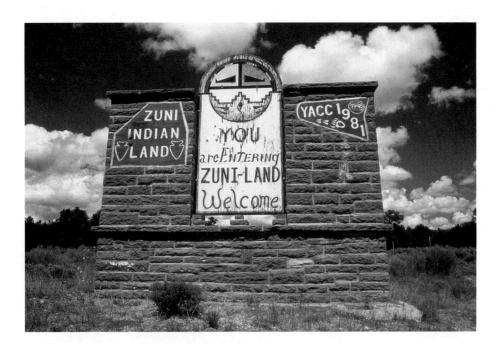

Figure 6.7 Although all of North America was once theirs alone, Native Americans have become now part of a larger cultural mix. In the United States, their areas of domination have been reduced to reservations found largely in the western half of the country and to the ethnic provinces shown in Figure 6.11. These are often areas to which Amerindian groups were relocated, not necessarily the territories occupied by their ancestors at the time of European colonization.

Amerindians were never a single ethnic or cultural group and cannot be compared to a European national immigrant group in homogeneity. Arriving over many thousands of years, from many different origin points, with different languages, physical characteristics, customs, and skills, they are in no way comparable to a culturally uniform Irish or Slovak ethnic group arriving during the 19th century or Salvadorans or Koreans during the 20th. Unlike most other minorities in the American amalgam, Amerindians have generally rejected the goal of full and complete assimilation into the national mainstream culture.

The reported Native American population increased sharply between 1960 and 2000, in part due to high fertility rates but also, importantly, to changing census racial classifications. Perhaps because of expanded ethnic awareness and pride, many more citizens now claim a Native American identity; in the 2000 census, about 2 million persons opted for the single Native American category, and another 2 million checked that and something else.

The English, particularly, became the **charter group,** the dominant first arrivals establishing the cultural norms and standards against which other immigrant groups were measured. It is understandable, then, in the light of Zelinsky's "doctrine," that English became the national language; English common law became the foundation of the American legal system; British philosophers influenced the considerations and debates leading to the American Constitution; English place names predominate in much of the country; and the influence of English literature and music remains strong. By their early arrival and initial dominance, the British established the majority culture of the Anglo American realm; their enduring ethnic impact is felt even today.

Somewhat comparable to the British domination in the East is the Hispanic influence in the Southwest. Spanish and Mexican explorers established settlements in New Mexico a generation before the Pilgrims arrived at Plymouth Rock. Spanish-speaking El Paso and Santa Fe were prospering before Jamestown, Virginia, was founded in 1607. Although subsequently incorporated into an expanding "Anglo"-controlled cultural realm and dominated by it, the early established Hispanic culture, reinforced by continuing immigration, has proved enduringly effective. From Texas to California, Spanish-derived social, economic, legal, and cultural institutions and traditions remain an integral part of contemporary life—from language, art, folklore, and names on the land through Spanish water law to land ownership patterns reflecting Spanish tenure systems.

Ethnic Clusters

Because the British already occupied much of the agricultural land of the East, other, later immigrant streams from Europe were forced to "leapfrog" those areas and seek settlement opportunities in still-available productive lands of the interior and western United States and Canada. The Scandinavians of the North Central states, the Germans in the Appalachian uplands, the upper Middle West, and Texas, various Slavic groups farther west on the Plains, and Italians and Armenians in California are examples of later arrivals occupying, ethnically influencing, and becoming identified with different sections of the United States even as they remained part of a larger cultural realm dominated by British roots. Such areas of ethnic concentration are known as **ethnic islands,** the dispersed and rural counterparts of urban ethnic neighborhoods (Figure 6.8).

Characterized usually by a strong sense of community, ethnic islands frequently placed their distinctive imprint on the rural

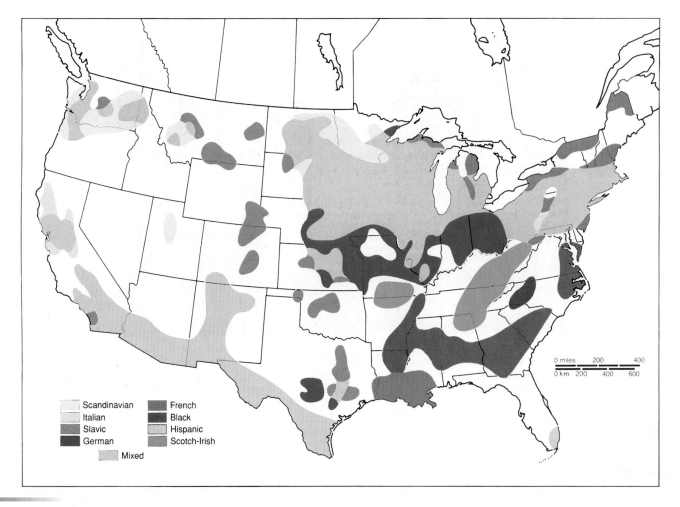

Figure 6.8 **Ethnic islands in the United States.**

Source: Redrawn with permission from Russel Gerlach, Settlement Patterns in Missouri *(Columbia: University of Missouri Press, 1986), p. 41.*

landscape by retaining home-country barn and house styles and farmstead layouts, while their inhabitants may have retained their own language, manner of dress, and customs. With the passing of the generations, rural ethnic identity has tended to diminish, and 20th-century adaptations and dispersions have occurred. When long-enduring through spatial isolation or group determination, ethnic islands have tended to be considered landscape expressions of folk culture rather than purely ethnic culture; we shall return to them in that context in Chapter 7.

Similar concentrations of immigrant arrivals are found in Canada. Descendants of French and British immigrants dominate its ethnic structure, both occupying primary areas too large to be considered ethnic islands. British origins are most common in all the provinces except Quebec, where 75% of the population is of French descent and over 80% of French Canadians make their home. French descendants are the second-largest ethnic group in Atlantic Canada and Ontario but fall to fifth or sixth position among minorities in the western provinces. Chinese have concentrated in British Columbia, Italians in Ontario and Quebec, and Ukrainians are the third-largest minority in the Prairie Provinces.

The ethnic diversity of that central portion of Canada is suggested by Figure 6.9.

European immigrants arriving in Anglo America by the middle of the 19th century frequently took up tracts of rural land as groups rather than as individuals, assuring the creation of at least small ethnic islands. German and Ukrainian Mennonites in Manitoba and Saskatchewan, for example; Doukhobors in Saskatchewan; Mennonites in Alberta; Hutterites in South Dakota, Manitoba, Saskatchewan, and Alberta; the Pennsylvania Dutch (whose name is a corruption of *Deutsch*, or "German," their true nationality); Frisians in Illinois; and other ethnic groups settled as collectives. They sometimes acted on the advice and the land descriptions reported by advance agents sent out by the group. In most cases, sizable extents of rural territory received the imprint of a group of immigrants acting in concert.

Such **cluster migration** was not unique to foreign colonies. In a similar fashion, a culturally distinctive American group, the Latter-day Saints (Mormons), placed their enduring mark as the first and dominant settlers on a large portion of the West, focusing on Utah and adjacent areas (Figure 6.10). In general, however,

Figure 6.9 **Ethnic diversity in the Prairie Provinces of Canada.** In 1991, 69% of all Canadians claimed some French or British ancestry. For the Prairie Provinces, with their much greater ethnic mixture, only 15% declared any British or French descent. Immigrants comprise a larger share of Canadian population than they do of the U.S. population. Early in the 20th century most newcomers located in rural western Canada and by 1921 about half the population of the Prairie Provinces was foreign born. Later immigrants concentrated in the major metropolitan centers. In 2001, some 40% of Toronto's population was foreign born and 35% of Vancouver's. In the period 1981 to 1991, 48% of Canada's immigrants were from Asia and only 25% from Europe, the traditionally dominant source region. From 1991 to 2001, the disparity increased: to 58% and 20%.

Source: D.G.G. Kerr, A Historical Atlas of Canada, 2nd edition, 1966. Thomas Nelson & Sons Ltd., 1966.

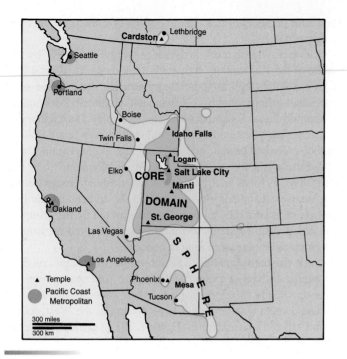

Figure 6.10 **The Mormon culture region** as defined by D. W. Meinig. To express the observed spatial gradations in Mormon cultural dominance and to approximate its sequential spread, Professor Meinig defined the Salt Lake City *core* region of Mormon culture as "a centralized zone of concentration . . . and homogeneity." The broader concept of *domain* identifies "areas in which the . . . culture is dominant" but less intensive than in the core. The *sphere* of any culture, Meinig suggests, is the zone of outer influence, where only parts of the culture are represented or where the culture's adherents are a minority of the total population.

Source: Redrawn with permission from Annals of the Association of American Geographers, *D. W. Meinig, Vol. 55, p. 214, Association of American Geographers, 1965.*

later in the century and in the less arable sections of the western United States, the disappearance of land available for homesteading and the changing nature of immigrant flows reduced the incidence of cluster settlement. Impoverished individuals rather than financially solid communities sought American refuge and found it in urban locations and employment.

While cluster migration created some ethnic concentrations of Anglo America—in the Carolinas, Wisconsin, Kansas, Nebraska, and Oklahoma, for example—others evolved from the cumulative effect of **chain migration**—the assemblage in one area of the relatives, friends, or unconnected compatriots of the first arrivals, attracted both by favorable reports and by familiar presences in specific locales of the New World (see also p. 78). Although such chain migration might not affect sizable districts, it could and did place a distinctive imprint on restricted rural ethnic islands and, particularly, urban areas. "Chinatown," "Little Sicily," and other urban enclaves, the concentration of Arab Americans in Dearborn, Michigan, and the Italian and Armenian farm communities of California's Central Valley, are examples of chain migrations and congregate settlement.

Black Dispersions

Some entire regions of North America—vastly larger than the distinctive ethnic islands—have become associated with larger ethnic

or racial aggregations numbering in the thousands or millions. Such **ethnic provinces** include French Canadians in Quebec; African Americans in the United States Southeast; Native Americans in Oklahoma, the Southwest, the Northern Plains, and Prairie Provinces; and Hispanics in the southern border states of the United States West (Figure 6.11). The identification of distinctive communities with extensive regional units persists, even though ethnicity and race have not been fully reliable bases for regionalization in North America. Cultural, ethnic, and racial mixing has been too complete to permit United States counterparts of Old World ethnic homelands to develop, even in the instance of the now-inappropriate association of African Americans with southern states.

African Americans, involuntary immigrants to the continent, were nearly exclusively confined to rural areas of the South and Southeast prior to the Civil War (Figure 6.12). Even after emancipation, most remained on the land in the South. During the first two-thirds of the 20th century, however, those established patterns of southern rural residence and farm employment

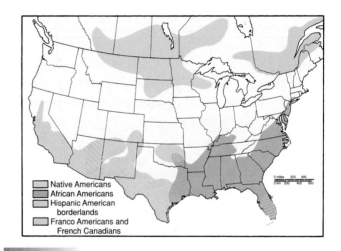

Figure 6.11 **Four North American ethnic groups and their provinces.** Note how this generalized map differs from the more detailed picture of ethnic distributions shown in Figure 6.8.

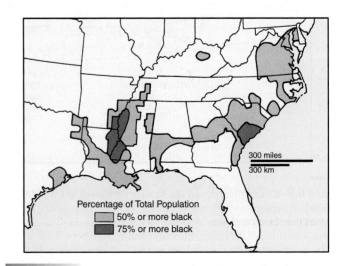

Figure 6.12 **African American concentrations, 1850.**

underwent profound changes. The decline of subsistence farming and share-cropping, the mechanization of southern agriculture, the demand for factory labor in northern cities starting with World War I (1914–1918), and the general urbanization of the American economy all induced black Americans to abandon the South in a "great migration" northward in search of manufacturing jobs and greater social equality.

Between 1940 and 1970, more than 5 million black Americans left their traditional southeastern concentration—the largest internal ethnic migration ever experienced in America. A modest return migration of, particularly, middle-class African Americans that began in the 1970s picked up speed during the 1980s and gave evidence of being a reverse "great migration" in the 1990s and early 21st century. That return movement, encouraged by an improving economic and racial environment in the South and by African Americans' enduring strong cultural and family ties, suggests a net inflow to the South of some 3 million African Americans between 1975 and 2010—more than half of the post-1940 out-migration.

The growing African American population (over 13% of all Americans in 2006) has become more urbanized than the general population; 86% were residents of metropolitan areas in 1999, compared with 75% for all Americans combined. Recent national economic trends, including industrial growth in the Sunbelt, have encouraged a reverse migration. Almost half of African Americans in 2004 resided within the former Confederacy states of the South (Figure 6.13). Prominent in that reverse flow are black professionals leaving such Northern strongholds as Baltimore and Philadelphia and settling in mostly black suburbs of Atlanta, Birmingham, Charlotte, and other Sunbelt metropolitan areas.

Black Americans, like Asian Americans and Hispanics, have had thrust on them an assumed common ethnicity that does not, in fact, exist. Because of prominent physical or linguistic characteristics, quite dissimilar ethnic groups have been categorized by the white, English-speaking majority in ways totally at odds with the realities of their separate national origins or cultural inheritances. Although the U.S. Census Bureau makes some attempt to subdivide Asian ethnic groups—Chinese, Filipino, and Korean, for example—these are distinctions not necessarily recognized by members of the white majority. But even the Census Bureau, in its summary statistics, has treated "Black" and "Hispanic Origin" as catchall classifications that suggest ethnic uniformities where none necessarily exist.

In the case of African Americans, such clustering is of decreasing relevance for two reasons. First,

(a)

(b)

Figure 6.13 **Evidences of African American Concentration, 2000.** (a) The top map shows the states where African Americans are most important to the total population of individual states. African Americans are particularly significant in the largely rural, relatively low-population states of the Southeast in a pattern reminiscent of their distribution in 1850 (Figure 6.12). (b) The bottom map shows the states that are most important to the total population of African Americans. This map shows the results of African Americans migrating in response to employment opportunities in the Northeast, Midwest, California, and the major urban centers of the Southeast. The South remained home to almost 55% of African Americans in 2000, reflecting both tradition and a pronounced return migration in the later 20th century.

immigration has made the black population increasingly heterogeneous. Between 1970 and 2000, the share of foreign-born in the black community rose from 1.3% to 7.8%. The immigrants originated in many countries of the Caribbean and Africa, with the largest percentages coming from Haiti (18%), Jamaica (15%), the Dominican Republic (7%), and Trinidad and Tobago (4%); Nigeria was a leading African immigrant origin. Census estimates are that by 2010 as many as 10% of black Americans will be recent immigrants from various regions of Africa or the Caribbean. Second, the earlier overwhelmingly rural Southern black community has become subdivided along socioeconomic rather than primarily regional lines, the result of its 20th-century spatial mobility encouraged by Northern industrial job opportunities first apparent during World War I and continuing through the 1960s. Government intervention, mandating and promoting racial equality, further deracialized the economic sector and opened the way for the creation of black urban middle and upper income and professional groups. No common native culture united the slaves brought to America; few of their transported traits or traditions could endure their generations of servitude. Now, by long residence and separate experiences, African Americans have become as differentiated as comparably placed ethnics of any other heritage.

Hispanic Concentrations

Similarly, the members of the multiracial, multinational, and multicultural composite population lumped by the Census Bureau into the single category of "Hispanic or Latino" are not a homogeneous group either. Indeed, it was the Census Bureau, not ethnicity or culture, that created the concept and distinct statistical and social category of "Hispanics." Prior to 1980 no such composite group existed; since then it has been statistically isolated from other ethnic or racial groupings with which its arbitrarily assigned members might otherwise identify. Although the Census assures that Hispanics "can be members of any race," it removes them officially from any other association. For example, although in 2000, 4 million California Hispanics—40% of their total number—specifically marked "white" as their race on the Census form, denying them that identity changed whites, statistically at least, from a 59.5% majority to a minority of the state's residents.

Hispanic Americans represent as much diversity within the assumed uniform group as they do between that group and the rest of the population. By commonly used racial categories, they may also be white, black, or Native American; nearly 60% of Hispanic Americans, in fact, report themselves to be white. Individually, they are highly diversified by country and culture of origin. Collectively, they also constitute the most rapidly growing minority component of U.S. residents—more than doubling in number between 1980 and 2000, accounting for 40% of the growth in the country's population during that period, and surpassing African Americans as the largest minority, as Table 6.5 indicates. Indeed, by 1990 Hispanics had already outnumbered blacks in four of the country's ten largest cities, and by 2000 they exceeded African Americans in seven of the top ten. By mid-2006 the Hispanic population had grown to 44.3 million—nearly 15% of U.S. population.

Mexican Americans account for about two-thirds of all Hispanic Americans (Table 6.6). About 8.8 million of them in 2000 had been born in Mexico, representing just under 30% of the total

Table 6.5

Actual and Projected United States Population Mix: 2000, 2025, and 2050

Population Group (One race options)	Percent of Total		
	2000	2025	2050
Non-Hispanic White	69.1	62.0	52.8
Hispanic or Latino	12.5	18.2	24.5
Black or African American	12.1	12.9	13.2
Asian/Pacific Islander	3.7	6.2	8.9
Native American	0.9	0.8	0.8

Note: Black, Asian, and Native American categories exclude Hispanics, who may be of any race.

Source: U.S. Bureau of the Census, Population Projection Program. Totals do not round to 100%.

Table 6.6

Composition of U.S. Hispanic Population, 2006

Hispanic Subgroup	Number (millions)	Percent
Mexican	28.3	64.0
Puerto Rican	3.7	8.6
Cuban	1.6	3.4
Dominican	1.2	2.8
Central American	3.5	7.6
South American	2.6	5.5
Other Hispanic origin[a]	3.0	7.7
Total Hispanic or Latino	**44.3**	**100**

[a]"Other Hispanics" includes those with origins in Spain or who identify themselves as "Hispanic," "Latino," "Spanish American," and so on.

Source: U.S. Bureau of the Census and Mumford Center, SUNY—Albany.

U.S. foreign-born population. Their highest concentrations are located in the southwestern states that constitute the ethnic province called the Hispanic American borderland (see Figure 6.11). Beginning in the 1940s, the Mexican populations in the United States became increasingly urbanized and dispersed, losing their earlier primary identification as agricultural *braceros* (seasonal laborers) and as residents of the rural areas of Texas, New Mexico, and Arizona. California rapidly increased its Mexican American populations (Figure 6.14), as did the Midwest, particularly the chain of industrial cities from southeastern Wisconsin through metropolitan Chicago to Detroit. Wherever they settled in the

Figure 6.14 A proudly assertive street mural in the Boyle Heights, Los Angeles, *barrio*. Half of Los Angeles' population in the early 21st century was Hispanic and overwhelmingly Mexican American. Their impact on the urban landscape—in choice of house colors, advertising signs, street vendors, and colorful wall paintings—is distinctive and pervasive.

each year, assuring strong Cuban presence in Florida, where 67% of Cuban Americans reside among a growing number of other, largely Central American immigrants, particularly in Miami's "Little Havana" community.

Early in the period of post-1959 Cuban influx, the federal government attempted a resettlement program to scatter the new arrivals around the United States. Some remnants of that program are still to be found in concentrations of Cubans in New York City, northern New Jersey, Chicago, and Los Angeles. The majority of early and late arrivals from Cuba, however, have settled in the Miami area. Nationally, 77% have located within metropolitan areas but outside of central cities.

Immigrants from the Dominican Republic, many of them undocumented and difficult to trace, appear to be concentrating in the New York City area. Within that same city, Central and South Americans have congregated in the borough of Queens, with the South American contingent, particularly Colombians, settling in the Jackson Heights section. Elsewhere, Central American Hispanics also tend to cluster. Los Angeles is estimated to hold some 35% of Central American immigrants; other concentrations include San Francisco, New York City, and Washington, D.C. Each concentration differs in its country of origin. Most Nicaraguans are found in the Miami area, most Hondurans in New Orleans. As noted, migrants from the Dominican Republic seek refuge in New York City; Salvadoran and Guatemalan migrants have dispersed themselves more widely, though they are particularly prominent in California.

Until recently, new arrivals tended to follow the paths of earlier arrivals from the home country. Chain migration and the security and support of an ethnically distinctive halfway community were as important for Hispanic immigrants as for their predecessors of earlier times and different cultures. Since the 2000 census recorded their established patterns of concentration, however, the share of Hispanics living in states and counties with large concentrations of Hispanics has been slipping. By 2004, Hispanics made up at least 5% of the population in 28 states, up from only 16 in 1990. The greater dispersion reflects many middle-class Hispanics following professional job opportunities throughout the country and moving to suburbs within and away from their former metropolitan concentrations. Many other dispersers are poorer, less-educated immigrants seeking jobs everywhere in construction, service industries, and retailing.

As the residential concentrations of the different Central American subgroups suggest, Hispanics as a whole are more urbanized than are non-Hispanic populations of the United States. In 2000, over 91% of Hispanic households were in metropolitan areas—nearly one-half in central cities—compared with 78% for non-Hispanic whites and 86% for blacks. Particularly the urbanized Hispanic population, it has been observed, appears confronted by two dominating but opposite trends. One is a drive toward conventional assimilation within American society. The other is consignment to a pattern of poverty, isolation, and, perhaps, cultural alienation from mainstream American life. Because of their numbers, which trend Hispanics follow will have significant consequences for American society as a whole.

To some observers, the very large and growing Mexican community poses a particular problem. Among other, earlier immigrant

United States, Mexican immigrants in 2000 represented a loss to their home country of 12% of its total labor force and 30% of its holders of doctorate degrees.

Mexican Americans, representing a distinctive set of cultural characteristics, have been dispersing widely across the United States, though increases in the South and Midwest have been particularly noticeable. In similar fashion, immigrants from equally distinctive South, Central, and Caribbean American countries have been spreading out from their respective initial geographic concentrations. Puerto Ricans, already citizens, first localized in New York City, now the largest Puerto Rican city anywhere in numerical terms. Since 1940, however, when 88% of mainland Puerto Ricans were New Yorkers, there has been an outward dispersal primarily to other major metropolitan areas of the northeastern part of the country. The old industrial cities of New Jersey (Jersey City, Newark, Paterson, Passaic, and Hoboken); Philadelphia, Pennsylvania; Bridgeport and Stamford, Connecticut; the Massachusetts cities of Lowell, Lawrence, and Brockton; and Chicago and other central cities and industrial satellites of the Midwest have received the outflow. Some 57% of Puerto Ricans reside in central cities, but in 2000, New York City retained only about one-quarter of the mainland Puerto Ricans.

Miami and Dade County, Florida, play the same magnet role for Cubans as New York City earlier did for Puerto Ricans. The first large-scale movement of Cuban refugees from the Castro revolution occurred between 1959 and 1962. There followed a mixed period lasting until 1980 when emigration was alternately permitted and prohibited by the Cuban government. Suddenly and unexpectedly, in April, 1980, a torrent of Cuban migration was released through the small port of Mariel. Although their flow was stopped after only 5 months, some 125,000 *Marielitos* fled from Cuba to the United States. A 1994 accord between the United States and Cuba allows for a steady migration of at least 20,000 Cubans groups, they point out, fluency or even knowledge of the ancestral language was effectively lost by the third generation. Yet large majorities of second-generation Mexicans appear to emphasize the need for their children to be fluent in Spanish and to maintain close and continuing identification with Mexican culture in general. Because language, culture, and identity are intertwined, the fear has been that past and continuing Mexican immigration will turn America into a bilingual, bi-cultural, and therefore divided, country. Countering those fears, a SUNY-Albany study revealed that English not only is the language of choice among the majority of the children and grandchildren of Hispanic immigrants, but is increasing its appeal to them as they steadily move toward English monolingualism. In 1990, 65% of third- and later-generation Mexican-American children spoke only English at home; by 2000 that figure had risen to 71%, and 72% of third-generation or later Hispanic children spoke English exclusively.

Asian Contrasts

Since the Immigration Act of 1965 and its abolition of earlier exclusionary immigration limits, the Asian American population has grown from 1.5 million to nearly 15 million (including mixed race options) in 2006; it is projected to grow to 25 million by 2020. Once largely U.S.-born and predominantly of Japanese and Chinese heritage, the Asian American population is now largely foreign-born and, through multiple national origins, is increasingly heterogeneous. Major sending home countries include Korea, the Philippines, Vietnam, India, Thailand, and Pakistan, in addition to continuing arrivals from China. Though second to Hispanics in numbers of new arrivals, Asians still comprised nearly one-third of the legal immigrant flow to the United States between 1990 and 2000.

Their inflow was encouraged, first, by changes in immigration law that dropped the older national origins quotas and favored family reunification as an admission criterion. Educated Asians, taking advantage of professional preference categories in the immigration laws to move to the United States (or remain here on adjusted student visas), could become citizens after 5 years and send for immediate family and other relatives without restriction. They, in turn, after 5 years, could bring in other relatives. Chain migration was an important agency. As a special case, the large number of Filipino Americans is related to U.S. control of the Philippines between 1899 and 1946. In the early part of the last century, Filipino workers were brought to Hawaii to work on sugar plantations, to California to labor on farms, or to Alaska to work in fish canneries. During World War II, Filipinos who served under the U.S. military were granted citizenship; immigration continues to be common today, especially for Filipino professionals.

Second, the flood of Southeast Asian refugees admitted during 1975–1980 under the Refugee Resettlement Program after the Vietnam War swelled the Asian numbers in the United States by over 400,000, with 2.4 million more Asian immigrants admitted between 1980 and 1990. At the start of the 21st century, nearly 28% of the U.S. foreign-born population were from Asia. Canada shows a similar increase in the immigrant flow from that continent. Although the annual share of immigrants coming from Asia to Canada never exceeded 5% during the 1950s, between 1991 and 2001, 58% of new arrivals were of Asian birth.

Table 6.7

U.S. Leading Asian Populations by Ethnicity,[a] 2000

Ethnicity	Number (000)	Percent of Asian American Total
Chinese	2734.8	23.0
Filipino	2364.8	19.9
Asian Indian	1899.6	16.0
Korean	1228.4	10.3
Vietnamese	1223.7	10.3
Japanese	1148.9	9.6
Cambodian	206.1	1.7
Pakistani	204.3	1.7
Laotian	198.2	1.6
Hmong	186.3	1.6
Thai	150.3	1.3
Taiwanese	144.8	1.2
Other Asian	208.6	1.8
Total	**11,898.8**	**100**

[a]Ethnicity as reported by respondents, including claimed combination ethnicities.
Source: U.S. Bureau of the Census.

Asia is a vast continent; successive periods of immigration have seen arrivals from many different parts of it, representing totally different ethnic groups and cultures. The major Asian American populations are detailed in Table 6.7, but even these groups are not homogeneous and cannot suggest the great diversity of other ethnic groups—Bangladeshi, Burmese, Nepalese, Sri Lankan, Mien, Indonesians of great variety, and many more—who have joined the American realm. Although settled in all sections of the country and, like Hispanic Americans, differently localized by ethnic group, Asian Americans as a whole are relatively concentrated in residence— far more so than the rest of the population. With the exception of Japanese Americans, most Asian Americans speak their native languages at home and maintain their distinctive ethnic cultures, values, and customs, suggesting either difficulties in fully assimilating into the American mainstream or purposefully resisting assimilation.

In 2000, about half of them resided in the West (and over 35% in California alone), where only 22% of all Americans lived; 36% of the whole population lived in the South, but only 19% of Asian Americans were found there. Japanese and Filipinos are particularly concentrated in the western states, where more than half of the Chinese Americans are also found. Only some 20% of all Asian Americans lived in the Northeast, but about one-third of the country's Asian Indians were localized there. Certain groups clearly indicate the tendency of Asian Americans to cluster: almost one-half of Filipinos are found in California, for example, as are 40% of the country's Vietnamese.

At a different scale, 18% of America's Koreans and 16% of its Filipinos found residence in the Los Angeles–Long Beach metropolitan area alone, and the largest Vietnamese community outside of Vietnam itself is in Orange County, south of Los Angeles. In whatever part of the country they settled, Asian Americans (and Pacific Islanders) were drawn to metropolitan areas, where 96% of them lived at the start of the century—more than half in suburban districts. Although their metropolitan affinities have remained constant, the trend over time has been for greater dispersal around the country. In 1990, the eight metropolitan areas with the largest concentrations had 47% of the Asian American population; by 2000, they held only 41%.

Immigrant Gateways and Clusters

Although new immigrants may ultimately seek residence in all parts of the United States, over the short term, immigrant concentrations rather than dispersals are the rule. Initially, most immigrants tend to settle near their points of entry (that is, nearest their country of origin) or in established immigrant communities. Family ties and job availability may replace or reinforce those primary draws. Five states—California, Texas, New York, Illinois, and New Jersey have experienced the largest increases in their foreign-born populations. Together, they housed (2000) almost 70% of America's total immigrant numbers, but only 36% of its native-born residents. Their attraction of newcomers, however, decreased over the last years of the 20th century; while they sustained 87% of the country's foreign-born gains in the 1980s, their share decreased to 60% of newcomer increases in the 1990s.

Certain metropolitan areas similarly experienced disproportionate immigrant gains during the 1990s. New York and Los Angeles received the most foreign-born, followed by San Francisco, Chicago, Miami, Dallas, Houston, and Washington. As a group, these eight metropolitan areas accounted for half of the country's foreign-born growth in the last decade of the 20th century and housed 57% of America's foreign-born population. In Canada, immigrants[5] are also concentrated in gateway cities. Of the immigrants arriving between 2001 and 2006, 40% settled in the Toronto metropolitan area. These magnet cities contain established immigrant networks that offer social and economic support to new arrivals drawn to them by chain migration flows. Those attractions are not permanent and census evidence suggests that immigrant diffusion is occurring in areas where the native-born labor supply does not satisfy market needs for both low-skilled and technically trained workers and as the socioeconomic condition of immigrants improves and their residential choices are less influenced by ethnic community considerations.

French Uniformity

The stamp of the French charter group on the ethnic province of French Canada is overwhelming. Quebec Province—with ethnic extensions into New Brunswick and northernmost Maine—is the only extensive region of North America (except northern Canadian Native American homelands) where regional delimitation on purely ethnic lines is possible or appropriate. In language, religion, legal principles, system of land tenure, the arts, cuisine, philosophies of

(a)

(b)

Figure 6.15 (*a*) The hotel Château Frontenac stands high above the lower older portion of Quebec City, where many streets show the architecture of French cities of the 18th century carried over to the urban heart of modern French Canada. (*b*) Rural Richelieu Valley in the Eastern Townships of Quebec Province.

life, and landscapes of rural and urban occupance, Quebec stands apart from the rest of Canada (Figure 6.15). Its distinctiveness and self-assertion have won it special consideration and treatment within the political structure of the country.

Although the *Canadiens* of Quebec were the charter group of eastern Canada and for some 200 years the controlling population, they numbered only some 65,000 when the Treaty of Paris ended the North American wars between the British and the French in 1763. That treaty, however, gave them control over three primary aspects of their culture and lives: language, religion, and land tenure. From these, they created their own distinctive and enduring ethnic province of some 1.5 million square kilometers (600,000 sq mi) and 7.4 million people, more than 80% of whom have French as their native tongue (see Figure 5.16) and are at least nominally Roman Catholic. Quebec City is the cultural heart of French Canada, though the bilingual Montreal metropolitan area with a population of 3.5 million is the largest center of Quebec Province. The sense of cultural identity prevalent throughout French Canada imparted a spirit of nationalism not similarly expressed in other ethnic provinces of North America. Laws and guarantees recognizing and strengthening the position of French language and culture within the province assure the preservation of this distinctive North American cultural region, even if the movement for full political separation from the rest of Canada is not successful.

Urban Ethnic Diversity and Segregation

"Little Havanas" and "Little Koreas" have joined the "Chinatowns," "Little Italys," and "Germantowns" of earlier eras as part of the American urban scene. The traditional practice of selective concentration of ethnics in their own frequently well-defined subcommunities is evidence of a much more inclusive, sharply defined social geography of urban America, in which ethnic neighborhoods have been a pronounced, enduring feature.

Protestant Anglo Americans created, from colonial times, the dominating host culture—the charter group—of urban North America. To that culture the mass migrations of the 19th and early 20th centuries brought individuals and groups representative of different religious and ethnic backgrounds, including Irish Catholics, eastern European Jews, and members of every nationality, ethnic stock, and distinctive culture of central, eastern, and southern Europe. To them were added, both simultaneously and subsequently, newcomers from Asia and Latin America and such urbanizing rural Americans as Appalachian whites and Southern blacks.

Each newcomer element sought both accommodation within the urban matrix established by the charter group and acceptable relationships with other in-migrant ethnic groups. That accommodation has characteristically been achieved by the establishment of ethnic communities or neighborhoods. These are areas within the city where a particular culture group aggregates, which it dominates, and which may serve as the core location from which diffusion or absorption into the host society can occur. The rapidly urbanizing, industrializing society of 19th-century America became a mosaic of such ethnic enclaves. Their maintenance as distinctive social and spatial entities depended on the degree to which the assimilation of their population occurred. Figure 6.16 shows the more recent ethnic concentrations that developed by the start of the 21st century in one major American city. The increasing subdivision of the immigrant stream and the consequent reduction in the size of identified enclaves make comparable maps of older U.S. cities such as New York and Chicago nearly unintelligibly complex.

Immigrant neighborhoods are a measure of the **social distance** that separates the minority from the charter group. The greater the perceived differences between the two groups, the greater the social distance and the less likely is the charter group to easily accept or assimilate the newcomer. Consequently, the ethnic community will endure longer as a place both of immigrant refuge and of enforced segregation.

Segregation is a shorthand expression for the extent to which members of an ethnic group are not uniformly distributed in relation to the rest of the population. A commonly employed measure quantifying the degree to which a distinctive group is segregated

is the segregation index or *index of residential dissimilarity*. It indicates the percentage difference between the distribution of two component groups of a population, with a theoretical range of values from 0 (no segregation) to 100 (complete segregation). For example, according to the 2000 Census, the index of dissimilarity in the New York City metropolitan area was a very high 81.8, meaning that nearly 82% of all blacks (or whites) would have to move to different census tracts before the two groups are equally distributed across the set of tracts. Evidence from cities throughout the world makes clear that most ethnic minorities tend to be sharply segregated from the charter group and that segregation on racial or ethnic lines is usually greater than would be anticipated from the socioeconomic levels of the groups involved. Further, the degree of segregation varies among cities in the same country and among different ethnic mixes within each city.

Among major U.S. metropolitan areas in 2000, for example, Chicago, Illinois, had a black–white segregation index of 81, while for Raleigh-Durham, North Carolina, it was 46. Within the Detroit metropolitan area, on the other hand, the black–white index of residential dissimilarity was 85, but the Hispanic–white and Asian–white indexes were much lower, each at 46. In the country as a whole in 2000, the typical white neighborhood was nearly 83% white, and the typical African American lived in a neighborhood that was 54% black. On average, Hispanics resided in areas 42% Hispanic and Asians in communities that were only 19% Asian. Collectively, blacks, Hispanics, and Asians lived in more integrated neighborhoods than did whites. Overall, a Brookings Institution study found, although segregation remains high in America, it steadily declined between 1970 and 2000. Nearly all the highly segregated cities of the Midwest and Northeast became slightly more integrated over the 30-year period while the newer, more rapidly growing cities of the West and South have become essentially less segregated and have reduced their already low levels of segregation over time.

Each world region and each country, of course, has its own patterns of national and urban immigration and immigrant residential patterns. Even when those population movements involve distinctive and contrasting ethnic groups, American models of spatial differentiation may not be applicable.

Foreign migrants to West European cities, for example, frequently do not have the same expectations of permanent residence and eventual amalgamation into the host society as their American counterparts. Many came under labor contracts with no initial legal assurance of permanent residence. Although many now have been joined by their families, they often find citizenship difficult to acquire; in Germany, even German-born children of "guest workers" are considered aliens. Their residential choices are consequently influenced by difficulties or disinterest in integration or amalgamation, a high degree of migrant self-identity, restriction to housing units or districts specially provided for them, and the locational pull of chain migration. Culture and religion are important in that regard as even small ethnically homogeneous groups, confined perhaps to part of a city block or to a single apartment building, help to maintain the lifestyle and support systems of home territories.

The Islamic populations from North Africa and Turkey tend to be more tightly grouped and defensive against the surrounding

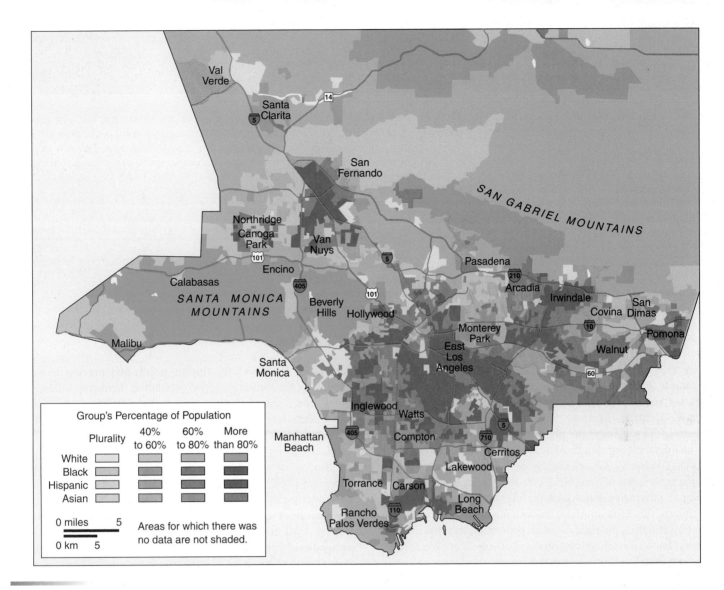

Figure 6.16 **Racial/ethnic patterns in Los Angeles County, 2000,** are greatly generalized on this map, which conceals much of the complex intermingling of different ethnic groups in several sections of Los Angeles city. However, the tendency of people to cluster in distinct neighborhoods by race and ethnicity is clearly evident.

Source: Adapted from The New York Times, *March 30, 2001, pg A18. Copyright © 2001 by The New York Times Co. Reprinted with permission.*

majority culture of western European cities than do African or south and east European Christian migrants. France, with some 5 million Muslim residents, most of them from North Africa, has tended to create bleak, distant outer city ghettoes in which Arab legal and illegal immigrants remain largely isolated from mainstream French life.

Racial and ethnic divisions appear particularly deep and divisive in Britain. A British government report of 2001 claimed that in Britain, whites and ethnic minorities lead separate lives with no social or cultural contact and no sense of belonging to the same nation. Residential segregation in public housing and inner-city areas was compounded by deep social polarization. The 7.1% (2001) of British population that was nonwhite—largely Caribbean and Asian in origin—and the white majority, the report concluded, "operate on the basis of a series of parallel lives . . .

that often do not seem to touch at any point," assigning blame for the situation on "communities choosing to live in separation rather than integration" (see "The Caribbean Map in London"). The Home Secretary observed on the basis of the report that many "towns and cities lack any sense of civic identity or shared values." A similar total minority segregation is evident in the Sydney, Australia, suburb of Redfern, which houses an Aboriginal population that rarely ventures out to work or mingle in the surrounding white city and that white Australians avoid and ignore.

Spatial segregation is growing in the developing countries as well. Rapid urbanization in multiethnic India has resulted in cities of extreme social and cultural contrasts. Increasingly, Indian cities feature defined residential colonies segregated by village and caste origins of the immigrants. Chain migration has eased the influx of newcomers to specific new and old city areas; language,

Although the movement [to England] from the West Indies has been treated as if it were homogeneous, the island identity, particularly among those from the small islands, has remained strong. . . . [I]t is very evident to anyone working in the field that the process of chain migration produced a clustering of particular island or even village groups in their British destination. . . .

The island identities have manifested themselves on the map of London. The island groups can still be picked out in the clusters of settlements in different parts of the city. There is an archipelago of Windward and Leeward islanders north of the Thames; Dominicans and St. Lucians have their core areas in Paddington and Notting Hill; Grenadians are found in the west in Hammersmith and Ealing; Montserratians are concentrated around Stoke Newington, Hackney and Finsburry Park; Antiguans spill over to the east in Hackney, Waltham Forest and Newham; south of the river is Jamaica.

That is not to say that Jamaicans are found only south of the river or that the only West Indians in Paddington are from St. Lucia. The mixture is much greater than that. The populations overlap and interdigitate: there are no sharp edges. . . . [Nevertheless, north of the river] there is a west-east change with clusters of Grenadians in the west giving way to St. Lucians and Dominicans in the inner west, through to Vincentians and Montserratians in the inner north and east and thence to Antiguans in the east.

Source: Ceri Peach, "The Force of West Indian Island Identity in Britain," in *Geography & Ethnic Pluralism*, eds. Colin Clarke, David Ley, and Ceri Peach. (London: George Allen & Unwin, 1984).

custom, religion, and tradition keep them confined. In Mumbai, for example, in Dharavi—considered the world's largest slum—Tamil, not Hindi, is spoken as the main language. Elsewhere, in Bangkok, Thailand, Burmese migrants are largely confined to the slum of Tlong Toey; the population of Hillbrow, a squatter slum in Johannesburg, South Africa, consists largely of Nigerian and French-speaking African immigrants; and the residents of the informal settlements of San José, Costa Rica, generally come from Nicaragua. International and domestic migration throughout ethnically diverse sub-Saharan Africa shows a repetitive pattern of residential segregation: the rural-to-urban population shift has created city neighborhoods defined on tribal and village lines. Worldwide in all continental and national urban contexts, the degree of immigrant segregation is at least in part conditioned by the degree of social distance felt between the newcomer population and the other immigrant and host societies among whom residential space is sought.

Constraints on assimilation and the extent of discrimination and segregation are greater for some minorities than for others. In general, the rate of assimilation of an ethnic minority by the host culture depends on two sets of controls: *external,* including attitudes toward the minority held by the charter group and other competing ethnic groups, and *internal* controls of group cohesiveness and defensiveness.

External Controls

When the majority culture or rival minorities perceive an ethnic group as threatening, the group tends to be spatially isolated by external "blocking" tactics designed to confine the rejected minority and to resist its "invasion" of already occupied urban neighborhoods. The more tightly knit the threatened group, the more adamant and overt are its resistance tactics. When confrontation measures (including, perhaps, threats and vandalism) fail, the invasion of charter-group territory by the rejected minority proceeds until a critical percentage of newcomer housing occupancy is reached. That level, the **tipping point,** may precipitate a rapid exodus by the former majority population. Invasion, followed by succession, then results in a new spatial pattern of ethnic dominance according to models of urban social geography developed for American cities and examined in Chapter 11, models less applicable to the European scene.

Racial or ethnic discrimination in urban areas generally expresses itself in the relegation of the most recent, most alien, most rejected minority to the poorest available housing. That confinement has historically been abetted by the concentration of the newest, least assimilated ethnic minorities at the low end of the occupational structure. Distasteful, menial, low-paying service and factory employment unattractive to the charter group is available to those new arrivals even when other occupational avenues may be closed. The dockworkers, street cleaners, slaughterhouse employees, and sweatshop garment workers of earlier America had and have their counterparts in other regions. In England, successive waves of West Indians and Commonwealth Asians took the posts of low-pay hotel and restaurant service workers, transit workers, refuse collectors, manual laborers, and the like; Turks in German cities and North Africans in France play similar low-status employment roles.

In the United States, there has been a spatial association between the location of such employment opportunities—the inner-city central business district (CBD) and its margins—and the location of the oldest, most dilapidated, and least desirable housing. Proximity to job opportunity and the availability of cheap housing near the CBD, therefore, combined to concentrate the U.S. immigrant slum near the heart of the 19th-century central city. In the second half of the 20th century, the suburbanization of jobs, the rising skill levels required in the automated offices of the CBD, and the effective isolation of inner-city residents by the absence of public transportation or their inability to pay for private transport maintained the association of the least competitive minorities and the least desirable housing area. But now those locations lack the promise of entry-level jobs formerly close at hand.

That U.S. spatial association does not necessarily extend to other cultures and urban environments. In Latin American cities, newest arrivals at the bottom of the economic and employment ladder are most apt to find housing in squatter or slum areas on the outskirts of the urban unit, prestigious housing claims room near the city center. European cities, too, have retained a larger proportion of upper income groups at the urban center than have their American counterparts, with a corresponding impact on the distribution of lower-status, lower-income housing. In French urban agglomerations, at least, the outer fringes frequently have a higher percentage of foreigners than the city itself.

Internal Controls

Although part of the American pattern of urban residential segregation may be explained by the external controls of host-culture resistance and discrimination, the clustering of specific groups into discrete, ethnically homogeneous neighborhoods is best understood as the result of internal controls of group defensiveness and conservatism. The self-elected segregation of ethnic groups can be seen to serve four principal functions—defense, support, preservation, and "attack."

First, it provides *defense,* reducing individual immigrant isolation and exposure by physical association within a limited area. The walled and gated Jewish quarters of medieval European cities have their present-day counterparts in the clearly marked and defined "turfs" of street gang members and the understood exclusive domains of the "black community," "Chinatown," and other ethnic or racial neighborhoods. In British cities, it has been observed that West Indians and Asians fill identical slots in the British economy and reside in the same sorts of areas, but they tend to avoid living in the *same* areas. West Indians avoid Asians; Sikhs isolate themselves from Muslims; Bengalis avoid Punjabis. In London, patterns of residential isolation even extend to West Indians of separate island homelands, as "The Caribbean Map in London" makes clear. Their own defined ethnic territory provides members of the group with security from the hostility of antagonistic social groups, a factor also underlying the white flight to "garrison" suburbs.

Second, the ethnic neighborhood provides *support* for its residents in a variety of ways. The area serves as a halfway station between the home country and the alien society, to which admittance will eventually be sought. It acts as a place of initiation and indoctrination, providing supportive lay and religious ethnic institutions, familiar businesses, job opportunities where language barriers are minimal, and friendship and kinship ties to ease the transition to a new society.

Third, the ethnic neighborhood may provide a *preservation* function, reflecting the ethnic group's positive intent to preserve and promote such essential elements of its cultural heritage as language and religion. The preservation function represents a disinclination to be totally absorbed into the charter society and a desire to maintain those customs and associations seen to be essential to the conservation of the group. For example, Jewish dietary laws are more easily observed by, or exposure to potential marriage partners within the faith is more certain in, close-knit communities than when individuals are scattered.

Finally, ethnic spatial concentration can serve what has been termed the *assertion* or *attack* function, a peaceful and legitimate search for, particularly, political representation by a concentration of electoral power. Voter registration drives among African and Hispanic Americans represent concerted efforts to achieve the promotion of group interests at all governmental levels.

Shifting Ethnic Concentrations

Ethnic communities once established are not necessarily, or even usually, permanent. For Europeans who came in the 19th and early 20th centuries and for more recent Hispanic and Asian immigrants, high concentrations were and are encountered in neighborhoods of first settlement (see "Colonies of Immigrants"). Second generation neighborhoods usually become far more mixed. The 2000 census reveals that older dominant urban ethnic groups in places called, for example, "Little Italy" rarely exceeded 50% as middle and upper-middle class members of the immigrant group move on. That mobility pattern appears to be repeating among Asian and Latino groups, but only or most clearly where those groups collectively account for a relatively small share of the total metropolitan area population. Black segregation and black communities, in contrast, appear more pronounced and permanent. Continuing racial or ethnic concentrations of 80% or 90% occur almost exclusively in African American neighborhoods where the dominant group remains isolated by segregation and white flight.

Ethnic congregations initially identified with particular central city areas are frequently or usually displaced by different newcomer groups (Figure 6.17). With recent diversified immigration, older homogeneous ethnic neighborhoods have become highly subdivided and polyethnic. In Los Angeles, for example, the great wave of immigrants from Mexico, Central America, and Asia has begun to push African Americans out of Watts and other well-established black communities, converting them from racially exclusive to multicultural areas. In New York, the Borough of Queens, once the stronghold of European ethnics, has now become home to more than 110 different, mainly non-European nationalities. In Woodside in Queens, Latin Americans and Koreans are prominent among the many replacements of the formerly dominant German and Irish groups. Elsewhere within the city, West Indians now dominate the old Jewish neighborhoods of Flatbush; Poles and Dominicans and other Central Americans have succeeded Germans and Jews in Washington Heights. Manhattan's Chinatown expands into old Little Italy, and a new Little Italy emerges in Bensonhurst.

Further, the new ethnic neighborhoods are intermixed in a way that enclaves of the early 20th century never were. The restaurants, bakeries, groceries, specialty shops, their customers and owners from a score of different countries and even different continents are now found within a two- or three-block radius. In the Kenmore Avenue area of East Los Angeles, for example, a half-square-mile (1.3 km^2) area of former Anglo neighborhood now houses over 9000 people representing Hispanics and Asians of widely varied origin along with Pacific Islanders, Amerindians, African Americans, and a scattering of native-born whites. Students in the neighborhood school come from 43 countries and speak 23 languages, a localized ethnic intermixture unknown in the communities of single ethnicity so characteristic of earlier stages

Figure 6.17 **Landscape evidence of shifting ethnic concentrations.** As Jews left North Minneapolis for the suburbs, they were succeeded by African Americans. This former Orthodox synagogue is one of the few reminders of the once vibrant Jewish presence. The building is now used by a non-denominational Protestant Christian congregation and the altered facade mixes carved lions guarding Hebrew scrolls, Stars of David, crosses and both Jewish and Christian messages.

 # Colonies of Immigrants

In the following extract from his 1904 book *Poverty,* Robert Hunter conveys a sense of the ethnic diversity found in American cities:

[In American cities] great colonies, foreign in language, customs, habits, and institutions, are separated from each other and from the distinctly American groups on national or racial lines. By crossing the Bowery one leaves behind him the great Jewish colony made up of Russians, Poles, and Roumanians and passes into Italy; to the northeast lies a little Germany; to the southwest a colony of Syrians; to the west lies an Irish community, a settlement of negroes, a remnant of the old native American stock; to the south lie a Chinese and a Greek colony. On Manhattan alone, either on the extreme west side or the extreme east side, there are other colonies of the Irish, the Jews, and the Italians, and, in addition, there is a large colony of Bohemians. In Chicago there are the same foreign poor. To my own knowledge there are four Italian colonies, two Polish, a Bohemian, an Irish, a Jewish, a German, a negro, a Chinese, a Greek, a Scandinavian, and other colonies. So it is also in Boston and many other cities. In New York alone there are more persons of German descent than persons of native descent, and the German element is larger than in any city of Germany except Berlin. There are nearly twice as many Irish as in Dublin, about as many Jews as in Warsaw, and more Italians than in Naples or Venice. . . .

To live in one of these foreign communities is actually to live on foreign soil. The thoughts, feelings, and traditions which belong to the mental life of the colony are often entirely alien to an American. The newspapers, the literature, the ideals, the passions, the things which agitate the community are unknown to us except in fragments. . . .

While there is a great movement of population from all parts of the old world to all parts of the new, the migration to the United States is the largest and the most conspicuous. Literally speaking, millions of foreigners have established colonies in the very hearts of our urban and industrial communities. . . . In recent years the flow of immigrants to the cities, where they are not needed, instead of to those parts of the country where they are needed, has been steadily increasing. Sixty-nine percent of the present immigration avows itself as determined to settle either in the great cities or in certain communities of the four great industrial states, Massachusetts, New York, Pennsylvania, and Illinois. According to their own statements, nearly 60 percent of the Russian and Polish Jews intend to settle in the largest cities. As a matter of fact, those who actually do settle in cities are even more numerous than this percentage indicates. As the class of immigrants, drawn from eastern and southern Europe, Russia, and Asia, come in increasing numbers to the United States, the tendency to settle in cities likewise increases.

Source: Robert Hunter, *Poverty.* (New York: Macmillan, 1904).

of immigration to the United States, as the excerpt "Colonies of Immigrants" suggests.

The changing ethnic spatial pattern is not yet clear or certain. Increasing ethnic diversity coupled with continuing immigration flow has, in some instances, expanded rather than reduced patterns of urban group segregation. The tendency for separate ethnic groups to cluster for security, economic, and social reasons cannot be effective if a great many relatively small numbers of different ethnic groups find themselves in a single city setting. Intermixture is inevitable when individual groups do not achieve the critical mass necessary to establish a true identifiable separate community. But as continuing immigration and natural increase allow groups to expand in size, they are able to create more distinctive self-selected ethnic clusters and communities. The 2000 census clearly shows the New York region, for example, to be more ethnically diverse and more segregated than was suspected during the 1990s, with multiple clearly recognizable enclaves and districts each with its own distinctive ethnic or racial composition and character. Immigration growth during the preceding decade yielded not only greater ethnic diversity but greater evident segregation as well.

Even when an ethnic community rejects or is denied assimilation into the larger society, it may both relocate and retain its coherence. "Satellite Chinatowns" are examples of migration from city centers outward to the suburbs or to outer boroughs—in Los Angeles' San Gabriel Valley, stretching in a 20-mile swath eastward from Alhambra and Monterey Park to West Covina and Diamond Bar; in San Francisco, from the downtown area along Grant Avenue to the Richmond district 3 miles away. In New York City, the satellite move was from the still-growing Canal Street area in lower Manhattan to Flushing, about 15 miles away (Figure 6.18) and to Elmhurst which, with immigrants from

114 different countries, is the city's most ethnically diverse neighborhood. Other growing, older ethnic communities—needing more space and containing newly affluent and successful members able to compete for better housing elsewhere—have followed a similar pattern of subdivision and relocation. One result has been termed the *ethnoburb,* a fully structured socioeconomic and political suburban community with a significant, though not necessarily exclusive, concentration of a single ethnic group. For some ethnics, assimilation in job and society does not reduce the need for community identity.

Typologies and Spatial Results

When both the charter group and the ethnic group perceive the social distance separating them to be small, the isolation caused by external discriminatory and internal cohesiveness controls is temporary, and ethnic residential clusters quickly give way to full assimilation. While they endure, the clusters may be termed **colonies,** serving essentially as points of entry for members of the particular ethnic group. They persist only to the extent that new arrivals perpetuate the need for them. In American cities, many European ethnic colonies began to lose their vitality and purpose with the reduction of European immigration flows after the 1920s.

When an ethnic cluster does persist because its occupants choose to preserve it, their behavior reflects the internal cohesiveness of the group and its desire to maintain an enduring **ethnic enclave** or neighborhood. When the cluster is perpetuated by external constraints and discriminatory actions, it has come to be termed a **ghetto.** The term ghetto was first used in Venice, Italy in the 16th century to refer to the area of the city where Jews were required to live. In reality, the colony, the enclave, and the ghetto are spatially similar. Figure 6.19 suggests the possible spatial expressions of these three recognized ethnic-cluster models.

Both discrimination and voluntarism determine the changing pattern of ethnic clustering within metropolitan areas. Where forced segregation limits residential choices, ethnic or racial minorities may be confined to the older, low-cost housing areas, typically close to the city center. Growing ethnic groups that maintain voluntary spatial association frequently expand the area of their dominance by growth outward from the core of the city in a radial pattern. That process has long been recognized in Chicago (Figure 6.20) and has, in that and other cities, typically been extended beyond the central city boundaries into at least the inner fringe of the suburbs.

African Americans have, traditionally, found strong resistance to their territorial expansion from the Anglo charter group, though white-black urban relations and patterns of black ghetto formation and expansion have differed in different sections of the country. A revealing typology of African American ghettos is outlined in Figure 6.21. In the South, the white majority, with total control of the housing market, was able to assign residential space to blacks in accordance with white, not black, self-interest. In the *early southern* ghetto of such pre-Civil War cities as Charleston and New Orleans, African Americans were assigned small dwellings in alleys

Figure 6.18 The Flushing, Queens, area of New York City contains one of the developing "satellite Chinatowns." Like those in other cities, it reflects both the pressures exerted by a growing Chinese community on their older urban enclaves and the suburbanization of an affluent younger generation that still seeks community coherence.

COLONY
▲ Initial clustering
• Subsequent dispersal

ENCLAVE
▨ Initial ethnic area
☐ Later ethnic areas and some dispersal (•) maintain contact with "core" of segregated area

GHETTO
▨ Initial
☐ Later expansion follows sector of least resistance

Figure 6.19 **Types of ethnic areas.** Unlike the truly suburban *ethnoburb*, the traditionally recognized ethnic concentrations shown here are all contained within the built-up area of the central city.

Source: David T. Herbert and Colin J. Thomas, Urban Geography, *London: David Fulton Publishers, 1987. Redrawn by permission.*

☐ Early American

Figure 6.20 **The outward expansion of racial and nationality groups in Chicago.** "Often," Samuel Kincheloe observed in the 1930s, "[minority] groups first settle in a deteriorated area of a city somewhere near its center, then push outward along the main streets." More recently, many—particularly young, innovative, and entrepreneurial—immigrants have avoided traditional first locations in central cities and from their arrival have settled in metropolitan area suburbs and outlying cities where economic opportunity and quality of life is perceived as superior to conditions in the primary inner city.

Source: The American City and its Church *by Samuel Kincheloe. Copyright 1938 by Friendship Press, New York.*

and back streets within and bounding the white communities where they worked as (slave) house and garden servants. The *classic southern* ghetto for newly free blacks was composed of specially built, low-quality housing on undesirable land—swampy, perhaps, or near industry or railroads—and was sufficiently far from better quality white housing to maintain full spatial and social segregation.

In the North, on the other hand, African Americans were open competitors with other claimants for space in a generalized housing market. The *early northern* ghetto represented a "toehold" location in high-density, aged, substandard housing on the margin of the central business district. The *classic northern* ghetto is a more recent expansion of that initial enclave to surround the CBD and to penetrate, through invasion and succession, contiguous zones as far as the numbers, rent-paying ability, and housing discrimination will allow. Finally, in new western and southwestern cities not tightly hemmed in by resistant white neighborhoods or suburbs, the black community may display a linear expansion from the CBD to the suburban fringe.

Native-Born Dispersals

Immigration flows to the United States during the last third of the 20th century—unlike those of earlier mass-immigration periods—have begun to affect both the broad regional ethnic makeup of the United States and the internal migration pattern of native-born Americans. The spatial consequence has been dubbed a "demographic balkanization," a pronounced and apparently reinforcing areal segmentation of population by race/ethnicity, economic status, and age across extended metropolitan areas and larger regions of the country.

Early 20th-century immigration streams resulted, as we have seen, in temporary ethnic segregation by urban neighborhoods

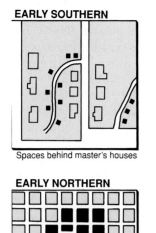

EARLY SOUTHERN

Spaces behind master's houses

CLASSIC SOUTHERN

"Other side of the tracks"

"New City"

CBD

Sector growth toward suburbia

EARLY NORTHERN

CBD

Foothold in inner city

CLASSIC NORTHERN

CBD

Compact inner city

Figure 6.21 **A typology of black ghettos in the United States.**

Source: David T. Herbert and Colin J. Thomas, Urban Geography, *London: David Fulton Publishers, 1987. Redrawn by permission.*

and between central cities and suburbs. Immigration legislation of 1965 dropped the national-origin quotas that had formerly favored European immigrants, replacing that with a more inclusive formula emphasizing family reunification. That change, plus economic and political pressures in many countries of Asia and Latin America, has swelled the influx of poorer, less-skilled Asians and Hispanics. Highly dependent on family members and friends for integration into the informal and formal American job market, the new arrivals are drawn to primary port-of-entry metropolitan areas by chain migration links. In those areas where immigrants account for most of the present and prospective population growth, the trend is toward increasingly multicultural, younger, and poorer residents and dominantly of Hispanic and Asian origins.

The high degree of areal concentration of recent immigrant groups initiated a selective native-born, particularly white, retreat, not only fleeing the cities for the suburbs but leaving entire metropolitan areas and states. California, with nearly one-quarter of its population foreign-born in the mid-1990s, saw a departure of one native-born white or black resident for nearly each foreign-born arrival. Individual urban areas echoed California's state experience. The New York, Chicago, Los Angeles, Houston, and Boston metropolitan areas—5 of the top 11 immigrant destinations—lost 9 native residents for every 10 immigrant arrivals. For whites, top destinations were to cities and states away from coastal and southern border immigrant entry points, from San Francisco to Houston in the West, Boston to Washington plus Miami in the East, and the Chicago district in the interior. African Americans, too, are leaving most of the high-immigration metropolitan areas, with Atlanta, Georgia, the preferred destination. A visible spatial consequence, then, of recent patterns of U.S. immigration and settlement is a decline of the older ideal and reality of immigrant assimilation and of racial and cultural urban mixtures. Instead, the emerging pattern is one of increasing wholesale segregation and isolation by metropolitan areas and segments of the country. Immigrant assimilation may now be more difficult than in the past and social and political divisions more pronounced and enduring.

Cultural Transfer

Immigrant groups arrive at their destinations with already existing sets of production techniques and skills. They bring established ideas of "appropriate" dress, foods, and building styles, and they have religious practices, marriage customs, and other cultural expressions in place and ingrained. That is, immigrants carry to their new homes a full complement of artifacts, sociofacts, and mentifacts. They may modify, abandon, or even pass these on to the host culture, depending on a number of interacting influences: (1) the background of the arriving group; (2) its social distance from the charter group; (3) the disparity between new home and origin-area environmental conditions; (4) the importance given by the migrants to the economic, political, or religious motivations that caused them to relocate; and (5) the kinds of encountered constraints that force personal, social, or technical adjustments on the new arrivals.

Immigrant groups rarely transferred intact all of their culture traits to North America. Invariably, there have been modifications as a result of the necessary adjustment to new circumstances or physical conditions. In general, if a transplanted ethnic trait was usable in the new locale, it was retained. Simple inertia suggested there was little reason to abandon the familiar and comfortable when no advantage accrued. If a trait or a cultural complex was essential to group identity and purpose—the religious convictions of the rural Amish, for example, or of urban Hasidic Jews—its retention was certain. But ill-suited habits or techniques would be abandoned if superior American practices were encountered, and totally inappropriate practices would be discarded. German settlers in Texas, for example, found that the vine and the familiar midlatitude fruits did not thrive there. Old-country agricultural traditions were, they discovered, not fully transferable and had to be altered.

Finally, even apparently essential cultural elements may be modified in the face of unalterable opposition from the majority population. Although American in origin, the Latter-day Saints (Mormons) were viewed as outsiders whose practice of polygamy was alien and repugnant. To secure political and social acceptance, church leaders denounced that facet of their religious belief. More recently, the some 30,000 Hmong and Mien tribespeople who settled in the Fresno, California, area after fleeing Vietnam, Thailand, and Laos found that their traditional practices of medicinal use of opium, of "capturing" young brides, and of ritual slaughtering of animals brought them into conflict with American law and customs and with the more Americanized members of their own culture group.

Every relocated ethnic group is subject to forces of attraction and rejection. The former tend toward assimilation into the host society; the latter, innate to the group, encourage retention of its self-identity. Acculturation tends to be responsive to economic advantage and to be accelerated if the immigrant group is in many basic traits similar to the host society, if it is relatively well educated, relatively wealthy, and finds political or social advantages in being "Americanized."

Rejection factors internal to the group that aid in the retention of cultural identification include the element of isolation. The immigrant group may seek physical separation in remote areas or raise barriers of a social nature to assure its separation from corrupting influences. Social isolation can be effective even in congested urban environments if it is buttressed by distinctive costume, beliefs, or practices (Figure 6.22). Group segregation may even result in the retention of customs, clothing, or dialects discarded in the original home area.

Rejection factors may also involve **culture rebound,** a belated adoption of group consciousness and reestablishment of identifying traits. These may reflect an attempt to reassert old values and to achieve at least a modicum of social separation. The wearing of dashikis, the popularity of Ghanian-origin kente cloth, or the celebration of Kwanzaa by American blacks seeking identification with African roots are examples of culture rebound. Ethnic identity is fostered by the nuclear family and ties of kinship, particularly when reinforced by residential proximity. It is preserved by such group activities as distinctive feasts or celebrations and by marriage customs; by ethnically identified clubs, such as the Turnverein societies of German communities or the Sokol movement of athletic and cultural centers among the Czechs; and by ethnic churches (Figure 6.23).

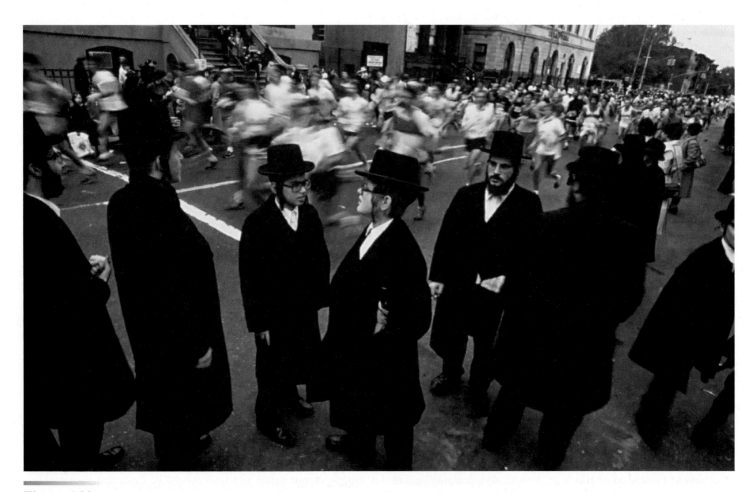

Figure 6.22 Ultra-orthodox Hasidim, seen here against the backdrop of the New York City marathon, segregate themselves by dress and custom, seek social isolation, and shun corrupting outside influences even in the midst of modern urban life.

Figure 6.23 These young girls, dressed in traditional garb for a Los Angeles Greek Orthodox Church festival, show the close association of ethnicity and religion in the American mosaic.

The Ethnic Landscape

Landscape evidence of ethnicity may be as subtle as the greater number and size of barns in the German-settled areas of the Ozarks or the designs of churches or the names of villages. The evidence may be as striking as the buggies of the Amish communities, the massive Dutch (really, German-origin) barns of southeastern Pennsylvania (Figure 6.24), or the adobe houses of Mexican American settlements in the Southwest. The ethnic landscape, however defined, may be a relic, reflecting old ways no longer pursued. It may contain evidence of artifacts or designs imported, found useful, and retained. In some instances, the physical or customary trappings of ethnicity may remain unique to one or a very few communities. In others, the diffusion of ideas or techniques may have spread introductions to areas beyond their initial impact. The landscapes and landscape evidences explored by cultural geographers are many and complex. The following paragraphs seek merely to suggest the variety of topics pursued in tracing the landscape impacts evident from the cultural diversity of Anglo America.

Land Survey

The charter group of any area had the option of designing a system for claiming and allotting land appropriate to its needs and traditions. For the most part, the English established land-division

Figure 6.24 The Pennsylvania Dutch barn, with its origins in southern Germany, has two levels. Livestock occupy the ground level; on the upper level, reached by a gentle ramp, are the threshing floor, haylofts, and grain and equipment storage. A distinctive projecting forebay provides shelter for ground-level stock doors and unmistakably identifies the Pennsylvania Dutch barn. The style, particularly in its primitive log form, was exported from its eastern origins, underwent modification, and became a basic form in the Upland (i.e., off the Coastal Plain) South, Ohio, Indiana, Illinois, and Missouri. An example of a distinctive ethnic imprint on the landscape, the Pennsylvania Dutch barn also became an example of cultural transfer from an immigrant group to the charter group.

policies in the Atlantic Seaboard colonies. In New England, basic land grants were for "towns," relatively compact blocks ideally 6 miles (9.7 km) square. The established central village, with its meeting house and its commons area, was surrounded by larger fields subdivided into strips for allocation among the community members (Figure 6.25). The result was a distinctive pattern of nucleated villages and fragmented farms.

From Pennsylvania southward, the original royal land grants were made to "proprietors," who in turn sold or allotted holdings to settlers. In the southern colonies, the occupants claimed land in amounts approved by the authorities but unspecified in location. The land evaluated as best was claimed first, poor land was passed over, and parcel boundaries were irregular and unsystematic. The *metes-and-bounds* system of property description of the region, based largely on landform or water features or such temporary landscape elements as prominent trees, unusual rocks, or cairns, led to boundary uncertainty and dispute (Figure 6.26). It also resulted in "topographic" road patterns, such as those found in Pennsylvania and other eastern states, where routes are often controlled by the contours of the land rather than the regularity of a geometric survey.

When independence was achieved, the federal government decided that the public domain should be systematically surveyed and subdivided before being opened for settlement. The resulting township and range *rectangular survey* system, adopted in the Land Ordinance of 1785, established survey lines oriented in the cardinal directions and divided the land into townships 6 miles (9.7 km) square, which were further subdivided into sections 1 mile (1.6 km) on a side (Figure 6.26). The resultant rectilinear system of land subdivision and ownership was extended to all parts of the United States ever included within the public domain, creating the basic checkerboard pattern of minor civil divisions, the regular pattern of section-line and quarter-line country roads, the block patterns of fields and farms, and the gridiron street systems of American towns and cities.

Elsewhere in North America, the French and the Spanish constituted charter groups and established their own traditions of land description and allotment. The French impress has been particularly enduring. The *long-lot* system was introduced into the St. Lawrence Valley and followed French settlers wherever they established colonies in the New World: the Mississippi Valley, Detroit, Louisiana, and elsewhere. The long lot was a surveyed elongated holding typically about 10 times longer than wide, stretching far back from a narrow river frontage (Figure 6.27). The back of the lot was indicated by a roadway roughly parallel to the line of the river, marking the front of a second series (or *range*) of long lots. The system had the advantage of providing each settler with a fair access to fertile land along the floodplain, lower-quality river terrace land, and remote poorer-quality back areas on the valley slopes serving as woodlots. Dwellings were built at the front

3 miles (4.8 km) long

Figure 6.25 Wethersfield, Connecticut: 1640–1641. The home lot and field patterns of 17th-century Wethersfield were typical of villages of rural New England.

Source: Charles M. Andrews, "The River Towns of Connecticut," in Johns Hopkins University Studies in Historical and Political Science, *7th series, VII-VIII-IX (1899), opposite p. 5.*

Figure 6.26 A contrast in survey systems. The original metes-and-bounds property survey of a portion of the Virginia Military District of western Ohio is here contrasted with the regularity of surveyor's townships, made up of 36 numbered sections, each one mile (1.6 km) on a side.

Source: Redrawn by permission from Original Survey and Land Subdivision, *Monograph Series No. 4, Norman J.W. Thrower, p. 46, Association of American Geographers, 1966.*

Figure 6.27 A portion of the Vincennes, Indiana–Illinois, topographic quadrangle (1944) showing evidence of original French long-lot survey. Note the importance of the Wabash River in both long-lot and Vincennes street-system orientations. This U.S. Geological Survey map was originally published at the fractional scale of 1:62,500.

Source: U.S. Geological Survey map.

of the holding, in a loose settlement alignment called a *côte,* where access was easy and the neighbors were close.

Although English Canada adopted a rectangular survey system, the long lot became the legal norm in French Quebec, where it controls land survey even in areas where river access is not significant. In the Rio Grande Valley of New Mexico and Texas, Spanish colonists introduced a similar long-lot system.

Settlement Patterns

While the metes and bounds and rectangular survey systems look very different (Figure 6.26), unlike long-lot systems they both produce the dispersed pattern of isolated farmsteads that typifies the rural United States. It is an arrangement conditioned by the block pattern of land survey, by the homesteading tradition of "proving up" claims through residence on them, and by the regular pattern of rural roads. Other survey systems, of course, permitted different culturally rooted settlement choices. The French and Hispanic long lots encouraged the alignment of closely spaced, but separated, farmsteads along river or road frontage (Figure 6.28). The New England village reflected the transplanting of an English tradition. Agricultural villages were found as well in Mormon settlement areas, in the Spanish American Southwest, and as part of the cultural landscapes established by early communistic or religious communities, such as the Oneida Community of New York; the Rappites's Harmony, Indiana; Fountaingrove, California; and other, mostly short-lived "utopias" of the 19th and early 20th centuries.

To encourage the settlement of the prairies, the Mennonites were granted lands in Manitoba not as individuals but as communities. Their established agricultural villages with surrounding communal fields (Figure 6.29) re-created in North America the landscape of their European homelands. (Ethnically German, some Mennonites had colonized in Russia and Ukraine before relocating in North America.)

MATHESON AREA **ABITIBI**

═══ Road ─── Lot boundary ■ Farmstead

0 miles   1   2
(3.2 km)

Figure 6.28 **Land survey in Canada.** Adjacent areas of Canada demonstrate the effects of different survey systems and cultural heritages on rural settlement patterns. The regular plots of Ontario in English Canada (left map) display the isolated farmsteads characteristic of much of rural Anglo America. The long-lot survey of Quebec in French Canada (right map) shows the lot-front alignments of rural dwellings.

Source: Redrawn by permission from Annals of the Association of American Geographers, *George I. McDermott, Vol. 51, p. 263, Association of American Geographers, 1961.*

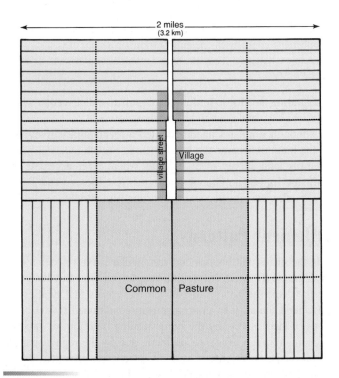

2 miles
(3.2 km)

village street | Village

Common | Pasture

Figure 6.29 **A transplanted ethnic landscape.** The German-speaking Mennonites settled in Manitoba in the 1870s and recreated the agricultural village of their European homeland. Individual farmers were granted strip holdings in the separate fields to be farmed in common with the other villagers. The farmsteads themselves, with elongated rear lots, were aligned along both sides of a single village street in an Old World pattern.

Source: Redrawn from Carl A. Dawson, Group Settlement: Ethnic Communities in Western Canada, *Vol. 7,* Canada Frontiers of Settlement *(Toronto: Macmillan Company of Canada, 1936), p. 111.*

Ethnic Regionalism

Other world regions display even more pronounced contrasts in the built landscape, reflecting the more entrenched homeland pattern of long-established ethnic regionalism. In areas of intricate mixtures of peoples—eastern and southeastern Europe, for example—different house types, farmstead layouts, even the use of color can distinguish for the knowledgeable observer the ethnicity of the local population. The one-story "smoking-room" house of the northern Slavs with its covered entrance hall and stables all under one roof marks their areas of settlement even south of the Danube River. Blue-painted one-story, straw-roofed houses indicate Croatian communities. In the Danube Basin, areas of Slovene settlement are distinguished by the Pannonian house of wood and straw-mud. In Spain, the courtyard farmstead marks areas of Moorish influence just as white stucco houses trimmed with dark green or ochre paint on the shutters indicates Basque settlement.

It is difficult to delineate ethnic regions of the United States that correspond to the distinctive landscapes created by sharply contrasting cultural groups in Europe or other world areas. The reason lies in the mobility of Americans, the degree of acculturation and assimilation of immigrants and their offspring, and the significance of other than ethnic considerations in shaping the activities, the associations, and the material possessions of participants in an urbanized, mass communication society. What can be attempted is the delimitation of areas in which particular immigrant-group influences have played a recognizable or determinant role in shaping tangible landscapes and intangible regional "character."

The "melting pot" producing a uniform cultural amalgam, we have seen, has been more American myth than reality. Therefore, there has occurred an inevitable, persistent disparity between the landscapes created by diverse immigrant groups and the national uniformity implicit either in the doctrine of first effective settlement or the concept of amalgamation. That disparity was summarized by Wilbur Zelinsky, as shown in Figure 6.30. The cultural areas are European in origin and can be seen as the expansionary product of three principal colonial culture hearths of the Atlantic Seaboard: the *New England,* the *South,* and the *Midland.* As the figure indicates, the "Middle West" is the product of the union of all three colonial regions. The popularly conceived American "West" probably exists not as a separate unit but as a set of subregions containing cross sections of national population with cultural mixing, but as yet with no achieved cultural uniformity.

REGION	APPROXIMATE DATES OF SETTLEMENT AND FORMATION	MAJOR SOURCES OF CULTURE (listed in order of importance)
NEW ENGLAND		
1a. Nuclear New England	1620–1750	England
1b. Northern New England	1750–1830	Nuclear New England, England
THE MIDLAND		
2a. Pennsylvania Region	1682–1850	England and Wales, Rhineland, Ulster, 19th-Century Europe
2b. New York Region or New England Extended	1624–1830	Great Britain, New England, 19th-Century Europe, Netherlands
THE SOUTH		
3a. Early British Colonial South	1607–1750	England, Africa, British West Indies
3b. Lowland or Deep South	1700–1850	Great Britain, Africa, Midland, Early British Colonial South, aborigines
3b-1. French Louisiana	1700–1760	France, Deep South, Africa, French West Indies
3c. Upland South	1700–1850	Midland, Lowland South, Great Britain
3c-1. The Bluegrass	1770–1800	Upland South, Lowland South
3c-2. The Ozarks	1820–1860	Upland South, Lowland South, Lower Middle West
THE MIDDLE WEST		
4a. Upper Middle West	1800–1880	New England Extended, New England, 19th-Century Europe, British Canada
4b. Lower Middle West	1790–1870	Midland, Upland South, New England Extended, 19th-Century Europe
4c. Cutover Area	1850–1900	Upper Middle West, 19th-Century Europe

REGION	APPROXIMATE DATES OF SETTLEMENT AND FORMATION	MAJOR SOURCES OF CULTURE (listed in order of importance)
THE WEST		
5a. Upper Rio Grande Valley	1590–	Mexico, Anglo America, aborigines
5b. Willamette Valley	1830–1900	Northeast U.S.
5c. Mormon Region	1847–1890	Northeast U.S., 19th-Century Europe
5d. Central California	(1775–1848) 1840–	(Mexico) Eastern U.S., 19th Century Europe, Mexico, East Asia
5e. Colorado Piedmont	1860–	Eastern U.S., Mexico
5f. Southern California	(1760–1848) 1880–	(Mexico) Eastern U.S., 19th and 20th-Century Europe, Mormon Region, Mexico, East Asia
5g. Puget Sound	1870–	Eastern U.S., 19th and 20th-Century Europe, East Asia
5h. Inland Empire	1880–	Eastern U.S., 19th and 20th-Century Europe
5i. Central Arizona	1900–	Eastern U.S., Southern California, Mexico
REGIONS OF UNCERTAIN STATUS OR AFFILIATION		
A. Texas	(1690–1836) 1821–	(Mexico) Lowland South, Upland South, Mexico, 19th-Century Central Europe
B. Peninsular Florida	1880–	Northeast U.S., the South, 20th-Century Europe, Antilles
C. Oklahoma	1890–	Upland South, Lowland South, aborigines, Middle West

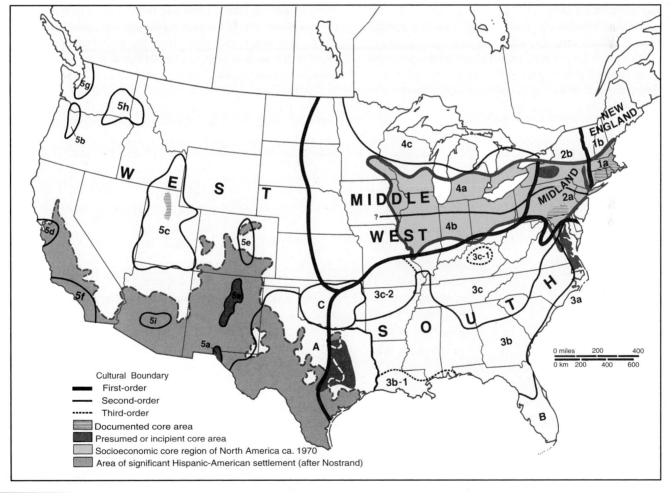

Cultural Boundary
First-order
Second-order
Third-order
Documented core area
Presumed or incipient core area
Socioeconomic core region of North America ca. 1970
Area of significant Hispanic-American settlement (after Nostrand)

Figure 6.30 Culture areas of the United States based on multiple lines of evidence.

Source: From Wilbur Zelinsky, The Cultural Geography of the United States, *Rev. ed., 1992, pp. 118–119. Redrawn by permission of Prentice-Hall, Inc., Upper Saddle River, NJ.*

Summary

Ethnic diversity is a reality in most countries of the world and is increasing in many of them. Immigration, refugee streams, guest workers, and job seekers all contribute to the mixing of peoples and cultures in an area. The mixing is not complete, however. Ethnicity—affiliation in a group sharing common identifying cultural traits—is fostered by territorial separation or isolation. In much of the world, that separation identifies home territories within which the ethnic group is dominant and with which it is identified. In societies of immigrants—Anglo America, for example—such homelands are replaced by ethnic colonies, enclaves, ghettos, and ethnoburbs of self-selected or imposed separation from the larger host society. Cluster migration helped establish such colonies in rural America; chain migration encouraged their development in cities.

The 19th- and early 20th-century American central city displayed pronounced areal segregation as immigrant groups established and clung to protective ethnic neighborhoods while they gradually adjusted to the host culture. A continual population restructuring of urban areas occurred as older groups underwent acculturation, amalgamation, or assimilation, and new groups entered the urban social mix. The durability of ethnic neighborhoods has depended, among other considerations, on the degree of social distance separating the minority group from the host culture and on the significance the immigrant group places on long-term maintenance of their own cultural identity. That is, ethnic communities have been the product of both external and internal forces.

In other world regions, similar spatial separation of immigrant groups by racial, cultural, national, tribal, or village origin within the alien city is common. In Europe, because of the uncertain legal and employment status of many foreign populations and the restricted urban housing market they enter, ethnic enclaves have taken a different form, extent, and level of segregation than has been the case in Anglo America.

Ethnicity is one of the threads of diversity in the spatial cultural fabric. Throughout the world, ethnic groups have imprinted their presence on the landscapes in which they have developed or to which they have transported their culture. In land division, house and farm building style, settlement patterns, and religious structures, the beliefs and practices of distinctive groups are reflected in the cultural landscape. Ethnicity is not, of course, the sole thread in the regional tapestry of societies. Folk culture joins ethnicity as a force creating distinctions between peoples and imparting special character to area. Countering those culturally based sources of separation is the behavioral unification and reduction of territorial distinctiveness that result from the homogenizing impact of popular culture. It is to these two additional strands in the cultural fabric—folk and popular culture—that we next turn our attention in Chapter 7.

KEY WORDS

acculturation 172
adaptation 168
amalgamation theory 172
assimilation 173
behavioral (cultural) assimilation 173
chain migration 178
charter group 176
cluster migration 177
colony 189
culture rebound 192

ethnic enclave 189
ethnic geography 165
ethnic group 165
ethnic island 176
ethnicity 166
ethnic province 178
ethnocentrism 166
first effective settlement 174
gene flow 168
genetic drift 168

ghetto 189
host society 167
natural selection 168
race 168
segregation 184
social distance 184
structural assimilation 173
tipping point 186

FOR REVIEW

1. How does *ethnocentrism* contribute to preservation of group identity? In what ways might an ethnic group sustain and support new immigrants?

2. How are the concepts of *ethnicity* and *culture* related?

3. What have been some of the principal time patterns of immigration flows into the United States? Into Canada? How are those patterns important to an understanding of present-day social conflicts in either or both countries?

4. How may *segregation* be measured? Does ethnic segregation exist in the cities of world areas outside of North America? If so, does it take different form than in American cities?

5. What forces external to ethnic groups help to create and perpetuate immigrant neighborhoods? What functions beneficial to immigrant groups do ethnic communities provide?

6. What kinds of land surveys were important in the allocation of property in the North American culture realm? With which *charter groups* were the different survey systems associated? How did survey systems affect settlement patterns?

KEY CONCEPTS REVIEW

1. **What are the implications and bases of "ethnicity," and how have historic immigration streams shaped Anglo American multiethnicity?** pp. 165–171.

Ethnicity implies a "people" or "nation," a large group classified according to common religious, linguistic, or other aspects of cultural origin or background, or, often, to racial distinctions. In common with nearly all countries, the United States and Canada are multiethnic. Past and current immigration streams—earlier primarily European, more recently Asian and Latin American—have intricately mixed their populations.

2. **How were the dominant Anglo American culture norms established, and how complete spatially and socially are its ethnic minorities integrated?** pp. 171–184.

The first effective settlers of Anglo America created its English-rooted charter culture to which other, later immigrant groups were expected to conform. Assimilation or acculturation has not been complete, and areal expressions of ethnic differentiation persist in America in the form of ethnic islands, provinces, or regional concentrations. French Canadian, black, Amerindian, Hispanic, Asian American, and other, smaller groups display recognizable areal presences. Among immigrant groups, those concentrations may result from cluster and chain migration.

3. **What patterns of ethnic diversity and segregation exist in the world's urban areas, and how are they created or maintained?** pp. 184–191.

Ethnic communities, clusters, and neighborhoods are found in cities worldwide. They are a measure of the social distance that separates minority from majority or other minority groups. Segregation measures the degree to which culture groups are not uniformly distributed within the total population. Although different world regions show differing patterns, all urban segregation is based on external restrictions of isolation and discrimination or ethnic group internal separatism controls of defense, mutual support, and cultural preservation. Ethnic colonies, enclaves, ghettos, and ethnoburbs are the spatial result.

4. **What have been some of the cultural landscape consequences of ethnic concentrations in Anglo America and elsewhere?** pp. 191–197.

Landscape evidence of ethnicity may be subtle or pronounced. In Anglo America, differing culturally based systems of land survey and allocation—such as metes-and-bounds, rectangular, or long lot—of earlier groups may still leave their landscape impacts. Clustered and dispersed rural settlement customs; house and barn types and styles; distinctive, largely urban, "Chinatowns," "Little Havanas," and other cultural communities; and even choices in dwelling-house colors or urban art are landscape imprints of multiethnicity in modern societies.

FOLK AND POPULAR CULTURE:

Diversity and Uniformity

7

Amish farmers, obedient to their cultural values, pursue traditional farming methods.

Key Concepts

A. Folk Culture

1. Anglo American hearths and folk building traditions, pp. 201–211.

2. Nonmaterial folk culture: foods, music, medicines, and folklore, pp. 211–215.

3. Folk regions and regionalism, pp. 215–217.

B. Popular Culture

4. The nature and patterns of popular culture: inside the mall and out, pp. 217–222.

5. Diffusion and regionalism in popular culture: drink and music, pp. 222–231.

*I*n rural and frontier America before 1850, the games people played were local, largely unorganized individual and team contests. Running, wrestling, weight lifting, shooting, or—if the Native American influence had been strong—shinny (field hockey), kickball, or lacrosse. In the growing cities, rowing, boxing, cricket, fencing, and the like involved the athletically inclined, sometimes as members of sporting clubs and sponsored teams. Everywhere, horse racing was an avid interest. In the countryside, sports and games relieved the monotony and isolation of life and provided an excuse, after the contests, for meeting friends, feasting, and dancing. Purely local in participation, games reflected the ethnic heritage of the local community—the games of the homeland—as well as the influence of the American experience. In the towns, they provided the outdoor recreation and exercise otherwise denied to shop-bound clerks and artisans. Without easy transportation, contests at a distance were difficult and rare; without easy communication, sports results were of local interest only.

The railroad and the telegraph changed all that. Teams could travel to more distant points, and scores could be immediately known to supporters at home and rivals in other cities. Baseball clubs were organized during the 1850s throughout the East and the Middle West. The establishment of the National Association of Base Ball Players in 1857 followed shortly after the railroad reached Chicago, and even before the Civil War, New York teams were competing throughout that state. After the war, the expanding rail network turned baseball into a national craze. The National League was organized in 1876; Chicago, Boston, New York, Washington, Kansas City, Detroit, St. Louis, and Philadelphia all had professional teams by the 1880s, and innumerable local leagues were formed. Horse racing, prizefighting, amateur and professional cycling races, and intercollegiate sports— football, baseball, rowing, and track and field contests—pitted contestants and drew crowds over long distances. Sports and games had been altered from small-group participations to national events. They were no longer purely local, traditional, informal expressions of community culture; rather, organized sport had emerged as a unifying, standardized expression of national popular culture (Figure 7.1).

Figure 7.1 Spectator sports emerged as a major element in American popular culture following the Civil War. The Cincinnati Red Stockings of 1869, shown in this print, were the first openly professional baseball team; the National League was established in 1876. Mark Twain, an early fan, wrote: "Baseball is the very symbol, the outward and visible expression of the drive and push and struggle of the raging, tearing, booming nineteenth century." Organized football was introduced as a college sport—also in 1869—when Rutgers played Princeton in the first intercollegiate game.

The kaleidoscope of culture presents an endlessly changing design, different for every society, world region, and national unit, and different over time. Ever present in each of its varied patterns, however, are two repeated fragments of diversity and one spreading color of uniformity. One distinctive element of diversity in many societies derives from *folk* culture—the material and nonmaterial aspects of daily life preserved by smaller groups partially or totally isolated from the mainstream currents of the larger society around them. A second source of diversity in composite societies, as we saw in Chapter 6, is surely and clearly provided by *ethnic* groups, each with its distinctive characterizing heritage and traditions and each contributing to the national cultural mix. Finally, given time, easy communication, and common interests, *popular* culture may provide a unifying and liberating color to the kaleidoscopic mix, reducing differences between formerly distinctive groups though perhaps not totally eradicating them. These three elements—folk, ethnic, and popular—of the cultural mosaic are intertwined. We will trace their connections particularly in the Anglo American context, where diversified immigration provided the ethnic mix, frontier and rural isolation encouraged folk differentiation, and modern technology produced the leveling of popular culture. Along the way, we will see evidences of their separate influences in other societies and other culture realms. And we shall also see the close interconnections between folk and popular culture and their inevitable impacts on each other.

Folk culture is often viewed as the absolute opposite of popular or mass culture. It is seen as the unchanging, rural way of life, largely relegated to nonmodern, "traditional" peoples untouched by outside influences. Where folk culture exists in developed countries like the United States, it is regarded as characteristic only of socially or geographically isolated groups—for example, the Amish, some Native American communities, or the presumably reclusive mountain folk of Appalachia. The prevailing notion is that if the artifacts, beliefs, and practices of folk culture are at all relevant to modern society, they serve only as reminders of the past to be relegated to museums or as touristic curiosities for outsiders seeking the quaint and exotic "other." The relationship between folk and popular culture is thus often portrayed as one of conflict between the two opposing forces of modernity and tradition in which, except for a few carefully protected human and material relics, folk culture is doomed to eventual extinction by the forces of modernization and globalization. As we shall see, reality is more complex, and the sharp contrast between folk and popular is more assumed than real.

Folk Cultural Diversity and Regionalism

Folk connotes traditional and nonfaddish, the characteristic or product of a homogeneous, cohesive, largely self-sufficient group that is essentially isolated from or resistant to outside influences, even of a larger society surrounding it. **Folk culture,** therefore, may be defined as the collective heritage of institutions, customs, skills, dress, and way of life of a small, stable, closely knit, usually rural community. Tradition controls folk culture, and resistance to change is strong. The homemade and handmade dominate in tools, food, music, story, and ritual. Buildings are erected without architect or blueprint, but with plan and purpose clearly in mind and by a design common to the local society using locally available building materials. When, as in Anglo America, folk culture may represent a modification of imported ideas and techniques, local materials often substitute for a less-available original substance even as the design concepts are left unchanged.

Although folk cultures are conservative and tend to resist innovations, they are not static. They often demonstrate flexibility and creativity when they encounter new or changing environmental or social circumstances and adapt their cultural practices accordingly. Indeed, all cultures were subsistence rural folk cultures until, in ancient hearth regions (p. 44), people built cities and developed a class hierarchy in which social and economic stratification began to differentiate the elite from commoners. The popular or mass culture that now so totally dominates modern life is a product of the industrialization and urbanization trends that began in the late 18th and early 19th centuries in Europe and the United States and recently, as an expression of globalization, has affected nearly every inhabited corner of the world. People everywhere tend to discard or alter elements of their folk culture when confronted with the attractions of modernity. Despite the claims of the folk or ethnic tourism trade in its efforts to sell "pristine" traditional cultures as a commodity, few if any groups remain, even in the developing world, that are still totally immersed in folk culture as their dominating way of life.

Yet folk cultural elements persist in all advanced societies. In Japan, traditional culture is tenaciously preserved in a highly industrialized and urbanized society that enthusiastically embraces nearly every fad produced by the Western culture they have adopted. And the popularity in the United States of folk-themed movies and CDs such as *Oh Brother, Where Art Thou?* the ever-present *Beverly Hillbillies* television reruns, and the proliferation of folk music and folk life festivals are evidence that folk culture is far from irrelevant to modern 21st-century society. Rather, it should be viewed as an underlying layer or substrate of popular culture, intersecting and influencing popular culture and conveying symbolic meaning.

Folk life in its unaltered form, however, is a cultural whole composed of both tangible and intangible elements. **Material culture** is made up of physical, visible things: everything from musical instruments to furniture, tools, and buildings. Collectively, material culture comprises the **built environment,** the landscape created by humans. At a different scale, it also constitutes the contents of household and workshop. **Nonmaterial culture,** in contrast, is the intangible part, the mentifacts and sociofacts expressed in oral tradition, folk song and folk story, and customary

behavior. Ways of speech, patterns of worship, outlooks and philosophies are parts of the nonmaterial component passed to following generations by teachings and examples.

Within Anglo America, true folk societies no longer exist; the universalizing impacts of industrialization, urbanization, and mass communication have been too pervasive for their full retention. Generations of intermixing of cultures, of mobility of peoples, and of leveling public education have altered the meaning of *folk* from the identification of a group to the recognition of a style, an article, or an individual preference in design and production. The Old Order Amish, with their rejection of electricity, the internal combustion engine, and other "worldly" accoutrements in favor of buggy, hand tools, and traditional dress are one of the least altered—and few—folk societies of the United States (Figure 7.2). Yet the Amish are very adept at dealing with the modern world, often with the assistance of their non-Amish (or "English") neighbors. For example, they own and operate successful cheese-making and furniture businesses; occasionally ride in, but do not drive, motor vehicles; use their "English" neighbors' telephones; and use propane gas to power their refrigerators instead of the electricity they are forbidden.

Canada, on the other hand, with as rich a mixture of cultural origins as the United States, has kept to much later date clearly recognizable ethnically unique folk and decorative art traditions. One observer has noted that nearly all of the national folk art traditions of Europe can be found in one form or another well preserved and practiced somewhere in Canada. From the earliest arts and crafts of New France to the domestic art forms and folk artifacts of the Scandinavians, Germans, Ukrainians, and others who settled in western Canada in the late 19th and early 20th centuries, folk and ethnic are intertwined through transference of traditions from homelands and their adaptation to the Canadian context.

Folk culture today is more likely to be expressed by individuals than by coherent, isolated groups. The collector of folk songs, the artist employing traditional materials and styles, the artisan producing in wood and metal products identified with particular groups or regions, the quilter working in modern fabrics the designs of earlier generations all are perpetuating folk culture: material culture if it involves "things," nonmaterial if the preserved tradition relates to song, story, recipe, or belief. In this respect, each of us bears the evidence of folk life. Each of us uses proverbs traditional to our family or culture; each is familiar with and can repeat childhood nursery rhymes and fables. We rap wood for luck and likely know how to make a willow whistle, how to plant a garden by phases of the moon, and what is the "right" way to prepare a favorite holiday dish.

When many persons share at least some of the same folk **customs**—repeated, characteristic acts, behavioral patterns, artistic traditions, and conventions regulating social life—and when those customs and artifacts are distinctively identified with any area long inhabited by a particular group, a *folk culture region* may be recognized. As with landscape evidence of ethnicity, folk culture in its material and nonmaterial elements may be seen to vary over time and space and to have hearth regions of origin and paths of diffusion.

(a)

(b)

Figure 7.2 (*a*) Motivated by religious conviction that the "good life" must be reduced to its simplest forms, Old Order Amish communities shun all modern luxuries of the majority secular society around them. Children use horse and buggy, not school bus or automobile, on their daily trip to this rural school in east central Illinois. (*b*) Distribution of Old Order Amish communities in the United States.

Source: (b) Redrawn by permission from Annals of the Association of American Geographers, *William K. Crowley, Vol. 68, p. 262, Association of American Geographers, 1978.*

Indeed, in many respects, ethnic geography and folk geography are extensions of each other and are logically intertwined. The variously named "Swiss" or "Mennonite" or "Dutch" barn (see Figure 6.24) introduced into Pennsylvania by German immigrants has been cited as physical evidence of ethnicity; in some of its many modifications and migrations, it may also be seen as a folk culture artifact of Appalachia. The folk songs of, say, western Virginia can be examined either as nonmaterial folk expressions of the Upland South or as evidence of the ethnic heritage derived from rural English forebears. In the New World the debt of folk culture to ethnic origins is clear and persuasive. With the passage of time, of course, the dominance of origins recedes and new cultural patterns and roots emerge.

Anglo American Hearths

Anglo America is an amalgam of peoples who came as ethnics and stayed as Americans or Canadians. They brought with them more than tools and household items and articles of dress. Importantly, they brought clear ideas of what tools they needed, how they should fashion their clothes, cook their food, find a spouse, and worship their deity. They knew already the familiar songs to be sung and stories to be told, how a house should look and a barn be raised. They came, in short, with all the mentifacts and sociofacts to shape the artifacts of their way of life in their new home (Figure 7.3). (Mentifacts, sociofacts, and artifacts are discussed in Chapter 2.)

Their trappings of material and nonmaterial culture frequently underwent immediate modification in the New World. Climates and soils were often different from their homelands; new animal and vegetable foodstuffs were found for their larders. Building

Figure 7.3 Reconstructed Plimoth Plantation. The first settlers in the New World carried with them fully developed cultural identities. Even their earliest settlements reflected established ideas of house and village form. Later, they were to create a variety of distinctive cultural landscapes reminiscent of their homeland areas, though modified by American environmental conditions and material resources.

materials, labor skills, and items of manufacture available at their origins were different or lacking at their destinations. What the newcomers brought in tools and ideas they began to modify as they adapted and adjusted to different American materials, terrains, and potentials. The settlers still retained the essence and the spirit of the old but made it simultaneously new and American.

The first colonists, their descendants, and still later arrivals created not one but many cultural landscapes of America, defined by the structures they built, the settlements they created, and the regionally varied articles they made or customs they followed. The natural landscape of America became settled, and superimposed on the natural landscape as modified by its Amerindian occupants were the regions of cultural traits and characteristics of the European immigrants (see "Vanished American Roots"). In their later movements and those of their neighbors and offspring, they left a trail of landscape evidence from first settlement to the distant interior locations where they touched and intermingled.

The early arrivers established footholds along the East Coast. Their settlement areas became cultural hearths, nodes of introduction into the New World—through *relocation diffusion*—of concepts and artifacts brought from the Old. Locales of innovation in a new land rather than areas of new invention, they were—exactly as their ancient counterparts discussed in Chapter 2—source regions from which relocation and *expansion diffusion* carried their cultural identities deeper into the continent (Figure 7.4). Later arrivals, as we have seen in Chapter 6, not only added their own evidence of passage to the landscape but often set up independent secondary hearths in advance of or outside of the main paths of diffusion.

Each of the North American hearths had its own mix of peoples and, therefore, its own landscape distinctiveness. French settlement in the lower St. Lawrence Valley re-created there the long lots and rural house types of northwestern France. Upper Canada was English and Scottish with strong infusions of New England folk housing carried by Loyalists leaving that area during the Revolutionary War. Southern New England bore the imprint of settlers from rural southern England, while the Hudson Valley

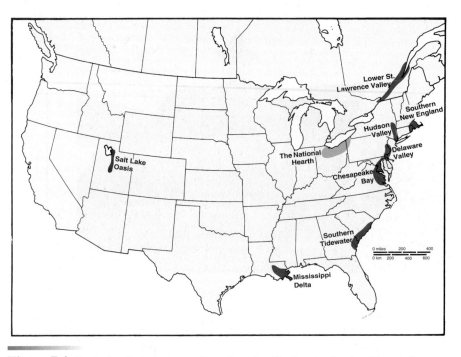

Figure 7.4 Early Anglo American culture hearths. The interior "national hearth," suggested by Richard Pillsbury, represents a zone of coalescence in the eastern Midwest, from which composite housing ideas dispersed farther into the interior.

Sources: Based on Allen G. Noble, Wood, Brick, and Stone, *Vol. 1 (Amherst: University of Massachusetts Press, 1984); and* Annals of the Association of American Geographers, *Richard Pillsbury, Vol. 60, p. 446, Association of American Geographers, 1970.*

hearth showed the impress of Dutch, Flemish, English, German, and French Huguenot settlers.

In the Middle Atlantic area, the Delaware River hearth was created by a complex of English, Scotch-Irish, Swedish, and German influences. The Delaware Valley below Philadelphia also received the eastern Finns, or Karelians, who introduced, according to one

Vanished American Roots

America, like every other world region, had its own primitive, naïve, and indigenous original architecture. But this was the architecture of Indians—the bark houses of the Penobscots, the long houses of the Iroquois, the tipis of the Crows, the mounds of the Mandans, the pueblos of the Zuñi, the hogans of the Navajos, the [plank] dwellings of Puget Sound.

(a) Bark house   (b) Long house   (c) Tipi
(d) Mound house   (e) Pueblo   (f) Hogan   (g) Plank house

Some of these were even elegant, many contained seeds of promise; but we swept them all aside. Indian words and Indian foods passed into the American culture but nothing important from the Indian architecture, save a belated effort to imitate the form but not the function of the pueblos. (The so-called "Spanish" architecture of the Hispanic borderlands and northern Mexico, however—adobe-walled with small windows and flat-roofs supported by wooden beams—was of Amerindian, not European, origin.)

Source: From John Burchard and Albert Bush-Brown, *The Architecture of America: A Social and Cultural History,* (Boston: Little, Brown and Company, 1961), p. 57. © 1961, The American Institute of Architects.

viewpoint, the distinctive "backwoods" lifestyles, self-sufficient economies, and log-building techniques and house designs of their forested homeland. It was their pioneering "midland" culture that was the catalyst for the rapid advance of the frontier and successful settlement of much of the interior of the continent and, later, of the Pacific Northwest.

Coastal Chesapeake Bay held English settlers, though Germans and Scotch-Irish were added elements away from the major rivers. The large landholdings of the area dispersed settlement and prevented a tightly or clearly defined culture hearth from developing, although distinctive house types that later diffused outward did emerge there. The Southern Tidewater hearth was dominantly English modified by West Indian, Huguenot, and African influences. The French again were part of the Delta hearth, along with Spanish and Haitian elements.

Later in time and deeper in the continental interior, the Salt Lake hearth marks the penetration of the distant West by the Mormons, considered an ethnic group by virtue of their self-identity through religious distinctiveness. Spanish American borderlands, the Upper Midwest Scandinavian colonies, English Canada, and the ethnic clusters of the Prairie Provinces could logically be added to the North American map of distinctive immigrant culture hearths.

The ethnic hearths gradually lost their identification with immigrant groups and became source regions of American architecture and implements, ornaments and toys, cookery and music. The evidence of the homeland was there, but the products became purely indigenous. In the isolated, largely rural American hearth regions, the ethnic culture imported from the Old World was partially transmuted into the folk culture of the New.

Folk Building Traditions and Hearths

People everywhere house themselves and, if necessary, provide protection for their domesticated animals. Throughout the world, native rural societies established types of housing, means of construction, and use of materials appropriate to their economic and family needs, the materials and technologies available to them, and the environmental conditions they encountered. Because all these preconditions are spatially variable, rural housing and settlement patterns are comparably varied, a diversity increasingly lost as standardization of materials (corrugated metal, poured concrete, cinder block, and the like) and of design replace the local materials and styles developed through millennia by isolated folk societies.

The world is not yet, of course, totally homogenized. The family compound of the Bambara of Mali (Figure 7.5) is obviously and significantly different from the farmstead of a North American rural family. The Mongol or Turkic *yurt* or *ger,* a movable low, rounded shelter of felt, skin, short poles, and rope, is a housing solution adapted to the needs and materials of nomadic herdsmen of the Asian grasslands (Figure 7.6a). A much different solution with different materials is reached by the Maasai, a similar nomadic herding society but of the grasslands of eastern Africa. Their temporary home was traditionally the *manyatta,* an immovable low, rounded hut made of poles, mud, and cow dung that was

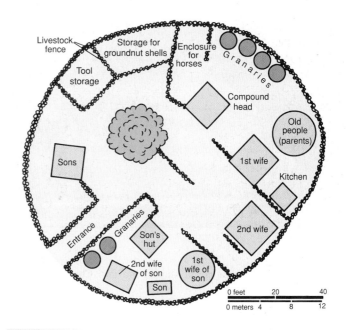

Figure 7.5 The extended family compound of the Bambara of Mali.

Source: Redrawn with permission from Reuben K. Udo, The Human Geography of Tropical Africa *(Ibadan: Heinemann Education Books (Nigeria) Ltd., 1982), p. 50.*

abandoned as soon as local grazing and water supplies were consumed (Figure 7.6b). As the structures in Figure 7.7 can only slightly suggest, folk housing solutions in design and materials provide a worldwide mosaic of nearly infinite diversity and ingenuity.

Within the Anglo American realm, although architectural diversity does not reach global proportions, the variety of ethnic and regional origins of immigrant streams and the differences in encountered environmental conditions assured architectural contrasts among the several settlement hearths of the New World. The landscapes of structures and settlements creating those contrasts speak to us of their creators' origins, travels, adaptations to new locales, and importations and retentions of the habits and customs of other places.

The folk cultural heritage is now passing; old farm structures are replaced or collapse with disuse as farming systems change. Old houses are removed, remodeled, or abandoned, and the modern, the popular, or the faddish everywhere replaces the evidences of first occupants. A close-knit community may preserve the past by resisting the present, but except where the efforts of preservationists have been successful in retaining and refurbishing one or a few structures or where outdoor museums and recreations have been developed, the landscapes—the voices—of the past are gradually lost. Many of those fading voices first took on their North American accents in the culture hearths suggested in Figure 7.4. They are still best heard in the house types associated with them.

Vernacular house styles—those built in traditional form but without formal plans or drawings—were part of the material culture of early colonists that met new conditions in America. In the Northeast, colder, snowier winters posed different environmental challenges than did the milder, frequently wetter climates of northwestern Europe, and American stone and timber were more accessible and more suitable construction materials than were the clay and thatch common in the homelands. In the American South,

(a)

(b)

Figure 7.6 (*a*) A Uighur *yurt* in Xinjiang Province, China; (*b*) the Maasai *manyatta*.

(a)

(b)

(c)

(d)

Figure 7.7 The common characteristics of preindustrial folk housing are an essential uniformity of design within a culture group and region, a lack of differentiation of interior space, a close adaptation to the conditions of the natural environment, and frequently ingenious use of available materials and response to the dictates of climate or terrain. (*a*) Stone house of Nepal; (*b*) Icelandic sod farm house; (*c*) reed dwelling of the Uros people on Lake Titicaca, Peru; (*d*) a Dogon village in Mali, West Africa; (*e*) traditional housing on Nias Island, off the west coast of Sumatra, Indonesia.

(e)

both climate and a new ethnic and cultural mix altered the styles of vernacular housing to forms suitable to the special needs of that region. In the Interior, the mix of still other European ethnic immigrants, indigenous cultural groups, and the extremes of a continental climate shaped emerging housing forms. In all areas and under different environmental conditions, however, traditional housing styles tended to persist, reflecting the imported cultures of new arrivals. Each separately colonized area produced its own distinctive vernacular housing mix, and a few served eventually as hearth districts from which its imported and developed house forms diffused.

The Northern hearths. In the north, the *St. Lawrence Valley* remains as one of the few areas with structural reminders of a French occupation that once spread widely but impermanently over eastern North America. There, in French Canada, beginning in the middle of the 17th century, three major house types were introduced, all styles still found in western France today (Figure 7.8); they were found as well in other areas of French settlement in North America—Louisiana, the St. Genevieve area of Missouri, and northern Maine. The rural southern English colonists who settled in *Southern New England* brought with them the heavily framed houses of their home counties: sturdy posts and stout horizontal beams sided by overlapping clapboards and distinguished by steep roofs and massive chimneys (Figure 7.9). The

Hudson Valley's complex mix of Dutch, French, Flemish, English, and German settlers produced a comparable mixture of common house forms. The Dutch were initially dominant and their side-gabled homes, all with a split "Dutch door" (whose separately opened upper half let air in and closed lower half kept children in and animals out), were characterized by a steep roof, often with flared eaves (Figure 7.10).

The Middle Atlantic hearths. The *Delaware Valley* and *Chesapeake Bay* were ethnically diverse sites of vernacular architecture more influential on North American housing styles than any other early settlement areas. The log cabin, later carried into Appalachia and the trans-Appalachian interior, evolved there (see "Log Cabin Myths and Facts") as did the vernacular *four-over-four* house—so called in reference to its basic two-story floor plan with four rooms up and four down. There, too, was introduced what would later be called the *I house*—a two-story structure one room deep with two rooms on each floor that became prominent in the Upper South and the Lower Middle West in the 19th century (Figure 7.11).

The Southern hearths. The southern settlement areas developed housing styles that were adapted to the climatic conditions and ethnic mixes distinguishing those areas from the northern colonial districts. In the *Southern Tidewater* along the southeastern Atlantic coastal region of South Carolina and Georgia, the malaria, mosquitoes, and extreme heat plaguing their inland plantations during the

(a)

(b)

Figure 7.8 Buildings of the Lower St. Lawrence hearth region. (*a*) The *Norman cottage* shows the steeply pitched hipped roofs and wide or upturned eaves of near-identical houses in the Normandy region of northern France; (*b*) the two-room *Quebec cottage* also has a steeply pitched (but gabled) roof with overhanging eaves; (*c*) the *Montreal house* was a larger stone structure found more in city than in countryside settings.

(c)

Figure 7.9 New England house types. (*a*) The characteristic second-floor overhang of the *garrison house* was a relict of medieval European urban house design; (*b*) the *saltbox* house showed an asymmetrical gable roof covering a lean-to addition for extra room; (*c*) the Georgian-style *New England large house* had up to ten rooms, a lobby entrance, and paired chimneys; (*d*) The *upright-and-wing* or *lazy-T* house (the wing represented a one-story extension of a basic gable-front house plan) was diffused widely in both rural and urban areas from western New York into the Middle West.

Figure 7.10 This New York *Dutch house* shares similarities, especially its outswept eaves, with the Quebec cottage of Canada's St. Lawrence Valley. The French Canadian house, with its roots in Normandy, and this Dutch American house of the Colonial Hudson Valley, with its roots in Flanders, issue from vernacular designs of the North European Plain.

summer caused the wealthy to prefer hot-season residence in coastal cities such as Charleston, where sea breezes provided relief. The result was the characteristic *Charleston single house* (Figure 7.12). The French, dominant in the Lower St. Lawrence Valley far to the north, established a second North American culture hearth in the *Mississippi Delta* area of New Orleans and along the lower Mississippi during the 18th century. There, French influences from Nova Scotia and the French Caribbean islands—Haiti, specifically—were mixed with Spanish and African cultural contributions. Again, heat and humidity were an environmental problem requiring distinctive housing solutions, one of which was the *shotgun* house, a folk cultural contribution that traces its roots to Africa and an introduction into America by free Haitian blacks who settled in the delta before the middle of the 19th century (Figure 7.13). Crossing cultural boundaries, the shotgun house after the Civil War became a common residence type for both poor blacks and whites migrating to cities in the South and Midwest in search of employment.

The Interior and Western hearths. Various immigrant groups, some from the eastern states, others from abroad—and all encountering still different environmental circumstances and building

(a)

(b)

Figure 7.11 House types of the Middle Atlantic hearths. (*a*) The *four-over-four house;* (*b*) the traditional or classic wood-frame *I house* with its two rooms on each floor separated by central hallways had a varying number of façade openings and, usually, end chimneys located in the standard gable roof, but all symmetrically organized. After the 1850s, its builders and building materials were brought by the new railroads to Indiana, Illinois, and Iowa (the *I*'s after which the house was named).

Log Cabin Myths and Facts

First settlers in New England and Virginia brought with them familiarity with timber framing, wattle-and-daub infilling, and thatch roofing. They did not know of and did not construct the log cabins that are now commonly associated with pioneer settlement throughout the Eastern Seaboard. Log buildings were familiar, however, to the Swedes, Germans, and most particularly the eastern Finns, who introduced them into the Delaware Valley area. In Pennsylvania and much of the rest of North America, log construction—employing various building traditions and techniques—marked an initial settlement period. Log housing was not glorified by those who built and occupied it, however. As soon as affluence permitted, the log cabin was replaced (or concealed behind a new façade) by housing of greater prestige or social acceptability. Harold R. Shurtleff explains how the log cabin assumed a bigger role in American folklore than it had in the hearts and minds of its builders.

[T]o deny that log cabins or log dwelling houses existed in the early English settlements,

or to maintain the fact that framed houses were built by the English without passing through a log cabin stage, is to take issue with an American belief that is both deep-seated and tenacious.

The reasons for this emotional basis for the Log Cabin Myth are not far to seek. In the nineteenth century Americans began to marvel at their own progress, and to make a virtue of their early struggles with the wilderness. The log cabin as a symbol of democracy was dramatized in two famous presidential campaigns, those of 1840 and 1860. In literature the popular "Log-Cabin to White House" series firmly fixed the log cabin as the proper scenario for the birth of a great American; as early as 1840 Daniel Webster was apologizing for not having been born in one, and as late as 1935, we are told, a "considerable legend" had already grown up around the "log-cabin origins" of Roy Harris, the Oklahoma composer. Thus, the log cabin came to be identified with "Old Hickory," "Tippecanoe," and Abraham Lincoln, with

democracy and the frontier spirit, and with the common man and his dream of the good life, and those persons, types, and forces of which Americans are justly proud. The log cabin, along with the Indian, the long rifle, and the hunting shirt is associated with one of the greatest of all conquests, the winning of the West. It gives us that sense of the dramatic which we seek in our history. . . . [W]e need not be surprised that careless historians projected it back into the earliest colonial settlements, or that many Americans today feel a sense of outrage when told that neither Captain John Smith [of Virginia colony] nor Governor Bradford [of Massachusetts Bay] nor any of the founding fathers dwelt in a log cabin, or ever saw one.

Source: Reprinted by permission of the publisher from *The Log Cabin Myth: A Study of the Early Dwellings of the English Colonists in North America* by Harold Shurtleff, edited and with an introduction by Samuel Eliot Morison, pp. 5–6, Cambridge, Mass.: Harvard University Press, copyright © 1939 by the President and Fellows of Harvard College, Copyright renewed 1967.

material sources—made their impress on local areas of the *Interior* and North American *West.* Settlers of many different origins on the Great Plains initially built sod dugouts or sod or rammed earth houses in the absence of native timber stands. Later, after the middle of the century, "balloon frame" construction, utilizing newly

available cheap wire nails and light lumber milled to standard dimensions, became the norm in the interior where heavy timbers for traditional post and beam construction were not available. The strong, low-cost housing the new techniques and materials made possible owed less to the architectural traditions of eastern America

Figure 7.12 The *Charleston single house* name related to its single row of three or four rooms ranged from front to back and lined on the outside of each floor by a long veranda or piazza along one side of the structure.

(a)

(b)

Figure 7.13 (*a*) This simple 3-room *shotgun house* in Baton Rouge, Louisiana, shows the design features typical of the class: long and narrow, one room wide, multiple rooms deep, a front-facing gable and porch, off-centered front and rear doors, and rooms connected by internal unaligned doors. A single shotgun house preserved in Tupelo, Mississippi, was the birthplace of Elvis Presley. (*b*) One variant of a shotgun cottage floor plan.

than it did to the simplicity and proportional dimensions imposed by the standardized materials. Midwest vernacular house types developed—including the one-story gabled rectangle, double-wing, and two-story foursquare farmhouses, quickly constructed by local carpenters or the farmers themselves.

The thick-walled *Spanish adobe house,* long and single-storied with a flat or low-pitched earth-covered roof entered Anglo America through the Hispanic borderlands (see Figure 6.11) but in most of its features owed more to indigenous Pueblo Indian design than to Spanish origins. In the Far West, Hispanic and Russian influences were locally felt, although housing concepts imported from the humid East predominated. In the Utah area, Mormon immigrants established the *central-hall house,* related to both the I house and the four-over-four house, as the dominant house type.

A variety of ethnic and architectural influences met and intermingled in the Pacific Northwest. French Canadians produced a closely knit ethnic settlement on the Willamette River at French Prairie (between Salem and Portland, Oregon). Chinese came to the coal mines of Vancouver Island in the 1860s; later, thousands were employed in the construction of the Northern Pacific Railroad. By the 1870s, an architecturally distinctive Chinatown was centered around the foot of Yesler Way and Occidental Avenue in Seattle, and similar enclaves were established in Tacoma, Portland, and other urban centers. But most immigrants to the British Columbia–Washington–Oregon regions were of Anglo American, not foreign birth, and the vast majority on the U.S. side came from midwestern roots, representing a further westward migration of populations whose forebears (or who themselves) were part of the Middle Atlantic culture hearths. Some—the earliest—carried to the Oregon and Washington forested regions the "midland" American backwoods pioneer culture and log-cabin tradition first encountered in the Delaware Valley hearth; others brought the variety of housing styles already well represented in the continental interior.

Architectural Diffusions

These vernacular architectural origins and movements were summarized by the cultural geographer Fred Kniffen (1900–1993), who thought that house types of the eastern United States and ultimately of much of Anglo America could be traced to three source regions on the Atlantic Coast, each feeding a separate diffusion stream: New England, Middle Atlantic, and Southern Coastal (Figure 7.14). *New England,* he argued, gave rise to a series of evolving house types based on a simple English original, variants of which spread westward with the settlers across New York, Ohio, Indiana, and Illinois and into Wisconsin and Iowa.

The principal contributions of the *Middle Atlantic* source region were the English *I house* and the Finnish-German log building. Its major diffusion directions were southward along the Appalachian Uplands, with offshoots in all directions, and westward across Pennsylvania. Multiple paths of movement from this hearth converged in the Ohio Valley Midwest, creating an interior "national hearth" of several intermingled streams (see Figure 7.4), and from there spread north, south, and west. In this respect, the narrow Middle Atlantic region played for vernacular architecture the same role its Midland dialect did in shaping the linguistic geography of the United States, as discussed on pages 133–134.

The earliest diffusion from the Middle Atlantic hearth was the backwoods frontier culture that carried rough log carpentry to all parts of the forested East and, eventually, westward to the northern Rockies and the Pacific Northwest. The identifying features of that

Figure 7.15 The "dogtrot" house.

Figure 7.14 **Architectural source areas and the diffusion of building methods** from the Atlantic Seaboard hearths. The map emphasizes log and frame construction as of 1850. The variation in the width of stream paths suggests the strength of the influence of the various hearths on vernacular housing away from the coast. The Southern Coastal Stream was limited in its influence to the coastal plain. The Delaware Valley hearth not only exerted a strong impact on the Upland South but also became—along with other Middle Atlantic hearths—the dominant vernacular housing source for the lower Middle West and the continental interior. By 1850, and farther to the west, new expansion cores were emerging around Salt Lake City, in coastal California, and in the Willamette Valley area of Oregon—all bearing the imprint of housing designs that first emerged in eastern hearths.

Sources: F. Kniffen, Annals of the Association of American Geographers, *Vol. 55:560, 1965; Fred Kniffen and Henry Glassie, "Building in Wood in the Eastern United States" in* Geographical Review 56:60, © 1966 The American Geographical *Society; and Terry G. Jordan and Matti Kaups,* The American Backwoods Frontier, *pp. 8–9, © 1989 The Johns Hopkins University Press.*

building tradition were the dogtrot and saddlebag house plans and double-crib barn designs. The basic unit of both house and barn was a rectangular "pen" ("crib" if for a barn) of four log walls that characteristically stood in tandem with an added second room that joined the first at the chimney end of the house. The resultant two-room central chimney design was called a *saddlebag house.* Another even more common expansion of the single-pen cabin was the *dogtrot* (Figure 7.15), a simple roofing-over of an open area left separating the two pens facing gable toward gable. Log construction techniques and traditions were carried across the intervening grasslands to the wooded areas of the mountains and the Pacific Coast during the 19th century. The first log buildings of settlements and farmsteads of the Oregon territory, for example, were indistinguishable from their eastern predecessors of the preceding century.

The third source area, in the Lower Chesapeake, spread its remarkably uniform influence southward as the *Southern Coastal Stream,* diffusing its impact inland along numerous paths into the Upland South (Figure 7.14). In that area of complex population

movements and topographically induced isolations, source area architectural styles were transformed into truly indigenous local folk housing forms. By 1850, diffusions from the eastern architectural hearths had produced a clearly defined folk housing geography in the eastern half of the United States and subsequently, by relocation and expansion diffusion, had influenced vernacular housing throughout Anglo America. The French and Caribbean influences of the *Delta Stream,* in contrast, were much more restricted and localized.

Nonmaterial Folk Culture

Houses burn, succumb to rot, are remodeled beyond recognition, or are physically replaced. Fences, barns, and outbuildings are similarly transitory features of the landscape, lost or replaced by other structures in other materials for other purposes as farms mechanize, consolidate, no longer rear livestock, are abandoned, or are subdivided for urban expansion. The folk housing and farm buildings that seem so solid a part of the built environment are, in reality, but temporary features of it. Impermanent, too, for the most part, are the tools and products of the folk craft worker. Some items of daily life and decoration may be preserved in museums or as household heirlooms; others may be exchanged among collectors of antiques. But inevitably, material folk culture is lost as the artifacts of even isolated groups increasingly are replaced by products of modern manufacture and standardized design.

In many ways, more permanent records of our folk heritages and differentials are to be found in the intangibles of our lives, in the nonmaterial folk culture that all of us possess and few recognize. Although ways of life change and the purposes of old tools are forgotten, favorite foods and familiar songs endure. Nonmaterial characteristics may more indelibly mark origins and flows of cultures and peoples than physical trappings outmoded, replaced, or left behind.

One important aspect of folk geography is the attention it pays to the spatial association of culture and environment. Folk societies, because of their subsistence, self-reliant economies, and limited technologies, are deemed particularly responsive to physical environmental circumstances. Thus, foodstuffs, herbs, and medicinal plants naturally available or able to be grown locally—as well as shelter—have been especially subject to folk geographic study. Less immediately connected to the environment, but important indicators of the backgrounds and memories of a social group, are the stories, fables, and music traditional to it and transmitted within it.

Another significant feature of nonmaterial folk culture is the ease and degree of its interconnections and transitions to popular cultural trends and adoptions. For example, the waltz originated in the early 17th century in the form of local peasant (folk cultural) dances of Austria and southern Germany. Performed at village festivals and taverns and featuring vigorous spinning motions in three-quarter time, the raucous waltz was passed by contagious diffusion to the town dwellers and aristocracy of an expanding Vienna. Denounced by civil and religious authorities as scandalous and vulgar, the waltz was modified and refined in cities and diffused rapidly throughout Europe and the Americas as an elite dance during the early 1800s; it was later adopted by the rising middle and urban working classes as perhaps the first really widespread fad of Western mass (popular) culture, remaining the favored social dance until overtaken around 1900 by Ragtime and other jazz-inspired dances—themselves originating as folk-cultural expressions.

Folk Food and Drink Preferences

Folk and Customary Foods

Cuisine, meaning the selection of foods and the style of cookery, is one of the most evident and enduring of the elements distinguishing cultural groups. Ethnic foods are the mainstay and the attraction of the innumerable fairs and "fests" held throughout the United States and Canada to celebrate the traditions of locally important groups. In the case of ethnic foods, of course, what is celebrated is the retention in a new environment of the food preferences, diets, and recipes that had their origin in a distant homeland. Folk food habits, on the other hand, are products of local circumstances; the dietary inputs are the natural foods derived from hunting, gathering, and fishing or the cultivated foods and domestic animals suited to the environmental conditions locally encountered.

The distinction between folk and ethnic is no clearer in foods than it is in other aspects of regional culture. Three observations may be made on this point. First, most societies have until recent times been intimately and largely concerned with food production on an individual and family basis. The close ties of people to environment—*folk* ties—are therefore particularly evident in food gathering and growing (Figure 7.16).

Second, most areas of the world have been occupied by a complex mix of peoples migrating in search of food and carrying food habits and preferences with them in their migrations. In the Americas, Australia, New Zealand, and a few other regions of recent colonization and diversified settlement, we are aware of these differing *ethnic* origins and the recipes and customs they imply. In other world regions, ethnic and cultural intermixture is less immediately

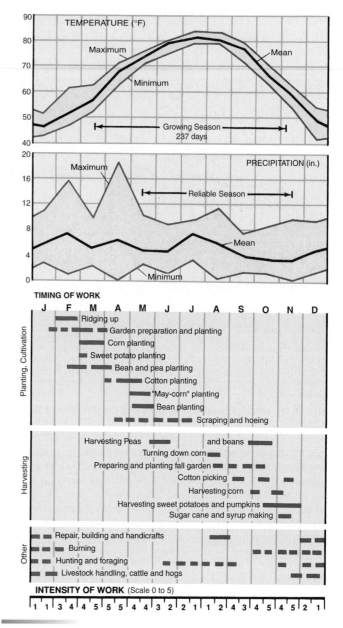

Figure 7.16 **The traditional "annual round" of folk culture farming** in the Upland South area of eastern Louisiana. The system and sequence of farming activities has varied little since the area was first settled around 1800. Frost danger dates and the phases of the moon are important in determining exact planting times. The corn, peas, and sweet potatoes assure the Upland farmer subsistence for family and animals. "The prudent folk farmer provides for subsistence first; then he turns to money crops"—in this case, cotton.

Source: Milton Newton, Jr., "The Annual Round in the Upland South: The Synchronization of Man and Nature through Culture," Pioneer America 3, No. 2 (Akron, Ohio: Pioneer Society of America, 1971), p. 65. Redrawn by permission.

apparent. In Korea, for example, what outsiders see as a distinctive ethnic cookery best known, perhaps, for *kimch'i*—brined, pickled, and spiced vegetables in endless combinations and uniquely Korean—also incorporates Japanese and Chinese foodstuffs and dishes.

Third, food habits are not just matters of sustenance but are intimately connected with the totality of *culture* or *custom.* People eat what is available and also what is, to them, edible. Sheep's brains and eyeballs, boiled insects, animal blood, and pig intestines, which are delicacies in some cultures, may be abominations to others unfamiliar with the culture that offers them as special treats to guests. Further, in most societies food and eating are considered a social, not just a personal, experience. Among Slavic peoples, to offer a guest bread and salt is a mark of esteem and welcome, and the bountiful and specially prepared meal as the mark of hospitality is common in nearly all cultures.

The interconnections between the folk, the ethnic, and the customary in food habits and preferences are evident in the Anglo American scene of mixed settlement and environmental diversity. Of course, the animals and plants nurtured, the basic recipes followed and flavorings added, and the specialized festive dishes of American folk groups have ethnic origins. Many originated abroad and were carried to and preserved in remote New World areas. Many were derived from the larder of the Amerindians and often varyingly used in different regional contexts. Turkey, squash, pumpkin, and cranberries were among them as was the corn (maize) that appeared with time as Southern grits, Southwestern tortillas, and everywhere south of Pennsylvania as the American replacement for wheat in the making of bread. Such classic American dishes as Brunswick stew (a thick stew made with vegetables and two meats, such as squirrel and rabbit or chicken), the clambake, smoked salmon, cornflakes, and beef jerky were originally Indian fare. Gradually, the environmental influences, isolation, and time spans implicit in the concept of folk culture created culinary distinctions among populations recognized as American rather than ethnic immigrants.

Shelves of cookbooks mark the general distinctions of folk cuisines of the United States and clearly suggest there is no clear separation between the traditional folk and modern popular in the realm of foods and cookery. Broad categories of New England, Creole, Southern, Chesapeake, Southwestern, and other regional cookery may be further refined into cookbooks containing Boston, Pennsylvania Dutch, Charleston, New Orleans, Tidewater, and other more localized recipes. Their number and diversity are ample proof of the diffusion into national and international popular culture of formerly spatially restricted folk cultural distinctions. Specific American dishes that have achieved fame and wide acceptance developed locally in response to food availability. New England seafood chowders and baked beans; southern pone, johnnycake, hush puppies, and other corn- (maize-) based dishes; the wild rice of the Great Lakes states; Louisiana crayfish (crawfish); southern gumbo; and salmon and shellfish dishes of the Pacific coast are but a few of many examples of folk foods and recipes originally and still characteristic of specific cultural areas but now also— through cookbooks, television cooking shows, and supermarket canned and frozen foods and produce displays of originally localized ingredients—made part of the modern national food experience. Other foods and recipes, once locally known, effectively disappear as the culture or foodstuff source is lost. The "fern pie" of Oregon's frontier past and "pigeon pie" made with the now-extinct passenger pigeon are among many examples.

Drink

In the United States, drink also represents an amalgam between ethnic imports and folk responses and emphases. A colonial taste for rum was based on West Indian and Tidewater sugarcane and molasses. European rootstock was introduced, with mixed results, to develop vineyards in most seaboard settlements; the native scuppernong grape was tried for wine making in the South. Peach, cherry, apple, and other fruit brandies were distilled for home consumption. Whiskey was a barley-based import accompanying the Scots and the Scotch-Irish to America, particularly to the Appalachians. In the New World, the grain base became native corn (maize), and whiskey making became a deeply rooted folk custom integral to the subsistence economy.

Whiskey also had cash economy significance. Small farmers of isolated areas far from markets converted part of their corn and rye crops into whiskey to produce a concentrated and valuable commodity conveniently transportable by horseback over bad roads (see "Transferability," p. 59). Such farmers viewed a federal excise tax imposed in 1791 on the production of distilled spirits as an intolerable burden not shared by those who could sell their grain directly. The tax led, first, to a short-lived tax revolt, the Whiskey Rebellion of 1794, in western Pennsylvania and, subsequently, to a tradition of moonshining—producing untaxed liquor in unlicensed stills. Figure 7.17 suggests the close association between its isolated Appalachian upland environment and illicit whiskey production in East Tennessee in the 1950s.

Folk Music

Folk music in North America is not merely intertwined with popular culture; it is the foundation on which American popular music is largely based. In turn, American popular music that was derived from folk sources exerts a global influence that since the late 1800s has fostered both popular and folk music genres throughout the rest of the world. And those folk sources continue to serve as inspirations and themes for the commercial music industry, films and film scores, musical theater, concert music, and television. Here again, the distinction between folk and popular culture is indistinct and largely meaningless.

Figure 7.17 In the mid-1950s, official estimates put weekly moonshine production at 24,000 gallons in mountainous eastern Tennessee, at 6000 gallons in partially hilly middle Tennessee, and at 2000 gallons in flat western Tennessee. The map shows the approximate number of stills seized each month at that time in East Tennessee. Each dot indicates one still.

Source: Redrawn by permission from Loyal Durand, "Mountain Moonshining in East Tennessee," Geographical Review 46 (New York: American Geographical Society, 1956), p. 171. Copyright © 1956 American Geographical Society.

North American folk music began as transplants of familiar Old World songs carried by settlers to the New World. Each group of immigrants established an outpost of a European musical community, making the American folk song, in the words of Alan Lomax, "a museum of musical antiques from many lands." But the imported songs became Americanized, hybridization between musical traditions occurred, and American experience added its own songs of frontier life, of farming, courting, and laboring (see "The American Empire of Song"). Eventually, distinctive American styles of folk music and recognizable folk song cultural regions developed (Figure 7.18).

The *Northern* song area—including the Maritime Provinces of Canada, New England, and the Middle Atlantic states—in general featured unaccompanied solo singing in clear, hard tones. Its ballads were close to English originals, and the British connection was continuously renewed by new immigrants, including Scots and Irish. The traditional ballads and current popular songs brought by British immigrants provided the largest part of the Anglo Canadian folk song heritage. On both sides of the border, the fiddle was featured at dances, and in the States, fife-and-drum bands became common in the early years of the Republic.

The *Southern Backwoods and Appalachian* song area, extending westward to East Texas, involved unaccompanied, high-pitched, and nasal solo singing. The music, based on English tradition and modified by Appalachian "hardscrabble" life, developed in isolation in upland and lowland settlement areas. Marked by moral and emotional conflict with an undercurrent of haunting melancholy, the backwoods style emerged in the modern period as the roots of the distinctive and popular genre of "country" music.

The northern and southern traditions abutted in a transition zone along the Ohio Valley but blended together across the Mississippi to create the *Western* song area. There, factual narrative songs reflected the experiences of cowboy, riverman,

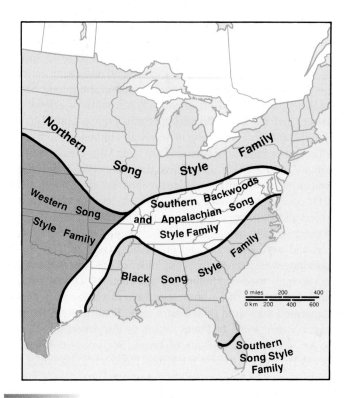

Figure 7.18 **Folk song regions of eastern United States.**
Alan Lomax has indirectly outlined folk culture regions of the eastern United States by defining areas associated with different folk song traditions.

Source: Redrawn "Map depicting folk song regions of the Eastern U.S." by Rafael Palacios, from Folk Songs of North America *by Alan Lomax. Copyright © 1960 by Alan Lomax. Used by permission.*

The American Empire of Song

The map sings. The chanteys surge along the rocky Atlantic seaboard, across the Great Lakes and round the moon-curve of the Gulf of Mexico. The paddling songs of the French-Canadians ring out along the Saint Lawrence and west past the Rockies. Beside them, from Newfoundland, Nova Scotia, and New England, the ballads, straight and tall as spruce, march towards the West.

Inland from the Sea Islands, slave melodies sweep across the whole South from the Carolinas to Texas. And out on the shadows of the Smoky and Blue Ridge mountains the old ballads, lonesome love songs, and hoedowns echo through the upland South into the

hills of Arkansas and Oklahoma. There in the Ozarks the Northern and Southern song families swap tunes and make a marriage.

The Texas cowboys roll the little doughies [sic] north to Montana, singing Northern ballads with a Southern accent. New roads and steel rails lace the Southern backwoods to the growl and thunder of Negro chants of labour—the axe songs, the hammer songs, and the railroad songs. These blend with the lonesome hollers of levee-camp mule-skinners to create the blues, and the blues, America's *cante hondo,* uncoils its subtle, sensual melancholy in the ear of all the states, then all the world.

The blues roll down the Mississippi to New Orleans, where the Creoles mix the musical gumbo of jazz—once a dirty word, but now a symbol of musical freedom for the West. The Creoles add Spanish pepper and French sauce and blue notes to the rowdy tantara of their reconstruction-happy brass bands, stir up the hot music of New Orleans and warm the weary heart of humanity. . . . These are the broad outlines of America's folk-song map.

Source: "Introduction" from *Folk Songs of North America* by Alan Lomax. Copyright © 1960 by Alan Lomax. Used by permission of Doubleday, a division of Random House, Inc.

sodbuster, and gold seeker. Natural beauty, personal valor, and feminine purity were recurring themes. Many songs appeared as reworked lumberjack ballads of the North or other modifications from the song traditions of the eastern United States.

Imported songs are more prominent among the traditional folk tunes of Canada than they are in the United States; only about one-quarter of Canadian traditional songs were composed in the New World. Most native Canadian songs—like their U.S. counterparts—reflected the daily lives of ordinary folk. In Newfoundland and along the Atlantic coast, those lives were bound up with the sea, and songs of Canadian origin dealt with fishing, sealing, and whaling. Particularly in Ontario, it was the lumber camps that inspired and spread folk music. Anglo Canadian songs show a strong Irish character in pattern and tune and traditionally were sung solo and unaccompanied.

The *Black* folk song tradition, growing out of racial and economic oppression, reflects a union of Anglo American folk song, English country dancing, and West African musical patterns. The African American folk song of the rural South or the northern ghetto was basically choral and instrumental in character; hands and feet were used to establish rhythm. A strong beat, a leader-chorus style, and deep-pitched mellow voices were characteristic.

Lomax dealt with and mapped only English-language folk song styles. To round out the North American scene, mention must also be made of French Canadian river and fur trader songs of the Northeast and the strong Mexican American musical tradition still vital and spreading in the Southwest.

Different folk music traditions metamorphosed and spread in the 20th century as distinctive styles of popular music. Jazz emerged in New Orleans in the later 19th century as a union of minstrel show ragtime and the blues, a type of southern black music based on work songs and spirituals. Urban blues—performed with a harsh vocal delivery accompanied by electric guitars, harmonicas, and piano—was a Chicago creation, brought there largely by artists from Mississippi. Country music spread from its southern white ancestral areas with the development of the radio and the phonograph in the 20th century. It became commercialized, electrified, and amplified but remained at core modified folk music. Bluegrass style, a high-pitched derivative of Scottish bagpipe sound and church congregation singing tradition, is performed unamplified, true to its folk origins. Bluegrass identification with commercial singing groups bearing identities derived from place names emphasizes the ties of the people, the performers, and the land in the folk tradition. As these examples of musical style and tradition show, the ethnic merges into the folk, and the folk blends into the popular—in music and in many other elements of culture.

The making of musical instruments is a recurring part of material folk culture traditions. For example, the zither was brought to the United States from northern and central Europe, but as the Pennsylvania Germans carried it southward into the southern Appalachians, it became the American-made three-or four-stringed strummed or plucked dulcimer. The banjo has clear African origins, but by the end of the 19th century it had become a characteristically American folk instrument, versions of which—five-stringed and fretless—were homemade throughout the Southern Uplands. The fiddle was the preeminent Canadian folk instrument and—along with the bagpipe in Scottish communities—was the most common accompaniment for dancing. Both instruments were frequently homemade.

The Oral Folk Tradition

Folklore is the oral tradition of a group. It refers to ways of talking and interacting and includes proverbs, prayers, common expressions, and particularly, superstitions, beliefs, narrative tales, and legends. It puts into words the basic shared values of a group and informally expresses its ideals and codes of conduct. Folklore serves, as well, to preserve old customs and tales that are the identity of the folk group. The Brothers Grimm recorded German fairy tales early in the 19th century to trace the old mythologies and beliefs of the German people, not for the entertainment of the world's children.

Immigrant groups settling in the Americas brought with them different well-developed folklore traditions, each distinctive not only to the ethnic group itself but even to the part of the home country from which it came. In the New World, the established folklores of home areas became intermixed. The countries of North and South America contain many coexisting and interacting folklore traditions brought by early European colonizers, by transported African slaves, and by later diversified immigrant groups from both Europe and Asia.

The imported folk traditions serve to identify the separate groups in pluralistic societies. In some instances, the retention of folk identity and belief is long term because particular groups—Pennsylvania Dutch, Old Order Amish, and the Hasidim of Brooklyn, for example—isolate themselves from mainstream American culture. Other groups—in Appalachia, the Missouri Ozarks, and the Louisiana bayous—may retain or develop distinctive folklore traditions because isolation was thrust on them by remoteness or terrain.

Where immigrant groups intermixed, however, as in most New World countries, *syncretism*—the merging or fusion of different traditions—is characteristic. Old World beliefs, particularly in magic, begin to recede and are lost to later generations. Proverbs begin to be shared, common short jokes replace long folk tales as both entertainment and devices of instruction or ridicule of deviant behavior, and literacy reduces dependence on the reports and repetitions of knowledgeable elders. **Folkways**—the learned behavior shared by a society that prescribes accepted and common modes of conduct—become those of the country as a whole as acculturation and popularization dictate the ways of life of all.

With the passage of time, too, a new folklore of legend, myth, and hero develops. In the United States, Washington and the cherry tree, Patrick Henry's plea for liberty, the exploits of Jim Bowie or Davy Crockett, the song of John Henry the steel-driving man, or tales of Paul Bunyan become the common property and heritage of all Americans—a new national folklore that transcends regional boundaries or immigrant origins.

Folk Cultural Regions of Eastern United States

A small set of hearths or source regions of folk culture origin and dispersal have been recognized for the eastern United States. They are indicated in Figure 7.19. The similarity of the hearth locations and diffusion routes to the pattern of ethnically based architectural regions and flows shown in Figure 7.14 is unmistakable and a reminder that in the American context, "folk" and "ethnic" are intertwined and interchangeable when traced back to first settlement. Frontier settlers

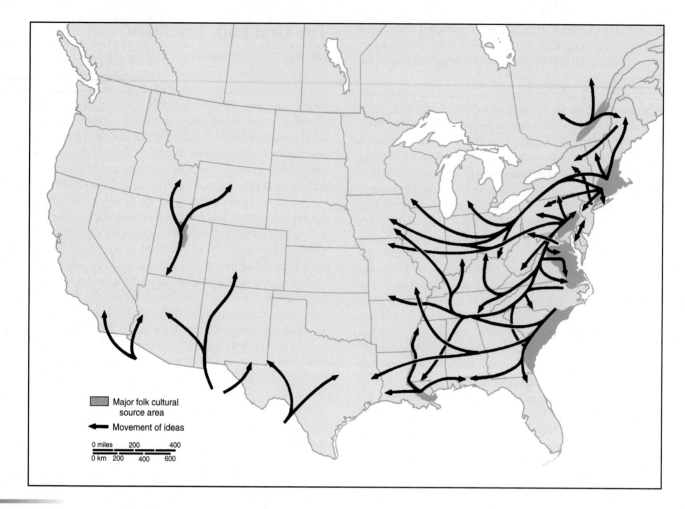

Figure 7.19 American folk culture hearths and diffusions.

Sources: Based on Henry Glassie, Pattern in the Material Folk Culture of the Eastern United States, *pp. 37–38, copyright © 1968 by the Trustees of the University of Pennysylvania; and Michael P. Conzen, ed.,* The Making of the American Landscape *(Winchester, Mass.: Unwin Hyman, 1990), 373.*

carrying to new, interior locations the artifacts and traditions of those hearth areas created a small set of indistinctly bounded eastern folk cultural regions (Figure 7.20). Although they have become blurred as folk traditions have died, their earlier contributions to American folk diversity remain clear.

From the small *Mid-Atlantic* region, folk cultural items and influences were dispersed into the North, the Upland South, and the Midwest. Southeastern Pennsylvania and the Delaware Valley formed its core and the Pennsylvania Dutch determined much of the Mid-Atlantic region's character. The eastern Finns added their log-building techniques and subsistence lifestyles. Furniture styles, log construction, decorative arts, house and barn types, and distinctive "sweet" cookery were among the purely European imports converted in the Mid-Atlantic hearth to American folk expressions.

The folk culture of the *Lowland South,* by contrast, derived from English originals and African admixtures. French influences in the Louisiana coastal extension and some down-slope migrations from the highland areas add to the amalgam. Dogtrot and I houses became common; English cuisine was adapted to include black-eyed peas, turnip greens, sweet potatoes, small-bird pies, and syrups from sugarcane and sorghum. African origins influenced the widespread use of the banjo in music.

The *Upland South* showed a mixture of influences carried up from the Tidewater and brought south from the Mid-Atlantic folk region along the Appalachian highlands by settlers of German and Scotch-Irish stock. The sheltered isolation of the Upland South and its Ozark outlier encouraged the retention of traditional folk culture long after it had been lost in more accessible and exposed locations. Log houses and farm structures, rail fences, traditional art and music, and home-crafted quilts and furniture make the Upland South region a prime repository of folk artifacts and customs in the United States.

The *North*—dominated by New England, but including New York State, English Canada, Michigan, and Wisconsin—showed a folk culture of decidedly English origin. The saltbox house and Boston baked beans in pots of redware and stoneware are among characteristic elements. The New England-British domination is locally modified by French Canadian and central European influences.

The *Midwest*—a conglomerate of inputs from the Upland South, from the North, and, particularly, from the Mid-Atlantic region—is the least distinctive, most intermixed and Americanized of the cultural regions. Everywhere the interior contains evidences, both rural and urban, of artifacts carried by migrants from the eastern hearths and by newly arriving European immigrants. Folk geography in the Midwest is more the occasional discovery of architectural relics more

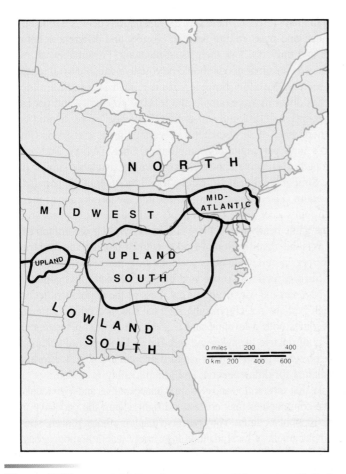

Figure 7.20 Material folk culture regions of the eastern United States.

Source: Redrawn with permission from Henry Glassie, Pattern in the Material Folk Culture of the Eastern United States, *p. 39, copyright © 1968 by the Trustees of the University of Pennsylvania.*

or less pure in form, though frequently dilapidated, or the recognition of such unusual cultural pockets as those of the Amish, than it is a systematic survey of a defined cultural region.

The Passing of Folk Cultural Regionalism

By the early 20th century, the impacts of immigrant beginnings, settlement diffusions, and ethnic modifications had made themselves felt in a pattern of regionally differentiated rural cultural landscapes. The cities of the eastern and midwestern parts of the country were socially a world apart from the farms. Brash and booming with the economic success of rampant industrialization, the cities were in constant flux. Building and rebuilding, adding and absorbing immigrants and rural in-migrants, increasingly interconnected by passenger and freight railroad and by the national economic unification important since the 1870s, they were far removed in culture, outlook, and way of life from the agricultural areas in which they were physically but not emotionally located.

It was in the countryside that the most pronounced effects of regional cultural differentiation were to be discerned. Although the flow of young people to the city, responding to the push of farm mechanization and the pull of urban jobs and excitement, was altering traditional social orders and rhythms, the automobile, electrical appliances, and the lively mass medium of radio had not as yet obscured the distinction between urban and rural. The family farm, kinship and community ties, the traditions, ways of life, and artifacts of small town and rural residence still existed as regionally varied composites. But those ways and artifacts, and the folk cultural regions they defined, were all being eroded and erased with the passage of time and the modernization of all segments of North American life and culture.

Regional character is a transient thing. New peoples, new economic challenges, and new technologies serve as catalysts of rapid change. By World War I and the Roaring Twenties, the automobile, the radio, motion pictures, and a national press began to homogenize America. The slowing of the immigrant stream and second-generation absorption of the common national culture served to blur and obliterate some of the most regionally distinctive cultural identifications. Mechanization, mass production, and mass distribution through mail order and market town diminished self-sufficiency and household crafts. Popular culture began to replace traditional culture in everyday life throughout the United States and Canada.

The leading American women's magazine of the middle 19th century was *Godey's Lady's Book,* featuring hand-colored pictures of the latest foreign and American fashions in clothing and articles about household furnishings in the newest styles. Its contents influenced ladies of fashion in cities and towns throughout the settled United States. The Montgomery Ward and Sears, Roebuck catalogs appearing in the late 19th century served the same purpose for more ordinary goods, garments, and classes of customers. Popular culture, based on fashions, standards, or fads developed in national centers of influence and prestige, became an important reality over wide areas and across social strata.

As we have seen, it is not realistic or valid to view folk and popular culture as opposites. Rather, transition and melding take place between them, often with folk cultural trends forming the inspiration and backdrop for developing popular cultural forms. There are, of

Patterns of Popular Culture

In 1728, Mary Stith of Virginia wrote to a friend, then in England, "When you come to London pray favour me in your choice of a suit . . . suitably dressed with . . . whatever the fashion requires." In the 1750s, George Washington wrote to his British agent, Thomas Knox, to request "two pair of Work'd Ruffles . . . ; if work'd Ruffles shou'd be out of fashion send such as are not . . . ," noting

"whatever Goods you may send me . . . you will let them be fashionable." In the 1760s, he asked another agent, Charles Lawrence, to "send me a Suit of handsome Cloth Cloaths. I have no doubts but you will choose a fashionable coloured Cloth as well as a good one and make it in the best taste. . . ." The American gentry might be distant and isolated, but they did not wish to be unstylish.

course, significant differences between them. Folk or ethnic culture suggests individuality, small group distinctiveness, and above all, tradition. **Popular culture,** in contrast, implies the general mass of people, primarily but not exclusively urban based, constantly adopting, conforming to, and quickly abandoning ever-changing common modes of behavior and fads of material and nonmaterial culture. Popular culture presumably substitutes for and replaces folk and ethnic differences.

For some, the term "popular culture" is not sufficiently precise to define the realities and trends of modern ways of life. They suggest a further distinction should be made between *popular culture* and *mass culture.* The former they view as participatory, involving people in active engagement in the activities and events that were formerly central in American life but now are diminished in relative importance. Amateur athletics; county-fair attendance; barn and ballroom dancing; viewing live theatrical and vaudeville performances; membership in community social, charitable, or political clubs; and the like exemplify the involvement and interaction of true popular culture. That kind of social and personal interaction, it is held, declined markedly after the middle of the 20th century. It was presumably largely replaced by a mass culture comprised of passive and solitary activities, typified by television viewing of game shows and sporting events in which the individual is manipulated and shaped by mass media without the necessity or opportunity to participate or interact with other participants.

Even the popular culture/mass culture contrast is incomplete and outdated. The mass culture of the latter part of the 20th century that locked millions of American viewers into sharing the "must see" offerings of variety shows, situation comedies, and evening newscasts on three national television networks had largely passed by the early 21st century. It was replaced by a culture of multiple entertainment and information niches and of personal rather than mass media. With hundreds of cable and satellite television channels to choose from, and with the proliferation of social-networking Internet sites demanding or encouraging personal involvement, contributions, and exchanges, the mass-culture era has been transformed into one of "microcultures" where everyone can restrict participation to those topics and groups of specific interest to themselves. The prospect is for individuals to interact electronically primarily with highly specialized likeminded persons, to become their own radio and television programmers, using their iPods, computer, and cell phone screens as personal media, and to lose interest in older forms of mass media and forego at least some of the contact with the larger society that is implied by older ideas of mass and popular culture.

Whether or not such a subdivision is useful, the basic characteristic of popular culture as a whole remains certain: it is pervasive, involving the vast majority of a population in similar consumption habits, exposing them to similar recreational choices, and leading them to similar behavioral patterns. Those restrictive similarities are the product of mass production of goods and services and their willing acceptance by the majority of the population as the normal, expected, and desired ingredients of daily life.

Many details of popular culture, we should remember, derive from regional folk cultural traits. For example, universally enjoyed popular and spectator sports such as soccer, football, golf, and tennis originated as local and regional folk games, many of them hundreds of years old. Similarly, musicologists easily trace most recent and current musical styles and fads to earlier folk and ethnic music genres.

In many respects, therefore, the distinctions between folk, ethnic, popular, and mass culture become blurred, and differences between local and universal lose their usual meaning. Presumably, all mass-produced consumer goods should be equally available to all segments of a society. We know, however, that regional tastes and consumption choices differ in, for example, the relative popularity and per capita consumption of different soft drinks (Dr Pepper more favored in the southern states than elsewhere) or various processed foods (Puerto Rico's high per capita consumption of Cheez Whiz). These mark regionally distinctive choices among widely available similar products. Similar "regionalism" can be found throughout the popular culture realm. The disinterest expressed until the last decade of the 20th century in soccer in the United States and the intense passion aroused by the game nearly everywhere else in the world is a common example, as is the identification of cricket with Britain and the countries of its former empire while other societies are unfamiliar with the game.

Such exceptions do not void the generalization that popular culture becomes the way of life of the mass of the population, reducing, though perhaps not eliminating, regional folk and ethnic differences. It becomes both a leveling and a liberating force, obliterating those locally distinctive lifestyles and material and nonmaterial cultures that develop when groups remain isolated and ethnocentric. Uniformity is substituted for differentiation, and group identity is eroded. For some people, that substitution and erosion is unacceptable, and individuals and whole communities may contest and fight against the pervasive influence of popular culture. They perceive that it promotes **placelessness**— the replacement of local identity and variety with a homogeneous and standardized landscape—and resist or reject, for example, the arrival of a Wal-Mart "big box" store, the multiplication of uniform highway strip malls, and the like. For those people and communities, the modernity of popular culture is viewed as destroying the sense of a traditional unique and identifiable locale. For others, however, the individual is liberated by popular culture through exposure to a much broader range of available opportunities— in clothing, foods, tools, recreations, and lifestyles—than ever were available in a cultural environment controlled by the restrictive and limited choices imposed by custom and isolation. Although broad areal uniformity may displace localisms, it is a cultural uniformity vastly richer in content and possibilities than any it replaces.

That uniformity is frequently, though not exclusively, associated with national populations: the American or Canadian way of life distinguished from the English, the Japanese, or others. Even these distinctions are eroding as popular culture in many aspects of music, movies, sports (soccer, for example), and the like becomes internationalized (Figure 7.21). Popular culture becomes dominant with the wide dissemination of common influences and with the mixing of cultures that force both ethnic and folk communities to become aware of and part of a larger homogeneous society. The result is a material and nonmaterial cultural mix that is not necessarily better or worse than the folk and ethnic cultures lost. It is, however, certainly and obviously different from the traits and distinctions of the past.

National Uniformities and Globalization

Landscapes of popular culture tend to acquire uniformity through the installation of standardized facilities. Within the United States, for example, national motel chains announced by identical signs,

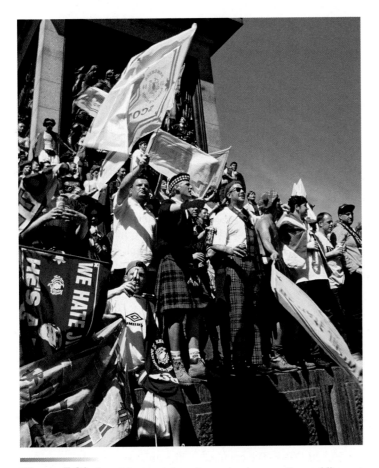

Figure 7.21 **Scottish soccer fans.** Soccer has become the world's most popular sport. The 2006 FIFA World Cup™ was broadcast on television stations in 214 countries and territories and had a cumulative television audience of over 26 billion. The final match between Italy and France had 715 million viewers—over 10 percent of the world's population.

Figure 7.22 Western fast-food chains, classics of standardized popular culture, have gone international—and bilingual—as this KFC outlet in Xian, China, reveals.

advertised by repetitious billboards, and featuring uniform facilities and services may comfort travelers with the familiar but also deny them the interest of regional contrast. Fast-food restaurants—franchised, standardized, and merchandised as identical—carry single logos, building designs, and menus across cultural boundaries and national borders (Figure 7.22). They provide the assurance of the known and the tolerable but insulate the palate from the regionally distinctive. Even food outlets identified with ethnics have lost their cultural character. The pizza has become American, not Italian (Figure 7.23), just as the franchised Mexican American taco and burrito have escaped their regional and ethnic confines and been carried nationwide. Chain gas stations, discount stores, and other enterprises carry on the theme of familiarity of outlet and standardization of product and service wherever one resides or journeys.

Many of these Anglo American elements of popular culture are oriented toward the automobile, the ubiquitous means of local and interregional travel. Advertisements' distinctiveness of design assures instant recaognition, and their clustering along highways and main streets guarantees that whatever the incidence of regional character still remaining, the public face of town and highway is everywhere the same—the

placelessness rejected by so many defending the local and unique (Figure 7.24).

Those uniformities are transitory. While folk cultures have ingrained traditions that change only slowly and locally, popular culture tends to change rapidly and uniformly over wide expanses. That is, popular culture diffuses rapidly, even instantaneously, in our age of immediate global communication and sharing of ideas through television, radio, and the Internet. Those same media and means assure the widespread quick replacement of the old fads with new. The globalization of popular culture is commonly recognized. In clothing styles and fashion trade names, near-universal display of American movies and television shows, worldwide acceptance of the cultural norms of urban life and western business conduct and institutions, and the global spread of soft drink signs and golden arches testify to the international standardization of life and the quick adoption of changing tastes and practices.

That standardization, of course, is not complete. National and regional cultural contrasts remain embedded in urban and rural landscapes, and seemingly universal popular icons are always differentially adapted and modified for easy acceptance by different national societies. The term **glocalization** describes this adaptation of globalized products to fit local contexts. Domino's and Pizza Hut, for example,

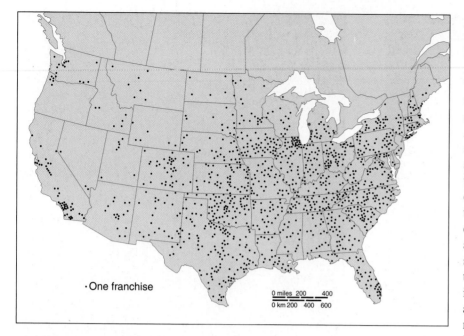

Figure 7.23 The locations of pizza parlors of a single national chain.

Source: Floyd M. Henderson and J. Russel, unpublished drawing.

Figure 7.24 For some, the advertisements for commercialized popular culture constitute visual blight.

phone to tell her mother that they plan to eat at a nearby McDonald's. Meanwhile, her brother sits at home, listening to the latest American music on his iPod while playing a game on the family's computer. The activities of both young people are evidence of the globalization of popular culture that is Western and particularly—though certainly not invariably—American in origin. U.S. movies, television shows, software, music, food, brand names, and fashions are marketed worldwide. They influence the beliefs, tastes, and aspirations of people in virtually every country, though their effect is most pronounced on the young. They, rather than their elders, want to emulate the stars they see in movies and on MTV and to adopt what they think are up-to-date lifestyles, manners, and modes of dress. They are also the group most apt to use English words and slang in everyday conversation, though the use of English as the worldwide medium of communication in economics, technology, and science is an even broader indication of current cultural merging.

Rapid introduction and quickly falling prices of high-tech communication and entertainment devices have had a profound effect on changing activities and lifestyles wherever personal freedom and Westernized economies, incomes, and cultures prevail. For example, the postal system and fixed-line telephone are increasingly passé, even more so in countries such as South Korea and Japan than in the United States. The computer with e-mail and instant messaging, the cell phone and text messages, and voice-over-Internet-protocol (VOIP) telephony have revolutionized local and long-distance communications. Computer chat rooms, blogs, and online communities both enlarge and focus interpersonal exchanges. Broadband gaming, iPods, cellular videos, and IPTV (Internet protocol TV) expand recreational and informational opportunities, and cell phone e-mail, Web browsing, video games, and more all are integral to new behavioral and communications practices and standards of, particularly, the younger and technologically at-ease age groups. And all are made possible for increasing numbers of people by quickly falling prices after their first introduction.

The globalization of popular culture (and the dominance of English in popular and professional use) is resented by many people, rejected by some, and officially opposed or controlled by certain governments. The Canadian government imposes minimum "Canadian content" requirements on television and radio broadcasters. Iran, Singapore, China, and other states, for example, attempt to restrict Western radio and television programming from reaching their people. Governments of many countries—Saudi Arabia, Myanmar, Laos, Yemen, China, and the United Arab Emirates among them—impose Internet surveillance and censorship and demand that U.S.-based search engines filter content to conform with official restrictions and limitations. China began regulating Internet access in the mid-1990s; more recently, even the Western European countries of Germany and France have demanded that American search engines exclude numerous disapproved websites from the German and French versions of their indexes.

In other instances, religious and cultural conservatives may decry what they see as the imposition of Western values, norms,

have a combined total of some 6000 overseas outlets in over 100 countries but do not serve a standard product worldwide. Pizza in India likely will be ordered with spicy chicken sausage or pickled ginger. In Japan, a best seller is pizza topped with potatoes, mayonnaise, and ham or bacon bits. Hong Kong customers prefer their pizza flavoring to be Cajun spices; Thais favor hot spices mixed with lemon grass and lime; in England preferred toppings include sweet corn and tuna; and in Australia, the number one topping for pizza is eggs. The store signs and designs may be universal; the product varies to fit local tastes.

Yet, on the world scene, globalized cultural amalgamation is increasingly evident though not universally welcomed. Imagine this scene: Wearing a Yankees baseball cap, a Gap shirt, Levis, and Reebok shoes, a middle-class teenager in Lima, Peru, goes with her friends to see the latest thriller. After the movie, she uses her cell and excesses through such mass culture industries as advertising, the media, professional sports, and the like. Whether or not movies, music, television programming, or clothing fads accurately reflect the essence of Western culture, critics argue that they force on other societies, as normal and unquestioned, alien values of materialism, innovation, self-indulgence, sexuality, and defiance of authority and tradition. More basically, perhaps, globalization of popular culture is seen as a form of dominance made possible by Western control of the means of communication and by self-proclaimed Western technical, educational, and social superiority. What may be accepted or sought by the young and better educated in many societies may simultaneously be strongly resisted by those of the same societies more traditional in outlook and belief.

Our Material Culture Focus

National economies have traditionally been perceived as being firmly based on the production of material things; industry was seen as the key to national strength. Since World War II, however, consumption rather than production has become the dominant engine driving the American economy. As a result, shopping is no longer thought of as a trivial female activity but as an expected and enjoyable pursuit regardless of gender or age, recognized and encouraged by common phrases such as "born to shop," "shop 'til you drop," or "buy 'til you die." The most prominent landscape expression of our commodity-driven popular culture, of course, is the shopping mall, sometimes dubbed the "palace of consumption."

The Shopping Mall

Within Anglo America and, increasingly, other world regions, the apparent exterior sameness of popular culture has been carried indoors into the design, merchants, and merchandise of the shopping mall. Major regional malls have been created in every part of North America that boasts a metropolitan population large enough to satisfy their carefully calculated purchasing-power requirements. Local and neighborhood malls extend the concept to smaller residential entities. With their mammoth parking lots and easy access from expressways or highways, America's 38,000 large and small malls are part of the automobile culture that helped create them after World War II (Figure 7.25). Increasingly, however, they stand in standardized separation from the world of movement and of regional contrast. Enclosed, temperature controlled, without windows or other acknowledgment of a world outside, some assume monumental size, approximating the retail space contained in the central business districts of older medium-sized and large cities (Figure 7.26). They cater to a full range of homogenized shopping and consuming wants with a repetitive assemblage of brand-name products available in a uniform collection of national or international chain outlets. Enclosed shopping malls have diffused through much of the world. The two largest shopping malls are located in China, the third largest is in the Philippines, and the fourth largest is in Dubai, United Arab Emirates.

Because the earlier, impersonal, massive enclosed malls gave a feeling of alienation and loss of belonging to a true community, North American developers have recently redesigned those older malls

Figure 7.25 The Carousel Center Mall in Syracuse, New York, with its extensive surrounding parking areas, typifies the gigantic enclosed regional malls of the late 20th century and now no longer in favor or being built.

Figure 7.26 Massive, enclosed, and buffered from its surroundings, the modern metropolitan shopping mall is an external and internal built environment that summarizes the contrasts between popular culture standardization and folk and ethnic cultural individuality. This mall is in the center city area of Philadelphia, Pennsylvania.

and constructed new ones as "new shopping towns" to replicate the landscape features of traditional urban places and evoke the sense of a distinctive community. Familiar urban landscape elements are expressed in these new-style malls, but in romanticized forms. The central corridors recall the Main Streets of the past, where shoppers jostle with friendly strangers. In the middle of the mall may be a large open space that functions as a simulated town square, often with benches and shrubbery imitating a city park or green space of a small-town center. The ever-present food court is simply an interior reproduction of sidewalk cafés of past urban places. These new-style shopping malls with their contrived sense of place are, it has been suggested, idealized Disneyland versions of the American myth of small-town intimacy, itself a product of popular culture. In addition to the climate control, a major difference is that a mall's

Figure 7.27 The Arbor Lakes lifestyle shopping center in the Minneapolis-St. Paul suburb of Maple Grove, Minnesota, creates a pseudo-Main Street ambience. Ironically, the nearby suburb of Edina, Minnesota, is home to Southdale, which was the country's first fully enclosed regional shopping mall when it opened in 1956.

central square is privately owned and controlled. Activities that would be allowed in a traditional city square such as rallies, proselytizing, and begging are usually not allowed in a mall since they aren't conducive to a pleasant shopping atmosphere.

That myth is accentuated in the recent popularity of *lifestyle centers.* The construction of large, enclosed malls has slowed to a virtual halt in the United States since 2000 and the phenomenon of vacant malls is on the rise. Instead of the enclosed regional mall, developers seem to prefer lifestyle centers, which numbered some 150 by the end of 2006. The new centers, differ from the older enclosed malls by being smaller outdoor or open-air assemblages with store-fronts facing the street or sidewalk (Figure 7.27). Rather than massive parking lots and a long walk past stores of no interest, customers in lifestyle centers are able to park near their destinations, shop, and leave without encountering the crowded interior space of traditional malls. Unlike the "placeless" environment associated with the massive enclosed mall, lifestyle centers possess a uniqueness, an ambience, and a "localized" feel of small towns, although most of the retailers and restaurants are national chains that would not be found in a typical small town.

The ubiquity of malls and the uniformity of their goods are clearly reflected in items of clothing. Fashion replaces personal preference, social position, occupation, or tradition as the arbiter of type or design of clothing. Whatever may be dictated nationally—miniskirt, designer jeans, or other fad—is instantly available locally, hurried to market by well-organized chains responding to well-orchestrated customer demand. A few national or international fashion centers dictate what shall be worn, a few designer names dominate the popularly acceptable range of choices. Since popular culture is, above all, commercialized culture, a market success by one producer is instantly copied by others. Thus, even the great number of individual shops within the mall is only an assurance of variations on the same limited range of clothing (or other) themes, not necessarily of diversity of choice. Yet, of course, the very wealth of variations and

separate items permits an individuality of choice and selection of image not possible within constrained and controlled folk or ethnic groups.

Even culture in the sense of the arts is standardized within the malls. Chain bookstores offer identical best-sellers and paperbacks; multiscreen cinemas provide viewing choice only among the currently popular films; gift shops have nationally identical selections of figurines and pressed glass; and art stores stock similar lines of prints, photographs, and posters. It has been noted that Americans, at least, spend more of their time within malls than anywhere else except home and work. It is not unlikely that a standardized popular culture is at least in part traceable to the homogenized shopping mall. By the late 1990s, the growing market dominance of a limited number of national chains of "super" stores and discount outlets— the Wal-Marts, Target stores, and the like—were noticeably eroding the customer volume at shopping malls of all sizes and further reducing the number and standardizing the array of clothing styles and brands and other common items universally available.

Outside the Mall

Other material and nonmaterial tastes and recreations are, in popular culture, subject to the same widespread uniformities as are the goods available within repetitive shopping complexes. Country music, we saw, was culturally associated with the Upland South. It has long since lost that regional exclusivity, and Nashville has become a product, not a place. By the late 1970s (Figure 7.28), no American with access to radio was denied exposure to electric guitar and melancholy lyric. The latest movies are simultaneously released throughout the country; the same children's toys and adults' games are everywhere instantly available to satisfy the generated wants.

Wilbur Zelinsky reported on the speed of diffusion of a manufactured desire:

> In August, 1958, I drove from Santa Monica, California, to Detroit at an average rate of about 400 miles (650 km) per day; and display windows in almost every drugstore and variety store along the way were being hastily stocked with hula hoops just off the delivery trucks from Southern California. A national television program the week before had roused instant cravings. It was an eerie sensation, surfing along a pseudo-innovation wave.[1]

Regional Differences

Of course, not all expressions of popular culture are spatially or socially uniform. Areal variations do exist in the extent to which particular elements in the general cultural pool are adopted. These variations impart aspects of regional and group differentiations of interest to geographers. For example, gaining momentum since 1980 has been a return to building new houses in traditional styles (Figure 7.29). This return to regional vernacular styles enhances regional identities and erases some of the homogeneity imposed by national trends and national homebuilders.

Spatial patterns in sports, for example, reveal that the games played, the migration paths of their fans and players, and the

[1]*The Cultural Geography of the United States.* Rev. ed. (Englewood Cliffs, N.J.: Prentice-Hall, 1992), p. 80, fn 18.

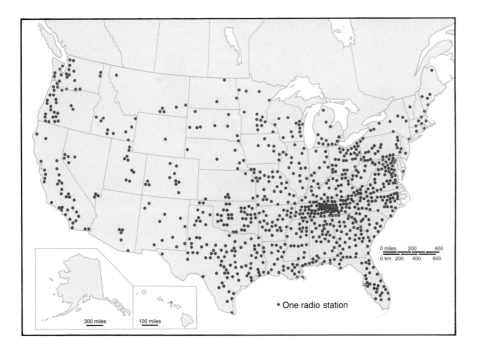

Figure 7.28 **Country music radio stations.**
Although still most heavily concentrated in the
Upland South, radio stations playing only country
music had become a national commonplace by the
late 1970s.

*Source: Redrawn by permission from George O. Carney, "From
Down Home to Uptown," Journal of Geography, 76 (Indiana, PA:
National Council for Geographic Education, 1977), p. 107.*

(a)

(b)

(c)

Figure 7.29 Revival of regional vernacular housing styles. (*a*) The
Kentlands neighborhood in suburban Washington, D.C., was developed
beginning in the 1980s following traditional 18th and early 19th century
Middle Atlantic designs. (*b*) A 1990s housing subdivision on Hilton Head
Island, South Carolina, revived the Charleston single house with its two-
story side porch. (*c*) An early 2000s suburban subdivision near Saint Paul,
Minnesota, featured revivals of common Midwestern vernacular house styles
such as the upright and wing.

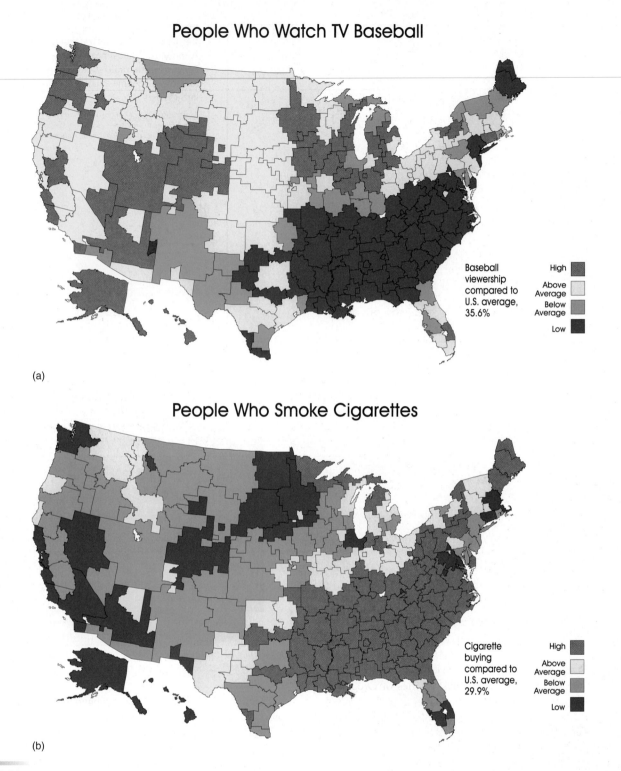

Figure 7.30 Regional variations in expressions of popular culture. (*a*) Part of the regional variation in television viewing of baseball reflects the game's lack of appeal in the African American community and, therefore, its low viewership in the Southeast and in metropolitan centers where, additionally, attendance at games is an alternative to watching TV. (*b*) Even bad habits regionalize. The country's cigarette belt includes notably many of the rural areas where tobacco is grown.

Source: From Michael J. Weiss, Latitudes and Attitudes: An Atlas of American Tastes, Trends, Politics and Passions, *Boston: Little, Brown and Company, 1994. Used by permission of the author.*

sports landscape constitutes part of the areal diversity of North American—and world—life. Figure 7.30a, for example, shows that television interest in professional baseball is not universal despite the sport's reputation as "the national pastime." Studies and maps of many regional differences in food and drink preferences, leisure activities, and personal and political tastes—a sampling is presented in Figure 7.30—are suggestive of the growing interest in how people behave and respond, not as echoes of the distant past but as participants in a vibrant and changing contemporary world that still retains evidence of regional contrast along with the commonalities of popular culture. (see "Lifestyle Segmentation").

Birds of a Feather…or, Lifestyle Segmentation

How does Starbucks or McDonald's decide where to open a new outlet? Will there be enough families with children to justify a play area? What sort of design theme and special menu items will work in this location? Why do some stores consistently outperform other locations? Geodemographic marketing, a marketing application of human geography, attempts to answer these and other related questions. Starting from the premise that "birds of a feather flock together" geodemographic market analysts at Claritas, Inc. argue that "you are where you live." Geodemographic marketing analysts point out that the U.S. population has clustered into lifestyle segments so that where a person lives is a useful predictor of the kind of car they will drive, their recreational pursuits, their household and personal purchases, the music they will listen to, and the magazines and newspapers they will read. Using GIS to map data from the U.S. Census and consumer spending records (now you know why store clerks ask for your phone number or zip code), geodemographic marketers have mapped and classified American neighborhoods. Claritas is one such company and has classified America's zip codes into 66 different lifestyle segments. Some of Claritas' lifestyle segments include:

Shotguns and Pickups: young, white working class couples with large families who live in small houses or trailer houses. This group has a median household income of $43,000. They are typically high school graduates and are likely to own pickup trucks, go hunting, shop at Lowes, and read *North American Hunter* magazine.

Young Digerati: affluent young families living in desirable urban neighborhoods filled with boutiques, fitness clubs, coffee shops, and microbreweries. The young digerati often have graduate degrees and are early adopters and leaders in the use of new technology. This group has a median household income of $85,700. They are likely to shop at Banana Republic, go snowboarding, watch independent films, and drive hybrid cars.

Multi-Culti Mosaic: lower middle-class, ethnically diverse families living in immigrant gateway neighborhoods. This group has a median household income of $35,200. They are likely to buy Spanish language music, shop at discount department stores, read *Jet* and drive a Nissan.

Blue Blood Estates: wealthy suburban families with a significant percentage of Asian Americans. This group consists mostly of professionals and business executives and has a median household income of $119,500. They are likely to drive expensive European automobiles, read architectural magazines, take ski vacations, and shop at Talbots.

The company realizes that the designations don't define the tastes and habits of everyone in a community, but maintains that the clusters summarize typical behavior. If you would like to know how Claritas has categorized your neighborhood, go to "http://www.claritas.com/MyBestSegments/Default.jsp and click on "Zip Code Look Up."

Drink and Music

Drink preferences and musical tastes yield other good instances of regional origins, specializations, diffusions, and differential adoption by social groups. The distribution of the approximately 1500 small-scale microbreweries in the United States, for example, is not geographically uniform across the country but instead exhibits regional concentrations (Figure 7.31). Their source or "hearth" as a popular culture innovation in the late 1980s was the West, specifically the Colorado Front Range cities, the greater San Francisco area, and the coastal cities of Oregon and Washington. The microbrew capital of the country is Portland, Oregon, with 30 or more microbreweries and brewpubs. During the 1990s, both the Northeast, and Wisconsin and Michigan of the Upper Midwest became prominent; in the late 1990s and into the 21st century, the economically dynamic cities of Georgia and the Carolinas were the sites of new microbrewery establishment. The popularity and consumption of microbrewed beer has been explained as an instance of *neolocalism*—the creation and maintenance of a place identity and attachment—that constitutes a rejection of a more homogeneous and uniform national and global culture represented, in this case, by major brands of beer, either domestic or imported. That neolocalism attachment to place is clearly expressed in microbrewery beer labels that are based on local history, famous local individuals or events, or locally identifiable nature scenes or distinctive structures such as windmill arrays (Figure 7.32).

Over the last quarter of the 20th century, specialty coffee establishments serving cappuccino, latte, mocha, and other variants have become common features of airports, shopping malls, bookstores, convenience stores, and mobile stands in urban places large and small. The American source locale of the specialty coffee culture was Seattle, Washington, in the Pacific Northwest, the original home of Starbucks, the most prominent corporate identity in the trade. Established in 1971, Starbucks in the early 21st century had some 6000 outlets in 30 countries, a dispersion and presence not universally appreciated (Figure 7.33). Although an unmistakable icon of popular culture, specialty coffee—whether Starbucks' or that of the many independent coffeehouses—is not part of *mass* culture. Rather, its consumption has become symbolic of social distinctions: those who consume it are self-identified as people with refined taste, differentiating them from other segments of the public who consume more pedestrian coffee. In addition, as in the case of microbreweries, place identity in a world ever-more homogenized and globalized is important in the specialty coffee phenomenon. Seattle possesses cachet in the American mind, and purchasing beans from Sumatra, Colombia, Kenya, or Ethiopia is not just a commercial transaction but a vicarious form of exotic tourism. Indeed, Starbucks gives with each purchase of beans a "coffee passport" accompanied by a visa stamp for the country "visited."

In popular music, too, regional and social taste and adoption differentials are evident. In a sense, music is symbolically expressive of the experiences and emotions of people with

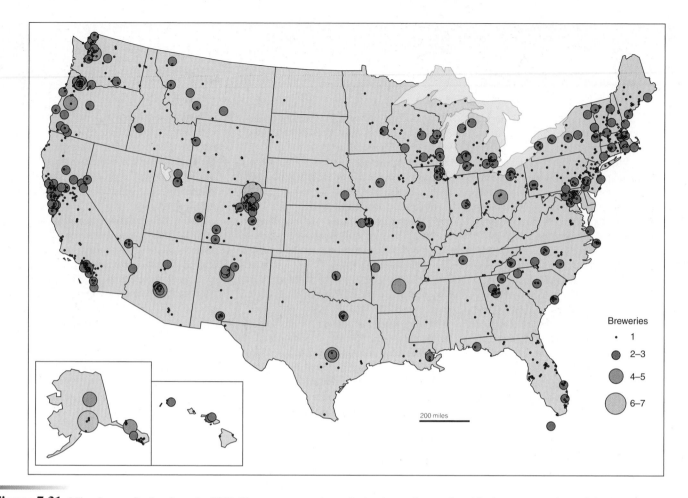

Figure 7.31 **Microbreweries by zip code, 2002.** Heavy concentrations of microbreweries are found in the source regions of the West.

Source: "Microbreweries as Tools of Local Identity" by Steven M. Schnell and Joseph F. Reese from Journal of Cultural Geography, Vol. 21, No. 1 (Fall/Winter 2003), figure 1, p. 50. Reprinted by permission of JCG Press.

particular spatial and group identifications. At the local scale, for example, both rap and grunge originated as expressions of the alienation felt by particular segments of the younger population in the Bronx and in Seattle, respectively. And regional musical expressions of culture include Cajun music of south Louisiana, Tejano music of the TexMex borderlands, and the polka of the Upper Midwest. To enter the popular and mass cultural spheres, however, particular regional genres of music must diffuse at the national and global scales and, in turn, be modified to express the collective cultural identities of people occupying different spaces and places.

That globalization and modification is clearly demonstrated by "world music," usually described as music strongly rooted in the folk and/or ethnic traditions of non-Western cultures but often blended with Western music to retain its sense of the exotic and yet be acceptable to Western tastes. Originally used to describe music from Africa and its diaspora in the New World, the term "world music" now more broadly includes the music of folk, ethnic, and frequently deprived minorities in any culture. Much of world music is hybrid in nature, a fusion of various music genres from different global origins.

In that blending process, local musical forms are "deterritorialized" and globalized, taking on transnational and cross-cultural characteristics not spatially tied to a single culture or state. World music, then, not only establishes African, West Indian, or Asian music in Western popular culture but creates new combinations and syncretisms such as Afro-Celtic, a fusion of African rhythms with traditional Celtic folk music, or reggae. World music also broadens the awareness and modifies the purity of such Western ethnic or folk genres as Celtic, zydeco, klezmer, Rom, bluegrass, jazz, and others. Whatever its folk, cultural, or national origin, world music represents a process of transformation of the musically unique and "other" into forms accepted by globalized popular culture.

Although popularly perceived as an authentic Jamaican music form, reggae displayed the cultural hybridity and deterritorialized qualities of world music even before that separate music category was recognized. Reggae is a fusion of African rhythms, earlier Caribbean music forms such as *ska* and *rock steady,* and European melodies with pronounced influences from modern American jazz, rhythm blues, and soul. As employed by Rastafarians (members of an African-originated religion associated with the poorer black

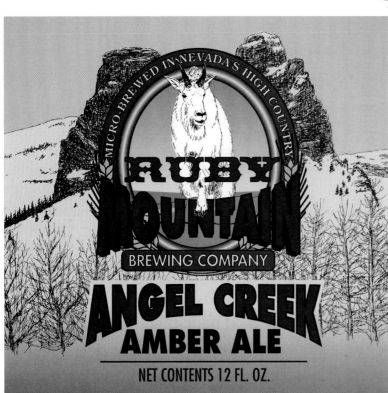

Figure 7.32 Scenes with nature and wildlife themes are common on microbrew beer labels from the West.

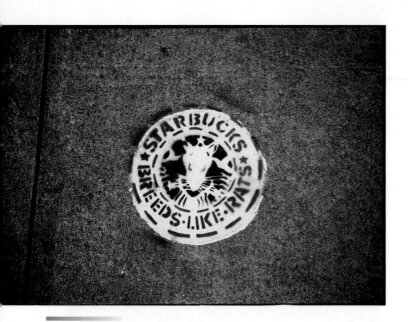

Figure 7.33 Anti-Starbucks graffito on a San Francisco sidewalk contesting the corporate homogenization of the urban landscape.

population of Jamaica), reggae lyrics often address issues of poverty, subordination, oppression, black pride, and pan-Africanism. The globalization of reggae music to become a popular cultural commodity, however, depended on contracts with the internationalized entertainment industry to package and market the reggae product.

Reggae first diffused to England from Jamaica in the early 1970s, taken up by Jamaicans who migrated there in the 1950s and 1960s. In Britain, lyrics were modified to express the place-specific diaspora experience of West Indian neighborhoods. Much like the commercialization of rock-and-roll from its black rhythm and blues roots in America, the mainstreaming of reggae in Britain involved its adoption by white British bands. In that process, reggae as a musical platform of cultural protest was transformed into a cultural commodity that helped reggae reach beyond the Afro-Caribbean community.

The emergence of reggae as a global commodity is identified with Bob Marley's 1972 album *Catch a Fire*. In recording sessions, however, London-based Island Records thought the album's music was too "Jamaican," and an alternative rock album with a strong roots reggae sound was produced. The global was thus fused with the local. To stress the local, however, the record and

Hip Hop Undergoes Globalization and Glocalization

Unlike the distant folk background of some world music, the beginnings of hip hop culture are recent and easily plotted on the map. Hip hop culture emerged in the Bronx borough of New York City in the 1970s at a time when the South Bronx was undergoing a massive downward spiral. The disruptive Cross-Bronx expressway had been sliced through the neighborhood, the middle-class was fleeing to the suburbs, manufacturing jobs were disappearing by the thousands, the city teetered on the edge of bankruptcy, and it had cut back essential services to the South Bronx. Many landlords responded by abandoning their tenement buildings, sometimes setting them afire to collect insurance money. Out of this urban wasteland environment arose hip hop culture. DJs at dance clubs and in street parties began stylized talking with a simple four-count beat—rapping—over a background of funk rock and disco music. Hip hop culture, which involves rap music, DJs, graffiti, and breakdancing, exhibits West African and Jamaican influences and is a contemporary expression of older forms of "talking music" such as spirituals, work songs, talkin'

country blues, and the rhythmic sermons of black preachers. From these beginnings, rap developed as underground "protest music" with lyrics voicing the experiences of socially and economically disadvantaged black and Latino youth—alienation, police harassment, drug use, sexual conduct, race relations, and the like. Themes of place, home, and identity abound in rap music with many songs depicting life in the "hood."

From its hearth in New York City, hip hop diffused to a second center in Los Angeles (particularly the suburb of Compton) where "gangsta" or "reality" rap developed. Subsequently, hip hop spread nationally to suburbs and corporate boardrooms, becoming the biggest-selling genre of popular music in America. Other centers of rap music have emerged, such as the South Coast region including Atlanta, New Orleans, Miami, and Memphis and a Midwest region centered on Detroit. Rap music has often been controversial due to lyrics and imagery that frequently celebrate violence, hopelessness, and the oppression of women. For example, among Tibetan immigrant youth the adoption of hip hop culture has generated objections because of negative

stereotypes and its associations with the black underclass. Hip hop has also diffused globally and undergone glocalization—adaptation to suit local cultures and experiences. In Cuba, popular rap lyrics have protested racial discrimination and inequality that wasn't supposed to exist in Castro's Cuba. In Mexico, rapper Control Machete has written lyrics that denounce U.S. border controls, while Columbian rap group La Etnia deals with poverty, prostitution, homelessness, and violence in their lyrics. In Germany, community centers became sites for the spread of hip hop culture among both native and immigrant youth. And from the Americas to South Africa, black youth have used hip hop as a way to forge a black identity that spans the Atlantic.

Sources: Arlene Tickner, "Aqui en el Ghetto: Hip Hop in Columbia, Cuba and Mexico," *Latin American Politics and Society*, 50, 2008, (3):121–146; Emily Yeh and Kunga Lama, "Hip-hop Gangsta or Most Deserving of Victims? Transnational Migrant Identities and the Paradox of Tibetan Racialization in the USA," *Environment and Planning A*, 2006, 38: 809–829; Marc Perry, "Global Black Self-Fashionings: Hip Hop as Diasporic Space," Identities: *Global Studies in Culture and Power*, 2008, 15: 635–664.

CD covers purposefully portrayed "dreadlocked revolutionaries" to authenticate their exotic place origins to Western consumers.

Vernacular Regions

Ordinary people have a clear view of space. They are aware of variations from place to place in the mix of phenomena, both physical and cultural. They use and recognize as meaningful such common regional names as Corn Belt, Sunbelt, and "the Coast." More important, people individually and collectively agree on where they live. They occupy regions that have reality in their minds and that are reflected in regional journals, in regional museums, and in regionally based names employed in businesses, by sports teams, or in advertising slogans.

These are **vernacular,** or **popular, regions;** they have reality as part of folk or popular culture rather than as political impositions or scholarly constructs. Geographers are increasingly recognizing that vernacular regions are significant concepts affecting the way people view space, assign their loyalties, and interpret their world. One geographer has drawn the boundaries of the large popular regions of North America on the basis of place names and locational identities found in the white pages of central-city telephone directories (Figure 7.34). The 14 large but subnational vernacular regions recognized accord reasonably well with cultural regions defined by more rigorous methods. However, particularly in the West, that accordance is not clearly demonstrated by comparison of the vernacular regions with Figure 6.30. Another, more subjective cultural regionalization of the United States is offered in Figure 7.35. The generalized "consensus" or vernacular regions suggested are based on an understood "sense of place" derived from current population and landscape characteristics as well as on historical differences that impart distinctive regional behaviors and attitudes.

Figure 7.34 **Vernacular regions of Anglo America** as determined by names of enterprises listed in central-city telephone directories. Regions are those in which a given term or a cluster of closely related terms (e.g., Southern, Southland, Dixie) outnumber all other regional or locational references.

Source: Redrawn by permission from Annals of the Association of American Geographers, W. Zelinsky, Vol. 70, p. 14, Fig. 9, Association of American Geographers, 1980.

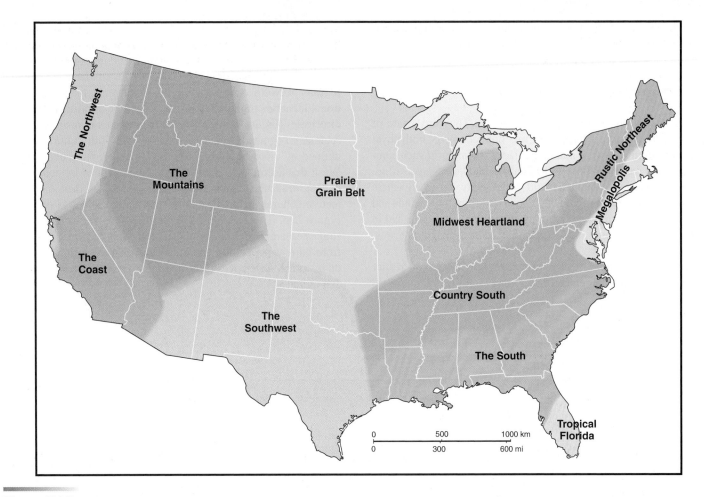

Figure 7.35 **Generalized U.S. culture regions.** "In spite of strong tendencies toward cultural homogenization and place obliteration, . . . regional identities persist," in the view of geographer Larry Ford, who suggests the 11 culture regions shown. Whatever the reasons for that persistence, "the different [culture] regions of the United States continue to have their own personalities and senses of place."

Summary

In the population mix that is the Anglo American, particularly U.S. society, we may recognize two culture-based sources of separation and one of unification. Ethnic culture and folk culture tend to create distinctions between peoples and to impart a special character to the areas in which their influences are dominant. Popular culture implies behavioral unification and the reduction of territorial distinctiveness.

Early arriving ethnic groups were soon Americanized, and their imported cultures were converted from the distinctly ethnic traits of foreigners to the folk cultures of the New World. The foothold settlements of first colonists became separate culture hearths in which imported architectural styles, food preferences, music, and other elements of material and nonmaterial culture were mixed, modified, abandoned, or disseminated along clearly traceable diffusion paths into the continental interior. Ethnic culture was transmuted to folk culture when nurtured in isolated

areas and made part of traditional America by long retention and by modification to accommodate local circumstances. Distinctive and bearing the stamp of restricted sections of the nation, those folk cultures contributed both to eastern regional diversity and to the diffusion streams affecting midwestern and western cultural amalgams.

The territorial and social diversities implied by the concepts of *ethnic* and *folk* are modified by the general unifying forces of *popular* culture. Fads, foods, music, dress, toys, games, and other introduced tastes tend to be adopted within a larger society, irrespective of the ethnic or folk distinctions of its parts. Sport interests and rivalries, as we saw at the opening of this chapter, become regional and national—and, increasingly, international—surmounting older limitations of distance. The more modernized and urbanized a country, the more it is uniformly subjected to the mass media and to common entertainment sources, and the more will popular culture subdue the remnant social distinctions still imparted by folk and ethnic customs. At the same time, the greater will be the choices made available to individuals newly freed from the limiting constraints of folk and ethnic traditions.

The threads of diversity traced in Chapter 6 and in this chapter are those of the traits and characteristics of small groups. We have focused on a single cultural realm and particularly a single country, the United States, because it is best known to most readers. However, the same patterns of cultural differentiation and unification could be observed for all other cultural realms and sizable countries.

If we were to do so, one recurring condition of material and nonmaterial cultural differentiation would become evident.

Much of human activity, including tools made and used, structures built, migrations undertaken, and social controls adopted, is related to economic life. Culture is conditioned by the necessities of production of food and material objects and, increasingly, of their exchange over space and between groups. Many of the threads in the fabric of cultural diversity—and, as well, many of its patterns of uniformity—are those woven by the traditions and technologies of livelihood. We must therefore next turn our attention to a consideration of the varied world of work and to the regional patterns of production and exchange revealed by that encompassing branch of human geography called *economic geography.*

KEY WORDS

built environment 202
custom 202
folk culture 202
folklore 215
folkways 215

glocalization 219
material culture 202
nonmaterial culture 202
placelessness 218

popular culture 218
popular region 229
vernacular house 205
vernacular region 229

FOR REVIEW

1. What contrasts can you draw between *folk culture* and *popular culture?* What different sorts of material and nonmaterial elements identify them? How are folk culture and popular culture interconnected and interrelated?

2. How many of the early settlement cultural hearths of North America can you name? Did early immigrants create uniform *built environments* within them? If not, why not?

3. When and under what circumstances did popular culture begin to erode the

folk and ethnic cultural differences between Americans? Thinking only of your own life and habits, what traces of folk culture do you carry? To what degree does popular culture affect your decisions on dress? On reading material? On recreation?

4. How are we able to recognize hearths and trace diffusions of folk cultural elements? Do items of popular culture have hearths and diffusion paths that are equally traceable? Why or why not?

5. What kinds of connections can you discern between the nature of the physical environment and the characteristics of different *vernacular house* styles in North America? In other parts of the world?

6. If, as some have observed, there is a close relationship between the natural environment and the artifacts of folk culture, is there likely to be a similar causal connection between the environment and expressions of popular culture? Why or why not?

KEY CONCEPTS REVIEW

1. **What is folk culture, and what folk culture hearths and building traditions are found in Anglo America?** pp. 201–211.
   Folk culture, often based on ethnic backgrounds, tends to be localized by population groups and areas. It acts to distinguish groups within mixed-

culture societies. In Anglo America, diversified immigrant groups settling different, particularly eastern, regions brought their own building traditions to "hearth" regions: those of the *North* in the northeastern United States and southeastern Canada, the *Middle Atlantic,* and the *South.*

2. **What elements and patterns of nonmaterial folk culture can we observe in Anglo America?** pp. 211–215.
   The universal elements of nonmaterial folk culture include food and drink preferences and ingredients, music, recreations,

The crop bloomed luxuriantly that summer of 1846. The disaster of the preceding year seemed over, and the potato, the sole sustenance of some 8 million Irish peasants, would again yield in the bounty needed. Yet within a week, wrote Father Mathew, "I beheld one wide waste of putrefying vegetation. The wretched people were seated on the fences of their decaying gardens . . . bewailing bitterly the destruction that had left them foodless." Colonel Gore found that "every field was black," and Father O'Sullivan noted that "the fields . . . appeared blasted, withered, blackened, and . . . sprinkled with vitriol. . . ." The potato was irretrievably gone for a second year; famine and pestilence were inevitable.

Within 5 years, the settlement geography of the most densely populated country in Europe was forever altered. The United States received a million immigrants, who provided the cheap labor needed for the canals, railroads, and mines that it was creating in its rush to economic development. New patterns of commodity flows were initiated as American maize for the first time found an Anglo-Irish market—as part of Poor Relief—and then entered a wider European market, which had also suffered general crop failure in that bitter year. Within days, a microscopic organism, the cause of the potato blight, had altered the economic and human geography of two continents.

Although the Irish famine of the 1840s was a spatially localized tragedy, it dramatically demonstrated how widespread and intricate are the interrelations between widely separated peoples and areas of the earth. It made vividly clear how fundamental to all human activity patterns are those rooted in economy and subsistence. While the preceding chapters in Part Two focused on traditional patterns of language, religion, ethnicity, and folk beliefs and customs, Part Three (chapters 8, 9, and 10) turns its attention to dynamic economic innovations that are reworking the spatial mosaic of culture. Food and raw material production still dominate the economies in some parts of the world, but increasingly people are engaged in activities that involve the processing of raw materials into finished products and the provision of personal, business, and professional services within an increasingly interconnected world economy. Changing patterns of subsistence, livelihood, exchange, and the pursuit of "development" are the focus of economic geography.

Simply stated, **economic geography** is the study of how people earn their living, how livelihood systems vary by area, and how economic activities are spatially interrelated and linked. It applies geography's general concern with spatial variation to the special circumstances of the production, exchange, and consumption of goods and services. In reality, of course, we cannot really comprehend the totality of the economic pursuits of nearly 7 billion human beings. We cannot examine the infinite variety of productive and service activities found everywhere on the earth's surface, nor can we trace all their innumerable interrelationships, linkages, and flows. Even if that level of understanding were possible, it would be valid for only a fleeting instant of time, for economic activities are constantly undergoing change.

Economic geographers seek consistencies. They attempt to develop generalizations that will aid in the comprehension of the maze of economic variations characterizing human existence. From their studies emerges a deeper awareness of the dynamic, interlocking diversity of human enterprise and of the impact of economic activity on all other facets of human life and culture.

From them, too, comes appreciation of the increasing interdependence of differing national and regional economic systems. The potato blight, although it struck only one small island, ultimately affected the economies of continents. In like fashion, the depletion of America's natural resources and the "deindustrialization" of its economy and conversion to postindustrial service and knowledge activities are altering the relative wealth of countries, flows of international trade, domestic employment and income patterns, and more (Figure 8.1).

The Classification of Economic Activity and Economies

The search for understanding of livelihood patterns is made more difficult by the complex environmental and cultural realities controlling the economic activities of humans. Many production patterns are rooted in the spatially variable circumstances of the *physical environment*. The staple crops of the humid tropics, for example, are not part of the agricultural systems of the midlatitudes; livestock types that thrive in American feedlots or on western ranges are not adapted to the Arctic tundra or to the margins of the Saharan desert. The unequal distribution of useful mineral deposits gives some regions and countries economic prospects and employment opportunities that are denied to others. Forestry and fishing depend on still other natural resources unequal in occurrence, type, and value.

Within the bounds of the environmentally possible, *cultural considerations* may condition economic or production decisions. For example, culturally based food preferences rather than environmental limitations may dictate the choice of crops or livestock. Maize is a preferred grain in Africa and the Americas; wheat in North America, Australia, Argentina, southern Europe and Ukraine; and rice in much of Asia. Pigs are not produced in Muslim areas, where religious belief prohibits pork consumption.

Level of *technological development* of a culture will affect its recognition of resources or its ability to exploit them. **Technology** refers to the totality of tools and methods available to and used by a culture group in producing items essential to its subsistence and comfort. Preindustrial societies have no knowledge of or need for the iron ore or coking coal underlying their hunting, gathering, or gardening grounds. *Political decisions* may encourage or discourage—through subsidies, protective tariffs, or production restrictions—patterns of economic activity. And, ultimately, production is controlled by *economic factors* of demand, whether that demand is expressed through a free market mechanism, government instruction, or the consumption requirements of a single family producing for its own needs.

Categories of Activity

Regionally varying environmental, cultural, technological, political, and market conditions add spatial details to more generalized ways of classifying the world's productive work. One approach to that categorization is to view economic activity as ranged along a continuum of both increasing complexity of product or service and increasing distance from the natural environment. Seen from that perspective, a small number of distinctive stages of production and service activities may be distinguished (Figure 8.2).

Figure 8.1 This oil tanker is part of a world of increasing economic interdependence. The United States imported 13.6 million barrels of oil per day in 2007, accounting for 66% of its consumption.

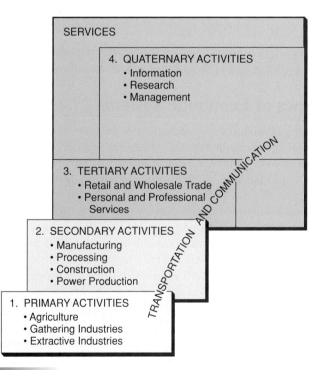

Figure 8.2 **The categories of economic activity.** The main sectors of the economy do not stand alone. They are connected and integrated by transportation and communication services and facilities not assigned to any single sector but common to all. Tertiary and quaternary activities involve services and are sometimes grouped together. Tertiary services focus on goods while quaternary services deal with information.

Primary activities are those that harvest or extract something from the earth. They are at the beginning of the production cycle, where humans are in closest contact with the resources and potentialities of the environment. Such activities involve basic foodstuff and raw material production. Hunting and gathering, grazing, agriculture, fishing, forestry, and mining and quarrying are examples. **Secondary activities** are those that add value to materials by changing their form or combining them into more useful—therefore more valuable—commodities. That provision of *form utility* may range from simple handicraft production of pottery or woodenware to the delicate assembly of electronic goods or space vehicles (Figure 8.3). Copper smelting, steel making, metalworking, automobile production, textile and chemical industries—indeed, the full array of *manufacturing and processing industries*—are included in this phase of the production process. Also included are the production of *energy* (the "power company") and the *construction* industry.

Tertiary activities consist of those business and labor specializations that provide *services* to the primary and secondary sectors and *goods* and *services* to the general community and to the individual. These include financial, business, professional, clerical, and personal services. They constitute the vital link between producer and consumer, for tertiary occupations importantly include the wholesale and retail *trade* activities—including "dot-com" Internet sales—necessary in highly interdependent societies. Tertiary activities also provide essential information to manufacturers: the knowledge of market demand without which economically justifiable production decisions are impossible.

In economically advanced societies a growing number of individuals and entire organizations are engaged in the processing and

Figure 8.3 These logs entering a lumber mill are products of *primary production.* Processing them into boards, plywood, or prefabricated houses is a *secondary activity* that increases their value by altering their form. The products of many secondary industries—sheet steel from steel mills, for example—constitute "raw materials" for other manufacturers.

dissemination of information and in the administration and control of their own or other enterprises. The term **quaternary** is applied to this fourth class of economic activities, a subset of service activities rendered by "white collar" professionals working in education, government, management, information processing, and research. Sometimes, the term **quinary activities** is used to recognize high-level decision-making roles in all types of large organizations, public or private. (The distinctions between tertiary, quaternary, and quinary activities are more fully developed in Chapter 9.) As Figure 8.2 suggests, transportation and communication services cut across the general categories of economic activity, unite them, and make possible the spatial interactions that all human enterprise requires (discussed in Chapter 3).

The term *industry*—in addition to its common meaning as a branch of manufacturing activity—is frequently employed as a substitute, identical in meaning to *activity,* as a designation of these categories of economic enterprise. That is, we can speak of the steel, or automobile, or textile "industry" with all the impressions of factories, mills, raw materials, and products each type of enterprise implies. But with equal logic we can refer in a more generalized way to the "entertainment" or the "travel" industries or, in the present context, to "primary," "secondary," and "tertiary" industries.

These categories of production and service activities or industries help us see an underlying structure to the nearly infinite variety of things people do to earn a living and to sustain themselves. But by themselves they tell us little about the organization of the larger economy of which the individual worker or establishment

is a part. For that broader organizational understanding we look to *systems* rather than *components* of economies.

Types of Economic Systems

Broadly viewed, national economies in the early 21st century fall into one of three major types of system: *subsistence, commercial,* or *planned.* None of these economic systems is "pure." That is, none exists in isolation in an increasingly interdependent world. Each, however, displays certain underlying characteristics based on its distinctive forms of resource management and economic control.

In a **subsistence economy,** goods and services are created for the use of the producers and their kinship groups. Therefore, there is little exchange of goods and only limited need for markets. In the **market (commercial) economies** that have become dominant in nearly all parts of the world, producers or their agents, in theory, freely market their goods and services, the laws of supply and demand determine price and quantity, and market competition is the primary force shaping production decisions and distributions. In the extreme form of **planned economies** associated with the communist-controlled societies that have now collapsed in nearly every country where they were formerly created or imposed, producers or their agents disposed of goods and services through government agencies that controlled both supply and price. The quantities produced and the locational patterns of production were strictly programmed by central planning departments.

With a few exceptions—for example, Cuba and North Korea—rigidly planned economies no longer exist in their classical form; they have been modified or dismantled in favor of free market structures or only partially retained in a lesser degree of economic control associated with governmental supervision or ownership of selected sectors of increasingly market-oriented economies. Nevertheless, their landscape evidence lives on. The physical structures, patterns of production, and imposed regional interdependencies they created continue to influence the economic decisions of successor societies.

In actuality, few people are members of only one of these systems. A farmer in India may produce rice and vegetables privately for the family's consumption but also save some of the produce to sell. In addition, members of the family may market cloth or other handicrafts they make. With the money derived from those sales, the Indian peasant is able to buy, among other things, clothes for the family, tools, and fuel. Thus, that Indian farmer is a member of at least two systems: subsistence and commercial.

In the United States, government controls on the production of various types of goods and services (such as growing wheat or tobacco, producing alcohol, constructing and operating nuclear power plants, and engaging in licensed personal and professional services) mean that the country does not have a purely market economy. To a limited extent, its citizens participate in a controlled and planned as well as in a free market environment. Many African, Asian, and Latin American market economies have been decisively shaped by governmental policies encouraging or demanding production of export commodities rather than domestic foodstuffs, or promoting through import restrictions the development of domestic industries not readily supported by the national

market alone. Example after example would show that there are very few people in the world who are members of only one type of economic system.

Inevitably, spatial patterns, including those of economic activities and systems, are subject to change. For example, the commercial economies of Western European countries, some with sizable infusions of planned economy controls, are being restructured by both increased free market competition and supranational regulation under the World Trade Organization and the European Union (see pp. 406–409). Many of the countries of Latin America, Africa, Asia, and the Middle East that traditionally were dominated by subsistence economies are now benefiting from technology transfer from advanced economies and integration into expanding global production and exchange patterns.

No matter what economic system prevails locally, in all systems transportation is a key variable. No advanced economy can flourish without a well-connected transport network. All subsistence societies—or subsistence areas of developing countries—are characterized by their isolation from regional and world routeways (Figure 8.4). That isolation restricts their progression to more advanced forms of economic structure.

Former sharp contrasts in economic organization are becoming blurred and national economic orientations are changing as globalization reduces structural contrasts in national economies. Still, both approaches to economic classification—by type of activity and by organization of economies—help us to visualize and understand changing world economic geographic patterns. In the remainder of this chapter, we will center our attention on the primary industries. In Chapter 9, we will consider secondary through quinary activity patterns.

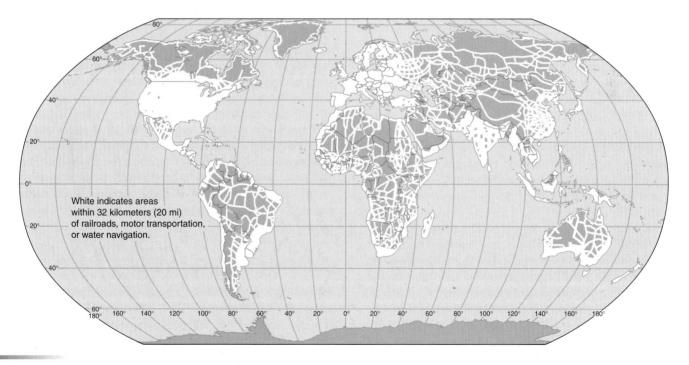

White indicates areas within 32 kilometers (20 mi) of railroads, motor transportation, or water navigation.

Figure 8.4 Patterns of access and isolation. Accessibility is a key measure of economic development and of the degree to which a world region can participate in interconnected market activities. Isolated areas of countries with advanced economies suffer a price disadvantage because of high transportation costs. Lack of accessibility in subsistence economic areas slows their modernization and hinders their participation in the world market.

Source: Hammond Inc. Used with permission

Primary Activities: Agriculture

Humankind's basic economic concern is producing or securing food resources sufficient in caloric content to meet individual daily energy requirements and so balanced as to satisfy normal nutritional needs. Those supplies may be acquired by the consumer directly through the primary economic activities of hunting, gathering, farming, and fishing (a form of "gathering") or indirectly through performance of other primary, secondary, or higher level economic endeavors that yield income sufficient to provide the earner and earner's family with income to obtain needed daily sustenance. Food and Agriculture Organization statistics show that, at the start of the 21st century, 2.57 billion people depended on agriculture, hunting, fishing, and forestry for their livelihoods, including those actively engaged in those activities and their dependents. These accounted for 42% of 2000 world population.

Since the middle of the 20th century, a recurring but unrealized fear has been that the world's steadily increasing population would exceed available or potential food supplies. Instead, although global population has more than doubled since 1950, the total amount of human food produced worldwide since then has also more than doubled. The Food and Agriculture Organization of the United Nations has set the minimum daily requirement for caloric intake per person at 2350. By that measure, annual food supplies are more than sufficient to meet world needs. That is, if total food resources were evenly distributed, everyone would have access to amounts sufficient for adequate daily nourishment. In reality, however, some one-eighth of the world's population—and one-sixth of the population of less developed countries—are inadequately supplied with food and nutrients. Conservatively, 54 countries fall below achieving the FAO minimum per capita requirement; they do not produce enough food to supply their populations nor have the economic means to close the gap through imports.

This stark contradiction between sufficient worldwide food supplies and widespread malnutrition reflects, among other reasons, inequalities in national and personal incomes; population growth rates; lack of access to fertile soils, credit, and education; local climatic conditions or catastrophes; and lack of transportation and storage facilities. By mid-century, the increasingly interconnected world population will expand to at least 9 billion, and concerns with individual states' food supplies will inevitably continue and remain, as well, a persistent international issue. World and regional issues of food supply and nutrition are explored in Chapter 10.

Before there was farming, *hunting* and *gathering* were the universal forms of primary production. These preagricultural pursuits are now practiced by at most a few thousands of persons worldwide, primarily in isolated and remote pockets within the low latitudes and among the sparse populations of very high latitudes. The interior of New Guinea, rugged areas of interior Southeast Asia, diminishing segments of the Amazon rain forest, and a few districts of tropical Africa and northern Australia still contain such preagricultural people. Much of the Arctic region, of course, is ill-suited for any form of food crop production. Hunter-gatherer numbers are few and declining, and wherever they are brought into contact with technologically more advanced cultures, their way of life is eroded or lost.

Agriculture, defined as the growing of crops and the tending of livestock whether for the subsistence of the producers or for sale or exchange, has replaced hunting and gathering as economically the most significant of the primary activities. It is spatially the most widespread, found in all world regions where environmental circumstances—including adequate moisture, good growing season length, and productive soils—permit (Figure 8.5). The United Nations estimates that more than one-third of the world's land area (excluding Greenland and Antarctica) is in some form of agricultural use, including permanent pastureland. Crop farming alone covers some 15 million square kilometers (5.8 million sq mi) worldwide, about 10% of the earth's total land area. In many developing economies, at least two-thirds of the labor force is directly involved in farming and herding. In some, such as Bhutan in Asia or Burkina Faso and Burundi in Africa, the figure is more than 90%. Overall, however, employment in agriculture is steadily declining in developing economies, echoing but trailing the trend in commercial economies, in which direct employment in agriculture involves only a small fraction of the labor force (Figure 8.6). (For the world pattern of the agricultural labor force early in this century, see Figure 10.10.) Indeed, a declining number or proportion of farm workers, along with farm consolidation and increasing output, are typical in all present-day highly developed commercial agricultural systems. On the other hand, agriculture remains a major component in the economies of many of the world's developing countries, producing for domestic markets and providing a major source of national income through exports (Figure 8.7).

It has been customary to classify agricultural societies on the twin bases of the importance of off-farm sales and the level of mechanization and technological advancement. *Subsistence, traditional* (or *intermediate*), and *advanced* are usual terms employed to recognize both aspects. These are not mutually exclusive but rather are recognized stages along a continuum of farm economy variants. At one end lies production solely for family sustenance, using rudimentary tools and native plants. At the other is the specialized, highly capitalized, near-industrialized agriculture for off-farm delivery that marks advanced economies. Between these extremes is the middle ground of traditional agriculture, where farm production is in part destined for home consumption and in part oriented toward off-farm sale, either locally or in national and international markets. We can most clearly see the variety of agricultural activities and the diversity of controls on their spatial patterns by examining the "subsistence" and "advanced" ends of the agricultural continuum.

Subsistence Agriculture

By definition, a *subsistence* economic system involves nearly total self-sufficiency on the part of its members. Production for exchange is minimal and any exchange is noncommercial; each family or close-knit social group relies on itself for its food and other most essential requirements. Farming for the immediate needs of the family is, even today, the predominant occupation of humankind. In most of Africa, south and east Asia, and much of Latin America, a large percentage of people are primarily concerned with feeding themselves from their own land and livestock.

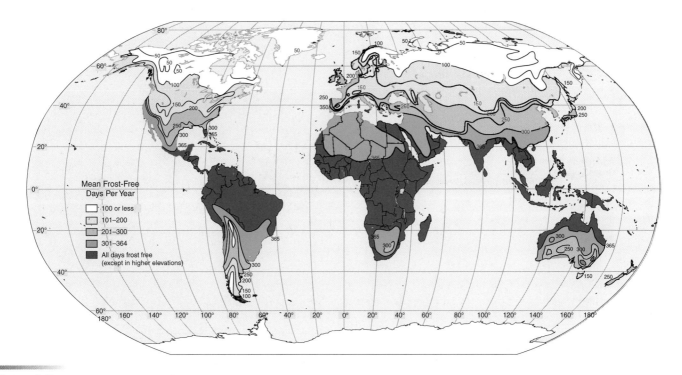

Figure 8.5 **Average length of growing season.** The number of frost-free days is an important environmental control on agriculture, as is the availability of precipitation sufficient in amount and reliability for crop production. Since agriculture is not usually practicable with less than a 90-day growing season, large parts of Russia and Canada have only limited cropping potential. Except where irrigation water is available, arid regions are similarly outside of the margins of regular crop production.

Source: Courtesy Wayne M. Wendland.

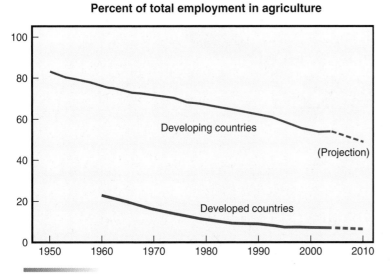

Percent of total employment in agriculture

Figure 8.6 In the developing economies worldwide, the percentage of the labor force in agriculture has been steadily declining—and is projected to decrease to even lower levels. In developed countries, too, a steady drop in agriculture's share of the labor force is evident and continuing.

Sources: FAO and World Bank.

Two chief types of subsistence agriculture may be recognized: *extensive* and *intensive*. Although each type has several variants, the essential contrast between them is realizable yield per unit of area used and, therefore, population-supporting potential. **Extensive subsistence agriculture** involves large areas of land

and minimal labor input per hectare. Both production per land unit and population densities are low. **Intensive subsistence agriculture** involves the cultivation of small landholdings through the expenditure of great amounts of labor per acre. Yields per unit area and population densities are both high (Figure 8.8).

Extensive Subsistence Agriculture

Of the several types of *extensive subsistence* agriculture—varying one from another in their intensities of land use—two are of particular interest: nomadic herding and shifting cultivation.

Nomadic herding, the wandering but controlled movement of livestock solely dependent on natural forage, is the most extensive type of land use system (Figure 8.8). That is, it requires the greatest amount of land area per person sustained. Over large portions of the Asian semidesert and desert areas, in certain highland zones, and on the fringes of and within the Sahara, a relatively small number of people graze animals for consumption by the herder group, not for market sale. Sheep, goats, and camels are most common, while cattle, horses, and yaks are locally important. The reindeer of Lapland were formerly part of the same system.

Whatever the animals involved, their common characteristics are hardiness, mobility, and an ability to subsist on sparse forage. The animals provide a variety of products: milk, cheese, blood, and meat for food; hair, wool, and skins for clothing; skins for shelter; and excrement for fuel. For the herder, they represent primary subsistence. Nomadic movement is tied to sparse and seasonal rainfall or to cold temperature regimes and to the areally varying appearance and exhaustion of forage. Extended stays in a

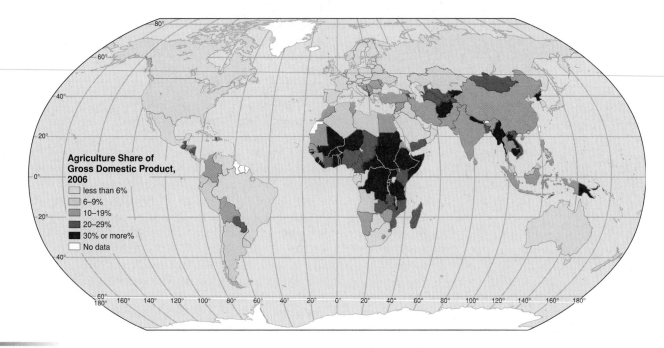

Figure 8.7 **Share of agriculture in gross domestic product, 2006.** Agriculture contributed 30% or more of gross domestic product (the total monetary output of goods and services of an economy) of more than 29 countries in 2006. Most were small, developing economies with less than US $500 in annual per capita income. Together, they held 11% of world population.

Source: The World Bank, World Development Indicators 2008.

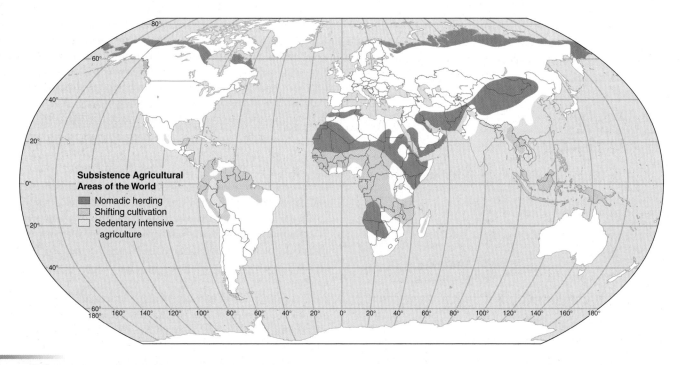

Figure 8.8 **Subsistence agricultural areas of the world.** Nomadic herding, supporting relatively few people, was the age-old way of life in large parts of the dry and cold world. Shifting or swidden agriculture maintains soil fertility by tested traditional practices in tropical wet and wet-and-dry climates. Large parts of Asia support millions of people engaged in sedentary intensive cultivation, with rice and wheat the chief crops.

given location are neither desirable nor possible. *Transhumance* is a special form of seasonal movement of livestock to exploit specific locally varying pasture conditions. Used by permanently or seasonally sedentary pastoralists and pastoral farmers, transhumance involves either the regular vertical alteration from mountain to valley pastures between summer and winter months or horizontal movement between established lowland grazing areas to reach pastures temporarily lush from monsoonal (seasonal) rains.

As a type of economic system, nomadic herding is declining. Many economic, social, and cultural changes are causing nomadic groups to alter their way of life or to disappear entirely. On the Arctic fringe of Russia, herders under communism were made members of state or collective herding enterprises. In northern Scandinavia, Lapps (Saami) are engaged in commercial more than in subsistence livestock farming. In the Sahel region of Africa on the margins of the Sahara, oases formerly controlled by herders have been taken over by farmers, and the great droughts of recent decades have forever altered the formerly nomadic way of life of thousands.

A much differently based and distributed form of extensive subsistence agriculture is found in all of the warm, moist, low-latitude areas of the world. There, many people engage in a kind of nomadic farming. Through clearing and use, the soils of those areas lose many of their nutrients (as soil chemicals are dissolved and removed by surface and groundwater—*leaching*—or nutrients are removed from the land in the vegetables picked and eaten), and farmers cultivating them need to move on after harvesting several crops. In a sense, they rotate fields rather than crops to maintain productivity. This type of **shifting cultivation** has a number of names, the most common of which are *swidden* (an English localism for "burned clearing") and *slash-and-burn*. Each region of its practice has its own name—for example, *milpa* in Middle and South America, *chitemene* in Africa, and *ladang* in Southeast Asia.

Characteristically, the farmers hack down the natural vegetation, burn the cuttings, and then plant such crops as maize (corn), millet (a cereal grain), rice, manioc or cassava, yams, and sugar-cane (Figure 8.9). Increasingly included in many of the crop combinations are such high-value, labor-intensive commercial crops as coffee, which provide the cash income that is evidence of the growing integration of all peoples into exchange economies. Initial yields—the first and second crops—may be very high, but they quickly become

Figure 8.9 An African swidden plot being fired. Stumps and trees left in the clearing will remain after the burn.

lower with each successive planting on the same plot. As that occurs, cropping ceases, native vegetation is allowed to reclaim the clearing, and gardening shifts to another newly prepared site. The first clearing will ideally not be used again for crops until, after many years, natural fallowing replenishes its fertility (see "Swidden Agriculture").

Less than 3% of the world's people are still predominantly engaged in tropical shifting cultivation on about one-seventh of the world's land area (Figure 8.8). Because the essential characteristic of the system is the intermittent cultivation of the land, each family requires a total occupance area equivalent to the garden plot in current use plus all land left fallow for regeneration. Population densities are traditionally low, for much land is needed to support few people. Here as elsewhere, however, population density must be considered a relative term. In actuality, although crude (arithmetic) density is low, people per unit area of *cultivated* land may be high.

Shifting cultivation is one of the oldest and most widely spread agricultural systems of the world. It is found on the islands of Borneo, New Guinea, and Sumatra but is now retained only in small parts of the uplands of Southeast Asia in Vietnam, Thailand, Myanmar, and the Philippines. Nearly the whole of Central and West Africa away from the coasts, Brazil's Amazon basin, and large portions of Central America were formerly all known for this type of extensive subsistence agriculture.

It may be argued that shifting cultivation is a highly efficient cultural adaptation where land is abundant in relation to population and levels of technology and capital availability are low. As those conditions change, the system becomes less viable. The basic change, as noted in Chapter 4, is that land is no longer abundant in relation to population in many of the less developed wet, tropical countries. Their growing populations have cleared and settled the forestlands formerly only intermittently used in swidden cultivation. The **Boserup thesis,** proposed by the economist Ester Boserup, is based on the observation that population increases necessitate increased inputs of labor and technology to compensate for reductions in the natural yields of swidden farming. It holds that population growth forces an increased use of technology in farming and—in a reversal of the Malthusian idea (p. 117) that the supply of essential foodstuffs is fixed or only slowly expandable—triggers the switch from extensive to intensive subsistence agriculture, which sharply increases food production.

Intensive Subsistence Systems

About 45% of the people of the world are engaged in intensive subsistence agriculture, which predominates in the areas shown in Figure 8.8. As a descriptive term, *intensive subsistence* is no longer fully applicable to a changing way of life and economy in which the distinction between subsistence and commercial is decreasing valid. Although families may still be fed primarily with the produce of their individual plots, the exchange of farm commodities within the system is considerable. Production of foodstuffs for sale in rapidly growing urban markets is increasingly vital for the rural economies of subsistence farming areas and for the sustenance of the growing proportion of national and regional populations no longer themselves engaged in farming. Nevertheless, hundreds of millions of Indians, Chinese, Pakistanis, Bangladeshis, and Indonesians plus further millions in other Asian, African, and Latin American countries

Swidden Agriculture

The following account describes shifting cultivation among the Hanunóo people of the Philippines. Nearly identical procedures are followed in all swidden farming regions.

When a garden site of about one-half hectare (a little over one acre) has been selected, the swidden farmer begins to remove unwanted vegetation. The first phase of this process consists of slashing and cutting the undergrowth and smaller trees with bush knives. The principal aim is to cover the entire site with highly inflammable dead vegetation so that the later stage of burning will be most effective. Because of the threat of soil erosion the ground must not be exposed directly to the elements at any time during the cutting stage. During the first months of the agricultural year, activities connected with cutting take priority over all others. It is estimated that the time required ranges from 25 to 100 hours for the average-sized swidden plot.

Once most of the undergrowth has been slashed, chopped to hasten drying, and spread to protect the soil and assure an even burn, the larger trees must be felled or killed by girdling (cutting a complete ring of bark) so that unwanted shade will be removed. The successful felling of a real forest giant is a dangerous activity and requires great skill. Felling in second growth is usually less dangerous and less arduous. Some trees are merely trimmed but not killed or cut, both to reduce the amount of labor and to leave trees to reseed the swidden during the subsequent fallow period.

The crucial and most important single event in the agricultural cycle is swidden burning. The main firing of a swidden is the culmination of many weeks of preparation in spreading and leveling chopped vegetation, preparing firebreaks to prevent flames escaping into the jungle, and allowing time for the drying process. An ideal burn rapidly consumes every bit of litter; in no more than an hour or an hour and a half, only smoldering remains are left.

The Hanunóo, swidden farmers of the Philippines, note the following as the benefits of a good burn: 1) removal of unwanted vegetation, resulting in a cleared swidden; 2) extermination of many animal and some weed pests; 3) preparation of the soil for dibble (any small hand tool or stick to make a hole) planting by making it softer and more friable; 4) provision of an evenly distributed cover of wood ashes, good for young crop plants and protective of newly-planted grain seed. Within the first year of the swidden cycle, an average of between 40 and 50 different types of crop plants have been planted and harvested.

The most critical feature of swidden agriculture is the maintenance of soil fertility and structure. The solution is to pursue a system of rotation of 1 to 3 years in crop and 10 to 20 in woody or bush fallow regeneration. When population pressures mandate a reduction in the length of fallow period, productivity of the region tends to drop as soil fertility is lowered, marginal land is utilized, and environmental degradation occurs. The balance is delicate.

Source: Based on Harold C. Conklin, *Hanunóo Agriculture*, FAO Forestry Development Paper No. 12.

remain small-plot, mainly subsistence producers of rice, wheat, maize, millet, or pulses (peas, beans, and other legumes). Most live in monsoon Asia, and we will devote our attention to that area.

Intensive subsistence farmers are concentrated in such major river valleys and deltas as the Ganges and the Chang Jiang (Yangtze) and in smaller valleys close to coasts—level areas with fertile alluvial soils. These warm, moist districts are well suited to the production of rice, a crop that under ideal conditions can provide large amounts of food per unit of land. Rice also requires a great deal of time and attention, for planting rice shoots by hand in standing fresh water is a tedious art (Figure 8.10). In the cooler and drier portions of Asia, wheat is grown intensively, along with millet and, less commonly, upland rice.

Rice is known to have been cultivated in parts of China and India for more than 7000 years. Today, wet, or lowland, rice is the mainstay of subsistence agriculture and diets of populations from Sri Lanka and India to Taiwan, Japan, and Korea. It is grown on more than 80% of the planted area in Bangladesh, Thailand, and Malaysia and on more than 50% in six other Asian countries. Almost exclusively used as a human food, rice provides 25% to 80% of the calories in the daily diet of some 3 billion Asians, or half the world's population. Its successful cultivation depends on the controlled management of water, relatively easy in humid tropical river valleys with heavy, impermeable, water-retaining soils though more difficult in upland and seasonally dry districts. Throughout

Asia, the necessary water management systems have left their distinctive marks on the landscape. Permanently diked fields to contain and control water, levees against unwanted water, and reservoirs, canals, and drainage channels to control its availability and flow are common sights. Terraces to extend level land to valley slopes are occasionally encountered as well (see Figure 4.23).

Intensive subsistence farming is characterized by large inputs of labor per unit of land, by small plots, by the intensive use of fertilizers, mostly animal manure, and by the promise of high yields in good years (see "The Economy of a Chinese Village"). For food security and dietary custom, *polyculture*—production of several different crops, often in the same field—is practiced. Vegetables and some livestock are part of the agricultural system, and fish may be reared in rice paddies and ponds. Food animals include swine, ducks, and chickens. Religion is a factor as well, since Muslims eat no pork, hogs are absent in their areas of settlement. Hindus generally eat little meat, mainly goat and lamb but not pork or beef. The large number of cattle in India are vital for labor, as a source of milk and cheese, and as producers—through excrement—of fertilizer and fuel.

Urban Subsistence Farming

Not all of the world's subsistence farming is based in rural areas. Urban agriculture is a rapidly growing activity, with some 800 million city farmers worldwide providing, according

Figure 8.10 Transplanting rice seedlings requires arduous hand labor by all members of the family. The newly flooded diked fields, previously plowed and fertilized, will have their water level maintained until the grain is ripe. This photograph was taken in Indonesia. The scene is repeated wherever subsistence wet-rice agriculture is practiced.

to United Nations figures, one-seventh of the world's total food production. Occurring in all regions of the world, developed and underdeveloped, but most prevalent in Asia, urban agricultural activities range from small garden plots, to backyard livestock breeding, to fish raised in ponds and streams. Using the garbage dumps of Jakarta, the rooftops of Mexico City, and meager dirt strips along roadways in Kolkata (Calcutta) or Kinshasa, millions of people are feeding their own families and supplying local markets with vegetables, fruit, fish, and even meat—all produced within the cities themselves and all without the expense and spoilage of storage or long-distance transportation.

In Africa where, for example, 2 of 3 Kenyan and Tanzanian urban families engage in farming, a reported 20% of urban nutritional requirement is produced in the towns and cities; in Accra, Ghana's capital, urban farming provides the city with 90% of its fresh vegetables. Early in the 21st century, city farming in Cuba produced 65% of the country's rice, 43% of its fruits and vegetables, and 12% of roots and fibers; altogether, some 165,000 urban Cubans annually produced 800,000 tons of fresh produce in 1999.

Urban agriculture occupies city land as well as city residents: in Bangkok, Thailand for example, some 60% of the metropolitan area is cultivated. A similar inclusion of adjacent rural land within urban boundaries is characteristic of China. There, based on an earlier mandate that socialist cities be self-sufficient, municipal boundaries were set to include large areas of rural land now worked intensively to supply the fruits, vegetables, fish, and the like consumed within the city proper. Chinese urban agriculture—by UN estimates providing 90% of the vegetable supply of cities—is, in reality, periurban (suburban) farming within city administrative control. Little or no backyard (or rooftop) land is available for food production within the densely developed Chinese city proper. In whatever form urban farming efforts are expressed, not all its area or yield is solely for local subsistence. An estimated 200 million global urban dwellers also produce food for sale to others.

In all parts of the developing world, urban-origin foodstuffs have reduced the incidence of adult and child malnutrition in cities rapidly expanding by their own birth rates and by the growing influx of displaced rural folk. City farming is, as well, a significant outlet for underemployed residents. In some cities, as many as one-fifth to two-thirds of all families are engaged in agriculture,

The Economy of a Chinese Village

The village of Nanching is in subtropical southern China on the Zhu River delta near Guangzhou (Canton). Its traditional subsistence agricultural system was described by a field investigator, whose account is here condensed. The system is still followed in its essentials in other rice-oriented societies.

In this double-crop region, rice was planted in March and August and harvested in late June or July and again in November. March to November was the major farming season. Early in March the earth was turned with an iron-tipped wooden plow pulled by a water buffalo. The very poor who could not afford a buffalo used a large iron-tipped wooden hoe for the same purpose.

The plowed soil was raked smooth, fertilizer was applied, and water was let into the field, which was then ready for the transplanting of rice seedlings. Seedlings were raised in a seedbed, a tiny patch fenced off on the side or corner of the field. Beginning from the middle of March, the transplanting of seedlings took place. The whole family was on the scene. Each took the seedlings by the bunch, ten to fifteen plants, and pushed them into the soft inundated soil. For the first thirty or forty days the emerald green crop demanded little attention except keeping the water at a proper

level. But after this period came the first weeding; the second weeding followed a month later. This was done by hand, and everyone old enough for such work participated. With the second weeding went the job of adding fertilizer. The grain was now allowed to stand to "draw starch" to fill the hull of the kernels. When the kernels had "drawn enough starch," water was let out of the field, and both the soil and the stalks were allowed to dry under the hot sun.

Then came the harvest, when all the rice plants were cut off a few inches above the ground with a sickle. Threshing was done on a threshing board. Then the grain and the stalks and leaves were taken home with a carrying pole on the peasant's shoulder. The plant was used as fuel at home.

As soon as the exhausting harvest work was done, no time could be lost before starting the chores of plowing, fertilizing, pumping water into the fields, and transplanting seedlings for the second crop. The slack season of the rice crop was taken up by chores required for the vegetables which demanded continuous attention, since every peasant family devoted a part of the farm to vegetable gardening. In the hot and damp period of late spring and summer, eggplant and several

varieties of squash and beans were grown. The green-leafed vegetables thrived in the cooler and drier period of fall, winter, and early spring. Leeks grew the year round.

When one crop of vegetables was harvested, the soil was turned and the clods broken up by a digging hoe and leveled with an iron rake. Fertilizer was applied, and seeds or seedlings of a new crop were planted. Hand weeding was a constant job; watering with the long-handled wooden dipper had to be done an average of three times a day, and in the very hot season when evaporation was rapid, as frequently as six times a day. The soil had to be cultivated with the hoe frequently as the heavy tropical rains packed the earth continuously. Instead of the two applications of fertilizer common with the rice crop, fertilizing was much more frequent for vegetables. Besides the heavy fertilizing of the soil at the beginning of a crop, usually with city garbage, additional fertilizer, usually diluted urine or a mixture of diluted urine and excreta, was given every ten days or so to most vegetables.

Source: Adapted from C. K. Yang, *A Chinese Village in Early Communist Transition* (Cambridge, Mass.: Massachusetts Institute of Technology, 1959).

a United Nations Development Programme study reports, with as many as one-third of them having no other source of income.

There are both positive and negative environmental consequences of urban agricultural activities. On the plus side, urban farming helps convert waste from a problem to a resource by reducing runoff and erosion from open dumps and by avoiding costs of wastewater treatment and solid waste disposal. In Khartoum, Sudan, for example, about 25% of the city's garbage is consumed by farm animals; in Kolkata (Calcutta), India, city sewage is used to feed some 3000 hectares (7400 acres) of lagoons which, in turn, produce some 6000 tons of fish annually. Nearly everywhere, human and animal wastes, vegetable debris, and table scraps are composted or applied to garden areas, and nearly everywhere, vegetable gardens and interspersed fruit trees, ornamental plants, and flowers enhance the often drab urban scene. Negative consequences also attend urban agriculture and frequently evoke restrictive governmental regulations and prohibitions. The widespread use of untreated human

waste as fertilizers exposes both producers and consumers to infectious diseases such as cholera and hepatitis.

Expanding Crop Production

Continuing population pressures on existing resources are a constant spur for ways to increase the food supply available both to the subsistence farmers of the developing economies and to the wider world as well. Two paths to promoting increased food production are apparent: (1) expand the land area under cultivation and (2) increase crop yields from existing farmlands.

The first approach—increasing cropland area—is not a promising strategy. Approximately 70% of the world's land area is agriculturally unsuitable, being too cold, too dry, too steep, or totally infertile. Of the remaining 30%, most of the area well suited for farming is already under cultivation, and of that area, millions of hectares annually are being lost through soil erosion, salinization, desertification, and the conversion of farm land to urban, industrial, and transportation uses in all developed and developing countries. Only the rain forests of Africa and the Amazon Basin of South America retain sizable areas of potentially farmable land. The soils of those regions, however, are fragile, are low in nutrients, have poor water retention, and are easily eroded or destroyed following deforestation.

When population pressures dictate land conversion, serious environmental deterioration may result. Clearing of wet tropical forests in the Philippines, the Amazon Basin, and Indonesia has converted dense woodland to barren desolation within a very few years as soil erosion and nutrient loss have followed forest destruction. In Southeast Asia, some 10 million hectares (25 million acres) of former forestland are now wasteland, covered by useless sawgrasses that supply neither forage, food, nor fuel. By most measures, world food output cannot reasonably be increased by simple expansion of cultivated areas.

Intensification and the Green Revolution

Increased productivity of existing cropland rather than expansion of cultivated area has been the key to the growth of agricultural production over the past few decades. Between 1974 and 2004, world total grain production rose nearly 70%. Crop output, however, varies considerably from year to year, adversely or favorably affected by weather, insect damage, plant diseases, and other growing season conditions. Overall, despite some 2.5 billion more people in the world, grain production per capita for the period 2003–2004 was nearly 3% above the 1974–1975 level. The vast majority of that production growth was due to increases in yields rather than expansions in cropland. For Asia as a whole, cereal yields grew by more than 40% between 1980 and the early 21st century, accounted for largely by increases in China and India; they grew by over 35% in South America. Two interrelated approaches to those yield increases mark recent farming practices.

First, throughout much of the developing world, production inputs such as water, fertilizer, pesticides, and labor have been increased to expand yields on a relatively constant supply of cultivable land. Irrigated area, for example, nearly doubled between 1960 and 2004 to comprise by the latter year some 17% of the world's cropland. Global consumption of fertilizers has dramatically increased since the 1950s, and inputs of pesticides and herbicides have similarly grown. Traditional practices of leaving land fallow (uncultivated) to renew its fertility have been largely abandoned, and double and triple cropping of land where climate permits has increased in Asia and even in Africa, where marginal land is put to near-continuous use to meet growing food demands.

Many of these intensification practices are part of the second approach, linked to the **Green Revolution**—the shorthand reference to a complex of seed and management innovations adapted to the needs of intensive agriculture and designed to bring larger harvests from a given area of farmland.

Using conventional plant breeding techniques of cross-pollination, University of Minnesota researcher Norman Borlaug developed a dwarf, high-yielding wheat variety at a Mexican research center in the 1940s. Borlaug was later awarded the Nobel Peace Prize and Mexico soon went from importing half its wheat to become a wheat exporter. Similarly, the International Rice Institute in the Philippines developed dwarf rice strains that yielded many more grains per plant. These high-yielding dwarf varieties respond dramatically to heavy applications of fertilizer, resist plant diseases, and can tolerate much shorter growing seasons than traditional native varieties can. Adopting the new varieties and applying the irrigation, mechanization, fertilization, and pesticide practices they require have created a new "high-input, high-yield" agriculture. Most poor farmers on marginal and rain-fed (nonirrigated) lands, however, have not benefited from the new plant varieties requiring irrigation and high chemical inputs.

Expanded food production made possible through the Green Revolution has helped alleviate some of the shortages and famines predicted for subsistence agricultural regions since the early 1960s, saving an estimated one billion people from starvation. According to World Bank calculations, more than 80% of people in developing countries now have adequate diets, versus 55% in 1950. As Figure 8.11 shows, however, not all world regions share those positive results. Although total food production has more than doubled in Africa since 1960, population growth has steadily reduced that continent's per capita food output. Although globally the *number* of undernourished people remains near the 900 million mark because of population growth, total world food supply has increased even faster than population and will continue to do so, the UN predicts, through at least 2030. However, a series of years beginning in 2000 in which production of all major grains fell substantially below consumption levels, materially reducing carry-over stocks and, therefore, endangering world food security, called the UN's prediction into question.

A price has been paid for Green Revolution successes. Irrigation, responsible for an important part of increased crop yields, has destroyed large tracts of land; excessive salinity of soils resulting from poor irrigation practices is estimated to have a serious effect on the productivity of 20 million to 30 million hectares (80,000–120,000 sq mi) of land around the world, out of a world total of some 270 million hectares of irrigated land. And the huge amount of water required for Green Revolution irrigation has led to serious groundwater depletion, conflict between agricultural and growing urban and industrial water needs in developing countries—many of which are in subhumid climates—and to worries about scarcity and future wars over water.

And very serious genetic consequences are feared from the loss of traditional and subsistence agriculture. With it is lost the food security that distinctive locally adapted native crop varieties (*land races*) provided and the nutritional diversity and balance that multiple-crop intensive gardening assured. Subsistence farming, wherever practiced, was oriented toward risk minimization. Many differentially hardy varieties of a single crop guaranteed some yield whatever adverse weather, disease, or pest problems might occur.

Commercial agriculture, however, aims at profit maximization, not minimal food security. Poor farmers unable to afford the capital investment the Green Revolution demands have been displaced by a commercial monoculture, one often oriented toward specialty and industrial crops designed for export rather than to food production for a domestic market. Traditional rural society has been disrupted, and landless peasants have been added to the urbanizing populations of affected countries. To the extent that land races are lost to monoculture, varietal distinction in food

(a)   (b)

Figure 8.11 **Trends in per capita food production, 1960–2004.** Globally, per capita production of food increased steadily over the 44-year span shown, with an average annual growth reaching 1.2% in the decade 1994 to 2004. Intensification and expansion of farming in Asia resulted both in greatly increased food production there and, despite continuing population growth, in expanding per capita availability. Population growth presented a different picture in Africa, where total production of food steadily grew over the graphed period, but per capita food supplies persistently declined. The nutrition problem in sub-Saharan Africa continues to the present, with stagnant food production levels but continuing population growth.

Source: Data from Food and Agriculture Organization.

crops is reduced. "Seed banks" rather than native cultivation are increasingly needed to preserve genetic diversity for future plant breeding and as insurance against catastrophic pest or disease susceptibility of inbred varieties (Figure 8.12).

The presumed benefits of the Green Revolution are not available to all subsistence agricultural areas or advantageous to everyone engaged in farming (see "Women and the Green Revolution"). Africa is a case in point (see Figure 8.11). Green Revolution crop improvements have concentrated on wheat, rice, and maize. Of these, only maize is important in Africa, where principal food crops include millet, sorghum, cassava, manioc, yams, cowpeas, and peanuts. Although new varieties of maize resistant to the drought and acidic soils common in Africa were announced in the middle 1990s, belated research efforts directed to other African crops, the continent's great range of growing conditions, and its abundance of yield-destroying pests and viruses have denied it the dramatic regionwide increases in food production experienced elsewhere in the developing world. No crop research or genetic modifications can fully compensate for an underlying limitation of African agricultural productivity: 80% of the continent's sub-Saharan farmland is severely depleted of the basic nutrients needed to grow crops, a condition which has been steadily worsening since the 1990s.

Some successes have been reported. The most widely cultivated tuber and second most important food staple in sub-Saharan Africa, cassava has been transformed from a low-yielding subsistence hedge against famine to a high-yielding cash crop. Between 1980 and 2005, total output more than doubled to about 110 million tons thanks to the introduction of new varieties developed by the International Institute of Tropical Agriculture. More recent experimental successes with a variety of genetically modified

(GM) crops promise other important yield improvements. Virus-resistant varieties of sweet potatoes and both white and yellow maize and faster-growing bananas are already available though not yet widespread and other food and fiber crops are receiving attention from African biotechnology scientists in Kenya, South Africa, and Egypt with contributions from American and other Western investigators. And in some physically favored areas benefiting in part from foreign investment but particularly reflecting local small farmer enterprise, encouraging pockets of crop specialization and growth in farm productivity, agribusiness creation, and rural income have been emerging. Uganda, for example, enjoys two growing seasons, ample rainfall, rich volcanic soils, and millions of small farmers rapidly expanding production of cash crops, most aimed at export markets in Asia, Europe, and North America. Output of a variety of specialty foodstuffs ranging from fish to rice, vanilla, sunflower seeds, roses, potatoes, and more has soared; Ugandan farm output and rural income increased by some 50 percent between 1995 and 2005.

In many areas showing greatest past successes, Green Revolution gains are falling off. Recent cereal yields in Asia, for example, are growing at only two-thirds of their 1970s rate: the UN's Food and Agriculture Organization now considers Green Revolution technologies "almost exhausted" of any further productivity gains in Asian rice cultivation. Little prime land and even less water remain to expand farming in many developing countries, and the adverse ecological and social consequences of industrial farming techniques arouse growing resistance. Nor does biotechnology—which many have hailed as a promising new Green Revolution approach—seem likely to fill the gap. Consumer resistance to genetically modified (GM) food crops, fear of the ecological consequences of such modification, the continuing

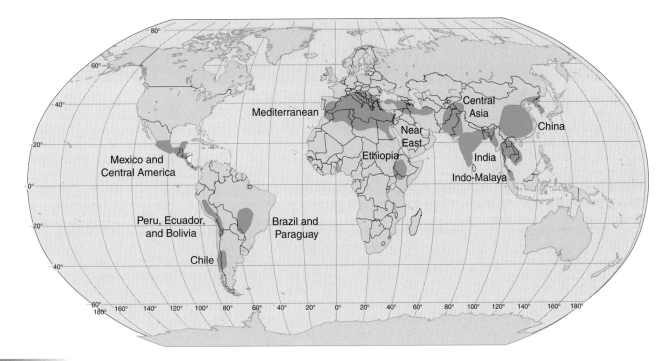

Figure 8.12 **Areas with high current genetic diversity of crop varieties.** Loss of crop varieties characterizes the commercial agriculture of much of the developed world. In place of the many thousands of species and subspecies (varieties) of food plants grown since the development of agriculture 15,000 or more years ago, fewer than 100 species now provide most of the world's food supply. Most of the diversity loss has occurred in the last 100 years. In the United States, for example, 96% of commercial vegetable varieties listed by the Department of Agriculture in 1903 are now extinct. Crop breeders, however, require genetic diversity to develop new varieties that are resistant to evolving plant pest and disease perils. That need necessitates the protection of plant stocks and environments in those temperate and subtropical zones where food plants were first domesticated and are home to the wild relatives of our current food crops. Comparable losses of species diversity are being felt in livestock as well. Half the livestock breeds that existed in Europe in 1900 are already extinct, and almost half the remainder are at risk or endangered.

Sources: J. G. Hawkes, The Diversity of Crop Plants, *(Cambridge, Mass.: Harvard University Press, 1983); and Walter V. Reid and Kenton R. Miller,* Keeping Options Alive: The Scientific Basis for Conserving Biodiversity *(Washington, DC: World Resources Institute, 1989), figure 5, p. 24.*

partial rejection of GM foods in the European Union market, and the high cost and restrictions on the new biotechnologies imposed by their corporate developers all conspire to inhibit the universal adoption of the new technologies in the developing world.

Nevertheless, the production of engineered crops is spreading rapidly. In 1996, the first year GM crops were commercially available, about 1.7 million hectares (4.3 million acres) were placed in biotechnology cultivation. By 2001, the area planted to GM crops had increased more than 30-fold and grew by another 140%—to 125 million hectares (309 million acres)—from 2001 to 2008. By the latter date, some 13.3 million farmers—12.3 million of them considered subsistence farmers—in 25 countries grew engineered crops. At least one-third of the global GM crop area in 2008 was located in developing countries; indeed, the percentage growth of GM acreage in the developing countries—notably Argentina, Brazil, China, India, and South Africa—was twice as high as in the industrial countries in the first years of this century. Globally, the principal GM crops have been GM soybeans, GM corn (including white corn for food in South Africa), transgenic cotton, and GM canola. Herbicide resistance (Roundup Ready soybeans) and insect resistance (Bt corn and cotton) have been the most important of the genetic crop modifications introduced and the ones responsible for the significant increase in productivity and reduction in costs of the crops involved.

Even in those world regions favorable for Green Revolution introductions, its advent has not always improved diets or reduced dependency on imported basic foodstuffs. Often, the displacement of native agriculture involves a net loss of domestic food availability. In many instances, through governmental directive, foreign ownership or management, or domestic market realities, the new commercial agriculture is oriented toward food and industrial crops for the export market or toward specialty crop and livestock production for the expanding urban market rather than food production for the rural population.

Commercial Agriculture

Few people or areas still retain the isolation and self-sufficiency characteristic of pure subsistence economies. Nearly all have been touched by a modern world of trade and exchange and have adjusted their traditional economies in response. Modifications of subsistence agricultural systems have inevitably made them more complex by imparting to them at least some of the diversity and linkages of activity that mark the advanced economic systems of the more developed world. Farmers in those systems produce not for their own subsistence but primarily for a market off the farm itself. They are part of integrated exchange economies in which agriculture is but one element in a complex structure that includes mining, manufacturing, processing, and the service activities of the tertiary, quaternary and quinary sectors. In those economies, farming activities presumably mark

Women farmers grow at least half of the world's food and up to 80% in some African countries. They are responsible for an even larger share of food consumed by their own families: 80% in sub-Saharan Africa, 65% in Asia, and 45% in Latin America and the Caribbean. Further, women comprise between one-third and one-half of all agricultural laborers in developing countries. For example, African women perform about 90% of the work of processing food crops and 80% of the work of harvesting and marketing.

Women's agricultural dominance in developing states is increasing, in fact, as male family members continue to leave for cities in search of paid urban work. In Mozambique, for example, for every 100 men working in agriculture, there are 153 women. In nearly all other sub-Saharan countries the female component runs between 120 and 150 per 100 men. The departure of men for near or distant cities means, in addition, that women must assume effective management of their families' total farm operations.

Despite their fundamental role, however, women do not share equally with men in the rewards from agriculture, nor are they always beneficiaries of presumed improvements in agricultural technologies and practices. Often, they cannot own or inherit the land on which they work, and they frequently have difficulty in obtaining improved seeds or fertilizers available to male farmers.

As a rule, women farmers work longer hours and have lower incomes than do male farmers. This is not because they are less educated or competent. Rather, it is due to restrictive cultural and economic factors. First, most women farmers are involved in subsistence farming and food production for the local market, which yields little cash return. Second, they have far less access than men to credit at bank or government-subsidized rates that would make it possible for them to acquire the Green Revolution technology, such as hybrid seeds and fertilizers. Third, in some cultures women cannot own land and so are excluded from agricultural improvement programs and projects aimed at landowners. For example, many African agricultural development programs are based on the conversion of communal land, to which women have access, to private holdings, from which they are excluded. In Asia, inheritance laws favor male over female heirs, and female-inherited land is managed by husbands; in Latin America, discrimination results from the more limited status held by women under the law.

At the same time, the Green Revolution and its greater commercialization of crops has generally required an increase in labor per hectare, particularly in tasks typically reserved for women, such as weeding, harvesting, and postharvest work. If women are provided no relief from their other daily tasks, the Green Revolution for them may be more burden than blessing. But when mechanization is added to the new farming system, women tend to be losers. Frequently, such predominantly female tasks as harvesting or dehusking and polishing of grain—all traditionally done by hand—are given over to machinery, displacing rather than employing women. Even the application of chemical fertilizers (a "man's task") instead of cow dung ("women's work") has reduced the female role in agricultural development programs. The loss of those traditional female wage jobs means that already poor rural women and their families have insufficient income to improve their diets even in the light of substantial increases in food availability through Green Revolution improvements.

If women are to benefit from the Green Revolution, new cultural norms—or culturally acceptable accommodations within traditional household, gender, and customary legal relations—will be required. These must permit or recognize women's landowning and other legal rights not now clearly theirs, access to credit at favorable rates, and admission on equal footing with males to government assistance programs.

Recognition of those realities fostered the Food and Agriculture Organization of the United Nations' "FAO Plan of Action for Women in Development (1996–2001)" and its "Gender and Development Plan (2002–2007)." Both aimed at stimulating and facilitating efforts to enhance the role of women as contributors and beneficiaries of economic, social, and political development. Objectives of the plans included promoting gender-based equity in access to, and control of, productive resources; enhancing women's participation in decision- and policy-making processes at all levels, local and national; and encouraging actions to reduce rural women's workload while enhancing their opportunities for paid employment and income.

production responses to market demand expressed through price and are related to the consumption requirements of the larger society rather than to the immediate needs of farmers themselves.

Production Controls

Agriculture within modern, developed economies is characterized by *specialization*—by enterprise (farm), by area, and even by country; by *off-farm sale* rather than subsistence production; and by *interdependence* of producers and buyers linked through markets. Farmers in a free market economy supposedly produce those crops that their estimates of market price and production cost indicate will yield the greatest return. Theoretically, farm products for which demand at a given price increases will command an increased market price. That, in turn, should induce increased production to meet the demand. In some developing countries, that market equilibrium is broken and the farm economy distorted when government policy requires uneconomically low food prices for urban workers. It may also suffer material distortion under governmental programs protecting local producers by inhibiting farm product imports or subsidizing production by guaranteeing prices for selected commodities.

Where free market conditions prevail, however, the crop or the mix of crops and livestock that individual commercial farmers produce is a result of an appraisal of profit possibilities. Farmers must assess and predict prices, evaluate the physical nature of farmland, and factor in the possible weather conditions. The costs of production (fuel, fertilizer, capital equipment, labor) must be reckoned. A number of unpredictable conditions may thwart farmers' aspirations for profit. Among them are the uncertainties of growing season conditions that follow the original planting decision, the total volume of output that will be achieved (and therefore the unit cost of production), and the supply and price situation that will exist months or years in the future, when crops are ready for market.

Beginning in the 1950s in the United States, specialist farmers and corporate purchasers developed strategies for minimizing those uncertainties. Processors sought uniformity of product quality and timing of delivery. Vegetable canners—of tomatoes, sweet corn, and the like—required volume delivery of raw products of uniform size, color, and ingredient content on dates that accorded with cannery and labor schedules. And farmers wanted the support of a guaranteed market at an assured price to minimize the uncertainties of their specialization and stabilize the return on their investment.

The solution was contractual arrangements or vertical integrations uniting contracted farmer with purchaser-processor. Broiler chickens of specified age and weight, cattle fed to an exact weight and finish, wheat with a minimum protein content, popping corn with prescribed characteristics, potatoes of the kind and quality demanded by particular fast-food chains, and similar product specification became part of production contracts between farmer and buyer-processor. In the United States, the percentage of total farm output produced under contractual arrangements or by vertical integration (where production, processing, and sales are all coordinated within one firm) rose from 19% in 1960 to well over one-third during the 1990s. For example, in 2003, about 72% of hogs were sold under some form of contract; in 1980, only 5% were sold that way. The term *agribusiness* is applied to the growing merging of the older, farm-centered crop economy and newer patterns of more integrated production and marketing systems.

Contract farming is spreading as well to developing countries, though it is often criticized as another adverse expression of globalization subjecting small-size farmers to exploitation by powerful Western agribusiness. The UN's FAO, however, argues that well-managed contract arrangements are effective in linking the small farmers of emerging economies with both foreign and local sources of advanced extension advice, seeds, fertilizers, machinery, and profitable markets at stable prices. The agency cites successful examples of contract farming in northern India, Sri Lanka, Nepal, Indonesia, Thailand, and the Philippines and sees in the arrangements a most promising approach to market-oriented production in areas still dominated by subsistence agriculture.

Even for family farmers not bound by contractual arrangements to suppliers and purchasers, the older assumption that supply, demand, and the market price mechanism are the effective controls on agricultural production is not wholly valid. In reality, those theoretical controls are joined by a number of nonmarket governmental influences that may be as decisive as market forces in shaping farmers' options and spatial production patterns. If there is a glut of wheat on the market, for example, the price per ton will come down and the area sown to it should diminish.

It will also diminish regardless of supply if governments, responding to economic or political considerations, impose acreage controls.

Distortions of market control may also be introduced to favor certain crops or commodities through subsidies, price supports, market protections, and the like. The political power of farmers in the European Union (EU), for example, secured for them generous product subsidies and for the EU immense unsold stores of butter, wine, and grains until 1992, when reforms began to reduce the surplus stockpiles even while increasing total farm spending. In Japan, the home market for rice is largely protected and reserved for Japanese rice farmers even though their production efficiencies are low and their selling price is high by world market standards. In the United States, programs of farm price supports, acreage controls, financial assistance, and other governmental involvements in agriculture have been of recurring and equally distorting effect (Figure 8.13).

A Model of Agricultural Location

Early in the 19th century, before such governmental influences were the norm, Johann Heinrich von Thünen (1783–1850) observed that lands of apparently identical physical properties were utilized for different agricultural purposes. Around each major urban market center, he noted, there developed a set of concentric land use rings of different farm products (Figure 8.14). The ring closest to the market specialized in perishable commodities that were both expensive to ship and in high demand. The high prices they could command in the urban market made their production an appropriate use of high-valued land near the city. Surrounding rings of farmlands farther away from the city were used for less perishable commodities with lower transport costs, reduced demand, and lower market prices. General farming and grain farming replaced the market gardening of the inner ring. At the outer margins of profitable agriculture, farthest from the single central market, livestock grazing and similar extensive land uses were found.

To explain why this should be so, von Thünen constructed a formal spatial model—the **von Thünen model**—perhaps the first developed to analyze human activity patterns. He concluded that the uses to which parcels were put was a function of the differing "rent" values placed on seemingly identical lands. Those differences, he claimed, reflected the cost of overcoming the distance separating a given farm from a central market town ("A portion of each crop is eaten by the wheels," he observed). The greater the distance, the higher was the operating cost to the farmer, since transport charges had to be added to other expenses. When a commodity's production costs plus its transport costs just equaled its value at the market, a farmer was at the economic margin of its cultivation. A simple exchange relationship ensued: the greater the transportation costs, the lower the rent that could be paid for land if the crop produced was to remain competitive in the market.

Since in the simplest form of the model, transport costs are the only variable, the relationship between land rent and distance from market can be easily calculated by reference to each competing crop's *transport gradient*. Perishable commodities such as fruits and vegetables would encounter high transport rates per unit of distance; other items such as grain would have lower rates. Land

Figure 8.13 Open storage of 1 million bushels of Iowa corn. In the world of commercial agriculture, supply and demand are not always in balance. Both the bounty of nature in favorable crop years and the intervention of governmental programs that distort production decisions can create surpluses for which no market is readily available.

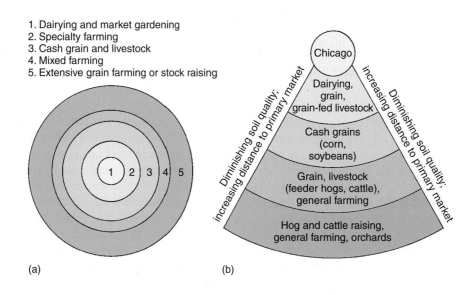

1. Dairying and market gardening
2. Specialty farming
3. Cash grain and livestock
4. Mixed farming
5. Extensive grain farming or stock raising

(a)

(b)

Figure 8.14 (*a*) **von Thünen's model.** Recognizing that as distance from the market increases, the value of land decreases, von Thünen developed a descriptive model of intensity of land use that holds up reasonably well in practice. The most intensively produced crops are found on land close to the market; the less intensively produced commodities are located at more distant points. The numbered zones of the diagram represent modern equivalents of the theoretical land use sequence von Thünen suggested over 175 years ago. As the metropolitan area at the center increases in size, the agricultural specialty areas are displaced outward, but the relative position of each is retained. Compare this diagram with Figure 8.18. (*b*) **A schematic view of the von Thünen zones** in the sector south of Chicago. There, farmland quality decreases southward as the boundary of recent glaciation is passed and hill lands are encountered in southern Illinois. On the margins of the city near the market, dairying competes for space with livestock feeding and suburbanization. Southward into flat, fertile central Illinois, cash grains dominate. In southern Illinois, livestock rearing and fattening, general farming, and some orchard crops are the rule.

Source: (b) Modified with permission from Bernd Andreae, Farming Development and Space: A World Agricultural Geography, *translated by Howard F. Gregor (Berlin; Hawthorne, N.Y.: Walter de Gruyter and Co., 1981).*

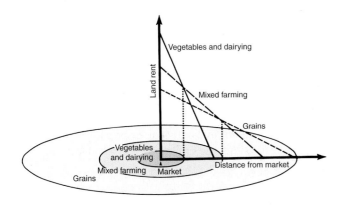

Figure 8.15 Transport gradients and agricultural zones.

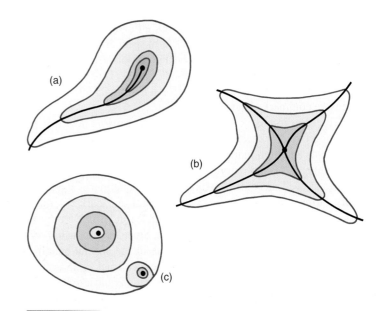

Figure 8.16 **Ring modifications.** Modifications of controlling conditions will alter the details but not change the underlying pattern of the *von Thünen rings.* For example, a growth in demand and therefore market price of a commodity would merely expand its ring of production. An increase in transport costs would contract the production area, while reductions in freight rates would extend it. (*a*) If transport costs are reduced in one direction, the circularity—but not the sequence—of the rings will be affected. (*b*) If several roads are constructed or improved, land use sequences assume a star-shaped or digitate outline. (*c*) The addition of a smaller outlying market results in the emergence of a set of von Thünen rings subordinate to it.

rent for any farm commodity decreases with increasing distance from the central market, and the rate of decline is determined by the transport gradient for that commodity. Crops that have both the highest market price and the highest transport costs will be grown nearest to the market. Less perishable crops with lower production and transport costs will be grown at greater distances away (Figure 8.15). Since in this model transport costs are uniform in all directions away from the center, a concentric zonal pattern of land use called the *von Thünen rings* results.

The von Thünen model may be modified by introducing ideas of differential transport costs (Figure 8.16), variations in topography or soil fertility, or changes in commodity demand and market price. With or without such modifications, von Thünen's analysis helps explain the changing crop patterns and farm sizes evident on the landscape at increasing distance from major cities, particularly in regions dominantly agricultural in economy. Farmland close to markets takes on high value, is used *intensively* for high-value crops, and is subdivided into relatively small units. Land far from markets is used *extensively* and in larger units.

In dominantly industrial and postindustrial economies, it has been suggested, the basic forces determining agricultural land use near cities are those associated with urban expansion itself, and von Thünen regularities are less predictable. Rather, irregularities and uncertainties of peripheral city growth, the encroachment on agricultural land by expansion from two or more cities, and the withholding of land from farming in anticipation of subdivision may locally reverse or invert the von Thünen intensity rings. Where those urbanizing forces dominate, the agricultural pattern often may be one of increasing—rather than decreasing—intensity with distance from the city.

Intensive Commercial Agriculture

Following World War II, agriculture in the developed world's market economies turned increasingly to concentrated methods of production. Machinery, chemicals, irrigation, and dependence on a restricted range of carefully selected and bred plant varieties and animal breeds all were employed in a concerted effort to wring more production from each unit of farmland.

The goal, of course, was to increase off-farm sales as American agriculture increasingly shifted from an objective of partial self-sufficiency to a total commitment to the commercial, exchange economy. Prior to 1950 most U.S. farms had a significant subsistence orientation; they were "general farms" growing a variety of crops, some for sale and some for feed for farmstead livestock—a milk cow or two, chickens for the pot and for household eggs, a few hogs and steers, partly for farm slaughter and use. Their extensive kitchen gardens supplied vegetables and fruits for farm family seasonal consumption and home canning. In 1949 the average American farm sold only $4,100 worth of products. By 2007, however, most farms had a full commitment to the market, average off-farm sales rose to more than $135,000, and farm families—like other Americans—shopped the supermarkets for their food needs. With the increases in capital investment and the need for larger farms to maximize return on that investment, many inefficient small farms have been abandoned. Consolidation has reduced the number and enlarged the size of farms still in production. From a high of 6.8 million in 1934, the number of U.S. farms dropped to 5.7 million in 1949 and, by 2007, to 2.2 million, with many of the smallest units "farms" only by courtesy of a generous Department of Agriculture definition.

The reorientation of farm production goals in the United States and in most other highly developed market economies has led to significant changes in regional farm production patterns. Reflecting the drive for enhanced, more specialized output and the investment of large amounts of capital (for machinery, fertilizers, and specialized buildings, for example), all modern agriculture is "intensive." But the several types of farm specializations differ in how much capital is invested per hectare of farmed land (and, of course, in the specifics of those capital inputs). Those differences underlie generalized distinctions between traditional intensive and extensive commerical agriculture.

The term **intensive commercial agriculture** is now usually understood to refer specifically to the production of crops that give high yields and high market value per unit of land. These include fruits, vegetables, and dairy products, all of which are highly perishable, as well as some "factory farm" production of livestock. Dairy farms and **truck farms** (horticultural or "market garden" farms that produce a wide range of vegetables and fruits) are found near most medium-sized and large cities. Since the product is perishable, transport costs increase because of the special handling that is needed, such as the use of refrigerated trucks and custom packaging. This is another reason for locations close to market. Note the distribution of truck and fruit farming in Figure 8.17, which also suggests the importance of climatic conditions in commercial fruit and vegetable growing.

Livestock-grain farming involves the growing of grain to be fed on the producing farm to livestock, which constitute the farm's cash product. In Western Europe, three-fourths of cropland is devoted to production for animal consumption; in Denmark, 90% of all grains are fed to livestock for conversion not only into meat but also into butter, cheese, and milk. Although livestock-grain farmers work their land intensively, the value of their product per unit of land is usually less than that of the truck farm. Consequently, in North America at least, livestock-grain farms are farther from the main markets than are horticultural and dairy farms.

Normally the profits for marketing livestock (chiefly hogs and beef cattle in the United States) are greater per pound than those for selling corn or other feed, such as alfalfa and clover. As a result, farmers convert their corn into meat on the farm by feeding it to the livestock, efficiently avoiding the cost of buying grain. They may also convert farm grain at local feed mills to the more balanced feed modern livestock rearing requires. Where land is too expensive to be used to grow feed, especially near cities, feed must be shipped to the farm. The grain-livestock belts of the world are close to the great coastal and industrial zone markets. The Corn Belt of the United States and the livestock region of Western Europe are two examples.

In the United States—and commonly in all developed countries—the traditional livestock and grain operations of small and family farms have been largely supplanted by very large scale concentrated animal feeding operations or "livestock factory farms" involving thousands or tens of thousands of closely quartered animals. From its inception in the 1920s, the intensive, industrialized rearing of livestock, particularly beef and dairy cattle, hogs, and poultry, has grown to dominate meat, dairy, and egg production. To achieve their objective of producing a marketable product in volume at the lowest possible unit cost, operators of livestock factory farms confine animals to pens or cages, treat them with antibiotics and vitamins to maintain health and speed growth, provide processed feeds that often contain the low-cost animal by-products or crop residue, and deliver them under contract to processors, packers, or their parent company (Figure 8.18). Although serious concerns have been voiced about animal waste management and groundwater, stream, and atmospheric pollution, contract-based concentrated feeding operations now provide almost all supermarket meat and dairy products. The location of this form of intensive commercial farming, however, is often determined not by land value or proximity to market but by land use restrictions and environmental standards imposed by state and county governments.

Extensive Commercial Agriculture

Farther from the market, on less expensive land, there is less need to use the land intensively. Cheaper land gives rise to larger farm units. **Extensive commercial agriculture** is typified by large wheat farms and livestock ranching.

There are, of course, limits to the land use explanations attributable to von Thünen's model. While it is true that farmland values decline westward with increasing distance from the northeastern market of the United States, they show no corresponding increase with increasing proximity to the massive West Coast market region until the specialty agricultural areas of the coastal states themselves are reached. The western states are characterized by extensive agriculture, but as a consequence of environmental, not distance, considerations. Climatic conditions obviously affect the productivity and the potential agricultural use of an area, as do associated soils regions and topography. In Anglo America, of course, increasing distance westward from eastern markets is by chance associated with increasing aridity and the beginning of mountainous terrain. In general, rough terrain and subhumid climates rather than simple distance from market underlie the widespread occurrence of extensive agriculture.

Large-scale wheat farming requires sizable capital inputs for planting and harvesting machinery—a large tractor might cost $300,000 and a combine (harvester) $ 500,000. However, the inputs per unit of land are low; wheat farms are very large. Nearly half the farms in Saskatchewan, for example, are more than 400 hectares (1000 acres). The average farm in Kansas is larger than 300 hectares, and in North Dakota, more than 525 hectares (1300 acres). In North America, the spring wheat (planted in spring, harvested in autumn) region includes the Dakotas, eastern Montana, and the southern parts of the Prairie Provinces of Canada. The winter wheat (planted in fall, harvested in midsummer) belt focuses on Kansas and includes adjacent sections of neighboring states (Figure 8.19). Argentina is the only South American country to have comparable large-scale wheat farming. In the Eastern Hemisphere, the system is fully developed only east of the Volga River in northern Kazakhstan and the southern part of Western Siberia, and in southeastern and western Australia. Because wheat is an important crop in many agricultural systems—today, wheat ranks first in total production among all the world's grains and accounts for more than 20% of the total calories consumed by humans collectively—large-scale wheat farms face competition from commercial and subsistence producers throughout the world (Figure 8.20).

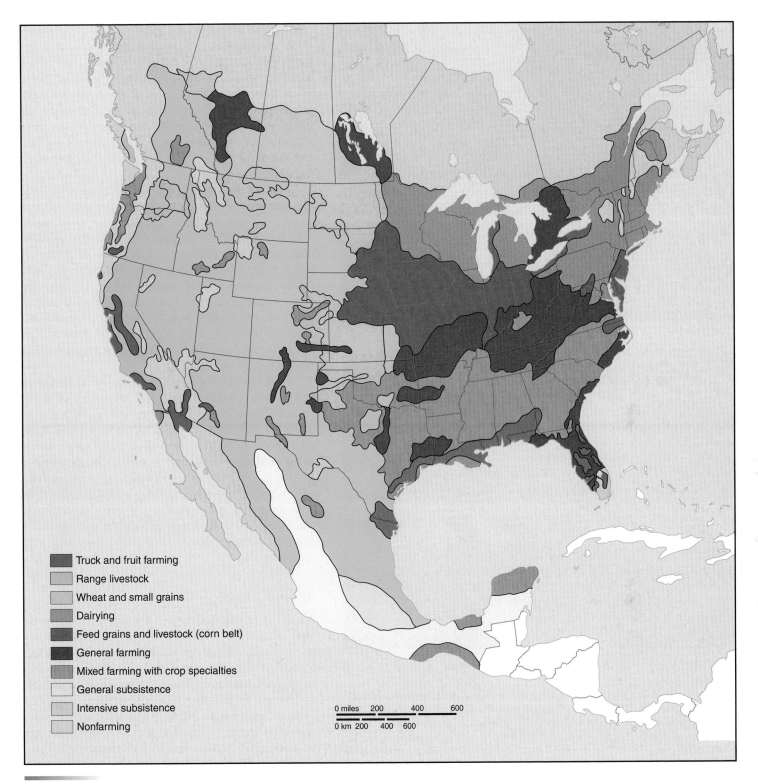

Figure 8.17 **Generalized agricultural regions of North America.**

Sources: U.S. Bureau of Agricultural Economics; Agriculture Canada; and Secretaría de Agricultura y Recursos Hidráulicos, Mexico.

Legend:
- Truck and fruit farming
- Range livestock
- Wheat and small grains
- Dairying
- Feed grains and livestock (corn belt)
- General farming
- Mixed farming with crop specialties
- General subsistence
- Intensive subsistence
- Nonfarming

0 miles   200   400   600
0 km 200 400 600

(a)

(b)

Figure 8.18 A hog factory-farm in Ohio. (*a*) On factory-style hog farms such as the one pictured here, thousands of animals are fed and raised indoors in large rectangular barns for the four or five months it takes them to grow to market weight of 250 pounds. (*b*) Feces and urine are washed through slots in the floor into pipes and trenches that carry the waste outdoors into holding pits known as waste lagoons.

Livestock ranching differs significantly from livestock-grain farming and, by its commercial orientation and distribution, from the nomadism it superficially resembles. A product of the 19th-century growth of urban markets for beef and wool in Western Europe and the northeastern United States, ranching has been primarily confined to areas of European settlement. It is found in the western United States and adjacent sections of

Mexico and Canada (see Figure 8.17); the grasslands of Argentina, Brazil, Uruguay, and Venezuela; the interior of Australia; the uplands of South Island, New Zealand; and the Karoo and adjacent areas of South Africa (Figure 8.21). All except New Zealand and the humid pampas of South America have semiarid climates. All, even the most remote from markets, were a product of improvements in transportation by land and sea, refrigeration of carriers, and of meat-canning technology.

In all of the ranching regions, livestock range (and the area exclusively in ranching) has been reduced as crop farming has encroached on their more humid margins, as pasture improvement has replaced less nutritious native grasses, and as grain fattening has supplemented traditional grazing. Recently, the mid-latitude demand for beef has been blamed for expanded cattle ranching and extensive destruction of tropical rain forests in Central America and the Amazon basin, although in recent years Amazon Basin deforestation has reflected more the expansion of soybean farming than of beef production.

In areas of livestock ranching, young cattle or sheep are allowed to graze over thousands of acres. In the United States, when the cattle have gained enough weight so that weight loss in shipping will not be a problem, they are sent to livestock-grain farms or to feedlots near slaughterhouses for accelerated fattening. Since ranching can be an economic activity only where alternative land uses are nonexistent and land quality is low, ranching regions of the world characteristically have low population densities, low capitalizations per land unit, and relatively low labor requirements.

Special Crops

Proximity to the market does not guarantee the intensive production of high-value crops should terrain or climatic circumstances hinder it. Nor does great distance from the market inevitably determine that extensive farming on low-priced land will be the sole agricultural option. Special circumstances, most often climatic, make some places far from markets intensively developed agricultural areas. Two special cases are agriculture in Mediterranean climates and in plantation areas (Figure 8.21).

Most of the arable land in the Mediterranean basin itself is planted to grains, and much of the agricultural area is used for grazing. *Mediterranean agriculture* as a specialized farming economy, however, is known for grapes, olives, oranges, figs, vegetables, and similar commodities. These crops need warm temperatures all year round and a great deal of sunshine in the summer. The Mediterranean agricultural lands indicated in Figure 8.21 are among the most productive in the world. Farmers can regulate their output in sunny areas such as these because storms and other inclement weather problems are infrequent. Also, the precipitation regime of Mediterranean climate areas—winter rain and summer drought—lends itself to the controlled use of water. Of course, much capital must be spent for the irrigation systems. This is another reason for the intensive use of the land for high-value crops that are, for the most part, destined for export to industrialized countries or areas outside the Mediterranean climatic zone and even, in the case of Southern Hemisphere locations, to markets north of the equator.

Climate is also considered the vital element in the production of what are commonly, but imprecisely, known as *plantation crops*. The implication of **plantation** is the introduction of a foreign element—investment, management, and marketing—into an indigenous culture and economy, often employing an introduced alien labor force. The plantation itself is an estate whose resident workers produce one or two specialized crops. Those crops, although native to the tropics, were frequently foreign to the areas of plantation establishment: African coffee and Asian sugar in the Western Hemisphere and American cacao, tobacco, and rubber in Southeast Asia and Africa are examples (Figure 8.22). Entrepreneurs in Western countries such as England, France, the Netherlands, and the United States became interested in the tropics partly because they afforded them the opportunity to satisfy a demand in temperate lands for agricultural commodities not producible in the market areas. Custom and convenience usually retain the term "plantation" even where native producers of local crops dominate, as they do in cola nut production in Guinea, spice growing in India or Sri Lanka, or sisal production in the Yucatán.

The major plantation crops and the areas where they are produced include tea (India and Sri Lanka), jute (India and Bangladesh), rubber (Malaysia and Indonesia), cacao (Ghana and Nigeria), cane sugar (Cuba and the Caribbean area, Brazil, Mexico, India, and the Philippines), coffee (Brazil and Colombia),

Figure 8.19 Contract harvesters follow the ripening wheat northward through the plains of the United States and Canada.

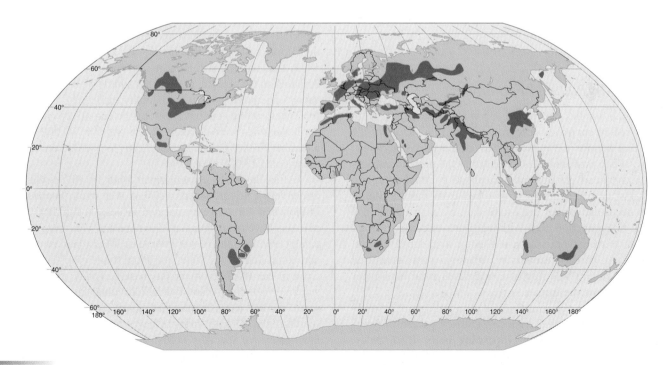

Figure 8.20 **Principal wheat-growing areas.** Only part of the world's wheat production comes from large-scale farming enterprises. In western and southern Europe, eastern and southern Asia, and North Africa, wheat growing is part of general or intensive subsistence farming. Recently, developing country successes with the Green Revolution and subsidized surpluses of the grain in Europe have altered traditional patterns of production and world trade in wheat.

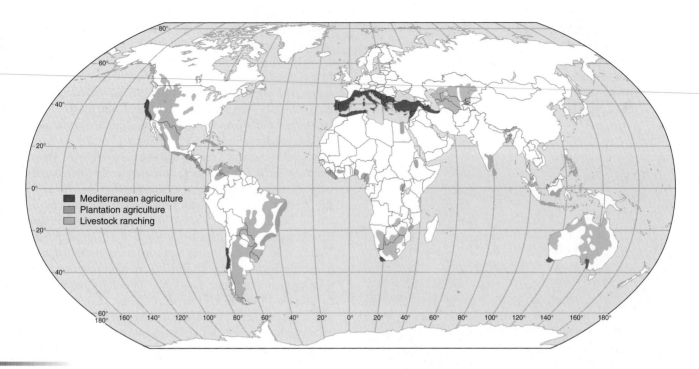

Figure 8.21 **Livestock ranching and special crop agriculture.** Livestock ranching is primarily a midlatitude enterprise catering to the urban markets of industrialized countries. Mediterranean and plantation agriculture are similarly oriented to the markets provided by advanced economies of western Europe and North America. Areas of Mediterranean agriculture—all of roughly comparable climatic conditions—specialize in similar commodities, such as grapes, oranges, olives, peaches, and vegetables. The specialized crops of plantation agriculture are influenced by both physical geographic conditions and present or, particularly, former colonial control of the area.

and bananas (Central America). As Figure 8.21 suggests, for ease of access to shipping, most plantation crops are cultivated along or near coasts since production for export rather than for local consumption is the rule.

Agriculture in Planned Economies

As their name implies, planned economies have a degree of centrally directed control of resources and of key sectors of the economy that permits the pursuit of governmentally determined objectives. When that control is extended to the agricultural sector, state and collective farms and agricultural communes replace private farms, crop production is divorced from market control or family need, and prices are established by plan rather than by demand or production cost. Although such extremes of rural control have in recent years been relaxed or abandoned in most formerly strictly planned economies, wherever past centralized control of agriculture was imposed, traditional rural landscapes were altered. Before the former Soviet Union's collapse in 1991, its rural landscape had been transformed from millions of prerevolutionary small farm holdings to a consolidated pattern of fewer than 50,000 centrally controlled operating units. Even today, because of inadequacies in farm registry and boundary descriptions and because of clouded ownership rights, the remnants of the old Soviet collective farm system still operate more than 90% of the country's farmlands but now respond to market opportunities, not centralized directives.

An incomplete progression from private and peasant agriculture, through collectivization, and back to what is virtually a private farming system took place in the planned economy of the People's Republic of China. After its assumption of power in 1949, the communist regime redistributed all farmlands to some 350 million peasants in inefficiently small (0.2 hectare, or 0.5 acre) subsistence holdings that were totally inadequate for the growing food needs of the country. Later, by the end of 1957, 90% of peasant households were collectivized into about 700,000 communes, a number further reduced in the 1970s to 50,000 communes averaging some 13,000 members.

After the death of Chairman Mao in 1976, what became effectively a private farming system was reintroduced when 180 million new farms were allocated to peasant families. Currently, peasants have renewable land use contracts valid for 30 years, but cannot own the land or sell their leases. Farmland remains owned and controlled by the state, and most staple crops are still sold at fixed prices to government purchasers. Today, production decisions are generally made by the individual farmer, based on the same market assessments that control capitalistic economies. Increasingly, China's farmers have turned to the production of labor-intensive specialty crops, such as fruits, vegetables, meat, pond-raised fish—not only for the country's rapidly expanding domestic market (Figure 8.23) but for export as well. China's per capita food production and availability have increased dramatically as this conversion to an agricultural market economy, rather than a subsistence or planned economy, has progressed.

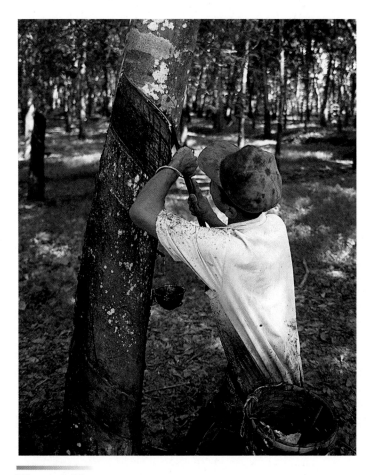

Figure 8.22 An Indonesian rubber plantation worker collects latex in a small cup attached to the tree and cuts a new tap just above the previous one. The scene typifies classical plantation agriculture in general. The plantation was established by foreign capital (Dutch) to produce a nonnative (American) commercial crop for a distant, midlatitude market using nonnative (Chinese) labor supervised by foreign (Dutch) managers. Present-day ownership, management, and labor may have changed, but the nature and market orientation of the enterprise remain.

Primary Activities: Resource Exploitation

In addition to agriculture, primary economic activities include fishing, forestry, and the mining and quarrying of minerals. These industries involve the direct exploitation of natural resources that are unequally available in the environment and differentially evaluated by different societies. Their development, therefore, depends on the occurrence of perceived resources, the technology to exploit their natural availability, and the cultural awareness of their value.

Fishing, forestry, and fur trapping are **gathering industries** based on harvesting the natural bounty of renewable resources that are in serious danger of depletion through overexploitation. Livelihoods based on these resources are areally widespread and involve both subsistence and market-oriented components. Mining and quarrying are **extractive industries,** removing nonrenewable metallic and nonmetallic minerals, including the mineral fuels,

Figure 8.23 Independent street merchants, shop owners, and peddlers in modern China are members of both a planned and a market system. Free markets and private vendors multiplied after government price controls on most food items were removed in May 1985. Increasingly, nonfood trade and manufacturing, too, are being freed of central government control and thriving in the private sector. As state-run companies shrank and laid off workers, privately owned businesses in 2007 accounted for two-thirds of China's economic output, and the private sector was growing twice as fast as the rest of the economy. The photo shows a row of outdoor poultry merchants in Wanxian, Sichuan Province.

from the earth's crust. They are the initial raw material phase of modern industrial economies.

Resource Terminology

Resources or **natural resources** are the naturally occurring materials that a human population, at any given state of economic development and technological awareness, perceives to be necessary and useful to its economic and material well-being. Their occurrence and distribution in the environment are the result of physical processes over which people have little or no direct control. The fact that things exist, however, does not mean that they are resources. To be considered such, a given substance must be *understood* to be a resource—and this is a cultural, not purely a physical, circumstance. Native Americans may have viewed the resource base of Pennsylvania, West Virginia, or Kentucky as composed of forests for shelter and fuel and as the habitat of the game animals (another resource) on which they depended for food. European settlers viewed the forests as the unwanted covering of the resource that *they* perceived to be of value: soil for agriculture. Still later, industrialists appraised the underlying coal deposits, ignored or unrecognized as a resource by earlier occupants, as the item of value for exploitation (Figure 8.24).

Resources may be classified as *renewable* or *nonrenewable.* **Renewable resources** are materials that can be consumed and then replenished relatively quickly by natural or by human-assisted processes. Food crops are renewable resources, for example, as are forests, grasslands, animals and fish, and other living things. Even renewable resources can be exhausted if exploited to extinction

Figure 8.24 The original hardwood forest covering these West Virginia hills was removed by settlers who saw greater resource value in the underlying soils. The soils, in their turn, were selectively stripped away for access to the still more valuable coal deposits below. Resources are as a culture perceives them, though their exploitation may consume them and, as coal refuse does here near Racine, destroy the potential of an area for alternate uses.

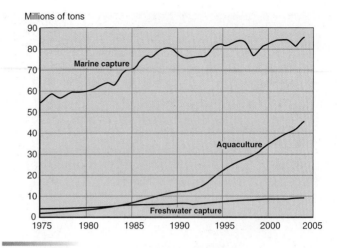

Millions of tons

Figure 8.25 **Officially recorded annual fish harvests, 1975–2004** rose irregularly from 66 million tons in 1975 to 140.5 million tons in 2004. On the basis of individual country reports, the FAO recorded fluctuating but slowly growing harvest totals up to 2002; the 1993 and 1998 dips are associated with ocean temperature changes produced by El Niño. Chinese admission of regular overreporting of, particularly, their marine capture suggests that world marine catch and composite harvest totals actually registered an irregular downward trend each year since 1988. A compensating adjustment to this graph would reduce 2004 total harvest and marine catch figures by some 9 million tons. The FAO estimates that 20 to 40 million tons per year of unintended marine capture of juvenile or undersized fish and nontarget species are discarded each year.

Source: Food and Agriculture Organization (FAO).

or destruction. Soils can be totally eroded, an animal species may be completely eliminated. That is, some resources are renewable only if carefully managed. The **maximum sustainable yield** of a resource is the maximum volume or rate of use that will not impair its ability to be renewed or to maintain the same future productivity. For fishing and forestry, for example, that level is marked by a catch or harvest equal to the net growth of the replacement stock. If that maximum exploitation level is exceeded, the renewable resource becomes a nonrenewable one—an outcome increasingly likely in the case of Atlantic cod and some other food fish species. **Nonrenewable resources** exist in finite amounts and either are not replaced by natural processes—at least not within any time frame of interest to the exploiting society—or are replaced at a rate slower than the rate of use.

Both types of resource are exploited by the nonagricultural primary industries. Fish as a food resource and forests as a source for building materials, cellulose, and fuel are heavily exploited renewable resources. Mining and quarrying extract from nature the nonrenewable minerals essential to industrialized economies.

Fishing

Although fish and shellfish account for only about 15% of all human animal protein consumption, an estimated one billion people—primarily in developing countries of eastern and south-eastern Asia, Africa, and parts of Latin America—depend on fish as their primary source of protein. Fish are also very important in the diets of most advanced states, both those with and those without major domestic fishing fleets. Although about 75% of the world annual fish harvest is consumed by humans, up to 25% is processed into fish meal to be fed to livestock or used as fertilizer. Those two quite different markets have increased both the demand

for and the annual harvest of fish. Indeed, so rapidly have pressures on the world's fish stocks expanded that evidence is unmistakable that at least locally, their *maximum sustainable yield* is actually or potentially being exceeded.

The annual fish supply comes from three sources:

1. the *inland catch,* from ponds, lakes, and rivers;
2. *fish farming,* in which fish are produced in a controlled and contained environment;
3. the *marine catch,* all wild fish harvested in coastal waters or on the high seas.

Inland waters supply less than 7% of the global fish catch (capture); fish farming, both inland and marine, accounts for some 32%. The other 61% or more of the total harvest comes from the world's ocean catch (Figure 8.25). And most of that catch is made in coastal wetlands, estuaries, and the relatively shallow coastal waters above the *continental shelf*—the gently sloping extension of submerged land bordering most coastlines and reaching seaward for varying distances up to 150 kilometers (about 100 miles) or more. Near shore, shallow embayments and marshes provide spawning grounds and river waters supply nutrients to an environment highly productive of fish. Increasingly, these areas are also seriously affected by pollution from runoff and ocean dumping, an environmental assault so devastating in some areas that fish and shellfish stocks have been destroyed with little hope of revival.

Commercial marine fishing is largely concentrated in northern waters, where warm and cold currents join and mix and where

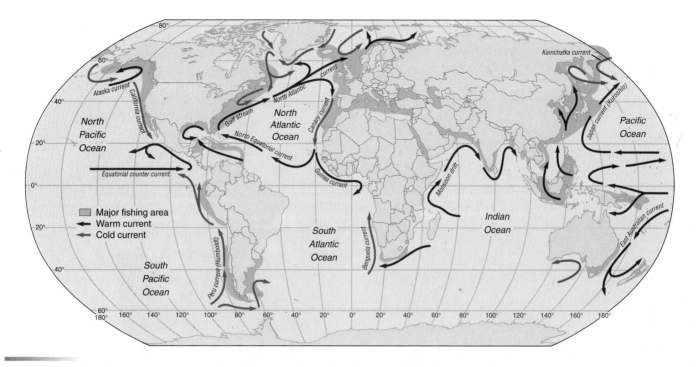

Figure 8.26 **The major commercial marine fisheries of the world.** The waters within 325 kilometers (200 miles) of the United States coastline account for almost one-fifth of the world's annual fish and shellfish harvests. Overfishing, urban development, and the contamination of bays, estuaries, and wetlands have contributed to the depletion of the fish stocks in those coastal waters.

such familiar food species as herring, cod, mackerel, haddock, and flounder congregate or "school" on the broad continental shelves and *banks*—extensive elevated portions of the shelf where environmental conditions are most favorable for fish production (Figure 8.26). Two of the most heavily fished regions are the Northeast Pacific and Northwest Atlantic, which together yield about 40% of the marine catch total. Tropical fish species tend not to school and, because of their high oil content and unfamiliarity, are less acceptable in the commercial market. They are, however, of great importance for local consumption. Traditional or "artisan" fishermen, nearly all working in inshore waters within sight of land, are estimated to number between 8 and 10 million worldwide. Their annual harvest of some 24 million tons of fish and shellfish is usually not included in world fishery totals. Only a very small percentage of total marine catch comes from the open seas that make up more than 90% of the world's oceans.

Modern technology and more aggressive fishing fleets of more countries greatly increased annual marine capture in the years after 1950. That technology included use of sonar, radar, helicopters, and satellite communications to locate schools of fish; more efficient nets and tackle; and factory trawlers to follow fishing fleets to prepare and freeze the catch. In addition, more nations granted ever-larger subsidies to expand and reward their marine trawler operations. The rapid rate of increase led to inflated projections of continuing or growing fisheries productivity and to optimism that the resources of the oceans were inexhaustible.

Quite the opposite has proved to be true. In fact, in recent years, the productivity of marine fisheries has declined because *overfishing* (catches above reproduction rates) and pollution of coastal waters have seriously endangered the supplies of traditional and desirable food species. Adjusted world total catch figures indicate that rather than the steady increase in capture rates shown on Figure 8.25, there has really been a decline of more than 660,000 tons per year since the late 1980s. This decline, coupled with growing world population, has caused a serious drop in the average per capita marine catch. The UN reports that all 17 of the world's major oceanic fishing areas are being fished at or beyond capacity; 13 are in decline. The plundering of Anglo American coastal waters has imperiled a number of the most desirable fish species; in 1993, Canada shut down its cod industry to allow stocks to recover, and U.S. authorities report that 67 North American species are overfished and 61 harvested to capacity.

Overfishing is partly the result of the accepted view that the world's oceans are common property, a resource open to anyone's use with no one responsible for its maintenance, protection, or improvement. The result of this "open seas" principle is but one expression of the so-called **tragedy of the commons**[1]—the economic reality that when a resource is available to all, each user, in the absence of collective controls, thinks he or she is best served by exploiting the resource to the maximum even though this exploitation means its eventual depletion. In 1995, more than 100 countries adopted a treaty—that became legally binding in 2001—to regulate fishing on the open oceans outside territorial waters. Applying to such species as cod, pollock, and tuna—that is, to migratory and high-seas species—the treaty requires fishermen to report the size of their catches to regional organizations

---

[1]The *commons* refers to undivided land available for the use of everyone; usually, it meant the open land of a village that all used as pasture. The *Boston Common* originally had this meaning.

Geography and Public Policy

Public Land, Private Profit

When U.S. President Ulysses S. Grant signed the Mining Act of 1872, the presidential and congressional goal was to encourage Western settlement and development by allowing any "hard-rock" miners (including prospectors for silver, gold, copper, and other metals) to mine federally owned land without royalty payment. It further permitted mining companies to gain clear title to publicly owned land and all subsurface minerals for no more than $12 a hectare ($5 an acre). Under those liberal provisions, mining firms have bought 1.3 million hectares (3.2 million acres) of federal land since 1872 and each year remove some $1.2 billion worth of minerals from government property. In contrast to the royalty-free extraction privileges granted to metal miners, oil, gas, and coal companies pay royalties of as much as 12.5% of their gross revenues for exploiting federal lands.

Whatever the merits of the 1872 law in encouraging economic development of lands otherwise unattractive to homesteaders, modern-day mining companies throughout the Western states have secured enormous actual and potential profits from the law's generous provisions. In Montana, a company claim to 810 hectares (2000 acres) of land would cost it less than $10,000 for an estimated $4 billion worth of platinum and palladium; in California, a gold mining company in 1994 sought title to 93 hectares (230 acres) of federal land containing a potential of $320 million of gold for less than $1200. Foreign as well as domestic firms may be beneficiaries of the 1872 law. In 1994, a South African firm arranged to buy 411 hectares (1016 acres) of Nevada land with a prospective $1.1 billion in gold from the government for $5100. A Canadian firm in 1994 received title to 800 hectares (nearly 2000 acres) near Elko, Nevada, that cover a likely $10 billion worth of gold—a transfer that Interior Secretary Bruce Babbitt dubbed

"the biggest gold heist since the days of Butch Cassidy." And in 1995, Mr. Babbitt conveyed about $1 billion worth of travertine (a mineral used in whitening paper) under 45 hectares (110 acres) of Idaho to a Danish-owned company for $275.

The "gold heist" characterization summarized a growing administration and congressional feeling that what was good in 1872 and today for metal mining companies was not necessarily beneficial to the American public that owns the land. In part, that feeling results from the fact that mining companies commit environmental sins that require public funding to repair or public tolerance to accept. The mining firms may destroy whole mountains to gain access to low-grade ores and leave toxic mine tailings, surface water contamination, and open-pit scarring of the landscape as they move on or disappear. Projected public cleanup costs of more than 500,000 abandoned mine sites, thousands of miles of damaged or dead streams, and several billion tons of contaminated waste are estimated at a minimum of $35 billion.

A congressional proposal introduced in 1993 would have required mining companies to pay royalties of 8% on gross revenues for all hard-rock ores extracted and prohibited them from outright purchase of federal land. The royalty provision alone would have yielded nearly $100 million annually at 1994 levels of company income. Mining firms claim that imposition of royalties might well destroy America's mining industry. They stress both the high levels of investment they must make to extract and process frequently low-grade ores and the large number of high-wage jobs they provide as their sufficient contribution to the nation. The Canadian company involved in the Elko site, for example, reports that since it acquired the claims in 1987 from their previous owner, it has expended over $1 billion, and in addition has made donations for town sewer lines and schools and created 1700 jobs. The American Mining Congress estimates the

proposed 8% royalty charge would cost 47,000 jobs out of 140,000, and even the U.S. Bureau of Mines assumes a loss of 1100 jobs.

Public resistance to Western mining activities is taking its toll. State and federal regulatory procedures, many dragging on for a decade or more, have discouraged opening new mines; newly enacted environmental regulations restricting current mining operations (for example, banning the use of cyanide in gold and silver refining) reduce their economic viability. In consequence, both investment and employment in U.S. mining is in steady decline, eroding the economic base of many Western communities.

Questions to Consider

1. Do you believe the 1872 Mining Law should be repealed or amended? If not, what are your reasons for arguing for retention? If so, would you advocate the imposition of royalties on mining company revenues? At what levels, if any, should royalties be assessed? Should hard-rock and energy companies be treated equally for access to public land resources? Why or why not?

2. Would you propose to prohibit outright land sales to mining companies? If not, should sales prices be determined by surface value of the land or by the estimated (but unrealized) value of mineral deposits it contains?

3. Do you think that cleanup and other charges now borne by the public are acceptable in view of the capital investments and job creation of hard-rock companies? Do you accept the industry's claim that imposition of royalties would destroy American metal mining? Why or why not?

4. Do you favor continued state and federal restrictions on mining operations, even at the cost of jobs and community economies? Why or why not?

region has virtually ceased in response to the decline of the U.S. steel industry. In commercial economies, cost and market controls dominate economic decisions. In planned economies, cost may be a less important consideration than other concerns such as goals of national development and resources independence.

Nonmetallic Minerals

From the standpoint of volume and weight of material removed, the extraction of nonmetallic earth materials is the most important branch of the extractive industries. The minerals mined are usually classified by their end use. Of widest distribution, greatest use, and

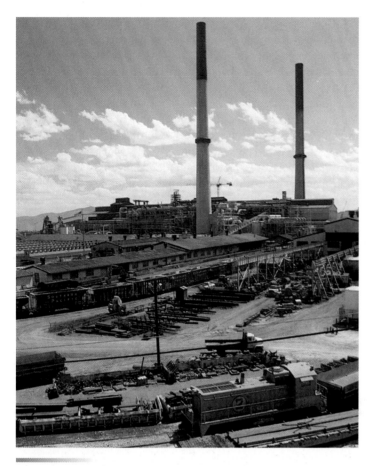

Figure 8.32 Copper ore concentrating and smelting facilities at the Phelps-Dodge mine in Morenci, Arizona. Concentrating mills crush the ore, separating copper-bearing material from the rocky mass containing it. The great volume of waste material removed assures that most concentrating operations are found near the ore bodies. Smelters separate concentrated copper from other, unwanted, materials such as oxygen and sulfur. Because smelting is also a "weight-reducing" (and, therefore, transportation-cost reducing) activity, it is frequently—though not invariably—located close to the mine as well.

least long-distance movement are those used for *construction:* sand and gravel, building stone, and the gypsum and limestone that are the ingredients of cement. Transportation costs play a great role in determining where low-value minerals will be mined. Minerals such as gravel, limestone for cement, and aggregate are found in such abundance that they have value only when they are near the site where they are to be used. For example, gravel for road building has value if it is at or near the road-building project, not otherwise. Transporting gravel hundreds of miles is an unprofitable activity (Figure 8.33).

The mined *fertilizer* minerals include potash and phosphate, which do move in international trade because of their unequal distribution and market value. *Precious* and *semiprecious* stones are also important in the trade of some countries, including South Africa and Sri Lanka.

Mineral Fuels

The advanced economies have reached that status through their control and use of energy. By the application of energy, the conversion of materials into commodities and the performance of services far beyond the capabilities of any single individual are made possible. Energy consumption goes hand in hand with industrial production and with increases in personal wealth. In general, the greater the level of energy consumption, the higher the gross national income per capita. Further, the application of energy can overcome deficiencies in the material world that humans exploit. High-quality iron ore may be depleted, but by massive applications of energy, the iron contained in rocks of very low iron content, such as taconite, can be extracted and concentrated for industrial uses.

Because of the association of energy and economic development, a basic disparity between societies is made clear. Countries that can afford high levels of energy consumption through production or purchase continue to expand their economies and to increase their levels of living. Those without access to energy or those unable to afford it see the gap between their economic prospects and those of the developed states growing ever greater.

Figure 8.33 The Vancouver, British Columbia, municipal gravel quarry and storage yard. Proximity to market gives utility to low-value minerals unable to bear high transportation charges.

Except for the brief and localized importance of waterpower at the outset of the Industrial Revolution, modern economic advancement has been heavily dependent on the *mineral fuels:* coal, petroleum, and natural gas. Also known as *fossil fuels,* these nonrenewable energy sources represent the capture of the sun's energy by plants and animals in earlier geologic time and its storage in the form of hydrocarbon compounds in sedimentary rocks within the earth's crust.

Coal was the earliest in importance and is still the most plentiful of the mineral fuels. As the first of the major industrial energy sources, coal deposits—as we shall see in Chapter 9—were formerly very important in attracting manufacturing and urbanization in industrializing countries. Although coal is a nonrenewable resource, world supplies are so great—on the order of 10,000 billion (10^{13}) tons—that its resource life expectancy is measured in centuries, not in the much shorter spans usually cited for oil and natural gas. Worldwide, the most extensive deposits are concentrated in the industrialized middle latitudes of the Northern Hemisphere (Table 8.1). Two countries, China and the United States, accounted for nearly 60% of total world coal output in 2007; industrializing China alone yielded more than 40% of world production. Russia and Germany, both with large domestic reserves, together produced less than 7%.

Coal is not a resource of constant quality, varying in *rank* (a measure—from lignite to anthracite—of increasing carbon content and fuel quality) and *grade* (a measure of its waste material content, particularly ash and sulfur). The value of a coal deposit depends on these measures and on its accessibility, which is a function of the thickness, depth, and continuity of the coal seam. Much coal can be mined relatively cheaply by open-pit (surface) techniques, in which huge shovels strip off surface material and remove the exposed coal (see Figure 13.21). Much coal, however, is available only by expensive and more dangerous shaft mining, as in Appalachia and most of Europe. In spite of their generally lower heating value, western U.S. coals are attractive because of their low sulfur content. They do, however, require expensive transportation to market or high-cost transmission lines if they are used to generate electricity for distant consumers (Figure 8.34).

Petroleum, first extracted commercially in the 1860s in both the United States and Azerbaijan, became a major power source and a primary component of the extractive industries only in the 20th century. The rapidity of its adoption as both a favored energy resource and a raw material important in a number of industries from plastics to fertilizers, along with the limited size and the speed of depletion of known and probable reserves, promise

Table 8.1

Proved Petroleum, Natural Gas, and Coal Reserves, January 1, 2008

	Share of World Total Petroleum (%)	Share of World Total Natural Gas (%)	Share of World Total Coal (%)
North America[a]	5.6	4.5	28.6
Europe	1.1	3.4	5.9
Former Soviet Union	*10.3*	*30.1*	*26.2*
Of which: Russian Federation	6.4	25.2	18.5
Others	4.0	4.9	7.7
Central and South America	8.7	4.4	1.9
Africa	9.5	8.2	5.8
Middle East[b]	61.0	41.3	0.2
Australia/New Zealand	0.3	1.4	9.1
Japan	–.–	–.–	–.–
China	1.3	1.1	13.5
Other Asia Pacific	2.0	5.7	7.8
Total World	100.0	100.0	100.0
Of which OPEC[c]	75.5	NA	NA

[a]Includes Canada, Mexico, U.S.A.
[b]Middle East includes Arabian Peninsula, Iran, Iraq, Israel, Jordan, Lebanon, Syria.
[c]OPEC: Organization of Petroleum Exporting Countries. Member nations are, by world region:
  South America: Venezuela
  Middle East: Iran, Iraq, Kuwait, Qatar, Saudi Arabia, United Arab Emirates (Abu Dhabi, Dubai, Ras-al-Khaimah, and Sharjah)
  North Africa: Algeria, Libya
  West Africa: Nigeria
  Asia Pacific: Indonesia

Source: Data from the BP Amoco *Statistical Review of World Energy,* 2008.

Figure 8.34 Long-distance transportation to eastern markets adds significantly to the cost of the low-sulfur western coal useful in meeting federal environmental protection standards. To minimize these costs, unit trains carrying only coal engage in a continuous shuttle movement between western strip mines and eastern utility companies.

that petroleum cannot continually retain its present position of importance in the energy budget of countries. No one has more than an educated guess of how much oil (or natural gas) remains in the world or how long it will last. By 2006, cautious estimates were that world production of conventional (easily extracted) oil would peak about 2016 and decline after that date. The U.S. Geological Survey, more optimistic, projected that world production will peak around 2040. Less optimistically, the international Association for the Study of Peak Oil & Gas (ASPO) in 2006 saw the peak coming in 2010. In a different form of assessment, British Petroleum reported the world had 1.2 trillion barrels of proven oil reserves at the end of 2007—enough to last for 42 years at the 2007 rate of extraction. Some respected oil experts, however, are convinced that price volatility marked by the sharp run-up in oil prices beginning in late 2004, carbon dioxide emissions concerns, and the steady drop in price of solar and other alternative energy sources, will reduce oil demand long before supply becomes an issue. On a world basis, petroleum accounted for 47% of commercial energy consumption in 1973, but had dropped to 36% by 2006 as a reflection of its increasing cost and of conservation measures to offset those increases.

Petroleum is among the most unevenly distributed of the major resources. Seventy-one percent of proved reserves are concentrated in just 7 countries; Iran and the Arab states of the Middle East alone control nearly two-thirds of the world total (Table 8.1). The distribution of petroleum supplies differs markedly from that of the coal deposits on which the urban-industrial markets developed, but the substitution of petroleum for coal did little to alter earlier patterns of manufacturing and population concentration. Because oil is easier and cheaper to transport than coal, it was moved in enormous volumes to the existing centers of consumption via intricate and extensive national and international systems of transportation, a textbook example of spatial interaction,

complementarity, and transferability (see Chapter 3 and Figure 3.2).

Natural gas has been called the nearly perfect energy resource. It is a highly efficient, versatile fuel that requires little processing and its emissions do not contribute to urban air pollution or acid precipitation, although they do contain carton dioxide. Geologists estimate that world recoverable gas reserves are sufficient to last to near the last third of the century at 2007 levels of consumption. *Ultimately recoverable reserves,* those that may be found and recovered at very much higher prices, might last another 200 years.

As we saw for coal and petroleum, reserves of natural gas are very unevenly distributed (Table 8.1). In the case of gas, however, inequalities of supply are not so readily accommodated by massive international movements. Like oil, natural gas flows easily and cheaply by pipeline, but unlike petroleum it does not move freely in international trade by sea. Transoceanic shipment involves costly equipment for liquefaction and for special vessels to contain the liquid under appropriate temperature conditions.

Where the fuel can be moved, even internationally, by pipeline, its consumption has increased dramatically. For the world as a whole, gas consumption rose more than 60% between 1974 and 2005, to more than 23% of global energy consumption.

Trade in Primary Products

International trade expanded more than eleven-fold between 1980 and 2005 to account for about 20% of all economic activity. Primary commodities—agricultural goods, minerals, and fuels—made up one-quarter of the total dollar value of those international flows. During much of the first half of the 20th century, the world distribution of supply and demand for those items in general resulted in an understandable pattern of commodity flow: from raw material producers located within less developed countries to processors, manufacturers, and consumers of the more developed ones (Figure 8.35). The reverse flow carried manufactured goods processed in the industrialized states back to the developing countries. That two-way trade presumably benefited the developed states by providing access to a continuing supply of industrial raw materials and foodstuffs not available domestically and gave less developed countries needed capital to invest in their own development or to expend on the importation of manufactured goods, food supplies, or commodities—such as petroleum—they did not themselves produce.

By the end of the century, however, world trade flows and export patterns of the emerging economies were radically changing. Raw materials greatly decreased and manufactured goods correspondingly increased in the export flows from developing states as a group. In 1990, nonmanufactured (unprocessed) goods accounted for 60% of their exports; by 2006, that share had been cut in four, and in a reversal, manufactured goods made up almost 65% of the export flows from the developing to the industrialized world. Even with that overall decline in raw material exports, however, trade in unprocessed goods remains dominant in the economic well-being of many of the world's poorer economies.

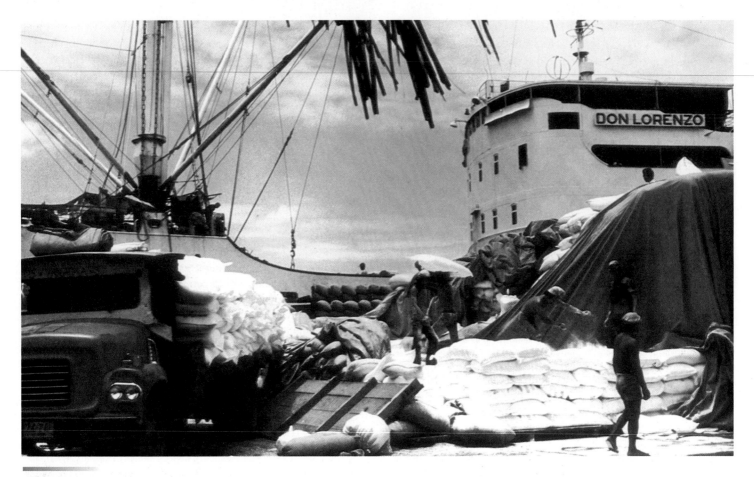

Figure 8.35 Sugar being loaded for export at the port of Cebu in the Philippines. Much of the developing world depends on exports of mineral and agricultural products to the developed economies for the major portion of its income. Fluctuations in market demand and price of some of those commodities can have serious and unexpected consequences.

Increasingly, the terms of the traditional trade flows on which they depend have been criticized as unequal and damaging to commodity-exporting countries.

Commodity prices are volatile; they may rise sharply in periods of product shortage or international economic growth. During much of the 1980s and 1990s, however, commodity price movements were downward, to the great detriment of material-exporting economies. Prices for agricultural raw materials, for example, dropped by 30% between 1975 and 2000, and those for metals and minerals decreased by almost 40%. Such price declines cut deeply into the export earnings of many emerging economies. Of the 141 developing countries, 95 rely on commodities for more than 50% of their export earnings and thus are vulnerable to commodity price volatility. Sub-Saharan African countries are particularly dependent on export earnings from a small number of mineral or agricultural commodities. For example, in 2002 Burundi earned 79% of its export income through coffee exports.

Whatever the current world prices of raw materials may be, raw material exporting states as a group have long expressed resentment at what they perceive as commodity price manipulation by rich countries and corporations to ensure low-cost supplies. Although collusive price-fixing has not been demonstrated, other disadvantages of being a commodity supply region are evident. Technology, for example, has provided industries in advanced countries with a vast array of materials that now can and do substitute for the ores and metals produced by developing states. Glass fibers replace copper wire in telecommunication applications; synthetic rubber replaces natural rubber; glass and carbon fibers provide the raw material for rods, tubes, sheet panels, and other products superior in performance and strength to the metals they replace; and a vast and enlarging array of plastics are the accepted raw materials for commodities and uses for which natural rivals are not even considered. That is, even as the world industrial economy expands, demands and prices for traditional raw materials remain depressed.

Whereas prices paid for developing country commodities tend to be low, prices charged for the manufactured goods offered in exchange by the developed countries tend to be high. To capture processing and manufacturing profits for themselves, some developing states have placed restrictions on the export of unprocessed commodities. Malaysia, the Philippines, and Cameroon, for example, have limited the export of logs in favor of increased domestic processing of sawlogs and exports of lumber. Some developing countries have also encouraged domestic manufacturing to reduce imports and to diversify their exports. Frequently, however, such exports meet with tariffs and quotas protecting the home markets of the industrialized states.

Many developing regions heavily dependent on commodity sales saw their share of global trade fall materially between 1970 and the early 21st century: sub-Saharan Africa from 3.8% to 1%,

Latin America from 5.6% to 3.3%, and the least developed states as a group from 0.8% to 0.4%. Those relative declines are understandable in the light of greatly expanding international trade in manufactured goods from China, Korea, Mexico, and other rapidly industrializing states and from the expansion of trade in both manufactured goods and primary products between the industrialized countries themselves within newly established regional free-trade zones. For example, the developed countries acquire some three-quarters by value of their agricultural imports and 70% of their industrial raw materials from one another, diminishing the prospects for developing country exports.

In 1964, in reaction to the whole range of perceived trade inequities, developing states promoted the establishment of the United Nations Conference on Trade and Development (UNCTAD). Its central constituency—the "Group of 77," expanded to 130 developing states—continues to press for a new world economic order based in part on an increase in the prices and values of exports from developing countries, a system of import preferences for their manufactured goods, and a restructuring of international cooperation to stress trade promotion and recognition of the special needs of poor countries. The World Trade Organization, established in 1995 (and discussed in Chapter 12) was designed in part to reduce trade barriers and inequities. It has, however, been judged by its detractors as ineffective on issues of importance to developing countries. Chief among the complaints is the continuing failure of the industrial countries significantly (or at all) to reduce protections for their own agricultural and mineral industries.

In 2001, members of the World Trade Organization met in Doha, Qatar, to begin negotiations on opening world markets in agriculture—of primary concern to developing states—and in industrial goods and trade in services—the principal interest of the fully developed countries. The "Doha Round" of discussions, with an original December 2004 deadline, continued over the next five years without reaching agreement. Despite the fact that agriculture makes up only 8% of world trade, it has been the road block in all global trade talks. Although the trade ministers of 149 countries at the December 2005 WTO meeting in Hong Kong did agree to the elimination of export subsidies on farm goods by the end of 2013, that interim agreement was criticized by developing states as insufficient and incomplete. In turn, the rich economies insisted that they needed to see significant concessions from poorer countries on trade in both manufactured goods and, particularly, services. The goals of greater equity in freer world trade flows, special consideration for the economic and developmental needs of poorer countries, and more fairness in international trade in primary products are yet to be achieved to the satisfaction of all parties.

Summary

How people earn their living and how the diversified resources of the earth are employed by different peoples and cultures are of fundamental concern in human geography. The economic activities that support us and our society are constant preoccupations that color our perception of the world and its opportunities. At the same time, the totality of our culture—technology, religion, customary behavior—and the circumstances of our natural environment influence the economic choices we discern and the livelihood decisions we make.

In seeking spatial and activity regularities in the nearly infinite diversity of human economic activity, it is useful to generalize about systems of economic organization and control and about classes of productive effort and labor specialization. We can observe, for example, that, broadly speaking, there are three types of economic systems: subsistence, commercial, and planned. The first is concerned with production for the immediate consumption of individual producers and family members. In the second, economic decisions ideally respond to impersonal market forces and reasoned assessments of monetary gain. In the third, at least some nonmonetary social rather than personal goals influence production decisions. The three system forms are not mutually exclusive; all societies contain some intermixture of features of at least two of the three pure types, and some economies have elements of all three. Recognition of each type's respective features and controls, however, helps us to understand the forces shaping economic decisions and patterns in different cultural and regional settings.

Our search for regularities is furthered by a classification of economic activities according to the stages of production and the degree of specialization they represent. We can, for example, decide all productive activity is arranged along a continuum of increasing technology, labor specialization, value of product, or sophistication of service. With that assumption, we can divide our continuum into primary activities (food and raw material production), secondary production (processing and manufacturing), tertiary activities (distribution and general professional and personal service), and the quaternary and quinary activities (administrative, informational, and technical specializations) that mark highly advanced societies of either planned or commercial systems.

Agriculture, the most extensively practiced of the primary industries, is part of the spatial economy of both subsistence and advanced societies. In the first instance—whether it takes the form of extensive or intensive, shifting or sedentary production—it is responsive to the immediate consumption needs of the producer group and reflective of the environmental conditions under which it is practiced. Agriculture in advanced economies involves the application of capital and technology to the productive enterprises; as one sector of an integrated economy, it is responsive to consumption requirements expressed through free or controlled markets. Its spatial expression reflects assessments of profitability and the dictates of social and economic planning.

Agriculture, fishing, forestry, trapping, and the extractive (mining) industries are closely tied to the uneven distribution of earth resources. Their spatial patterns reflect those resource potentials, but they are influenced as well by the integration of all societies and economies through the medium of international trade and mutual dependence. The flows of primary products and of manufactured goods suggest the hierarchy of production, marketing, and service activities, which will be the subject of Chapter 9.

KEY WORDS

agriculture 238
aquaculture 260
Boserup thesis 241
commercial economy 236
economic geography 234
extensive agriculture 239, 252
extractive industry 257
gathering industry 257
Green Revolution 245
intensive agriculture 239, 252
market economy 236

maximum sustainable yield 258
natural resource 257
nomadic herding 239
nonrenewable resource 258
planned economy 236
plantation 255
primary activity 235
quaternary activity 236
quinary activity 236
renewable resource 257

resource 257
secondary activity 235
shifting cultivation 241
subsistence economy 236
technology 235
tertiary activity 235
tragedy of the commons 259
truck farm 252
usable reserves 263
von Thünen model 249

FOR REVIEW

1. What are the distinguishing characteristics of the economic systems labeled *subsistence, commercial,* and *planned?* Are they mutually exclusive, or can they coexist within a single political unit?

2. What are the ecological consequences of the different forms of *extensive subsistence* land use? In what world regions are such systems found? What, in your opinion, are the prospects for these land uses and for the way of life they embody?

3. How is *intensive subsistence* agriculture distinguished from *extensive subsistence* cropping? Why,

in your opinion, have such different land use forms developed in separate areas of the warm, moist tropics?

4. Briefly summarize the assumptions and dictates of von Thünen's agricultural model. How might the land use patterns predicted by the model be altered by an increase in the market price of a single crop? A decrease in the transportation costs of one crop but not of all crops?

5. What is the basic distinction between a *renewable* and a *nonrenewable* resource? Under what circumstances might the distinction between the two be blurred or obliterated?

6. What economic and ecological problems can you cite that do or might affect the viability and productivity of the *gathering industries* of forestry and fishing? What is meant by the *tragedy of the commons?* How is that concept related to the problems you discerned?

7. Why have the mineral fuels been so important in economic development? What are the mineral fuels, and what are the prospects for their continued availability? What economic and social consequences might you anticipate if the price of mineral fuels should double? If it should be cut in half?

KEY CONCEPTS REVIEW

1. **How are economic activities and national economies classified?**
   pp. 234–237.
   The innumerable economically productive activities of humans are influenced by regionally varying environmental, cultural, technological, political, and market conditions. Understanding the world's work is simplified by thinking of economic activity as arranged along a continuum of increasing complexity of product or service and increasing distance from nature. Primary industries (activities) harvest or extract something from the

earth. Secondary industries change the form of those harvested items. Tertiary activities render services, and quaternary efforts reflect professional or managerial talents. Those activity stages are carried out within national economies grouped as subsistence, commercial, or planned.

2. **What are the types and prospects of subsistence agriculture?**
   pp. 237–247.
   Subsistence farming—food production primarily or exclusively for the producers' family needs—still remains the predominant occupation of humans on a worldwide basis. Nomadic

herding and shifting ("swidden") cultivation are extensive subsistence systems. Intensive subsistence farming involves large inputs of labor and fertilizer on small plots of land. Both rural and urban subsistence efforts are increasingly marked by some production for market; they have also benefited from Green Revolution crop improvements.

3. **What characterizes commercial agriculture, and what are its controls and special forms?**
   pp. 247–257.
   The modern integrated world of exchange and trade increasingly

implies farming efforts that reflect broader market requirements, not purely local or family needs. Commercial agriculture is characterized by specialization, off-farm sale, and interdependence of farmers and buyers linked through complex markets. The von Thünen model of agricultural location suggests that intensive forms of commercial farming—fruits, vegetables, dairy products, and livestock-grain production—should be located close to markets. More extensive commercial agriculture, including large-scale wheat farms and livestock ranches, are by model and reality at more distant locations. Special crops may by value or uniqueness defy these spatial determinants; Mediterranean and plantation agriculture are examples.

4. **What are the special characteristics and problems of nonagricultural primary industries?** pp. 257–267.
The "gathering" industries of fishing, forestry, and trapping and the "extractive" industries of mining and quarrying involve the direct exploitation of areally variable natural resources. Resources are natural materials that humans perceive as necessary and useful. They may be renewable—replenished—by natural processes or nonrenewable once extracted and used. Overexploitation can exceed the maximum sustainable yield of fisheries and forests and eventually destroy the resource. Such destruction is assured in the case of nonrenewable minerals and fuels when their total or economically feasible supply is exhausted.

5. **What is the status and nature of world trade in primary products?** pp. 267–269.
The primary commodities of agricultural goods, fish, forest products, furs, and minerals and fuels account for nearly one-third of the dollar value of international trade. Traditional exchange flows of raw materials outward from developing states that then imported manufactured goods from advanced economies have changed in recent years. Increasingly, the share of manufactured goods in developing world exports is growing, and dependence on income from raw material sales is dropping. However, material-exporting states argue that current international trade agreements are unfavorable to exporters of agricultural products and ores and minerals.

LIVELIHOOD AND ECONOMY:

From Blue Collar to Gold Collar

9

A Juarez, Mexico, *maquiladora* factory of a major American transnational corporation.

Key Concepts

1. What principles or considerations guide manufacturing locational decisions, pp. 273–280, and how those considerations have been selectively incorporated in different industrial location theories, pp. 280–282.

2. How other nontheoretical considerations including transnational ownership affect, distort, or reinforce classical locational controls, pp. 282–288.

3. The older world patterns of manufacturing regions, pp. 288–295 and how they have been affected by the special locational characteristics of high-tech industries, pp. 296–298.

4. What the identifying characteristics of tertiary, quaternary, and quinary service activities are, pp. 298–301, and how their recent development impacted world economic patterns and international trade, pp. 301–304.

Route 837 connects the four U.S. Steel plants stretched out along the Monongahela River south of Pittsburgh. Once, in the late 1960s, 50,000 workers labored in those mills, and Route 837 was choked with the traffic of their cars and of steel haulers' trucks. By 1979, fires were going out in the furnaces of the aging mills as steel imports from Asia and Europe flowed unchecked into domestic markets long controlled by American producers. By the mid-1980s, with employment in the steel plants of the "Mon" Valley well below 5000, the highway was only lightly traveled and only occasionally did anyone turn at the traffic lights into the closed and deserted mills.

At the same time, traffic was building along many highways in the northeastern part of the country. Four-lane Route 1 was clogged with traffic along the 42 kilometers (26 miles) of the "Princeton Corridor" in central New Jersey as that stretch of road in the 1980s had more office space, research laboratories, hotels, conference centers, and residential subdivisions planned and under construction than anywhere else between Washington, D.C. and Boston. Farther to the south, around Washington itself, traffic grew heavy along the Capital Beltway in Virginia, where vast office building complexes, defense-related industries, and commercial centers were converting rural land to urban uses. And east of New York City, traffic jams were monumental around Stamford, Connecticut, in Fairfield County, as it became a leading corporate headquarters town with 150,000 daily in-commuters.

By the early 1990s, traffic in Fairfield County had thinned as corporate takeovers, leveraged buyouts, and "downsizing" reorganizations reduced the number and size of companies and their need for both employees and office space. Vacancies exceeded 25% among the office buildings and research parks so enthusiastically built during the 1970s and 1980s, and vacant "corporate campuses" lined stretches of formerly clogged highways. But soon traffic was building elsewhere in the country as millions of Americans during the 1990s gained technology-related jobs in California's "Silicon Valley," and a whole series of other widely spaced emerging "high-tech" hot spots clustered around such industries as computers, lasers, software, medical devices, and biotechnology. And by the late 1990s, all sections of the United States again were experiencing the traffic volumes that economic prosperity induces, only once more to endure job losses, office vacancies, economic reversals, and altered traffic flows following the "dotcom" bubble collapse of the early 21st century.

These contrasting and fluctuating patterns of traffic flow symbolize the ever-changing nature and structure of the Anglo American space economy. The smokestack industries of the 19th and early 20th centuries have declined, replaced by research park industries, shopping centers, and office building complexes that in their turn experience variable prosperity and adversity. The continent's economic landscape and employment structure are continually changing (Figure 9.1). And North America is not alone. Change is the ever-present condition of contemporary economies, whether of the already industrialized, advanced countries or of those newly developing in an integrated world marketplace. Resources are exploited and exhausted; markets grow and decline; patterns of economic advantage, of labor skills, of industrial investment and productive capacity undergo alteration as countries and regions differentially develop, prosper, or experience reversals and decline. Such changes have profound impact on the spatial structure and processes of economic activity.

Figure 9.1 This derelict, abandoned Massey-Ferguson tractor factory in Brantford, Ontario—a brownfield site—typifies the structural changes occurring in "postindustrial" economies. For heavy industrial jobs lost to deindustrialization, replacement employment must be found in the tertiary or quaternary service industries. Some cities have been successful in attracting service jobs and redeveloping brownfield sites for commercial, housing, or recreational uses. In Brantford, this site remains derelict.

Components of the Space Economy

All human activity has spatial expression. In the economic sphere we recognize regions of industrial concentration, areas of employment and functional specialization, and specific factory sites and store locations. As geographers, we assume an underlying logic to those spatial economic patterns and seek, through observation and theory, an understanding and explanation of them.

Primary industries are tied to the natural resources they gather or exploit. Location is therefore predetermined by the distribution of minerals, fuels, forests, fisheries, or natural conditions affecting agriculture and herding. The later (beyond primary) stages of economic activity, however, are increasingly divorced from the conditions of the physical environment. In them, processing, distribution, communication, and management permit enterprise location in response to cultural and economic rather than physical influences. They are movable, rather than spatially tied activities. The locational decisions made and the economic patternings that result differ with the type or level of economic activity in question. Secondary industries involved in material processing and goods production have different spatial constraints than do the retailing activities of tertiary industry or the research parks or office complexes of quaternary and quinary activities. At every industrial or activity level, however, it is assumed that a recurring set of economic controls may be identified.

Concepts and Controls

The controls that are assumed to exist are rooted in observations about human spatial behavior in general and economic behavior in particular. We have already explored some of those assumptions in earlier discussions. We noted, for example, that the intensity of spatial interaction decreases with increasing separation of places—distance decay, we called it. We observed the importance of complementarity and transferability in the assessment of resource value and trade potential. Von Thünen's model of agricultural land use, you will recall, was rooted in conjectures about transportation cost and land value relationships.

Such simplifying assumptions help us to understand a presumed common set of controls and motivations guiding human economic behavior. We assume, for example, that people are *economically rational;* that is, given the information at their disposal, they make locational, production, or purchasing decisions in light of a perception of what is most cost-effective and advantageous. Behavioral research concludes that while people are not truly rational in the theoretical economic sense, neither are they insane or incompetent. The acceptance of rationality, they conclude, is proper if one also accepts the reality that individuals respond to behavioral traits— envy, rivalry, impulsiveness, forgetfulness of past mistakes, positive wishful thinking, and the like—at odds with purely rational actions or decisions. With those appreciations of behavioral human nature, economic rationality is still the accepted theoretical starting point.

From the standpoint of producers or sellers of goods or services, it is assumed each is intent on *maximizing profit.* To reach that objective, each may consider a host of production and marketing costs and political, competitive, and other limiting factors— and, perhaps, respond to individual behavioral quirks—but the ultimate goal of profit-seeking remains clear. Finally, we assume that in commercial economies the best measure of the correctness of economic decisions is afforded by the *market mechanism.*

At root, that market control mechanism is measured by *price*—the price of land (rent), of labor (wages), of a college course (tuition), or of goods at the store. In turn, price is seen as a function of *supply* and *demand.* In large, complex economies where there are many producers, sellers, and buyers, and many alternative products competing in the marketplace, price is the neutral measure of comparative value and profitability. The theoretical relationship between supply, demand, and price is simple. If demand for a good or service exceeds its available supply, scarcity will drive up the price it can command in the marketplace. That increased price will enhance the profitability of the sale, which will encourage existing producers to increase output or induce new producers or sellers to enter the market (Figure 9.2a). That is, *the higher the price of a good, the more of it will be offered in the market.*

When the price is very high, however, relatively few people are inclined to buy. To dispose of their increased output, old and new producers of the commodity are forced to reduce prices to enlarge the market by making the good affordable to a larger number of

Figure 9.2 Supply, demand, and market equilibrium. The regulating mechanism of the market may be visualized graphically. (*a*) The *supply curve* tells us that as the price of a good increases, more of that good will be made available for sale. Countering any tendency for prices to rise to infinity is the market reality that the higher the price, the smaller the demand as potential customers find other purchases or products more cost-effective. (*b*) The *demand curve* shows how the market will expand as prices are lowered and goods are made more affordable and attractive to more customers. (*c*) *Market equilibrium* is marked by the point of intersection of the supply and demand curves and determines the price of goods, the total demand, and the quantity bought and sold.

potential customers. That is, *at lower prices, more of a good will be purchased* (Figure 9.2b). If the price falls too low, production or sale becomes unprofitable and inefficient suppliers are forced out of business, reducing supply. **Market equilibrium** is marked by the price at which supply equals demand, satisfying the needs of consumers and the profit motivation of suppliers (Figure 9.2c).

These and other modifying concepts and controls of the economist treat supply, demand, and price as if all production, buying, and selling occurred at a single point. But as geographers, we know that human activities have specific locational settings and that neither people, nor resources, nor opportunities are uniformly distributed over the earth. We appreciate that the place or places of production may differ from the locations of demand. We understand that there are spatial relations and interactions based on supply, demand, and equilibrium price. We realize there is a *geography* of supply, a *geography* of demand, and a *geography* of cost.

Secondary Activities: Manufacturing

If we assume free markets, rational producers, and informed consumers, then locational production and marketing decisions should be based on careful consideration of spatially differing costs and opportunities. In the case of primary industries—those tied to the environment—points or areas of possible production are naturally fixed. The only decision is whether or not to exploit known resources. In the instance of secondary and higher levels of economic activity, however, the locational decision is more complex. It involves the weighing of the locational "pulls" of a number of cost considerations and profit prospects.

On the *demand* side, the distribution of populations and of purchasing power defines general areas of marketing opportunities. The regional location of tertiary—sales and service—activities may be nearly as fixed as are primary industries, though specific site decisions are more complex. On the *supply* side, decision making for manufacturers involves a more intricate set of equations. Manufacturers must consider costs of raw materials, distance from them and from markets, wages of labor, outlays for fuel, capital availability and rates, and a host of other inputs to the production and distribution process. It is assumed that the nature and the spatial variability of those myriad costs are known and that rational location decisions leading to profit maximization are based on that knowledge. For market economies, both observation and theory tend to support that assumption.

Locational Decisions in Manufacturing

Secondary activities involve transforming raw materials into usable products. Dominant among them is manufacturing in all of its aspects, from pouring iron and steel to stamping out plastic toys, assembling computer components, or sewing dresses. In every case, the common characteristics are the application of power and specialized labor to the production of standardized commodities in factory settings: in short, the characteristics of industrialization.

Manufacturing poses a different locational problem than does the gathering of primary commodities. It involves the assembly and the processing of inputs and the distribution of the output to other points and therefore presents the question of where the processing should take place. The answer may require multiple spatial levels of consideration. The first is regional and addresses the comparative attractions for different types of industry of different sections of the country or even of different countries at the international scale. Later decision stages become more focused, localized, and specific to an individual enterprise. They involve assessment of the special production and marketing requirements of particular industrialists and of the degree to which those requirements can or will be met at different subregional scales—at the state (in the U.S.), community, and individual site levels. That is, we can ask at one level why northeastern United States-southeastern Canada exerted an earlier pull on industry in general and, at other decision stages, why specific sites along the Monongahela Valley to the south of Pittsburgh in Pennsylvania were chosen by U.S. Steel Corporation for its mills.

In framing responses, one needs to consider a wide range of industrial pulls and attractions and the modifying influence of a number of physical, political, economic, and cultural constraints. For a great many searches, two or several alternate locations would be equally satisfactory. In very practical financial terms, locational decisions at the state, community, and site levels may ultimately be based on the value of inducements that are offered by rival areas and agencies competing for the new or relocated manufacturing plant (See "Contests and Bribery," p. 287). In both practice and theory, locational factors recognized and analyzed are complexly interrelated, change over time in their relative significance, and differ between industries and regions. But all of them are tied to *principles of location* that are assumed to operate under all economic systems, though to be determinant, perhaps, only in free market, or commercial, economies.

Principles of Location

The principles, or "ground rules," of location are simply stated.

1. Certain input costs of manufacturing are **spatially fixed costs,** that is, are relatively unaffected in their amount or relative importance no matter where the industry is located within a generalized regional or national setting. Wage rates set by national or areawide labor contracts are an example. Fixed costs have no implication for comparative locational advantage.

2. Other input costs of manufacturing are **spatially variable costs;** that is, they show significant differences from place to place in both their amount and their relative contribution to the total cost of manufacturing (Figure 9.3). These will influence locational choices.

3. The ultimate aim of the economic activity is *profit maximization.* In an economic environment of full and perfect competition, the profit objective is most likely to be achieved if the manufacturing enterprise is situated at the *least total cost* location. Under conditions of imperfect competition, considerations of sales and market may be more important than production costs in fixing "best" locations.

4. Since among the totality of production costs some inputs are approximately the same irrespective of location, fixed costs are not of major importance in determining optimum, or least-cost, locations. Rather, the industrialist bases the locational

Variable, or | locational, cost

Fixed, or | basic, cost

Distance ←——————→ O ←——————→ Distance

Least-cost location

Figure 9.3 **The spatial implications of fixed and variable costs.**
Spatially fixed (or *basic*) costs represent the minimum price that must
be paid at any location for the necessary inputs of production of a given
item. Here, for simplicity, a single raw material is assumed and priced at
its cheapest source. *Spatially variable* (*locational*) costs are the additional
costs incurred at alternate locations in overcoming distance, attracting
labor, purchasing the plant site, and so forth. In the example, only the
transportation cost of the single material away from its cheapest (source)
location is diagrammed to determine *O,* the optimal or least-cost location.

search on the minimization of variable costs. The locational
determinant is apt to be the cost that is an important component of total costs and shows the greatest spatial variation.

5. Transportation charges—the costs of accumulating inputs and of
distributing products—are highly variable costs. As such, they
(rather than the commodity transported) may become the locational determinant, imparting an unmistakable *orientation*—a term
describing locational tendencies—to the plant siting decision.

6. Individual establishments rarely stand alone; they are part
of integrated manufacturing sequences and environments in
which *interdependence* increases as the complexity of industrial processes increases. The economies of structural and
spatial interdependence may be decisive locational determinants for some industries. *Linkages* between firms may
localize manufacturing in areas of industrial agglomeration
where common resources—such as skilled labor—or multiple
suppliers of product inputs—such as automobile component
manufacturers—are found.

These principles are generalized statements about locational tendencies of industries. Their relative weight, of course, varies among
industries and firms. Their significance also varies depending on the
extent to which purely economic considerations—as opposed, say, to
political or environmental constraints—dictate locational decisions.

Raw Materials

All manufactured goods have their origins in the processing of
raw materials, but only a few industries at the early stages of the
production cycle use raw materials directly from farms or mines.
Most manufacturing is based on the further processing and shaping
of materials already treated in some fashion by an earlier stage of
manufacturing located elsewhere. In general, the more advanced
the industrial economy of a nation, the smaller is the role played
by truly *raw* materials in its economic structure.

For those industries in which unprocessed commodities are a
primary input, however, the source and characteristics of the raw
materials upon which they are based are important indeed. The
quality, amount, or ease of mining or gathering of a resource may
be a locational determinant if cost of raw material is the major variable and multiple sources of the primary material are available. Raw
materials may attract the industries that process them when they are
bulky, undergo great weight loss in the processing, or are highly
perishable. Copper smelting and iron ore beneficiation are examples
of weight- (impurity-) reducing industries localized by their ore supplies (see pp. 263–264). Pulp, paper, and sawmills are, logically,
found in areas within or accessible to timber. Fruit and vegetable
canning in California, midwestern meat packing, and Florida orange
juice concentration and freezing are different but comparable examples of raw **material orientation.** The reason is simple; it is cheaper
and easier to transport to market a refined or stabilized product than
one filled with waste material or subject to spoilage and loss.

Multiple raw materials might dictate an intermediate plant
location. Least cost may be determined not by a single raw material
input but by the spatially differing costs of accumulating several
inputs. Steel mills at Gary, Indiana, or Cleveland, Ohio, for example, were not based on local raw material sources but on the minimization of the total cost of collecting at a point the necessary ore,
coking coal, and fluxing material inputs for the production process
(Figure 9.4). Steel mills along the U.S. East Coast—at Sparrows
Point, Maryland, or the Fairless Works near Philadelphia—were
localized where imported ores were unloaded from ocean carriers,
avoiding expensive transshipment costs. In this latter avoidance,
both the Great Lakes and the coastal locations are similar.

Power Supply

For some industries, power supplies that are immobile or of low transferability may serve to attract the activities dependent upon them. Such
was the case early in the Industrial Revolution when water power sites
localized textile mills, and fuel (initially charcoal, later coking coal)
drew the iron and steel industry. Metallurgical industries became concentrated in such coal-rich regions as the Midlands of England, the
Ruhr district of Germany, and the Donets Basin of Ukraine.

Massive charges of electricity are required to extract aluminum from its processed raw material, *alumina* (aluminum oxide).
Electrical power accounts for between 30% and 40% of the cost of
producing the aluminum and is the major variable cost influencing
plant location in the industry. The Kitimat plant on the northwest
coast of Canada or the Bratsk plant near Lake Baikal in eastern
Siberia are examples of industry placed far from raw material
sources or market but close to vast supplies of cheap power—in
these instances, hydroelectricity.

Labor

Labor also is a spatial variable affecting location decisions and industrial development. Traditionally, three different considerations—price,
skill, and amount—of labor were considered to be determinant sin-
gly or in combination. For many manufacturers today, an increasingly important consideration is *labor flexibility,* implying more
highly educated workers able to apply themselves to a wide variety
of tasks and functions. For some activities, a cheap labor supply is a

Figure 9.4 Material flows in the steel industry. When an industrial process requires the combination of several heavy or bulky ingredients, an intermediate point of assembly of materials is often a least-cost location. In the earlier 20th century, the iron and steel industry of the eastern United States showed this kind of localization—not at the source of any single input but where coking coal, iron ore, and limestone could be brought together at the lowest price.

necessity. For others, labor skills may constitute the locational attraction and regional advantage. Machine tools in Sweden, precision instruments in Switzerland, optical and electronic goods in Japan are examples of industries that have created and depend on localized labor skills. In an increasingly high-tech world of automation, electronics, and industrial robots, labor skills—even at high unit costs—are often more in demand than an unskilled, uneducated workforce.

In some world areas, of course, labor of any skill level may be poorly distributed to satisfy the developmental objectives of government planners or private entrepreneurs. In the former Soviet Union, for example, long-standing economic plans called for the fuller exploitation of the vast resources of sparsely populated Siberia, an area generally unattractive to a labor force more attuned to the milder climates and greater amenities of the settled European portion of the country. At the same time, labor surpluses were growing in Soviet Central Asia, where resources were few and rates of natural population increase were high, but whose Muslim populations resisted resettlement outside of their homeland areas.

Market

Goods are produced to supply a market demand. Therefore, the size, nature, and distribution of markets may be as important in industrial location decisions as are raw material, energy, labor, or other inputs.

Market pull, like raw material attraction, is at root an expression of the cost of commodity movement. When the transportation charges for sending finished goods to market are a relatively high proportion of the total value of the good (or can be significantly reduced by proximity to market), then the attraction of location near to the consumer is obvious and **market orientation** results.

The consumer may be either another firm or the general public. When a factory is but one stage in a larger manufacturing process—firms making wheels, tires, windshields, bumpers, and the like in the assembly of automobiles, for example—location near the next stage of production is an obvious advantage. The advantage is increased if that final stage of production is also near the ultimate consumer market. To continue our example, automobile assembly plants have been scattered throughout the North American realm in response to the existence of large regional markets and the cost of distribution of the finished automobile. This market orientation is further reflected by the location in North America of auto manufacturing or assembly plants of Asian and European motor vehicle companies, although both foreign and domestic firms again appear to be reconcentrating the industry in the southeastern part of the United States.

People themselves, of course, are the ultimate consumers. Large urban concentrations represent markets, and major cities have always attracted producers of goods consumed by city dwellers. Admittedly, it is impossible to distinguish clearly between urbanites as market and urbanites as labor force. In either case, many manufacturing activities are drawn to major metropolitan centers. Certain producers are, in fact, inseparable from the immediate markets they serve and are so widely distributed that they are known as **ubiquitous industries.** Newspaper publishing, bakeries, and dairies, all of which produce a highly perishable commodity designed for immediate consumption, are examples.

Transportation

Transportation has been so much the unifying thread of all of these references to "factors" of industrial location that it is difficult to isolate its separate role. In fact, some of the earlier observations about manufacturing plant orientations can be restated in purely transportation cost terms. For example, copper smelting or iron ore beneficiation—described earlier as examples of raw material orientation—may also be seen as industries engaged in *weight reduction* designed to minimize transportation costs by removal of waste material prior to shipment. Some market orientation is of the opposite nature, reflecting *weight-gaining* production. Soft drink bottlers, for example, add large amounts of water to small amounts of concentrated syrup to produce a bulky product of relatively low value. All transport costs are reduced if only the concentrate is shipped to local bottlers, who add the water that is available everywhere and distribute only to local dealers. The frequency of this practice suggests the inclusion of soft drink bottlers among the ubiquitous industries.

No matter the specific characterization of attraction, modern industry is intimately and inseparably tied to transportation systems. The Industrial Revolution is usefully seen as initially and simultaneously a transportation revolution as successive improvements in the technology of movement of peoples and commodities enlarged the effective areas of spatial interaction and made integrated economic development and areal specialization possible.

All advanced economies are well served by a diversity of transport media (see Figure 8.4); without them, all that is possible is local subsistence activity. All major industrial agglomerations are simultaneously important nodes of different transportation media, each with its own characteristic advantages and limitations.

Water transportation is the cheapest means of long-distance freight movement (Figure 9.5), with low operating and right-of-way costs. Inland waterway improvement and canal construction marked the first phase of the Industrial Revolution in Europe and was the first stage of modern transport development in the United States. Even today, river ports and seaports have locational attractiveness for industry unmatched by alternative centers not served by water carriers, and where water routes are in place, as in northwestern Europe or the Great Lakes–Mississippi systems of the United States, they are vital elements in regional industrial economies.

Railroads efficiently move large volumes of freight over long distances at low fuel and labor costs (Figure 8.34). They are, however, inflexible in route, slow to respond to changing industrial locational patterns, and expensive to construct and maintain. When for any reason traffic declines below minimum revenue levels, rail service may be considered uneconomic and the lines abandoned—a response of American railroads, which abandoned over 125,000 miles of line between 1930 and 2000.

High-volume, high-speed *motor trucks* operating on modern roadway and expressway systems have altered the competitive picture to favor highways over railways in many intercity movements in modern economies. Road systems provide great flexibility of service and are more quickly responsive than railroads to new traffic demands and changing origin and destination points. Intervening opportunities are more easily created and regional integration more cheaply achieved by highway than by railroad (or waterway systems).

Increasingly in the United States and elsewhere, greater transport cost efficiencies and time savings are achieved by the use of freight containers. Hauling a truck trailer on a railroad flatcar ("piggybacking") or on ship deck serves to minimize total freight rates and transport times. Such *multimodal freight* movements seek the advantages of the most efficient carrier for each stage of the journey from cargo origin point to final destination through the use of internationally standardized shipping containers, which are tracked by computer. The containers with undisturbed content may be transferred to ships for international ocean carriage, to railroads for long-haul land movement, and to truck trailers for shorter-haul distances and pickup and delivery. Their use is increasingly common: on long "trailer-on-flat-car" trains and in the growing volume of international ocean trade (Figure 9.6).

Figure 9.5 The pattern of carrier efficiency. Different transport media have cost advantages over differing distances. The usual generalization is that when all three media are available for a given shipment, trucks are most efficient and economical over short hauls of up to about 500 kilometers (about 300 miles), railroads have the cost advantage over intermediate hauls of 500 to 3200 kilometers (about 300 to 2000 miles), and water (ship or barge) movement over longer distances (and, often, over shorter distances where speed of delivery of nonperishable commodities is not a consideration). The differing cost curves represent the differing amounts of fixed or variable costs incurred by each transport medium, as further illustrated in Figure 9.8.

Figure 9.6 Cargo Containers in Shanghai Docks, China. Standardized cargo containers have revolutionized shipping, sharply reducing shipping times and making possible the increased economic interdependence in the world economy. In 2007, China exported 1.22 trillion dollars worth of goods, with the largest categories being electrical machinery and equipment, power generation equipment, clothing, iron and steel, and toys. Chinese exports rose 390% between 2000 and 2007.

Pipelines provide efficient, speedy, and dependable transportation specifically suited to the movement of a variety of liquids and gases. They serve to localize along their routes the industries—particularly fertilizer and petrochemical plants—that use the transported commodity as raw material. In contrast, *air transport* has little locational significance for most industries despite its growing importance in long-distance passenger and high-value package freight movement. It contributes, of course, to the range of transport alternatives available to large population centers in industrially advanced nations and may increase the attractiveness of airport sites for high-tech and other industries shipping or receiving high-value, low-bulk commodities. It is not, however, an effective competitor in the usual patterns of freight flow (see "A Comparison of Transport Media").

Transportation and Location

Figure 9.7 indicates the general pattern of industrial orientation related to variable transportation costs. In their turn, those costs are more than a simple function of the distance that goods are carried. Rather, they represent the application of differing **freight rates,** charges made for loading, transporting, and unloading of goods. Freight rates are said to *discriminate* between commodities on the basis of their assumed ability to bear transport costs in relation to their value. In general, manufactured goods have higher value and greater fragility, require more special handling, and can bear higher freight charges than can unprocessed bulk commodities. The higher transport costs for finished goods are therefore seen as a major reason for the increasing market orientation of industry in advanced economies with high-value manufacturing.

In addition to these forms of rate discrimination, each shipment of whatever nature must bear a share of the **fixed costs** of the company's investment in land, plant, and equipment and the assigned *terminal* and *line-haul* costs of the shipment. **Terminal costs** are charges associated with loading, packing, and unloading of a shipment and of the paperwork and shipping documents it entails. **Line-haul** or *over-the-road costs* vary with the individual shipments and are the expenses involved in the actual movement of commodities once they have been loaded. They are allocated to each shipment according to equipment used and distance traveled. Total transport costs represent a combination of all pertinent charges and are curvilinear rather than linear functions of distance. That is, carrier costs have a tendency to decline as the length of haul increases because scale economies in long-haul movement permit the averaging of total costs over a greater number of miles. The result is the *tapering principle* diagrammed in Figure 9.8.

A Comparison of Transport Media

Mode	Uses	Advantages	Disadvantages
Railroad	Intercity medium- to long-haul bulk and general cargo transport.	Fast, reliable service on separate rights-of-way; essentially nonpolluting; energy efficient; adapted to steady flow of single commodities between two points; routes and nodes provide intervening development opportunities.	High construction and operating costs; inflexibility of routes; underutilized lines cause economic drain.
Highway carrier	Local and intercity movement of general cargo and merchandise; pickup and delivery services; feeder to other carriers.	Highly flexible in routes, origins, and destinations; individualized service; maximum accessibility; unlimited intervening opportunity; high speed and low terminal costs.	Low energy efficiency; contributes to air pollution; adds congestion to public roads; high maintenance costs; inefficient for large-volume freight.
Inland waterway	Low-speed haulage of bulk, nonperishable commodities.	High energy efficiency; low per mile costs; large cargo capacity.	High terminal costs; low route flexibility; not suited for short haul; possible delays from ice or low water levels.
Pipelines	Continuous flows of liquids, gases, or suspended solids where volumes are high and continuity is required.	Fast, efficient, dependable; low per mile costs over long distances; maximum safety.	Highly inflexible in route and cargo type; high development cost.
Airways	Medium- and long-haul of high-value, low-bulk cargo where delivery speed is important.	High speed and efficiency; adapted to goods that are perishable, packaged, of a size and quantity unsuited to other modes; high route flexibility; access to areas otherwise inaccessible.	Very expensive; high mileage costs; some weather-related unreliability; inconvenient terminal locations; no intervening opportunities between airports.
Intermodal containerization	Employs standardized closed containers to move a shipment by any combination of water, rail, and truck without unpacking between origin and final destination.	Speed and efficiency of transit and lower shipping costs when multiple carriers are needed; reduced labor charges and pilferage losses.	Requires special terminals and handling machinery to load, off-load, and transfer containers.

Figure 9.7 **Spatial orientation tendencies.** *Raw material orientation* is presumed to exist when there are limited alternative material sources, when the material is perishable, or when—in its natural state—it contains a large proportion of impurities or nonmarketable components. *Market orientation* represents the least-cost solution when manufacturing uses commonly available materials that add weight to the finished product, when the manufacturing process produces a commodity much bulkier or more expensive to ship than its separate components, or when the perishable nature of the product demands processing at individual market points.

Source: Adapted from Interpreting the City: An Urban Geography, *Truman A. Hartshorn. Copyright © 1980 John Wiley & Sons, Inc. Reproduced with permission of John Wiley & Sons, Inc.*

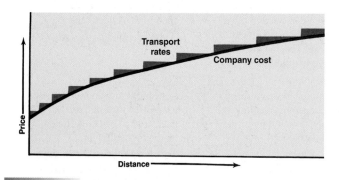

Figure 9.8 **The tapering principle.** The actual costs of transport, including terminal charges and line costs, increase at a decreasing rate as fixed costs are spread over longer hauls. The "tapering" of company cost is differently expressed among media because their mixes of fixed and variable costs are different, as Figure 9.5 diagrams. Note that actual rates charged move in stepwise increments to match the general pattern and level of company costs.

One consequence of the necessary assignment of fixed and terminal costs to *every* shipment regardless of distance moved is that factory locations intermediate between sources of materials and final markets are less attractive than location at either end of a single long haul. That is, two short hauls cost more than a single continuous haul over the same distance (Figure 9.9).

Figure 9.9 **The short-haul penalty.** Plant locations intermediate between material and market are generally avoided because of the realities of transportation pricing that are shown here. Two short hauls simply cost more than a single long haul because two sets of fixed costs must be assigned to the interrupted movement.

Two exceptions to this locational generalization are of practical interest. **Break-of-bulk points** are sites where goods have to be transferred or transshipped from one carrier to another—at ports, for example, where barge or ocean vessel must be unloaded and cargo reloaded to railcar or truck, or between railroad and truck line. When such transfer occurs, an additional fixed or terminal cost is levied against the shipment, perhaps significantly increasing its total transport costs (piggyback transfers reduce, but do not eliminate, those handling charges). There is a tendency for manufacturing to concentrate at such points to avoid the additional charges. As a traffic-generating inducement, **in-transit privilege** may be granted to a manufacturer by a transportation agency through the quotation of a special single rate from material source to market for a movement that may be interrupted for processing or manufacturing *en route.* Such a special rate obviously removes the cost disadvantage of two short hauls and, by equalizing shipping costs between locations, tends to reduce the otherwise dominant attractions of either material or market locations.

Industrial Location Theories

In practice, enterprise locational decisions are based not on the impact of a single selected industrial factor but on the interplay and balance of a number of considerations. Implicit in our review has been the understanding that each type or branch of industry has its own specific set of significant plant siting conditions. For secondary activities as a whole, therefore, a truly bewildering complex of locational determinants exists. Theorists beginning in the first third of the 20th century set themselves the task of sorting through that complex in the attempt to define its underlying structure. The economic world they surveyed at that time, dominated by railroads, based on heavy industry and ideas of national industrial self-sufficiency, no longer is fully consistent with a globalized economy reflecting political, competitive, and social decisions of, for example, the World Trade Organization, transnational corporations, environmental protection agencies, and the like. Nevertheless, the logical systems and concepts they developed and the spatial conclusions they reached still are relevant in understanding present-day industrial locational decisions. Although a full review of all of their contributions is beyond our scope and interest, it is useful to survey briefly the three fundamental approaches to the problem of plant location those theorists proposed—*least-cost theory, locational interdependence theory,* and *profit-maximization approaches*—and the different conclusions they reach.

Least-Cost Theory

The classical model of industrial location theory, the **least-cost theory,** is based on the work of Alfred Weber (1868–1958) and sometimes called **Weberian analysis.** It explains the optimum location of a manufacturing establishment based on minimizing three basic expenses: relative transport costs, labor costs, and agglomeration costs. **Agglomeration** refers to the clustering of productive activities and people for mutual advantage. Such clustering can produce "agglomeration economies" through shared facilities and services. Diseconomies such as higher rents or wage levels resulting from competition for these resources may also occur.

Weber concluded that transport costs are the major consideration determining location. That is, the optimum location will be found where the costs of transporting raw materials to the factory and finished goods to the market are at their lowest. He noted, however, if variations in labor or agglomeration costs are sufficiently great, a location determined solely on the basis of transportation costs may not in fact be the optimum one.

Weber made five controlling assumptions: (1) An area is completely uniform physically, politically, culturally, and technologically. This is known as the **uniform,** or **isotropic, plain** assumption. (2) Manufacturing involves a single product to be shipped to a single market whose location is known. (3) Inputs involve raw materials from more than one known source location. (4) Labor is infinitely available but immobile in location. (5) Transportation routes are not fixed but connect origin and destination by the shortest path; and transport costs directly reflect the weight of items shipped and the distance they are moved.

Given these assumptions, Weber derived the least transport cost location by means of the *locational triangle* (Figure 9.10). It diagrams the cost consequences of fixed locations of materials and market and of movement in any direction of a given weight of commodity at a uniform cost per unit of distance. In Figure 9.10a, S_1 and S_2 are the two material sources for a product consumed at M. The problem is to locate the *optimum point of production* where the total ton-distance involved in assembling materials and distributing the product is at a minimum. Each corner of the triangle exerts its pull; each has a defined cost of production should it be chosen as the plant site. If we assume that the material weights are cut in half during manufacturing (so that the finished product weighs the same as each of the original raw materials), then location at either S_1 or S_2 on the diagram would involve a $3 shipping charge from the other raw material source plus $3 to move the product, for a total delivered cost at market of $6. If the market were selected as the plant site, two raw material shipments—again totaling $6—would be involved.

Weberian analysis, however, aims at the least transport cost location, which most likely will be an intermediate point somewhere within the locational triangle. Its exact position will depend on distances, the respective weights of the raw material inputs, and the final weight of the finished product, and may be either material or market oriented (Figure 9.10b). Material orientation reflects a sizable weight loss during the production process; market orientation indicates a weight gain. The optimum placement of P can be found by different analytical means, but the easiest to visualize is by way of a mechanical model of weights and strings (Figure 9.11).

Locational Interdependence Theory

When the locational decision of one firm is influenced by locations chosen by its competitors, a condition of **locational interdependence** exists. It influences the manner in which competitive firms with

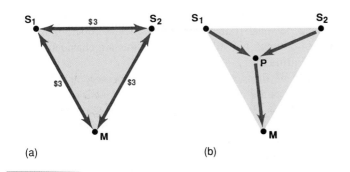

(a)   (b)

Figure 9.10 Weber's locational triangle with differing assumptions. (*a*) With one market, two raw material sources, and a finished product reflecting a 50% material weight loss, production could appropriately be located at S_1, S_2, or M since each length of haul is the same. In (*b*) the optimum production point, P, is seen to lie within the triangle, where total transport costs would be less than at corner locations. The exact location of P would depend on the weight-loss characteristics of the two material inputs if only transport charges were involved. P would, of course, be pulled toward the material whose weight is most reduced.

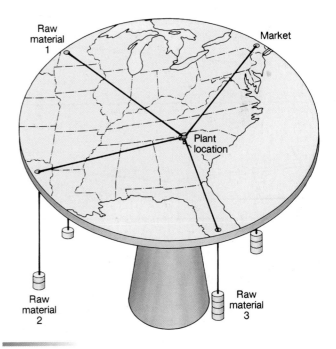

Figure 9.11 Plane table solution to a plant location problem. This mechanical model, suggested by Alfred Weber, uses weights to demonstrate the least transport cost point where there are several sources of raw materials. When a weight is allowed to represent the "pull" of raw material and market locations, an equilibrium point is found on the plane table. That point is the location at which all forces balance each other and represents the least-cost plant location.

identical cost structures arrange themselves in space to assure themselves a measure of *spatial monopoly* in their combined market. In locational interdependence theory, the concern is with *variable revenue analysis* rather than, as in the Weber model, with variable costs.

The simplest case concerns the locational decisions of two firms in competition with each other to supply identical goods to customers evenly spaced along a linear market. The usual example cited is of two ice cream vendors, each selling the same brand at the same price along a stretch of beach having a uniform distribution of people. All will purchase the same amount of ice cream (that is, demand is *inelastic*—is not sensitive to a change in the price) and will patronize the seller nearer to them. Figure 9.12 suggests that the two sellers would eventually cluster at the midpoint of the linear market (the beach) so that each vendor could supply customers at the extremities of the market without yielding locational advantage to the single competitor.

This is a spatial solution that maximizes return but does not minimize costs. The lowest total cost location for each of the two vendors would be at the midpoint of his or her half of the beach, as shown at the top of Figure 9.12, where the total effort expended by customers walking to the ice cream stands (or cost by sellers

delivering the product) is least. To maximize market share, however, one seller might decide to relocate immediately next to the competitor (Figure 9.12b), dominating now three-fourths of the entire beach market. The logical retaliation would be for the second vendor to jump back over the first to recapture market share. Ultimately, side-by-side location at the center line of the beach is inevitable and a stable placement is achieved since neither seller can gain any further advantage from moving. But now the customers collectively have to walk farther to satisfy their ice cream hunger than they did initially; that is, total acquisition cost or delivered price (ice cream purchase plus effort expended) has increased.

The economist Harold Hotelling (1895–1973), who is usually associated with the locational interdependence approach, expanded the conclusion about clustered ice cream sellers to a more generalized statement explaining industrial concentration by multiple producers under conditions of identical production costs and inelastic market demand. However, if the market becomes sensitive to price, sales to more distant customers will be discouraged and producers seeking to maximize sales will again separate rather than aggregate. The conclusion then is that price sensitivity (elasticity of demand) will encourage industrial dispersion.

Profit-Maximization Approaches

For many theorists, the simplicities and rigidities of the least-cost and the locational interdependence explanations are unrealistically restrictive. Ultimately, they maintain, the correct location of a production facility is where the net profit is greatest. They propose employing a **substitution principle** that recognizes that in many industrial processes it is possible to replace a declining amount of one input (e.g., labor) with an increase in another (e.g., capital for automated equipment) or to increase transportation costs while simultaneously reducing land rent. With substitution, a number of different points may be appropriate manufacturing locations. Further, they suggest, a whole series of points may exist where total revenue of an enterprise just equals its total cost of producing a given output. These points, connected, mark the **spatial margin of profitability** and define the larger area within which profitable operation is possible (Figure 9.13). Location anywhere within the margin assures some profit and tolerates both imperfect knowledge and personal (rather than economic) considerations. Such less-than-optimal, but still acceptable, sites are considered **satisficing locations.**

For some firms, spatial margins may be very broad because transport costs are a negligible factor in production and marketing. Such firms are said to be **footloose**—that is, neither resource nor market oriented. For example, both the raw materials and the finished product in the manufacture of computers are so valuable, light, and compact that transportation costs have little bearing on where production takes place.

Other Locational Considerations and Controls

The behavior of individual firms seeking specific production sites under competitive commercial conditions forms the basis of most classical industrial location theory. But such theory no longer fully

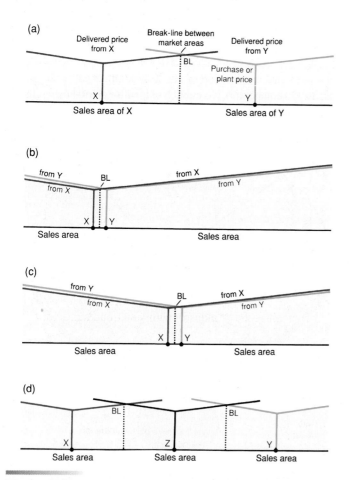

Figure 9.12 Competitive locations in a linear market (Hotelling model). (*a*) The initial *socially optimal* locations (*b*) that minimize total distribution costs will be vacated in the search for market advantage (*c*), eventually resulting in *competitive equilibrium* at the center of the market (*d*). Spatial dispersion will again occur if two or more competitors either encounter elasticity of demand or subdivide the market by agreement.

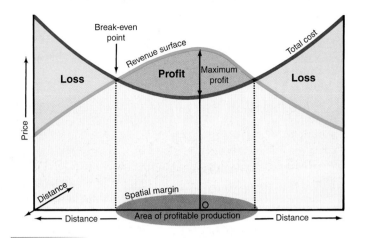

Figure 9.13 **The spatial margin of profitability.** In the diagram, *O* is the single optimal profit-maximizing location, but location anywhere within the area defined by the intersects of the total cost and total revenue surfaces will permit profitable operation. Some industries will have wide margins; others will be more spatially constricted. Skilled entrepreneurs may be able to expand the margins farther than less able industrialists. Importantly, a *satisficing* location may be selected by reasonable estimate even in the absence of the totality of information required for an *optimal* decision.

explains world or regional patterns of industrial localization or specialization. Moreover, it does not account for locational behavior that is uncontrolled by objective "factors," influenced by new production technologies and corporate structures, or directed by noncapitalistic planning goals.

Traditional theories (including many variants not reviewed here) sought to explain location decisions for plants engaged in mass production for mass markets where transportation lines were fixed and transport costs relatively high. Both conditions began to change significantly during the last years of the 20th century. Assembly line production of identical commodities by a rigidly controlled and specialized labor force for generalized mass markets—known as "**Fordism**" to recognize Henry Ford's pioneering development of the system—became less realistic in both market and technology terms. In its place, post-Fordist *flexible manufacturing* processes based on smaller production runs of a greater variety of goods aimed at smaller, niche markets than were catered to by traditional manufacturing have become common. At the same time, information technology applied to machines and operations, increasing flexibility of labor, and declining costs for transportation services that were increasingly viewed from a cost-time rather than a cost-distance standpoint have materially altered underlying assumptions of the classical theories.

Agglomeration Economies

Geographical concentration of economic, including industrial, activities is the norm at the local or regional scale. The cumulative and reinforcing attractions of industrial concentration and urban growth are recognized locational factors, but ones not easily quantified. Both cost-minimizing and profit-maximizing theories, as we have seen, make provision for *agglomeration,* the spatial concentration of people and activities for mutual benefit. That is, both recognize that areal grouping of industrial activities may

produce benefits for individual firms that they could not experience in isolation. Those benefits—**agglomeration economies,** or **external economies**—accrue in the form of savings from shared transport facilities, social services, public utilities, communication facilities, and the like. Collectively, these and other installations and services needed to facilitate industrial and other forms of economic development are called **infrastructure.**

Areal concentration may also create pools of skilled and ordinary labor, of capital, ancillary business services, and, of course, a market built of other industries and urban populations. New firms, particularly, may find significant advantages in locating near other firms engaged in the same activity, for labor specializations and support services specific to that activity are already in place. Some may find profit in being near other firms with which they are linked either as customers or suppliers.

A concentration of capital, labor, management skills, customer base, and all that is implied by the term *infrastructure* will tend to attract still more industries from other locations to the agglomeration. In Weber's terms, that is, economies of association distort or alter locational decisions that otherwise would be based solely on transportation and labor costs, and once in existence, agglomerations will tend to grow (Figure 9.14). Through a **multiplier effect,** each new firm added to the agglomeration will lead to the further development of infrastructure and linkages. As we shall see in Chapter 11, the "multiplier effect" also implies total (urban) population growth and thus the expansion of the labor pool and the localized market that are part of agglomeration economies.

Agglomeration—concentration—of like industries in small areas dates from the early industrial age and continues with many of the newest industries. Familiar examples include the town of Dalton, Georgia, in or near which were found all but one of the top 20 United States carpet makers, and Akron, Ohio, which, before 1930, held almost the entire 100 or so tire manufacturers of the country. Silicon Valley dating from the 1960s and other more recent high-tech specialized concentrations simply continue the tradition.

Admittedly, agglomeration can yield disadvantages as well as benefits. Overconcentration can result in diseconomies of congestion, high land values, pollution, increased governmental regulation, and the like. When the costs of aggregation exceed the benefits, a firm will actually profit by relocating to a more isolated position, a process called **deglomeration.** It is a process expressed in the suburbanization of industry within metropolitan areas or the relocation of firms to nonmetropolitan locations.

Just-in-Time and Flexible Production

Agglomeration economies and tendencies are also encouraged by newer manufacturing policies practiced by both older, established industries and by newer post-Fordist plants.

Traditional Fordist industries required the on-site storage of large lots of materials and supplies ordered and delivered well in advance of their actual need in production. That practice permitted cost savings through infrequent ordering and reduced transportation charges and made allowances for delayed deliveries and for inspection of received goods and components. The assurance of supplies on hand for long production runs of standardized outputs was achieved at high inventory and storage costs.

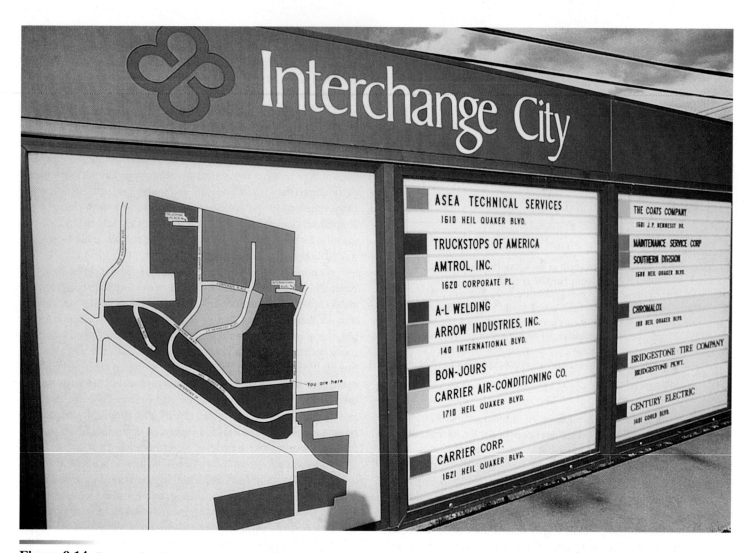

Figure 9.14 On a small scale, the planned industrial park furnishes its tenants external agglomeration economies similar to those offered by large urban concentrations to industry in general. An industrial park provides a subdivided tract of land developed according to a comprehensive plan for the use of (frequently) otherwise unconnected firms. Since the park developers, whether private companies or public agencies, supply the basic infrastructure of streets, water, sewage, power, transport facilities, and perhaps private police and fire protection, park tenants are spared the additional cost of providing these services themselves. In some instances, factory buildings are available for rent, still further reducing firm capital outlays. Counterparts of industrial parks for manufacturers are the office parks, research parks, science parks, and the like for "high-tech" firms and for enterprises in tertiary and quaternary services.

Just-in-time (JIT) manufacturing, in contrast, seeks to reduce inventories for the production process by purchasing inputs for arrival just in time to use and producing output just in time to sell. Rather than costly accumulation and storage of supplies, JIT requires frequent ordering of small lots of goods for precisely timed arrival and immediate deployment to the factory floor. Just-in-time manufacturing is often associated with Toyota, whose engineers developed the concept from American management consultants and watching American companies. Such "lean manufacturing" based on frequent purchasing of immediately needed goods demands rapid delivery by suppliers and encourages them to locate near the buyer. Recent manufacturing innovations thus reinforce and augment the spatial agglomeration tendencies evident in the older industrial landscape and deemphasize the applicability of older single-plant location theories.

JIT is one expression of a transition from mass-production Fordism to more *flexible production systems.* That flexibility is designed to allow producers to shift quickly and easily between different levels of output and, importantly, to move from one factory process or product to another as market demand dictates. Flexibility of that type is made possible by new technologies of easily reprogrammed computerized machine tools and by computer-aided design and computer-aided manufacturing systems. These technologies permit small-batch, just-in-time production and distribution responsive to current market demand as monitored by computer-based information systems.

Flexible production to a large extent requires significant acquisition of components and services from outside suppliers rather than from in-house production. For example, modular assembly, where many subsystems of a complex final product enter the plant already assembled, reduces factory space and worker requirements. The premium that flexibility places on proximity to component suppliers adds still another dimension to industrial agglomeration tendencies. "Flexible production regions" have, according to some observers, emerged in response to the new flexible production strategies and interfirm dependencies. Those regions, it is claimed, are usually some distance—spatially or socially—from established concentrations of Fordist industrialization.

Comparative Advantage, Outsourcing, and Offshoring

The principle of *comparative advantage* and the practices of *outsourcing* and *offshoring* are of growing international importance in decisions regarding industrial location. They are interconnected in that each reflects cost advantages of specialization and each is dependent on free trade and the free flow of information. **Comparative advantage** tells us that areas and countries can best improve their economies and living standards through specialization and trade. These benefits will follow if each area or country concentrates on the production of those items for which it has the greatest relative advantage over other areas or for which it has the least relative disadvantage, and imports all other goods. This principle is basic to the understanding of regional specializations and it applies as long as areas have different relative advantages for two or more goods and free trade exists between them.

The logic of comparative advantage was recognized by economists in the 19th century when specialization and exchange involved shipments of grain, coal, or manufactured goods whose relative costs of production in different areas were clearly evident. Today, when other countries' comparative advantages may reflect lower costs for labor, land, and capital, the application of the principle is seen in a much less favorable light by some critics. They observe that manufacturing activities may relocate from higher-cost market country locations to lower-cost foreign production sites, taking jobs and income away from the consuming country to the apparent detriment of that country's prosperity. However, other observers argue that the domestic economic consequences of such voluntary **outsourcing**— producing parts or products abroad for domestic sale—by American manufacturers are no different from those resulting from successful competition by foreign companies or from industrial locational decisions favoring one section of the country over others.

Outsourcing has also come to mean subcontracting production and service sector work to outside, often nonunion, domestic companies. In 2005, U.S. companies outsourced an estimated $4 trillion in goods and services, a 50% increase since the start of the century; outsourcing in the American context is growing at an estimated 15% to 20% yearly pace. Roughly one-half of the 2005 total value of outsourcing related to manufacturing; about one-third of that share involved foreign suppliers. The other half was domestic, involving purchases—including service sector activities—from American suppliers. In manufacturing, outsourcing has become an important element in just-in-time acquisition of preassembled components for snap-together fabrication of finished products, often built only to fill orders actually received from customers. Reducing parts inventories and introducing build-to-order production demands a high level of flexible freight movement increasingly supplied by "logistics" firms that themselves may become involved in packaging, labeling, and even manufacturing products for client companies. When comparative advantage and outsourcing are exploited by individual corporations, one expression of flexible production systems is evident in the erosion of the rigid spatial concentration of manufacturing assumed by classical location theory.

A clear example of that impact is evident in the changing nature of automobile manufacturing. Formerly, motor vehicle companies were largely self-contained production entities controlling raw material inputs through their own steel and glass plants and producing themselves all parts and components required in the assembly of their products. Since late 1992, that self-containment has been abandoned because car companies have divested themselves of raw material production facilities and have in large part sold off their in-house parts production. Increasingly, they are purchasing parts and subassemblies from independent, often distant, suppliers. In fact, some observers of the changing vehicle production scene predict that established automobile companies will eventually convert themselves into "vehicle brand owners," retaining for themselves only such essential tasks as vehicle design, engineering, and marketing. All else, including final product assembly, is projected to be done through outsourcing to parts suppliers. Similar trends are already evident in consumer electronics, where a third of manufacturing (2005) is estimated to be outsourced.

A distinctive regional illustration of more diversified industrial deconcentration through outsourcing is found along the northern border of Mexico. In the 1960s Mexico enacted legislation permitting foreign (specifically, American) companies to establish "sister" plants, called *maquiladoras,* within 20 kilometers (12 miles) of the U.S. border for the duty-free assembly of products destined for reexport. By 2003 more than 3000 such assembly and manufacturing plants had been established to produce a diversity of goods including electronic products, textiles, furniture, leather goods, toys, and automotive parts. The plants generated direct and indirect employment for more than a million Mexican workers (Figure 9.15) and for large numbers of U.S. citizens, employees of growing numbers of American-side *maquila* suppliers and of diverse service-oriented businesses spawned by the "multiplier effect." The North American Free Trade Agreement (NAFTA), which created a single Canadian–United States–Mexican production and marketing community, turns outsourcing in the North American context from a search abroad for low-cost production sites to a review of best locations within an enlarged unified economic environment.

On the broader world scene, outsourcing often involves production of commodities by developing countries that have benefited from the transfer of technology and capital from industrialized states and that use their new facilities and skills to improve productivity in areas formerly dominated by the profitable home production and exports of a rich world state. For example, electrical and electronic goods from China and Southeast Asia compete with and replace in the market similar goods formerly produced by Western firms. Such replacements, multiplied by numerous new country origins of the whole range of producer and consumer goods in world trade, have resulted in new global patterns of industrial regions and specializations. They have also strikingly changed the developing world's share of gross global output, growing from an estimated 20% in the mid-20th century to nearly one-half in 2005, measured by purchasing power parity (see p. 313–314). That improvement reflected, in part, the fact that manufacturers' share of their exports grew from less than half in 1990 to nearly two-thirds in 2006. For some observers, that change is ample proof of the beneficial impact of comparative advantage on the world economy.

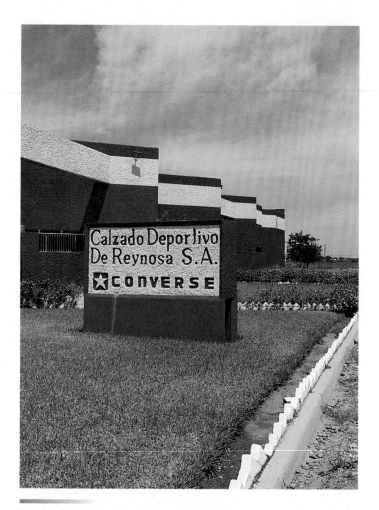

Figure 9.15 American manufacturers, seeking lower labor costs, began in the 1960s to establish light manufacturing, component production, and assembly operations along the international border in Mexico. *Outsourcing* to such plants as this Converse Sport Shoe factory at Reynosa has moved a large proportion of American electronics, small appliance, toy, and garment industries to offshore subsidiaries or contractors in Asia and Latin America. More than a quarter-million Mexican *maquilador* jobs and 350 plants were lost between 2000 and 2004, however, largely to competition from lower-cost, more-efficient Chinese and other Asian producers. Comparative advantage is not a permanent condition.

Outsourcing not only involves manufacturing activity and blue-collar jobs but also, as we shall see later in this chapter, may be used by companies to reduce their service worker costs as well. When that reduction involves janitorial and similar services spatially tied to the home establishment, no adverse domestic employment consequences are felt. When, however, lower-paid foreign workers can satisfactorily replace technical, professional, and white-collar workers, the outsourcing action is known as service *offshoring* and has the immediate effect of exporting the jobs of highly paid skilled workers.

Offshoring is the practice of either hiring foreign workers or, commonly, contracting with a foreign third-party service provider to take over and run particular business processes or operations, such as call centers or accounting, billing, and similar nonproduction "back office" aspects of manufacturing. Offshoring has become an increasingly standard cost-containment strategy,

reflecting the recent steep decline in communication costs, the ease of Internet use, and the growing technical proficiencies of foreign labor pools. With an ever-increasing portion of the developing world acquiring the education and experience to provide skilled professional services of almost every kind at a level comparable to that formerly available only in advanced countries, traditional notions of comparative advantage are disappearing in the face of a new era of *hypercompetition,* at least in business and professional services. India in particular has emerged as the dominant competitor and beneficiary of services offshoring, echoing China's position as the preferred destination of production outsourcing.

The exploitation of comparative advantage and utilization of outsourcing and offshoring, by transferring technology from economically advanced to underdeveloped economies is transforming the world economy by introducing a *new international division of labor* (NIDL). In the 19th century and the first half of the 20th century, the division of labor invariably involved exports of manufactured goods from the "industrial" countries and of raw materials from the "colonial" or "undeveloped" economies. Roles have now altered. Manufacturing no longer is the mainstay of the economy or employment structure of Europe or Anglo America, and the world pattern of industrial production is shifting to reflect the growing dominance of countries formerly regarded as subsistence peasant societies that are now emerging as the source areas for manufactured goods of all types produced competitively for the world market. In recognition of that shift, the NIDL builds on the current trend toward the increased subdivision of manufacturing processes into smaller steps (and a similar fragmentation of stages of professional services). That subdivision permits multiple outsourcing and offshoring opportunities based on differential land and capital costs and skill levels available in the globalized world economy, opportunities effectively exploited by transnational corporations.

Imposed Considerations

Locational theories dictate that in a pure, competitive economy, the costs of material, transportation, labor, and plant should be controlling in locational decisions. Obviously, neither in the United States nor in any other market economy do the idealized conditions exist. Other constraints—some representing cost considerations, others political or social impositions—also affect, perhaps decisively, the locational decision process. Land use and zoning controls, environmental quality standards and regulations, governmental area-development inducements, local tax abatement provisions or developmental bond authorizations, noneconomic pressures on quasi-governmental corporations, and other considerations constitute attractions or repulsions for industry outside of the context and consideration of pure theory (see "Contests and Bribery"). If these noneconomic forces become compelling, the assumptions of the commercial economy classification no longer apply, and locational controls reminiscent of those enforced by centrally planned economies become determining.

No other imposed considerations were as pervasive as those governing industrial location in planned economies. The theoretical controls on plant location decisions that apply in commercial economies were not, by definition, determinant in the centrally planned Marxist economies of Eastern Europe and the former

Geography and Public Policy

Contests and Bribery

In 1985, it cost Kentucky over $140 million in incentives—some $47,000 a job—to induce Toyota to locate an automobile assembly plant in Georgetown, Kentucky. That was cheap. By 1993, Alabama spent $169,000 per job to lure Mercedes-Benz to that state, Mississippi agreed to $400 million in spending and tax rebates to Nissan in 2001, and in 2002 Georgia gave DaimlerChrysler $320 million in incentives in successful competition with South Carolina to secure the company's proposed new factory. Earlier, Kentucky bid $350,000 per job in tax credits to bring a Canadian steel mill there.

The spirited auction for jobs is not confined to manufacturing. A University of Minnesota economist calculates that his state will have spent $500,000 for each of the 1500 or more permanent jobs created by Northwest Airlines at two new maintenance facilities. Illinois gave $240 million in incentives ($44,000 per job) to keep 5400 Sears, Roebuck employees within the state, and New York City awarded $184 million to the New York Mercantile Exchange and more than $30 million each to financial firms Morgan Stanley and Kidder, Peabody to induce them to stay in the city. For some, the bidding between states and locales to attract new employers and employment gets too fierce. Kentucky withdrew from competition for a United Airlines maintenance facility, letting Indianapolis have it when Indiana's offered package exceeded $450 million. By 2004, following a slowdown in air travel, United walked away from a fully completed operational facility, leaving the city and state with $320 million of bonded debt and a complex of empty hangars and office buildings.

Inducements to lure companies are not just in cash and loans—though both figure in some offers. For manufacturers, incentives may include workforce training, property tax abatement, subsidized costs of land and building or their outright gifts, below-market financing of bonds, and the like. Similar offers are regularly made by states, counties, and cities to wholesalers, retailers, major office worker and other service activity employers. The total annual loss of city and state tax revenue through abatements, subsidies, grants, and the like to benefit retained or attracted firms has been estimated at $30 billion to $40 billion. The objective, of course, is not just to secure the new jobs represented by the attracted firm but to benefit from the general economic stimulus and employment growth that those jobs—and their companies—generate. Auto parts manufacturers are presumably attracted to new assembly plant locations; cities grow and service industries of all kinds—doctors, department stores, restaurants, food stores—prosper from the investments made to attract new basic employment.

Not everyone is convinced that those investments are wise, however. A poll of Minnesotans showed a majority opposed the generous offer made by the state to Northwest Airlines. In the late 1980s, the governor of Indiana, a candidate for Kentucky's governorship, and the mayor of Flat Rock, Michigan, were all defeated by challengers who charged that too much had been spent in luring the Suburu-Isuzu, Toyota, and Mazda plants, respectively. Established businesses resent what often seems neglect of their interests in favor of spending their tax money on favors to newcomers. The Council for Urban Economic Development, surveying the escalating bidding wars, has actively lobbied against incentives, and many academic observers note that industrial attraction amounts to a zero-sum game: unless the attracted newcomer is a foreign firm, whatever one state achieves in attracting an expanding U.S. company comes at the expense of another state.

Some doubt that inducements matter much, anyway. Although, sensibly, companies seeking new locations will shop around and solicit the lowest-cost, best deal possible, their site choices are apt to be determined by more realistic business considerations: access to labor, suppliers, and markets; transportation and utility costs; weather; the nature of the workforce; and overall costs of living. Only when two or more similarly attractive locations have essentially equal cost structures might such special inducements as tax reductions or abatements be determinants in a locational decision.

Questions to Consider

1. As citizen and taxpayer, do you think it is appropriate to spend public money to attract new employment to your state or community? If not, why not? If yes, what kinds of inducements and what total amount offered per job seem appropriate to you? What reasons support your opinion?

2. If you believe that "best locations" for the economy as a whole are those determined by pure location theory, what arguments would you propose to discourage locales and states from making financial offers designed to circumvent decisions clearly justified on abstract theoretical grounds?

Soviet Union. In those economies, plant locational decisions were made by government agencies rather than by individual firms.

Bureaucratic rather than company decision making did not mean that location assessments based on factor cost were ignored; it meant that central planners were more concerned with other than purely economic considerations in the creation of new industrial plants and concentrations. Important in the former Soviet Union, for example, was a controlling policy of the *rationalization* of industry through full development of the resources of the country wherever they were found and without regard to the cost or competitiveness of such development. Inevitably, although the factors of industrial production are identical in capitalist and non-capitalist economies, the philosophies and patterns of industrial location and areal development will differ between them. Since major capital investments are relatively permanent additions to the landscape, the results of their often noneconomic political or philosophical decisions are fixed and will long remain to influence industrial regionalism and competitive efficiencies into the post-communist present and future. Those same decisions and rigidities continue to inhibit the transition by the formerly fully planned economies to modern capitalist industrial techniques and flexibilities.

Transnational Corporations

Outsourcing is but one small expression of the growing international structure of modern manufacturing and service enterprises. Business and industry are increasingly stateless and economies borderless as giant **transnational corporations (TNCs)**—private firms that have established branch operations in nations foreign to their headquarters' country—become ever-more important in the globalizing world space economy. In 2005, about 77,000 transnational (also known as *multinational*) companies controlled more than 770,000 foreign affiliates employing about 62 million workers.

Measured by value added (not total sales), 29 of the world's top 100 economic entities in 2003 were corporations, not countries. The great majority of them, all TNCs, are engaged in secondary industries. That is, except for a few resource-based firms they are principally involved in producing and selling manufactured goods. Although as we shall see, tertiary and quaternary activities have also become international in scope and transnational in corporate structure, the locational and operational advantages of multicountry operation were first discerned and exploited by manufacturers. Because of their outsourced purchases of raw materials, parts and components, and services, the total number of worldwide jobs associated with TNCs in 2005 reached 150 million or more.

TNCs are increasingly international in origin and administrative home, based primarily in a growing number of both economically advanced and newly industrializing countries. In 2004, 85 of the world's 100 largest TNCs had home offices in the European Union, the United States, and Japan. However, cash-rich multinationals of such developing world states as China, Taiwan, India, Korea, Mexico, and Brazil, for example, were moving up on the list. Through their own surging growth and through mergers and acquisitions, formerly developing world regional players—often state owned or controlled—have emerged as major global forces.

The direct impact of TNCs is limited to relatively few countries and regions. **Foreign direct investment** (FDI)—the purchase or construction of factories and other fixed assets by TNCs—has been a significant engine of globalization, reaching some $1.2 trillion in 2006. In the late 20th and very early 21st century, however, less than 30% of FDI flows went to developing countries and the majority of that share was concentrated in 10 to 15 states, mainly in South, Southeast, and East Asia (China was the largest developing country recipient) and in Latin America and the Caribbean. An estimated 42% of world FDI inflows went to developing countries in 2005, the largest share ever up to that year, suggesting their increasing attractiveness for TNC investment. The portion of FDI going to the 50 least developed countries as a group—including nearly all African states—has been small but steadily increasing, from a low of 1% in 1994 to almost 5% in 2004. Notably, investment outflows from companies based in India, Brazil, South Africa, Malaysia, and China (among others) have swelled, rising from $3 billion in 1991 to $40 billion in 2004, with one-third of the 2004 total going to other developing countries.

Because 80% of the world's more than 6-billion consumers live in the expanding developing nations, TNCs based in newly industrializing countries have the strength of familiarity with those markets and have an advantage in supplying them with goods and services that are usually cheaper to purchase, simpler and more familiar in operation, and more effectively distributed than those of many Western rival TNCs. Nevertheless, despite poor countries' hopes for foreign investment to spur their economic growth, the vast majority of FDI flows not to the poor or developing worlds but to the rich.

The advanced-country destination of those capital flows is understandable: TNCs are actively engaged in merging with or purchasing competitive established firms in already developed foreign market areas, and cross-border mergers and acquisitions have been the main stimulus behind FDI. In 2004, in the manufacturing sector alone, 135,000 mergers and acquisitions were announced worldwide. Because most transnational corporations operate in only a few industries—computers, electronics, petroleum and mining, motor vehicles, chemicals, and pharmaceuticals—the worldwide impact of their consolidations is significant. Some dominate the marketing and distribution of basic and specialized commodities. In raw materials, a few TNCs account for 85% or more of world trade in wheat, maize, coffee, cotton, iron ore, and timber, for example. In manufactures, the highly concentrated world pharmaceutical industry is dominated by just six firms, and the world's 15 major automobile producers at the start of the 21st century, it has been predicted, will fall to five or 10 by 2015.

Because they are international in operation with multiple markets, plants, and raw material sources, TNCs actively exploit the principle of comparative advantage and seize opportunities for outsourcing and offshoring. In manufacturing they have internationalized the plant-siting decision process and multiplied the number of locationally separated operations that must be assessed. TNCs produce in that country or region where costs of materials, labor, or other production inputs are minimized, or where existing efficient company-owned factories can be easily expanded to produce for a global, rather than simply a national, market. At the same time, they can maintain operational control and declare taxes in localities where the economic climate is most favorable. Research and development, accounting, and other corporate activities are placed wherever economical and convenient.

TNCs have become global entities because global communications make it possible (Figure 9.16). Many have lost their original national identities and are no longer closely associated with or controlled by the cultures, societies, and legal systems of a nominal home country. At the same time, their multiplication of economic activities has reduced any earlier identifications with single products or processes and given rise to "transnational integral conglomerates" spanning a large spectrum of both service and industrial sectors.

World Manufacturing Patterns and Trends

Whether locational decisions are made by private entrepreneurs or central planners—and on whatever considerations those decisions are based—the results over many years have produced a distinctive

Figure 9.16 The world's transnational corporations increased in number from some 7000 in 1970 to about 62,000 in 2004. Ninety of the top 100 TNCs are headquartered in the *Triad*—the European Union, the United States, and Japan. Their recognition and impact, however, are global, as suggested by these billboards advertising just a sample of leading TNCs in distant settings. Corporate names and headquarters countries are followed by billboard locations in parentheses.

world pattern of manufacturing. While Figure 9.17 suggests a large number of industrial concentrations, in fact four regions are commonly recognized as most significant: *Eastern Anglo America, Western and Central Europe, Eastern Europe,* and *Eastern Asia.* Together, the industrial plants within these established regional clusters account for an estimated three-fifths of the world's manufacturing output by volume and value.

Their continuing dominance is by no means assured. The first three—those of Anglo America and Europe—were the beneficiaries of an earlier phase in the development and spread of manufacturing following the Industrial Revolution of the 18th century and lasting until after World War II. The countries within them now are increasingly "postindustrial" and traditional manufacturing and processing are of declining relative importance.

The fourth—the East Asian district—is part of the wider, newer pattern of world industrialization that has emerged in recent years, the result of massive international *cultural convergence* (p. 46) and technology transfers in the latter half of the 20th century and early in the 21st. The older rigid economic split between the developed and developing worlds has rapidly weakened as the full range of industrial activities from primary metal processing

(e.g., the iron and steel industries) through advanced electronic assembly has been dispersed from, or separately established within, an ever-expanding list of countries.

Such states as Mexico, Brazil, China, and others of the developing world have created industrial regions of international significance, and the contribution to world manufacturing activity of the smaller newly industrializing countries (NICs) has been growing significantly. The spreading use of efficient and secure containerized shipment of high-value goods to Anglo American and European markets has been a major contributor to their competitive success. Even economies that until recently were overwhelmingly subsistence or dominated by agricultural or mineral exports have become important players in the changing world manufacturing scene. Foreign branch plant investment in low-wage Asian, African, and Latin American states has not only created their industrial infrastructures but also increased their gross national products and per capita incomes sufficiently to permit expanded production for growing domestic—not just export—markets.

Much of that new plant investment and expanded developing country industrial production has concentrated within the great number of *export processing zones* (EPZs) recently created within

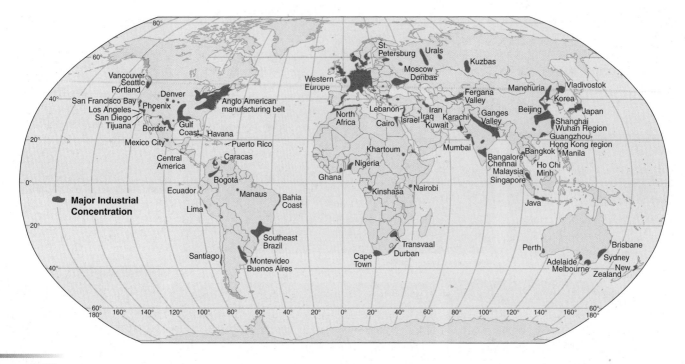

Figure 9.17 **World industrial regions.** Industrial districts are not as continuous or "solid" as the map suggests. Manufacturing is a relatively minor user of land even in areas of greatest concentration.

those countries. An EPZ may be either a delimited geographical area or, frequently, an export-oriented manufacturing enterprise located anywhere within a host country that benefits from special investment incentives. These incentives usually include exemptions from customs duties, preferential treatment from various regulatory and financial regulations, and the provision of high-quality infrastructure—airports, highways, telecommunications, and electric and water facilities—usually provided by the local or national governments. Enterprises operating within or as an EPZ usually enjoy preferential conditions under which they can import equipment, components, and raw materials duty-free to produce goods mainly for export. And exports from those zones generally are afforded tariff reductions or duty-free entry into receiving European and North American markets. Because of their obvious production-site advantages, therefore, EPZs are both favored locations for transnational corporation outsourcing and the promoted device with which developing countries compete for TNC foreign investment.

Nevertheless, those smaller Asian, African, and Latin American countries separately and collectively figure less prominently in world manufacturing volumes and values than do the Anglo American and European industrial regions that still remain major components on the world economic landscape and are now matched by the Eastern Asian region of more recent origin. Because of either their traditional or newly emerging world significance, each of those Western and Eastern Hemisphere industrial regions warrants a closer look.

Anglo America

The importance of manufacturing in Anglo America has been steadily declining. In 1960, the 28% of the labor force engaged in manufacturing generated nearly one-third of the region's wealth.

In the early 21st century, manufacturing employment had dropped to about 16% of a much larger labor force, and manufacturing contributed about 14% of the gross domestic product of the Anglo American realm.

Manufacturing is found particularly in the urbanized sections of North America, but is not uniformly distributed. Its primary concentration is in the northeastern part of the United States and adjacent sections of southeastern Canada, the *Anglo American Manufacturing Belt* (Figure 9.18). That district contains the majority of the urban population of the two countries, their densest and best-developed transportation network, the largest number of their manufacturing establishments, and the preponderance of heavy industry.

Anglo American manufacturing began early in the 19th century in southern New England, where waterpowered textile mills, iron plants, and other small-scale industries began to free Canada and the new United States from total dependence on European—particularly English—sources. The eastern portion of the manufacturing belt contained early population centers, a growing canal and railroad network, a steady influx of immigrant skilled and unskilled labor, and concentrations of investment capital to invest in new manufacturing enterprises. The U.S. eastern seaboard remains an important producer of consumer goods, light industrial, and high-technology products on the basis of its market and developed labor skills. Its core is *Megalopolis,*[1] a 1000-kilometer- (600-mile-) long city system stretching from southern Maine to Norfolk, Virginia, with a great array of market-oriented industries and thousands of individual industrial plants.

The heart of the Anglo American manufacturing belt developed across the Appalachians in the interior of the continent. The

---

[1]*Megalopolis* or *conurbation* is an extended urbanized area formed by the gradual merger of several individual cities.

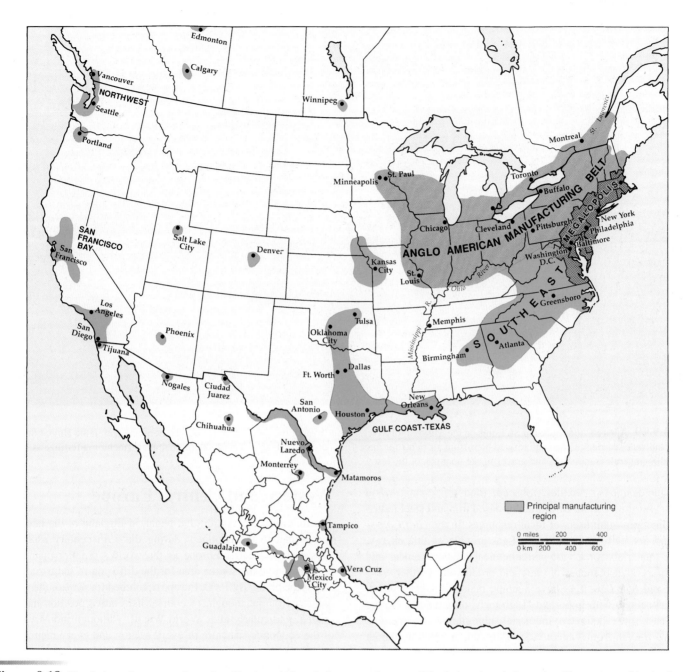

Figure 9.18 North American manufacturing districts. Although the preponderance of North American industry is still concentrated in Anglo America, Mexican manufacturing activity is rapidly growing and diversifying—for both expanding domestic and export markets. While Mexico City alone yields nearly half of the country's manufacturing output volume, industrial plants are also localized in the Central Plateau area and along the northern border with the United States, where most *maquiladoras* have been established.

Ohio River system and the Great Lakes provided the early—and still important—"highways" of the interior (Figure 9.19), supplemented later by canals and, after the 1850s, by the railroads that tied together the agricultural and industrial raw materials, the growing cities, and multiplying manufacturing plants of the interior with markets and materials throughout the country. The early heavy metallurgical emphasis—the U.S. Steel plants of the Monongahela Valley are an example—has declined and been succeeded early in the 21st century by advanced material processing and fabrication plus high-tech manufacturing, creating a renewed and modernized diversified industrial base.

The Canadian portion of the Anglo American manufacturing belt lies close to neighboring U.S. industrial districts. About one-half of Canada's manufacturing labor force is localized in southern Ontario. With Toronto as the hub, the industrial belt extends westward to Windsor, across from Detroit. Another third of Canadian manufacturing employment is found in Quebec, with Montreal as the obvious core but with energy-intensive industries—particularly aluminum plants and paper mills—along the St. Lawrence River.

By the 1990s, manufacturing employment and volume was declining everywhere in the Anglo American economy. What remained showed a pattern of relocation to Western and Southern zones reflecting national population shifts and changing material and product orientations.

Figure 9.19 A barge "tow" passing St. Louis on the Mississippi River. About 15% of the total ton-miles of freight movement in the United States is by inland water carriers. Crude and refined petroleum accounts for three-fifths of the tonnage. Farm products, chemicals (including fertilizers), and nonmetallic minerals (sand, rock, and gravel) make up much of the rest.

In the *Southeast,* textiles, tobacco, food processing, wood products, furniture, and a Birmingham-based iron and steel industry became important users of local resources. In the *Gulf Coast–Texas district,* petroleum and natural gas provide wealth, energy, and raw materials for a vast petrochemical industry; sulfur and salt support other branches of chemical production. Farther west, *Denver* and *Salt Lake City* have become major, though isolated, industrial centers with important "high-tech" orientations. On the West Coast, three distinctive industrial subregions have emerged. In the *Northwest,* from Vancouver to Portland, orientation to both a regional and a broader Asian-Pacific market is of greater significance than are the primary domestic markets of Canada and the United States. Seattle's aircraft production and the software industry of the Northwest are, by their high-value products, largely unaffected by transport costs to world markets. The *San Francisco Bay district* is home to Silicon Valley and the electronics/computer/high-tech manufacturing that name implies. Food specializations there (wine, for example) for a national market have their counterpart farther south in the *Los Angeles–San Diego corridor,* where fruits and vegetables are grown and packed. More important, however, is diversified, particularly consumer-goods, production for the rapidly growing California and western market.

North America's fastest growing industrial region lies along the U.S.-Mexican border. Called *la frontera* by its Mexican workers and extending 2100 miles from the Pacific Ocean to the Gulf of Mexico, this subregion served us earlier as an example of "outsourcing" and comparative advantage (p. 285) based on its low wages, easy access to U.S. markets, and less stringent environmental regulations.

Western and Central Europe

The Industrial Revolution that began in England in the late 1700s and spread to the continent during the 19th century established Western and Central Europe as the world's premier manufacturing region and the source area for the diffusion of industrialization across the globe. By 1900, Europe accounted for 80% of the world's industrial output though, of course, its relative position has since eroded, particularly after World War II. Although industry is part of the economic structure of every section and every metropolitan complex of Europe, the majority of manufacturing output is concentrated in a set of distinctive districts stretching from the Midlands of England in the west to the Ural Mountains in the east (Figure 9.20).

Waterpowered mechanical spinning and weaving in the textile industry of England began the Industrial Revolution, but it was steam power, not waterpower, that provided the impetus for the full industrialization of that country and of Europe. Consequently, coal fields, not rivers, were the sites of the new manufacturing districts in England. London, although remote from coal deposits, became the largest single manufacturing center of the United Kingdom, its consumers and labor force potent magnets for new industry.

Technologies developed in Britain spread to the continent. The coal fields distributed in a band across northern France, Belgium, central Germany, the northern Czech Republic, southern Poland, and eastward to southern Ukraine, as well as iron ore deposits, localize the metallurgical industries to the present day. Other pronounced industrial concentrations focus on the major metropolitan districts and capital cities of the countries of Europe.

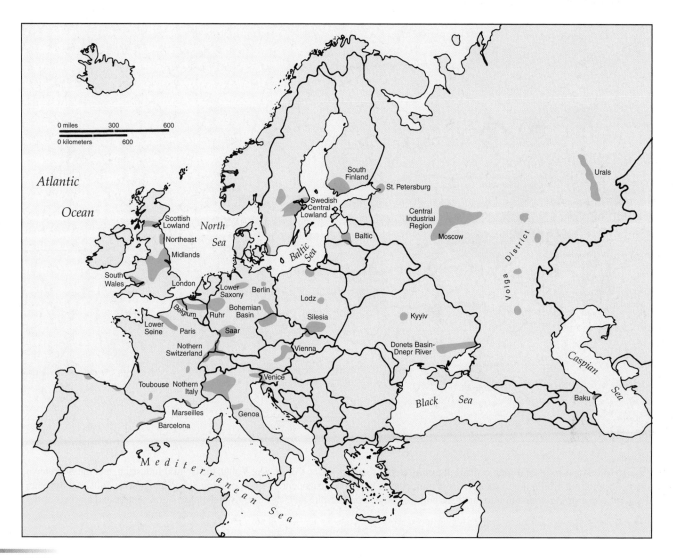

Figure 9.20 The industrial regions of Europe.

The largest and most important single industrial area of Europe extends from the French–Belgian border to western Germany. Its core is Germany's Ruhr, a compact, highly urbanized industrial concentration of more than 50 major cities housing iron and steel, textiles, automobiles, chemicals, and all the metal-forming and metal-using industries of modern economies. In France, heavy industry located near the iron ore of Nancy and the coal of Lille, and the aerospace industry is concentrated in Toulouse. Like London, Paris lacks raw materials, but with easy access to the sea and to the domestic market, it became the major manufacturing center of France. Farther east, the Saxony district began to industrialize as early as the 1600s, in part benefiting from labor skills brought by immigrant artisans from France and Holland. Those skills have been preserved in a district noted for the quality of its manufactured goods.

Western Europe is experiencing a deindustrialization accompanied by massive layoffs of workers in coal mining because of declining demand and in iron mining because of ore depletion. Iron and steel, textiles, and shipbuilding—the core industries of the Industrial Revolution—have been particularly hard hit. As in the Anglo American Manufacturing Belt, a restructuring of the Western European economy is introducing new industrial and service orientations and employment patterns.

Eastern Europe

Between the end of World War II and 1990, Eastern European industrial concentrations, such as that of Silesia in Poland and the Czech portion of the Bohemian Basin (Figure 9.20), were largely cut off from their earlier connections with the larger European market and economy. Instead, they were controlled by centralized industrial planning and tied to the regional economic plans imposed by the Soviet Union. Since its fall, Eastern European states have struggled with a generally poorly conceived, technologically antiquated, uneconomic industrial structure that, in its creation and operation, was unresponsive to market realities.

Farther east, in Russia and Ukraine, two distinctly different industrial orientations predominate, both dating from Czarist times and strengthened under Soviet-era planning. One emphasis is on light industrial, market-oriented production primarily focused on Russia's Central Industrial Region of Greater Moscow and surrounding areas

Figure 9.21 Industrial regions under central planning in the former Soviet Union. The Volga, the Central Industrial, and the St. Petersburg (Leningrad) concentrations within the former Soviet manufacturing belt were dependent on transportation, labor, and market pulls. All the other planned industrial regions had a strong orientation to materials and were developed despite their distance from the population centers and markets of the west.

(Figure 9.21). The other orientation is heavy industrial. Its Czarist beginnings were localized in the southern Ukrainian Donets Basin-Dnepr River district where coking coal, iron ore, fluxing materials, and iron alloys are found near at hand. Under the Stalinist Five-year plans, with their emphasis on creation of multiple sources of supply of essential industrial goods, heavy industry was also developed elsewhere in the Soviet Union. The industrial districts of Russia's Volga, Urals, Kuznetsk Basin, Baikal, and Far East regions, and the industrial complexes of the Caucasus, Kazakhstan, and Central Asia resulted from those Soviet programs first launched in 1928.

Eastern Asia

The Eastern Asian sphere is rapidly becoming the most productive of the world's industrial regions (Figure 9.22). Japan has emerged as the overall second-ranked manufacturing nation. China—building on a rich resource base, massive labor force, and nearly insatiable market demand—is industrializing rapidly and ranks among the top 10 producers of a number of major industrial commodities; by 2006 China's economy had become the world's fourth largest, after the United States, Japan, and Germany. South Korea, Taiwan, Singapore, and (before its inclusion in China's mainland economy in 1997) Hong Kong, were recognized as "the four tigers," swiftly industrializing Asian economies that have become major presences in markets around the world.

Japanese industry was rebuilt from near total destruction during World War II to its present leading position in some areas of electronics and other high-tech production. That recovery was accomplished largely without a domestic raw material base and primarily with the export market in mind. Dependence on imports of materials and exports of product has encouraged a coastal location for most factories. The industrial core of modern Japan is the heavily urbanized belt from Tokyo to northern Kyushu (Figure 9.22).

When the communists assumed control of China's still war-damaged economy in 1949, that country was essentially unindustrialized. Most manufacturing was small-scale production geared to local subsistence needs. A massive industrialization program initiated by the new regime greatly increased the volume, diversity, and dispersion of manufacturing in China. Until 1976, domestic needs rather than foreign markets were the principal concern of an industrial development totally controlled by the state and the communist party. From the late 1970s, manufacturing activities were freed from absolute state control and industrial output grew rapidly with most dramatic gains coming not from state enterprises but from quickly multiplying rural collectives.

By the start of the 21st century, however, it was foreign direct investment, foreign firm outsourcing of production to low-cost Chinese suppliers, and relocation to China of manufacturing and assemblage of a host of consumer electronics, clothing, toys, and industrial equipment from other Asian countries

Figure 9.22 The industrial districts of Eastern Asia.

that propelled China to the forefront among East Asian and developing countries worldwide as an industrial powerhouse. Simultaneously, China's economic planners actively shuttered inefficient and uneconomic state-owned enterprises (SOEs) that had been the mandated industrial units of the Communist past. Between 1997 and 2002, 27 million workers in SOEs were laid off, and further plant closings followed. China's admission in 2001 to the World Trade Organization (see Chapter 12) further enhanced the competitive position of an economy already accounting for 10.1% of total world exports of manufactured goods in 2006.

Unlike Japan, China possesses a relatively rich and diversified domestic raw material base of ores and fuels. Resource distribution in part accounts for the spatial pattern of industry, though urban agglomerations and market orientations are equally important (Figure 9.22). Coastal and port locations have industrialized most dramatically. The main dynamos of China's industrial and economic transformation have been Shanghai and the lower reaches of the Yangtze River in the East District and Shenzhen and Guangzhou in the Xi Jiang delta of the Central South. To relieve pressure on those and other rapidly expanding industrial areas and to create a new northern equivalent zone of major growth,

the development of the Binhai New Area along the coast east of Tianjin was announced in 2006.

Three smaller East Asian economies—Taiwan, South Korea, and Singapore—have outgrown their former "developing country" status to become advanced industrialized states. Their rise to prominence has been rapid, and their share of market in those branches of industry in which they have chosen to specialize has increased dramatically. Although the specifics of their industrial successes have differed, in each case an educated, trainable labor force; economic and social systems encouraging industrial enterprise; and national programs directed at capital accumulation, industrial development, and export orientation fueled the programs.

Their ranks have recently been joined by an expanded list of other industrial "tigers"—nations demonstrating the capacity for rapid, sustained economic growth. At the least, the new Asian tiger group includes Malaysia and Thailand and may soon be joined by the Philippines, Indonesia, and Vietnam. Other Asian manufacturing concentrations are also emerging as important participants in the world's industrial economy. India, for example, benefits from expanding industrial bases centered in metropolitan Bangalore, Mumbai (Bombay), Delhi, Kolkata (Calcutta), and elsewhere, each with its own developing specializations.

High-Tech Patterns

Major industrial districts of the world developed over time as entrepreneurs and planners established traditional secondary industries according to the pulls and orientations predicted by classical location theories. Those theories are less applicable in explaining the location of the latest generation of manufacturing activities: the high-technology—or *high-tech*—processing and production that is increasingly part of the advanced economies. For these firms, new and different patterns of locational orientation and advantage have emerged based on other than the traditional regional and site attractions.

High technology is more a concept than a precise definition. It probably is best understood as the application of intensive research and development efforts to the creation and manufacture of new products of an advanced scientific and engineering character.[2] Professional—"white collar"—workers make up a large share of the total workforce. They include research scientists, engineers, and skilled technicians. When these high-skill specialists are added to administrative, supervisory, marketing, and other professional staffs, they may greatly outnumber actual production workers in a firm's employment structure. In the world of high-tech, that is, the distinction between secondary (manufacturing) and quaternary (knowledge) activities and workers is increasingly blurred.

Although only a few types of industrial activity are generally reckoned as exclusively high-tech—electronics, communication, computers, software, pharmaceuticals and biotechnology, aerospace, and the like—advanced technology is increasingly a part of the structure and processes of all forms of industry. Robotics on the assembly line, computer-aided design and manufacturing, electronic controls of smelting and refining processes, and the constant development of new products of the chemical industries are cases in point. Indeed, in the United States in 2004 an average of some 5% of total employment among all industry was in technology-oriented occupations.

The impact of high-tech industries on patterns of economic geography is expressed in at least three ways. First, high-tech activities are becoming major factors in employment growth and manufacturing output in the advanced and newly industrializing economies. Restricting the count only to those defined as truly high-tech industries, there were 14.4 million American wage and salary jobs in 2002, about 11% of the total nonfarm jobs in the economy. Furthermore, during the decade 1992–2002, employment in the high-tech industries increased 7.5%, accounting for 5% of total employment growth. That increase was, however, less than the nearly 20% job growth in the economy as a whole; high-tech employment is important but it is not the dominating economic force it is sometimes claimed to be. Looking forward, the U.S. Bureau of Labor Statistics in 2005 projected that high-tech industry employment would grow more slowly than the average for all industries up to 2012, although it also expected that output (not jobs) in high-tech industries would likely grow rapidly. In the manufacturing sector alone, the BLS foresees high-tech manufacturing declining faster than overall manufacturing as physical production continues to move out of the country. The United Kingdom, Germany, Japan, and other advanced countries have had similar

high-tech employment courses while high-tech manufacturing has been established and grown most dramatically in the newly industrializing countries of South, Southeast, and East Asia, beneficiaries initially of outsourcing and offshoring but also, more recently, of independent, vigorous, and successful competition in the world market.

The products of high- and medium-high-technology manufacturing represent a significant share of total gross value added (GVA)[3] for many individual countries. Data for 2003 indicate they accounted for about 21% of GVA in Ireland, 14% in South Korea, almost 13% in Germany, and 10% in Finland, but only about 7% in the United States and the United Kingdom. Global data are incomplete, but suggest the great disparity between countries in the importance of high-tech products in their exports of manufactured goods.

A second impact is more clearly spatial. High-tech industries have tended to become regionally concentrated in their countries of development, and within those regions, they frequently form self-sustaining, highly specialized agglomerations (Figure 9.23). California, for example, has a share of U.S. high-tech employment far in excess of its share of American population. Along with California, the Pacific Northwest (including British Columbia), New England, New Jersey, Texas, and Colorado all have proportions of their workers in high-tech industries above the national average. And within these and other states or regions of high-tech concentration, specific locales have achieved prominence: "Silicon Valley" of Santa Clara County near San Francisco; Irvine and Orange County south of Los Angeles; the "Silicon Forest" near Seattle; North Carolina's Research Triangle; Utah's "Software Valley"; Routes 128 and 495 around Boston; "Silicon Swamp" of the Washington, D.C. area; Ottawa, Canada's "Silicon Valley North"; or the Canadian Technology Triangle west of Toronto are familiar Anglo American examples.

Within such concentrations, specialization is often the rule: medical technologies in Minneapolis and Philadelphia, biotechnology around San Antonio, computers and semiconductors in eastern Virginia and at "Silicon Hills" in Austin, Texas, biotechnology and telecommunications in New Jersey's Princeton Corridor, telecommunications and Internet industries near Washington, D.C. Elsewhere, Scotland's Silicon Glen, England's Sunrise Strip and Silicon Fen, Wireless Valley in Stockholm, China's Zhong Guancum in suburban Beijing and the High-Tech Industries Zone in Xian, and Hitec City at Hyderabad, Pune, and Bangalore, India, are other examples of industrial landscapes characterized by low, modern, dispersed office-plant-laboratory buildings rather than by massive factories, mills, or assembly structures, freight facilities, and storage areas.

The older distributional patterns of high-tech industries suggest they respond to different localizing forces than those controlling traditional manufacturing industries. At least five locational tendencies have been recognized: (1) Proximity to major universities or research facilities and to a large pool of scientific and technical labor skills; (2) avoidance of areas with strong labor unionization where contract rigidities might slow process innovation and workforce flexibility; (3) locally available venture capital and entrepreneurial daring; (4) location in regions and major metropolitan areas with favorable "quality of life" reputations—climate, scenery, recreation, good universities, and an employment base sufficiently

---

[2]The Congressional Office of Technology describes high-technology firms as those "engaged in the design, development, and introduction of new products and/or innovative manufacturing processes through the systematic application of scientific and technical knowledge."

[3]Gross value added is linked to gross domestic product; the link can get defined as GVA + taxes on products - subsidies on products = GDP.

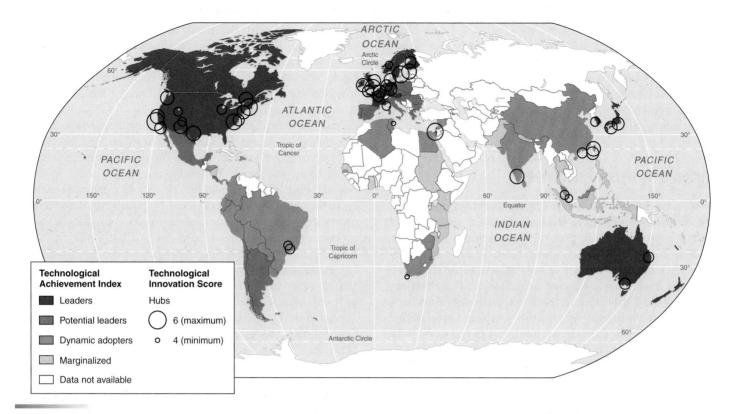

Figure 9.23 **Global Hubs of Technological Innovation.** The technology innovation hubs shown with circles were identified by *Wired* magazine in 2000 based on the presence of research universities, research laboratories, established technology companies, venture capital, and entrepreneurial activity. The highest scoring regions were Silicon Valley (California), Boston (Massachusetts), Stockholm (Sweden), Israel, Research Triangle (North Carolina), and London (U.K.). The technological achievement index was generated by the United Nations.

Source: United Nations Human Development Report, 2001. *Adapted by permission from Bradshaw, White, Dymond, and Chacko, Contemporary World Regional Geography, 2009.*

large to supply needed workers and provide job opportunities for professionally trained spouses; (5) availability of first-quality communication and transportation facilities to unite separated stages of research, development, and manufacturing and to connect the firm with suppliers, markets, finances, and the government agencies so important in supporting research. Essentially all of the major high-tech agglomerations have developed on the semirural peripheries of metropolitan areas but far from inner-city problems and disadvantages. Many have emerged as self-sufficient areas of subdivisions, shopping centers, schools, and parks in close proximity to company locations and business parks that form their core. While the New York metropolitan area is a major high-tech concentration, most of the technology jobs are suburban, not in Manhattan; the periphery's share of computer-related employment in the region amounted to 80% at the end of the 20th century.

Agglomerating forces are also important in this new industrial locational model. The formation of new firms is frequent and rapid in industries where discoveries are constant and innovation is continuous. Since many are "spin-off" firms founded by employees leaving established local companies, areas of existing high-tech concentration tend to spawn new entrants and to provide necessary labor skills. Agglomeration, therefore, is both a product and a cause of spatial associations.

Not all phases of high-tech production must be concentrated, however. The spatial attractions affecting the professional, scientific, and knowledge-intensive aspects of high tech have little

meaning for many of the component manufacturing and assembly operations, which may be highly automated or require little in the way of labor skills. These tasks, in our earlier locational terminology, are "foot-loose"; they require highly mobile capital and technology investments but may be advantageously performed by young women in low-wage areas at home or—more likely—in countries such as Taiwan, Singapore, Malaysia, or Mexico. Contract manufacturers totally divorced spatially and managerially from the companies whose products they produce accounted in 2005 for an estimated 15% to 20% of the output of electronics hardware. Most often the same factory produces similar or identical products under a number of different brand names.

Through such manufacturing transfers of technology and outsourcing, therefore, high-tech activities are spread to newly industrializing countries—from the center to the periphery, in the developmental terms we will explore in Chapter 10. This globalization through areal transfer and dispersion represents a third impact of high-tech activities on world economic geographic patterns already undergoing significant but variable change in response to the new technologies. The United States was consistently the world's leading producer of high-tech products from 1980 to 2002, contributing about one-third of the total world high-tech output. In 2001 the European Union's share of world high-tech production was 23%, a decline from its share in the early 1980s. On the other hand, Asia's market share steadily increased over the last two decades of the 20th century, led first by Japan in the 1980s and then by South

Korea, Taiwan, and China in the 1990s. By 2001, South Korea produced 7.1% and China 8.7% of world high-tech output. Such summary figures tend to conceal relative national importance in particular types of high-tech production and trade. For example, in 2005 China had surpassed the United States in exporting information-technology goods, such as laptop computers, mobile phones, and digital cameras.

Tertiary and Beyond

Primary activities, you will recall, gather, extract, or grow things. *Secondary* industries, we have seen in this chapter, give form utility to the products of primary industry through manufacturing and processing efforts. A major and growing segment of both domestic and international economic activity, however, involves *services* rather than the production of commodities. These **tertiary activities** consist of business and labor specializations that provide services to the primary and secondary sectors, to the general community, and to the individual. They imply pursuits other than the actual production of tangible commodities.

As we have seen, regional and national economies undergo fundamental changes in emphasis in the course of their development. Subsistence societies exclusively dependent on primary industries may progress to secondary stage processing and manufacturing activities. In that progression, the importance of agriculture, as an employer of labor or contributor to national income, declines as manufacturing expands. Many parts of the formerly underdeveloped world have made or are making that developmental transition, as we shall review in Chapter 10.

The advanced countries that originally dominated the world manufacturing scene, in contrast, saw their former industrial primacy reduced or lost during the last third of the 20th century. Rising energy and labor costs, the growth of transnational corporations, transfer of technology to developing countries, and outsourcing of processing or assembly have all changed the structure and pattern of the world economy. The earlier competitive manufacturing advantages of the developed countries could no longer be maintained and new economic orientations emphasizing service and information activities became the replacement. Based on sector contribution to their gross domestic products, it is the advanced economies that have most completely made that transition and are often referred to as "postindustrial" (Table 9.1).

Perhaps more than any other major country economy, the United States has reached postindustrial status. Its primary sector component fell from 66% of the labor force in 1850 to 1% in 2006, and the service sector rose from 18% to 83% (Figure 9.24). Of the more than 15 million new jobs created in the United States between 1996 and 2006, effectively all occurred in services. Comparable changes are found in other countries. Early in the 21st century, between 65% and 80% of jobs in such economies as Japan, Australia, Canada, Israel, and all major Western European countries were also in the services sector; Russia and Eastern Europe averaged rather less.

The significance of tertiary activities to national economies and the contrast between more developed and less developed

Table 9.1

Stage of Economic Development and the Structure of Output

Country Category	Percent of Gross Domestic Product, 2006			
	Agriculture	**Industry[a]**	**Manufacturing[b]**	**Services**
Least Developed				
Liberia	66	16	12	18
Mali	37	24	3	39
Newly Industrialized				
Malaysia	9	50	30	41
Thailand	11	45	35	45
Industrial				
Czech Republic	3	39	27	58
Ireland	2	36	25	62
Postindustrial				
Australia	3	28	11	69
United States	1	23	14	76

[a]Includes mining, manufacturing, construction, and utilities
[b]Also included in "Industry"
Source: The World Bank, *World Development Indicators* 2008.

states are made clear not just by employment but also by the differential contribution of services to the gross domestic products of states. The relative importance of services displayed in Figure 9.25 shows a marked contrast between advanced and subsistence societies. The greater the service share of an economy, the greater is the integration and interdependence of that society. That share has grown over time among most regions, and all national income categories as all economies have shared to some degree in world developmental growth (Table 9.2). Indeed, the expansion of the tertiary sector in modernizing East Asia, South Asia, and the Pacific was more than twice the world average in the 1990s. In Latin America and the Caribbean, services accounted for 62% of total output in 2006.

Tertiary and *service,* however, are broad and imprecise terms that cover a range of activities from neighborhood barber to World Bank president. The designations are equally applicable both to traditional low-order personal and retail activities and to higher-order knowledge-based professional services performed primarily for other businesses, not for individual consumption.

Logically, the composite tertiary category should be subdivided to distinguish between those activities answering to the daily living and support needs of individuals and local communities and those involving professional, administrative, or financial management tasks at regional, national, and international scales. Those differing levels and scope of activity represent different locational principles and quite different roles in their contribution to domestic and world economies.

To recognize such fundamental contrasts, we can usefully restrict the term "tertiary" specifically to those lower-level services largely related to day-to-day needs of people and to the usual range of functions found in smaller towns and cities worldwide. We can then assign higher-level, more specialized information research, and management activities to distinctive "quaternary" and "quinary" categories (see Figure 8.2) with quite different and distinctive characteristics and significance.

Tertiary Services

Some services are concerned with the wholesaling or retailing of goods. They fulfill the exchange function of advanced economies and provide the market transactions necessary in highly interdependent societies. In commercial economies, tertiary activities also provide vitally needed information about market demand, without which economically justifiable production decisions are impossible.

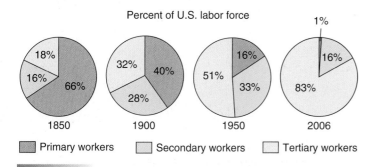

Percent of U.S. labor force

Figure 9.24 The changing sectoral allocation of the U.S. labor force is a measure of the economic development of the country. Its progression from a largely agricultural to postindustrial status is clearly evident.

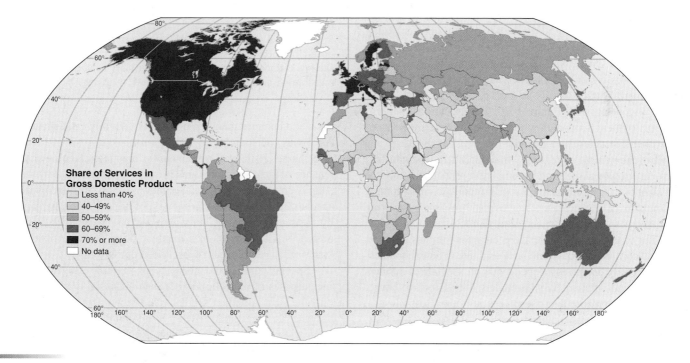

Figure 9.25 Services accounted for 69% of global GDP in 2006, up sharply from about 50% twenty years earlier. As the map documents, the contribution of services to individual national economies varied greatly; Table 9.2 indicates all national income categories shared to some degree in the expansion of service activities.

Source: World Bank, World Development Indicators.

Table 9.2

Contribution of the Service Sector to Gross Domestic Product

Country Group	Percentage of GDP		
	1960	1980	2006
Low income	32	30	52
Middle income	47	46	54
High income	54	59	72
United States	58	63	76
World		55	69

Source: Data from World Bank, World Development Indicators, 2008.

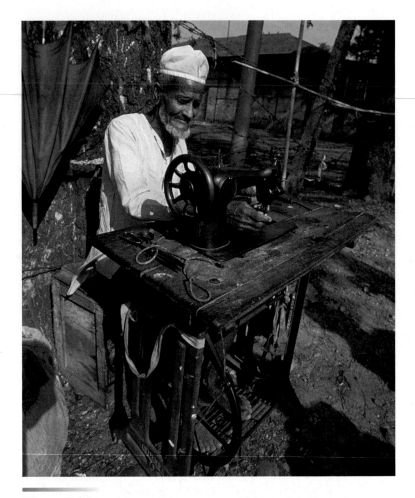

Figure 9.26 Low-level services are most efficiently and effectively performed where demand and purchasing power are concentrated, as this garment repairman in a Bangladesh city marketplace demonstrates. Such informal sector employment—street vendors, odd-job handymen, open-air dispensers of such personal services as barbering, shoe shining, clothes mending, and the like—usually escapes governmental registration and is not included in official service employment totals.

The locational controls for tertiary enterprises are rather simpler than those for the manufacturing sector. Service activities are by definition market oriented. Those dealing with transportation and communication are concerned with the placements of people and commodities to be connected or moved; their locational determinants are therefore the patterns of population distribution and the spatial structure of production and consumption.

Most tertiary activities, however, are concerned with personal and business services performed in shops, restaurants, and company and governmental offices that cluster in cities large and small. The supply of those kinds of low-level services of necessity must be identical to the spatial distribution of *effective demand*—that is, wants made meaningful through purchasing power. Retail and personal services are localized by their markets, because the production of the service and its consumption are simultaneous occurrences. Retailers and personal service providers tend to locate, therefore, where market density is greatest and multiple service demands are concentrated (Figure 9.26). Their locational patterns and the employment support they imply are important aspects of urban economic structure and are dealt with in Chapter 11.

In all of the world's increasingly interdependent postindustrial societies, the growth of the service component reflects not only the development of ever more complex social, economic, and administrative structures, it also indicates changes made possible by growing personal incomes and alterations in family structure and individual lifestyle. For example, in subsistence economies families produce, prepare, and consume food within the household. Urbanizing industrial societies have increasing dependence on specialized farmers growing food and wholesalers and retailers selling food to households that largely prepare and consume it at home. Postindustrial America increasingly opts to purchase prepared foods in restaurants, fast-food, or carry-out establishments with accelerating growth of the tertiary food service workers that change demands. People are still fed, but the employment structure has altered.

Part of the growth in the tertiary component is statistical, rather than functional. We saw in our discussion of modern industry that "outsourcing" was increasingly employed as a device to reduce costs and enhance manufacturing and assembly efficiencies. In the same way, outsourcing of services formerly provided in-house is also characteristic of current business practice. Cleaning and maintenance of factories, shops, and offices—formerly done by the company itself as part of internal operations—now are subcontracted to specialized service providers. The jobs are still done, perhaps even by the same personnel, but worker status has changed from "secondary" (as employees of a manufacturing plant, for example) to "tertiary" (as employees of a service company).

Special note should be made of *tourism*—travel undertaken for purposes of recreation rather than business. It has become not only the most important single tertiary sector activity but is, as well, the world's largest industry in jobs and total value generated. On a worldwide basis, tourism accounts for some 250 million recorded jobs and untold additional numbers in the informal economy. Altogether, 15% or more of the world's workforce is engaged in providing services to the recreational traveler, and the total economic value of tourism goods and services in 2004 reached about $4.5 trillion, or some 8% of the world's gross domestic product.

In middle- and high-income countries, tourism supports a diversified share of domestic expenditures through transportation-related costs, roadside services, entertainment, national park visits, and the like. International tourism, on the other hand, generates new income and jobs of growing importance in developing states since one-fifth of all international tourists now travel from an industrial country to a developing one. International tourist arrivals numbered 808 million in 2005, more than a third of them destined for the less developed low- and middle-income countries. The inbound flow produced some 7% of all foreign earnings of developing states in 2004 and—in the form of goods and services such as meals, lodging, and transport of foreign travelers—comprised about 45% of their total "service exports." For half of the world's 50 poorest countries, tourism had become by 2004 the leading service export sector.

Whatever the origins of tertiary employment growth, the social and structural consequences are comparable. The process of development leads to increasing labor specialization and economic interdependence within a country. That was true during the latter part of the 20th century for all economies, as Table 9.2 attests. Carried to the postindustrial stage of advanced technology-based economies and high per capita income, the service component of both the gross domestic product (see Figure 9.25) and the employed labor force rises to dominance.

Quaternary and Quinary Activities

Available statistics unfortunately do not always permit a clear distinction between *tertiary* service employment that is a reflection of daily lifestyle or corporate structural changes and the more specialized, higher-level *quaternary* and *quinary* activities.

The **quaternary** sector may be seen realistically as an advanced form of services involving specialized knowledge, technical skills, communication ability, or administrative competence. These are the tasks carried on in office buildings, elementary and university classrooms, hospitals and doctors' offices, theaters, accounting and brokerage firms, and the like. With the explosive growth in demand for and consumption of information-based services—mutual fund managers, tax consultants, software developers, statisticians, and more at near-infinite length—the quaternary sector in the most highly developed economies has replaced all primary and secondary employment as the basis for economic growth. In fact, more than half of all workers in rich economies are in the "knowledge sector" alone—in the production, storage, retrieval, or distribution of information.

Quaternary activities performed for other business organizations often embody "externalization" of specialized services similar to the outsourcing of low-level tertiary functions. The distinction between them lies in the fact that knowledge and skill-based free-standing quaternary service establishments can be spatially divorced from their clients; they are not tied to resources, affected by the environment, or necessarily localized by market. They can realize cost reductions through serving multiple clients in highly technical areas and permit client firms to utilize specialized skills and efficiencies to achieve competitive advantage without the expense of adding to their own labor force.

Often, of course, when high-level personal contacts are required, the close functional association of client and service firms within a country encourages quaternary locations and employment patterns similar to those of the headquarters distribution of the primary and secondary industries served. But the transportability of quaternary services also means that many of them can be spatially isolated from their client base. In the United States, at least, these combined trends have resulted both in the concentration of certain specialized services—merchant banking or bond underwriting, for example—in major metropolitan areas and, as well, in a regional diffusion of the quaternary sector to accompany a growing regional deconcentration of the client firm base. Similar locational tendencies have been noted even for the spatially more restricted advanced economies of, for example, England and France.

Information, administration, and the "knowledge" activities in their broadest sense are dependent on communication. Their spatial dispersion has been facilitated by the underlying technological base of most quaternary activities: electronic digital processing and telecommunication transfer of data. That technology permits many "back-office" tasks to be spatially far distant from the home office locations of either the service or client firms. Insurance claims, credit card charges, mutual fund and stock market transactions, and the like, are more efficiently and economically recorded or processed in low-rent, low-labor cost locations—often in suburbs or small towns and in rural states—than in the financial districts of major cities. Production and consumption of such services can be spatially separated in a way not feasible for tertiary, face-to-face activities.

Finally, there are the **quinary activities,** the "gold collar" professions of the chapter title, another separately recognized subdivision of the tertiary sector representing the special and highly paid skills of top business executives, government officials, research scientists, financial and legal consultants, and the like. These people find their place of business in major metropolitan centers, in and near major universities and research parks, at first-rank medical centers, and in cabinet and department-level offices of political capitals. Within their cities of concentration they may be highly localized by prestigious street addresses (Park Avenue, Wall Street) or post offices (Princeton, New Jersey), or by notable "signature" office buildings (Transamerica Building, Seagram Building). Their importance in the structure of advanced economies far outweighs their numbers.

The list of tertiary, quaternary, and quinary employment is long. Its diversity and familiarity remind us of the complexity of modern life and of how far removed we are from the subsistence economies. As societies advance economically, the share of employment and national income generated by the primary, secondary, and composite tertiary sectors continually changes; the spatial patterns of human activity reflect those changes. The shift is steadily away from production and processing, and toward the trade, personal, and professional services of the tertiary sector and the information and control activities of the quaternary and quinary. That transition is the essence of the now-familiar term *postindustrial.*

Services in World Trade

Just as service activities have been major engines of national economic growth, so too have they become an increasing factor in international trade flows and economic interdependence.

Between 1980 and 2004, services increased from 15% of total world trade to nearly 20%. The fastest growing segment of that increase was in such private services as financial, brokerage, and leasing activities, which had grown to almost 50% of all commercial services trade by the early 21st century. As in the domestic arena, rapid advances and reduced costs in information technology and electronic data transmission have been central elements in the internationalization of services, as wired and wireless communication costs have been reduced to negligible levels. Many services considered nontradable even late in the 1990s are now actively exchanged at long distance, as the growth of services offshoring clearly shows.

Developing countries have been particular beneficiaries of the new technologies. Their exports of services—valued at more than $420 billion in 2004—grew at an annual 15% rate in the 1990s, twice as fast as service exports from industrial regions, and continued at a 16% increase rate from 2000 to 2005. The increasing tradability of services has expanded the international comparative advantage of developing states in relatively labor-intensive long-distance service activities such as mass data processing, computer software development, and the like. At the same time, they have benefited from increased access to efficient, state-of-the-art equipment and techniques transferred from advanced economies.

That integration has increasingly moved to higher levels of economic and professional services. The cost and efficiency advantages of outsourcing skilled functions—such as paralegal and legal services, accountancy, medical analysis and technical services, and research and development work in a nearly unlimited range of businesses—are now widely understood and appreciated. Wired and wireless transmission of data, documents, medical and technical records, charts, X-rays, and the like make distant quaternary and higher-level services immediately and efficiently accessible. Further, many higher-level services are easily subdivided and performable in sequence or simultaneously in multiple locations. The well-known "follow the sun" practices of software developers who finish a day's tasks only to pass on work to colleagues elsewhere in the world are now increasingly used by professionals in many other fields. When the practice involves highly educated and talented specialists receiving developing world compensation levels, the cost attractions for developed country companies are irresistible. The necessary levels of education and technical expertise themselves are, to an ever greater extent, more apt to have been acquired not by expensive training in European or North American universities but rather through distant learning programs and professional school contacts through the Internet.

The concentration of computer software development around Bangalore and Hyderabad has made India a major world player in software innovation, for example, whereas there and elsewhere in that country, increasing volumes of back-office work for Western insurance, financial, and accounting companies and airlines are being performed. Customer interaction services ("call centers") formerly based in the United States are now increasingly relocated to India, employing workers trained to speak to callers in perfect American English. Claims processing for life and health insurance firms formerly were concentrated in English-speaking Caribbean states though increasingly such business process outsourcing (BPO) has shifted to India, Eastern Europe, and increasingly to China. In all such cases, the result is an acceleration in the transfer rate of technology in such expanding areas as information and telecommunications services and an increase in the rate of developing-country integration in the world economy.

Many of the current developing-country gains in international quaternary services are the result of increased foreign direct investment (FDI) in the services sector. Those flows accounted for three-fifths of all FDI in the early years of the 21st century. The majority of such investment, however, is transferred among the advanced countries themselves rather than between industrial and developing states. In either case, as transnational corporations use mainframe computers around the clock for data processing, they can exploit or eliminate time zone differences between home office countries and host countries of their affiliates. Such cross-border intrafirm service transactions are not usually recorded in balance of payment or trade statistics, but materially increase the volume of international services flows.

Despite the increasing share of global services trade held by developing countries, world trade—imports plus exports—in services is still overwhelmingly dominated by a very few of the most advanced states (Table 9.3). The country and category contrasts are great, as a comparison of the "high-income" and "low-income" groups documents. At a different level, the single small island state of Singapore had a larger 2004 share (1.9%) of world services trade than all of sub-Saharan Africa (1.4%).

Table 9.3

Shares of World Trade in Commercial Services (Exports, 2006)

Country or category	% of World
United States	14.4
United Kingdom	8.2
Germany	6.0
France	4.2
Japan	4.2
Spain	3.8
Italy	3.5
China (with Hong Kong)	3.3
High-income states	72.4
Low-income states	4.0
Sub-Saharan Africa	1.3
European Monetary Union	31.5

Sources: Data from World Bank, World Development Indicators, 2008.

(a)

(b)

Figure 9.27 (*a*) **The hierarchy of international financial centers,** topped by New York and London, indicates the tendency of highest-order quaternary activities to concentrate in a few world and national centers. (*b*) At the same time, the multiplication of offshore locations where "furtive money" avoiding regulatory control and national taxes finds refuge suggests that dispersed convenience sites also serve the international financial community. In 2002 under international pressure, most of the tax havens agreed to greater openness and less protective secrecy.

Source: Peter Dicken, Global Shift, *4th Edition. New York: Guilford Press, 2003, Figures 13.8 and 13.10.*

The same cost and skill advantages that enhance the growth and service range of quaternary firms and quinary activities on the domestic scene also operate internationally. Principal banks of all advanced countries have established foreign branches, and the world's leading banks have become major presences in the primary financial capitals. In turn, a relatively few world cities have emerged as international business and financial centers whose operations and influence are continuous and borderless, while a host of offshore banking havens have emerged to exploit gaps in regulatory controls and tax laws (Figure 9.27). Accounting firms, advertising agencies, management consulting companies, and similar establishments of primarily North American or European origin have increasingly established their international presence, with main branches located in principal business centers worldwide. Those advanced and specialized service components help swell the dominating role of the United States and European Union in the structure of world trade in services.

Summary

The spatial patterns of the world's manufacturing regions represent the landscape evidence of industrial location theories. Those theories are based on assumed regularities of human economic behavior that is responsive to profit and price motivations and on simplifying assumptions about fixed and variable costs of manufacturing and distribution. In commercial economies, market mechanisms and market prices guide investment and production decisions.

Industrial cost components considered theoretically important are raw materials, power, labor, market accessibility, and transportation. Weberian analysis argues that least-cost locations are optimal and are strongly or exclusively influenced by transportation charges. Locational interdependence theory suggests that firms situate themselves to assure a degree of market monopoly in response to the location of competitors. Profit maximization concepts accept the possibility of multiple satisficing locations within a spatial margin of profitability. Agglomeration economies and the multiplier effect may make attractive locations not otherwise predicted for individual firms, while comparative advantage may dictate production, if not location, decisions of entrepreneurs. Location concepts developed to explain industrial distributions under Fordist production constraints have been challenged as new just-in-time and flexible production systems introduce different locational considerations.

Major industrial districts of Eastern Anglo America, Western and Central Europe, Eastern Europe, and Eastern Asia contain the vast majority of global secondary industrial activity. The most advanced countries, however, are undergoing deindustrialization as newly industrializing countries with more favorable cost structures compete for markets. In the advanced economies, tertiary, quaternary, and quinary activities become more important as secondary-sector employment and share of gross national income decline. The new high-tech and postindustrial spatial patterns are not necessarily identical to those developed in response to theoretical and practical determinants of manufacturing success.

The nearly empty highway of the Monongahela Valley and the crowded expressways of high-tech and office park corridors are symbols of those changes in North America. As economic activity becomes less concerned with raw materials and freight rates, it becomes freer of the locational constraints of an older industrial society. Increasingly, skills, knowledge, communication, and population concentrations are what attract and hold the newer economic sectors in the most advanced economies. At the same time, much of the less developed world is striving for the transfer of manufacturing technology from developed economies and for the industrial growth seen as the path to their future prosperity. Those aspirations for economic development and the contrasts they imply in the technological subsystems of the countries of the world are topics of concern in Chapter 10.

 ## KEY WORDS

FOR REVIEW

1. What are the six *principles of location* outlined in this chapter? Briefly explain each and note its contribution to an entrepreneur's spatial search.

2. What is the difference between *fixed* and *variable* costs? Which of the two is of interest in the plant locational decision? What kinds of variable costs are generally reckoned as most important in locational theory?

3. What role do prices play in the allocation of resources in commercial economies? Are prices a factor in resource allocation in planned economies? What differences in locational patterns of industry are implicit in the different treatment of costs in the two economies?

4. *Raw materials, power, labor, market,* and *transportation* are "factors of location" usually considered important in industrial placement decisions. Summarize the role of each, and cite examples of where each could be decisive in a firm's location.

5. What were Weber's controlling assumptions in his theory of plant location? What "distortions" did he recognize that might alter the locational decision?

6. With respect to plant siting, in what ways do the concepts and conclusions of *locational interdependence theory* differ from those of *least-cost theory?*

7. What is the *spatial margin of profitability?* What is its significance in plant location practice?

8. How have the concepts or practices of *comparative advantage* and *outsourcing* affected the industrial structure of advanced and developing countries?

9. In what ways are the locational constraints for *high-tech* industries significantly different from those of more basic secondary activities?

10. As high-tech industries and *quaternary* and *quinary* employment become more important in the economic structure of advanced nations, what consequences for economic geographic patterns do you anticipate? Explain.

KEY CONCEPTS REVIEW

1. **What are the principal elements of locational theory, and how do different classical theories employ them?** pp. 280–282.
   Costs of raw materials, power, labor, market access, and transportation are the assumed controls governing industrial location decisions. They receive different emphases and imply different conclusions in the theories considered here. *Least-cost* (Weber) analysis concludes transport costs are the fundamental consideration; *locational interdependence* (Hotelling) considers that location of competitors determines a firm's siting decision; *profit maximization* maintains a firm should locate where profit is maximized by utilizing the substitution principle.

2. **How do agglomeration, just-in-time, comparative advantage, and TNC control affect traditional location theory outcomes?** pp. 282–288.
   By sharing infrastructure, agglomerating companies may reduce their individual total costs, while JIT supply flows reduce their inventory capital and storage charges.

   Comparative advantage recognizes that different regions or nations have different industrial cost structures. Companies utilize *outsourcing* of part of their production to exploit those differences. Transnational corporations distribute their operations based on comparative advantage: manufacturing in countries where production costs are lowest; performing research, accounting, and other service components where economical or convenient; and maintaining headquarters in locations that minimize taxes. Outsourcing and TNC practices evade the single location implications of classical location theories.

3. **What influences high-tech activity location, and what is the impact of high-tech growth on established world manufacturing regions?** pp. 296–298.
   Long-established industrial regions of Eastern Anglo America and of Western, Central, and Eastern Europe developed over time in response to predications of classical location analysis. Eastern Asia, the most recently developed major industrial region, has been influenced by both classical locational pulls and outsourcing and high-tech locational needs. High-tech industries tend to create regionally specialized agglomerations reflecting proximity to scientific research centers, technically skilled labor pools, venture capital availability, quality of life environments, and superior transport and communication facilities. Their emergence has altered traditional industrial emphases and distributional patterns.

4. **What are the functional and locational characteristics of tertiary, quaternary, and quinary service activities** pp. 298–301, **and how are they reflected in world trade patterns?** pp. 301–304.
   Tertiary industries include all nongoods production activities

and provide services to goods producers, the general community, and individuals. Subdivided for easier recognition, the general tertiary category contains: (*a*) low-level personal and professional services, retailing of goods, and the like involved in daily life and market-oriented functions. This subcategory is also called *tertiary*. (*b*) The *quaternary* sector comprises advanced forms of services suggested by the term "knowledge industries" that are performed in classrooms, hospitals, accounting and brokerage firms, corporate office buildings, etc. (*c*) *Quinary* activities include highly specialized and advanced services of research scientists, highest-level corporate executives and governmental officials, and the like. The growing world trade in services, made possible by plummeting costs of information transmission, has altered international economic relations and encouraged cultural and functional integration.

PATTERNS OF DEVELOPMENT AND CHANGE

10

Women learning about microcredit at a Karnataka, India meeting.

Key Concepts

1. Definitions and explanations of development and underdevelopment, pp. 308–313.

2. Economic measures and models of development: income, energy, farming and food, and stages of growth, pp. 313–326.

3. Noneconomic measures of development: education, services, health, and cultural satisfaction, and their relationship to economic indices, pp. 326–332.

4. Women's roles and rewards: the determinants of the pattern of gender relationships, pp. 332–336.

*T*he Hindu funeral pyres burned day and night; Muslims were buried five and more together in common graves. Countless dead cattle, buffalo, and dogs were hastily gathered and dumped in pits. In a sense, on that unseasonably cold December night in central India, all had died for economic development (Figure 10.1). Some 40% of the Indian population exists in poverty. Eager to attract modern industry to its less developed states, to create additional industrial and urban employment, and to produce domestically the chemicals essential to its drive for agricultural self-sufficiency, the Indian government in 1969 granted Union Carbide Corporation a license to manufacture pesticides at a new plant built on vacant land on the outskirts of Bhopal. A principal ingredient was deadly methyl isocyanate gas, the silent killer that escaped from its storage tank that winter night of 1984 after a sudden and unexplained buildup of its temperature and pressure.

To assure the plant's success, Union Carbide had been exempted from many local taxes, and land, water, and power costs were heavily subsidized. To yield maximum benefit to the local economy and maximum transfer of technology and skills, 50% ownership in the enterprise was retained for Indian investors along with total local control of construction and operation of the plant. The 1000 jobs were considered so important by the state and local governments that despite six accidents and one death in the years before the night of disaster, reports critical of plant safety and operation were shelved and ignored. A local official who had called for the removal of the factory to a more isolated area was himself removed from office.

By the time of the fatal accident, Bhopal had grown from 300,000 to more than 900,000 people. More than 130,000 residents lived in the slums and shantytowns they built for themselves just across the street from a factory they thought produced "plant medicine" to keep crops healthy; they were the principal victims. Before the week was over, almost 3000 people had died. Another 300,000 had been affected by exposure to the deadly poison, and perhaps 150,000 of those suffer long-term permanent disabilities—blindness, sterility, kidney and liver infections, and brain damage.

Development as a Cultural Variable

Whatever its immediate cause of equipment failure or operator error, the tragedy of Bhopal—seen by opponents of globalization as an emblem of the evils of multinationalism—is witness to the lure of economic development so eagerly sought that safety and caution are sacrificed to achieve it. That lure is nearly irresistible for those countries and regions that look to industrialization and urban employment as their deliverance from traditional economies no longer able to support their growing populations or to satisfy their hopes for an improved quality of life.

Any view of the contemporary world quickly shows great—almost unbelievable—contrasts from place to place in levels of economic development and people's material well-being. Variations in these are indicative of the tools, energy sources, and other *artifacts* (p. 46) differing societies employ in production and the kinds of economic activities in which they engage, and underlie the social organizations and behavior patterns they have developed.

Figure 10.1 Burning the dead at Bhopal. At the time of the tragedy, India was more prepared than many developing countries to accept the transfer of advanced technology. In 1984, it ranked among the top 15 countries in manufacturing output and supplied most basic domestic needs from its own industry. India still sought modern plants and processes and, particularly, industry supporting agricultural improvement and expansion.

A look around tells us that these interrelated economic and social structures are not shared by all societies; they vary between cultures and countries. The ready distinction that we make between the "Gold Coast" and the "slum" indicates that different groups have differential access to the wealth, tools, and resources of the global and national societies of which they are a part.

At an international scale, we distinguish between "advanced" or "rich" nations, such as Canada or Switzerland, and "less developed" or "poor" countries, like Bangladesh or Burkina Faso, though neither class of states may wish those adjectives applied to its circumstances. Development differentials exist within countries, too. The poverty of drought- and hunger-plagued northeastern Brazil stands in sharp contrast to the prosperous, industrialized modernity of São Paulo state or city (Figure 10.2), while in the United States, farmers of the hillsides of Appalachia live in a different economic and cultural reality than do midwestern cash grain farmers.

Dividing the Continuum: Definitions of Development

Countries display different levels of development. **Development** in that comparative sense means simply the extent to which the human and natural resources of an area or country have been brought into full productive use. It may also carry in common usage the implications of economic growth, modernization, and improvement in levels of material production and consumption. For some, it also suggests changes in traditional social, cultural, and political structures to resemble more nearly those displayed in countries and economies deemed "advanced." For others, "development" and "underdevelopment" as concepts and measurable conditions were post–World War II inventions of Western cultural thought and economic institutions. Their creation presumably permitted viewing the global scene as an orderly structure or system,

parts of which did not conform to Western standards of wealth, well-being, and achievement. Once visualized in this manner, the perceived conditions of underdevelopment could be addressed by international institutions such as the World Bank and accepted as valid by the non-Western societies to which they were applied. Those who view development theory in this negative light see it as a conscious and effective means of exerting Western influence and control over postcolonial societies.

Whatever the philosophical merits of the two viewpoints, many of the attributes of development under its usual economic definition can be quantified by reference to statistics of national production, per capita income, energy consumption, nutritional levels, labor force characteristics, and the like. Taken together, such variables might calibrate a scale of achievement against which the level of development of a single country may be compared.

Such a scale would reveal that countries lie along a continuum from the least advanced in technology or industrialization to the most developed in those and similar characteristics. Geographers (and others) attempt to classify and group countries along the continuum in ways that are conceptually revealing and spatially informative. The extremes are easy; the middle ground is less clear-cut, and the terminology referring to it is mixed.

In the broadest view, "developed" countries stand in easy contrast to the "underdeveloped," "less developed," or "developing" world. (*Developing* was the term introduced by President Harry S. Truman in 1949 as a replacement for *backward*, the unsatisfactory and unflattering reference then in use.) **Underdevelopment** from a strictly economic point of view suggests the possibility or desirability of applying additional capital, labor, or technology to the resource base of an area to permit the present population to improve its material well-being or to allow populations to increase without a deterioration in their quality of life.

The catch-all category of *underdeveloped,* however, does not tell us in which countries such efforts at improvement have occurred or been effective. With time, therefore, more refined subdivisions of development have been introduced, including such indistinctly

(a)

(b)

Figure 10.2 (*a*) The modern high-rise office and apartment buildings of prosperous São Paulo (*b*), a city that generates over one-third of Brazil's national income, stand a world apart from the poverty and peasant housing of northeastern Brazil. The evidences and benefits of "development" are not equally shared by all segments of any country or society.

relative terms as *moderately, less,* or *least developed* countries.[1] Since development is commonly understood to imply industrialization and to be reflected in improvements in national and personal income, the additional terms *newly industrializing countries* (NICs) (which we encountered in Chapter 9) and *middle income countries* have been employed. More recently, *emerging economy* has become a common designation, providing a more positive image than "underdeveloped." In a corruption of its original meaning, the term *Third World* is still occasionally applied to the developing countries as a group, though when first used that designation was a purely political reference to nations not formally aligned with a "First World" of industrialized free market (capitalist) nations or a "Second World" of centrally controlled (communist bloc) economies. And the name *Fourth World* has sometimes been attached to the UN-recognized group of least developed states. Further, some development workers have altered the term Third World to "Two-Thirds World" or "Majority World" as a reminder that most of the world's population resides in the developing countries.

Because all these terms and categories are used and clearly suggest the possibility of a country progressing from a lower to a higher developmental status, one would expect agreement on which

category is applicable to a specific country and when a state can be seen to have advanced from a lesser to a greater degree of development. Unfortunately, neither conclusion is valid. Different international agencies reach different conclusions: for the United Nations, Singapore and South Korea are "developing" or "emerging" economies; for the International Monetary Fund, they are "advanced economies." On the reasonable basis of per capita wealth (gross domestic product per head), Singapore ("emerging") in 2006 surpassed New Zealand ("advanced"), and Hong Kong and South Korea ("developing") equaled or exceeded Portugal and Greece ("developed"). And to equate "advanced" with "industrialized" economies, which is commonly done, seems meaningless because industry accounts for an ever shrinking component of the labor force in the United States.

In 1980 the contrasting terms *North* and *South* were introduced (by the Independent Commission on International D evelopment Issues, commonly called the Brandt Report[2]) as a broad and not wholly accurate generalization to emphasize the distinctions between the rich, advanced, developed countries of the Northern Hemisphere (to which Australia and New Zealand are added)—the *North*—and, roughly, all the rest of the world—the *South* (Figure 10.3). This split agreed with the United Nations classification that placed all

---

[1]In 1971, the General Assembly of the UN listed 24 "least developed" countries identified by per capita gross domestic product, share of manufacturing in GDP, and adult literacy. In later years the criteria were changed to reflect: low national income (per capita GDP under $900); weak human assets (a composite index based on health, nutrition, and educational measures); and high economic vulnerability (a composite index based on instability of agricultural production and inadequate diversification of a small economy). In addition, population of a "least developed country" had to be below 75 million. The list of those countries—also recognized as "poorest" countries has grown over the years and reached 50 in 2004. Only one country, Botswana, has ever "graduated" from the list. See Figure 10.3.

[2]*North-South: A Programme for Survival.* The Commission was established in 1977 at the suggestion of the chairman of the World Bank. Under its charge, "global issues arising from economic and social disparities of the world community" were to be studied and "ways of promoting adequate solutions to the problems involved in development" were to be proposed. The former Soviet Union was at that time included within the North; since the breakup of the Soviet Union in 1991, Georgia, Uzbekistan, and other former Soviet republics in Asia have been classified as "less developed" by the United Nations.

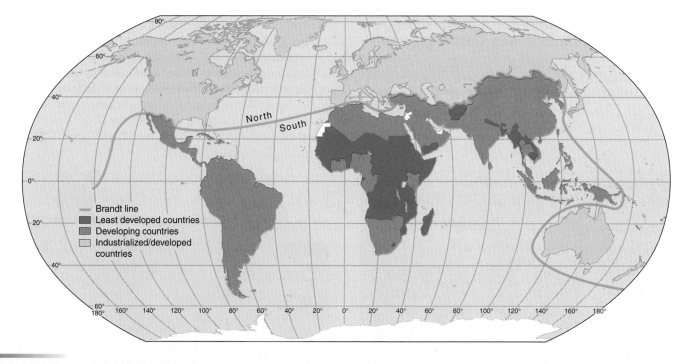

Figure 10.3 Comparative development levels. The "North–South" line of the 1980 *Brandt Report* suggested a simplified world contrast of development and underdevelopment based largely on degree of industrialization and per capita wealth recorded then. Following the dissolution of the USSR in 1991, the former Central Asian and Transcaucasian Soviet republics were added to the "South." In 2004 the United Nations Economic and Social Council and the UN Conference and Trade and Development (UNCTAD) expanded to 50 the list of "least developed countries." The inclusive category of "developing countries" ignores recent significant economic and social gains in several Asian and Latin American states, raising them now to "industrialized/developed" status. Some "least developed" states are small island countries not shown at this map scale.

Sources: UNCTAD and United Nations Development Program.

of Europe and North America, plus Australia, Japan, New Zealand, and the former USSR in a *more developed country* category, with all other states classed as *less developed countries* (LDCs).

The variety of terms devised—not all of them accurately descriptive or acceptable to those countries designated—represent honest efforts to categorize countries whose developmental circumstances are defined by a variety of economic and social measures along a continuum of specific or composite characteristics. In the remainder of this chapter, broad developmental contrasts between countries or regions will conform to the "North-South" and the UN "more developed-less developed" categorizations. Our primary attention in maps and text, however, will be given to the developing countries of the "South."

The terminology of development is usually applied to country units, but it is equally meaningful at the regional and local levels within them, for few countries are uniformly highly developed or totally undeveloped. Many emerging economies contain pockets—frequently the major urban centers—of productivity, wealth, and modernity not shared by the rest of the state. For example, Mexico is a leading NIC, but more than 50% of its industrial workers and more than 60% of value of manufacturing are located in metropolitan Mexico City. Many other parts of the country and, particularly, its Indian population, remain untouched by the development concentrated in the capital city. Similarly, the Mumbai (Bombay) agglomeration, with less than 2% of India's population, generates one-sixth of the country's gross domestic product. Even within the most advanced societies, some areas and populations remain outside the mainstream of progress and prosperity enjoyed by the majority. Fourth World deprivation is not just a whole country concept.

Explanations of Underdevelopment

It is one thing to devise categories of relative development and to assign countries to them; it is quite another to see in those categories an explanation of their spatial pattern. Why are different countries arranged as they are along the continuum of advancement? What conditions underlie their relative degrees of development? Are those conditions common to all countries at the same level of technology? And do those conditions have spatial expression and spatial explanation?

The Brandt Report hints at one frequent but simplistic spatial explanation: Development is a characteristic of the rich "North"—the midlatitudes, more precisely; poverty and underdevelopment are tropical conditions. Proponents of the latitudinal explanation support their conviction not only by reference to such topical maps as Figures 10.7, 10.10, or 10.12, but by noting that rich countries—some 35 in number—have 93% of their population resident in temperate or "snow belt" zones; 42 of the world's poorest states have 56% of their people in tropical latitudes and 18% in arid zones. They also note that observable differences in development and wealth exist within individual countries. Brazilians of the southeastern temperate highlands, for example, have average incomes several times higher than their compatriots of tropical Amazonia. Annual average incomes of Mexicans of the temperate north far exceed those of southern Yucatán. Australians of the tropical north are poorer than Australians of the temperate south. Unfortunately for the search for easy explanation, many of the poorer nations of the "South" lie partially or wholly within

the midlatitudes or at temperate elevations—Afghanistan, North Korea, and Mongolia are examples—while equatorial Singapore and Malaysia prosper. Location, many argue forcefully, is not destiny, although tropical regions admittedly face the major ecological handicaps of low agricultural productivity and high incidence of plant, animal, and human disease.

Other generalizations seem similarly inconclusive: (1) Resource poverty is cited as a limit to developmental possibilities. Although some developing countries are deficient in raw materials, others are major world suppliers of both industrial minerals and agricultural goods—bauxite, cacao, and coffee, for example. Admittedly, a developing world complaint is that their materials are underpriced in the developed world markets to which they flow or are restricted in that flow by tariffs and subsidized destination country competitors. Those, however, are matters of marketing, politics, and economics, not of resources. Further, economists have long held that reliance on natural resource wealth and exports by less developed countries undermines their prospects for growth by interfering with their development of industry and export-oriented manufacturing. (2) Overpopulation and overcrowding are frequently noted as common denominators of national underdevelopment, but Singapore prospers with some 7000 per square kilometer (18,000 per sq mi) while impoverished Mali is empty with 11 per square kilometer (28 per sq mi) (Figure 10.4). (3) Former colonial status is often blamed for present underdevelopment. The accusation is arguably valid for countries where—as in sub-Saharan Africa and southern Asia—colonizers left largely intact

Figure 10.4 Landlocked and subject to severe droughts, Mali is one of the poorest of the "least developed" countries. Low densities of population are not necessarily related to prosperity, or high densities to poverty. Mali has only 11 people per square kilometer (28 per sq mi); Japan has 338 per square kilometer (876 per sq mi). These Dogon women crossing a parched millet field near Sanga are on their way to get water—a time- and energy-consuming daily task for many least developed country women. Even in more humid South Africa, rural women on average spend 3 hours and 10 minutes each day fetching water, according to a government survey.

the indigenous populations but created political structures and physical infrastructures suited more for exploitation for mother country profit than for balanced economic, social, and political development for the long-term benefit of the colony itself. In cases in which the colonists were expatriates of an already advanced state and largely replaced the original inhabitants—as in the ex-colonies of Australia, New Zealand, Canada, or the United States—the association of colonial past with present underdevelopment is, of course, inapplicable.

Although there appears to be no single, simple explanation of Third World status, just as there is no single measure of underdevelopment that accounts for every Third World case, the Harvard Institute for International Development did attempt to quantify differences in national economic development. It argued that "physical geography" is one of four factors influencing global patterns of growth; the least developed countries are almost without exception located in ecological zones that pose serious health conditions—including much shorter life spans—not found in the midlatitudes and have agricultural limitations that are very different from those of wealthy states. The other three factors are initial economic level, government policy, and demographic change. The Institute's conclusions were that landlocked countries grew more slowly than coastal economies, that—because of poor health and unproductive farming—tropical states were slower to develop than temperate zone ones, and that sparse natural resources and transport isolation inhibited growth possibilities and rates.

These physical differences and environmental limitations, the Institute found, were far less explanatory of national growth rates than were market economies, prudent fiscal policies, and the rule of laws prohibiting corruption, breach of contract, expropriation of property, and the like. These are circumstances and controls independent of locational or resource differentials. That conclusion is buttressed by a United Nations report concluding that "good government," including protection of property rights under a stable political and legal system, is the top priority in poverty-fighting and the key to sustainable development. These are, however, conditions reflective of western market economy standards that are not necessarily acceptable to all cultures.

The Core-Periphery Argument

Core-periphery models are based on the observation that within many spatial systems sharp territorial contrasts exist in wealth, economic advancement, and growth—in "development"—between economic heartlands and outlying subordinate zones. Wealthy urban cores and depressed rural peripheries, or prospering "high-tech" concentrations and declining "rust belts," are contrasts found in many developed countries. On the international scene, core-periphery contrasts are discerned between, particularly, Western Europe, Japan, and the United States as prosperous cores and the Fourth World as underdeveloped periphery. At all spatial scales, the models assume that at least partially and temporarily the growth and prosperity of core regions is at the expense of exploited peripheral zones.

That conclusion is drawn from the observation that linkages and interactions exist between the contrasting parts of the system.

As one variant of the model suggests, if for any reason (perhaps a new industrial process or product) one section of a country experiences accelerated economic development, that section by its expanding prosperity becomes increasingly attractive for investors and other entrepreneurs. Assuming national investment capital is limited, growth in the developing core must come at the expense of the peripheries of the country.

A process of **circular and cumulative causation** thus set in motion continues to polarize development and, according to economist Gunnar Myrdal, leads to a permanent division between prosperous (and dominating) cores and depressed (and exploited) peripheral districts that are milked of surplus labor, raw materials, and profits. In its *dependency theory* form (p. 326), this version of the core-periphery argument sees the developing world as effectively held captive by the leading industrial nations. It is drained of wealth and deprived of growth by remaining largely a food and raw material exporter and an importer of manufactured commodities—and frequently suffering price discrimination in both their sales and purchases. A condition of *neocolonialism* is said to exist in which economic and even political control is exercised by developed states over the economies and societies of legally independent countries of the underdeveloped world.

A more hopeful variant of the model observes that regional income inequalities exist within all countries but that they tend to be greater in less developed countries than in the developed ones. That is, within market economies, income disparities tend to be reduced as developmental levels increase. Eventually, it is argued, income convergence will occur as **trickle-down effects,** or **spread effects,** work to diffuse benefits outward from the center in the form of higher prices paid for needed materials or through the dispersion of technology to branch plants or contract suppliers in lower-cost regions of production. On the international scale, such spread effects should work to reduce the dominance of formerly exploitative cores and equalize incomes between world regions. The increasing wealth of the newly industrializing economies and the penetration of European and American markets by, for example, Asian-produced goods ranging from cheap textiles to expensive automobiles and high-technology electronics are cited in support of this model variant.

Core-periphery models stress economic relationships and spatial patterns of control over production and trade. Indeed, the usual measures and comparisons of development are stated in economic terms. As we shall see later in this chapter, noneconomic measures may also be employed, though usually not without reference to their relationships to national or per capita income or to other measures of wealth and productivity. We shall also see that composite measures of developmental level are perhaps more useful and meaningful than those restricted to single factors or solely to matters of either economy or social welfare.

And finally, we should remember that "development" is a culturally relative term. It is usually interpreted in western, democratic, market economy terms that presumably can be generalized to apply to all societies. Others insist that it must be seen against the background of diverse social, material, and environmental conditions that differently shape cultural and economic aspirations of different peoples, many of whom specifically reject those western cultural and economic standards.

Millennium Development Goals

In September 2000, 189 member states of the United Nations adopted the Millennium Declaration to help the world's poorest countries make measured progress toward reducing or eliminating within their borders by 2015 extreme poverty in its many social and economic dimensions. The eight interlinked goals and 18 associated measurement targets they identified—the Millennium Development Goals (MDGs)—were the outgrowth of a series of international conferences in the 1990s on children, population and development, human rights, women, social development, AIDs, and development financing.

The MDGs are quantified objectives for addressing extreme poverty in its many guises; they aim to eradicate extreme hunger and monetary poverty; achieve universal primary education; promote gender equality and empower women; reduce child mortality; improve maternal health; combat HIV/AIDs, malaria, and other diseases; ensure environmental sustainability; and create a global partnership for development. The achievement of the goals, according to the founding document, depends on a commitment by developing countries to take primary responsibility for their own development by strengthening their financial management and controls, effectively mobilizing their local resources, and initiating or improving the delivery of basic public services; key actions are to respect human rights and root out corruption. Donor (advanced) countries were charged not only with providing funds adequate to reach the MDGs but also to ensure that aid-recipient countries create "transparent, credible, and properly costed" national development strategies.

Although significant progress in achieving many of the goals has been made, that progress has not been uniform across the world or the individual goals. Assessments by the UN's Human Development Program leaders in 2005 were that the "overall report card makes for depressing reading" and that many countries were failing to make steady (or any) progress toward achieving the MDGs or reducing the already deep inequalities between and within countries. A September 2005 "Millennium + 5" summit expressed disappointment in progress made since the original Millennium agreement in 2000 and failed to agree on a strong program addressing the developing world's continuing developmental needs. Nevertheless, the MDGs and their target measures remain as progress guidelines and benchmarks followed by international agencies.

Economic Measures of Development

Two common measures are used to gauge economic activity—gross domestic product (GDP), which was introduced in Chapters 8 and 9, and **gross national income (GNI)**. Gross domestic product is the total market value of all final goods and services produced annually within the borders of a country. Gross national income adds to GDP the total foreign income earned by its citizens (gross national income was formerly known as gross national product). To compare the living standards in different countries, we make three adjustments to GNI. First we convert each country's currency into a single measure, typically U.S. dollar equivalents. Second, we divide by the number of people in a country to get GNI per capita. Third, we note that market rates of currency exchange fluctuate with business cycles and trading patterns and do not necessarily correspond to prices in a particular country. For example, you may have noticed that prices for most goods and services are lower in developing countries, and if you've traveled to Scandinavia you've noticed that prices are much higher than in the United States. Thus, a **purchasing power parity (PPP)** correction is often applied to GNI to account for price differences. Let's say a Big Mac costs $3.50 in the United States and 35 pesos in Mexico. Then, in terms of purchasing power, one peso equals 10 cents. Of course, the actual purchasing power parity calculation uses a bundle of goods rather than Big Macs.

The developing low- and middle-income countries as a group have made significant progress along the continuum of economic development. Between 1990 and 2004, their economies collectively grew at an average annual rate of 4.2% compared to 2.5% per year for the industrial states. As a result of those growth differentials and of overall changes in the composition of their gross domestic products, the less developed states were in a decisively different relative position early in the 21st century than they were a century earlier. In 1913, on the eve of World War I, the 20 or so countries now known as the rich industrial economies produced almost 80% of world manufacturing. In 1950, the United States alone accounted for around half of world output, about the share produced by all the developed economies together in 2002.

The last half of the 20th and early years of the 21st century, indeed, witnessed a remarkable expansion of the "core" of economically advanced states and a substantial reordering of world economic power and national rankings. By the purchasing power measure the emerging world—the South—now accounts for more than half of global economic output; even by current exchange rates, the former "underdeveloped" world now contributes nearly 30% of world production and accounted for half the growth in global output in 2006. By a variety of measures, economic power is shifting away from the more developed economies of the North (North America, western Europe, Japan, and Australasia, basically) toward the emerging states, particularly in Asia. By 2006, developing countries held the majority of the world's foreign exchange reserves, consumed more than half of the world's energy, and accounted for nearly 45% of all exports (up from 20% in 1970). That growing developing world prosperity is rather broadly spread. Africa, of course, lags seriously behind, the widely recognized new powerhouses of China, Brazil, India, and Russia.

Particularly after 1950, the spread effects of technology transfer, industrialization, and expanding world trade substantially reduced—though have not yet eliminated—the core-periphery contrasts in productivity and structure of gross domestic product that formerly seemed insurmountably great. Significantly, manufactured goods early in 2006 accounted for about 60% of all merchandise exports of developing countries as a group—including the rapidly industrializing and exporting economies of the East Asian "tigers" (fast-growing economies, such as Singapore, South Korea, and Taiwan)—up from only 5% in 1955. Their growing importance in manufacturing exports clearly marks the restructuring of the economies of many developing states away from subsistence agriculture and primary commodity production. Not all developing regions have experienced that restructuring, of course; the share of manufacturing in exports for sub-Saharan Africa was still less than one-third in 2006.

In 1965, 30% of the developing countries' combined income came from agriculture and another 30% from industry. By 2006, agriculture's share had dropped to 10% while industry grew to account for nearly 40% of their collective national earnings; over the same span, services increased from less than 40% to more than one-half of earnings. Not all of the employment shifts and structural changes within developing countries, however, are accounted for by official statistics. In all countries, at least a portion of goods and services is produced and workers supported by the **informal** (shadow, gray, underground) **economy.**

The informal economy in developing countries as a group, a 2002 World Bank study estimated, was equivalent to 41% of their official gross domestic product. Even in the rich West European countries, the share of the informal economy reached 18%. The proportion of economic activity escaping official notice and thus not part of published GNI totals varies greatly among regions and states.

In Africa, the average size of the informal economy was 42% of GNI. Zimbabwe, Tanzania, and Nigeria had by far the largest informal sector with between 58% and 59% of GNI; the figure dropped to 28% in South Africa. In Asia, Thailand at 53% of GNI is the developing country most affected by informal sector activity; China (13%) and Vietnam (16%) are the least impacted. Bolivia, at 67% of GNI, is the gray economy leader in Latin America, where the informal sector accounted on average for 41% of gross national income. Whether undertaken to avoid taxes or to hide illegal enterprises or whether it simply reflects the efforts and employment of those unable to find jobs with registered businesses, informal economic activity obviously distorts government statistics on total employment and GDP and their agricultural, industrial, and service components (Figure 10.5).

The International Monetary Fund and the World Bank now use purchasing power parity, which takes account of what money actually buys in each country. When the new PPP measure was introduced in 1993, it gave a clearer picture of the world economy and radically changed traditional assessments of it. Immediately, the relative economic importance of the emerging economies

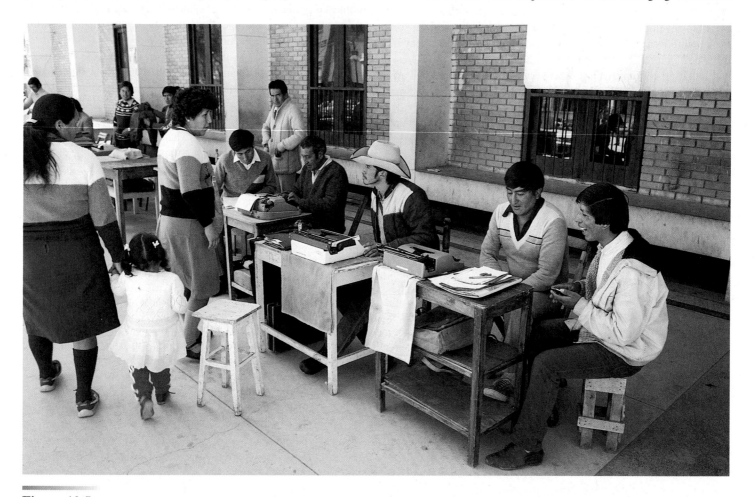

Figure 10.5 "Informal sector" initiative by street typists for hire in Huancayo, Peru. Between 1965 and 2000, the percentage of the labor force in agriculture dropped precipitously in all countries of Latin America. That decline was not matched by a proportional increase in jobs in manufacturing and other industries. In Peru, employment in agriculture fell from 50% to less than 8% of the total, but the share of workers in industry remained constant at about 20%. Many of the former rural workers found urban work in the informal or shadow economy sector, the generator of 60% of all new Latin American jobs in the 1990s. They became errand runners, street vendors, odd-job handymen, open-air dispensers of such personal services as barbering, shoe shining, clothes mending, letter-writing, and the like, as well as unregistered workers in small-scale construction and repair shops. For Latin America as a whole, the UN reports, 74% of the female and 55% of the male labor force worked in the informal economy early in this century. For developing countries as a group, informal sector employment made up 37% of total jobs; it reached 45% in Africa and 33% in Asia. See also Figure 9.26.

ballooned. Using purchasing power parity, East Asia's share of world 2004 output jumped from 7% to 18%, and the revised 2005 contribution for all developing states vaulted from one-quarter to slightly more than one-half. That is, the developing economies are finally returning to the dominant economic position they held for most of history before being overwhelmed by the productive capacity of the industrialized states in the late 19th century; even as late as 1820, the emerging economies accounted for more than 70% of global GDP at PPP. If present trends hold, the World Bank forecasts, by 2020 the current "rich world's" share of global output could shrink to less than two-fifths.

Impressive as the shifts in global economic balance between the industrial and developing countries may be, they do little to reduce the contrasts that remain between the richest of the North and the poorest of the South. While as a group the least developed and developing countries—187 of them by UN definition—are catching up to the developed world in total productivity, a good part of the aggregate gain is lost in per capita terms (see "Poverty and Development"). With the South's (excluding China) population increasing at nearly a 2% per annum rate, growing national prosperity has to be—at least statistically—divided among an increasing number of claimants. In the early 1990s, the South

Poverty and Development

According to the World Bank and the United Nations Human Development Programme (UNDP), of the world's 6.2 billion people (2002), 2.6 billion—some 42%—lived on less than $2.00 per day. More than 1 billion—about a sixth of the world total—experienced "absolute poverty." These folk existed on an income of less than $1 per day ($440 per year in purchasing power parity), a figure below which, it is usually reckoned, people are unable to buy adequate food, shelter, and other necessities. As a hopeful measure of progress, this is a smaller number and a smaller percentage of the world's population than were abjectly poor in 1990. About 43% of the very poor lived in South Asia and another 29% in sub-Saharan Africa. East Asia and the Pacific accounted for 21% of those in absolute poverty and Latin America and the Caribbean added another 5%.

Although the dollar definition of poverty is applied as if it were a worldwide constant, in reality poverty is comprised of two separate elements that are regional variables. One of these is the reasonably objective observation that you are impoverished if you can't afford a minimum standard of nutrition. The other element is more subjective and equates poverty with inability to buy basic goods that other citizens of your country regard as necessities. The UNDP has attempted to combine these separate elements in devising a human poverty index (HPI) that, first, identifies poverty populations by the simple income test and then concentrates on measuring deprivation in three essential dimensions of human life: longevity (percentage of people not expected to live to age 40); knowledge (percentage of adults who are illiterate); and deprivation in living standards (measured by access to safe water, access to health services, and percentage of malnourished children under 5).

By these standards, the world made significant progress in reducing human poverty in the 1990s. In developing countries, the percentage of newly born people not expected to survive to age 40 declined from 20% to 14% during the decade. Adult illiteracy dropped from 35% to 28% and access to safe water increased from 68% to 78%. The purchasing power income poverty rate, even at the $1-a-day standard, dropped from 17% of world population in 1970 to about 7% in 2000. Income poverty declined during the 1990s in every developing region, though the decline was not uniform and ranged from 11 percentage points in East Asia to only 0.3 percentage points in sub-Saharan Africa.

The UNDP reports that some countries have made notable progress. Malaysia reduced income absolute poverty (the $1 per day level) from 50% in 1960 to less than 2% in 2003, China from 33% in 1978 to 17%, and India from 54% in 1974 to 35% in 2003. In contrast, in Niger, the African country lowest on the human poverty index scale in 2003, more than 60% of residents lived in conditions of absolute poverty, though Mali held the record that year with 72.3% of its population living on less than $1 a day and 90.6% below the $2 a day level. In the Western Hemisphere, Haiti has the highest HPI, and Guatemala is the Latin American poverty leader. In Asia, Bangladesh is worst off among South Asian states and Yemen leads the Arab world.

Poverty is an areal variable within countries. In Burkina Faso and Zambia, rural poverty fell and urban poverty rose during the 1990s. In Mexico between 1989 and 1994, overall poverty declined modestly, but there were large variations across regions within the country. In Thailand, the incidence of poverty in the rural northeast was almost double the national

average in 1992. The World Bank notes that, in general, poverty tends to be associated with distance from cities and the seacoast.

Africa is a continuing problem region. Because of its rapid population growth, stagnation or decline in per capita food production, weakness in infrastructure and facilities systems, periodic drought, and devastating civil wars, in sub-Saharan Africa the number of very poor people increased from 217 million in 1987 to more than 300 million in 2002. The World Bank projects that the sub-Saharan region will have 360 million people or 40% of its population in poverty in 2010.

One key to improving both the economic and social lot of the "poorest of the poor," the World Bank and United Nations argue, is to target public spending on their special needs of education and health care and to pursue patterns of investment and economic growth that can productively employ the underutilized and growing labor force so abundant in the least developed countries. These identified socio-economic needs are important elements in the UN's interlocked Millennium Development Goals. Another needed solution, many argue, is for rich creditor countries and international lending agencies to provide relief from the massive burden of interest and principal repayments owed by the group of 38 or more highly indebted poor countries (HIPCs).[a] Major steps to that goal have been taken by the International Monetary Fund, the World Bank, and the finance ministers of large donor countries. In 2005 they reached agreement on plans to erase as much as $55 billion in debt owed by impoverished nations based on their per capita incomes and adherence to "sound" economic policies and standards of good government.

---

[a]See "Does Foreign Aid Help?", p. 325.

had to apportion its recalculated one-third share of *gross global product* (the total value of goods and services produced by the world economy) among more than three-fourths of world population. By 2005, the South's population had increased by one billion to more than 80% of the world total. Because of that growth, the number of persons worldwide living in poverty hardly changed during the interim. And the very rich, in contrast, continue to get richer. Average income in the richest 20 countries early in the century was 39 times the average in the poorest 20 (at market rates of exchange)—a gap that had doubled over the preceding 40 years, and the average income of the top 20% of the world's population was about 50 times the average income of the bottom 20%.

As core-periphery theorists suggest, the industrial economies still (2004) account for more than 70% of world total and merchandise exports and dominate the international financial markets. Further, the South's economies are far more (though decreasingly) oriented toward raw material production than are those of the developed world. For example, in 1965, more than 80% of the exports from developing countries—but less than one-third of those from industrial market countries—were minerals and agricultural products. By 2002, the disparity had materially lessened; minerals and agricultural goods represented only 25% by value of the developing countries'[3] merchandise exports and 10% of those from industrial market economies.

The Diffusion of Technology

Composite figures mask the disparities that exist within the ranks of developing countries. The world's 50 "least developed" states in 2003 produced just 0.6% of global wealth, measured at market exchange rates. In contrast, the small, industrialized "four tigers"—Hong Kong, Singapore, South Korea, and Taiwan—alone contributed more than 3% to gross world product. Obviously, there are differences within the developing world in the successful application of technology to the creation of wealth.

Technology refers to the totality of tools and methods available to and used by a culture group in producing items essential to its subsistence and comfort. We saw in Chapter 2 how in antiquity there emerged *culture hearths*—centers of technological innovation, of new ideas and techniques that diffused or were carried out from the core region. Innovation is rarely a single event; as cultures advance, needs multiply and different solutions develop to meet expanding requirements. The ancient hearths (see Figure 2.15) were locales of such multiple invention and innovation. Their modern counterparts are the highly urbanized, industrialized advanced nations whose creativity is recorded by patent registrations and product and process introductions. The changing rate of innovation over time is suggested by Figure 2.20.

In all periods there has existed between hearths and outlying regions a **technology gap,** a contrast in the range and productivity of artifacts introduced at the core and those known or employed at the periphery. That gap widened at an accelerating rate as technology moved farther away from the shared knowledge of earlier periods. During the Industrial Revolution, the technological distance between cottage hand looms of 18th-century English villagers and the power looms of their neighboring factories was one of

Figure 10.6 Early in the Industrial Revolution, new techniques that diffused most readily from the English hearth were those close to handicraft production processes. In some industries, the important innovation was the adoption of power and volume production, not radically new machines or products. For textiles and similar light industries, capital requirements were low and workers required little training in new skills. The picture shows carding, drawing, and spinning machinery built by memory in the United States in 1790 by Samuel Slater, an Englishman who introduced the new technology despite British prohibitions on exports of drawings or models of it.

only moderate degree (Figure 10.6). Far greater is the gap between the range of traditional crafts known throughout the world and the modern technologies of the most advanced societies. It is much more difficult now for a less developed society to advance to the "state of the art" by its own efforts than it was for British colonies or the rest of Europe to re-create the textile or iron-making industries first developed in England.

The persistence and expansion of the technology gap suggest that the idea of **cultural convergence**—the increasing similarity in technologies and ways of life among societies at the same levels of development—does not as well unite the most and the least advanced economies. In the modern world, as we saw in Chapter 2 (p. 46), there is a widespread sharing of technologies, organizational forms, and developed cultural traits. But not all countries are at the same developmental state. Not all are equally able to draw on advanced technology to create the same products with identical efficiency and quality, although there is increasing awareness of the existence of those products and the benefits of their use.

The technology gap matters. At any given level of technology, the resources of an area will have a limited population supporting capacity. As population growth approaches or exceeds those limits, as it has in many less developed areas of the globe, poverty, famine, and political and social upheaval can result. Understandably, all countries aspire to expand their resource base, increase its support levels through application of improved technologies, or enter more fully into an income-producing exchange relationship with other world regions through economic development. Their objective is a **technology transfer,** placing in their own territory and under their own control the productive plants and processes marking the more advanced countries. The chemical plant of Bhopal was one item in a technology transfer sought by the state of Madhya Pradesh and the government of India, one step in the process of moving the region and country further along the continuum from less developed to more developed status.

---

[3]Excluding high-income petroleum exporting countries.

Not all technology, of course, is equally transferable. Computers, information management techniques, cell phones, and the like easily make the move between advanced and emerging economies. Other technologies, particularly in the life sciences, materials innovation, and energy, are more specific to the markets, monetary resources, and needs of the rich countries and not adapted to those of the less developed states. Even where transfer is feasible, imported innovations may require domestic markets sufficient to justify their costs, markets that poor countries will not possess at their current national income levels. And the purchase of technology presumes recipient country export earnings sufficient to pay for it, again a condition not met by the poorest states.

Developing countries have, in a form of reverse flow, contributed to scientific and engineering innovation. Advanced technologies and scientific breakthroughs depend on public and private research institutions and corporate research and development departments common in the rich states. Many of the advances produced by those agencies have been made by poor-country scientists working in the rich-country laboratories. Indian and Chinese technologists and engineers, for example, are major components in the workforce of all the high-tech concentrations discussed in Chapter 9 (p. 296), though many are increasingly returning to do innovative research and development in their home countries.

The Complex of Development

Technology transfer is only one aspect of economic development. The process as a whole intricately affects all facets of social and economic life. The terms *level of living* and *standard of living* bring to mind some of the ways in which economic advancement implies both technological and societal change, including amount of personal income, levels of education, food consumption, life expectancy, and the availability of health care. The complexity of the occupational structure, the degree of specialization in jobs, the ways in which natural resources are used, and the level of industrialization are also measures of development and of the innovation or adoption of technology within a society.

Relative Characteristics of Development

Less Developed

1. Per capita incomes are low, and capital is scarce.

2. Wealth is unevenly distributed within individual countries (e.g., in Colombia 2.6% of population owns 40% of the national wealth, and in Gabon 1% owns 56% of total wealth).

3. Primary industries (farming, forestry, quarrying, mining, fishing) dominate national economies.

4. High proportion (more than 50%) of the labor force is engaged in agriculture.

5. Farming is mostly at the subsistence level and is characterized by hand labor methods and underemployment. Farm holdings are small, mechanization is limited, and crop yields are low.

6. Populations are dominantly rural, though impoverished urban numbers are growing.

7. Birth and death rates are high, and life expectancy is low. There tends to be a high proportion of children. Rates of natural increase are high.

8. Inadequate or unbalanced diets resulting from a relatively low consumption of protein; hunger and malnutrition are common.

9. Infectious, respiratory, and parasitic diseases are common; medical services are poor.

10. Overcrowding, poor housing, few public services, and bad sanitation yield poor social conditions.

11. Poor educational facilities and high levels of illiteracy hinder scientific and technological advancement. (In sub-Saharan Africa, 40% of adult population is illiterate.)

12. Women may be held in inferior position in society.

Developed

1. Per capita incomes are high, and capital is readily available.

2. Wealth within individual countries is comparatively evenly distributed (e.g., in Canada, 10% of the population owns 24% of national wealth).

3. Manufacturing and service industries dominate national economies.

4. Very small proportion (less than 10%) of population is engaged in agriculture.

5. Farming is mostly commercial, efficient, and highly mechanized.

Farm holdings are generally large, and crop yields are high.

6. Populations are predominantly urban, with nearly 80% living in towns and cities.

7. Birth and death rates are low, and life expectancy is high. There is often a high proportion of people over 65 years of age. Rates of natural increase are low.

8. Generally adequate supplies of food and balanced diets; overeating is sometimes a problem.

9. Primary diseases are related to age and lifestyle; good medical services are available.

10. Social conditions are generally good, with adequate housing space and a high level of public health facilities and sanitation.

11. Highly developed educational facilities and low levels of illiteracy are the norm. Technical proficiency is advanced.

12. Women are increasingly treated on equal terms with men.

Source: Adapted from *Elements of Human Geography*, 2nd ed. by Charles Whynn-Hammond. p. 171. Copyright 1985 by Taylor & Francis Books (UK).

The generalized summary table "Relative Characteristics of Development" outlines some of the many implications and attributes of development. It also makes clear why no single measure is sufficient to assess the comparative stage of economic development or level of living of a society. We might, for example, simplistically assume that national contrasts in average per capita income would serve to measure the level of living in all of its aspects; but personal income figures are particularly hard to compare across national borders. An income of (U.S.) $50,000 in Sweden is taxed at a much higher rate than a similar income in the United States. But social welfare programs, higher education, and medicine receive greater central governmental funding in Sweden; the American family must set aside a larger portion of its income for such services.

Further, identical incomes will be spent on different amounts and types of goods and services in different countries. Americans, because of lower prices, spend a smaller proportion of their personal income on food than do the residents of most European states or Japan; those living in upper latitudes must buy fuel and heavy clothing not necessary in tropical household budgets; and price levels may vary widely in different economies for similar essential goods. Of course, national average personal income figures do not indicate how earnings are distributed among the citizenry. In some countries, the wealthiest 5% of the population control more than 50% of the income, whereas in others, revenues are more uniformly distributed.

To broaden the limited view afforded by per capita income figures, therefore, a variety of more specific and descriptive measures has been employed to suggest national levels of development. Each such measure can present only part of a total picture of developmental status. Taken together, however, the comparative criteria tend to show a high, but not perfect, correlation that collectively supports the accepted North-South global split. The primarily economic measures discussed here are among those commonly accepted as most revealing of the relative progress of countries of the "South" along the scale of development. They are (1) gross national income and purchasing power parity (PPP) per capita, (2) per capita energy consumption, (3) percent of the workforce engaged in agriculture, and (4) calorie intake per capita.

Gross National Income and PPP per Capita

Gross national income (GNI) per capita is a frequently used indicator of a country's economic performance (Figure 10.7). Like any other single index of development, gross national income tells only part of a complex story. Indeed, its concept, and that of the related gross domestic product, is under increasing attack for its assumed distortions of reality. One group, including environmentalists, argues that the GNI overstates the wealth of a society by ignoring the cost of ecological damage and the drain modern economies place on natural resources. An opposing group holds that GNI understates the strength of economic growth by overlooking much of the quality and productivity improvements brought by technology (safer automobiles, faster, more powerful computers, etc.).

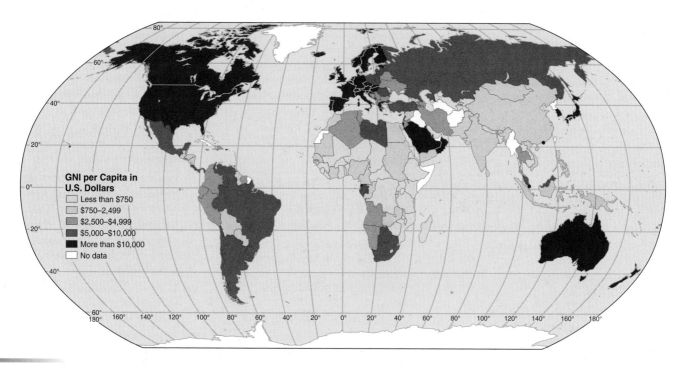

Figure 10.7 Gross national income per capita, 2007. GNI per capita is a frequently employed summary of degree of economic advancement, though high incomes in sparsely populated, oil-rich countries may not have the same meaning in developmental terms as do comparable per capita values in industrially advance states. The map implies an unrealistic precision. For many states, when uncertain GNI is divided by unreliable population totals, the resulting GNI per capita is at best a rough approximation that varies between reporting agencies. A comparison of this map and Figure 10.10 presents an interesting study in regional contrasts.

Sources: Data from World Bank and Population Reference Bureau.

Of course, gross national income per capita is not a personal income figure, but simply a calculated assignment of each individual's share of a national total. Change in total population or in total national income will alter the average per capita figure but need have no impact on the personal finances of any individual citizen. Nor is per capita GNI a totally realistic summary of developmental status. It tends to distort a more inclusive picture of underdevelopment by overemphasizing the purely monetary circumstances of countries and not accurately representing the economic circumstances of countries with dominantly subsistence economies, for example, many of the nations of Asia and Africa with low income figures.

As expected, the countries with the highest GNI per capita are those in northwestern Europe, where the Industrial Revolution began, and in the midlatitude colonial areas—North America, Australia, and New Zealand—to which the new technologies were first transplanted. In the middle position are found many of the countries of Latin America and of southern and eastern Europe. Large sections of Africa and Asia, in contrast, are at the low end of average income figures, since the money value of the nontraded goods and services that subsistence farmers provide for themselves and their communities goes unrecorded in the GNI. That problem is partly resolved, you will recall, by calculating what are sometimes called "real per capita gross domestic products," but more usually summarized as *purchasing power parities* (see Figure 10.8 and p. 313).

Energy Consumption per Capita

Per capita energy consumption is a common measure of technological advancement of nations because it loosely correlates with per capita income, degree of industrialization, and use of advanced technology. In fact, the industrialized countries use about 10 times more energy on a per capita basis than developing economies do. The consumption rather than the production of energy is the concern. Many of the highly developed countries consume large amounts of energy but produce relatively little of it. Japan, for example, must import from abroad the energy supplies its domestic resource base lacks. In contrast, many less developed countries have very high per capita or total energy production figures but primarily export the resource (petroleum). Libya, Nigeria, and Brunei are cases in point. Most of the less and least developed countries depend less on commercial forms of inanimate energy (petroleum, coal, lignite, natural gas, hydropower, etc.) than they do on animate energy (human and animal labor) and the firewood, crop residues, dung, peat, and other domestic fuels on which subsistence populations must depend. Both rudimentary and some advanced technologies are locally and gradually improving that picture as solar stoves, waste matter converters (Figure 10.9), solar photovoltaic panels, and the like come into use.

The advanced countries developed their economic strength through the use of cheap energy and its application to industrial

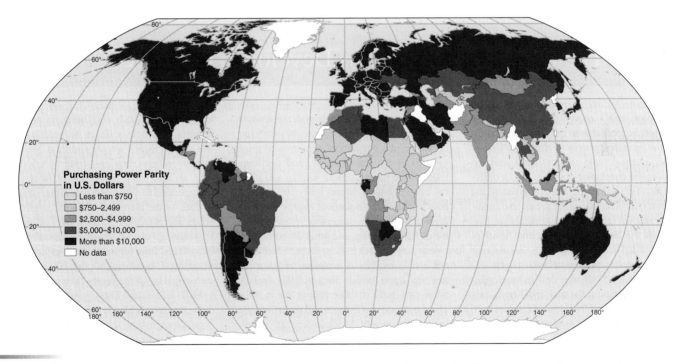

Figure 10.8 **Purchasing power parity (PPP), 2007.** When local currency measures of gross national income or gross domestic product are converted into purchasing power parities, there is a twofold revision of the usual view of world economic status. The first result is a sharp increase in developing countries' share of total world output. Second, the abject poverty suggested by per capita gross national income or gross domestic product is seen to be much reduced in many developing countries. India, for example, showed a 2007 gross national income per capita at market exchange rates of $950; in purchasing power parity, the figure rose to $2740. Compare this map with Figure 10.7 to see how PPP changes our impressions of some countries' economic status.

Sources: Data from World Bank and United Nations.

A widely cited model for economic advancement was proposed in 1960 by W. W. Rostow (1916–2003). Generalizing on the "sweep of modern history," Rostow theorized that all developing economies may pass through five successive stages of growth and advancement. *Traditional societies* of subsistence agriculture, low technology levels, and poorly developed commercial economies can have only low productivity per capita. The *preconditions for takeoff* are established when those societies, led by an enterprising elite, begin to organize as political rather than kinship units and to invest in transportation systems and other productive and supportive infrastructure.

The *takeoff* to sustained growth is the critical developmental stage, lasting perhaps 20 to 30 years, during which rates of investment increase, new industries are established, resources are exploited, and growth becomes the expected norm. The *drive to maturity* sees the application of modern technology to all phases of economic activity; diversification carries the economy beyond the industrial emphases first triggering growth, and the economy becomes increasingly self-sufficient. Finally,

when consumer goods and services begin to rival heavy industry as leading economic sectors and most of the population has consumption levels far above basic needs, the economy has completed its transition to the *age of mass consumption*. More recently—and referring to most advanced economies (and discussed in Chapter 9)—a sixth stage, the *postindustrial,* has been recognized. Services replace industry as the principal sector of the economy, professional and technical skills assume preeminence in the labor force, and information replaces energy as the key productive resource.

Rostow's expectations of an inevitable progression of development proved illusory. Many LDCs remain locked in one of the first two stages of his model, unable to achieve the takeoff to self-sustained growth despite importation of technology and of foreign aid investment funds from the more developed world (see "Does Foreign Aid Help?"). Indeed, it has become apparent to many observers that despite the efforts of the world community, the development gap between the most and the least advanced countries may widen rather than narrow over time. A case in point is sub-Saharan

Geography and Public Policy

Does Foreign Aid Help?

A 1998 World Bank report on "Assessing Aid" concluded that the raw correlation between rich country aid and developing country growth is near zero. Simply put, more aid does not mean more growth, certainly not for countries with "bad" economic policies (high inflation, large budget deficits, corrupt bureaucracy); for them, the report claims, aid actually retards growth and does nothing to reduce poverty. Other studies similarly have found no clear link between aid and faster economic development. The $1 trillion that rich countries and international agencies gave and loaned to poor ones between 1950 and 2002 did not have the hoped-for result of eliminating poverty and reducing economic and social disparities between the rich and poor countries of the world.

In part, that was because economic growth was not necessarily a donor country's first priority. During the Cold War, billions flowed from both the Soviet Union and the United States to prop up countries whose leaders favored the donor state agendas. Even today, strategic considerations may outweigh charitable or developmental aims. Israel gets a major share of American aid for historical reasons; Egypt, Lebanon, Pakistan, and Colombia get sizable portions for political and strategic reasons; and Afghanistan and Iraq, after 2003, received billions for rehabilitation and

restructuring. Up until 2005, America, in fact, spent only 40% of its modest foreign aid budget on assistance to poorer states.

About one-quarter of all aid from whatever national source has been tied to purchases which must be made in the donor country, and additional large shares flow, regardless of need or merit, to former colonies of donor countries. In part, a World Bank report admits, aid failures reflect the fact that the bank and its sister agencies have wasted billions on ill-conceived projects.

More optimistic conclusions are drawn by other observers who note that: (a) foreign aid tends to reduce poverty in countries with market-based economic policies but is ineffective where those policies do not exist; (b) aid is most effective in lowering poverty if it is given to poor, rather than less poor, countries; and (c) aid targeted to specific objectives—eradication of a disease or Green Revolution crop improvement, for example—is often remarkably successful, though spending on food aid or on aid tied to purchases from donor countries is of little use.

Although some countries—Botswana, the Republic of Korea, China, different Southeast Asian states—made great progress thanks to development assistance, a large number of others saw their prospects worsen and their economies decline. Slow growth and rising populations lowered their per capita incomes, and poor use of aid and loans failed to improve

their infrastructures and social service levels. Most critical for the economic and social development prospects of those countries was that the financing offered to them over the years in the hopes of stimulating new growth became a burden of unmanageable debt.

So great and intractable did their debt problem become that the international community recognized a whole class of countries distinguished by their high-debt condition: Heavily Indebted Poor Countries (HIPCs) that were so far in debt that many of them were paying more in interest and loan payments to industrialized countries and international agencies than they were receiving in exports to or aid from those sources. Gradually, the rich world accepted that debt relief, not lectures on capitalism, is the better approach to helping the world's poor countries and people. In 1996 the World Bank, the International Monetary Fund, and other agencies launched the first HIPC initiative, identifying 41 very poor countries and acknowledging that their total debt burden (including the share owed to international institutions) must be reduced to sustainable levels. In the following years, differing definitions of "sustainable" and criteria for debt relief were adopted but remained rooted in the requirement that benefiting countries must face an unsustainable debt burden, maintain good economic policies, and prepare a blueprint laying out how the country will

Africa; between 1975 and 2000, per capita income declined by almost 1% a year, leaving all but a tiny elite significantly poorer at the end of the period. Over the same years, income per head in the industrial market economies grew at a 1.8% annual rate. The 1960s, 1970s, and 1980s were all proclaimed by United Nations resolutions as "Development Decades." They proved instead to be decades of disappointment, at least by economic measures. Between 1990 and 2004, however, the picture brightened for the developing world as a whole. Average per capita income growth in developing countries in the 1990s was 1.5%, about three times the rate in the 1980s; between 2000 and 2004 their average per capita income growth increased to 3.4%, double the rate for high-income states. Even sub-Saharan Africa posted growth in the 2000–2004 period. For many, faith in the likelihood of growth—even if not in definable "stages of development"—was renewed.

Other development theories and models try to address these realities. The concept of the "Big Push" concludes that underdeveloped economies can break out of their poverty trap by coordinated investment in both basic—but high wage—industries and infrastructure, creating simultaneously an expanding consumer base and steadily falling costs and rising volumes of production. These, in turn, encourage creation of backward- and forward-linked industries, further cost reductions, faster growth, and perhaps the industrial specializations that foster agglomeration economies and trade expansion.

Another viewpoint holds that national growth rate differentials are rooted in differing investments in "human capital," an ill-defined composite of skills, habits, schooling, and knowledge that—more importantly than labor force numbers or capital availability—contributes to successful economic development and sustained growth. Technological progress in recent decades, it is pointed out, has been notably dependent on more educated workforces equipped with high levels of capital investment. The current deep global imbalance in literate and technically trained people has been called the most potent force of divergence in well-being between the rich world and the poor.

A corollary concept concludes that for least developed or newly industrializing countries, incentives encouraging foreign direct investment and technology transfer are the most important policy.

fight poverty and promote health and educational programs, and how savings from debt relief will help. After 2000, both debt relief and continuing flows of aid were also tied to the UN's Millennium Development Goals.

Official donor country development assistance increased by $12 billion from 2000 to 2004; $8 billion of that was pledged by the United States. By the end of 2004, 27 of 38 eligible countries had been accepted into the HIPC debt relief program. The debt reduction packages approved for the 27 states—23 of them in Africa—aimed to remove more than $40 billion in debt, about half of what the countries owed. Funds freed from debt service were to be spent on social services and other MDGs by the beneficiary states.

In a dramatic new approach, in 2004 Britain's prime minister Tony Blair offered a plan to cancel 100% of the foreign debts owed by the world's poorest states, freeing them to spend on social and infrastructure improvements rather than on interest payments on their massive loans. Mr. Blair's proposal began to bear fruit in September of 2005 when the finance ministers of the world's richest countries agreed to wipe out up to $55 billion in debt owed by impoverished states. Initially affecting only about 18 countries, eventually as many as 35 states could qualify for debt relief. No longer restricted to HIPCs, the 2005 agreement was simply based on a country's per capita income and a determination that the beneficiary government follow "sound" economic policies and meet standards for good governance. Part of the philosophy behind the debt forgiveness was to clean the slate and shift future aid away from loans and to outright grants.

The expressed hope of the international community now is that the answer to the question "Does foreign aid help?" will finally be "Yes." In a reconsideration of its former pessimism, the World Bank now concludes that, indeed, the answer is affirmative. It feels that foreign aid has been instrumental in increasing life expectancy at birth in developing countries by 20 years since 1960, cutting adult illiteracy in half since 1970, reducing the number of people in abject poverty by 200 million since 1980 even as world population increased by 2 billion, and more than doubling the per capita income in developing countries since 1965. The expectation now is that massive debt forgiveness will be reflected in accelerating social and economic improvement in emerging economies and further reduce the disparities between their conditions and those of more affluent developed states.

Questions to Consider

1. In light of World Bank and other studies concluding aid does not always correlate with development or poverty reduction in recipient countries, do you think the rich world and international agencies should halt all further monetary assistance to developing states? Why or why not?

2. Do you think donor countries such as the United States should completely ignore all self-interest including, for example, extra generosity toward friendly or politically compatible states, in making aid decisions? Why or why not?

3. Do you think international programs of forgiveness of debts contracted by sovereign states is appropriate or fair to lending countries and their citizens? Why or why not?

4. One widely held opinion is that money now spent on direct and indirect foreign aid more properly should be spent on domestic programs dealing with poverty, unemployment, homelessness, inner-city decay, inequality, and the like. An equally strongly held contrary view is that foreign aid should take priority, for it is needed to address world and regional problems of overpopulation, hunger, disease, destruction of the environment, and civil and ethnic strife those conditions foster. Assuming you had to choose one of the two polar positions, which view would you support, and why?

When imported ideas and technology that help create "human capital" labor and intellectual skills are combined with domestic industrial control, encouragement of education, and local research and development, there will certainly follow industrial specializations, massive exports, and rising levels of living—as presumably they did for Taiwan, Singapore, and the other surging Asian economies.

Obviously, not all less developed countries have been able to follow that same path to success. Indeed, those countries where the poorest 20% of the world's people live were, in 2004, 50 times worse off than those where the richest fifth live, and the gap between the two groups had doubled since the early 1960s. *Dependency theory* holds that these differentials are not accidental but the logical result of the ability and necessity of developed countries and power elites to exploit and subjugate other populations and regions to secure for themselves a continual source of new capital. This exploitation of poor countries by rich countries has its roots in colonialism and the slave trade. Today, transnational corporations, the theory contends, tend to dominate through their investments key areas of developing state economies. They introduce technologies and production facilities to further their own corporate goals, not to further the balanced development of the recipient economies.

Development aid where proffered, dependency theory holds, involves a forced economic reliance on donor countries and economies that continues an imposed cycle in which, in a sense, selective industrialization leads not to independent growth but to further dependent underdevelopment.

Infrastructure for development such as roads, water supplies, hydroelectric dams, and electric transmission lines typically requires outside financing. The two major international lending agencies, the International Monetary Fund (IMF) and the World Bank, were the outcome of a conference held at Bretton Woods, New Hampshire, near the end of World War II. The IMF is mostly concerned with lending to governments to address balance-of-payment issues and facilitate international trade. The World Bank has focused on lending for development, beginning with the restoration of war devastated countries of Europe, and then shifting its attention to the world's developing countries. Unfortunately, many expensive World Bank-financed development projects have been disappointing failures while developing countries have accumulated foreign debts that approach or even exceed their annual GNI. When the IMF and World Bank have refinanced development debts, they have required structural adjustment programs that institute economic and government reforms, some of which have led to cuts in education, health care, or social services. Suffering on the part of the world's poor in order to finance debts owed to the world's richest nations, has sparked controversy and dissatisfaction with conventional development models.

Balancing these polar extremes, we have seen, is the emerging world reality of accelerating economic growth for the developing countries as a group. Their present status as collective generators of one-half of world output and 25% of world trade clearly suggests that, development theories aside, the best stimulus for economic development has been the widespread relaxation of restrictive economic and political controls on all economies and on international trade flows in the past generation. Transnational corporations, technology transfer, pro-development national policies, trade restriction relaxations, and selective foreign aid and lending have all played a part. But the major impetus to the transition to Rostow's *takeoff* to sustained growth appears to be near worldwide conversion from controlled to free market economies, a conversion to economic and cultural globalization resented, rejected, and resisted by many individuals and groups.

Noneconomic Measures of Development

Development is measured by more than economic standards, though income and national wealth strongly affect the degree to which societies can invest in education, sanitation, health services, and other components of individual and group well-being. Indeed, the relationship between economic and social measures of development is direct and proportional. The higher the per capita gross national income is, for example, the higher the national ranking tends to be in such matters as access to safe drinking water, prevalence of sanitary waste treatment, availability of physicians and hospital beds, and educational and literacy levels.

In contrast, the relationship between social-economic and demographic variables is usually inverse. Higher educational or income levels, that is, are usually associated with lower infant mortality rates, birth and death rates, rates of natural increase, and the like. However it is measured, the gap between the most and least developed countries in noneconomic characteristics is at least as great as it is in their economic-technological circumstances. Table 10.1 suggests that the South as a whole has made progress in reducing its disadvantages in some human well-being measures. In others, however, the gap between rich and poor remains or is increasing, and disparities still persist after the three UN "development decades."

Education

A literate, educated labor force is essential for the effective transfer of advanced technology from the developed to developing countries. Yet in the poorest societies half or more of adults are illiterate; for the richest, the figure is 1% or less (Figure 10.14). The problem in part stems from a national poverty that denies funds sufficient for teachers, school buildings, books, and other necessities of the educational program. In part it reflects the lack of a trained pool of teachers and the inability to expand their number rapidly enough to keep up with the ever-increasing size of school-age populations. In African countries worst hit by the AIDS epidemic, deaths among established teachers exceeded the supply of new teachers entering the profession beginning in the late 1990s. For the same number of potential pupils, the richest countries may have 20 to 25 times as many teachers as do the poorest countries. In Norway in 2004, there was 1 teacher for every 10 primary school children; in Congo Republic the ratio was 1 to 83. Commitment appears as important as wealth in determining student-teacher ratios; Israel had more teachers per 1000 students than did richer Canada or the United Kingdom.

Lack of facilities and teachers, family poverty that makes tuition fees prohibitive and keeps millions of school-age children in full-time work, and national poverty that underfunds all levels of education together combine to restrict school enrollment in poor countries to a fraction of normal rich country expectations. Whatever the enrollment percentages were in individual

Table 10.1

The Narrowing North–South Disparity in Human Development, 1960 to 2004

	North		South		Absolute Disparity	
	1960	**2004**	**1960**	**2004**	**1960**	**2004**
Life expectancy (years)	69	78	46	62	23	16
Adult literacy (%)	95	97	46	67	49	30
Nutrition (daily calorie supply as % of requirement)	124	141	90	114	34	27
Infant mortality (per 1000 live births)	37	7	149	62	112	55
Child mortality (under age 5)	46	7	216	90	170	83
Access to safe water (% of population)	100	100	40	78	60	22

Sources: United Nations Development Programme, World Bank, and UNICEF.

countries, girls were less apt to be in school than were boys. In 2004, the UN estimated that 121 million children worldwide were being denied formal education; 54% of them were girls. More than 50 million primary-school-age girls were out of school in sub-Saharan Africa and South Asia alone. And the disparity in many countries increases with age, because girls are less likely than boys to progress to secondary school. The implicit economic and social development consequences are evident in the correlations that have been established between levels of female education and, for example, birth rates and family size preferences, family nutrition practices and health maintenance, and life expectancies.

Public Services

Development implies more than industrial expansion or agricultural improvement. The quality of public services and the creation of facilities to assure the health of the labor force are equally significant evidences of national advancement. Safe drinking water

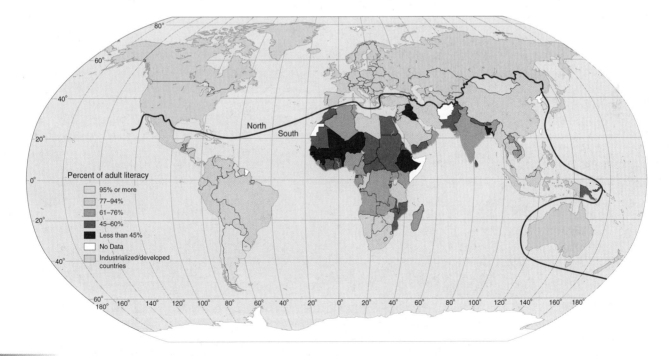

Figure 10.14 The South: Adult literacy rate, 2003, as a percentage of the adult population (over 15 years of age) able to read and write short, simple statements relating to their everyday life. With almost no exceptions, adult literacy is 95% or more in countries of the North. With only a few exceptions, literacy rates in all countries of the South improved dramatically during the 1990s. For developing countries as a group, 80% of adults were literate in 2003 compared with 64% in 1990; for least developed countries the improvement was from 45% literate at the start of the 1990s to 54% literate in 2003.

Source: Data from United Nations Development Programme, Human Development Report 2005.

and the sanitary disposal of human waste are particularly important in maintaining human health (see Figure 4.18). As Table 10.1 notes, disparities in access to safe water are being steadily reduced between developed and developing countries. Similar improvements have been registered for access to improved sanitation. Even in the least developed countries, more than one-third of the population had basic hygienic sanitation in 2002, up from less than one-quarter in 1990. But worldwide, more than 40% of all people—2.6 billion in 2001—lacked that access, mostly in rural areas.

The accepted presence of pure water and sanitary toilets in the North and their frequent or general absence in, particularly, rural areas and urban slums in the less developed world present a profound contrast between the two realms. Only half of the rural populations of the predominantly rural least developed states had access in 2002 to water safe to drink. Within the expanding cities of the developing countries more than a half-billion people lived in shantytowns and slums devoid of either adequate water supply or sanitary disposal facilities or both (Figure 10.15). Worldwide, more than a billion people lacked a dependable sanitary supply of water (Figure 10.16) and water-related diseases kill approximately 10 million people every year. Yet, significant progress has been made; during the 1980s and 1990s about 2 billion people worldwide were added to the ranks of those with access to potable waters. By 2004, the UN reported, some 83% of all people had access to clean water, up from 76% in 1990, though more than 40% of sub-Saharan Africans still relied on unsafe drinking water supplies.

Health

Access to medical facilities and personnel is another spatial variable with profound implications for the health and well-being of populations. Within the less developed world, vast numbers of people are effectively denied the services of physicians. While in industrial countries, on average (2005), one physician served 270 people, the figure for low income developing countries was more than 2500. For sub-Saharan Africa as a whole, the ratio is about 10,000 to 1. In the developing world, there are simply too few trained health professionals to serve the needs of expanding populations. Those few who are in practice tend to congregate in urban areas, or leave for better pay in developed countries. Rural clinics are few in number and the distance to them so great that many rural populations are effectively denied medical treatment of even the most rudimentary nature.

Increasingly, those sorts of health-related contrasts between advanced and developing countries have become matters of international concern and attention (see "Poverty and Development" p. 315). Indeed, three of the eight Millennium Development Goals (see p. 313) deal directly with child mortality, maternal health, and eradication of disease. We saw in Chapter 4 how important for developing states, population growth is the transfer of advanced technologies of medicine and public health: insecticides, antibiotics, and immunization, for example. Most recently, childhood diseases and deaths in developing countries have come under coordinated attack by the World Health Organization under the Task Force for Child Survival program (Figure 10.17). Gains have been impressive. If the

Figure 10.15 Because they have no access to safe drinking water or sanitary waste disposal, impoverished populations of a developing country's unserved rural districts and urban slums—like this one in Capetown, South Africa—are subject to water-borne and sanitation-related diseases.

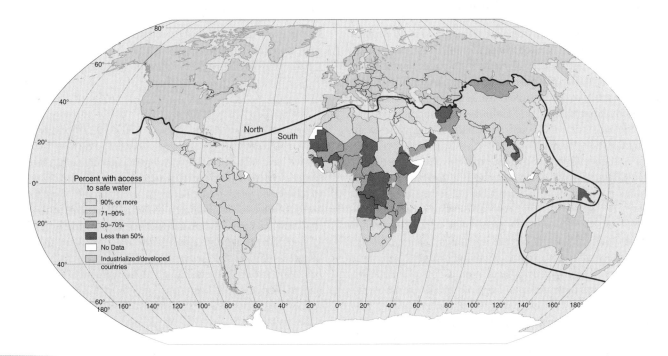

Figure 10.16 Percentage of population with access to safe drinking water, 2002. Between 1975 and 2002, access to safe water increased by more than two-thirds to make potable water available to 92% of urban residents in developing countries and 70% of rural folk (though only to 58% of total populations in the least developed states). By the early 21st century, thanks to WHO, United Nations, and World Bank programs and to targeted foreign aid, much of the developing world was approaching the levels of safe water availability formerly found only in industrialized states of the North.

Source: Data from UNICEF, State of the World's Children 2004.

Figure 10.17 The World Health Organization (WHO) is the agency of the United Nations that helps bring modern preventive health care, safe water, and sanitation to the less developed world. WHO workers help to fight certain diseases, advise on nutrition and living conditions, and aid developing countries in strengthening their health services. When the organization launched its Expanded Programme on Immunization in 1974, only 5% of the world's children were immunized against measles, diphtheria, polio, tetanus, whooping cough, and tuberculosis, diseases claiming 7 million young lives annually. In the early 1990s, more than 70% of children in developing countries were vaccinated against basic childhood diseases following an accelerated campaign by UNICEF and WHO. But by 2002, poor countries reported that only 56% of their children received such immunization because of a falloff in financial support from wealthy nations. In response to the slowdown, in 1999, a Global Alliance for Vaccines and Immunization was formed by national and international agencies, philanthropies, and pharmaceutical companies to revive the earlier efforts. The UN Children's Fund reported in 2004 that some 85% of the children of the developing world lived in countries again making significant progress toward reducing malnutrition and preventing diseases. Pictured is preventive health care in a Micronesian clinic.

1960 worldwide infant mortality rate had remained in 2000, 15 million more children would have died than in fact did. Yet stark contrasts between most developed and least developed societies remain. Based on the mortality levels for children under 5 in industrialized countries in 2004 (7 per thousand), the United Nations estimated that more than 90% of the approximately 11 million infant and child deaths in developing countries (122 per thousand) in that year were preventable.

Taken at their extremes, advanced and developing countries occupy two distinct worlds of disease and health. One is affluent; its death rates are low, and the chief killers of its mature populations are cancers, heart attacks, and strokes. The other world is impoverished, often crowded, and prone to disease. The deadly dangers of its youthful populations are infectious, respiratory, and parasitic diseases made more serious by malnutrition.

In 1978, the World Health Organization endorsed preventive health care as an attainable goal and adopted "health for all by the year 2000" as its official target. It was to be reached through primary health care: low technologies aimed at disease prevention in poorer nations. Although substantial improvements in global health were made by the target year and disparities between the developed and developing worlds had been reduced, gaps had actually widened between the developing world as a whole and its "least developed" components, and health gains have actually been reversed in some states. The World Health Assembly of 1998, recognizing the continuing challenges, renewed the global commitment to "health for all" and established new targets for the early 21st century.

The general determinants of health are well known: enough purchasing power to secure the food, housing, and medical care essential to it; a healthful physical environment that is both sanitary and free from infectious disease; and a particularly female educational level sufficient to comprehend the essentials of nutrition and hygiene. Family planning, health, and infrastructure and economic developmental programs have begun to increase the numbers in the developing world that now have access to at least rudimentary health services.

Unfortunately, resurgence of old diseases and emergence of new ones may disrupt or reverse the hoped-for transition to better health in many world areas (See "Our Delicate State of Health," p. 106). Almost 10% of world population now suffer from one or more tropical diseases, many of which—malaria, affecting 200 to 300 million people with up to 3 million deaths annually, is an example—were formerly thought to be eradicable but now are spreading in drug-resistant form. One such scourge, tuberculosis, is appearing as a major concern among particularly poorer populations outside tropical regions. Low income countries are also hard hit by the spread of AIDS (acquired immune deficiency syndrome). In 2007, one-third of persons living with HIV/AIDS were in sub-Saharan Africa.

The high and rising costs of modern medications place unbearable burdens on strained budgets of developing states. Those costs increasingly must include health care for the rapidly growing number of their elderly citizens and for those exposed to the health risks that come with economic development and industrialization: higher consumption of alcohol, tobacco, and fatty foods, pollution, motor vehicle accidents, and the like. The World Health Organization is concerned that health services in poor developing countries may be overwhelmed by the twin burdens of poverty-related illness and health problems of industrialization and urbanization; heart disease and cancer now claim as many developing world as industrial world lives.

Aggregate Measures of Development and Well-Being

As we have seen, no single measure adequately summarizes the different facets of national development or gives a definitive comparison of countries on the continuum of development. Composite measures to achieve that summary aim can, of course, be devised from the growing body of comparative statistics regularly published by United Nations agencies, the World Bank, and other sources. Many of those—Figure 10.3 is an example—have been criticized for being based too strongly on economic and infrastructural indicators: gross national income, per capita income, sectoral structure of national economies, import and export data, miles of railroad or paved highways, and the like.

Development, it is maintained, is more than the purely economic and physical, and personal development may have little or nothing to do with objective statistical measures. The achievement of development must also be seen in terms of individual and collective well-being: a safe environment, freedom from want, opportunity for personal growth and enrichment, and access to goods and services beyond the absolute minimum to sustain life (see "Measuring Happiness"). Health, safety, educational and cultural development, security in old age, political freedom, and similar noneconomic criteria are among the evidences of comparative developmental level that are sought in composite statistics. Also sought is a summary statistic of development that is value free; that is, the input data should not measure development by expenditure patterns or performance standards that are ethnocentric or colored by political agendas. The values of one culture—for example, in housing space per person, in educational levels achieved, or in distribution of national income—are not necessarily universally applicable or acceptable, and a true comparative statistic should not imply that they are.

Seeking a value-free measure of the extent to which minimum human needs are being satisfied among the world's countries, the Overseas Development Council devised a Physical Quality of Life Index (PQLI). Three indicators—infant mortality, life expectancy, and literacy—are each scored 0–100, with 0 an explicitly "worst" performance. A national achievement level is calculated by averaging the three indicators. The PQLI is but one of many attempts to recognize that national development and human welfare are complex achievements not measurable by a single indicator. Each approach has attempted to integrate into a composite index a larger or smaller number of national variables detailing physical, economic, political, and social conditions specific to country units. On the basis of the national rankings they derived, each has explicitly or implicitly ranked the countries of the world on a continuum from least to most developed.

One such ranking gaining increasing recognition is employed by the United Nations Development Programme. Its "human development index" (HDI) combines purchasing power (not just dollar amount of per capita GNI), life expectancy, and literacy (Figure 10.18). The HDI reflects the Programme's conviction that

Measuring Happiness

Is there a spatial pattern to happiness? And is it related to spatial patterns of development, underdevelopment, high-incomes, or poverty? Psychologists have long used surveys of reported well-being to study happiness, and some economists have explored the relationships between economic variables and measures of life satisfaction. The results are fascinating, complicated, and sometimes surprising. Within a country, those with higher incomes tend to report greater happiness, but as standards of living rise, happiness does not necessarily increase. Generally, higher income countries have higher reported levels of happiness, but the many exceptions suggest other cultural factors are important influences. Putting Ruut Veenhoven at Erasmus University in the Netherlands has compiled "The World Database of Happiness," containing the results of surveys of life enjoyment drawn from 155 countries. Following is a sample of top-ranked countries, middle-range countries, and bottom-ranked countries on surveys administered since the year 2000 asking people to rate their "satisfaction with life as a whole" on a 0 to 10 scale. While the United States ranked fairly high on the life satisfaction survey with an average rating of 7.0, Canadians report even higher levels of life satisfaction with an average of 7.6, and Mexicans were even happier yet. The top five nations for life satisfaction include three prosperous European countries known for their high quality of life (Iceland, Denmark, and Switzerland) but also two developing countries with much lower incomes than the rest (Columbia and Mexico). Further, Puerto Rico, which was not included in the rankings because it is not a country, had a score that would have put it in second place. Many Asian countries cluster in the middle range, even though their incomes range by a factor of nearly ten. The countries with the lowest happiness ratings are mostly in Africa, although one, Belarus—a former Soviet republic, has incomes much higher than its level of happiness would suggest.

Country	Happiness Score (0–10)	GNI/Capita (US$), 2007
Happiest Countries		
Iceland	8.5	$34,060
Denmark	8.4	$36,740
Columbia	8.1	$6,640
Switzerland	8.1	$43,080
Mexico	8.0	$12,580
Middle Range Countries		
Philippines	6.3	$3,730
Iran	6.3	$10,800
India	6.0	$2,740
China	5.9	$5,370
South Korea	5.9	$24,750
Least Happy Countries		
Belarus	4.2	$10,740
Chad	4.2	$1,280
Togo	4.1	$800
Zimbabwe	3.3	No Data
Tanzania	3.2	$1,200

Sources: Veenhoven, R., *Average happiness in 145 nations 2000–2008,* World Database of Happiness, Rank Report 2009-la, URL: *worlddatabaseofhappiness.eur.ni,* Graham, Carol, 2005. "The Economics of Happiness," *World Economics,* Vol. 6 (3):41–55.

the important human aspirations are leading a long and healthy life, receiving adequate education, and having access to assets and income sufficient for a decent quality of life. The arbitrary weighting of the three input variables—longevity (measured by life expectancy at birth), knowledge (indicated by weighted measures of adult literacy and mean years of schooling), and income (based on a poverty-adjusted statistic of gross domestic product per capita)—makes the derived national rankings subjective rather than fully objective. The HDI, like all attempts at measuring developmental levels of countries and categorizing their variations

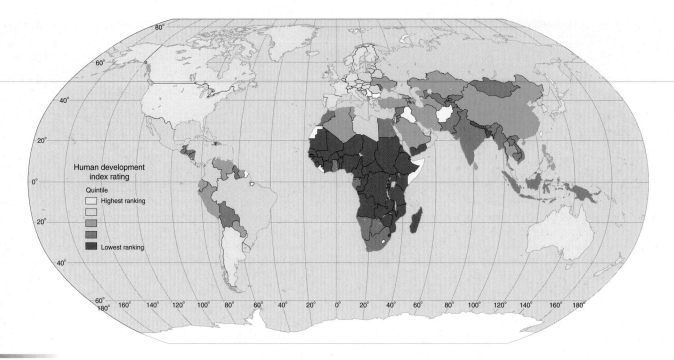

Figure 10.18 **Country rankings according to the Human Development Index, 2003** of the United Nations Development Programme. Since the index is intended to measure the absence of deprivation, it discounts incomes higher than needed to achieve an acceptable level of living and therefore is uninformative in comparing the levels of development of the richest countries. The four measures that are used by the UNDP—life expectancy, adult literacy, combined school enrollment ratios, and real (PPP) income—are highly correlated with one another. For that reason, it has been noted, the rankings derived by the HDI differ only slightly from income rankings adjusted for purchasing power parity; the Indian minister for human resources in 2002 objected that the HDI ignored "spiritual happiness" and "intellectual advances." Fifth quintile countries, at the bottom of the Human Development Index, closely match the "least developed" countries recognized by the UN and shown on Figure 10.3.

Source: "Human Development Index," country rankings are made and reported by United Nations Development Programme in its annual Human Development Report.

in qualities of life and human welfare, is a recognition both of the complexity of the economic and social structures involved and of the need to focus developmental efforts.

The UN Development Programme has also developed a reverse image of poverty in its Human Poverty Index (HPI). While the HDI measures average *achievement,* the HPI measures *deprivation* in the same three measures of development underlying the HDI. For the poverty index, the benchmarks of concern are probability of not surviving to age 40; exclusion from full social intercourse because of illiteracy; and deprivation of a decent level of living as measured by lack of safe water access and percentage of underweight small children. The Human Poverty Index is discussed in more detail in "Poverty and Development" (p. 315).

The Role of Women

Many of the common measures of development and change within and between countries take no account of the sex and age structures of the societies examined. Gross national income per capita, literacy rates, percentage of labor force in agriculture, and the like are statistics that treat all members (or all adult members) of the society uniformly. Yet among the most prominent strands in the fabric of culture are the social structures (*sociofacts*) and relationships that establish distinctions between males and females in the duties assigned and the rewards afforded to each.

Because gender relationships and role assignments vary among societies, the status of women is a cultural spatial variable. Because so much of that variation is related to the way economic roles and production and reward assignments are allocated by sex, we might well assume a close tie between the status of women in different societies and their level and type of economic development. Further, it would be logical to believe that advancement in the technological sense would be reflected in an enhancement of the status and rewards of both men and women in developing countries. Should that prove true, it would logically follow that contrasts between the developed and developing world in gender relationships and role assignments would steadily diminish.

The pattern that we actually observe is not quite that simple or straightforward, for gender relationships and role assignments are only partially under the control of the technological subsystem. **Gender** in the cultural sense refers to socially created—not biologically based—distinctions between femininity and masculinity. Therefore, religion and custom play their own important roles. Further, it appears that at least in the earlier phases of technological change and development, women generally lose rather than gain in status and rewards. Only recently and only in the most developed countries have gender-related contrasts been reduced within and between societies.

Hunting and gathering cultures observed a general egalitarianism; each sex had a respected, productive role in the kinship group (see Figure 2.11). Gender is more involved and changeable in agricultural societies (see "Women and the Green Revolution," p. 248).

The Agricultural Revolution—a major change in the technological subsystem—altered the earlier structure of gender-related responsibilities. In the hoe agriculture found in much of sub-Saharan Africa and in South and Southeast Asia, women became responsible for most of the actual field work, while still retaining their traditional duties in child rearing, food preparation, and the like.

Plow agriculture, on the other hand, tended to subordinate the role of women and diminish their level of equality. Women may have hoed, but men plowed, and female participation in farm work was drastically reduced. This is the case today in Latin America and, increasingly, in sub-Saharan Africa where women are often more visibly productive in the market than in the field (Figure 10.19). As women's agricultural productive role declined, they were afforded less domestic authority, less control over their own lives, and few if any property rights independent of male family members.

Western industrial—"developed"—society emerged directly from the agricultural tradition of the subordinate female who was not considered an important element in the economically active population, no matter how arduous or essential the domestic tasks assigned, and who was not afforded full access to education or similar amenities of an advancing society. European colonial powers introduced that attitude along with economic development into Third World cultures. Only within the later 20th century, and then largely in the more developed countries, has that subordinate role pattern changed.

The rate and extent of women's participation in the labor force has expanded everywhere in recent years. Since 1970, both the percentage of the total labor force who are women and the percentage of women who are economically active[4] increased in nearly every world region—developed and developing (Figure 10.20). Women's increased participation in the workforce reflects several

[4]The International Labour Office defines "economically active" work as that "producing significant amounts of 'economic' (that is, marketable) goods, or of visible income." Included in the "economically active population" are all employed and unemployed persons seeking employment and all wage earners, unpaid family workers, and members of producers' cooperatives.

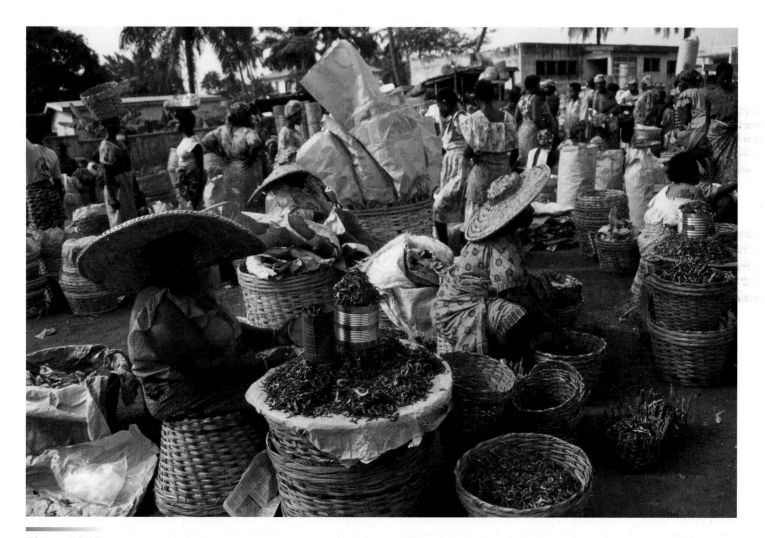

Figure 10.19 Women dominate the once-a-week *periodic* markets in nearly all developing countries. Here they sell produce from their gardens or the family farm and often offer processed goods for sale (to which their labor has added value)—oil pressed from seeds or, in Niger, for example, from peanuts grown on their own fields; cooked, dried, or preserved foods; simple pottery and baskets; or decorated gourds. In West Africa, the Caribbean, and Asia, between 70% and 90% of all farm and marine produce is traded by women. The market shown here is in the West African country of Ghana. More than half of the economically active women in sub-Saharan Africa and southern Asia and about one-third in northern Africa and the rest of Asia are self-employed, working primarily in the informal sector. In the developed world, only about 14% of active women are self-employed.

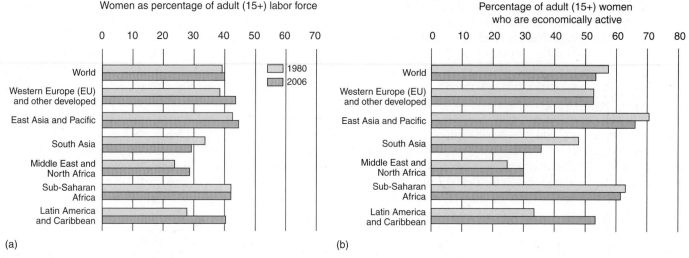

Figure 10.20 (*a*) **Women's share of the labor force.** Worldwide, women were recorded by the World Bank at 40% of the total labor force in 2006 and comprised 40% or more of the workers in all areas except South Asia and the Middle East and North Africa. Female employment growth was relatively greatest in Latin America and the Caribbean between 1980 and 2006. (*b*) **Women's economic activity rates** showed a mixed pattern of change between and within many world regions. More than half the world's female labor force lived in Asia and the Pacific area in 2006 and worldwide 53% of women participated in the workforce. Although the regional share of economically active women varies widely, it stands at 46% for the lowest income states and at 53% for the developing world as a whole. Except for South Asia and the Middle East–North Africa zone, women made up over half of the labor force everywhere.

Source: World Bank, World Development Indicators 2008.

changing conditions. Women have gained greater control over their fertility, thus increasing their opportunities for education and employment. Further, attitudes toward employed women have changed and public policies on, for example, child care, maternity benefits, and the like, are more favorable. Economic growth, including the expansion of service sector jobs open to women, was also important in many regions. Permissive attitudes and policies with regard to micro and small enterprises, including financing and credit programs, have in some areas played a major role in encouraging women entrepreneurs (see "Empowering Women Financially").

Considering all work—paid and unpaid economic activity and unpaid housework—women spend more hours per day working than do men in all developing and developed regions except Anglo America and Australia. In developing countries, the UN estimates, when unpaid agricultural work and housework are considered along with wage labor, women's work hours exceed men's by 30% and may involve at least as arduous—or heavier—physical labor. The FAO reports "rural women in the developing world carry 80 tons or more of fuel, water and farm produce for a distance of 1 km during the course of a year. Men carry much less . . ." Everywhere women are paid less than men for comparable employment, but in most world regions the percentage of economically active women holding wage or salaried positions is about equal to the rate for men. Exceptions are Latin America, where a higher proportion of active women than men are wage earners, and Africa, where wage-earning opportunities for women are few; in several African states, less than 10% of economically active women are wage earners.

Despite these and similar widely applicable generalizations, the present world pattern of gender-related institutional and economic role assignments is varied. It is influenced by a country's level of economic development, by the persistence of the religious and customary restrictions its culture imposes on women, and by the specific nature of its economic—particularly agricultural—base. The first control is reflected in contrasts between the developed and developing world; the second and third are evidenced in variations within the developing world itself.

The differential impact of these and other conditions is evident in Figure 10.21. The pattern shows a distinct gender-specific regionalization among the countries of the developing world. Among the Arab or Arab-influenced Muslim areas of western Asia and North Africa, the recorded proportion of the female population that is economically active is low. Religious tradition restricts women's acceptance in economic activities outside of the home, a tradition that results in probable under-reporting of female employment by the countries involved. The same cultural limitations do not apply under the different rural economic conditions of Muslims in southern and southeastern Asia, where labor force participation by women in Indonesia and Bangladesh, for example, is much higher than it is among the western Muslims.

In Latin America, women have been overcoming cultural restrictions on their employment outside the home and their active economic participation has been increasing. That participation is occurring almost entirely outside of the agricultural realm, where the high degree of farm labor tenancy as well as custom limits the role of females. Sub-Saharan Africa, highly diverse culturally and economically, in general is highly dependent on female farm labor and market income. The historical role of strongly independent, property-owning females formerly encountered under traditional agricultural and village systems, however, has increasingly been replaced by subordination of women with modernization of agricultural techniques and introduction of formal, male-dominated financial and administrative farm-sector institutions.

Empowering Women Financially

The Fourth World Conference on Women held in Beijing during September, 1995, called on all governments to formulate strategies, programs, and laws designed to assure women their full human rights to equality and development. The Conference's final declaration, reinforced at the "Beijing Plus Five" Conference held at The United Nations in June, 2000, detailed recommended policies in the areas of sexuality and child-bearing, violence against women, discrimination against girls, female inheritance rights, and family protection. Its particular emphasis, however, focused on efforts to "ensure women's equal access to economic resources including land, credit, . . . and markets as a means to further advancement and empowerment of women and girls."

That special economic emphasis was reinforced by the UN Food and Agriculture Organization's "Gender and Development Plan (2002–2007)," which aimed at stimulating efforts to enhance gender-based equity in the control of productive resources and providing women with access to credit to enable them to engage as creators and owners of small-scale manufacturing, trade, or service businesses. Still later, the UN General Assembly designated 2005 as the "International Year of Microcredit" to further the same objectives.

Two-thirds of the total amount of work women do is unpaid, but that unpaid work amounts to an $11 trillion addition to the total world economy. The Beijing Conference declaration was a recognition that women's economic contribution would be even greater—and of more social and personal benefit—were governments to grant them equal opportunity through financial support to engage as owners in small-scale manufacturing, trade, or service enterprises. In fact, both the model and proof of success in granting women access to credit were already in place.

In 1976, a Bangladeshi economist, Muhammad Yunus, wandered into a poor village and got an idea that has captured international interest and changed accepted beliefs and practices of banking in developing countries. The concept behind the Grameen Bank he established is simple: if individual borrowers are given access to credit, they will be able to identify and engage in viable income-producing activities such as pottery making, weaving, sewing, buying and marketing simple consumer goods, or providing transportation and other basic services.

Declaring that "Access to credit should be a human right," Mr. Yunus was a pioneer in extending "microcredit" for "microenterprises" with women emerging as the primary borrowers and beneficiaries of Grameen Bank's practice of lending money without collateral and at low rates of interest. Under the original Grameen concept, to be eligible for the average loan of about U.S. $160, women without assets must join or form a "cell" of five unrelated women, of whom only two can borrow at first though all five are responsible for repayment. When the first two begin to repay, two more can borrow, and so on. As a condition of the loan, clients must also agree to increase their savings, observe sound nutritional practices, and educate their children.

By 2005, the bank had made over 5 million loans in 40,000 villages in Bangladesh alone. More than 96% of the borrowers are women, and repayment rates reach above 95%. The average household income of Grameen Bank members has risen to about 59% higher than that of nonmembers in the same villages, with the landless benefiting most and marginal landowner families following closely. Because of enterprise incomes resulting from the lending program, there has been a sharp reduction in the number of Grameen Bank members living below the poverty line—to 20% compared with nearly 60% for nonmembers. There has also been a marked shift from low-status agricultural labor to self-employment in simple manufacturing and trading. That shift has encouraged a borrower and lender recognition that larger loans are needed to enable increasingly entrepreneurial women to build small businesses, hire employees, acquire office and manufacturing equipment, and the like. In consequence, some lenders now approve loans of several thousand dollars, though such larger loans are still much in the minority.

The Grameen concept has spread from its Bangladesh origins to elsewhere in Asia and to Latin America, Eastern Europe, and Africa. In 2007, some 10,000 microcredit institutions worldwide had reached more than 113 million clients, including 67 million first-time borrowers who were among the world's poorest people. Of those poorest clients, 84.5% are women. But the women recipients still represent only a faction of the estimated 500 to 600 million women worldwide who have virtually no access to credit—or to the economic, social, educational, and nutritional benefits that come from its availability. It is that globally enormous number of women now effectively denied credit equality that the resolutions of the Fourth World Conference on Women and the FAO and UN General Assembly plans and programs seek to benefit.

A "gender empowerment measure" (GEM) devised by the United Nations Development Programme emphasizes female participation in national economic, political, and professional affairs. The GEM rankings are heavily biased toward measures that technologically advanced, career-oriented, Western cultures consider indicative of gender equality and progress; they do not consider the standards and values accepted in other cultural settings. As calculated, the GEM shows that gender equality in political, economic, and professional activities is not necessarily related to level of national wealth or development. According to the measure, some developing countries—China, for example, where women are afforded a large share of legislative seats and political administrative positions—outperform industrialized South Korea. In most countries, women are in a distinct minority in the exercise of economic power and decision making. Unfortunately, GEM rankings have been calculated for relatively few countries—only 80 in 2004. For countries for which sufficient data are available, however, a set of indicators has been combined to establish a more inclusive "gender-related development index" and ranking (Figure 10.22). Based on the differentials between men and women in life expectancy, literacy rates and school enrollment ratios, and earned income, it clearly displays regional differentials in the relative position of women in different cultures and world areas.

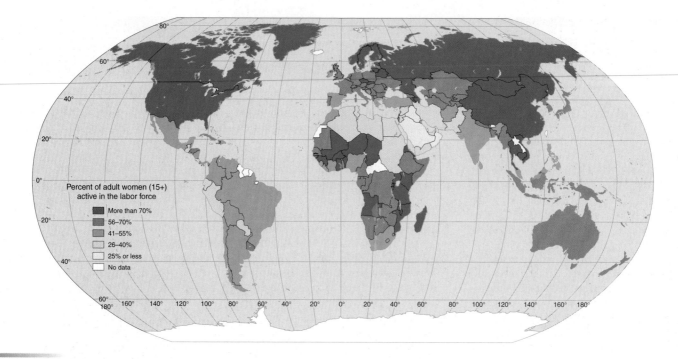

Figure 10.21 **Economically active women, 2004.** Since female participation in the labor force is reported by individual countries with differing definitions of "economically active," international comparisons may be misleading. The International Labor Office definition is given as a footnote on page 000. Because a higher proportion of the female than the male labor force is engaged in the "informal" sector, their recorded presence in the workplace is officially understated. The ILO maintains that "in many developing areas . . . the number of women in the labor force . . . is much larger than that given in official statistics."

Sources: International Labour Office and World Bank, World Development Indicators 2006.

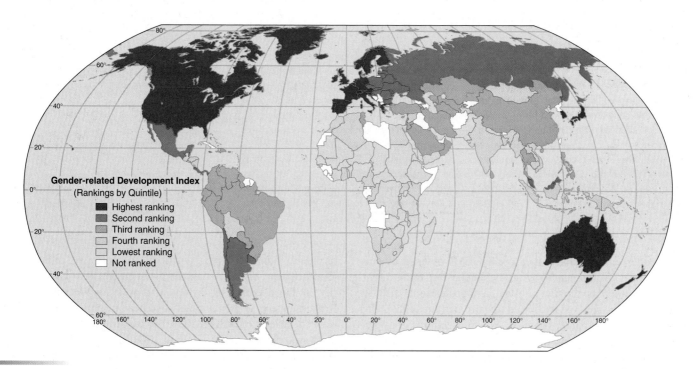

Figure 10.22 The **gender-related development index (GDI)** is a composite index that attempts to measure inequalities of achievements between men and women through differences in their life expectancies at birth, literacy levels and educational attainments, and female and male earned income shares. The greater the gender achievement disparities, the lower is a country's GDI. Analysis of the measured achievements and resulting rankings suggests that, first, no society treats its women as well as its men and, second, gender equality does not depend on the overall income level of a country.

Source: 2003 rankings from United Nations Development Programme, Human Development Report 2005. *Rankings are adjusted for each annual edition.*

Summary

Development as a concept and process implies change and improvement. It suggests the fuller and more productive use of the resources of an area through the application of advanced levels of technology. The result is presumed to be improved conditions of life and well-being for constant or growing populations and, for the society undergoing development, a fuller integration into—and more equal share of—the world space economy.

Development in that light can be seen as a cultural variable with a distinctive spatial patterning. No two countries have exactly the same position on the continuum of development in all of its many different possible economic and noneconomic measures. For this reason, precise classification of countries by developmental level is impossible, and a variety of general descriptive terms has been introduced, including the following: developed, developing, underdeveloped, least (or less) developed, Third or Fourth World, and the like. Whatever the terms, the overall world pattern of development is clear: The advanced and relatively wealthy countries of the economic core are those of Europe, North America, Japan, Australia, and New Zealand and a small but growing number of newly industrialized countries with high incomes and quality of life—Taiwan, South Korea, Singapore, and the like. The rest of the world is considered to be "developing" on the economic periphery, where individual countries are progressing at different rates and with different degrees of success.

A variety of comparative economic and noneconomic data are available to help identify the relative position of individual countries. *Gross national income* and *purchasing power parity per capita* document the basic core-periphery pattern while making clear the diversity among the developing countries in the monetary success of their economies. *Per capita consumption of commercial energy* reveals the immense size of the technology gap between most and least developed states, for energy use may be loosely equated with modern industrial plant and transportation facilities. A high percentage of a country's *workforce in agriculture* is associated with less developed subsistence economies with low labor productivity and low levels of national wealth. The price of underdevelopment—and of the relative poverty it implies—is malnutrition. Although the correlation is not exact, countries registering *average caloric intake* below daily requirements are also countries registering poorly on all purely economic measures of development.

Earlier hopes that underdevelopment was simply the common starting point in a series of expected and inevitable stages of advancement have been dashed. Many countries appear unable to accumulate the capital, develop the skills, or achieve the technology transfer necessary to carry them along the path to fuller economic development and prosperity. Without that development, countries score poorly on noneconomic measures such as literacy, safe water, and conditions of health. With it, they can—as the experience of newly industrializing countries demonstrates—experience growing cultural and technological convergence with the most advanced states. That convergence, in fact, is increasing, and the share of the *gross world product* attributable to what is still called the "developing" world continues to grow and amounted to more than 50% in 2006.

Development implies pervasive changes in the organizational and institutional structuring of peoples and space. Urbanization of populations and employment has invariably accompanied economic development, as has a more complete and rigorous political organization of space. We turn our attention in Chapters 11 and 12 to these two important expressions of human geographic variation, beginning first with an examination of city systems and of the spatial variations observable in the structure of urban units.

KEY WORDS

circular and cumulative causation 312	gross national income (GNI) 313	technology gap 316
core-periphery model 312	informal economy 314	technology transfer 316
cultural convergence 316	purchasing power parity (PPP) 313	trickle-down effect 312
development 309	spread effect 312	underdevelopment 309
gender 332	technology 316	

FOR REVIEW

1. How does the *core-periphery* model help us understand observed contrasts between developed and developing countries? In what way is *circular and cumulative causation* linked either to the perpetuation or the reduction of those contrasts? How does the concept of *trickle-down effects,* or *spread effects,* explain the equalization of development and incomes on a regional or international scale?

2. What are some of the reasons that have been given to explain why some countries are *developed* and others are *underdeveloped?*

3. What different ways and measures do we have to indicate degrees of

development of particular countries or regions? Do you think these measures can be used to place countries or regions into uniform *stages of development?*

4. Why should any country or society concern itself with *technology transfer* or with the *technology gap?* What do these concepts have to do with either development or societal well-being?

5. What kinds of material and nonmaterial economic and noneconomic contrasts can you cite

that differentiate more developed from less developed societies?

6. Assume you are requested to devise a composite index of national development and well-being. What *kinds* of characteristics would you like to include in your composite? Why? What specific *measures* of those characteristics would you like to cite?

7. Why is energy *consumption* per capita considered a reliable measure of level of national economic development?

If a country has a large per capita *production* of energy, can we assume that it also has a high level of development? Why or why not?

8. Have both males and females shared equally in the benefits of economic development in its early stages? What are the principal contrasts in the status of women between the developed and developing worlds? What regional contrasts within the developing world are evident in the economic roles assigned to women?

KEY CONCEPTS REVIEW

1. **How do we define development and explain the occurrence or persistence of underdevelopment?** pp. 308–313.
   Development implies improvement in economic and quality-of-life aspects of a society. It presumably results from technology transfer from advanced to developing states and, through consequent cultural convergence, promises the full integration of the developing society into the larger modern world order. When that stage of advancement is reached, transition from the world economic and social "periphery" to its "core" has been achieved. Persistence of underdevelopment is usually attributed to failure of a culture or region to accumulate capital, develop skills, or achieve technology transfers to improve its prosperity or quality of life.

2. **What economic measures mark a country's stage of development or its progress from underdevelopment?** pp. 313–326.
   Gross national income and purchasing power parity per capita, per capita

commercial energy consumption, percentage of labor force in agriculture, and average daily caloric intake are common, accepted measures of development. Attempts to model the process of development have led to inconclusive and contrasting theories of inevitable "stages of growth," optimistic "Big Push" ideas of coordinated investment, and pessimistic "dependency theory" concepts of perpetual exploitation of underdeveloped regions.

3. **What are noneconomic aspects of development, and how are they related to measures of economic growth?** pp. 326–332.
   Education, sanitation, and health services are among many noneconomic indices of development that are strongly related to income and national wealth. The higher a country's ranking on purely economic measures, the more it can and does spend on improvement of quality-of-life conditions for its citizens. Similarly, the higher those expenditures are, the lower on average are national rates of infant mortality,

births and deaths, rates of natural increase, and the like. "Happiness" or satisfaction of such cultural wants as social support, aesthetic and sensory needs, and creativity outlets also figure as importantly into well-being assessments as do gross domestic product or energy consumption.

4. **What conditions underlie the varying world pattern of women's roles, status, and rewards?** pp. 332–336.
   The status of women is a cultural spatial variable reflecting gender relationships characteristic of different societies. The world pattern of gender-related institutional and economic role assignments and rewards appears strongly influenced by national levels of economic development and by the persistence of customary and religious restrictions on women. With few exceptions, women worldwide spend more hours per day working than do men; everywhere they are paid less for comparable work. A general world trend is toward greater equality for women in political and economic opportunities and status.

Part Four

URBAN SYSTEMS AND URBAN STRUCTURES

11

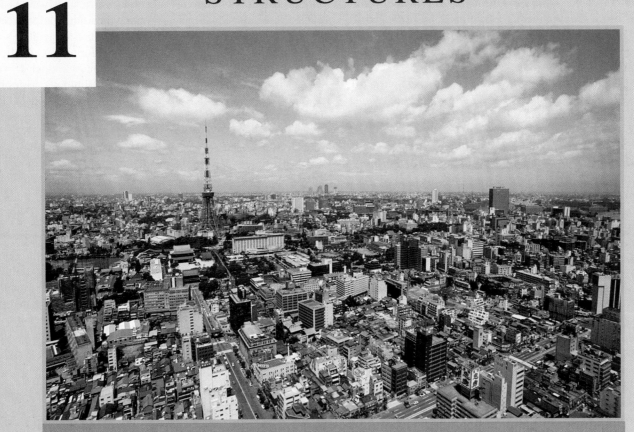

Tokyo, Japan, the world's most populous urban agglomeration.

Key Concepts

1. The nature of cities in an urbanizing world: origins, definitions, and locations, pp. 340–346.

2. The economic base and systems of cities: functions, hierarchies, and networks, pp. 346–353.

3. Inside the city: land uses, social areas, and patterns of change, pp. 354–369.

4. World urban diversity: European and non-Western cities, pp. 369–380.

airo was a world-class city in the 14th century. Situated at the crossroads of Africa, Asia, and Europe, it dominated trade on the Mediterranean Sea. By the early 1300s, it had a population of half a million or more, with 10- to 14-story buildings crowding the city center. A Cairo chronicler of the period recorded the construction of a huge building with shops on the first floors and apartments housing 4000 people above. One Italian visitor estimated that more people lived on a single Cairo street than in all of Florence. Travelers from all over Europe and Asia made their way to Cairo, and the shipping at its port of Bulaq outdistanced that of Venice and Genoa combined. The city contained more than 12,000 shops, some specializing in luxury goods from all over the world—Siberian sable, chain mail, musical instruments, luxurious cloth, and exotic songbirds. Travelers marveled at the size, density, and variety of Cairo, comparing it favorably with Venice, Paris, and Baghdad.

Today, Cairo is a vast, sprawling metropolis, plagued by many of the problems common to the urbanization of developing countries in which population growth has far outstripped economic development. The 1970 population of Egypt was 35.3 million; it had grown to more than 75 million by 2006, thanks to improved health care in general, a dramatic drop in infant mortality, a continuing high total fertility rate, and a lengthening of life expectancy. An estimated 12 million people reside in the Cairo greater metropolitan area; the metro area contains 45% of all Egyptian urban dwellers and 20% of the entire population of the country. Cairo city alone holds 11 million residents at a density of more than 32,000 per square kilometer (12,000 per sq mi). And the city continues to grow, spreading onto valued farmland and decreasing food production for the country's increasing population.

A steady stream of migrants arrives daily in Cairo where, they hope, opportunities will be available for a better and brighter life than in the crowded countryside. The city is the symbol of modern Egypt, a place where young people are willing to undergo deprivation for the chance to "make it." But real opportunities continue to be scarce. The poor, of whom there are millions, crowd into row after row of apartment houses, many of them poorly constructed. Tens of thousands more live in rooftop sheds or small boats on the Nile; a half million find shelter living between the tombs in the Northern and Southern Cemeteries—known as the Cities of the Dead—on Cairo's eastern edge. On occasion, buildings collapse; the earthquake of October 12, 1992, measuring 5.9 on the Richter scale, did enormous damage, leveling thousands of structures.

One's first impression when arriving in central Cairo is of opulence, a stark contrast to what lies outside the city center. High-rise apartments, regional headquarters buildings of multinational corporations, and modern hotels stand amid clogged streets, symbols of the new Egypt (Figure 11.1). New suburban developments and exclusive residential communities create enclaves for the wealthy whose plush apartments are but a short distance from the slums housing a largely unemployed 20% of Cairo's population. Like cities nearly everywhere in the developing world, Cairo has experienced explosive growth that finds an increasing proportion of the country's population housed in an urban area without the economy or facilities to support them

all. Street congestion and idling traffic generate air pollution now worse than that of Mexico City, long the holder of that world record. Both the Nile River and the city's treated drinking water show dangerous levels of lead and cadmium, the unwanted by-products of the local lead smelter.

Cairo is a classic case of an urban explosion that sees an increasing proportion of the world's population housed within a growing number of both very large and mid-size cities. Urban population overall is growing more rapidly than the population as a whole and, by most estimates, by larger annual increments than ever before. In this chapter we turn to urbanization, which has always accompanied economic advancement. Among their other purposes cities serve as concentrations of people and activities to facilitate social interaction and the efficient exchange of information, goods, and services. Manufacturing and trade imply concentrations of workers, managers, merchants, and supporting institutions. Cities exist as functional nodes within a broader, hierarchical system of cities. Cities are also unique places with complex internal arrangements of land uses and social groups. In this chapter we begin by examining systems of cities and then turn our attention to life inside cities in different parts of the world.

An Urbanizing World

Figure 11.2 gives evidence that the growth of cities and major metropolitan areas was astounding in the 20th century. Some 411 metropolitan areas each had in excess of 1 million people by 2000; in 1900, there were only 12. Expectations are for 564 "million cities" in 2015. As many as 19 metropolises had populations of 10 million or more people in 2007, the United Nations calls them *megacities* (Figure 11.3). In 1900, none was of that size and in 1975 there were just 3.

Figure 11.1 Sprawling Cairo, Egypt. The population growth in the greater metropolitan area—from some 3 million in 1970 to an estimated 15 million today—has been mirrored in most developing countries. The rapid expansion of urban areas and populations brings housing shortages, inadequate transportation and other infrastructure development, unemployment, poverty, and environmental deterioration.

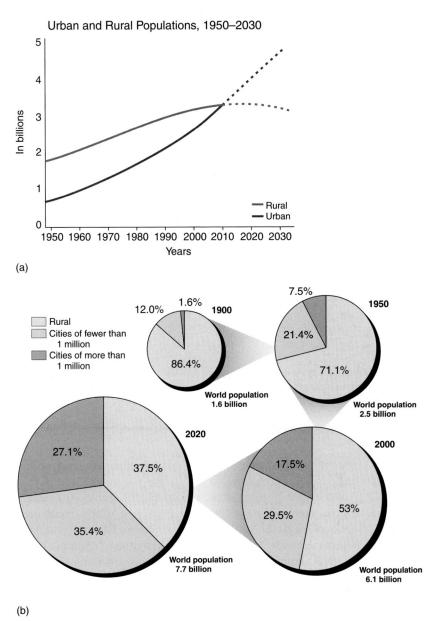

Urban and Rural Populations, 1950–2030

(a)

Rural
Urban

1900
1.6%
12.0%
86.4%
World population
1.6 billion

Rural
Cities of fewer than 1 million
Cities of more than 1 million

1950
7.5%
21.4%
71.1%
World population
2.5 billion

2020
27.1%
37.5%
35.4%
World population
7.7 billion

2000
17.5%
29.5%
53%
World population
6.1 billion

(b)

Figure 11.2 **Trends of world urbanization** document the steady decline in rural population proportions throughout the 20th century. *(a)* Since 1950, the growth rate of the rural component has slackened compared to the urban rate; by 2008, world urban numbers overtook the rural. *(b)* The United Nations estimates that virtually all the population growth expected during 2000–2020 will be concentrated in the urban areas of the world and that small and medium-sized cities will increase more rapidly than will megacities.

Source: United Nations, World Urbanization Prospects: The 2003 Revision and 2007 Revision, Population Reference Bureau, and other sources.

It follows, of course, that since the world's total population has greatly increased over the centuries, so too would its urban component—from 3% in 1800 to half in 2008. The urban share of the total has grown everywhere as urbanization has spread to all parts of the globe. Indeed, in 2008, for the first time in history, more people were living in cities than in rural areas.

The amount of urban growth differs from continent to continent and from region to region, but nearly all countries have two things in common: the proportion of their people living in cities

is rising, and the cities themselves are large and growing. The UN projects that urban majorities will exist in essentially all regions of the world by 2015 or 2020 and will reach more than 60% of the world's population by 2030 (Table 11.1).

The vast majority of urban growth will occur in low- to middle-income countries of the developing world. Industrialization spurred the earlier rapid urbanization in the present highly developed regions of Western Europe and North America. In many of the still-developing countries, however, urban expansion is only partly the result of the transition from agricultural to industrial economies. Rather, in many of those areas people flock to cities as refugees from impoverished rural districts; by their numbers and high fertility rates they accelerate city expansion. Even the high-income, highly developed states—with low or negative rates of natural population increase—will experience multicultural expansion from international migrants seeking livelihood opportunities in their cities. Worldwide in 2006 there were at least 200 million international migrants, and almost all migrants—whatever their destination country—seek refuge in cities. The result everywhere is growing urban multiculturalism with attendant problems of social fragmentation and minority segregation, isolation, and poverty, affecting primarily the largest cities of the inflow state.

Megacities and Merging Metropolises

The emergence of megacities aroused dire predictions that there would soon be cities of totally unmanageable size—25 million inhabitants or more. Those size predictions now appear to have been overblown in many cases, reflecting simple extrapolation. In reality megacity growth rates and sizes are below those earlier anticipated. Largest cities have proved not to be the fastest growing agglomerations. Megacities in 1975 held 2% of world population; in 2006, they contained only 4% and are expected to hold less than 5% by 2015. Although data are not totally conclusive, the earlier rapid expansion of many megacities has been slowing and some of the largest may now, in fact, be stabilized or even losing population. While megacities such as São Paulo, Brazil, and Mexico City may, indeed, have stopped growing, mid-size cities such as Curitiba (Brazil) and Monterrey (Mexico) within the same countries are expanding, with at least part of their growth representing out-migrants from the megacities and government programs encouraging investment and population retention within smaller towns and mid-sized cities.

When separate major metropolitan complexes of whatever size expand along the superior transportation facilities connecting them, they may eventually meet, bind together at their outer margins, and create the extensive metropolitan regions or **conurbations** suggested on Figure 11.3. Where this increasingly common pattern

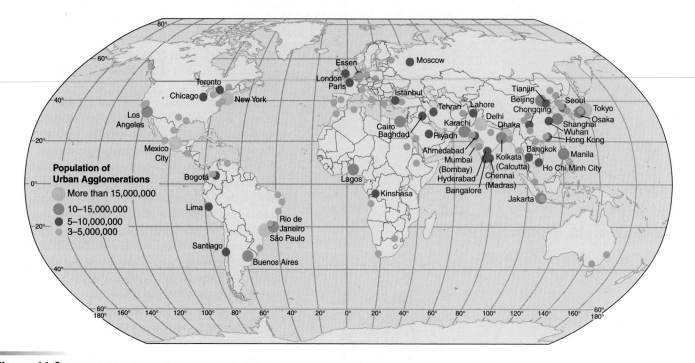

Figure 11.3 **Metropolitan areas of 3 million or more in 2006.** Only metropolitan areas with a population of 5 million or more are named. Massive urbanized districts are no longer characteristic only of the industrialized, developed countries. They are now found on every continent, in all latitudes, as part of most economics and societies. Not all cities in congested areas are shown.

Source: Data from United Nations Population Division.

Table 11.1

Estimated Urban Share of Total Population, Selected Areas: 1950, 2005, and 2030

Region or Country	1950	2005	2030
North America	64	79	87
Latin America and Caribbean	42	76	85
Europe	51	74	80
Russia	45	73	78
Oceania	61	72	75
China	13	37	61
Southeast Asia	15	38	61
Africa	15	36	54
More developed	53	76	82
Less developed	18	42	57
World	29	47	61

Sources: United Nations Population Division and Population Reference Bureau.

of continuous urbanization made up of multiple centers that have come together at their edges.

A major North American example, *Megalopolis* (already encountered in Chapter 9, page 290), is a nearly continuous urban string that stretches from north of Boston (southern Maine) to south of Washington, D.C. (southern Virginia). Other North American present or emerging conurbations shown on Figure 11.4 include: the southern Great Lakes region stretching from north of Milwaukee through Chicago and eastward to Detroit, Cleveland, and Pittsburgh; the Coastal California zone of San Francisco–Los Angeles–San Diego–Tijuana, Mexico; the Canadian "core region" conurbation from Montreal to Windsor, opposite Detroit, Michigan, where it connects with the southern Great Lakes region; the Vancouver–Willamette strip ("Cascadia") in the West, and the Gulf Coast and the Coastal Florida zones in the Southeast. Outside North America, examples of conurbations are numerous and growing, still primarily in the most industrialized European and East Asian (Japanese) districts, but forming as well in the other world regions where urban clusters and megacities emerged in developing countries still primarily rural in residential pattern.

Settlement Roots

The major cities of today had humbler origins, their roots lying in the clustered dwellings which everywhere have been the rule of human settlement. People are gregarious and cooperative. Even Stone Age hunters and gatherers lived and worked in groups, not as single individuals or isolated families. Primitive cultures are

has emerged, the urban landscape can no longer be described in simple terms. No longer is there a single city with a single downtown area set off by open countryside from any other urban unit in its vicinity. Rather, we must now recognize extensive regions

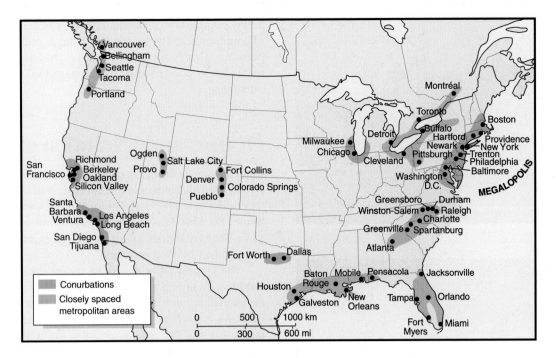

Figure 11.4 Megalopolis and other Anglo American conurbations. The northeast U.S. Boston-to-Norfolk urban corridor comprises the original and largest *Megalopolis* and contains the economic, political, and administrative core of the United States. A Canadian counterpart core region anchored by Montreal and Toronto connects with U.S. contributions through Buffalo, New York, and Detroit, Michigan. For some of their extent, conurbations fulfill their classic definition of continuous built-up urban areas. In other portions, they are more statistical than landscape entities, marked by counties that qualify as "urban" or "metropolitan" even though land uses may appear dominantly rural.

communal for protection, cooperative effort, sharing of tasks by age and sex, and for more subtle psychological and social reasons. Communal dwelling became the near-universal rule with the advent of sedentary agriculture wherever it developed, and the village became the norm of human society.

In most of the world still, most rural people live in nucleated settlements, that is, in villages or hamlets, rather than in dispersed dwellings or isolated farmsteads. Only in Anglo America, parts of northern and western Europe, and in Australia and New Zealand do rural folk tend to live apart, with houses and farm buildings located on land that is individually worked. Elsewhere in the world, villages and hamlets were and are the settlement norm, though with size and form varied by region and culture. Intensity of agricultural land use, density of population, complexity and specialization of life and livelihood, and addition of functions other than the purely residential affected the size, distribution, external form, and internal structure of settlements (Figures 11.5 and 11.6).

Rural settlements in developing countries are often expressions of subsistence economic systems in which farming and fishing cultures produce no more than their individual families can consume. When trade does develop between two or more rural settlements, they begin to take on new physical characteristics as their inhabitants

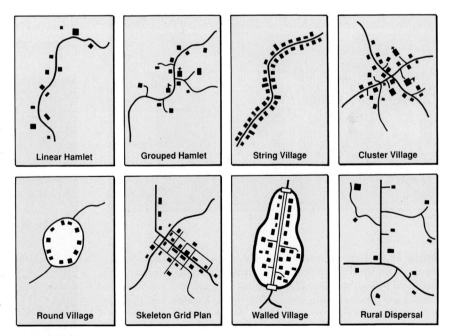

Figure 11.5 Basic settlement forms. The smallest organized rural clusters of houses and nonresidential structures are commonly called *hamlets,* and may contain only 10–15 buildings. *Villages* are larger agglomerations, although not as sizable or functionally complex as urban *towns.* The distinction between village and town is usually a statistical definition that varies by country.

Source: Redrawn from Introducing Cultural Geography, *2d ed., by J. E. Spencer and W. L. Thomas. Coypright © 1978 John Wiley & Sons, Inc. Reproduced with permission of John Wiley & Sons, Inc.*

(a)

(b)

(c)

Figure 11.6 Rural settlements in largely subsistence economies vary from the rather small populations characteristic of compact African villages, such as (*a*) the Zulu village, or kraal, in South Africa to more dispersed and populous settlements such as (*b*) the Nepalese high pasture summer village of Konar, to (*c*) very large, densely populated Indian rural communities.

engage in additional types of occupations. The villages lose the purely social and residential character of subsistence agricultural settlements and assume urban features. The beginnings of urbanization are seen in the types of buildings that are erected and in the heightened importance of the main streets and of the roads leading to other settlements. No longer are the settlements

nearly completely self-contained; they become part of a system of communities. The location of villages relative to one another becomes significant as the once self-sufficient rural settlements become towns and cities engaged in urban activities and interchange.

Origins and Evolution of Cities

Cities are among the oldest marks of civilization; indeed, "city" and "civilization" have the same Latin root, *civis*. Dating from at least 6000 years ago, they originated in—or diffused from—the culture hearths that first developed sedentary agriculture (Figures 2.15 and 11.7). They are as well among the newest experiences of a growing share of the world's population.

The earliest cities depended on the creation of agricultural surpluses. Many early cities included farms within their walls, but the main distinction between the city and the countryside stemmed from the nonagricultural pursuits of most urban dwellers. This meant that food had to be provided to the urban population by the **hinterland**—the productive area surrounding a population center. Those in the nascent town who were not involved in farming were free to specialize in other activities—metal working, pottery making, cloth weaving, perhaps—producing goods for other urbanites and for the farm population on which they depended. Still others became scribes, merchants, priests, soldiers, and the like, providing the services and refining the power structure on which the organized urban and rural society depended.

Social organization and a defined power structure, reflected in a religious hierarchy and civil administration, were essential in urban development. Ancient cities centered on a principal temple or palace district housing the priests, the ruler, public storehouses

Figure 11.7 Aerial view of Erbil, Iraq. The site of modern Erbil—the ancient Assyrian city of Arabilu—has been continuously inhabited for about 8000 years. The debris of millennia of urban settlement gradually raised the level of the land surface, producing a *tell,* or occupation mound. The city—one of the oldest in the world—literally was constantly rebuilt at higher elevations on the accumulation of refuse of earlier occupants.

Figure 11.8 By Europe's Middle Ages, the ancient need for city protection remained, but fortifications and defensive structures had assumed elaborate and massive forms unknown and unneeded before siege weapons and siege warfare put all cities in jeopardy. The walls of Ávila, Spain, shown here, were built in the 12th century, extending 2500 meters (8200 ft) and encircling the entire city at that time; the modern part of Ávila lies outside.

Figure 11.9 The densely built historic medieval section of Florence, Italy, is dominated by the Cathedral Santa Maria del Fiore. Florence prospered in the late Middle Ages as a center for textiles, artisanal craft industries, trade and banking. It reached a population of 95,000 in 1300 before the plague decimated its population. In the 15th century it was the center for the rediscovery of classical culture and was home to artists such as Botticelli, Leonardo da Vinci, and Michelangelo.

and granaries, public baths, perhaps schools, and certainly a central marketplace. Cities became the seats of local and regional power, exercising control over the rural hinterland and extracting agricultural surplus from it for redistribution in the city. If possible, ancient cities were located in spots easy to defend—on hilltops, often—but nearly always in addition the community built walls and perimeter defenses to enhance its protection (Figure 11.8). The massive protective walls of early cities, however, could also limit the expansion of prospering, growing communities. Some cities, like Rome, went through multiple rounds of wall construction, with each new outer wall extending the urban area within which functions could be located and workers housed.

Among those functions and workers were those engaged in long-distance trade, exchanging local goods and materials for raw materials and special products not easily or at all obtainable locally. Merchants, wholesalers, clerks, scribes, carters, river men and sailors, and those who produced the vessels and supplied the necessary trade support services came to characterize and dominate the functional base of the city. The importance of city location on navigable waterways, always a key to urban economic success, became ever more important.

In Europe and Asia, from about the 11th to the 18th century, local and distant trade, production of consumer goods by craftsmen organized into protective guilds, and increasing use of water-powered mills for grinding grain, fulling cloth, sawing timber, and the like moved cities from their ancient agriculturally based roots to intricate involvement in nearly modern forms of interregional and international economy. Massive trade fairs, international banking houses, and cooperative leagues of cities were precursors of the global marketing, stock exchanges and clearinghouses, and regional trade alliances of today. (Figure 11.9).

With the Industrial Revolution, another shift in economic orientation took place. Industrialization accelerated urbanization, initially in Europe, then elsewhere where European control

or influence was extended. Powered by water or steam, the new machinery in factories—operated by paid laborers, not by independent guild members—introduced mass production of standardized goods; it inevitably led, as well, to increasing economic and social stratification of urban populations. Cities, once centered on the temple or the palace, once surrounded by walls, once focused on the marketplace and the river or sea front, changed utterly; their economic fortunes now centered on the factories, the canals, the railroads, and the housing required by their hired workers.

The Nature of Cities

Whether ancient or modern, all cities show regularities appropriate to their time and place of existence. First, all perform functions—have an economic base—generating the income necessary to support themselves and their contained population. Second, none exists in a vacuum; each is part of a larger society and economy with which it has essential reciprocal connections. That is, each is a unit in a system of cities and a focus for a surrounding nonurban area. Third, each urban unit has a more or less orderly internal arrangement of land uses, social groups, and economic functions. These arrangements may be partially planned and controlled and partially determined by individual decisions and market forces. Finally, all cities, large or small, ancient or modern, have experienced problems of land use, social conflict, and environmental concern. Yet cities, though flawed, remain the capstone of our cultures, the organizing focuses of modern societies and economies, the magnet of people everywhere.

All urban settlements exist for the efficient performance of functions required by the society that creates them. They reflect the saving of time, energy, and money that the agglomeration of people and activities implies. The more accessible the producer to the consumer, the worker to the workplace, the citizen to the town hall, the worshiper to the church, or the lawyer or doctor to the client, the more efficient is the performance of their separate activities, and the more effective is the integration of urban functions.

Because all urban functions and people cannot be located at a single point, cities themselves must take up space, and land uses and populations must have room within them. Because interconnection is essential, the nature of the transportation system will have an enormous bearing on the total number of services that can be performed and the efficiency with which they can be carried out. The totality of people and functions of a city constitutes a distinctive cultural landscape whose similarities and differences from place to place are the subjects for urban geographic analysis.

The Location of Urban Settlements

Urban centers are functionally connected to other cities and to rural areas. In fact, the reason for the existence of an urban unit is not only to provide services for itself, but for others outside of it. The urban center is a consumer of food, a processor of materials, and an accumulator and dispenser of goods and services. But it must depend on outside areas for its essential supplies and as a market for its products and activities.

In order to adequately perform the tasks that support it and to add new functions as demanded by the larger economy, the city must be efficiently located. That efficiency may be marked by centrality to the area served. It may derive from the physical characteristics of its site. Or placement may be related to the resources, productive regions, and transportation network of the country, so that the effective performance of a wide array of activities is possible.

In discussing urban settlement location, geographers usually mention the significance of site and situation, concepts already introduced in Chapter 1 (see p. 8 and Figures 1.6 and 1.7). You will recall that *site* refers to the exact terrain features associated with the city, as well as—less usefully—to its absolute (globe grid) location. Classifications of cities according to site characteristics have been proposed, recognizing special placement circumstances. These include *break-of-bulk* locations such as river crossing points where cargoes and people must interrupt a journey; *head-of-navigation* or *bay head* locations where the limits of water transportation are reached; and *railhead* locations where a railroad ended. In Europe, security and defense—island locations or elevated sites—were considerations in earlier settlement placements. Waterpower sites of earlier stages and coalfields of later phases of the Industrial Revolution were noted in Chapters 8 and 9 and represent a union of environmental and cultural–economic considerations.

If site suggests absolute location, situation indicates relative location that places a settlement in relation to the physical and cultural characteristics of surrounding areas. Very often it is important to know what kinds of possibilities and activities exist in the area near a settlement, such as the distribution of raw materials, market areas, agricultural regions, mountains, and oceans. Although in many ways more important than site in understanding the functions and growth potentials of cities, situation is more nearly unique to each settlement and does not lend itself to easy generalization.

The site or situation that originally gave rise to an urban unit may not remain the essential ingredient for its growth and development for very long. Agglomerations originally successful for whatever reason may by their success attract people and activities totally unrelated to the initial localizing forces. By what has been called a process of "circular and cumulative causation" (see p. 312), a successful urban unit may acquire new populations and functions attracted by the already existing markets, labor force, and urban facilities. In the same way, a site that originally favored the success of the new urban unit—on a navigable river or coal field, perhaps—may with the passage of time no longer be important in supporting any or all of its current economic activities.

The Economic Base

We saw that from their ancient beginnings, cities depended on close reciprocal relationships with their hinterlands. They provided the market where rural produce could be exchanged for the goods produced and the defense or religious functions performed by the city. Such rural service functions remain important. However, not all of the activities carried on within a city are intended to connect that city with the outside world. Some are necessary simply to support the city itself. Together, these two levels of activity make up the **economic base** of an urban settlement. Understanding the growth or decline of cities hinges on grasping the relationship between the two sectors.

Part of the employed population of an urban unit is engaged either in the production of goods or the performance of services for areas and people outside the city itself. They are workers engaged in "export" activities, whose efforts result in money flowing into the community. Collectively, they constitute the **basic sector** of the city's total economic structure.

Other workers support themselves by producing goods or services for residents of the urban unit itself. Their efforts, necessary to the well-being and the successful operation of the settlement, do not generate new money for it but comprise a **nonbasic sector** of its economy. These people are responsible for the internal functioning of the urban unit. They are crucial to the continued operation of its stores, professional offices, city government, local transit, and school systems.

The total economic structure of an urban area equals the sum of its basic and nonbasic activities. In actuality, it is difficult to classify work as belonging exclusively to one sector or the other. Some part of the work of most people involves financial interaction with residents of other areas. Doctors, for example, may have mainly local patients and thus are members of the nonbasic sector, but the moment they provide a service to someone from outside the community, they bring new money into the city and become part of the basic sector.

Variations in basic employment structure among urban units characterize the specific functional role played by individual cities. Most centers perform many export functions, and the larger the urban unit, the more multifunctional it becomes. Nonetheless, even in cities with a diversified economic base, one or a very small number of export activities tends to dominate the structure of the community and to identify its operational purpose within a system of cities. Figure 11.10 indicates the functional specializations of some large U.S. metropolitan areas.

Assuming it were possible to divide with complete accuracy the employed population of a city into totally separate basic and service (nonbasic) components, a ratio between the two employment groups could be established.

This *basic/nonbasic ratio* shown in Figure 11.11 indicates that as a settlement increases in size, the number of nonbasic personnel grows faster than the number of new basic workers. In cities with a population of 1 million, the ratio is about two nonbasic workers for every basic worker. This means that adding ten new basic employees expands the labor

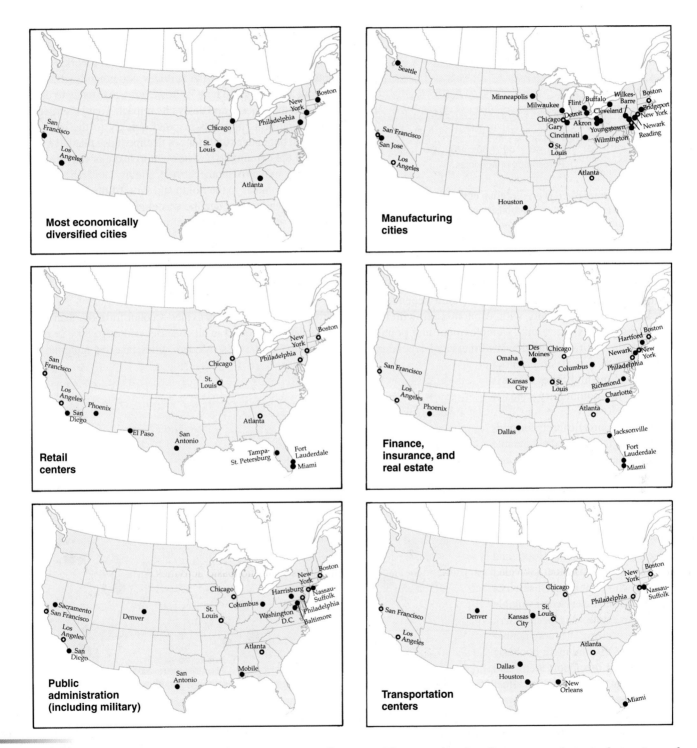

Figure 11.10 **Functional specialization of selected U.S. metropolitan areas.** Five categories of employment were chosen to show patterns of specialization for some U.S. metropolitan areas. In addition, the category "Most Economically Diversified" includes representative examples of cities with a generally balanced employment distribution. Since their "balance" implies performance of a variety of functions, the diversified cities are included as open circles on the other specialization maps. Note that the most diversified urban areas tend to be the largest.

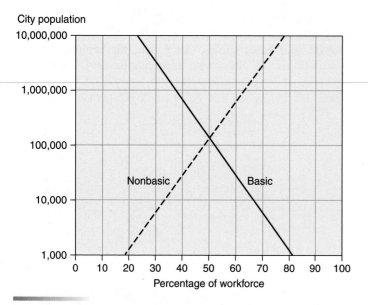

Figure 11.11 **A generalized representation of the proportion of the workforce engaged in basic and nonbasic activities.** As settlements become larger, a greater proportion of the workforce is employed in nonbasic activities. Larger centers are therefore more self-contained.

force by 30 (10 basic, 20 nonbasic). The resultant increase in total population is equal to the added workers plus their dependents. A **multiplier effect** associated with economic growth thus exists. The term means that a city's employment and population grow with the addition of nonbasic workers and dependents as a supplement to new basic employment. The size of the multiplier effect is determined by the community's basic/nonbasic ratio.

The changing numerical relationships shown in Figure 11.11 are understandable when we consider how settlements add functions and grow in population. A new industry selling services to other communities requires new workers who thus increase the basic workforce. These new employees in turn demand certain goods and services, such as clothing, food, and medical assistance, which are provided locally. Those who perform such services must themselves have services available to them. For example, a grocery clerk must also buy groceries. The more nonbasic workers a city has, the more nonbasic workers are needed to support them, and the application of the multiplier effect becomes obvious.

The growth of cities may be self-generating—"circular and cumulative"—in a way related not to the development of industries that specialize in the production of material objects for export, like automobiles and paper products, but

to the attraction of what would be classified as *service* activity. Banking and legal services, a sizable market, a diversified labor force, extensive public services, and the like may generate additions to the labor force not basic by definition, but nonbasic. In recent years, service industries have developed to the point where new service activities serve older ones. For example, computer systems firms aid banks in developing more efficient computer-driven banking systems.

In much the same way as settlements grow in size and complexity, so do they decline. When the demand for the goods and services of an urban unit falls, obviously fewer workers are needed and both the basic and the services components of a settlement system are affected. There is, however, a resistance to decline that impedes the process and delays its impact. That is, settlements can grow rapidly as migrants respond quickly to the need for more workers, but under conditions of decline those that have developed roots in the community are hesitant to leave or may be financially unable to move to another locale. Figure 11.12 shows that in the 1990s urban areas in the South and West of the United States were growing, while some decline was evident in the Northeast and the Midwest regions; that regional pattern has largely continued into the 21st century.

The Functions of Cities

Urban-based economic activities account for more than 50% of the gross national product in all countries and up to 80% or more in the more urbanized states. Modern cities take on multiple functions.

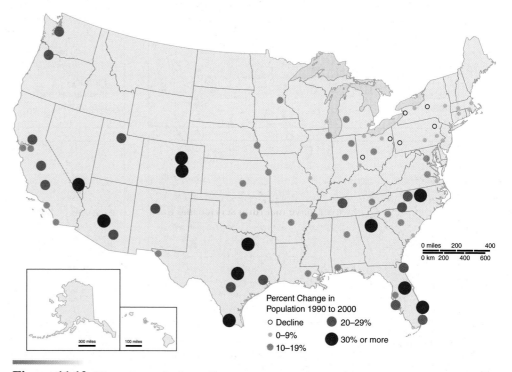

Figure 11.12 **The pattern of metropolitan growth and decline in the United States, 1990–2000.** Shown are metropolitan areas with 600,000 or more population in 2000. The cities of the southern and southwestern Sun Belt showed the greatest relative growth. Only modest growth, stability, or decline generally marked the Northeast and Midwest.

Source: Data from U.S. Bureau of the Census.

These include manufacturing, retailing, wholesaling, transportation, public administration, housing cultural and educational institutions and, of course, the housing of their own citizens. Most cities, however, specialize in, or are dominated by, only one or a very few of the full range of economic activities. Only a relatively few very large members of a national system of cities are importantly multifunctional and truly diversified.

No matter what their size, cities exist for the efficient performance of necessary functions. Those functions reflect cities' roles as transportation nodes, central places, and special-functional cities. All centers provide the first two functions; some may be dominated by special functions or, at least, include them within their composite economic structure. Each class has its own characteristic spatial arrangement; together, the three classes help explain the distributional pattern and the size and functional hierarchies of the entire city system.

The spatial pattern of *transportation centers* is that of alignment—along seacoasts, major and minor rivers, canals, or railways. Routes of communication form the orienting axes along which cities developed and on which at least their initial functional success depended (Figure 11.13). *Special-function cities* are those engaged in mining, manufacturing, or other activities the localization of which is related to raw material occurrence, agglomeration economies, or the circular and cumulative attractions of constantly growing market and labor concentrations. Special-function cities show a pattern of urban clustering—as the mining and manufacturing cities of the Ruhr district of Germany, the Midlands of England, or the Donets Basin in Ukraine, for example.

Beginning with the Industrial Revolution of the 18th century, manufacturing industries were a major impetus for urban growth. The handicraft production of goods was, of course, always a part of the functional base of even the earliest urban units. Only with the rise of mass production, however, did industry become a primary basic urban function, producing wealth and, through the *multiplier effect,* expanding the numbers of basic and nonbasic workers through the export of manufactured goods throughout the larger economy.

A common property of all settlements is centrality, no matter what their recognized functional specializations. Every urban unit provides goods and services for a surrounding area tributary to it. For many, including mining or major manufacturing centers, service to tributary areas is only a very minor part of their economic base. Some settlements, however, have that rural service and trade function as their dominant role, and these make up the third simplified category of cities: *central places.*

Cities as Central Places

Central places are nodes for the distribution of economic goods and services to surrounding nonurban populations. For as long as cities have existed, they have served as marketplaces, not only for their own residents, but also for the population beyond the city limits. Small cities provide a range of goods and services that suffice for most everyday needs. But specialized "higher-order" expensive or unique commodities and skilled specialized services can be found only in the largest centers. To serve the rural populations, central places show size and spacing regularities unrelated to the

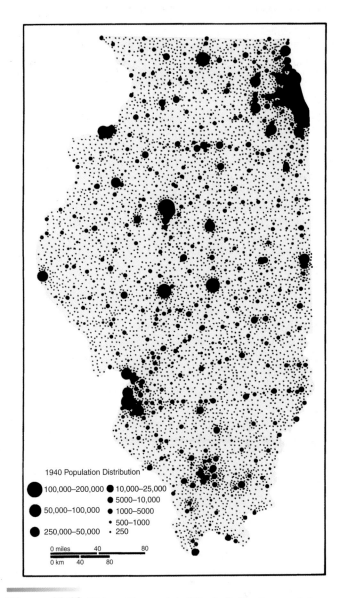

1940 Population Distribution

Figure 11.13 **Urban alignments in Illinois.** Railroads preceded settlement in much of the Anglo American continental interior, and urban centers were developed—frequently by the railroad companies themselves—as collecting and distributing points expected to grow as the farm populations increased. Located at constant 8-to 10-kilometer (5-to 6-mile) intervals in Illinois, the rail towns were the focal points of an expanding commercial agriculture. The linearity of the town pattern in 1940, at the peak of railroad influence, unmistakably marks the rail routes. Also evident are such special-function clusterings as the Chicago and St. Louis metropolitan districts and the mining towns of Southern Illinois. In addition to the linear and cluster patterns, the smallest towns show the uniform distribution characteristic of central places.

patterns of alignment and clustering characteristic of transportation and special function cities. Instead, they display a regularity of distribution, with towns of about the same size and performing about the same number and kind of functions located about the same distance from each other.

The geographer Walter Christaller developed **central place theory** to explain those observed settlement size and spacing regularities (see "Central Place Theory"). He observed a pattern of interdependent small, medium, and larger towns that together

In 1933, the German geographer **Walter Christaller** attempted to explain the size and spacing regularities he observed for towns in Southern Germany. In doing so he developed a framework, called *central place theory,* that provided the descriptive understandings he sought. Christaller did recognize that his explanatory theory would best describe an idealized and somewhat artificial situation with the following characteristics:

1. Towns that provide the surrounding rural agricultural population with such fundamental goods as groceries and clothing would develop on a uniform plain with no topographic barriers, channelization of traffic, or variations in farm productivity.

2. The rural population would be dispersed in an even pattern across that plain.

3. The characteristics of the people would be uniform; that is, they would possess similar tastes, demands, and incomes.

4. Each kind of product or service available to the dispersed population would have its own *threshold,* or minimum number of consumers needed to support its supply. Because such goods as sports cars or fur coats are either expensive or not in great demand, they would have a high threshold, while a fewer number of customers within smaller tributary areas would be sufficient to support a small grocery store.

5. Consumers would purchase goods and services from the nearest opportunity (store or supplier).

When all of Christaller's assumptions are considered simultaneously, they yield the following results:

1. Since each customer patronizes the nearest center offering the needed goods, the agricultural plain is automatically divided into noncompeting market areas—*complementary regions*—where each individual town (and its merchants) has a sales monopoly.

2. Those market areas will take the form of a series of hexagons that cover the entire plain, as shown in the diagram.

  - ◉ A central place
  - ● B central place
  - ● C central place

Complementary regions and the pattern of central places. The two A central places are the largest on this diagram of one of Christaller's models. The B central places offer fewer goods and services for sale and serve only the areas of the intermediate-sized hexagons. The many C central places, which are considerably smaller and more closely spaced, serve still smaller market areas. The goods offered in the C places are also offered in the B and A places, but the latter offer considerably more and more specialized goods. Notice that places of the same size are equally spaced.

Source: Arthur Getis and Judith Getis, "Christaller's Central Place Theory." Journal of Geography, *1966. Used with permission of the National Council for Geographic Education.*

There will be a central place at the center of each of the hexagonal market areas.

3. The size of the market area of a central place will be proportional to the number of goods and services offered from that place and the largest central places (with the largest market areas) will supply all the goods and services the consumers in that area demand and can afford.

4. As the diagram indicates, the central place pattern shows a "nesting" of complementary regions in which part or all of multiple lower-order service areas are contained within the market area of a higher-order center.

In addition, Christaller reached two important conclusions. First, towns at the same size (functional level) in the central place system will be evenly spaced, and larger towns (higher-order places) will be farther apart than smaller ones. This means that many more small than large towns will exist. In the diagram, the ratio of the number of small towns to towns of the next larger size is 3 to 1. This distinct, steplike series of towns in discrete classes differentiated by both size and function is called a *hierarchy of central places.*

Second, the system of towns is interdependent. If one central place were eliminated, the entire system would have to readjust. Consumers need a variety of products and services, each of which has a different minimum number of customers required to support it. The towns containing many goods and services become regional retailing centers, while the smaller central places serve just the people in their immediate vicinity. The higher the threshold of a desired product, the farther, on average, the consumer must travel to purchase it.

could provide the goods and services needed by a dispersed rural population. Small towns, Christaller postulated, would serve as marketplaces for frequently required "low order" commodities and services, while expensive luxury goods would be available only in larger communities that were central to a number of surrounding small towns. People, that is, would have to travel only short distances for basic things, such as groceries or haircuts, and longer distances for expensive and infrequently demanded goods and services, such as luxury automobiles or specialized medical treatments.

Christaller's explanation and description of the urban size and spacing regularities he observed have been shown to be generally applicable in widely differing regions of the world. When varying incomes, cultures, physical landscapes, and transportation systems are taken into consideration, his theory holds up rather well. It is particularly applicable, of course, to agricultural areas with a uniform distribution of consumers and purchasing power. If we combine a Christaller-type approach with the ideas of industrial location that help us understand the cluster patterns of special-function cities (see Chapter 9) and the alignments of transportation-based cities, we have a fairly good understanding of the distribution of most towns and cities.

The interdependence of small, medium, and large cities can also be seen in their influence on each other. A small city may influence a local region of some 1000+ square kilometers (400 sq mi) if, for example, its newspaper is delivered to that district. Beyond that area, another city may be the dominant influence. **Urban influence zones** are the areas outside of a city that are still affected by it. As the distance away from a community increases, its influence on the surrounding countryside decreases (recall the idea of distance decay discussed in Chapter 3, p. 60). The sphere of influence of an urban unit is usually proportional to its size.

A large city located, for example, 100 kilometers (62 miles) away from a small city may influence that and other smaller communities through its banking services, TV stations, professional sports teams, and large shopping malls. There is an overlapping hierarchical arrangement, and the influence of the largest cities is felt over the widest areas, a "market area" dominance basic to central place theory.

Intricate relationships and hierarchies are common. Consider Grand Forks, North Dakota, which for local market purposes dominates the rural area immediately surrounding it. However, Grand Forks is influenced by political decisions made in the state capital, Bismarck. For a variety of cultural, commercial, and banking activities, Grand Forks is influenced by Minneapolis. As a center of wheat production, Grand Forks and Minneapolis are subordinate to the grain market in Chicago. Of course, the pervasive agricultural and other political controls exerted from Washington, D.C., on Grand Forks, Minneapolis, and Chicago indicate how large and complex are urban zones of influence.

Systems of Cities

The recognition of transportation, special function, and central place cities helps us visualize and understand patterns of urban size, spacing, and distribution. It also reminds us that cities are interdependent. Any given urban unit may have few or multiple functions and those are influenced by its location and size and—very strongly—by its distance from, size of, and functions of other cities.

The Urban Hierarchy

Perhaps the most effective way to recognize how systems of cities are organized is to consider the **urban hierarchy,** a ranking of cities based on their size and functional complexity. One can measure the numbers and kinds of functions each city or metropolitan area provides. The hierarchy is then like a pyramid; a few large and complex cities are at the top and many smaller, simpler ones are at the bottom. There are always more smaller cities than larger ones.

When a spatial dimension is added to the hierarchy as in Figure 11.14, it becomes clear that an areal system of metropolitan centers, large cities, small cities, and towns exists. Goods, services, communications, and people flow up and down the hierarchy. The few high-level metropolitan areas provide specialized functions for large regions while the smaller cities serve smaller districts. The separate centers interact with the areas around them, but since cities of the same level provide roughly the same services, those of the same size tend not to serve each other unless they provide some very specialized activity, such as housing the political capital of a region or a major hospital or university. Thus,

Figure 11.14 A functional hierarchy of U.S. metropolitan areas. Only the major metropolitan areas are shown. The hierarchy includes smaller urban districts (not shown) that depend on or serve the larger centers.

Source: Redrawn from P. L. Knox, ed., The United States: A Contemporary Human Geography. *Harlow, England. Longman, 1988, Fig. 5.5, p. 144.*

the settlements of a given level in the hierarchy are not independent but interrelated with communities of other levels in that hierarchy. Together, all centers at all levels in the hierarchy constitute an urban system.

World Cities

Standing at the top of national systems of cities are a relatively few agglomerations that may be called **world cities.** These large urban centers are control points for international production, marketing, and finance. When manufacturing dominated the economy, much of what an individual company did—production, management, sales, accounting, etc.—took place in a single city, often in the same building. Now, the globalized economy and transnational corporations have scattered those functions and jobs across the world. But all those activities must be coordinated somewhere, and that place is the world city. Collectively, world cities have been termed the "control and command centers" of the global economy.

London, New York, and Tokyo have been generally recognized as the three dominant world cities. They contain the highest number of transnational service offices and headquarters of multinational corporations, and they dominate commerce in their respective parts of the world. Each is directly linked to a number of other primary and secondary level world cities. All are bound together in complex networks that control the organization and management of the global system of finance, production, and trade. Figure 11.15 shows the links between the dominant centers and some of the major and secondary world cities, which include Paris, Hong Kong, Singapore, Milan, Toronto, Chicago, and Los Angeles. These cities are all interconnected by advanced communication systems between governments, major corporations, stock and futures exchanges, securities and commodity markets, major banks, and international organizations.

Major transnational corporations themselves spur world city development and dominance. The growing size and complexity of transnational corporations dictate their need to outsource central managerial functions to specialized service firms to minimize the complexity of control over dispersed operations. Those specialized service agencies—legal, accounting, financial, etc.—in their turn need to draw on the very large pools of expertise, information, and talent available only in world cities.

Rank-Size and Primacy

The development of city systems on a global scale invites inquiry about the organization of city systems within regions or countries. The observation that there are many more small than large cities within an urban system ("the larger the fewer") is itself a statement about city hierarchies we normally expect. In some countries, especially those with complex economies and a long urban history, the city size hierarchy is summarized by the **rank-size rule.** It tells us that the nth largest city of a national system of cities will be $1/n$ the size of the largest city. That is, the second largest settlement will be $1/2$ the size of the largest, the 10th biggest will be $1/10$ the size of the first-ranked city. Although no national city system exactly meets the requirements of the rank-size rule, that of Russia and the United States closely approximates it.

Rank-size ordering is less applicable to countries with developing economies or where the city system is dominated by

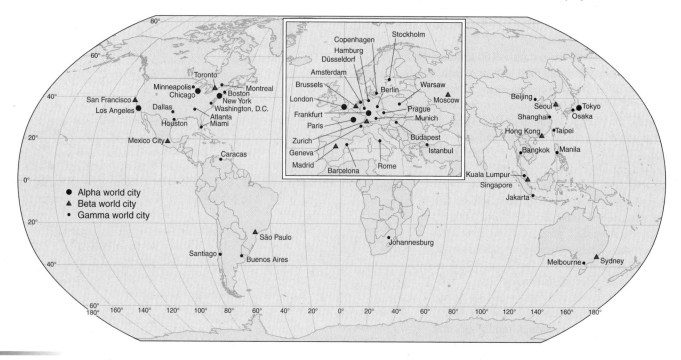

Figure 11.15 A classification of world (or global) cities based on international business services of advertising, accounting, banking, and law. These cities are bound together in complex networks, all interconnected by the flow of financial and economic information. A classification based on a different set of economic activities would yield a slightly different list but a similar hierarchy.

Source: Adapted from P. J. Taylor, D. R. F. Walker, and J. V. Beverstock, "Firms and their Global Service Networks," In S. Sassen, ed. (2002), Global Networks, Linked Cities, *New York: Routledge, pp. 93–115*

a **primate city,** one that is far more than twice the size of the second ranked city. In fact, there may be no obvious "second city" at all, for a characteristic of a primate city hierarchy is one very large city, few or no intermediate-sized cities, and many subordinate smaller settlements. For example, Seoul (at 10.3 million in 2006) contains over 20% of the total population and one-quarter of the urban population of South Korea, Luanda has well over one-half of Angola's urban folk, and Bangkok has 45% of Thailand's.

The capital cities of many developing countries display that kind of overwhelming primacy. In part, their primate city pattern is a heritage of their colonial past, when economic development, colonial administration, and transportation and trade activities were concentrated at a single point (Figure 11.16); Nairobi

(Kenya), Dakar (Senegal), and many other African capital cities are examples.

In other instances—Egypt (Cairo) or Mexico (Mexico City), for example—development and population growth have tended to concentrate disproportionately in a capital city whose very size attracts further development and growth. Many European countries—Austria, the United Kingdom, and France are familiar examples—also show a primate structure, often ascribed to the former concentration of economic and political power around the royal court in a capital city that was, perhaps, also the administrative and trade center of a larger colonial empire.

Network Cities

In recent years a new kind of urban spatial pattern has begun to appear, one seemingly divorced from the more recognized hierarchical orderings of cities we have reviewed. A **network city** evolves when two or more previously independent nearby cities, potentially complementary in functions, strive to cooperate by developing between them high-speed transportation corridors and communications infrastructure.

For example, since the reunion of Hong Kong and China proper in 1997, an infrastructure of highway and rail lines and of communications improvements has been developed to help integrate Hong Kong with Guangzhou, the huge, rapidly growing industrial and economic hub on the mainland. In Japan, three distinctive, nearby cities—Kyoto, Osaka, and Kobe—are joining together to compete with the Tokyo region as a major center of commerce. Kyoto, with its temples and artistic treasures, is the cultural capital of Japan; Osaka is a primary commercial and industrial center; and Kobe is a leading port. Their complementary functional strengths are reinforced by high speed rail transport connecting the cities and by a new airport (Kansai) designed to serve the entire region.

In Europe, the major cities of Amsterdam, Rotterdam, and The Hague, together with intermediate cities such as Delft, Utrecht, and Zaanstad, are connected by high speed rail lines and a major airport. Each of these cities has special functions not duplicated in the others and planners have no intention of developing competition between them. This region—called the Randstad—is second only to London in its popularity for international head offices, putting it in a strong position to compete for dominant world city status.

No similar network city has yet developed in the United States. The New York-Philadelphia, the Chicago-Milwaukee, the San Francisco-Oakland, or the Los Angeles-San Diego city pairings do not yet qualify for network city status since there has been no concerted effort to bring their competing interests together into a single structure of complementary activities.

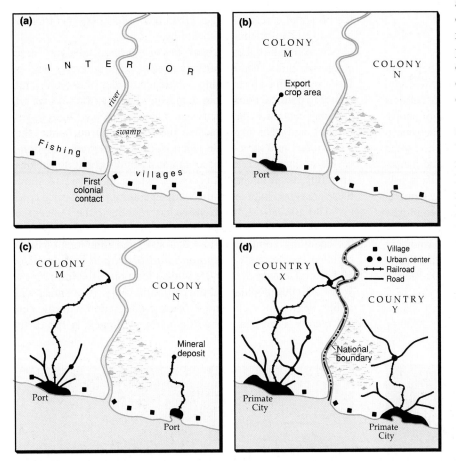

Figure 11.16 Primate city evolution. At first colonial contact (*a*) settlements are coastal and unconnected with each other. Joining a newly productive hinterland by European-built railroad to a new colonial port (*b*) begins to create a pattern of core-periphery relations and to focus European administration, trade, and settlement at the port. Mineral discoveries and another rail line in a neighboring colony across the river (*c*) mark the beginnings of a new set of core-periphery relationships and of a new multifunctional colonial capital nearby but unconnected by land with its neighbor. With the passage of time and further transport and economic development, two newly independent nations (*d*) display *primate city* structures in which further economic and population growth flows to the single dominating centers of countries lacking balanced regional transport networks, resource development, and urban structures. Both populations and new functions continue to seek locations in the primate city where their prospects for success are greatest.

Source: Adapted from E. S. Simpson, The Developing World: An Introduction. *(Harlow, Essex, England: Longman Group UK Limited, 1987.)*

Inside the City

The structure, patterns, and spatial interactions of systems of cities make up only half of the story of urban settlements. The other half involves the distinctive cultural landscapes that are the cities themselves. An understanding of the nature of cities is incomplete without a knowledge of their internal characteristics. So far, we have explored the origins and functions of cities within hierarchical urban systems. Now we look into the city itself to better understand how its land uses are distributed, how social areas are formed, and how institutional controls such as zoning regulations affect its structure. We will begin on familiar ground and focus our discussion primarily on United States cities. Later in this chapter we will review urban land use patterns and social geographies in different world settings. First, however, it is important to understand the common terms we will use throughout this section.

Defining the City Today

Urban units are not of a single type, structure, or size. Their common characteristic is that they are nucleated, nonagricultural settlements. At one end of the size scale, urban areas are hamlets or small towns with at most a single short main street of shops; at the opposite end, they are complex multifunctional metropolitan areas or megacities (Figure 11.17). The word *urban* is often used to describe such places as a town, city, suburb, and metropolitan area, but it is a general term, not used to specify a particular type or size of settlement. Although the terms designating the different types of urban settlement, like *city*, are employed in common speech, not everyone uses them in the same way. What is recognized as a city by a resident of rural Vermont or West Virginia might not at all be afforded that name and status by an inhabitant of California or New Jersey. One should keep in mind, as well, that the same term may be understood or defined differently in different parts of the world. In the United States, the Census Bureau describes an *urban* place as having 2500 or

more inhabitants. In Greece, *urban* refers to municipalities in which the largest population center has 10,000 or more inhabitants and Nicaragua uses the term to denote administrative centers with streets, lights, and at least 1000 inhabitants. It is useful in this chapter to agree on the meanings of terms commonly used but varyingly interpreted.

The words **city** and **town** denote nucleated settlements, multifunctional in character, including an established central business district and both residential and nonresidential land uses. Towns are smaller in size and have less functional complexity than cities, but they still have a nuclear business concentration. **Suburb** implies a subsidiary area, a functionally specialized segment of a larger urban complex. It may be dominantly or exclusively residential, industrial, or commercial, but by the specialization of its land uses and functions, a suburb is not self-sufficient. Suburbs can, however, be independent political entities. A **central city** is the principal core of a larger urban area, separately incorporated and ringed by its dependent suburbs.

Some or all of these urban types may be associated into larger composite units. The **urbanized area** is a continuously built-up landscape defined by building and population densities with no reference to political boundaries. It may be viewed as the *physical city* and may contain a central city and many contiguous cities, towns, suburbs, and other urban tracts. A **metropolitan area,** on the other hand, refers to a large-scale *functional* entity, perhaps containing several urbanized areas, discontinuously built-up but nonetheless operating as an integrated economic whole. Figure 11.18 shows these areas in a hypothetical American county.

The Bureau of the Census has redefined the concept of "metropolitan" from time to time to summarize the realities of the changing population, physical size, and functions of urban regions. The current *metropolitan statistical areas* are comprised of a central county or counties with at least one urbanized area of at least 50,000 population, plus adjacent outlying counties with a high degree of social and economic integration with the central county as measured by commuting volumes. A list of the

(a)

(b)

Figure 11.17 The differences in size, density, and land use complexity are immediately apparent between (*a*) New York City and (*b*) a small town (Amityville, NY). Clearly, one is a city, one is a town, but both are *urban* areas.

Figure 11.18 **A hypothetical spatial arrangement of urban units within a metropolitan area.** Sometimes official limits of the central city are very extensive and contain areas commonly considered suburban or even rural. On the other hand, older eastern U.S. cities (and some such as San Francisco in the West) more often have restricted limits and contain only part of the high-density land uses and populations of their metropolitan or urbanized areas.

largest U.S. metropolitan statistical areas in 2004 is given in Table 11.2.

Patterns of Urban Land Use

A recurring pattern of land use arrangements and population densities exists within urban areas. There is a certain sameness in the way cities are internally organized, especially within one particular culture region, such as Anglo America or Western Europe. Accessibility, a competitive market in land, and the innumerable individual residential, commercial, and industrial locational decisions made and changed over time have been major persisting variables shaping Anglo America's unplanned internal urban land use patterns. Dominating them, however, and giving rise to two sharply different urban land use layouts were the transportation technologies—first, mass transit systems and later the automobile—available during successive periods of urban growth.

The pedestrian and pack animal movement of people and goods within the small, compact pre-industrial city could no longer serve the increasing number of people and functions seeking accommodation within the expanding industrial city of the late 19th and early 20th centuries. Mass transit lines—horse car, cable car, electric streetcar lines, eventually elevated and subway rail systems—were successively installed and extended; they controlled the development and layout of cities in, particularly, the northeastern United States, southeastern Canada, and older cities of the Interior and West. Radiating outward from the town center,

the transit systems immediately gave differential accessibility to the different areas of the growing city. Properties along and near the lines were usable and valuable because reachable; land between the radiating transit routes and beyond easy walking distance from them was unusable and left vacant. The result was a compact, high-density central city with a sharp break at its margins between urban and nonurban uses (Figure 11.19).

After the 1940s, however, automotive transportation became dominant in the movement of people and goods. The compact older mass transit city of the East was fundamentally changed and, in

Figure 11.19 Town houses such as these in the Back Bay of Boston as well as apartment buildings and duplexes were a characteristic response to the price and scarcity of developable urban land in the era before automobiles became widely available. Where detached single-family dwellings were built, they were typically on smaller lots than became the norm once widespread automobile use allowed cities to spread outward in the second half of the 20th century.

the rapidly urbanizing West and Southwest, succeeded by the low-density unfocused urban and suburban sprawl of the automobile city. The land use contrast between the two periods of development is not absolute, of course, and the ever-changing 21st-century American city shows the intermingling of their two influences.

The Central Business District

Within the older central city, the radiating mass transit lines focused on the original city center, giving that area the highest accessibility within the growing urban complex and, therefore, the greatest attraction for those functions profiting most from a central location. Building lots within the emerging **central business district** (CBD), as a result of their scarcity and accessibility, could command high rental and purchase prices.

In the absence of effective zoning and land use controls up through the first quarter of the 20th century, the value of American urban land was determined by competitive bidding among potential users. Public uses—parks, municipal buildings, schools—were allocated land according to criteria other than ability to pay. In the private market, however, uses with the greatest need and demand for accessibility bid most for, and occupied, the most central parcels within the CBD. Those uses were typically the department stores and other retail outlets catering to the shopping needs of the majority of urban residents. The urban core, that is, became the highest-order central place (see p. 349) within the central place hierarchy of the mass transit city. Slightly less accessible parcels— because more distant from the *hot corner* or peak intersection of mass transit convergence—generally became sites for tall office

buildings (skyscrapers), the principal hotels, and similar land uses that helped produce the distinctive skyline of the older, high-order commercial city.

Outside the Central Business District

Outside the core area of the city, comparable but lower-order commercial aggregations developed at the outlying intersections—transfer points—of the mass transit network. Industry controlled parcels adjacent to essential cargo routes: rail lines, waterfronts, rivers, or canals. Strings of stores, light industries, and high-density apartment structures could afford and benefit from location along high-volume transit routes. The least accessible locations within the city were left for the least-competitive users: low-density residences. A diagrammatic summary of this repetitive allocation of space among competitors for urban sites is shown in Figure 11.20.

The competitive bidding for land should yield—in theory, at least—two separate but related distance–decay patterns: both land values and population densities decrease as distance from the CBD increases. Land values decline in distinct pattern: within the central business district there is a sharp drop in values a short distance from the hot corner, the most accessible and costly parcel of the CBD; then the values decline less steeply to the margins of the built-up urban area. With the exception of a tendency to form a *hollow at the center,* the CBD, the population density pattern of the central city showed a comparable distance–decay arrangement, as suggested by Figure 11.21. The low population density at the city center, of course, reflected the superior rent-paying abilities of commercial and industrial users, displacing residential uses outward. With time, as transportation made lower-priced and larger lots available on the fringes of cities, the wealthy and middle class moved away from the city center, shifting outward the zones and flattening the curve of higher residential density (Figure 11.22).

The regularities of the older mass-transit central cities were not fully maintained or replicated in the evolving eastern or newer western United States cities of the later 20th century. The density and land use structures of the newer cities and growth areas of older centers have been influenced primarily or exclusively by the automobile and motor truck, not by mass-transit and rail freight systems. They spread more readily, evolved at lower densities, and therefore display less tightly structured and standardized land use patterns than did their older early 20th-century predecessors. Even so, the patterns we have been discussing have not been totally erased and since the early 20th-century have been the basis of descriptions of urban land use and social structure offered by geographers, land economists, and sociologists alike.

Models of Urban Form

Generalized models—simplified graphic and descriptive summaries— of urban growth and land use patterns began to appear during the 1920s and 1930s. While those models generalized what

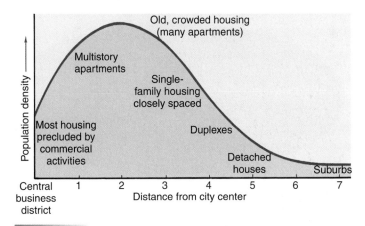

Figure 11.21 **A summary population density curve.** As distance from the area of multistory apartment buildings increases, the population density declines.

Figure 11.20 **Generalized urban land use pattern.** The model depicts the location of various land uses in an idealized city where the highest bidder gets the most accessible land.

characterized by stagnation and deterioration and contains high-density, low-income slums, rooming houses, and perhaps ethnic ghettoes. Next outward is a zone of workers' homes, usually smaller, older homes on small lots. The third zone houses better residences, single-family homes or higher-rent apartments for those able to exercise choice in housing location and afford the longer journey to CBD employment. Finally, just beginning to emerge when this model was proposed, was an outer zone of low-density suburban development.

The concentric zone model is dynamic. Each type of land use and each residential group tends to move outward into the next outer zone as the city matures and expands. That movement was seen as part of a ceaseless process of invasion and succession that yielded a restructured land use pattern and population segregation

admittedly was a tremendously varied urban universe, they did help explain some regularities in city growth and structure. More recently, urban geographers have begun to offer models that address the newer patterns of the decentralized automobile city.

The common starting point of the classical models is the distinctive central business district found in every older central city. The core of this area displays the intensive land use development already discussed: the major shopping concentration, tall office buildings, and streets crowded by pedestrians. Framing the core is a fringe area of warehousing, transportation terminals, and light industries. Just beyond the fringe, residential land uses begin.

The **concentric zone model** (Figure 11.23a) was developed by University of Chicago sociologists to explain the structuring of American cities in the 1920s. It describes the urban community as a set of nested rings of mostly residential diversity at increasing distances in all directions from the CBD fringe. The first, a zone of transition, is

Figure 11.22 **Population density gradients for Cleveland, Ohio, 1940–1990.** The progressive depopulation of the central core and flattening of the density gradient over time to the city margin is clearly seen as Cleveland passed from mass transit to automobile domination. The Cleveland pattern is consistent with conclusions drawn from other urban density studies: density gradients tend to flatten over time, and the larger the city, the flatter the gradient.

Source: Anupa Mukhopadhyay and Ashok K. Dutt, "Population Density Gradient Changes of a Postindustrial City—Cleveland, Ohio 1940–1990," GeoJournal 34:517, No. 4, 1994. Redrawn by permission of Kluwer Academic Publishers and Ashok K. Dutt.

(a) Concentric Zone Model

(b) Sector Model

①	Central business district
②	Wholesale, light manufacturing
③	Low-class residential
④	Medium-class residential
⑤	High-class residential
⑥	Heavy manufacturing
⑦	Outlying business district
⑧	Residential suburb
⑨	Industrial

(c) Multiple-Nuclei Model

Figure 11.23 Three classic models of the internal structure of cities.

Source: Redrawn from "The Nature of Cities" by C.D. Harris and E.L. Ullman in volume no. 242 of The Annals of the American Academy of Political and Social Science. *Copyright © 1945 The American Academy of Political and Social Science, Philadelphia, PA. Used by permission of the publisher and authors.*

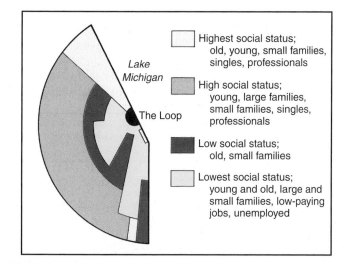

Figure 11.24 **A diagrammatic representation of the major social areas of the Chicago region.** The central business district of Chicago is known as the "Loop."

Source: Redrawn with permission from Phillip Rees, "The Factorial Ecology of Metropolitan Chicago" M. A. Thesis, University of Chicago, 1968.

by income level. The social patterning of Chicago (Figure 11.24) shows some accordance with this model.

The **sector model** (Figure 11.23b) devised in the 1930s by the land economist Homer Hoyt focuses on transportation arterials. It posits that high-rent residential areas are dominant in city expansion and grow outward from the city center along major transportation routes such as streetcar and elevated railroad lines or suburban commuter routes. As cities grow, the model suggests, the highest-income groups move into new homes in new neighborhoods located along the extending transit lines radiating outward from the center of the city. Middle-income housing follows and clusters around the residences of the wealthy, and low-income populations occupy districts adjacent to the areas of industry and associated transportation, such as freight railroad lines.

The sector model is also dynamic, marked by a *filtering down* process as older areas are abandoned by the outward movement of their original higher-income inhabitants, with the lowest-income populations (closest to the city center and furthest from the current location of the wealthy) becoming the inheritors of the least-desirable vacated areas. The expansion of the city is radial, not circular, as in the concentric zone model. The accordance of the sector model with the actual pattern that emerged in Calgary, Canada, is suggested in Figure 11.25.

The basic assumption of the concentric circle and sector models—that urban growth and development proceeded outward from a single central core—was countered by the **multiple-nuclei model** (Figure 11.23c) proposed by geographers Chauncy Harris and Edward Ullman. In their view, large cities developed by peripheral spread from several nodes of growth, not just one. Certain activities have specific locational requirements: the retail district

Figure 11.25 The land use pattern in and around Calgary, Alberta, in 1981. Physical and cultural barriers and the evolution of cities over time tend to result in a sectoral pattern of similar land uses. Calgary's central business district was the focus for many of the sectors.

Source: Revised and redrawn with permission from P. J. Smith, "Calgary: A Study in Urban Patterns" in Economic Geography, *Vol. 38, p. 328. Copyright © 1962 Clark University, Worcester, MA.*

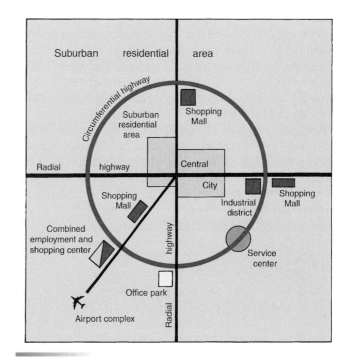

Figure 11.26 Metropolitan peripheral model. The galactic city's multiple downtowns and special function nodes and corridors are linked by the metropolitan expressway systems in this conceptualization proposed by Chauncy Harris.

Source: Reprinted with permission from Urban Geography, *Vol. 18, No. 1, pp. 15–35. © Bellwether Publishing, Ltd. 8640 Guilford Road, Suite 200, Columbia MO 21046. All rights reserved.*

needs accessibility; a port function needs a waterfront site; heavy industry requires level land adjacent to railroads. Peripheral expansion of the separate nuclei eventually leads to coalescence and the meeting of incompatible land uses along the lines of juncture. The urban land use pattern, therefore, is not regularly structured from a single center in a sequence of circles or a series of sectors but based on separately expanding clusters of contrasting activities.

Although the society, economy, and technology these three models summarized have now been superseded, the physical patterns they explained remain as vestiges and controls on the current landscape of older central cities. Many cities prior to 1950 resembled the concentric zonal or sector models with a clearly defined and dominant CBD, but both new and expanding older cities grew more sprawled and complex in the automobile era following World War II. The multiple-nuclei model gives a better insight into metropolitan area structuring of the more recent past and present, but should be supplemented by newer visualizations of contemporary metropolitan complexes or "galactic cities."

The **peripheral model** (Figure 11.26) take into account the major changes in urban form that have taken place since World War II, especially the suburbanization of various central city functions. The peripheral model focuses on the peripheral belt that lies within the metropolitan area, but outside the central city itself. Functions of peripheral belt communities are defined not by their relationship to the metropolitan center, but to other parts of the peripheral zone.

In these models, circumferential highways and expressways outside the central city make large tracts of land available for development in the low-density sprawl characteristic of individual rather than mass transit movement of people. Residences are segregated by price level into relatively homogenous suburban clusters, and individual nodes in the peripheral belt are

centers for employment or services: shopping malls; industrial parks; distribution and warehouse concentrations; office parks; airport-associated clusters containing hotels, meeting facilities, car rental agencies, and the like.

Much of the life of the residents of the periphery takes place outside the central city, as they shop for food, clothing, and services in the shopping malls, seek recreation in country clubs and entertainment complexes, and find employment in outlying industrial or office parks. The periphery, however, remains a functional part of the metropolitan complex and not free-standing or self-sufficient.

The models of urban form just discussed aid our understanding of urban structure and development, but it must be stressed that a model is not a map, and that many cities contain elements and characteristics of more than a single model.

Social Areas of Cities

Vestiges of the classical models of American city layout are evident in the observed social segregation within urban areas. The larger and more economically and socially complex cities are, the stronger is the tendency for their residents to segregate themselves into groups based on *social status, family status,* and *ethnicity.* In a large metropolitan region with a diversified population, this territorial behavior may be a defense against the unknown or the unwanted, a desire to be among similar kinds of people, a response to income constraints, or a result of social and institutional barriers. Most people feel more at ease when they are near those with whom they can easily identify. In traditional societies, these groups are the families and tribes. In modern society, people tend to group according to income or occupation (social status), stages in the life cycle (family status), and language or race (ethnic characteristics) (see "Birds of a Feather" in Chapter 7).

Many of these social area groupings are fostered by the size and the value of available housing. Land developers, especially in cities, produce homes of similar quality in specific areas. Of course, as time elapses, there is a change in the condition and quality of that housing. Land uses may change and new groups may replace previous tenants, leading to the evolution of new neighborhoods of differently similar social characteristics.

Social Status

The social status of an individual or a family is determined by income, education, occupation, and home value, though it may be measured differently in different cultures. In the United States, high income, a college education, a professional or managerial position, and high home value constitute high status. High home value can mean an expensive rental apartment or a large house with extensive grounds. A good housing indicator of social status is persons per room. A low number of persons per room tends to indicate high status. Low status characterizes people with low-income jobs living in low-value housing.

Social status patterning agrees with the sector model. In most cities, people of similar status are grouped in sectors that fan out from the innermost urban residential areas (Figure 11.27). If the number of people within a given social group increases, they tend to move away from the central city along an arterial connecting them with the old neighborhood. Major transport routes leading to the city center are the usual migration routes out from the core.

Today, social status divisions are often perpetuated between separate municipalities, which may differ greatly in relative income. Many residential developments are also income-segregated because their houses are of similar value. To preserve the upscale nature of a development and protect land values, self-governing community associations may be formed to enact and enforce land use restrictions (see "The Gated Community"). Pervasive and detailed, these restrictions may specify such things as the size, construction, and color of exterior walls and fences, the size and permitted uses of rear and side yards, and the design of outside lights and mailboxes. Some go so far as to tell residents what trees they may plant, what pets they may raise, and where they may park their boats or recreational vehicles.

Family Status

As the distance from the city center increases, the average age of the adult residents declines, or the size of their family increases, or both. Within a particular sector—say, that of high status—older people whose children do not live with them and young professionals without families, tend to live close to the city center. In contrast, young families seeking space for child rearing locate farther from the city center, while singles and empty-nesters

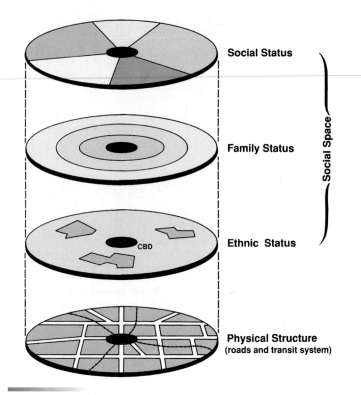

Figure 11.27 The social geography of American and Canadian cities.

Source: Redrawn with permission from Robert A. Murdie, Factorial Ecology of Metropolitan Toronto. *Research Paper 116. Department of Geography* Research Series, *University of Chicago, 1969.*

may covet more the accessibility of the cultural and business life of the urban core. However, where inner-city life is unpleasant, there is a tendency for older people to migrate to the suburbs or to retirement communities. The arrangement that emerges is a concentric circle patterning according to family status, as Figure 11.27 suggests.

Ethnicity

For some groups, ethnicity is a more important residential location determinant than is social or family status. Areas of homogeneous ethnic identification appear in the social geography of cities as separate clusters or nuclei, reminiscent of the multiple-nuclei concept of urban structure. For some ethnic groups, cultural segregation is both sought and vigorously defended, even in the face of pressures for neighborhood change exerted by potential competitors for housing space, as we saw in Chapter 6. The durability of "Little Italys" and "Chinatowns" and of Polish, Greek, Armenian, and other ethnic neighborhoods in many American cities is evidence of the persistence of self-maintained segregation.

Certain ethnic or racial groups, especially African Americans, have had segregation forced on them. Every city in the United States has one or more black areas that in many respects may be considered cities within a city, with their own self-contained social geographies of social status, income, and housing quality. Social and economic barriers to movement outside the area have

The Gated Community

Approximately one in six Americans—some 50 million people—lives in a master-planned community. Particularly characteristic of the fastest growing parts of the country, most of these communities are in the South and West, but they are increasingly common everywhere. In many regions, more than half of all new houses are being built in private developments. Master-planned communities in the United States trace their modern start back to the 1960s, when Irvine, California, and Sun City, Arizona, were built, but their roots can be found much earlier. Tuxedo Park, New York, for example, was planned and built in 1886 as a fully protected, socially exclusive community, and in the 1920s Kansas City's Country Club District was established as a restricted residential development with land use controlled by planning and deed restrictions and a self-governing homeowners association providing a variety of governmental, cultural, and recreational services.

A subset of the master-planned community is the **gated community,** a fenced or walled residential area with checkpoints staffed by security guards and access limited to designated individuals and identified guests. By 2005, 10 million Americans were living in these middle- and high-income gated communities within communities. With private security forces, surveillance systems monitoring common recreational areas such as community swimming pools, tennis courts, and health clubs and—often—with individual home security systems, the walled enclaves provide a sense of refuge from high crime rates, drug abuse, and other social problems of urban America.

Gated and sheltered communities are not just an American phenomenon but are increasingly found in all parts of the world. More and more guarded residential enclaves have been sited in such stable Western European states as Spain, Portugal, and France. Developers in Indian cities have also used gated communities to attract wealthy residents. Trying to appeal to Indians returning to that country after years in areas like the Boston high-tech corridor and Silicon Valley, developers have built enclaves with names like Regent Place and Golden Enclave that boast American-style two-story houses and barbecues in the backyards.

Elsewhere, as in Argentina or Venezuela in South America or Lebanon in the Near East—with little urban planning, unstable city administration, and inadequate police protection—not only rich but also middle-class citizens are opting for protected residential districts. In China and Russia, the sudden boom in private and guarded settlements reflects in part a new form of post-communist social class distinction, while in South Africa gated communities serve as effective racial barriers.

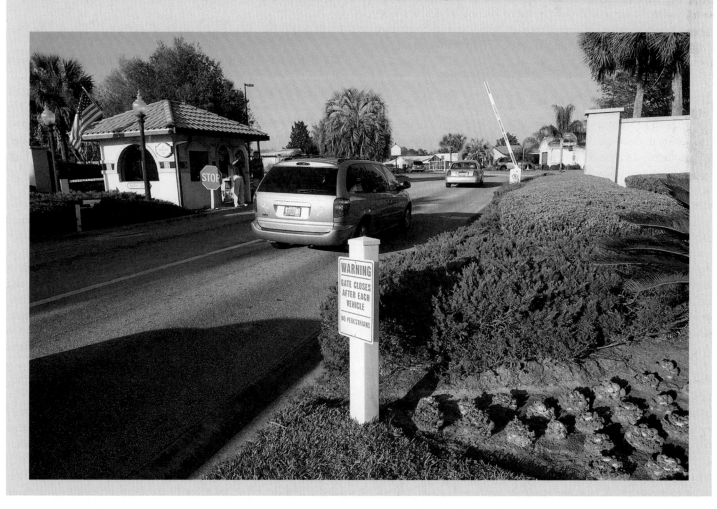

always been high, as they also have been for Hispanics and other non-English-speaking minorities.

As whites and Asians increase their household incomes, they tend to move to neighborhoods that match their economic standing. Due to persistent residential segregation, census data document, blacks with similar income growth are less able to move to less segregated neighborhood settings. Although segregation in 2000 was slightly lower nationally than in 1990, at the start of the 21st century the average city black lived in a census tract that was more than 75% minority and three-fifths black in racial composition. Figure 6.16 (p. 185) illustrates the concentration of blacks, Hispanics, and other ethnic groups in Los Angeles. Elsewhere, black segregation varies by region. Black-white separation is highest in metropolitan areas in the Northeast and Midwest; greatest integration is found in the metropolitan South and West and, notably, in military towns like Norfolk, Virginia, and San Diego.

Of the three social geographic patterns depicted on Figure 11.27, family status has undergone the most widespread change in recent years. Today, the suburbs house large numbers of singles and childless couples, as well as two-parent families. Areas near the central business district have become popular for young professionals. Gay couples and families often choose to live in urban centers as well. The city structure is constantly changing, reflecting changes in family and employment makeup. For example, there are now large numbers of new jobs for professionals in the suburbs and central business districts, but not in between. With more women in the workforce than ever before, and as a result of multiple-earner families, residential site selection has become a more complex undertaking.

Institutional Controls

Over the past century, and particularly since World War II, institutional controls have strongly influenced the land use arrangements and growth patterns of most United States cities. Indeed, the governments—local and national—of most Western urbanized societies have instituted myriad laws to control all aspects of urban life with particular emphasis on the ways in which individual property and city areas can be developed and used. In the United States, emphasis has been on land use planning, subdivision control and zoning ordinances, and building, health, and safety codes. All have been designed to assure a legally acceptable manner and pattern of urban development, and all are based on broad applications of the police powers of municipalities to assure public health, safety, and well-being even when private property rights are infringed.

These nonmarket controls on land use are designed to minimize incompatibilities (residences adjacent to heavy industry, for example), provide for the creation in appropriate locations of public uses (the transportation system, waste disposal facilities, government buildings, parks), and private uses (colleges, shopping centers, housing) needed for and conducive to a balanced, orderly community. In theory, such careful planning should prevent the emergence of slums, so often the result of undesirable adjacent uses, and should stabilize neighborhoods by reducing market-induced pressures for land use change.

Zoning ordinances and land use planning have sometimes been criticized as being unduly restrictive and unresponsive to changing land use needs and patterns of economic development. Zoning and subdivision control regulations that specify large lot sizes for residential buildings and large house-floor areas have been particularly criticized as devices to exclude from upper-income areas lower-income populations or those who would choose to build or occupy other forms of residences: apartments, special housing for the aged, and so forth. Bitter court battles have been waged, with mixed results, over "exclusionary" zoning practices that in the view of some serve to separate rather than to unify the total urban structure and to maintain or increase diseconomies of land use development. All institutional controls, of course, interfere with the market allocation of urban land, as do the actions of real estate agents who "steer" people of certain racial and ethnic groups into neighborhoods that the agent thinks are appropriate.

In most of Asia there is no zoning, and it is quite common to have small-scale industrial activities operating in residential areas. Even in Japan, a house may contain living space and several people doing piecework for a local industry. In both Europe and Japan, neighborhoods have been built and rebuilt gradually over time to contain a wide variety of building types from several eras intermixed on the same street. In Anglo America, such mixing is much rarer and is often viewed as a temporary condition in a process of transition to total redevelopment.

Changes in Urban Form

The 20th century started with mass transit dominating the physical and social structure of the American city. It ended with the automobile everywhere controlling the movement of people and determining the pattern and fate of cities and metropolitan areas. In the course of that century, and particularly after its middle years, new technological, physical, and institutional structures were created fostering fundamental change in the frameworks within which individual city and metropolitan area development and change occurred.

First, the improvement of the automobile increased its reliability, range, and convenience, freeing its user from dependence on fixed-route public transit for access to work, home, or shopping. The new transport flexibility opened up vast new acreages of nonurban land to urban development. That flexibility of movement of people and, through semitrailer and pickup trucks, of heavy and light freight, was augmented by the substantial completion during the 1970s of the interstate highway system and its supplements, the major metropolitan expressways. The improved routeways allowed sites 30 to 45 kilometers (20 to 30 mi) or more distant to be considered acceptable commuting distance between workplace and home and freed warehouses and industries from dependence on railside locations.

Second, during the 1930s and after World War II (1939–1945), both the Federal Housing Administration and the Veterans Administration, by easing the terms of home mortgage requirements, vastly increased the number of persons eligible to own their home rather than rent a house or apartment. Those agencies stimulated a housing boom by offering much more generous mortgage loan terms than had private bankers previously, when buyers had to provide large down payments (sometimes 50% or more) and repay their high interest loans within a short time, often 10 years or less. The VA program permitted veterans to purchase homes with virtually no down payment and both the VA and FHA lengthened low interest repayment periods to 15 to 25 years or more. Finally, the acceptance of a maximum 40-hour work week in 1938 guaranteed millions of Americans the time for a commuting journey not possible when workdays of 10 or more hours 6-days a week were common.

These structural and economic changes altered the prevailing patterns of accessibility and behavior and significantly modified the land value curve and population density gradient established in the mass transit city. Over the past half-century or more, U.S. metropolitan areas have experienced massive decentralization of people and activities as residents, businesses, and industries moved outward into suburbs. The end of the 20th century and early years of the 21st have, however, witnessed a slight reversal of those trends with some population and economic return to the core areas of many cities.

Suburbanization

Demand for housing, pent up by years of economic depression and wartime restrictions, was loosed in a flood after 1945, and a massive suburbanization altered the existing land use and functional patterns of urban America. Between 1950 and 1990, the two most prominent patterns of population growth were the *metropolitanization* of people and, within metropolitan areas, their *suburbanization*.

Suburban expansion reached its maximum pace during the decade of the 1970s when developers were converting open land to urban uses at the rate of 80 hectares (200 acres) an hour. High energy prices of the 1970s slowed the rush to the suburbs, but during the 1980s suburbanization again continued apace. In much of the recent outward flow, the tendency has been as much for "filling in" as for continued sprawl.

Residential land uses led the initial rush to the suburbs. Typically, uniform but spatially discontinuous housing developments were built beyond the boundaries of most older central cities. The new design was an unfocused sprawl because it was not tied to mass transit lines and the channelized pattern of nodes and links they imposed. It also represented a massive relocation of purchasing power to which retail merchants were quick to respond. The planned major regional shopping center became the suburban counterpart of higher-order central places and the outlying commercial districts of the central city. Smaller shopping malls and strip shopping centers gradually completed the retailing hierarchy.

Faced with a newly suburbanized labor force, industry followed the outward move, attracted as well by the economies derived from modern single-story plants with plenty of parking space for employees. Industries no longer needed to locate near railway facilities; freeways presented new opportunities for lower-cost, more flexible truck transportation. Service industries were also attracted by the purchasing power and large, well-educated labor force now present in the suburbs, and complexes of office buildings developed, like the shopping malls, at freeway intersections

Figure 11.28 **A history of urban sprawl.** In Chicago, as in most larger and older U.S. cities, the slow peripheral expansion recorded during the late 19th and early 20th centuries suddenly accelerated as the automobile suburbs began developing after 1945. The red line marks the Chicago city boundary.

Source: Revised with permission from B. J. L. Berry, Chicago: Transformation of an Urban System, *1976, with additions from other sources.*

and along freeway frontage roads and major connecting highways. The growth pattern for the Chicago area illustrating these features of peripheral spread is shown on Figure 11.28.

In time, in the United States, new metropolitan land use and functional patterns emerged that could no longer be satisfactorily explained by the classic ring, sector, or multiple-nuclei models. Yet traces of the older generation concepts seemingly remained applicable. Multiple nuclei of specialized land uses appeared, expanded, and coalesced. Sectors of high-income residential use continued their outward extension beyond the central city limits, usurping the most scenic and most desirable suburban areas and segregating them by price and zoning restrictions. As shown in Figure 11.29, middle-, lower-middle-, and lower-income groups found their own income-segregated portions of the fringe. Ethnic minorities were frequently relegated to the inner city and to some older industrial suburbs although increasingly immigrants are locating in suburbs as their first step on arrival in the country, and a growing share of native-born minorities are also suburbanizing. In the country's largest metropolitan areas, minorities accounted for nearly one-third of suburbanites in 2006, up from 19% in 1990. In all metropolitan fringe areas, blacks and other minorities irrespective of income levels are apt to live in suburban racial and ethnic enclaves. Unlike the depressed segregated neighborhoods

Industrial park

CBD and major regional
shopping center

Regional shopping
center

Low income

Lower middle and
middle income

High income

Figure 11.29 **A diagram of the present-day United States metropolitan area.** Note that aspects of the concentric zone, sector, and multiple-nuclei patterns are evident and carried out into the suburban fringe. The "major regional shopping centers" of this earlier, mid-1970s model are increasingly the cores of newly developing "outer cities."

Source: Figure 4.10 (redrawn) from The North American City, *4th ed. by Maurice Yeates. Copyright © 1990 by Harper & Rowe, Publishers, Inc.*

of central cities, however, suburban segregation in *ethnoburbs* (see p. 189) appears to be a residential choice of more affluent minorities.

By the 1990s, a new urban America had emerged on the perimeters of the major metropolitan areas. With increasing sprawl and the rising costs implicit in the ever-greater spatial separation of the functional segments of the fringe, peripheral expansion slowed, the supply of developable land was reduced (with corresponding increases in its price), and the structural and population density of land development increased. No longer dependent on the central city, the suburbs were reborn as vast collectively self-sufficient outer cities, marked by landscapes of industrial parks, skyscraper office clusters, massive retailing complexes, and a proliferation of apartment and condominium districts and gated communities.

The new suburbia began to rival older central business districts in size and complexity. Collectively, the new centers surpassed the central cities as generators of employment and income. Together with the older CBDs, the suburbs perform the many tertiary and quaternary services that mark the postindustrial metropolis. During the 1980s, more office space was created in the suburbs than in the central cities of America. Tysons Corner, Virginia (between Arlington and Reston), for example, became

the ninth largest central business district in the United States. Regional and national headquarters of leading corporations, banking, professional services of all kinds, major hotel complexes and recreational centers—all formerly considered immovable keystones of central business districts—became parts of the new outer cities. Sometimes called **edge cities,** they are defined by their large nodes of concentrated office and commercial structures and characterized by having more jobs than residents within their boundaries.

Edge cities now exist in all regions of urbanized Anglo America. The South Coast Metro Center in Orange County, California; the City Post Oak-Galleria center on Houston's west side; King of Prussia and the Route 202 corridor northwest of Philadelphia; the Meadowlands, New Jersey, west of New York City; and Schaumburg, Illinois, in the western Chicago suburbs are but a very few examples of the new urban forms. The metropolis has become polynucleated and urban regions are increasingly "galactic"—that is, galaxies of economic activity nodes organized primarily around the freeway systems as suggested in Figure 11.26a. Commuting across the galaxy is far more common than journeys-to-work between suburbs and central cities. In recent years, suburban outliers and edge cities are coalescing, creating continuous metropolitan belts on the pattern shown in Figure 11.4.

On the leading edges of that pattern are the outer suburbs or "exurbs," vast sprawling areas of centerless growth beyond the pull of central cities or edge cities. That unfocused low-density development continues and increases population segregation by income and further disperses places of employment and the intermittent commercial developments that always follow dispersing purchasing power. Early in the 21st century, one-third of all jobs are located beyond a 10-mile radius of central city or edge city central business districts, nearly 40% of all commuting trips are within and between suburbs and exurbs, and 90% of the office space built in America during the 1990s and early 2000s was built in outer suburbia and beyond. The aging inner suburbs of the late 20th century are now beginning to suffer the transfer of wealth and erosion of functions that earlier afflicted the center cities themselves.

The emerging nearly formless sprawl has earned the negative name of "spread city," defined by the New York Regional Plan Association as "not a true city because it lacks centers, nor a suburb because it is not a satellite of any city, nor is it truly rural because it is loosely covered with houses and urban facilities." The recent evolution of North American metropolitan areas has led to a radical revisioning of traditional urban structure models. Geographers studying Los Angeles have proclaimed the obsolescence of the older models of urban structure, most of which were based on Chicago with its dominant central business district and concentric rings of growth. Instead, they describe what they call post-modern urbanism, which is marked by radical fragmentation into a collage of theme parks, gated communities, corporate citadels, ethnoburbs, street warfare zones, consumption opportunities, spectacle sites, and edge cities—with no organizing center, no edge, and only a communications network and highway system to hold it together.

Decline of the Central City

The superior accessibility that determined the success and internal structure of the mass transit city faded with the advent of the cheap and reliable automobile and motor truck and development of interstate highways, metropolitan expressways, and air transportation. The dominance of the central business district was based on its being the focus of urban mass transit (streetcar, subway, elevated) systems and intercity rail lines. When its accessibility eroded with the decline or abandonment of those carrier networks, central cities lost their primary situational advantage and the foundation of their internal land use patterns. The dynamic that provided functional superiority to central cities increasingly worked to their detriment. Populations moved out, functions and jobs dispersed to the fringes following the relocating labor force and its purchasing power, and the central city was increasingly viewed as aging, congested, and inefficient. Once vibrant industrial districts were left behind as blighted, polluted sites—*brownfield* sites.

The redistribution of population caused by suburbanization resulted not only in the spatial but also in the political segregation of social groups of the metropolitan area. The upwardly mobile resident of the city—younger, wealthier, and better educated—took advantage of the automobile and the freeway to leave the central city. The poorer, older, least-advantaged urbanites were left behind (Figure 11.30). The central cities and the suburbs became increasingly differentiated. Large areas within those cities now contain only the poor and minority groups, including women (see "Women in the City"), a population little able to pay the rising costs of the social services that their numbers, neighborhoods, and condition require.

The services needed to support the poor include welfare payments, social workers, extra police and fire protection, health delivery systems, and subsidized housing. Central cities, by themselves, are unable to support such an array and intensity of social services since they have lost the tax bases represented by suburbanized commerce, industry, and upper-income residential uses. Lost, too, are the job opportunities that were formerly a part of the central city structure. Increasingly, the poor and minorities are trapped in a central city without the possibility of nearby employment and are isolated by distance, immobility, and unawareness—by *spatial mismatch*—from the few remaining low-skill jobs, which are now largely in the suburbs.

The population shift and the abandonment of the central city by commercial and industrial functions have nearly destroyed the traditional active, open auction of urban land that led to the replacement of obsolescent uses and inefficient structures in a continuing process of urban modernization. In the vacuum left by the departure of private investors, the federal government, particularly after the landmark Housing Act of 1949, initiated urban renewal programs that remade inner city areas in the 1950s and 1960s. Under a wide array of programs, slum areas were cleared, public housing was built (Figure 11.31), cultural

Figure 11.30 A derelict slum in Detroit. Some areas of large cities—abandoned by their former occupants and unwanted for traditional land market resale and private redevelopment—now stand vacant or house only the poor, the destitute, and the homeless.

complexes and industrial parks were created, and city centers were reconstructed.

With the continuing erosion of the urban economic base and the disadvantagous restructuring of the central city population mix, however, the hard-fought governmental battle to maintain or revive the central city is frequently judged to be a losing one. Cities such as Detroit, Michigan; Toledo, Ohio; and Bridgeport, Connecticut, experienced multiple failed attempts at urban renewal. Public assistance programs have not reduced the central city burden of thousands of homeless people (see "The Homeless"), and central city economies, with their limited unskilled job opportunities, and inadequate resources for social services appeared to many observers to offer few or no prospects for change.

Structural and functional deterioration (but not the homeless problem) primarily afflicted older, eastern American cities. In the western United States, the experience of the central city has been rather different. During the latter part of the 20th century, the most dramatic U.S. urban growth rates were in the Mountain and Pacific West. In 1940 little more than half of all Westerners lived in cities; by 2005 more than 90% were urbanites. Arizona, California, Nevada, and Utah all have a higher percentage of city dwellers than New York, and the majority of the fastest growing U.S. metropolitan areas are in the West.

For the most part, these newer "automobile" metropolises were able to expand physically to keep within the central city boundaries the new growth areas on their peripheries. Nearly without exception they placed few restrictions on physical expansion. That unrestricted growth has often resulted in the coalescence of separate cities into ever-larger metropolitan complexes.

Unlike cities in the East and Midwest, cities in the West were usually allowed by their state legislatures to expand their

Urban space is not identically viewed or uniformly accessible to men and women; fear of rape and sexual harassment, for example, may restrict women's mobility within some areas and times of urban movement and deny them the same access to public space enjoyed by men. Maurice Yeates has noted that women's needs, problems, and patterns with respect to urban social space are quite different from men's.

In the first place, women are more numerous in large central cities than are men. Washington, D.C. probably is the most female-dominant (numerically) of any city in North America, with a "sex ratio" of eighty-seven (or 115 females for every 100 males). In Minneapolis it is eighty-four. The preponderance of women in central cities is related to an above-average number of household units headed by women, and to the larger numbers of women among the elderly.

A second characteristic is that women, along with their children, constitute the bulk of the poor. This feminization of poverty among all races is a consequence of the low wage rates, part-time work, and lack of security of employment in many "women's jobs." Central cities, with their low-cost but often low-quality rental housing units, house the vast majority of poor women.

A third spatial characteristic of women in urban areas is that they have shorter journeys to work and rely more heavily upon public transportation than do men, a reflection of the lower incomes received by women, the differences in location of "female jobs," and the concentration of women in the central cities. Women on the whole simply cannot afford to spend as much on travel costs as men and make greater use of public transportation, which in the United States is usually inferior and often dangerous. The concentration of employment of women in clerical, sales, service jobs, and nursing also influences travel distances because these "women's jobs" are spread around the metropolitan area more than "men's jobs," which tend to be concentrated. It might well be argued that the more widespread location of "women's jobs" helps maintain the relative inaccessibility of many higher-paid "men's jobs" to a large number of women.

Given the allocation of roles, the resulting inequities, and the persistence of these inequities, there are spatial issues that impinge directly upon women. One is that many women find that their spatial range of employment opportunities is limited as a result of the inadequate availability of child-care facilities within urban areas. A second spatial issue relates to the structure of North American metropolitan areas and to the design of housing in general. North American cities are the outcome of male-dominant traits. Suburbs, in particular, reflect a male-paid work and female-home/children ethos. The suburban structure militates against women by confining them to a place and role in which there are very few meaningful choices. It has been argued that suburban women really desire a greater level of accessibility to a variety of conveniences and services, more efficient housing units, and a range of public and private transportation that will assure higher levels of mobility. These requirements imply higher-density urban areas.

Source: Text excerpt from *The North American City*, 5th ed., by Maurice Yeates. Copyright © 1997. Reprinted by permission of Pearson Education, Inc., Upper Saddle River, NJ 07458.

borders so that central cities were able to capture new growth taking place at the urban periphery. This allowed western cities to grow into ever-larger metropolitan complexes but it also meant that central cities had a mixture of both new and older housing and poor and middle-class residents within their borders. The speed and volume of growth in the West means city governments face the economic, social, and environmental consequences of unrestricted outward expansion. Scottsdale, Arizona, for example, covered a single square mile (2.6 sq km) in 1950; by the end of the 1990s it grew to nearly 200 square miles (500 sq km), four times the physical size of San Francisco. Phoenix, with which Scottsdale has now coalesced, surpasses in sprawl Los Angeles, which has three times as many people. The phenomenal growth of Las Vegas, Nevada, has similarly converted vast areas of desert landscape to low-density urban use (Figure 11.32).

Increasingly, central cities and metropolitan areas of both East and West are seeking to restrain rather than encourage physical growth. Portland, Oregon, drew a "do not pass" line around itself in the late 1970s, prohibiting urban conversion of surrounding forests, farmlands, and open space. Even with its vigorously enforced "Smart growth" policies, however, Portland has been unable to stop some suburbanization of rural land in the face of continuing population growth although at least part of that growth was accommodated by higher densities per square mile rather than by low-density sprawl.

Central City Renewal and Gentrification

Central cities were often dismissed in the 1980s as anachronisms in the coming age of fax machines, the Internet, mobile phones, and the like that would eliminate the need for the face-to-face interaction intrinsic to cities. Instead, communications have become centralizing concerns of knowledge-based industries and activities such as finance, entertainment, health care, and corporate management that depend on dense, capital-intensive information technologies concentrated in geographically centralized markets. Cities—particularly large metropolitan cores—provide the first-rate telecommunications and fiber optics infrastructures and the access to skilled workers, customers, investors, research, educational, and cultural institutions needed by the modern, postindustrial economy.

As a reflection of cities' renewed attractions, employment and gross domestic product in the country's 50 largest urban areas

Figure 11.31 Faulty towers. Many elaborate—and massive—public housing projects have been failures. Chicago's Robert Taylor Homes, completed in 1962, consisted of 28 identical 16-story buildings, the largest public housing project in the world and the biggest concentration of poverty in America. The 4400 apartments occupied a 3.2-kilometer-long (2-mi) stretch of South State Street, a concrete curtain that concealed from passing traffic the vandalism and crime that wracked the project. The growing awareness that public high-rise developments intended to revive the central city do not meet the housing and social needs of their inhabitants led to razing over 100,000 of the more than 1.3 million public housing units in cities around the country by 2006, including the Robert Taylor Homes.

grew significantly in the 1990s, reversing stagnation and decline in the preceding decade. Demand for downtown office space was met by extensive new high-rise and skyscraper construction and urban renewal, and even manufacturing has revived in the form of small and midsize companies providing high-tech equipment and processes. These, in turn, support a growing network of suppliers and specialized services with "circular and cumulative" growth the result.

Part of the new vigor of central cities comes from its new residents. Between 1980 and 2000, some 15 million immigrants arrived in the United States, most concentrating in "gateway" cities where they have become deeply rooted in their new communities by buying and renovating homes in inner-city areas, spending money in neighborhood stores, and most importantly establishing their own businesses (Figure 11.33a). They also are important additions to the general urban labor force, providing the skilled and unskilled workers needed in expanding office-work, service, and manufacturing sectors.

Another part of central city residential revival is found in **gentrification,** the rehabilitation of housing in the oldest and now deteriorated inner-city areas by middle- and high-income groups (Figure 11.33b). Welcomed by many as a positive, privately financed force in the renewal of depressed urban neighborhoods, gentrification also has serious negative social and housing impacts on the low-income, frequently minority families that are displaced. Gentrification is another expression of the continuous remaking of urban land use and social patterns in accordance with the rent-paying abilities of alternate potential occupants. Yet the rehabilitation and replacement of housing stock that it implies yield inflated rents and prices that push out established residents, disrupt the social networks they have created, and totally alter the characteristics and services of their home areas.

The districts usually targeted for gentrification are those close to downtown jobs, with easy access to transit, low housing costs, and interesting older architecture. Gentrification is often led by artists who lack financial resources but exert a great deal of cultural influence. The replacement influx of younger, wealthier professionals has helped revitalize and repopulate inner city zones already the destination of growing numbers of urbanites. A study of 26 cities nationwide found each expecting its downtown population to grow by 2010, some by double-digit percentages.

The reason for that expected and actual growth lies in demographics. Young professionals are marrying and having children later or, often, are divorced, never-married, or same-sex couples. For them—a growing proportion of Americans—suburban life and shopping malls hold few attractions, while central city residence offers high-tech and executive jobs within walking or biking distance and cultural, entertainment, and boutique shopping opportunities

Geography and Public Policy

The Homeless

In the past quarter century, the number of homeless people in the United States has risen dramatically. Now every large city is apt to have hundreds or even thousands of people who lack homes of their own. One sees them pushing shopping carts containing their worldly goods, lining up at soup kitchens or rescue missions, and sleeping in parks or doorways. Reliable estimates of their numbers simply do not exist; official counts place the numbers of homeless Americans anywhere between 600,000 and 3 million.

Their existence and persistence raise a multitude of questions; the answers, however, are yet to be agreed upon by public officials and private Americans. Who are the homeless, and why have their numbers increased? Who should be responsible for coping with the problems they present? Are there ways to eliminate homelessness?

Some people believe the homeless are primarily the impoverished victims of a rich and uncaring society. They view them as ordinary people, but ones who have had a bad break and been forced from their homes by job loss, divorce, domestic violence, or incapacitating illness. They point to the increasing numbers of families, women, and children among the homeless, less visible than the "loners" (primarily men) because they tend to live in cars, emergency shelters, or doubled-up in substandard buildings. Advocates of the homeless argue that government policies of the 1980s and 1990s that led to a dire shortage of affordable housing were partly to blame for the homeless problem. Federal outlays for building low-income and subsidized housing were more than $30 billion in 1980 but dropped by three-quarters to $7.5 billion a decade later. During the same period, city governments pursued policies of destruction of low-income housing, especially single-room-occupancy hotels. In addition, federal regulations and reduced state funding for mental hospitals cast institutionalized patients onto the streets to join people displaced by gentrification, job loss, or rising rents.

A contrary view is presented by those who see the homeless chiefly as people responsible for their own plight. In the words of one commentator, the homeless are "deranged, pathological predators who spoil neighborhoods, terrorize passersby, and threaten the commonweal." They point to studies showing that nationally between 66% and 85% of all homeless suffer from alcoholism, drug abuse, or mental illness, and argue that people are responsible for the alcohol and drugs they ingest; they are not helpless victims of disease.

Communities have tried a number of strategies to cope with their homeless populations. Some set up temporary shelters, especially in cold weather; some subsidize permanent housing and/or group homes. They encourage private, nonprofit groups to establish soup kitchens and food banks. Others attempt to drive the homeless out of town or at least to parts of town where they will be less visible. They forbid loitering in city parks or on beaches after midnight, install sleep-proof seats on park benches and bus stations, and outlaw aggressive panhandling.

Neither point of view appeals to those who believe that homelessness is more than simply a lack of shelter, that it is a matter of a mostly disturbed population with severe problems that requires help getting off the streets and into treatment. What the homeless need, they say, is a "continuum of care"—an entire range of services that includes education; treatment for drug and alcohol abuse and mental illness; and job training.

Questions to Consider

1. What is the nature of the homeless problem in the community where you live or with which you are most familiar?

2. Where should responsibility for the homeless lie: at the federal, state, or local governmental level? Is it best left to private groups such as churches and charities? Or is it ultimately best recognized as a personal matter to be handled by homeless individuals themselves? What reasons form or support your response?

3. Some people argue that giving money, food, or housing but no therapy to street people makes one an "enabler" or accomplice of addicts. Do you agree? Why or why not?

4. One columnist has proposed quarantining male street people on military bases and compelling them to accept medical treatment. Those who resist would be charged with crimes of violence and turned over to the criminal justice system. Do you believe the homeless should be forced into treatment programs or institutionalized against their will? If so, under what conditions?

A homeless man finds shelter on a bench near the White House in Washington, D.C.

Figure 11.32 Urban sprawl in the Las Vegas, Nevada, metropolitan area. Like many western U.S. cities, Las Vegas has spread out over great expanses of desert in order to keep pace with its rapidly growing population. The fastest growing metropolitan area of the United States in the 1990s, Las Vegas increased from a little more than 850,000 people in 1990 to 1.84 million by 2007, an increase of 162%.

World Urban Diversity

The city, Figure 11.3 reminds us, is a global phenomenon. It is also a regional and cultural variable reflecting diverse heritages and economies. The descriptions and models that we have used in this chapter to study the functions, land use arrangements, suburbanization trends, and other aspects of the United States city do not always apply to the structures and patterns of cities in other parts of the world. Those cities have been created under different historical, cultural, and technological circumstances. They have developed different functional and structural patterns, some so radically different from our United States model that we would find them unfamiliar and uncharted landscapes indeed. Even Canadian cities differ significantly from their counterparts in the United States (see "The Canadian City"). The city is universal; its characteristics are cultural and regional.

The West European City

Although each is unique historically and culturally, Western European cities as a group share certain common features. They have a much more compact form and occupy less total area than American cities of comparable population and most of their residents are apartment dwellers. Residential streets of the older sections tend to be narrow, and front, side, or rear yards or gardens are rare.

European cities also enjoy a long historical tradition. Medieval origins, Renaissance restructurings, and industrial period growth has given the cities of Western Europe distinctive features. Despite wartime destructions and postwar redevelopments, many still bear the impress of past occupants and technologies, even back to Roman times in some cases. An irregular system of narrow streets may be retained from the random street pattern developed in medieval times of pedestrian and pack-animal movement. Main streets radiating from the city center and cut by circumferential "ring roads" tell us the location of primary roads leading into town through the gates in city walls now gone and replaced by circular boulevards. Broad thoroughfares, public parks, and plazas mark Renaissance ideals of city beautification and the esthetic need felt for processional avenues and promenades.

European cities were developed for pedestrians and still retain the compactness and character appropriate to walking. The sprawl of American suburban zones is generally absent. At the same time, compactness and high density do not necessarily mean skyscraper skylines. Much of urban Europe predates the steel frame building and the elevator. City skylines tend to be low, three to five stories in height, sometimes (as in central Paris) held down by building ordinance (Figure 11.34), or by prohibitions on

close at hand. The younger group has been joined by "empty-nesters," couples who no longer have children living at home and who find big houses on suburban lots no longer desirable. By their interests and efforts these two groups have largely or completely remade and upgraded such old city neighborhoods as the Mill District of Minneapolis, the Armory District of Providence, R.I., the Denny Regrade and Belltown of Seattle, Main St./Market Square district of Houston, and many others throughout the country.

Individual home buyers and rehabbers opened the way; commercial developers followed, greatly increasing the stock of quality housing in downtown areas—but often only after local, state, or federal government made the first investments in slum clearance, park development, cultural center construction, and the like. Columbus, Ohio, for example, built a hockey arena downtown and a soccer stadium north of the CBD, promoted rehabilitation of several neighborhoods near the city center, and aided the development of a stretch of art galleries that now dominate the northern part of the main street of the CBD. Milwaukee built a riverside walk and attracted $50 million in private investment. Indianapolis city officials are emptying housing projects in the Chatham Arch neighborhood and selling them to developers for conversion into apartments and condominiums. And as whole areas are gentrified or redeveloped residentially, other investment flows into nearby commercial activities. For example, Denver's LoDo district, once a skid row, has been wholly transformed into a thriving area of shops, restaurants, and sports bars along with residential lofts.

(a)

(b)

(c)

Figure 11.33 Revitalized central cities. (*a*) New entrepreneurs in New York City. Many Latin American and Asian immigrants have established their own businesses, fixing, making, or selling things, adding to the vitality of central cities. Some work out of sidewalk stalls; others have stores. According to the U.S. Census Bureau, 36% of New York City residents were born abroad. (*b*) Gentrified housing in Old Town in Alexandria, Viriginia, near Washington, D.C. Gentrification is especially active in the major urban centers of the eastern United States, from Boston south along the Atlantic Coast to Charleston, South Carolina, and Savannah, Georgia. (*c*) Former mills along the Mississippi River in Minneapolis, Minnesota, have been converted to loft-style condominiums and offices that are some of the most sought after in the region. The City of Minneapolis initiated the conversion of derelict mills by cleaning pollution and building riverfront parks and trails.

private structures exceeding the height of a major public building, often the central cathedral. Where those older restrictions have been relaxed, however, taller office buildings have been erected—such as in the financial districts of London and Frankfurt, Germany.

Compactness, high densities, and apartment dwelling encouraged the development and continued importance of public transportation, including well-developed subway systems. The private automobile has become much more common of late, though most central city areas have not yet been significantly restructured with wider streets and parking facilities to accommodate it. The automobile is not the universal need in Europe that it has become in American cities. Home and work are generally more closely spaced in Europe—often within walking or bicycling distance—while most sections of towns have first-floor retail and business establishments (below upper-story apartments) bringing both places of employment and retail shops within convenient distance of residences.

In many cities, the historic core is now increasingly gentrified and residential units for the middle class, the self-employed,

Figure 11.34 Even in their central areas, many European cities show a low profile, like that of Paris seen here. Although taller buildings—20, 30, even 50 or more stories in height—have become more common in major European cities since World War II, they are not the universal mark of central business districts that they have become in the United States, nor are they necessarily welcomed symbols of city progress and pride.

and the older generation of skilled artisans share limited space with preserved historic buildings, monuments, and tourist attractions. Many are at the same time affected by the processes of decentralization; some of their residents now choose to live in suburban locations as car ownership and use becomes more commonplace.

The old city fortifications may mark the boundary between the core and the surrounding transitional zone of substandard housing, 19th-century industry, and recent immigrants. European governments used the strategy of grouping industrial developments, working-class homes, and public housing in peripheral or suburban areas outside the city core.

The West European city is not characterized by inner-city deterioration and out-migration. Its core areas tend to be stable in population and attract, rather than repel, the successful middle class and upwardly mobile. Nor does it always feature the ethnic neighborhoods of U. S. cities although some, like London, do (see The Caribbean Map in London, page 186). Non-European immigrant communities, where present in a city, tend to be clustered in older working class districts or in peripheral public housing apartment blocks. Segregation of new immigrants into peripheral suburban apartments has been a particular problem in France as it leads to social isolation and a lack of opportunities for youth.

Eastern European Cities

Cities of Eastern Europe, including Russia and the former European republics of the Soviet Union, once part of the communist world, make up a separate urban class. These postcommunist cities share many of the traditions and practices of West European cities, but differ from them in the centrally administered planning principles that were, in the communist period (1945–1990), designed to shape and control both new and older settlements. For reasons both ideological and practical, the particular concerns were, first, to limit the size of cities to avoid supercity growth and metropolitan sprawl; second, to ensure an internal structure of neighborhood equality and self-sufficiency; and third, to segregate land uses. The planned Eastern European city fully achieved none of these objectives, but by attempting them it has emerged as a distinctive urban form.

The planned city of the communist era is compact, with relatively high building and population densities reflecting the nearly universal apartment dwelling, and with a sharp break between urban and rural land uses on its margins. It depends heavily on public transportation. During the communist period, the Eastern European city differed from its Western counterpart in its purely governmental rather than market control of land use and functional patterns. That control dictated that the central area of cities (the Central Cultural District, or CCD) should be reserved for public use, not occupied by retail establishments or office buildings on the Western, capitalist model. A large central square used for assemblies and celebrations ringed by administrative and cultural buildings was the preferred pattern. Nearby, space was provided for a large recreational and commemorative park. In the Russian prototype, neither a central business district nor major outlying business districts were required or provided. Residential areas were expected to be largely self-contained in the provision of at least low-order goods and services, minimizing the need for a journey to centralized shopping locations.

Residential areas were made up of *microdistricts,* assemblages of uniform apartment blocks housing perhaps 10,000 to 15,000 persons, surrounded by broad boulevards, and containing centrally sited nursery and grade schools, grocery and department stores, theaters, clinics, and similar neighborhood necessities and amenities (Figure 11.35a). Plans called for effective separation of residential quarters from industrial districts by landscaped buffer zones, but in practice many microdistricts were built by factories for their own workers and were located immediately adjacent to the workplace. Because microdistricts were most easily and rapidly constructed on open land at the margins of expanding cities, high residential densities have been carried to the outskirts of town (Figure 11.35b).

These characteristic patterns will change in the decades to come as market principles of land allocation are adopted. Now that private interests can own land and buildings, the urban areas of postcommunist Eastern Europe may take on forms similar to those of the Western European city. In Moscow, the prototypical communist-era Eastern European city, a recent spate of building is rapidly remaking a landscape and skyline once dominated by Soviet-style drab gray concrete monoliths. Glass and metal apartment buildings, modernistic Western-style shopping malls, gated communities of luxury apartments and individual houses, and commercial and residential redesign and redevelopment within existing older structures are the 21st-century trend experienced as well in other major Russian and Eastern European cities. Currently in all major Eastern European cities the trend is to restore historic buildings, construct more spacious privately owned apartments and single-family houses for the newly rich and middle-class. Meanwhile, population decline due to low birth rates (see Appendix B) and out migration in pursuit of better paying jobs in Western Europe has led to shrinking cities in Eastern Europe (Figure 11.36) and problems of high vacancy rates in the less desirable, mass-produced apartment tower blocks of the communist era.

Rapidly Growing Cities of the Developing World

The fastest growing cities and the fastest growing urban populations are found in the developing world (Figure 11.36). Industrialization has come to most of them only recently. Modern technologies in transportation and public facilities are sparsely available, and the structures of cities and the cultures of their inhabitants are far different from the urban world familiar to North Americans. The developing world is vast in extent and diverse in its physical and cultural content; generalizations about it or its urban landscapes lack certainty and universality.

The backgrounds, histories, and current economies and administrations of developing world cities vary greatly. Some are ancient, having been established many centuries before the more developed

The Canadian City

Even within the seemingly homogeneous culture realm of the United States and Canada, cities in the two countries show subtle but significant differences. Although the urban expression is similar in the two countries, it is not identical. The Canadian city, for example, is more compact than its U.S. counterpart of equal population size, with a higher density of buildings and people and a lesser degree of suburbanization of populations and functions.

Space-saving and multiple-family housing units are more the rule in Canada, so a similar population size is housed on a smaller land area with much higher densities, on average, within the central area of cities. The Canadian city is better served by and more dependent on mass transportation than is the U.S. city. Because Canadian metropolitan areas have only one-quarter as many miles of expressway lanes per capita as U.S. metropolises—and at least as much resistance to constructing more—suburbanization of peoples and functions is less extensive north of the border than south.

The differences are cultural, as well. Cities in both countries are ethnically diverse (Canadian communities, in fact, have the higher proportion of foreign born), but U.S. central cities exhibit far greater internal distinctions in race, income, and social status, and more pronounced contrasts between central city and suburban residents. That is, there has been much less "flight to the suburbs" by middle-income Canadians. As a result, the Canadian city shows greater social stability, higher per capita average income, more retention of shopping facilities, and more employment opportunities and urban amenities than its U.S. central city counterpart. In particular, it does not have the rivalry from well-defined competitive edge cities of suburbia that so spread and fragment United States metropolitan complexes.

Vancouver, British Columbia has embraced high-density living and a strong central business district as solutions to the traffic, land-use, and environmental problems of urban sprawl. The commercial and civic buildings of Vancouver, British Columbia's central business district are nearly obscured by the high-rise condominiums and apartments that have been built on former brownfield sites along the False Creek waterfront. Vancouver's central business district is well served by public transit and walking and bicycle trails . On average, Canadian metropolitan areas are almost twice as densely populated as those of the United States. Further, on a per capita basis, Canadian urbanites are two and a half times more likely to use public transportation than American city dwellers.

cities of Europe and Anglo America. Some are still pre-industrial, with only a modest central commercial core; they lack industrial districts, public transportation, or any meaningful degree of land use separation. Others, though increasingly Western in form, are only beginning to industrialize. And some have taken on industrial, commercial, and administrative functions on the Western model and, at least in their central areas, assumed as well the appearance of fully modern urban centers (Figure 11.37).

(a)

(b)

Figure 11.35 (*a*) This scene from Bucharest, Romania, clearly shows important recurring characteristics of the East European socialist-era city design: mass transit service to boulevard-bordered "superblocks" of self-contained apartment-house microdistricts with their own shopping, schools, and other facilities. (*b*) High-density apartment houses bordered by wheat fields mark the urban margin of Poprad, Slovakia; the Tatra Mountains are in the background.

Despite the variety of urban forms found in such diverse regions as Latin America, Africa, the Middle East, and South and Southeast Asia, we can identify some features common to most of them. First, most of what are currently categorized as developing countries have a colonial legacy, and several major cities were established principally to serve the needs of the colonizing country. The second aspect is that of underdevelopment of urban facilities. The tremendous growth these cities are generally experiencing as their societies industrialize has left many of them with inadequate physical infrastructure and public utilities and no way to keep up with population growth. Third, most cities in developing countries are now characterized by neighborhoods hastily built by new migrants, away from city services, and often occupying land illegally. Such squatter settlements are a large and growing component of these cities and reflect both the city's relative opportunity and poverty. Finally, in many cases, governments have responded with drastic remedies, sometimes going so far as to move the national capital away from the overcrowded primate city to a new location or to create entirely new cities to house planned industrial or transportation functions.

Colonial and Noncolonial Antecedents

Cities in developing countries originated for varied reasons and continue to serve several functions based on their position as market, production, government, or religious centers. Their legacy and purpose influence their urban form.

Many are the product of colonialism, established as ports or outposts of administration and exploitation, built by Europeans on a Western model current at the time of their development. For example, the British built Kolkata (Calcutta), New Delhi, and Mumbai (Bombay) in India and Nairobi and Harare (formerly Salisbury) in Africa. The French developed Hanoi and Ho Chi Minh City (Saigon) in Vietnam, Dakar in Senegal, and Bangui in the Central African Republic. The Dutch planned Jakarta (former Batavia) in Indonesia as their main outpost, Belgium placed Kinshasa (formerly Leopoldville) in what is now the Democratic Republic of the Congo, and the Portuguese founded a number of cities in Angola and Mozambique.

Urban structure is a product not just of the time when a city was founded, or of who the founders were, but also of the role it plays in its own cultural setting. Land use patterns in capital cities reflect the centralization of government functions and the concentration of wealth and power in a single city of a country (Figure 11.38a). The physical layout of a religious center is conditioned by the religion it serves, whether Hinduism, Buddhism, Islam,

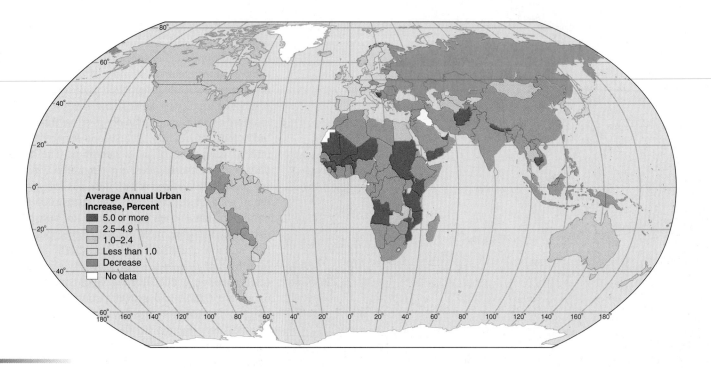

Figure 11.36 **Average annual urban population growth rates, 1990–2004.** In general, developing countries show the highest percentage increases in their urban populations, and the already highly urbanized and industrialized countries have the lowest—less than 1% per year in most of Europe. Demographers anticipate that population increases in cities in developing countries will be the distinguishing demographic trend of the 21st century. In contrast to their patterns of growth, the cities of Russia and most of the states formerly within its empire have experienced population decline since the breakup of the Soviet Union in 1991. An urban growth rate of 5% means that a country's city population will double in just 14 years.

Source: Data from United Nations Population Division.

Christianity, or other faith. Typically, a monumental structure—a temple, mosque, or cathedral—and associated buildings rather than government or commercial offices occupy the city center. Multifunctional centers display a greater diversity of land uses and structures (Figure 11.38b). Traditional market centers for a wide area (Timbuktu in Mali and Lahore in Pakistan), or cultural capitals (Addis Ababa in Ethiopia and Cuzco in Peru), have land use patterns that reflect their special functions. Similarly, port cities such as Dubai (United Arab Emirates), Haifa (Israel), or Shanghai (China) have a land use structure different from that of an industrial or mining center such as Johannesburg (South Africa). Adding to the complexity is the fact that cities with a long history reflect the changes wrought by successive rulers and/or colonial powers, and that as some of the megacities in the developing world have grown, they have engulfed nearby towns and cities.

Even within a single culture realm, then, urban forms display significant variation. For example, for South Asia, which includes Afghanistan, Pakistan, India, Nepal, Bhutan, and Bangladesh, geographers have developed several different descriptive models to characterize colonial cities, traditional bazaar cities, planned cities, and cities that are intermixtures of these. Still other models describe land use patterns in smaller cities that developed originally as hill stations (resorts), railway colonies, or military encampments.

Yet, by observation and consensus, some common features of developing-world cities are recognizable. For example, wherever automobiles or modern transport systems are an integral part of the modernizing city, the metropolis begins to take on Western

characteristics. Also, all of the large cities have modern centers of commerce, not unlike their Anglo American counterparts (see Figure 11.37).

All, too, wherever located, have experienced massive in-migrations from rural areas. Many, particularly in sub-Saharan Africa, have absorbed large numbers of foreign immigrants seeking asylum or economic opportunity. Most have had even faster rates of natural increase than of immigration. The predicted consequences, according to the UN, will be the concentration of nearly all of the global population increase between 2000 and 2030 within the urban areas of the world's least developed countries. Many of those populations are and will continue to be impacted by the negative effects of a globalizing world economy that features massive transfers of money and jobs to cities and countries at least temporarily able to offer the cheapest labor for the "footloose" operations of transnational corporations. UN-Habitat has termed the economic consequences a "race to the bottom" that yields widespread urbanization of poverty as jobs gained by temporary local advantages are lost to other locales offering superior—if transitory—inducements. Increased urban poverty and greater social and economic inequality and segregation are the foreseen consequences for much of the urbanizing developing countries. In all their cities, large numbers of people support themselves in the "informal" sector—as food vendors, peddlers of cigarettes or trinkets, street-side barbers or tailors, errand runners or package carriers—outside the usual forms of wage labor (Table 11.3 and Figure 10.5).

Figure 11.37 Downtown Nairobi, Kenya, is a busy, modern urban core, complete with high-rise commercial buildings.

Urban Primacy and Rapid Growth

The developing countries have experienced disproportionate population concentrations in their national and regional capitals. Few developing countries have mature, functionally complex, small and medium-size centers. The primate city dominates their urban systems (see Figure 11.16). One-fifth of all Nicaraguans live in metropolitan Managua, and Libreville contains a third of the populace of Gabon. Vast numbers of surplus, low-income rural populations have been attracted to these developed seats of wealth and political centrality in the hope of finding a job.

Whatever their relative or absolute size within their respective states, large cities of the developing world typically produce a significant share of the gross domestic income (GDI) of their countries. Within Latin America, for example, Lima contributes 44% of Peru's GDI and São Paulo yields 37% of Brazil's. Major cities of Asia show comparable relative economic importance: Bangkok is credited with 38% of Thailand's gross domestic income and Manila, Philippines; Karachi, Pakistan; and Shanghai, China, contributed 25%, 18%, and 12% to the GDI of their countries, the UN reported in 2001. Despite its inadequate infrastructure, Mumbai generates one-sixth of the GDI of India.

Many cities, including the primate city, in developing countries with rapidly growing economies have a vibrant and modern city center and elite residential sector (Figure 11.39). Such districts contain amenities that could be found in major Western centers and are the places where the wealthiest members of society work and often live. This is also the part of the city that businesspeople, officials, tourists, and other visitors are most likely to see. Some, particularly Asian, cities have made great investments in these city centers, often as much for prestige as for practical purposes. In fact, the booming cities of Asia now are leaders in skyscraper construction; of the world's ten tallest buildings in 2009, the eight newest were located in East or Southeast Asia, and just two were in the United States.

Yet the presence of gleaming downtowns cannot disguise the fact that most of these cities simply cannot keep pace with the massive growth they are experiencing (Figure 11.40). The less-developed world as a whole had 44% of its population urban in 2007; the UN anticipates that urban component will rise to 57% by 2030, promising unceasing pressure on governments to provide adequately for the housing, employment, and public service needs of that burgeoning population. In many individual cities, growth rates appear unsustainable; Lagos, Nigeria, for

(a)

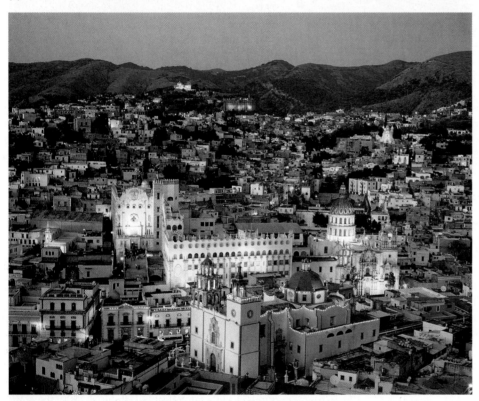
(b)

Figure 11.38 Developing-world cities vary greatly in structure and appearance, reflecting their differing culture regions, histories, and functions, (*a*) Monumental government buildings mark single-function Brasilia, capital city of Brazil, whereas (*b*) the central area of multifunctional Guanajuato, Mexico, is dominated by religious structures.

example, had a 2007 population estimated at 9.5 million and a UN estimated growth rate between 4% and 7% yearly. By one calculation, Lagos adds some 600,000 people each year, the same as crowding in an additional Baltimore, Maryland, or Abilene, Texas, population each 12 months. The massive rural-to-urban movement contributing to such growth rates and population increases is augmented by the additional births produced by the youthful immigrants. In 2005, China had within its cities 114 to 150 million unregistered migrants from the countryside, providing cheap factory and construction labor for the country's booming economy but swelling, as well, the number of homeless and impoverished urbanites.

Squatter Settlements

Most developing world cities are now and seem likely to continue to be ringed by vast squatter settlements high in density and low in public facilities and services. With regional variations (Table 11.4), slum dwellers account for about 43% of the urban population in developing regions, and squatter slums early in this century held at least a billion people—about a third of the world's city dwellers. The UN predicts slums will house some two billion by 2030. Then, as now, their most vulnerable and deprived residents will be women and children as the urban "feminization of poverty" expresses itself in large parts of the developing world.

Between one-third and two-thirds of the population of most developing world cities is crowded into shantytowns and squatter settlements built by the inhabitants, often in defiance of officialdom. These unofficial communities—*favela* in Brazil, *barrio* in Mexico, *kampung* in Indonesia, *gecekondu* in Turkey, or *katchiabadi* in Pakistan—usually have little or no access to publicly provided services such as water supply, sewerage and drainage, paved roads, and garbage removal. In such megacities as Rio de Janeiro (Figure 11.41), São Paulo, Mexico City, Bangkok, Chennai (Madras), Cairo, or Lagos, millions find refuge in the shacks and slums of the "informal housing sector." Crumbling tenements house additional tens of thousands, many of whom are eventually forced into shantytowns by the conversion of tenements into commercial property or high-income apartments.

No more than 20% of the new housing in Third World cities is produced by the formal housing sector; the rest develops informally, ignoring building codes, zoning restrictions, property rights, and infrastructure standards. Informal settlements house varying percentages of these populations, but for low-income developing countries as a whole in

Table 11.3

Relative Importance of the Informal Economy in Employment (percent)

	Africa	Asia	Latin America and Caribbean
Non-agricultural employment	78	45–85	57
Urban employment	61	40–60	40
Total new job creation	93	—	83

Source: From Cities Alliance, *2004 Annual Report,* Table 1, p. 7

Figure 11.39 High-rise buildings near Ipanema Beach in Rio de Janeiro, Brazil, make up part of the city's elite residential sector that extends outward from the central business district. This spine of high-quality development is well served with sewers and other urban services in contrast with the favelas elsewhere in Rio de Janeiro (Figure 11.41).

Table 11.4

Slum Dwellers' Share of Total Urban Population

Region	Percent
Sub-Saharan Africa	72
South Central Asia	58
East Asia	36
Western Asia	33
Latin America and Caribbean	32
North Africa	28
Southwestern Asia	28
Developing regions	*43*
Developed regions	*6*

Source: UN-Habitat, *The Challenge of Slums,* 2003.

the early 21st century, only one formal housing unit was being added for every nine new households, and between 70% and 90% of all new households found shelter in shanties or slums.

Overcrowding often transforms peripheral squatter settlements into vast zones of disease and squalor subject to constant danger from landslides, fire, and flooding. The informality and often illegality of the squatter housing solution means that those who improvise and build their own shelters lack registration and recognized ownership of their domiciles or the land on which they stand. Without such legal documentation, no capital accumulation based on housing assets is possible and no collateral for home improvement loans or other purposes is created.

As many as half of the 3 million residents in Nairobi, Kenya, live in slums, most without electricity, running water, or sewers; in that city's sprawling slum district of Mathare Valley, some 250,000 people are squeezed into 15 square kilometers (6 sq mi) and are increasing by 10,000 inhabitants per year. Such impoverished squatter districts exist around most major cities in Africa, Asia, and Latin America; in 2006, a reported 20 million people in the five great conurbations of South Asia—Delhi, Dhaka, Karachi, Kolkata, and Mumbai—existed in slum conditions, and over 99% of the urban population of Chad and Ethiopia are slum dwellers. With some of the fastest urban growth rates, Sub-Saharan African cities are case studies of slum development and poverty to accompany the skyscraper modernization of many of their capital city cores. Early in the 21st century, 72% of the region's urbanites were slum dwellers; they were, in addition, afflicted with low life expectancies, high levels of infant and child mortality, HIV/AIDS prevalence, and illiteracy, particularly among women and girls.

Sometimes residents of squatter settlements have successfully lobbied governments for water, sewers, roads and other infrastructure and over time have become more established neighborhoods. Although improvements in sanitary conditions are occurring

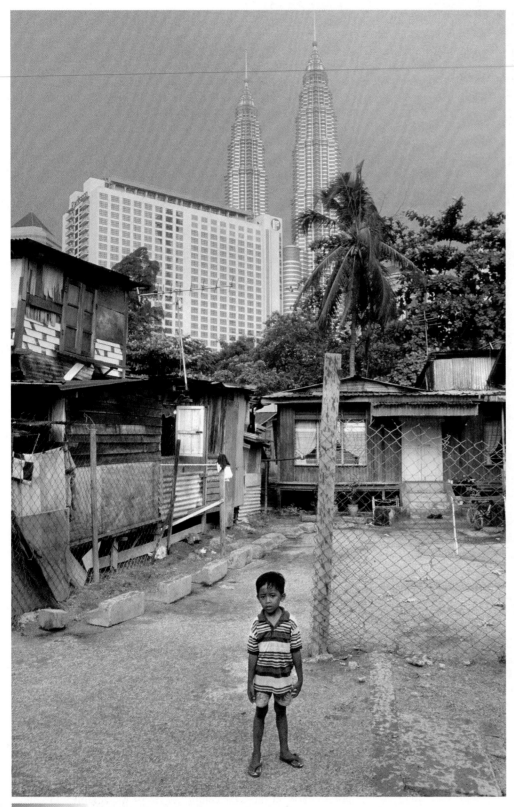

(83% of sub-Saharan urban people have access to improved drinking water supplies and 73% use adequate sanitary facilities), the UN anticipates continuing pressure on city infrastructure as slum populations, at present rates of increase, are likely to double every 15 years. The land use result of inner city slum concentrations in all developing world regions has frequently been the creation of an *inverse concentric zone* pattern in which the elite and upper class reside in central areas and social status declines with increasing distance from the center.

Latin American City Model

While Latin American cities have their own unique characteristics, many of the traits common to cities in the developing world can be observed in the **Latin American city model** (Figure 11.42). At the center is the traditional market area, key government and religious buildings, and a modern central business district. Extending outward from the center is a commercial spine that features high status establishments and terminates at a suburban mall. The spine features amenities such as tree-lined boulevards, is well-served with sewers and urban services, and is surrounded by an elite residential sector. Residential zones generally decrease in status with distance from the center since the inner city has a positive connotation. The zone of maturity has the better quality residences, while the zone of in-situ accretion is mixed in status but undergoing improvement. Squatter settlements are found at the urban periphery and in disamenity zones such as near dumps, in flood-prone areas, or on slopes too steep for conventional development. An industrial corridor terminates at a peripheral industrial park and a circumferential roadway (*perférico*) connects the industrial park and suburban mall.

Figure 11.40 Dualism of prosperity and poverty in Kuala Lumpur, Malaysia. In the background, the Petronas Towers—completed in 1998 and for 6 years the world's tallest—and the Radisson Hotel rise in sharp contrast to the downtown shanties in their shadow.

Figure 11.41 A *favela* in Rio de Janeiro, Brazil. These homes are built out of scrap wood and sheet metal and have no city services such as sewers, running water, electricity, or street maintenance.

Planned Cities

Some national capitals have been removed from their earlier primate city sites and relocated outside the core regions of their countries. The objective has been to achieve the presumed advantages of national territorial centrality or to encourage more uniform national development; examples include Islamabad (Pakistan), Brasilia (Brazil), Abuja (Nigeria), and Putrajay (Malaysia). Other relocations have been planned or announced, including a 2004 decision to relocate South Korea's capital 150 kilometers (93 mi) to the southeast of Seoul.

A number of developing countries have also created or are currently building some new cities intended to draw population away from overgrown metropolises; others are designed to house transportation facilities or industrial agglomerations. For example, China's capital, Beijing, is establishing 11 satellite cities in its suburbs to accommodate 5.7 million people, relieving pressure on the capital city itself. Thailand opened Suvarnabhumi, a major airport an hour outside of Bangkok, intended to become the air transport hub for Southeast Asia with a new city nearby planned as a major new industrial center for the nation. China, India, Malaysia, and other Asian industrializing states are also planning—or have constructed—high-tech manufacturing and service centers, catering to the outsourcing needs and market opportunities of a globalizing economy (Figure 11.43).

Figure 11.42 **The Latin American City Model** shows the wealthy living in the inner city and along a commercial spine that extends outward in one sector. Income generally declines with distance from the central business district.

Source: Larry R. Ford, "A New and Improved Model of Latin American City Structure," Geographical Review 86 (1996): 438.

Figure 11.43 The Cyber Gateway Building in Hyderabad's Hitec City. The complex houses firms like the multinational software companies Microsoft, IBM, and Toshiba, as well as Indian companies like Wipro, which provides information technology services and product design. Hitec City also houses professional schools in business and information technology.

Summary

The city is the essential focus of activity for every society advanced beyond the subsistence level. Although they are among the oldest marks of civilization, only in the past decade have cities become the home of the majority of the world's people. Virtually all population growth worldwide in the first decades of the 21st century will be captured by cities in the developing world.

All settlements growing beyond their village origins take on functions uniting them to the countryside and to a larger system of settlements. As they grow, they become functionally complex. Their economic structure, composed of both *basic* and *nonbasic* activities, may become diverse. Basic activities represent the functions performed for the larger economy and urban system; nonbasic activities satisfy the needs of the urban residents themselves. Functional classifications distinguish the economic roles of urban centers, while simple classification of them as transportation and special-function cities or as central places helps define and explain their functional and size hierarchies and the spatial patterns they display within a system of cities.

Systems of cities are reflected in the urban hierarchy and in part described by the rank-size rule, primacy, and central place theory. When a city is far larger than all others in its country, it is termed a primate city. Many countries display this dominating city pattern, but there are only a few *world cities* dominating the global economy.

Repetitive physical and social patterns are found inside Anglo American cities. At the core, the central business district, localized originally by mass transit line convergence, has highest land values and accessibility. Outside the CBD, lower order commercial centers are also transport-route oriented. Residential uses occupy less valuable and less accessible land. These patterns inspired geographers to summarize early 20th-century urban form by the concentric zone, sector, and multiple-nuclei models, modified by 21st-century recognition of metropolitan peripheral models. The period following World War II brought massive changes in urban organization, with the decline and regeneration of the central city accompanied by the rise and expansion of suburbs. Urban social patterns have been influenced by the tendency for urban dwellers to sort themselves spatially by family status, social status, and ethnicity. In Western countries, these patterns are also influenced by governmental controls that help determine land uses.

Urbanization is a global phenomenon, and Anglo American models of city systems, land use, and social area patterns differ substantially from cities in the rest of the world, reflecting diverse heritages and economic structures. Western European cities differ from those in Eastern Europe, where land uses reflect earlier communist principles of city structure. Explosive growth in developing-world cities is rendering them unable to provide all their residents with employment, housing, safe water, sanitation, and other minimally essential services and facilities.

KEY WORDS

basic sector 346
brownfields 365
central business district (CBD) 356
central city 354
central place 349
central place theory 349
Christaller, Walter 349
city 354
concentric zone model 357
conurbation 341
economic base 346

edge city 364
gated community 361
gentrification 367
hinterland 344
Latin American city model 378
metropolitan area 354
multiple-nuclei model 358
multiplier effect 348
network city 353
nonbasic (service) sector 354

peripheral model 359
primate city 353
rank-size rule 352
sector model 358
suburb 354
town 354
urban hierarchy 351
urban influence zone 351
urbanized area 354
world city 352

FOR REVIEW

1. Consider the city or town in which you live, attend school, or with which you are most familiar. In a brief paragraph, discuss that community's *site* and *situation*. Point out the connection, if any, between its site and situation and the basic functions that it earlier or now performs.

2. Describe the *multiplier effect* as it relates to the population growth of urban units.

3. Is there a hierarchy of retailing activities in the community with which you are most familiar? Of how many and of what kinds of levels is that hierarchy composed? What localizing forces affect the distributional pattern of retailing within that community?

4. Briefly describe the urban land use patterns predicted by the *concentric circle,* the *sector,* and the *multiple-nuclei* models of urban development. Which one, if any, best corresponds to the growth and land use pattern of the community most familiar to you?

5. In what ways do *social status, family status,* and *ethnicity* affect the residential choices of households? What expected distributional patterns of urban social areas are associated with each? Does the social geography of your community conform to the predicted pattern?

6. How has suburbanization damaged the economic base and the financial stability of the United States central city?

7. In what ways does the Canadian city differ from the pattern of its U.S. counterpart?

8. Why are metropolitan areas in developing countries expected to grow larger than many Western metropolises by 2015 or 2020?

9. What are *primate cities?* Why are primate cities so prevalent in the developing world? Why are they so overburdened in populations and functions? How are some governments attempting to reduce their relative importance in their national systems of cities?

10. How are cities in the developing world influenced by their colonial pasts?

KEY CONCEPTS REVIEW

1. **What common features define the origin, nature, and locations of cities?** pp. 340–346.
   Cities arose 4000–6000 years ago as distinctive evidence of the growing cultural and economic complexity of early civilizations. Distinct from the farm villages of subsistence economies, true cities provided an increasing range of functions—religious, military, trade, production, etc.—for their developing societies. Their functions and importance were affected by the sites and situations chosen for them. The massive recent increase in number and size of cities worldwide reflects the universality of economic development and total population growth in the latter 20th century.

2. **How are cities structured economically and how are systems of cities organized?** pp. 346–353.
   The economic base of a city—the functions it performs—is divided between basic and nonbasic (or service) activities. Through a multiplier effect, adding basic workers increases both the number of service workers and the total population of a city. The amount of growth reflects the base ratio characteristic of the city. Cities may be hierarchically ranked by their size and functional complexity. Rank-size, primate, and central place hierarchies are commonly cited but distinctly different.

3. **How are cities structured internally and how do people distribute themselves within them?** pp. 354–369.

Cities are themselves distinctive land use and cultural area landscapes. In the United States, older cities show repetitive land use patterns that are largely determined by land value and accessibility considerations. Classical land use models include the concentric circle, sector, and multiple nuclei patterns. Distinct social area arrangements have been equated with those land use models. Newer cities and growing metropolitan areas have created different land use and social area structures with suburbs, edge cities, and galactic metropolises as recognized urban landscape features.

4. **Are there world regional and cultural differences in the land use and population patterns of major cities?** pp. 369–380.

Cities are regional and cultural variables; their internal land use and social area patterns reflect the differing historical, technological, political, and cultural conditions under which they developed. We are most familiar with the U.S. city, but we can easily recognize differences between it and Western European, Eastern European, and developing world cities, themselves of great regional, physical, and cultural complexity.

THE POLITICAL ORDERING OF SPACE

12

The Palace of Westminster or the Houses of Parliament, located on the north bank of the River Thames in London, is the seat of the government of the United Kingdom of Great Britain and Northern Ireland.

Key Concepts

1. National political units: geographic characteristics and boundary concerns, pp. 384–397.

2. Nationalism, unifying centripetal, and destabilizing centrifugal forces, pp. 397–403.

3. International political systems: the UN, maritime law, and regional alliances, pp. 403–410.

4. Local and regional political forms: representation and fragmentation, pp. 410–416 .

They met together in the cabin of the little ship on the day of the landfall. The journey from England had been long and stormy. Provisions ran out, a man had died, a boy had been born. Although they were grateful to have been delivered to the calm waters off Cape Cod that November day of 1620, their gathering in the cramped cabin was not to offer prayers of thanksgiving but to create a political structure to govern the settlement they were now to establish (Figure 12.1). The Mayflower Compact was an agreement among themselves to "covenant and combine our selves togeather into a civill Body Politick . . . to enacte, constitute, and frame such just and equall Lawes, Ordinances, Acts, Constitutions, and Offices . . . convenient for ye Generall good of ye Colonie. . . ." They elected one of their company governor, and only after those political acts did they launch a boat and put a party ashore.

The land they sought to colonize had for more than 100 years been claimed by the England they had left. The New World voyage of John Cabot in 1497 had invested their sovereign with title to all of the land of North America and a recognized legal right to govern his subjects dwelling there. That right was delegated by royal patent to colonizers and their sponsors, conferring upon them title to a defined tract and the authority to govern it. Although the Mayflower settlers were originally without a charter or patent, they recognized themselves as part of an established political system. They chose their governor and his executive department annually by vote of the General Court, a legislature composed of all freemen of the settlement.

As the population grew, new towns were established too distant for their voters to attend the General Court. By 1636, the larger towns were sending representatives to cooperate with the executive branch in making laws. Each town became a legal entity, with election of local officials and enactment of local ordinances the prime purpose of the town meetings that are still common in New England today.

The Mayflower Compact, signed by 41 freemen as their initial act in a New World, was the first step in a continuing journey of political development for the settlement and for the larger territory of which it became a part. From company patent to crown colony to rebellious commonwealth under the Continental Congress to state in a new country, Massachusetts (and Plimoth Plantation) were part of a continuing process of the political organization of space.

That process is as old as human history. From clans to kingdoms, human groups have laid claim to territory and have organized themselves and administered their affairs within it. Indeed, the political organizations of society are as fundamental an expression of culture and cultural differences as are forms of economy or religious beliefs. Geographers are interested in that structuring because it is both an expression of the human organization of space and closely related to other spatial evidences of culture, such as religion, language, and ethnicity.

Political geography is the study of the organization and distribution of political phenomena, including their impact on other spatial components of society and culture. Nationality is a basic element in cultural variation among people, and political geography traditionally has had a primary interest in country units, or *states* (Figure 12.2). Of particular concern have been spatial patterns that reflect the exercise of central governmental control, such as questions of boundary delimitation. Increasingly, however, attention has shifted both upward and downward on the political scale. On the world scene, international alliances, regional compacts, and producer cartels—some requiring the surrender of at least a portion of national sovereignty—have increased in prominence since World War II, representing new forms of spatial interaction. At the local level, voting patterns, constituency boundaries and districting rules, and political fragmentation have directed public attention to the significance of area in the domestic political process.

In this chapter, we discuss some of the characteristics of political entities, examine the problems involved in defining jurisdictions, seek the elements that lend cohesion to a political entity, explore the implications of partial surrender of sovereignty, and consider the significance of the fragmentation of political power. We begin with states (countries) and end with local political systems.

Emphasis in this chapter on political entities should not make us lose sight of the reality that states are rooted in the operations of the economy and society they represent, that social and economic disputes are as significant as border confrontations, and that in some regards transnational corporations and other nongovernmental agencies may exert more influence in international affairs than do the separate states in which they are housed or operate. Some of those expanded political considerations are alluded to in the discussions that follow; others were developed more fully in Chapter 9.

Figure 12.1 Signing the Mayflower Compact, probably the first written plan for self-government in America. Forty-one adult males signed the Compact aboard the *Mayflower* before going ashore.

Figure 12.2 These flags, symbols of separate member states, grace the front of the United Nations building in New York City. Although central to political geographic interest, states are only one level of the political organization of space.

National Political Systems

One of the most significant elements in human geography is the nearly complete division of the earth's land surface into separate country units, as shown on the Countries of the World map inside this book's cover. Even Antarctica is subject to the rival territorial claims of seven countries, although these claims have not been pressed because of the Antarctic Treaty of 1959 (Figure 12.3). Another element is that this division into country units is relatively recent. Although countries and empires have existed since the days of ancient Egypt and Mesopotamia, only in the last century has the world been almost completely divided into independent governing entities. Now people everywhere accept the idea of the state and its claim to sovereignty within its borders as normal.

States, Nations, and Nation-States

Before we begin our consideration of political systems, we need to clarify some terminology. Geographers use the words *state* and *nation* somewhat differently than the way they are used in every-day speech; sometimes confusion arises because each word has more than one meaning. A state can be defined as either (1) any of the political units forming a federal government (e.g., one of the United States) or as (2) an independent political entity holding sovereignty over a territory (e.g., the United States). In this latter sense, *state* is synonymous with *country* or *nation.* That is, a nation can also be defined as (1) an independent political unit holding sovereignty over a territory (e.g., a member of the United Nations). But it can also be used to describe (2) a community of people with a common culture and territory (e.g., the Kurdish nation). The second definition is *not* synonymous with state or country.

To avoid confusion, we shall define a **state** on the international level as an independent political unit occupying a defined, permanently populated territory and having full sovereign control over its

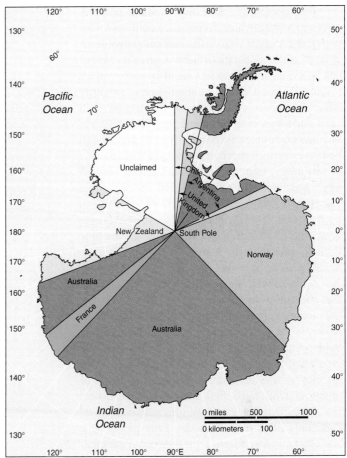

Figure 12.3 **Territorial claims in Antarctica.** Seven countries claim sovereignty over portions of Antarctica, and those of Argentina, Chile, and the United Kingdom overlap. The Antarctic Treaty of 1959 froze those claims for 30 years, banned further land claims, and made scientific research the primary use of the continent. The treaty was extended for 50 years in 1991. Antarctica is neither a sovereign state—it has no permanent inhabitants or local government—nor a part of one.

internal and foreign affairs. We will use *country* as a synonym for the territorial and political concept of "state." Not all recognized territorial entities are states. Antarctica, for example, has neither established government nor permanent population, and it is, therefore, not a state. Nor are *colonies* or *protectorates* recognized as states. Although they have defined extent, permanent inhabitants, and some degree of separate governmental structure, they lack full control over all of their internal and external affairs. More importantly, they lack recognition as states by the international community, a decisive consideration in the proper use of the term "state."

We use nation in its second sense, as a reference to people, not to political structure. A **nation** is a group of people with a common culture occupying a particular territory, bound together by a strong sense of unity arising from shared beliefs and customs. Language and religion may be unifying elements, but even more important are an emotional conviction of cultural distinctiveness and a sense of ethnocentrism. The Cree nation exists because of its cultural uniqueness, not by virtue of territorial sovereignty.

The composite term **nation-state** properly refers to a state whose territorial extent coincides with that occupied by a distinct nation or people or, at least, whose population shares a general sense of cohesion and adherence to a set of common values (Figure 12.4a). That is, a nation-state is an entity whose members feel a natural connection with each other by virtue of sharing language, religion, or some other cultural characteristic strong enough both to bind them together and to give them a sense of distinction from all others outside the community. Although all countries strive for consensus values and loyalty to the state, few can claim to be true nation-states since few are or have ever been wholly uniform ethnically. Iceland, Slovenia, Poland, and the two Koreas are often cited as acceptable examples.

A *binational* or *multinational state* is one that contains more than one nation (Figure 12.4b). Often, no single ethnic group dominates the population. In the constitutional structure of the former Soviet Union before 1988, one division of the legislative branch of the government was termed the Soviet of Nationalities. It was composed of representatives from civil divisions of the Soviet Union populated by groups of officially recognized "nations": Ukrainians, Kazakhs, Tatars, Estonians, and others. In this instance, the concept of nationality was territorially less than the extent of the state.

Alternatively, a single nation may be dispersed across and be predominant in two or more states. This is the case with the *part-nation state* (Figure 12.4c). Here, a people's sense of nationality exceeds the areal limits of a single country. An example is the Arab nation, which dominates 17 states.

Finally, there is the special case of the *stateless nation,* a people without a state. The Kurds, for example, are usually regarded as the largest stateless nation containing some 20 million people divided among six states and dominant in none (Figure 12.4d). Kurdish nationalism has survived over the centuries, and many Kurds nurture a vision of an independent Kurdistan. Other stateless nations include the Roma (Gypsies) and Basques.

Figure 12.4 Types of relationships between states and nations. (*a*) **Nation-states.** Poland and Slovenia are examples of states occupied by a distinct nation or people. (*b*) **A multinational state.** Switzerland shows that a common ethnicity, language, or religion is not necessary for a strong sense of nationalism. (*c*) **A part-nation state.** The Arab nation extends across and dominates many states in northern Africa and the Middle East. (*d*) **A stateless nation.** An ancient group with a distinctive language, the Kurds are concentrated in Turkey, Iran, and Iraq. Smaller numbers live in Syria, Armenia, and Azerbaijan.

The Evolution of the Modern State

The concept and practice of the political organization of space and people arose independently in many parts of the world. Certainly, one of the distinguishing characteristics of very early culture hearths—including those shown on Figure 2.15—was the political organization of their peoples and areas. The larger and more complex the economic structures they developed, the more sophisticated became their mechanisms of political control and territorial administration.

Our Western orientations and biases may incline us to trace ideas of spatial political organization through their Near Eastern Mediterranean, and Western European expressions. Mesopotamian and classical Greek city states, the Roman Empire, and European colonizing kingdoms and warring principalities were, however, not unique. Southern, southeastern, and eastern Asia had their counterparts, as did sub-Saharan Africa and the Western Hemisphere. Although the Western European models and colonization strongly influenced the forms and structures of modern states in both hemispheres, the cultural roots of statehood run deeper and reach further back in many parts of the world than European example alone suggests.

The now universal idea of the modern state was developed by European political philosophers in the 18th century. Their views advanced the concept that people owe allegiance to a state and the people it represents rather than to its leader, such as a king or feudal lord. The new concept coincided in France with the French Revolution and spread over Western Europe, to England, Spain, and Germany.

Many states are the result of European expansion during the 17th, 18th, and 19th centuries, when much of Africa, Asia, and the Americas was divided into colonies. Usually these colonial claims were given fixed and described boundaries where none had earlier been formally defined. Of course, precolonial native populations had relatively fixed home areas of control within which there was recognized dominance and border defense and from which there were, perhaps, raids of plunder or conquest of neighboring "foreign" districts. Beyond understood tribal territories, great empires arose, again with recognized outer limits of influence or control: Mogul and Chinese; Benin and Zulu; Incan and Aztec. Upon them where they still existed, and upon the less formally organized spatial patterns of effective tribal control, European colonizers imposed their arbitrary new administrative divisions of the land. In fact, groups that had little in common were often joined in the same colony (Figure 12.5). The new divisions, therefore, were not usually based on meaningful cultural or physical lines. Instead, the boundaries simply represented the limits of the colonizing empire's power.

As these former colonies have gained political independence, they have retained the idea of the state. They have generally accepted—in the case of Africa, by a conscious decision to avoid precolonial territorial or ethnic claims that could lead to war—the borders established by their former European rulers (Figure 12.6).

Figure 12.5 **The discrepancies between ethnic groups and country boundaries in Africa.** Cultural boundaries were ignored by European colonial powers. The result was significant ethnic diversity in nearly all African countries and conflict between countries over borders.

Source: Redrawn from World Regional Geography: A Question of Place *by Paul Ward English, with James Andrew Miller. Copyright © 1977 Harper & Row. Used by permission of the author.*

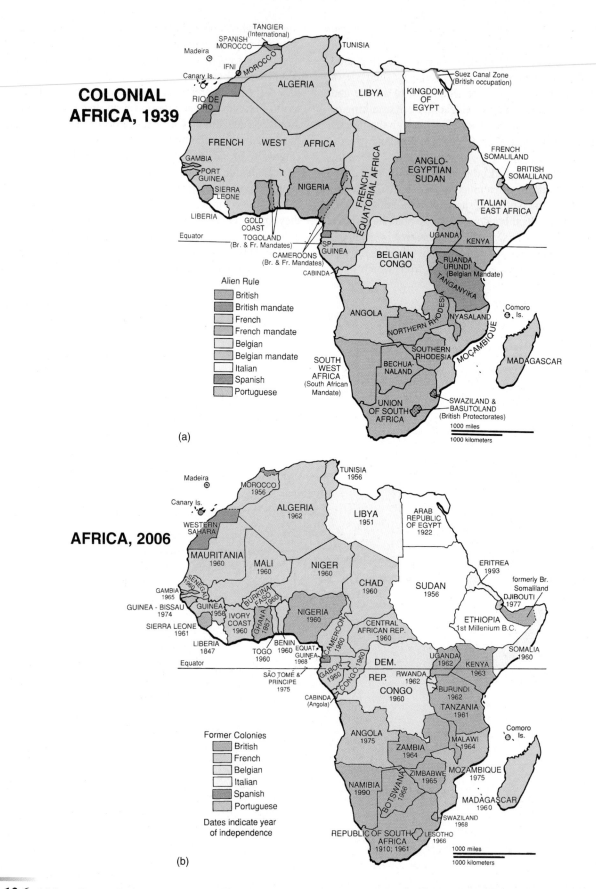

Figure 12.6 Africa—from colonies to states. (*a*) **Africa in 1939** was a patchwork of foreign claims and alien rule, some dating from the 19th century, others of more recent vintage. For example, Germany lost its claim to South West Africa, Tanganyika, Togoland, and the Cameroons after World War I, and Italy asserted control over Ethiopia during the 1930s. (*b*) **Africa in 2006** was a mosaic of separate states. Their dates of independence are indicated on the map. French West Africa and French Equatorial Africa have been extensively subdivided, and Ethiopia and Somaliland emerged from Italian control. Most of the current countries retain the boundaries of their former colonial existence, though the continent's structure of political influence and regional power has changed through civil wars and neighboring state interventions. These marked the decline of earlier African principles of inviolability of borders and noninterference in the internal affairs of other states.

The problem that many of the new countries face is "nation building"—developing feelings of loyalty to the state among their arbitrarily associated citizens. For example, the Democratic Republic of the Congo, the former Belgian Congo, contains some 270 frequently antagonistic ethnic groups. Julius Nyerere, then president of Tanzania, noted in 1971, "These new countries are artificial units, geographic expressions carved on the map by European imperialists. These are the units we have tried to turn into nations."

The idea of separate statehood grew slowly at first and, more recently, has accelerated rapidly. At the time of the Declaration of Independence of the United States in 1776, there were only some 35 empires, kingdoms, and countries in the entire world. By the beginning of World War II in 1939, their number had only doubled to about 70. Following that war, the end of the colonial era brought a rapid increase in the number of sovereign states. From the former British Empire and Commonwealth, there have come the independent countries of India, Pakistan, Bangladesh, Malaysia, Myanmar (Burma), and Singapore in Asia, and Ghana, Nigeria, Kenya, Uganda, Tanzania, Malawi, Botswana, Zimbabwe, and Zambia in Africa. Even this extensive list is not complete. A similar process has occurred in most of the former overseas possessions of the Netherlands, Spain, Portugal, and France. By 1990, independent states totaled some 180, and their number increased again following—among other political geographic developments—the disintegration during the 1990s of the USSR, Czechoslovakia, and Yugoslavia, which created more than 20 countries where only three had existed before (Figure 12.7).

Challenges to the State

The state and nation-state have long been the focus of political geography, and we shall keep that focus in much of the following discussion. But we should also realize that the validity of that state-centric view of the world is increasingly under assaults from multiple new agents of economic and social power. Among them are:

- The globalization of economies and the emergence of transnational corporations whose economic and production decisions are unrelated to the interests of any single state, including their home office state. Those decisions—outsourcing of production and services, for example—may be detrimental to the employment structure, tax base, and national security of any single state and limit the applicability of national economic planning and control.

- The proliferation of international and supranational institutions initially concerned with financial or security matters but all representing the voluntary surrender of some traditional state autonomy. The World Trade Organization, regional trade blocs like the North American Free Trade Association, the European Union, and a host of other international conventions and agreements all limit the independence of action of each of their members and thus diminish absolute state primacy in economic and social matters.

- The emergence and multiplication of nongovernmental organizations (NGOs) whose specific interests and collective actions cut across national boundaries and unite people sharing common concerns about, for example, globalization, the environment, economic and social injustice, AIDS efforts, and the like. The well-publicized protests and pressures exerted by NGOs channel social pressures to influence or limit governmental actions.

- The massive international migration flows that tend to undermine the state as a cultural community with assured and expected common values and loyalties. The Internet, cheap telephone calls, and easy international travel permit immigrant retention of primary ties with their home culture and state, discouraging their full assimilation into their new social environment or the transfer of loyalties to their adopted country.

- The increase in nationalist and separatist movements in culturally composite states, weakening through demands for independence or regional autonomy the former unquestioned primacy of the established state.

Some of these agents and developments have been touched on in earlier chapters; others will be reviewed in this, particularly in the section on Centrifugal Forces (p. 399–403). All represent recent and strengthening forces that, in some assessments of political geographic reality, weaken the validity of a worldview in which national governments and institutionalized politics are all-powerful.

Geographic Characteristics of States

Every state has certain geographic characteristics by which it can be described and that set it apart from all other states. A look at the world political map inside the cover of this book confirms that every state is unique. The size, shape, and location of any one state combine to distinguish it from all others. These characteristics are of more than academic interest, because they also affect the power and stability of states.

Figure 12.7 After the former USSR dissolved in 1991, 15 newly independent countries emerged from the 15 republics that once comprised it.

A new form of state organization, *regional* government or *asymmetric federalism,* is emerging in Europe as formerly strong unitary states acknowledge the autonomy aspirations of their several subdivisions and grant to them varying degrees of local administrative control while retaining in central hands authority over matters of nationwide concern, such as monetary policy, defense, foreign relations, and the like. That new form of federalism involves recognition of regional capitals, legislative assemblies, administrative bureaucracies, and the like. The asymmetric federalism of the United Kingdom, for example, now involves separate status for Scotland, Wales, and Northern Ireland, with their own capitals at Edinburgh, Cardiff, and Belfast, respectively. That of Spain recognizes Catalonia and the Basque country with capitals in Barcelona and Vitoria, respectively. In Canada, the establishment of the self-governing Inuit arctic territory of Nunavut (see p. 174, footnote 2) in 1999 has been followed by other recognized Indian claims of home territory land use control: that of the Haida in British Columbia, the Dogrib (Tlicho) in the Northwest Territories, and the Cree in northern Quebec, for example.

All other things being equal, a capital located in the center of the country provides equal access to the government, facilitates communication to and from the political hub, and enables the government to exert its authority easily. Many capital cities, such as Washington, D.C., were centrally located when they were designated as seats of government but lost their centrality as the state expanded.

Some capital cities have been relocated outside of peripheral national core regions, at least in part to achieve the presumed advantages of centrality. Two examples of such relocation are from Karachi inland to Islamabad in Pakistan and from Istanbul to Ankara, in the center of Turkey's territory. A particular type of relocated capital is the *forward-thrust capital* city, one that has been deliberately sited in a state's interior to signal the government's awareness of regions away from an off-center core and its interest in encouraging more uniform development. In the late 1950s, Brazil relocated its capital from Rio de Janeiro to the new city of Brasília to demonstrate its intent to develop the vast interior of the country. The West African country of Nigeria has been building the new capital of Abuja near its geographic center since the late 1970s, with relocation there of government offices and foreign embassies in the early 1990s.

The British colonial government relocated Canada's capital six times between 1841 and 1865, in part seeking centrality to the mid-19th-century population pattern and in part seeking a location that bridged that colony's cultural divide (Figure 12.12). A Japanese law of 1997 calling for the relocation out of Tokyo of the parliament building, Supreme Court, and main ministries by 2010 is more related to earthquake fears and a search for seismic safety than to enhanced convenience or governmental efficiency. Putrajaya, the new administrative seat of Malaysia 25 miles south of the present capital, Kuala Lumpur; Astana, the new national capital of Kazakhstan located on a desolate stretch of Siberian steppe; and Naypyidaw, a desolate, rocky site 200 miles north of Myanmar's present capital of Yangon (Rangoon) are other examples of recent new national capital creations.

Figure 12.12 Canada's migratory capital. Kingston was chosen as the first capital of the united Province of Canada in preference to either Quebec, capital of Lower Canada, or Toronto, that of Upper Canada. In 1844, governmental functions were relocated to Montreal where they remained until 1849, after which they shifted back and forth—as the map indicates—between Toronto and Quebec. An 1865 session of the provincial legislature was held in Ottawa, the city that became the capital of the Confederation of Canada in 1867.

Source: Redrawn with permission from David B. Knight, A Capital for Canada *(Chicago: University of Chicago, Department of Geography,* Research Paper No. 182, 1977*), Figure 1. p. vii.*

Boundaries: The Limits of the State

We noted earlier that no portion of the earth's land surface is outside the claimed control of a national unit, that even uninhabited Antarctica has had territorial claims imposed upon it (see Figure 12.3). Each of the world's states is separated from its neighbors by *international boundaries,* or lines that establish the limit of each state's jurisdiction and authority. Boundaries indicate where the sovereignty of one state ends and that of another begins (Figure 12.13).

Within its own bounded territory, a state administers laws, collects taxes, provides for defense, and performs other such governmental functions. Thus, the location of the boundary determines the kind of money people in a given area use, the legal code to which they are subject, the army they may be called upon to join, and the language and perhaps the religion children are taught in school. These examples suggest how boundaries serve as powerful reinforcers of cultural variation over the earth's surface.

Territorial claims of sovereignty, it should be noted, are three-dimensional. International boundaries mark not only the outer limits of a state's claim to land (or water) surface, but are also projected downward to the center of the earth in accordance with international consensus allocating rights to subsurface resources. States also project their sovereignty upward, but with less certainty because of a lack of agreement on the upper limits of territorial airspace. Properly viewed, then, an international boundary is a line without breadth; it is a vertical interface between adjacent state sovereignties.

Before boundaries were delimited, nations or empires were likely to be separated by *frontier zones,* ill-defined and fluctuating areas marking the effective end of a state's authority. Such zones were often uninhabited or only sparsely populated and were liable to change with shifting settlement patterns. Many present-day international boundaries lie in former frontier zones, and in that sense the boundary line has replaced the broader frontier as a marker of a state's authority.

Natural and Geometric Boundaries

Geographers have traditionally distinguished between "natural" and "geometric" boundaries. **Natural** (or **physical**) **boundaries** are those based on recognizable physiographic features, such as mountains, rivers, and lakes. Although they might seem to be attractive as borders because they actually exist in the landscape and are visible dividing elements, many natural boundaries have proved to be unsatisfactory. That is, they do not effectively separate states.

Many international boundaries lie along mountain ranges, for example in the Alps, Himalayas, and Andes, but while some have proved to be stable, others have not. Mountains are rarely total barriers to interaction. Although they do not invite movement, they are crossed by passes, roads, and tunnels. High pastures may be used for seasonal grazing, and the mountain region may be the source of water for irrigation or hydroelectric power. Nor is the definition of a boundary along a mountain range a simple matter. Should it follow the crests of the mountains or the *water divide* (the line dividing two drainage areas)? The two are not always the same. Border disputes between China and India are in part the result of the failure of mountain crests and headwaters of major streams to coincide (Figure 12.13).

Rivers can be even less satisfactory as boundaries. In contrast to mountains, rivers foster interaction. River valleys are likely to be agriculturally or industrially productive and to be densely populated. For example, for hundreds of miles the Rhine River serves as an international boundary in Western Europe. It is also a primary traffic route lined by chemical plants, factories, and power stations and dotted by the castles and cathedrals that make it one of Europe's major tourist attractions. It is more a common intensively used resource than a barrier in the lives of the nations it borders.

The alternative to natural boundaries are **geometric** (or **artificial**) **boundaries.** Frequently delimited as segments of parallels of latitude or meridians of longitude, they are found chiefly in Africa, Asia, and the Americas. The western portion of the United States–Canada border, which follows the 49th parallel, is an example of a geometric boundary. Many such were established when the areas in question were colonies, the land was only sparsely settled, and detailed geographic knowledge of the frontier region was lacking.

Boundaries Classified by Settlement

Boundaries can also be classified according to whether they were laid out before or after the principal features of the cultural landscape were developed. An **antecedent boundary** is one drawn across an area before it is well populated, that is, before most of the cultural landscape features were put in place. To continue our earlier example, the western portion of the United States–Canada boundary is such an antecedent line, established by a treaty between the United States and Great Britain in 1846.

(a) (b)

Figure 12.13 International boundaries. (*a*) **The U.S.-Canada border** at Peace Arch International Park between Blaine, Washington, and Douglas, British Columbia. (*b*) **The U.S.-Mexico border** near Tijuana, Mexico.

Boundaries drawn after the development of the cultural landscape are termed **subsequent.** One type of subsequent boundary is **consequent** (also called *ethnographic*), a border drawn to accommodate existing religious, linguistic, ethnic, or economic differences between countries. An example is the boundary drawn between Northern Ireland and Eire (Ireland). Subsequent **superimposed boundaries** may also be forced on existing cultural landscapes, a country, or a people by a conquering or colonizing power that is unconcerned about preexisting cultural patterns. The colonial powers in 19th-century Africa superimposed boundaries upon established African cultures without regard to the tradition, language, religion, or tribal affiliation of those whom they divided (see Figure 12.5).

When Great Britain prepared to leave the Indian subcontinent after World War II, it was decided that two independent states would be established in the region: India and Pakistan. The boundary between the two countries, defined in the partition settlement of 1947, was thus both a *subsequent* and a *superimposed* line. As millions of Hindus migrated from the northwestern portion of the subcontinent to seek homes in India, millions of Muslims left what would become India for Pakistan. In a sense, they were attempting to ensure that the boundary would be *consequent,* that is, that it would coincide with a division based on religion.

If a former boundary line that no longer functions as such is still marked by some landscape features or differences on the two sides, it is termed a **relic boundary** (Figure 12.14). The abandoned castles dotting the former frontier zone between Wales and England are examples of a relic boundary. They are also evidence of the disputes that sometimes attend the process of boundary making.

Boundary Disputes

Boundaries create many possibilities and provocations for conflict. Since World War II, almost half of the world's sovereign states have been involved in border disputes with neighboring

Figure 12.14 Like Hadrian's Wall in the north of England or the Great Wall of China, the Berlin Wall was a demarcated boundary. Unlike them, it cut across a large city and disrupted established cultural patterns. The Berlin Wall, therefore, was a *subsequent superimposed* boundary. The dismantling of the wall in 1990 marked the reunification of Germany; what remains standing as a historic monument is a *relic* boundary.

countries. Just like householders, states are far more likely to have disputes with their neighbors than with more distant parties. It follows that the more neighbors a state has, the greater the likelihood of conflict. Although the causes of boundary disputes and open conflict are many and varied, they can reasonably be placed into four categories.

1. **Positional disputes** occur when states disagree about the interpretation of documents that define a boundary and/or the way the boundary was delimited. Such disputes typically arise when the boundary is antecedent, preceding effective human settlement in the border region. Once the area becomes populated and gains value, the exact location of the boundary becomes important. The boundary between Argentina and Chile, originally defined during Spanish colonial rule and formalized by treaty in 1881, was to follow "the most elevated crests of the Andean Cordillera dividing the waters" between east- and west-flowing rivers. Because the southern Andes had not been adequately explored and mapped, it was not apparent that the crest lines (highest peaks) and the watershed divides do not always coincide. In some places, the water divide is many miles east of the highest peaks, leaving a long, narrow area of some 52,000 square kilometers (20,000 sq mi) in dispute (Figure 12.15). In Latin America as a whole, the 21st century began with at least 10 unresolved border disputes, some dating back to colonial times.

2. **Territorial disputes** over the ownership of a region often, though not always, arise when a boundary that has been superimposed on the landscape divides an ethnically homogeneous population. Each of the two states then has some justification for claiming the territory inhabited by the ethnic group in question. We noted previously that a single nation may be dispersed across several states (see Figure 12.4d). Conflicts can arise if the people of one state want to annex a territory whose

population is ethnically related to that of the state but now subject to a foreign government. This type of expansionism is called **irredentism** and is often a consequence of superimposed boundaries. In the 1930s, Hitler used the existence of German minorities in Czechoslovakia and Poland to justify German invasion and occupation of those countries. More recently, Somalia has had many border clashes with Ethiopia over the rights of Somalis living in that country, and the area of Kashmir has been a cause of dispute and open conflict between India and Pakistan since the creation of the two countries (Figure 12.16).

3. Closely related to territorial conflicts are **resource disputes.** Neighboring states are likely to covet the resources—whether they be valuable mineral deposits, fertile farmland, or rich fishing grounds—lying in border areas and to disagree over their use. In recent years, the United States has been involved in disputes with both its immediate neighbors: with Mexico over the shared resources of the Colorado

Figure 12.15 Territory once disputed by Argentina and Chile in the Southern Andes Mountains. The treaty establishing the boundary between the two countries preceded adequate exploration and mapping of the area, leaving the precise location of the mountain crests and watershed divides in doubt. Friction over the disputed territory nearly led to war before an accord was reached in 1902. Subsequent disputes over details were resolved in an accord signed in 1998.

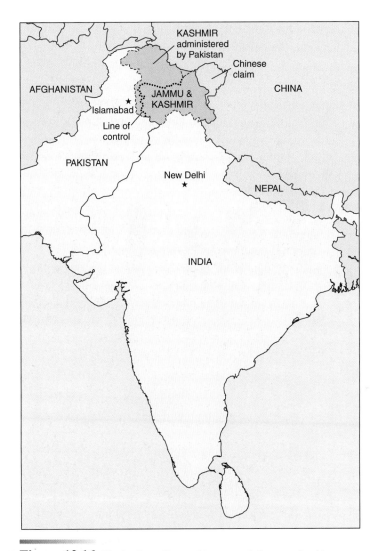

Figure 12.16 Kashmir, a disputed area, was left unresolved by the British when they dismantled their empire and partitioned India and Pakistan in 1947. At the time of partition the leader of the princely state of Kashmir chose to join India despite the Muslim majority in the Kashmir—giving both countries a claim to the territory. The dispute has sparked two wars between India and Pakistan and the territory has a *de facto* partition along a Line of Control that has been patrolled by United Nations peacekeepers since 1949.

River and Gulf of Mexico and with Canada over the Georges Bank fishing grounds in the Atlantic Ocean.

One of the causes of the 1990–1991 war in the Persian Gulf was the huge oil reservoir known as the Rumaila field, lying mainly under Iraq with a small extension into Kuwait (Figure 12.17a). Because the two countries were unable to agree on percentages of ownership of the rich reserve, or a formula for sharing production costs and revenues, Kuwait pumped oil from Rumaila without any international agreement. Iraq helped justify its invasion of Kuwait by contending that the latter had been stealing Iraqi oil in what amounted to economic warfare.

4. **Functional disputes** arise when neighboring states disagree over policies to be applied along a boundary. Such policies may concern immigration, the movement of traditionally nomadic groups, customs regulations, or land use. U.S. relations with

Mexico, for example, have been affected by the increasing number of illegal aliens and the flow of drugs entering the United States from Mexico (Figure 12.17b).

Centripetal Forces: Promoting State Cohesion

At any moment in time, a state is characterized by forces that promote unity and national stability and by others that disrupt them. Political geographers refer to the former as **centripetal forces.** These are factors that bind together the people of a state, that enable it to function and give it strength. **Centrifugal forces,** on the other hand, destabilize and weaken a state. If centrifugal forces are stronger than those promoting unity, the very existence of the state will be threatened. In the sections that follow, we examine four centripetal (uniting) forces—nationalism, unifying institutions, effective organization and administration of government, and systems of transportation and communication—to see how they can promote cohesion.

Nationalism

One of the most powerful of the centripetal forces is **nationalism,** an identification with the state and the acceptance of national goals. Nationalism is based on the concept of allegiance to a single country and the ideals and the way of life it represents; it is an emotion that provides a sense of identity and loyalty and of collective distinction from all other peoples and lands.

States purposely try to instill feelings of allegiance in their citizens, for such feelings give the political system strength. People who have such allegiance are likely to accept common rules of action and behavior and to participate in the decision-making process establishing those rules. In light of the divisive forces present in most societies, not everyone, of course, will feel the same degree of commitment or loyalty. The important consideration is that the majority of a state's population accepts its ideologies, adheres to its laws, and participates in its effective operation. For many countries, such acceptance and adherence has come only recently and partially; in some, it is frail and endangered.

Recall that true nation-states are rare; in only a few countries do the territory occupied by the people of a particular nation and the territorial limits of the state coincide. Most countries have more than one culture group that considers itself separate in some important way from other citizens. In a multicultural society, nationalism helps integrate different groups into a unified population. This kind of consensus nationalism has emerged in countries such as the United States and Switzerland, where different culture groups have joined together to create political entities commanding the loyalties of all their citizens.

States promote nationalism in a number of ways. *Iconography* is the study of the symbols that help unite people. National anthems and other patriotic songs; flags, national sports teams, and officially designated or easily identified flowers and animals; and rituals and holidays are all developed by states to promote nationalism and attract allegiance (Figure 12.18). By ensuring that all citizens, no matter how diverse the population may be, will have at least these symbols in common, they impart a sense of belonging to a political entity called, for example, Japan or Canada. In some

(a)

(b)

Figure 12.17 (*a*) **The Rumaila oil field.** One of the world's largest petroleum reservoirs, Rumaila straddles the Iraq-Kuwait border. Iraqi grievances over Kuwaiti drilling were partly responsible for Iraq's invasion of Kuwait in 1990. (*b*) To stem the flow of undocumented migrants entering California from Baja California, the United States in 1993 constructed a fence 3 meters (10 feet) high along the border. While American construction crews worked on the north side of the wall, protesters who opposed the wall painted graffiti on its south side. As of early 2009, approximately 670 miles of fence had been constructed in high priority sections along the approximately 2,000-mile United States–Mexico border.

countries, certain documents, such as the Magna Carta in England or the Declaration of Independence in the United States, serve the same purpose. Royalty may fill the need: in Sweden, Japan, and the United Kingdom, the monarchy functions as the symbolic focus of allegiance. Such symbols are significant, for symbols and beliefs are major components of the ideological subsystem (p. 46) of every culture. When a society is very heterogeneous, composed of people with different customs, religions, and languages, belief in the national unit can help weld them together.

Unifying Institutions

Institutions as well as symbols help to develop the sense of commitment and cohesiveness essential to the state. Schools, particularly elementary schools, are among the most important of these. Children learn the history of their own country and relatively little about other countries. Schools are expected to instill the society's goals, values, and traditions, to teach the common language that conveys them, and to guide youngsters to identify with their country.

Other institutions that advance nationalism are the armed forces and, sometimes, a state church. The armed forces are of necessity taught to identify with the state. They see themselves as protecting the state's welfare from what are perceived to be its enemies. In about one-quarter of the world's countries, the faith of the majority of the people has by law been designated the state religion. In such cases, the religion may become a force for cohesion, helping unify the population. This is true of Buddhism in Thailand, Hinduism in Nepal, Islam in Pakistan, and Judaism in Israel. In countries like these, the religion and the church are so identified with the state that belief in one is transferred to allegiance to the other.

The schools, the armed forces, and the church are just three of the institutions that teach people what it is like to be members of a state. As institutions, they operate primarily on the level of the sociological subsystem of culture, helping to structure the outlooks and behaviors of the society. But by themselves, they are not enough to give cohesion, and thus strength, to a state. Indeed, each of the institutions we have discussed can also be a destabilizing centrifugal force.

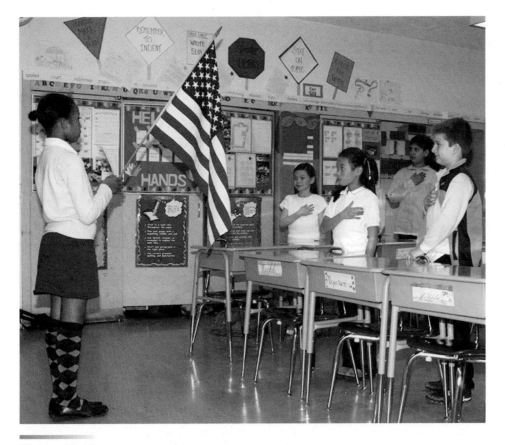

Figure 12.18 The ritual of the pledge of allegiance is just one way in which schools in the United States seek to instill a sense of national identity in students.

Organization and Administration

A further bonding force is public confidence in the effective organization of the state. Can it provide security from external aggression and internal conflict? Are its resources distributed and allocated in such a way as to be perceived to promote the economic welfare of all its citizens? Are all citizens afforded equal opportunity to participate in governmental affairs (see "Legislative Women")? Do institutions that encourage consultation and the peaceful settlement of disputes exist? How firmly established are the rule of law and the power of the courts? Is the system of decision making responsive to the people's needs?

The answers to such questions, and the relative importance of the answers, will vary from country to country, but they and similar ones are implicit in the expectation that the state will, in the words of the Constitution of the United States, "establish justice, insure domestic tranquility, provide for the common defence, [and] promote the general welfare. . . . " If those expectations are not fulfilled, the loyalties promoted by national symbols and unifying institutions may be weakened or lost.

Transportation and Communication

A state's transportation network fosters political integration by promoting interaction between areas and by joining them economically and socially. The role of a transportation network in uniting a country has been recognized since ancient times. The saying that all roads lead to Rome had its origin in the impressive system of roads that linked Rome to the rest of its empire. Centuries later, a similar network was built in France, joining Paris to the various departments of the country. Often the capital city is better connected to other cities than the outlying cities are to one another. In France, for example, it can take less time to travel from one city to another by way of Paris than by direct route.

Roads and railroads have played a historically significant role in promoting political integration. In the United States and Canada, they not only opened up new areas for settlement but increased interaction between rural and urban districts. Because transportation systems play a major role in a state's economic development, it follows that the more economically advanced a country is, the more extensive its transport network is likely to be (see Figure 8.4). At the same time, the higher the level of development, the more resources there are to be invested in building transport routes. The two reinforce one another.

Transportation and communication, while encouraged within a state, are frequently curtailed or at least controlled between them as a conscious device for promoting state cohesion through limitation on external spatial interaction (Figure 12.19). The mechanisms of control include restrictions on trade through tariffs or embargoes, legal barriers to immigration and emigration, and limitations on travel through passports and visa requirements.

Centrifugal Forces: Challenges to State Authority

State cohesion is not easily achieved or, once gained, invariably retained. Destabilizing *centrifugal forces* are ever-present, sowing internal discord and challenges to the state's authority (see "Terrorism and Political Geography"). Transportation and communication may be hindered by a country's shape or great size, leaving some parts of the state not well integrated with the rest. A country that is not well organized or administered stands to lose the loyalty of its citizens. Institutions that in some states promote unity can be a divisive force in others.

Organized religion, for example, can be a potent centrifugal force. It may compete with the state for people's allegiance—one reason the former USSR and other communist governments suppressed religion and promoted atheism. Conflict between majority and minority faiths within a country—as between Catholics and Protestants in Northern Ireland or Hindus and Muslims in Kashmir and Gujarat State in India—can destabilize social order. Opposing sectarian views within a single, dominant faith can also promote civil conflict. Recent years have seen particularly Muslim militant

Women, a majority of the world's population, in general fare poorly in the allocation of such resources as primary and higher education, employment opportunities and income, and health care. That their lot is improving is encouraging. In nearly every developing country, women have been closing the gender gap in literacy, school enrollment, and acceptance in the job market.

But in the political arena—where power ultimately lies—women's share of influence is increasing only slowly and selectively. In 2006, fewer than 15 countries out of a world total of more than 200 had women as heads of government: presidents or prime ministers. Nor did they fare much better as members of parliaments. Women in early 2008 held just 18% of all the seats in the world's legislatures.

Only in 42 countries did women in 2008 occupy one-quarter or more of the seats in the lower or single legislative House. Of these, Rwanda and Sweden were the leaders with 51% and 47%, respectively, of their members female. A number of countries had no female representatives at all. In contrast, in at least 51 countries women make up less than 10% of the legislature.

Although in the Parliament of the European Union women comprised 31% of members in 2007, they held only 13% of the seats in the Greek parliament and 12% of France's National Assembly. Japan made an even poorer showing with but a 9% female membership. Arab states average only 8%. Nor did the United States show a very significant number of women members. At the start of the 111th Congress (2009–2011), only 18 women served in the Senate (18% female) and 77 in the House of Representatives (18% female). At that time, both numbers were at their highest-ever levels. American women have made greater electoral gains in state legislatures than at the national level in recent years. At the state level, women's legislative membership has increased from 4% in 1969 to 24% in 2006, though wide disparities exist among the states.

In the later 1990s, women's legislative representation began to expand materially in many developed and developing democracies, and their "fair share" of political power began to be formally recognized or enforced. In Western countries, particularly, improvement in female parliamentary participation has become a matter of plan and pride for political parties and, occasionally, for governments themselves.

Political parties from Mexico to China have tried to correct female underrepresentation, usually by setting quotas for women candidates, and a few governments—including Belgium and Italy—have tried to require their political parties to improve their balance. France went further than any other country in acknowledging the right of women to equal access to elective office when in 1999 it passed a constitutional amendment requiring *parité*—parity or equality. A year later, the National Assembly enacted legislation requiring the country's political parties to fill 50% of the candidacies in all elections in the country (municipal, regional, and European Parliament) with women, or lose a corresponding share of their state-provided campaign funding. India similarly proposed to reserve a third of the seats in parliament for women.

Quotas are controversial, however, and often are viewed with disfavor even by avowed feminists. Some argue that quotas are demeaning because they imply women cannot match men on merit alone. Others fear that other groups—for example, religious groups or ethnic minorities—would also seek quotas to guarantee their proportionate legislative presence.

A significant presence of women in legislative bodies makes a difference in the kinds of bills that get passed and the kinds of programs that receive governmental emphasis. Regardless of party affiliation, women are more apt than their male counterparts to sponsor bills and vote for measures affecting child care, elderly care, women's health care, medical insurance, and bills affecting women's rights and family law.

---

groups attempt to overturn official or constitutional policies of secularism or replace a government deemed insufficiently ardent in its imposition of religious laws and regulations. Islamic fundamentalism led to the 1979 overthrow of the Shah of Iran; more recently, Islamic militancy has been a destabilizing force in, among other countries, Afghanistan, Algeria, Iraq, Tunisia, Egypt, and Saudi Arabia.

Nationalism, in contrast to its role as a powerful centripetal agency, is also a potentially disruptive centrifugal force. The idea of the nation-state (see p. 386) is that states are formed around and coincide with nations. It is a small step from that to the notion that every nation has the right to its own state or territory.

Centrifugal forces are particularly strong in countries containing multiple nationalities and unassimilated minorities, racial or ethnic conflict, contrasting cultures, and a multiplicity of languages or religions. Such states are susceptible to nationalist challenges from within their borders. A country whose population is not bound by a shared sense of nationalism is split by several local primary allegiances and suffers from **subnationalism.** That is, many people give their primary allegiance to traditional groups or nations that are smaller than the population of the entire state.

Any country that contains one or more important national minorities is susceptible to challenges from within its borders if the minority group has an explicit territorial identification and believes that its right to *self-determination*—the right of a group to govern itself in its own state or territory—has not been satisfied. A dissident minority that has total or partial secession from the state as its primary goal is said to be guided by **separatism** or **autonomous nationalism.** In recent years, such nationalism has created currents of unrest within many countries, even long-established ones.

Canada, for example, houses a powerful secessionist movement in French-speaking Quebec, the country's largest province. In October, 1995, a referendum to secede from Canada and become a sovereign country failed in Quebec by a razor-thin margin. Quebec's nationalism is fueled by strong feelings of

Figure 12.19 Canadian–U.S. railroad discontinuity. Canada and the United States developed independent railway systems connecting their respective prairie regions with their separate national cores. Despite extensive rail construction during the 19th and early 20th centuries, the pattern that emerged even before recent track abandonment was one of discontinuity at the border. Note how the political boundary restricted the ease of spatial interaction between adjacent territories. Many branch lines approached the border, but only eight crossed it. In fact, for more than 480 kilometers (300 miles), no railway bridged the boundary line. The international border—and the cultural separation it represents—inhibits other expected degrees of interaction. Telephone calls between Canadian and U.S. cities, for example, are far less frequent than would be expected if distance alone were the controlling factor.

collective identity and distinctiveness and by a desire to protect its language and culture, and by the conviction that the province's ample resources and advanced economy would permit it to manage successfully as a separate country.

In Western Europe, five countries (the United Kingdom, France, Belgium, Italy, and Spain) house separatist political movements whose members reject total control by the existing sovereign state and who claim to be the core of a separate national entity (Figure 12.20). Their basic demand is for *regional autonomy,* usually in the form of self-government or "home rule" rather than complete independence. Accommodation of those demands has resulted in some degrees of **devolution**—the transfer of some central powers to regional or local governments—and in the forms of asymmetric federalism discussed earlier (p. 394) with the United Kingdom and Spain as examples.

Separatist movements affect many states outside of Western Europe. Many countries containing disparate groups that are more motivated by enmity than affinity have powerful centripetal tendencies. The Basques of Spain and the Bretons of France have their counterparts in the Palestinians in Israel, the Sikhs in India, the Moros in the Philippines, the Tamils in Sri Lanka, and many others. Separatist movements are expressions of **regionalism,** minority group self-awareness and identification with a region rather than with the state.

The countries of Eastern Europe and the republics of the former Soviet Union have seen many instances of regionally rooted nationalist feelings. Now that the forces of ethnicity, religion, language, and culture are no longer suppressed by communism, ancient rivalries are more evident than at any time since World War II. The end of the Cold War aroused hopes of decades of peace. Instead, the collapse of communism and the demise of the USSR spawned dozens of smaller wars. Numerous ethnic groups

large and small are asserting their identities and what they perceive to be their right to determine their own political status.

The national independence claimed in the early 1990s by the 15 former Soviet constituent republics did not assure the satisfaction of all separatist movements within them. Many of the new individual countries are themselves subject to strong destabilizing forces that threaten their territorial integrity and survival. The Russian Federation itself, the largest and most powerful remnant of the former USSR, has 89 components, including 21 "ethnic republics" and a number of other nationality regions. Many are rich in natural resources, have non-Russian majorities, and seek greater autonomy within the federation. Some, indeed, want total independence. One, the predominantly Muslim republic of Chechnya, in 1994 claimed the right of self-determination and attempted to secede from the federation, provoking a bloody civil war that escalated again in 1996 and 1999.

As the USSR declined and disbanded, it lost control of its communist satellites in Eastern Europe. That loss and resurgent nationalism led to a dramatic reordering of the region's political map. East Germany was reunited with West Germany in 1990 and 3 years later, the people of Czechoslovakia agreed to split their country into two separate, ethnically based states: the Czech Republic and Slovakia. More violently, Yugoslavia shattered into five pieces in 1991–1992, but with the exception of Slovenia, the boundaries of the five new republics did not match the territories occupied by nationalities, a situation that plunged the region into war as nations fought to redefine the boundaries of their countries. One tactic used to transform a multinational area into one containing only one nation is **ethnic cleansing,** the killing or forcible relocation of less powerful minorities. It occurred in Croatia, Bosnia-Herzegovina, and the Kosovo province of southern Serbia.

"Where were you when the world stopped turning?" Asks Alan Jackson in his song about the September 11, 2001, terrorist attacks on the United States. You probably know the answer to his question, and you probably always will. Of course, the world didn't really stop turning, but that's how it felt to millions of Americans with no previous exposure to terrorism.

What is terrorism? How does it relate to political geography? Do all countries experience terrorism? Is terrorism new? Is there a way to prevent it? Attempting to answer these questions, difficult as they are, may help us understand the phenomenon.

Terrorism is the calculated use of violent acts against civilians and symbolic targets to publicize a cause, intimidate or coerce a civilian population, or affect the conduct of a government. *International terrorism,* such as the attacks of September 11, 2001, include acts that transcend national boundaries. International terrorism is intended to intimidate people in other countries. *Domestic terrorism* consists of acts by individuals or groups against the citizens or government of their own country. *State terrorism* is committed by the agents of a government. *Subnational terrorism* is committed by nongovernmental groups. Whatever its agency or level, terrorism is a weapon designed to intimidate populations and, often, to influence government actions or policies.

State terrorism is probably as old as the concept of a state. As early as 146 B.C., for example, Roman forces sacked and completely destroyed the city of Carthage, burning it to the ground, slaughtering its population, and sowing salt on the fields so that no crops could grow. Governments have used systematic policies of violence and intimidation to further dominate and control their own populations. Nazi Germany, the Pol Pot regime in Cambodia, and Stalinist Russia are 20th-century examples of state terrorism. Heads of state ordered the murder, imprisonment, or exile of enemies of the state—politicians, intellectuals, dissidents—anyone who dared to criticize the government. In Rwanda, the former Yugoslavia, and Saddam Hussein's Iraq, state terrorism aimed against ethnic and religious minorities provided the government with a method of consolidating power; in each case, genocide, or mass murder of ethnic minority groups, was the result.

Subnational terrorism is of more recent vintage, coinciding with the rise of the nation-state. Subnational terrorism can be perpetrated by those who feel wronged by their own or another government. For example, ethnic groups in a minority who feel that the central government has taken their territory and absorbed them into a larger political entity, such as the Basques in Spain, have used terrorist activities to promote their cause and resist the government. Ethnic and religious groups that have been split by national boundaries imposed by others, such as Palestinian Arabs in the Middle East, have used terrorism to make governance impossible. Political, ethnic, or religious groups or individuals who feel oppressed by their own government, such as the Oklahoma City bombers in the United States, have committed acts of domestic terrorism.

Nearly every country has experienced some form of terrorism at some point since the mid-19th century. These acts have been as various as the anarchist assassinations of political leaders in Europe during the 1840s and in the United States in the late 19th century, the abduction of Canadian government officials by the Front Libération du Québec (FLQ) in 1970, and the release of sarin gas in the Tokyo subways in 1995 by the group Aum Shinrikyo.

The political and religious aims of these attackers, however, can cause confusion on the world stage. In 2001, the Reuters News Agency told its reporters to stop using the word *terrorism,* because "one person's terrorist is another's freedom fighter." The definition of terrorism rests on the ability to define motives and the outlook of the observer.

Although it may be difficult to distinguish among types of terrorism, it is even more difficult to prevent it. Generally speaking, governments and international bodies respond to terrorist acts in one of four ways:

1. Reducing or addressing the causes of terrorism. In some cases, political change can reduce a terrorist threat. For example, the 1998 Good Friday Agreement in Northern Ireland led to a reduction of terrorist acts; the Spanish government's granting of some regional autonomy to the Basques helped lessen the violent actions of the ETA (Basque separatists) and reduced the support of many Basque people for such acts.

2. Increasing international cooperation in the surveillance of subnational groups. Spurred by terrorist crimes in Bahrain and Saudi Arabia, the Arab Gulf States agreed in 1998 to exchange intelligence regarding terrorist groups, to share information regarding anticipated terrorist acts, and to assist each other in investigating terrorist crimes.

3. Increasing security measures in a country. In the United States, following September 11, 2001, the government organized a Department of Homeland Security, federalized air traffic screening, and increased efforts to reduce financial support for foreign terrorist organizations. In concert, the European Union froze the assets of any group on its list of terrorist organizations.

4. Using military means, either unilaterally or multilaterally, against terrorists or governments that sponsor terrorists. Following the September 11, 2001, World Trade Center and Pentagon assaults, the United States led a coalition of countries in attacking the government of Afghanistan, which had harbored Osama bin Laden's al-Qaeda terrorist organization.

Each response to terrorism is expensive, politically difficult, and potentially harmful to the life and liberty of citizens. Governments must decide which response or combination of responses is likely to have the most beneficial effect.

More peacefully, several European governments have recently moved in the direction of regional recognition and devolution. In France, 22 regional governments were established in 1986; Spain has a program of devolution for its 17 "autonomous communities," a program that Portugal is beginning to emulate. Italy, Germany, and the Nordic countries have, or are developing, similar recognitions of regional communities with granted powers of local administration and relaxation of central controls.

(a)

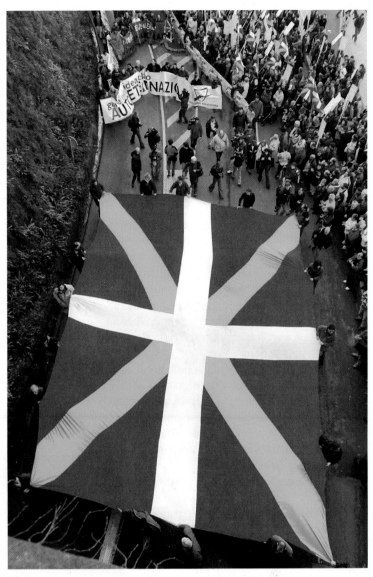

(b)

Figure 12.20 (*a*) **Regions in Western Europe seeking autonomy.**
Despite long-standing state attempts to assimilate these historic nations
culturally, each contains a political movement that has sought or is seeking
a degree of self-rule recognizing its separate identity. Separatists on the
island of Corsica, for example, want to secede from France, and separatists
in Catalonia demand independence from Spain. The desires of nationalist
parties in both Wales and Scotland were partially accommodated by
the creation in 1999 of their own parliaments and a degree of regional
autonomy, an outcome labeled "separation but not divorce" from the
United Kingdom. (*b*) Demonstrators carry a giant Basque flag during a
march to call for independence for the Basque region.

The two preconditions common to all separatist movements
are *territory* and *nationality*. First, the group must be concentrated
in a core region that it claims as a national homeland and seek
to regain control of land and power that it believes were unjustly
taken from it. Second, certain cultural characteristics must provide a basis for the group's perception of separateness, identity,
and unity. These might be language, religion, or distinctive group
customs and institutions that promote feelings of group identity at
the same time that they foster exclusivity. Normally, these cultural
differences have persisted over several generations and have survived despite strong pressures toward assimilation.

Other characteristics common to many separatist movements
are a *peripheral location* and *social* and *economic inequality*.
Troubled regions tend to be peripheral, often isolated in rural
pockets, and their location away from the seat of central government engenders feelings of alienation and exclusion. Further, the
dominant culture group is often seen as an exploiting class that
has suppressed the local language, controlled access to the civil
service, and taken more than its share of wealth and power. Poorer

regions complain that they have lower incomes and greater unemployment than prevail in the rest of the state and that "outsiders"
control key resources and industry. Separatists in relatively rich
regions believe that they could exploit their resources for themselves and do better economically without the constraints imposed
by the central state.

Cooperation among States

The modern state is fragile and, as we have seen, its primacy may
be less assured in recent years. In many ways, countries are now
weaker than ever before. Many are economically frail, others are
politically unstable, and some are both. Strategically, no country
is safe from military attack, for technology now enables countries
to shoot weapons halfway around the world. Some people believe
that no national security is possible in the nuclear age.

Recognizing that a country cannot by itself guarantee either
its prosperity or its own security, many states have opted to

cooperate with others. These cooperative ventures are proliferating quickly, and they involve countries everywhere. They are also adding a new dimension to the concept of political boundaries, because the associations of states themselves have limits that are marked by borders of a higher spatial order than those between individual states. Such boundaries as the current division between NATO (North Atlantic Treaty Organization) and non-NATO states, or between the European Union area and other European countries represent a different scale of the political ordering of space.

Supranationalism

Associations among states represent a new dimension in the ordering of national power and national independence. Recent trends in economic globalization and international cooperation suggest to some that the sovereign state's traditional responsibilities and authorities are being diluted by a combination of forces and partly delegated to higher-order political and economic organizations. Corporations and even nongovernmental economic and communication agencies often operate in controlling ways outside of nation-state jurisdiction.

The rise of transnational corporations dominant in global markets, for example, limits the economic influence of individual countries. Cyberspace and the Internet are controlled by no one and are largely immune to the state restrictions on the flow of information exerted by many governments. Those information flows help create and maintain the growing number of international *nongovernmental organizations* (*NGOs*), estimated at more than 20,000 in number and including such well-known groups as Greenpeace, Amnesty International, and Doctors without Borders. NGOs, through petitions, demonstrations, court actions, and educational efforts, have become effective influences on national and international political and economic actions. And increasingly, individual citizens of any country have their lives and actions shaped by decisions not only of local and national authorities, but by those of regional economic associations (e.g., the North American Free Trade Agreement), multinational military alliances (e.g., NATO), and global political agencies (the United Nations).

The roots of such multistate cooperative systems are ancient—for example, the leagues of city states in the ancient Greek world or the Hanseatic League of free German cities in Europe's medieval period. The creation of new ones has been particularly active since 1945. They represent a world trend toward a **supranationalism** comprised of associations of three or more states created for mutual benefit and to achieve shared objectives. Although many individuals and organizations decry the loss of national independence

that supranationalism entails, the many supranational associations in existence early in the 21st century are evidence of their attraction and pervasiveness. Almost all countries, in fact, are members of at least one—and most are members of many—supranational groupings. All at least are members of the United Nations.

The United Nations and Its Agencies

The United Nations (UN) is the only organization that tries to be universal, and even it is not all-inclusive. With its membership expanded from 51 countries in 1945 to 192 by 2009, when Montenegro was admitted, the UN is the most ambitious attempt ever undertaken to bring together the world's nations in international assembly and to promote world peace. Stronger and more representative than its predecessor, the League of Nations, it provides a forum where countries may discuss international problems and regional concerns and a mechanism, admittedly weak but still significant, for forestalling disputes or, when necessary, for ending wars (Figure 12.21). The United Nations also sponsors 40 programs and agencies aimed at fostering international cooperation with respect to specific goals. Among these are the World Health Organization (WHO), the Food and Agriculture Organization (FAO), and the United Nations Educational, Scientific, and Cultural Organization (UNESCO). Many other UN agencies and much of the UN budget are committed to assisting member states with matters of economic growth and development.

Figure 12.21 United Nations peacekeeping forces on duty in East Timor (Timor Leste). Under the auspices of the UN, soldiers from many different countries staff peacekeeping forces and military observer groups in many world regions in an effort to halt or mitigate conflicts. Demand for peacekeeping and observer operations is indicated by recent deployment of UN forces in Bosnia, Croatia, Cyprus, Eritrea, Haiti, Kosovo, Lebanon, Pakistan/India, Sierra Leone, Somalia, and elsewhere.

Member states have not surrendered sovereignty to the UN, and the world body is legally and effectively unable to make or enforce a world law. Nor is there a world police force. Although there is recognized international law adjudicated by the International Court of Justice, rulings by this body are sought only by countries agreeing beforehand to abide by its arbitration. The United Nations has no authority over the military forces of individual countries.

A pronounced change both in the relatively passive role of the United Nations and in traditional ideas of international relations has begun to emerge. Long-established rules of total national sovereignty that allowed governments to act internally as they saw fit, free of outside interference, are fading as the United Nations increasingly applies a concept of "interventionism." The Persian Gulf War of 1991 was UN authorized under the old rules prohibiting one state (Iraq) from violating the sovereignty of another (Kuwait) by attacking it. After the war, the new interventionism sanctioned UN operations within Iraq—to protect Kurds in that country. Later, the UN intervened with troops and relief agencies in Somalia, Bosnia, and elsewhere, invoking an "international jurisdiction over inalienable human rights" that prevails without regard to state frontiers or sovereignty considerations.

Whatever the long-term prospects for interventionism replacing absolute sovereignty, for the short term the United Nations remains the only institution where the vast majority of the world's countries can collectively discuss matters of international political and economic concerns and attempt peacefully to resolve their differences. It has been particularly influential in formulating a law of the sea.

Maritime Boundaries

Boundaries define political jurisdictions and areas of resource control. But claims of national authority are not restricted to land areas alone. Water covers about two-thirds of the earth's surface, and increasingly countries have been projecting their sovereignty seaward to claim adjacent maritime areas and resources. A basic question involves the right of states to control water and the resources that it contains. The inland waters of a country, such as rivers and lakes, have traditionally been considered within the sovereignty of that country. Oceans, however, are not within any country's borders. Are they, then, to be open to all states to use, or may a single country claim sovereignty and limit access and use by other states?

For most of human history, the oceans remained effectively outside individual national control or international jurisdiction. The seas were a common highway for those daring enough to venture on them, an inexhaustible larder for fishermen, and a vast refuse pit for the muck of civilization. By the end of the 19th century, however, most coastal countries claimed sovereignty over a continuous belt 3 or 4 nautical miles wide (a *nautical mile,* or *nm,* equals 1.15 statute miles, or 1.85 km). At the time, the 3-nm limit represented the farthest range of artillery and thus the effective limit of control by the coastal state. Though recognizing the rights of others to innocent passage, such sovereignty permitted the enforcement of quarantine and customs regulations, allowed national protection of coastal fisheries, and made claims of neutrality effective during other people's wars. The primary concern was with security and unrestricted commerce. No separately codified

laws of the sea existed, however, and none seemed to be needed until after World War I.

A League of Nations Conference for the Codification of International Law, convened in 1930, inconclusively discussed maritime legal matters and served to identify areas of concern that were to become increasingly pressing after World War II. Important among these was an emerging shift from interest in commerce and national security to a preoccupation with the resources of the seas, an interest fanned by the *Truman Proclamation* of 1945. Motivated by a desire to exploit offshore oil deposits, the federal government under this doctrine laid claim to all resources on the continental shelf contiguous to its coasts. Other states, many claiming even broader areas of control, hurried to annex their own adjacent marine resources. Within a few years, a quarter of the earth's surface was appropriated by individual coastal countries.

An International Law of the Sea

Unrestricted extensions of jurisdiction and disputes over conflicting claims to maritime space and resources led to a series of United Nations conferences on the Law of the Sea. Meeting over a period of years, delegates from more than 150 countries attempted to achieve consensus on a treaty that would establish an internationally agreed-upon "convention dealing with all matters relating to the Law of the Sea." The meetings culminated in a draft treaty in 1982, the **United Nations Convention on the Law of the Sea** (UNCLOS).

The convention delimits territorial boundaries and rights by defining four zones of diminishing control (Figure 12.22):

- A *territorial sea* of up to 12 nm (19 km) in breadth over which coastal states have sovereignty, including exclusive fishing rights. Vessels of all types normally have the right of innocent passage through the territorial sea, though under certain circumstances, noncommercial (primarily military and research) vessels can be challenged.

- A *contiguous zone* to 24 nm (38 km). Although a coastal state does not have complete sovereignty in this zone, it can enforce its customs, immigration, and sanitation laws and has the right of hot pursuit out of its territorial waters.

- An **exclusive economic zone** (**EEZ**) of up to 200 nm (370 km) in which the state has recognized rights to explore, exploit, conserve, and manage the natural resources, both living and nonliving, of the seabed and waters (see Figure 12.23 and "Specks and Spoils"). Countries have exclusive rights to the resources lying within the continental shelf when this extends farther, up to 350 nm (560 km), beyond their coasts. The traditional freedoms of the high seas are to be maintained in this zone.

- The *high seas* beyond the EEZ. Outside any national jurisdiction, they are open to all states, whether coastal or landlocked. Freedom of the high seas includes the right to sail ships, fish, fly over, lay submarine cables and pipelines, and pursue scientific research. Mineral resources in the international deep seabed area beyond national jurisdiction are declared the common heritage of humankind, to be managed for the benefit of all the peoples of the earth.

By the end of the 1980s, most coastal countries, including the United States, had used the UNCLOS provisions to proclaim and

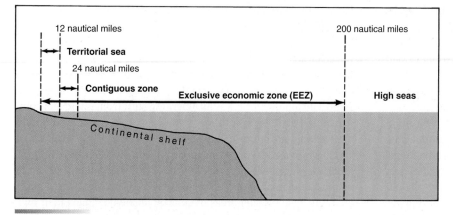

Figure 12.22 Territorial claims permitted by the 1982 United Nations Convention on the Law of the Sea (UNCLOS).

reciprocally recognize jurisdiction over 12-nm territorial seas and 200-nm economic zones. Despite reservations held by the United States and a few other industrial countries about the deep seabed mining provisions, the convention received the necessary ratification by 60 states and became international law in 1994.

UN Affiliates

Other fully or essentially global supranational organizations with influences on the economic, social, and cultural affairs of states and individuals have been created. Most are specialized international agencies, autonomous and with their own differing memberships but with affiliated relationships with the United Nations and operating under its auspices. Among them are the Food and Agriculture Organization (FAO), the International Bank for Reconstruction and Development (World Bank), the International Labor Organization (ILO), the United Nations Children's Fund (UNICEF), the World Health Organization (WHO), and—of growing economic importance—the World Trade Organization (WTO).

The WTO, which came into existence at the start of 1995, has become one of the most significant of the global expressions of supranational economic control. It is charged with enforcing the global trade accords that grew out of years of international negotiations under the terms of the General Agreement on Tariffs and Trade (GATT). The basic principle behind the WTO is that the member countries (153 as of August 2009, with additional states preparing for membership or seeking admission) should work to cut tariffs, dismantle nontariff barriers to trade, liberalize trade in services, and treat all other countries uniformly in matters of trade. Any preference granted to one should be available to all.

Increasingly, however, regional rather than global trade agreements are being struck, and free trade areas are proliferating. Only a few WTO members are not already part of some other regional trade

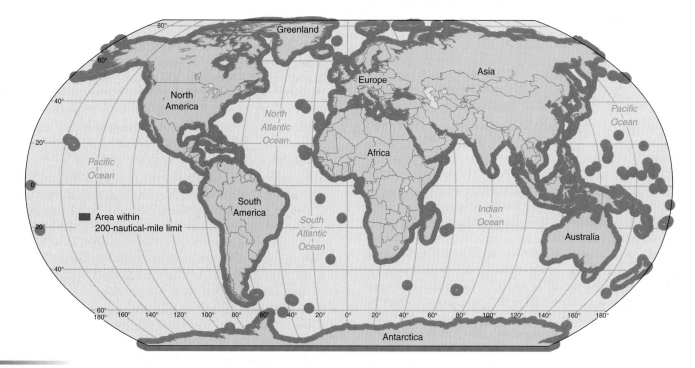

Figure 12.23 The 200-nautical mile exclusive economic zone (EEZ) claims of coastal states. The provisions of the Law of the Sea Convention have in effect changed the maritime map of the world. Three important consequences flow from the 200-nm EEZ concept: (1) islands have gained a new significance (see "Specks and Spoils"), (2) countries have a host of new neighbors, and (3) the EEZ lines result in overlapping claims. EEZ lines are drawn around a country's possessions as well as around the country itself. Every island, no matter how small, has its own 200-nm EEZ. This means that although the United States shares continental borders only with Canada and Mexico, it has maritime boundaries with countries in Asia, South America, and Europe. All told, the United States may have to negotiate some 30 maritime boundaries, which is likely to take decades. Other countries, particularly those with many possessions, will have to engage in similar lengthy negotiations.

Specks and Spoils

The Convention on the Law of the Sea gives to owners of islands claims over immense areas of the surrounding sea and, of course, to the fisheries and mineral resources in and under them. Tiny specks of land formerly too insignificant in size or distant in location to arouse the emotions of any nation now are avidly sought and fervently claimed. Remote Rockall, a British islet far west of Scotland, was used by Britain in 1976 to justify extending its fishing rights claim farther into the North Atlantic than otherwise was possible. Argentina nearly went to war with Chile in 1978 over three islands at the tip of South America at the Atlantic end of the Beagle Channel. Chile had lodged its claim of ownership hoping to gain access to known South Atlantic fish resources and hoped-for petroleum deposits. In 1982, Argentina seized the Falkland Islands from Britain, ostensibly to reclaim the Malvinas (their Spanish name) as national territory, but with an underlying economic motive as well. British forces retook the islands and subsequently used sovereignty over them to claim a sea area three times as large as Britain. Japan has encased a disappearing islet in concrete to maintain territorial claims endangered through erosion of the speck of land supporting them.

The Paracel and Spratly Islands, straddling trade routes in the South China Sea, have attracted more attention and claimants than most island groups, thanks to presumed large reserves of oil and gas in their vicinities. The Japanese seized the Paracels from

China during World War II and at its end surrendered them to Nationalist Chinese forces that soon retreated to Taiwan. South Vietnam took them over until 1974, when they were forcibly ejected by the mainland Chinese. In 1979, a united Vietnam reasserted its claims, basing them on 17th- and 18th-century maps. China countered with reference to 3rd-century explorations by its geographers and maintained its control.

The location of the Paracels to the north, near China, in the South China Sea places them in a different and less difficult status than that of the Spratlys, whose nearest neighbors are the Philippines and Malaysia. Mere dots in the sea, the largest of the Spratlys is about 100 acres—no more than one-eighth the size of New York's Central Park. But under the Convention on the Law of the Sea, possession of the island group would confer rights to the resources (oil, it is hoped) found beneath about 400,000 square kilometers (150,000 sq mi) of sea. That lure has made rivals of six governments and posed the possibility of conflict. Until early in 1988, Vietnam, the Philippines, Malaysia, Taiwan, and tiny Brunei had all maintained in peaceful coexistence garrisons on separate islets in the Spratly group. Then China landed troops on islands near the Vietnamese holdings, sank two Vietnamese naval ships, and accused Vietnam of seizing "Chinese" territory on the pretext of searching for their missing sailors. Although China agreed in 1992 that ownership disputes in the Spratlys should be resolved without violence,

it also, in 1993, passed a law repeating its claims to all the islands and its determination to defend them. In early 1995, China occupied "Mischief Reef," close to—and already claimed by—the Philippines, but in late 2002 agreed with other Southeast Asian countries to avoid future disputes over the islands.

Assertions of past discovery, previous or present occupation, proximity, and simple wishful thinking have all served as the basis for the proliferating claims to seas and seabeds. The world's oceans, once open and freely accessible, are increasingly being closed by the lure of specks of land and the spoils of wealth they command.

association. Such areal associations, some argue, make world trade less free by scrapping tariffs on trade among member states but retaining them separately or as a group on exchanges with nonmembers.

Regional Alliances

In addition to their membership in such international agencies, countries have shown themselves willing to relinquish some of their independence to participate in smaller multinational systems. These groupings can be economic, military, or political, and many have been formed since 1945. Cooperation in the economic sphere seems to come more easily to states than does military and political collaboration.

Economic Alliances

Among the oldest, most powerful, and far-reaching of the regional economic alliances are those that have evolved in Europe,

particularly the European Union and its several forerunners. Shortly after the end of World War II, the Benelux countries (Belgium, the Netherlands, and Luxembourg) formed an economic union to create a common set of tariffs and to eliminate import licenses and quotas. Formed at about the same time were the Organization for European Cooperation (1948), which coordinated the distribution and use of Marshall Plan funds, and the European Coal and Steel Community (1952), which integrated the development of that industry in the member countries. A few years later, in 1957, the *European Economic Community (EEC)*, or *Common Market*, was created, composed at first of only six states: France, Italy, West Germany, and the Benelux countries.

To counteract these Inner Six, as they were called, other countries in 1960 formed the European Free Trade Association (EFTA). Known as the Outer Seven, they were the United Kingdom, Norway, Denmark, Sweden, Switzerland, Austria, and Portugal (Figure 12.24). Between 1973 and 1986, three members (the United

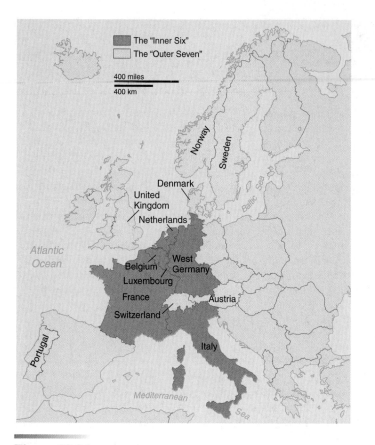

Figure 12.24 The original Inner Six and Outer Seven of Europe.

Kingdom, Denmark, and Portugal) left EFTA for membership in the Common Market and were replaced by Iceland and Finland.

The **European Union (EU)** grew out of the Common Market. It added new members slowly at first, as Greece, Spain, and Portugal joined during the 1980s; Austria, Finland, and Sweden joined in 1995. As it gathered momentum, more countries were admitted to the EU during the early 2000s, including the island states of Malta and Cyprus and 10 former Soviet bloc nations from Estonia in the north to Bulgaria and Slovenia in the South (Figure 12.25). These additions brought the number of member nations to 27, increased the EU's total population to some half-billion people, and expanded its economy to rival that of the United States. The European Union is now the world's largest and richest bloc of nation-states.

Over the years, members of the European Union have taken many steps to integrate their economies and coordinate their policies in such areas as transportation, agriculture, and fisheries. A council of ministers, a commission, a European parliament, and a court of justice give the European Union supranational institutions with effective ability to make and enforce laws. By January 1, 1993, the EU had abolished most remnant barriers to free trade and the free movement of capital and people among its members, creating a single European market. In another step toward economic and monetary union, the EU's single currency, the *euro,* replaced separate national currencies in 1999. And all applicant members in 2002 added 80,000 pages of EU law to their own legal systems.

We have traced this European development history, not because the full history of the EU is important to remember, but simply to illustrate the fluid process by which regional alliances are made. Countries come together in an association, some drop out, and others join. New treaties are made, and new coalitions emerge. Indeed, a number of such regional economic and trade associations have been added to the world supranational map. None are as encompassing in power and purpose as the EU, but all represent a cession of national independence to achieve broader regional goals.

NAFTA, the North American Free Trade Agreement launched in 1994, links Canada, Mexico, and the United States in an economic community aimed at lowering or removing trade and movement restrictions among the countries. It is perhaps the best known to North American students. The Americas as a whole, however, have other similar associations with comparable trade enhancement objectives, though frequently they—in common with other world regional alliances—have social, political, and cultural interests also in mind. CARICOM (Caribbean Community and Common Market), for example, was established in 1974 to further cooperation among its members in economic, health, cultural, and foreign policy arenas. MERCOSUR—the Southern Cone Community Market—which unites Brazil, Argentina, Uruguay, and Paraguay in the proposed creation of a customs union to eliminate levies on goods moving among them, is a South American example.

A similar interest in promoting economic, social, and cultural cooperation and development among its members underpins the Association of Southeast Asian Nations (ASEAN), formed in 1967. A similar, but much less wealthy African example is ECOWAS, the Economic Community of West African States. The Asia Pacific Economic Cooperation (APEC) forum includes China, Japan, Australia, Canada, and the United States among its 18 members and has a grand plan for "free trade in the Pacific" by 2020. More restricted bilateral and regional preferential trade arrangements have also proliferated, numbering more than 250 by 2006, up from only 50 in 1990, with another 60 or so under negotiation. They create a maze of rules, tariffs, and commodity agreements that result in trade restrictions and preferences contrary to the free trade intent of the World Trade Organization.

Some supranational alliances, of course, are more cultural and political in orientation than these cited agencies. The League of Arab States, for example, was established in 1945 primarily to promote social, political, military, and foreign policy cooperation among its 22 members. In the Western Hemisphere, the Organization of American States (OAS) founded in 1948 concerns itself largely with social, cultural, human rights, and security matters affecting the hemisphere. A similar concern with peace and security underlay the Organization of African Unity (OAU) formed in 1963 by 32 African countries and, by 2001, expanded to 53 members and renamed the African Union.

Economic interests, therefore, may motivate the establishment of most international alliances, but political, social, and cultural objectives also figure largely or exclusively in many. Although the alliances themselves may change, the idea of supranational associations has been permanently added to the national political and global realities of the 21st century. The world map pattern those alliances create must be recognized to understand the current international order.

Three further points about regional international alliances are worth noting. The first is that the formation of a coalition in one area

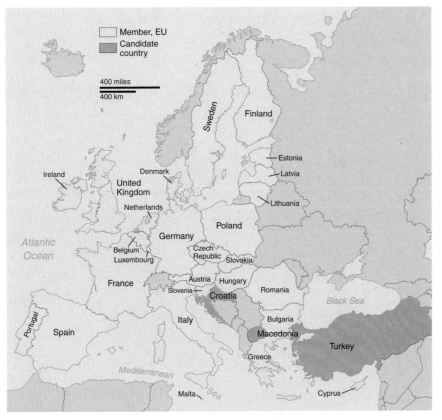

Figure 12.25 The 27 members of the European Union (EU). The admission of Romania and Bulgaria on January 1, 2007, marked the end of EU expansion according to the European Commission until "further institutional reform" increased its absorption capacity. The EU earlier stipulated that in order to join, a country must have stable institutions guaranteeing democracy, the rule of law, human rights and protection of minorities; a functioning market economy; and the ability to accept the obligations of membership, including the aims of political, economic, and monetary union.

often stimulates the creation of another alliance by countries left out of the first. Thus, the union of the Inner Six gave rise to the treaty among the Outer Seven. Similarly, a counterpart of the Common Market was the Council of Mutual Economic Assistance (CMEA), also known as Comecon, which linked the former communist countries of Eastern Europe and the USSR through trade agreements.

Second, the new supranational unions tend to be composed of contiguous states (Figure 12.26). This was not the case with the recently dissolved empires, which included far-flung territories. Contiguity facilitates the movement of people and goods. Communication and transportation are simpler and more effective among adjoining countries than among those far removed from one another, and common cultural, linguistic, historical, and political traits and interests are more to be expected in spatially proximate countries.

Finally, it does not seem to matter whether countries are alike or distinctly different in their economies, as far as joining economic unions is concerned. There are examples of both. If the countries are dissimilar, they may complement each other. This was one basis for the European Common Market. Dairy products and furniture from Denmark are sold in France, freeing that country to specialize in the production of machinery and clothing. On the other hand, countries that produce the same raw

materials hope that by joining together in an economic alliance, they might be able to enhance their control of markets and prices for their products. The Organization of Petroleum Exporting Countries (OPEC), mentioned in Chapter 8, is a case in point. Other attempts to form commodity cartels and price agreements between producing and consuming nations include the International Tin Agreement, the International Coffee Agreement, and others.

Military and Political Alliances

Countries form alliances for other than economic reasons. Strategic, political, and cultural considerations may also foster cooperation. *Military alliances* are based on the principle that unity assures strength. Such pacts usually provide for mutual assistance in the case of aggression. Once again, action breeds reaction when such an association is created. The formation of the North Atlantic Treaty Organization (NATO), a defensive alliance of many European countries and the United States, was countered by the establishment of the Warsaw Treaty Organization, which joined the USSR and its satellite countries of Eastern Europe. Both pacts allowed the member states to base armed forces in one another's territories, a relinquishment of a certain degree of sovereignty uncommon in the past.

Military alliances depend on the perceived common interests and political goodwill of the countries involved. As political realities change, so do the strategic alliances. NATO was created to defend Western Europe and North America against the Soviet military threat. When the dissolution of the USSR and the Warsaw Pact removed that threat, the purpose of the NATO alliance became less clear. Since the 1990s, however, the organization has added seven members and has taken on a greater role in peacekeeping activities (Figure 12.27).

All international alliances recognize communities of interest. In economic and military associations, common objectives are clearly seen and described, and joint actions are agreed on with respect to the achievement of those objectives. More generalized mutual concerns or appeals to historical interest may be the basis for primarily *political alliances*. Such associations tend to be rather loose, not requiring their members to yield much power to the union. Examples are the Commonwealth of Nations (formerly the British Commonwealth), composed of many former British colonies and dominions, and the Organization of American States, both of which offer economic as well as political benefits.

There are many examples of abortive political unions that have foundered precisely because the individual countries could not agree on questions of policy and were unwilling to subordinate individual interests to make the union succeed. The United Arab Republic, the Central African Federation, the Federation of Malaysia and Singapore, and the Federation of the West Indies fall within this category.

Although many such political associations have failed, observers of the world scene speculate about the possibility that

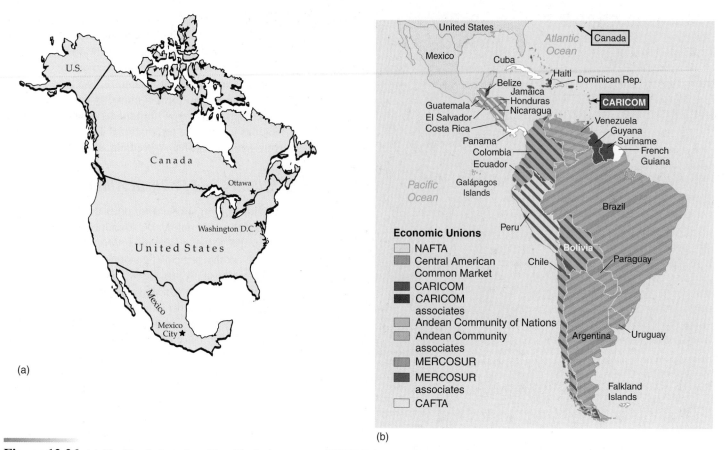

(a)

(b)

Figure 12.26 (*a*) **The North American Free Trade Agreement (NAFTA)** is intended to unite Canada, the United States, and Mexico in a regional free trade zone. Under the terms of the treaty, tariffs on all agricultural products and thousands of other goods were to be eliminated by the end of 1999. In addition, all three countries are to ease restrictions on the movement of business executives and professionals. If fully implemented, the treaty will create one of the world's richest and largest trading blocs. (*b*) **Western Hemisphere economic unions** in 2009. In addition to these subregional alliances, President George H. W. Bush in 1990 proposed a "free trade area of the Americas" to stretch from Alaska to Cape Horn.

"superstates" will emerge from one or more of the economic or political alliances that now exist. Will a "United States of Europe," for example, under a single government be the logical outcome of the successes of the EU? No one knows, but as long as the individual state is regarded as the highest form of political and social organization (as it is now) and as the body in which sovereignty rests, such total unification is unlikely.

Local and Regional Political Organization

The most profound contrasts in cultures tend to occur among, rather than within, states, one reason political geographers traditionally have been primarily interested in country units. The emphasis on the state, however, should not obscure the fact that for most of us it is at that local level that we find our most intimate and immediate contact with government and its influence on the administration of our affairs. In the United States, for example, an individual is subject to the decisions and regulations made by the school board, the municipality, the county, the state, and, perhaps, a host of special-purpose districts—all in addition to the laws and regulations issued by the federal government and its agencies. Among other things,

local political entities determine where children go to school, the minimum size lot on which a person can build a house, and where one may legally park a car. Adjacent states of the United States may be characterized by sharply differing personal and business tax rates; differing controls on the sale of firearms, alcohol, and tobacco; variant administrative systems for public services; and different levels of expenditures for them (Figure 12.28).

All of these governmental entities are *spatial systems*. Because they operate within defined geographic areas and because they make behavior-governing decisions, they are topics of interest to political geographers. In the concluding sections of this chapter, we examine two aspects of political organization at the local and regional level. Our emphasis will be on the U.S. and Canadian scene simply because their local political geography is familiar to most of us. We should remember, however, Anglo American structures of municipal governments, minor civil divisions, and special-purpose districts have counterparts in other regions of the world.

The Geography of Representation: The Districting Problem

There are more than 85,000 local governmental units in the United States. Slightly more than half of these are municipalities, townships, and counties. The remainder are school districts, water-control

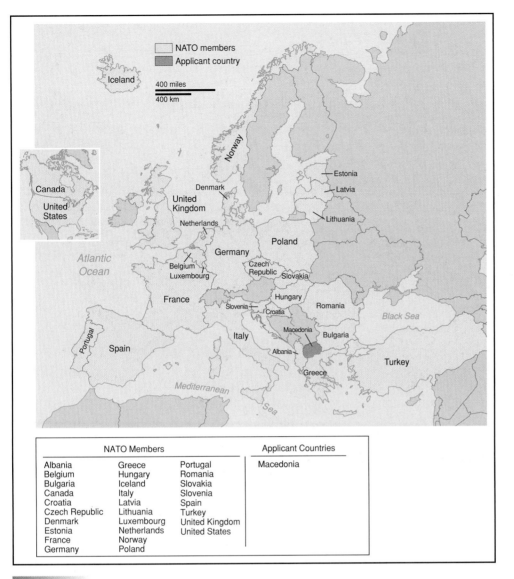

NATO Members			Applicant Countries
Albania	Greece	Portugal	Macedonia
Belgium	Hungary	Romania	
Bulgaria	Iceland	Slovakia	
Canada	Italy	Slovenia	
Croatia	Latvia	Spain	
Czech Republic	Lithuania	Turkey	
Denmark	Luxembourg	United Kingdom	
Estonia	Netherlands	United States	
France	Norway		
Germany	Poland		

Figure 12.27 The NATO military alliance in 2009 had 28 members. Countries that have recently joined the alliance include Estonia, Latvia, Lithuania, Slovakia, Romania, Bulgaria, and Slovenia in 2004 and Albania and Croatia in 2009. Proponents of expansion argue that NATO is necessary in order to create a zone of stability and security throughout Europe. Opponents contend that enlargement is a divisive move that will cast a shadow over the future of relations with Russia, which is opposed to expansion so close to its borders.

districts, airport authorities, sanitary districts, and other special-purpose bodies. Around each of these districts, boundaries have been drawn. Although the number of districts does not change greatly from year to year, many boundary lines are redrawn in any single year. When the size or shape of a district is based on population numbers or distribution, such *redistricting* or *reapportionment* is made necessary by shifts in population, as areas gain or lose people.

For example, every 10 years following the U.S. census, updated figures are used to redistribute the 435 seats in the House of Representatives among the 50 states. Redrawing the Congressional districts to reflect population changes is required by the Constitution, the intention being to make sure that each legislator represents roughly the same number of people. Since 1964, Canadian provinces and territories have entrusted redistricting for federal offices to independent electoral boundaries commissions. Although a few states in the United States also have independent, nonpartisan boards or commissions draw district boundaries, most rely on state legislatures for the task. Across the United States, the decennial census data are also used to redraw the boundaries of legislative districts within each state as well as those for local offices, such as city councils and county boards.

The analysis of how boundaries are drawn around voting districts is one aspect of **electoral geography,** which also addresses the spatial patterns yielded by election results and their relationship to the socioeconomic characteristics of voters. In a democracy, it might be assumed that election districts should contain roughly equal numbers of voters, that electoral districts should be reasonably compact, and that the proportion of elected representatives should correspond to the share of votes cast for a given political party. Problems arise because the way in which the electoral boundary lines are drawn can maximize, minimize, or effectively nullify the representational power of a group of people.

Gerrymandering is the practice of drawing the boundaries of voting districts so as to unfairly favor one political party over another, to fragment voting blocs, or to achieve other nondemocratic objectives (Figure 12.29). A number of strategies have been employed over the years for that purpose. *Stacked* gerrymandering involves drawing circuitous boundaries to enclose pockets of strength or weakness of the group in power; it is what we usually think of as "gerrymandering." The *excess vote* technique concentrates the votes of the opposition in a few districts, which they can win easily, but leaves them few potential seats elsewhere. Conversely, the *wasted vote* strategy dilutes the opposition's strength by dividing its votes among a number of districts.

Assume that X and O represent two groups with an equal number of voters but different policy preferences. Although there are equal numbers of Xs and Os, the way electoral districts are drawn affects voting results. In Figure 12.30a, the Xs are concentrated in one district and will probably elect only one representative of four. The power of the Xs is maximized in Figure 12.30b, where they may control three of the four districts. The voters are evenly divided in Figure 12.30c, where the Xs have the opportunity to elect two of the four representatives. Finally, Figure 12.30d shows how both political parties might agree to delimit the electoral districts to provide "safe

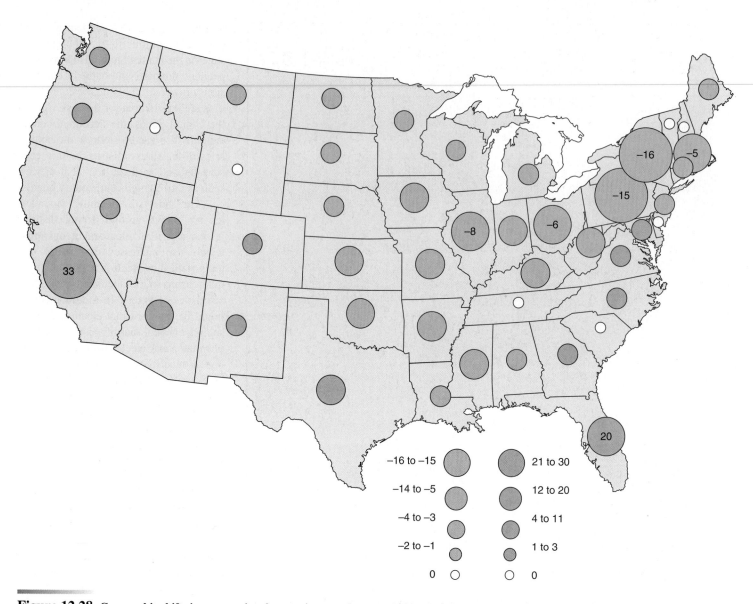

Figure 12.28 **Geographic shifts in congressional apportionment between 1930 and 2000** illustrate dramatic population movements to the South and West. Seats in the U.S. House of Representatives are reapportioned after each census with the goal of achieving an equitable distribution based on population while maintaining at least one member for each state. Since 1930, New York has lost 16 seats and Pennsylvania 15 while California has gained 33, Florida gained 20, and Texas gained 11. After the 2000 census, twelve seats were shifted. Alaska and Hawaii are not shown because they were not states in 1930. Data: Office of the Clerk, U.S. House of Representatives.

seats" for incumbents. Such partitioning offers little chance for change.

Figure 12.30 depicts a hypothetical district, compact in shape with an even population distribution and only two groups competing for representation. In actuality, voting districts are often oddly shaped because of such factors as the city limits, current population distribution, and transportation routes—as well as past gerrymandering. Further, in any large area, many groups vie for power. Each electoral interest group promotes its version of fairness in the way boundaries are delimited. Minority interests, for example, seek representation in proportion to their numbers so that they will be able to elect representatives who are concerned about and responsive to their needs (see "Voting Rights and Race").

In practice, gerrymandering is not always and automatically successful. First, a districting arrangement that appears to

be unfair may be appealed to the courts. Further, voters are not unthinking party loyalists; key issues may cut across party lines, scandal may erode, or personal charm increase votes unexpectedly; and the amount of candidate financing or number of campaign workers may determine election outcome if compelling issues are absent.

The Fragmentation of Political Power

Boundary drawing at any electoral level is never easy, particularly when political groups want to maximize their representation and minimize that of opposition groups. Furthermore, the boundaries that we may want for one set of districts may *not* be those that we want for another. For example, sewage districts must take natural drainage features into account, whereas police districts may

THE GERRY-MANDER. (Boston, 1811.)

Figure 12.29 The original gerrymander. The term *gerrymander* originated in 1811 from the shape of an electoral district formed in Massachusetts while Elbridge Gerry was governor. When an artist added certain animal features, the district resembled a salamander and quickly came to be called a gerrymander.

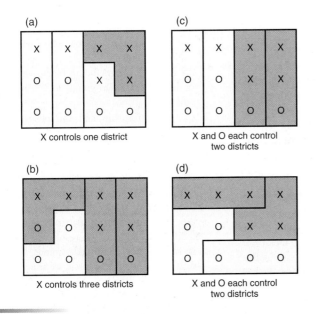

(a)
X controls one district

(c)
X and O each control two districts

(b)
X controls three districts

(d)
X and O each control two districts

Figure 12.30 Alternative districting strategies. *Xs* and *Os* might represent Republicans and Democrats, urban and rural voters, blacks and whites, or any other distinctive groups.

be based on the distribution of the population or the number of miles of street to be patrolled, and school attendance zones must consider the numbers of school-aged children and the capacities of individual schools.

As these examples suggest, the United States is subdivided into great numbers of political administrative units whose areas of control are spatially limited. The 50 states are partitioned into more than 3000 counties ("parishes" in Louisiana), most of which are further subdivided into townships, each with a still lower level of governing power. This political fragmentation is further increased by the existence of nearly 88,000 special-purpose districts whose boundaries rarely coincide with the standard major and minor civil divisions of the country or even with each other (Figure 12.31). Each district represents a form of political allocation of territory to achieve a specific aim of local need or legislative intent.

Canada, a federation of ten provinces and three territories, has a similar pattern of political subdivision. Each of the provinces contains minor civil divisions—municipalities—under provincial control, and all (cities, towns, villages, and rural municipalities) are governed by elected councils. Ontario and Quebec also have counties that group smaller municipal units for certain purposes. In general, municipalities are responsible for police and fire protection, local jails, roads and hospitals, water supply and sanitation, and schools, duties that are discharged either by elected agencies or appointed commissions.

Most Anglo Americans live in large and small cities. In the United States these, too, are subdivided, not only into wards or precincts for voting purposes but also into special districts for such functions as fire and police protection, water and electricity supply, education, recreation, and sanitation. These districts almost never coincide with one another, and the larger the urban area, the greater the proliferation of small, special-purpose governing and taxing units. Although no Canadian community has quite the multiplication of governmental entities plaguing many U.S. urban areas, major Canadian cities may find themselves with complex and growing systems of similar nature. Even before its major expansion on January 1, 1998, for example, Metropolitan Toronto had more than 100 identified authorities that could be classified as "local governments."

The existence of such a great number of districts in metropolitan areas may cause inefficiency in public services and hinder the orderly use of space. *Zoning ordinances,* for example, controlling the uses to which land may be put, are determined by each municipality and are a clear example of the effect of political decisions on the division and development of space. Unfortunately, in large urban areas, the efforts of one community may be hindered by the practices of neighboring communities. Thus, land zoned for an industrial park or shopping mall in one city may abut land zoned for single-family residences in an adjoining municipality. Each

Geography and Public Policy

Voting Rights and Race

Irregularly shaped Congressional voting districts were created by several state legislatures after the 1990 census to make minority representation in Congress more closely resemble minority presence in the state's voting-age population. Most were devised to contain a majority of black voters, but what opponents called racial gerrymandering was in a few cases utilized to accommodate Hispanic majorities. States that intentionally created majority-minority districts after the 1990 census included Florida, Georgia, Illinois, Louisiana, North Carolina, Texas, and Virgina. All represented a deliberate attempt to balance voting rights and race; all were specifically intended to comply with the federal Voting Rights Act of 1965, which provides that members of racial minorities shall not have "less opportunity than other members of the electorate . . . to elect representatives of their choice."

Because at least some of the newly created districts had very contorted boundaries, on appeal by opponents they have been ruled unconstitutional by the Supreme Court and have been redrawn. The state legislatures' attempts at fairness and adherence to Congressional mandate contained in the Voting Rights Act were held not to meet such other standards as rough equality of district population size, reasonably compact shape, and avoidance of disenfranchisement of any class of voters. The conflicts reflected the uncertainty of exactly what were the controlling requirements in voting district creation.

In North Carolina, for example, although 24% of the 1990 population of that state was black, past districting had divided black voters among a number of districts, with the result that blacks had not elected a single Congressional representative in the 20th century. In 1991, the Justice Department ordered North Carolina to redistrict so that at least two districts would contain black majorities. Because of the way the black population was distributed, the only way to form black-majority districts was to string together cities, towns, and rural areas in very elongated sinuous belts. The two newly created districts had slim (53%) black majorities.

The redistricting in North Carolina and other states had immediate effects. Black membership in the House of Representatives increased from 26 in 1990 to 39 in 1992; blacks constituted nearly 9% of the House as against 12% in the total population. Within a year, those electoral gains were threatened as lawsuits challenging the redistricting were filed in a number of states. The chief contention of the plaintiffs was that the irregular shapes of the districts were a product of racial gerrymandering and amounted to reverse discrimination against whites.

In June, 1993, a sharply divided Supreme Court ruled in *Shaw v. Reno* that North Carolina's 12th Congressional District might violate the constitutional rights of white voters and ordered a district court to review the case. The 5–4 ruling gave evidence that the country had not yet reached agreement on how to comply with the Voting Rights Act. It raised a central question: Should a state maximize the rights of racial minorities or not take racial status into consideration? A divided Court provided answers in 1995, 1996, and 1997 rulings that rejected Congressional redistricting maps for Georgia, Texas, and North Carolina on the grounds that "race cannot be the predominant factor" in drawing election district boundaries.

The difficulty in interpreting and complying with the Act is illustrated by the fact that although the Supreme Court in 1996 ruled North Carolina's 12th Congressional District unconstitutional, federal courts in 1998 and 1999 rejected alternate district designs. In *Easley v. Cromartie* (2001) the Court approved both a redrawn 12th District and using race as a redistricting consideration as long as it was not the "dominant and controlling" one. Some research suggests that race-based redistricting results in more polarized politics with some districts more solidly liberal and others more solidly conservative. Results of elections since some majority-minority districts were dismantled by the courts suggest that minorities can win even if their group is not in the majority in a district. While the use of GIS in redistricting has increased the speed and power with which officials can evaluate alternative districting schemes, it has not resolved what are fundamentally ethical issues regarding race, democracy, and electoral geography.

Questions to Consider

1. Do you believe that race should be a consideration in the electoral process? Why or why not? If so, should voting districts be drawn to increase the likelihood that representatives of racial or ethnic minorities will win elections? If not, how can one be certain that the voting power of minorities will not be unacceptably diluted?

2. With which of the following arguments in *Shaw v. Reno* do you agree? Why? ". . . Racial gerrymandering, even for remedial purposes, may balkanize us into competing racial factions; it threatens to carry us further from the goal of a political system in which race no longer matters." (Justice Sandra Day O'Connor) ". . . Legislators will have to take race into account in order to avoid dilution of minority voting strength." (Justice David Souter).

3. One of the candidates in North Carolina's 12th Congressional District said, "I love the district because I can drive down I-85 with both car doors open and hit every person in the district." Given a good transportation and communication network, how important is it that voting districts be compact?

4. Critics of "racial gerrymandering" contend that blacks have been and can continue to be elected in white-majority districts and, further, that white politicians can and do adequately represent the needs of all, including black, voters in their districts. Do you agree? Why or why not?

5. Given partisanship and the desire of incumbent legislators to protect their own seats, is there an inherent conflict in having legislators draw district boundaries? Defend your answer.

6. After the 1990 census, more than 130 suits were filed in 40 states challenging either the states' overall redistricting plans or individual districts. The result was that, in many cases, courts determined final district boundaries. Does it seem democratic for a judge elected in one district to draw up a redistricting plan for an entire state? Defend your answer.

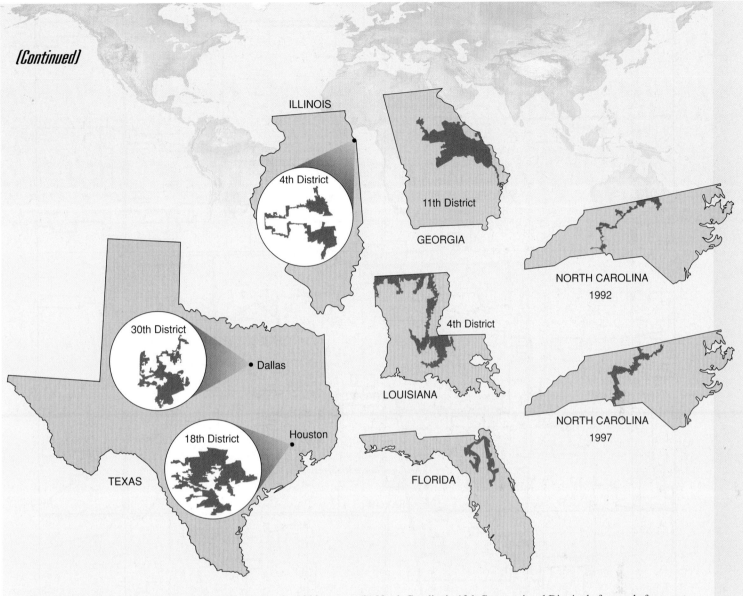

(a) Majority-minority congressional districts drawn after the 1990 census. (b) North Carolina's 12th Congressional District before and after court challenges.

community pursues its own interests, which may not coincide with those of its neighbors or the larger region.

Inefficiency and duplication of effort characterize not just zoning but many of the services provided by local governments. The efforts of one community to avert air and water pollution may be, and often are, counteracted by the rules and practices of other towns in the region, although state and national environmental protection standards are now reducing such potential conflicts. Social as well as physical problems spread beyond city boundaries. Thus, nearby suburban communities are affected when a central city lacks the resources to maintain high-quality schools or to attack social ills. The provision of health care facilities, electricity and water, transportation, and recreational space affects the whole region and, many professionals think, should be under the control of a single consolidated metropolitan government.

The growth in the number and size of metropolitan areas has increased awareness of their administrative and jurisdictional problems. Too much governmental fragmentation and too little local control are both seen as metropolitan problems demanding attention and solution. The one concern is that multiple jurisdictions prevent the pooling of resources to address metropolitan-wide needs. The other is that local community needs and interests are subordinated to social and economic problems of a core city for which outlying communities feel little affinity or concern.

Figure 12.31 **Political fragmentation in Champaign County, Illinois.** The map shows a few of the independent administrative agencies with separate jurisdictions, responsibilities, and taxing powers in a portion of a single Illinois county. Among the other such agencies forming the fragmented political landscape are Champaign County itself, a forest preserve district, a public health district, a mental health district, the county housing authority, and a community college district.

Summary

The sovereign state is the dominant entity in the political subdivision of the world. It constitutes an expression of cultural separation and identity as pervasive as that inherent in language, religion, or ethnicity. A product of 18th-century political philosophy, the idea of the state was diffused globally by colonizing European powers. In most instances, the colonial boundaries they established have been retained as their international boundaries by newly independent countries.

The greatly varying physical characteristics of states contribute to national strength and stability. Size, shape, and relative location influence countries' economies and international roles, while national cores and capitals are the heartlands of states. Boundaries, the legal definition of a state's size and shape, determine the limits of its sovereignty. They may or may not reflect preexisting cultural landscapes and in any given case may or may not prove to be viable. Whatever their nature, boundaries are at the root of many international disputes. Maritime boundary claims, particularly as reflected in the UN Convention on the Law of the Sea, add a new dimension to traditional claims of territorial sovereignty.

State cohesiveness is promoted by a number of centripetal forces. Among these are national symbols, a variety of institutions, and confidence in the aims, organization, and administration of government. Also helping to foster political and economic integration are transportation and communication connections. Destabilizing centrifugal forces, particularly ethnically based separatist movements, threaten the cohesion and stability of many states.

Although the state remains central to the partitioning of the world, a broadening array of political entities affects people individually and collectively. Recent decades have seen a significant increase in supranationalism, in the form of a number and variety of global and regional alliances to which states have surrendered some sovereign powers. At the other end of the spectrum, expanding Anglo American urban areas and governmental responsibilities raise questions of fairness in districting procedures and of effectiveness when political power is fragmented.

KEY WORDS

antecedent boundary 395
artificial boundary 395
autonomous nationalism 400
centrifugal force 397
centripetal force 397
compact state 391
consequent (ethnographic) boundary 395
core area 392
devolution 401
electoral geography 411
elongated state 391
enclave 391
ethnic cleansing 401
European Union (EU) 408
exclave 391

exclusive economic zone (EEZ) 405
fragmented state 391
functional dispute 397
geometric boundary 395
gerrymandering 411
irredentism 396
nation 385
nationalism 397
nation-state 386
natural boundary 395
perforated state 391
physical boundary 395
political geography 384
positional dispute 396

prorupt state 391
regionalism 401
relic boundary 395
resource dispute 396
separatism 400
state 395
subnationalism 400
subsequent boundary 395
superimposed boundary 395
supranationalism 404
territorial dispute 396
terrorism 402
United Nations Convention on the Law of the Sea 405

FOR REVIEW

1. What are the differences between a *state,* a *nation,* and a *nation-state?* Why is a colony not a state? How can one account for the rapid increase in the number of states since World War II?

2. What attributes differentiate states from one another? How do a country's size and shape affect its power and stability? How can a piece of land be both an *enclave* and an *exclave?*

3. How can boundaries be classified? How do they create opportunities for conflict? Describe and give examples of three types of border disputes.

4. How does the *United Nations Convention on the Law of the Sea* define zones of diminishing national control? What are the consequences of the concept of the 200-nm *exclusive economic zone?*

5. Distinguish between *centripetal* and *centrifugal* political forces. What are some of the ways national cohesion and identity are achieved?

6. What characteristics are common to all or most regional autonomist movements? Where are some of these

movements active? Why do they tend to be on the periphery rather than at the national core?

7. What types of international organizations and alliances can you name? What were the purposes of their establishment? What generalizations can you make regarding economic alliances?

8. Why does it matter how boundaries are drawn around electoral districts? Theoretically, is it always possible to delimit boundaries "fairly"? Support your answer.

9. What reasons can you suggest for the great political fragmentation of the United States? What problems stem from such fragmentation?

KEY CONCEPTS REVIEW

1. **What are the types and geographic characteristics of countries and the nature of their boundaries?** pp. 384–397.
   States are internationally recognized independent political entities. When culturally uniform, they may be termed nation-states. Their varying physical characteristics of size, shape, and location have implications for national power and cohesion. Boundaries define the limits of states' authority and underlie many international disputes.

2. **How do states maintain cohesiveness and instill nationalism?** pp. 397–403.
   Cohesiveness is fostered through unifying institutions, education, and efficient transport and communication systems. It may be eroded by minority group separatist wishes and tendencies.

3. **Why are international alliances proliferating, and what objectives do they espouse and serve?** pp. 403–410.
   In an economically and technologically changing world, alliances are presumed to increase the security and prosperity of states. The UN claims to represent and promote worldwide cooperation; its Law of the Sea regulates use and claims of the world's oceans. Regional alliances involving some reduction of national independence promote economic, military, or political objectives of groups of states related spatially or ideologically. They are expressions of the growing trend toward *supranationalism* in international affairs.

4. **What problems are evident in defining local political divisions in Anglo America, and what solutions have been proposed or instituted?** pp. 410–416.
   The great political fragmentation within, particularly, the United States reflects the creation of special-purpose units to satisfy a local or administrative need. States, counties, townships, cities, and innumerable special-purpose districts all have defined and often overlapping boundaries and functions. Voting rights, reapportionment, and local political boundary adjustments represent areas of continuing political concern and dispute. In the United States, racial gerrymandering is a current legal issue in voting district definition.

Part Five

HUMAN IMPACTS ON NATURAL SYSTEMS

13

High rise buildings and fishing boats form the background of a garbage littered beach in Mumbai, India.

Key Concepts

1. Climates and biomes: problems of global warming, acid rain, and ozone change, pp. 420–431.

2. Abuses of land and vegetation: deforestation, desertification, and soil erosion, pp. 431–437.

3. Problems of water supply and water quality, pp. 437–441.

4. Disposal of solid and toxic wastes, pp. 440–450.

*W*hen the daily tides come in, a surge of water high as a person's head moves up the rivers and creeks of the world's largest delta, formed where the Ganges and Brahmaputra rivers meet the Bay of Bengal in the South Asian country of Bangladesh. Within that Wisconsin-sized country that is one-fifth water, millions of people live on thousands of alluvial islands known as "chars." These form from the silt of the rivers and are washed away by their currents and by the force of cyclones that roar upstream from the bay during the annual cyclone period. As the chars are swept away so, too, are thousands and tens of thousands of their land-hungry occupants who fiercely battled each other with knives and clubs to claim and cultivate them.

Late in April of 1991, an atmospheric low-pressure area moved across the Malay Peninsula of Southeast Asia and gained strength in the Bay of Bengal, generating winds of nearly 240 kilometers (150 miles) per hour. As it moved northward, the storm sucked up and drew along with it a wall of water 6 meters (20 feet) high. At 1:00 A.M. on April 30, with a full moon and highest tides, the cyclone and its battering ram of water slammed across the chars and the deltaic mainland. When it had passed, some of the richest rice fields in Asia were gray with the salt that ruined them, islands totally covered with paddies were left as giant sand dunes, others—densely populated—simply disappeared beneath the swirling waters. An estimated 500,000 lives were lost to the storm and to subsequent starvation, disease, and exposure.

Each year lesser variants of the tragedy are repeated; each year survivors return to rebuild their lives on old land or new still left after the storms or created as the floods ease and some of the annual 2.5 billion tons of river-borne silt is deposited to form new chars. Deforestation in the Himalayan headwaters of the rivers increases erosion there and swells the volume of silt flowing into Bangladesh. Dams on the Ganges River in India alter normal flow patterns, releasing more water during floods and increasing silt deposits during seasonal droughts. And, always, population growth adds to the number of desperate people seeking homes and fields on lands more safely left as the realm of river and sea.

Physical Environments and Cultural Impacts

The people of the chars live with an immediate environmental contact that is not known to most of us in the highly developed, highly urbanized countries of the world. In fact, much of the content of the preceding chapters has detailed ways that humans isolate themselves from the physical environment and superimpose cultural landscapes on it to accommodate the growing needs of their growing numbers.

Many cultural landscape changes are minor in themselves. The forest clearing for swidden agriculture or the terracing of hillsides for subsistence farming are modest alterations of nature. Plowing and farming the prairies, harnessing major river systems by dams and reservoirs, building cities and their connecting highways, or opening vast open-pit mines are much more substantial modifications. In some cases the new landscapes are apparently completely divorced from the natural ones that preceded them—as in enclosed, air-conditioned shopping malls and office towers. The original minor modifications have cumulatively become totally new cultural creations.

But suppression of the physical landscape does not mean eradication of human–environmental interactions. They continue, though in altered form, as humans increasingly become the active and dominant agents of environmental change. More often than not, the changes we have set in motion create unplanned cultural landscapes and unwanted environmental conditions. We have altered our climates, polluted our air and water and soil, destroyed natural vegetation and land contours while stripping ores and fuels from the earth. At the same time, we have found it increasingly difficult and costly to provide with food and resources our growing populations.

Environment is an overworked word that means the totality of things that in any way affect an organism. Humans exist within a natural environment—the sum of the physical world—that they have modified by their individual and collective actions. Human impacts on the environment can be summarized through the simple **IPAT** equation: $I = PAT$; where: I (Impact on the environment) equals P (Population) multiplied by A (Affluence as measured by per capita income) multiplied by T (a Technology factor). As indicated by the IPAT equation, population growth and rising standards of living both lead to greater use of natural resources and greater production of wastes. However, the technology factor in the equation accounts for the very different impacts associated, for example, with various sources of energy such as coal, nuclear, or wind energy. Further, in many instances increased standards of living have led to improvements in local air and water quality because rising prosperity has allowed societies to invest in pollution controls and cleaner technologies. Unfortunately, some changes aimed at improving the quality of the local environment such as shifting to taller smokestacks or shipping toxic wastes to distant landfills come at the expense of the environment elsewhere or at the expense of the global environment (Figure 13.1). Each of the factors in the IPAT equation relate to topics in human geography—population geography, economic geography, and the various technologies societies use to house, feed, and transport themselves. Thus, adverse consequences of human impact on the environment are the unforeseen creations of the cultural landscapes we have been examining and analyzing, and their study highlights the unity of physical and human geography.

Even in the absence of humans, those conditions were marked by constant alteration and adjustment that nonetheless preserved intact the **biosphere** (or **ecosphere**), the thin film of air, water, and earth within which all organisms live. This biosphere is composed of three overlapping, interrelated parts: (1) the *atmosphere,* a light blanket of air enveloping the earth, with more than half of its mass within 6.5 kilometers (4 miles) of the surface and 98% within 26 km (16 mi); (2) the *hydrosphere,* the surface and subsurface waters in oceans, rivers, lakes, glaciers, and groundwater; and (3) the *lithosphere,* the upper reaches of the earth's crust containing the soils that support plant life, the minerals that plants and animals require for life, and the fossil fuels and ores that humans exploit.

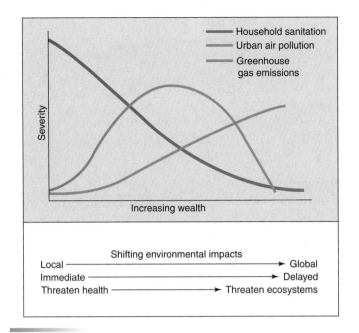

Figure 13.1 **The geographic scale of environmental impacts** shifts as incomes rise. For the world's poor, the primary environmental problems are disposing of human wastes and ensuring clean water supplies. As standards of living increase, communities can afford water and sewage treatment systems but also increase their consumption of raw materials, synthetic chemicals, and fossil fuel energy. This tends to shift environmental problems from local, immediate threats to human health to longer-term, delayed global impacts on ecosystems such as destruction of the ozone layer, acid precipitation, and global climate change.

Source: Graph from World Energy Assessment, UNDP, 2000, Figure 3.10, p.95.

The biosphere is an intricately interlocked system, containing all that is needed for life, all that is available for life to use, and, presumably, all that ever will be available. The ingredients of the ecosphere must be and are constantly recycled and renewed in nature: plants purify the air; the air helps to purify the water; plants and animals use the water and the minerals, which are returned to the system for reuse. Anything that upsets the interplay of the ecosphere or diminishes its ability to recycle itself or to sustain life endangers all organisms within it, including humans.

Climates, Biomes, and Change

The structure of the ecosphere is not eternal and unchanging. On the contrary, alteration is the constant rule of the physical environment and would be so even in the absence of humans and their distorting impacts. Climatic change, year-to-year variations in weather patterns, fires, windstorms, floods, diseases, or the unexplained rise and fall of predator and prey populations all call for new environmental configurations and forever prevent the establishment of a single, constant "balance of nature."

Remember that we began to track cultural geographic patterns from the end of the last continental glaciation, some 11,000–12,000 years ago. Our starting point, then, was a time of environmental change when humans were too few in number and primitive in

technology to have had any impact on the larger structure of the biosphere. Their numbers increased and their technologies became vastly more sophisticated and intrusive with the passage of time, but for nearly all of the period of cultural development to modern times, human impact on the world environment was absorbed and accommodated by it with no more than local distress. The rhythm and the regularity of larger global systems proceeded largely unaffected by people.

Over the millennia since the last glaciation—with a few periods of unusual warming or cooling as the exceptions—a relatively stable pattern of climatic regions emerged, a global system of environmental conditions within which human cultures developed and differentiated. That pattern reflected enduring physical controls and balances: the tilt of the earth's axis; the earth's rotation and its movement about the sun; its receipt of energy from the sun and the seasonal variations in energy received in the Northern and Southern Hemispheres; the reradiation of some of that received energy back through the atmosphere in the form of heat and, in finer detail, the pattern of land and water distribution and of ocean and atmospheric currents.

In combination these and other controls determine global patterns of temperature and precipitation, the basic variables in world climatic systems. The continual warmth of the tropical (equatorial) regions contrasts with the seasonal temperature variations of the midlatitudes, where land and water contrasts also affect the temperatures recorded even at the same latitude. Summers become cooler and shorter farther toward the poles until, finally, permanent ice cap conditions prevail. Precipitation patterns are more complex than are those of temperature but are important constituents of regional environmental variation.

The pattern of global climates that these physical controls established (Figure 13.2) also established a pattern of biomes. **Biomes** are major communities of plants and animals occupying extensive areas of the earth's surface in response to climatic conditions. We know them by such descriptive names as *desert, grassland* or *steppe* or as the *tropical rain forest* and *northern coniferous forest* that we met in Chapter 8. Biomes, in turn, contain smaller, more specialized **ecosystems:** self-contained, self-regulating, and interacting communities adapted to local combinations of climate, topography, soil, and drainage conditions.

Ecosystems have long felt the destructive hand of humans and the cultural landscapes they made. We saw in Chapter 2 the results of human abuse of the local environment in the Chaco Canyon and Easter Island deforestations. Forest removal, over-grazing, and ill-considered agriculture turned lush hillsides of the Mediterranean Basin into sterile and impoverished landscapes by the end of the Roman Empire.

At a global scale, however, human impact was minimal. Long-term and short-term deviations from average conditions were induced by natural, not cultural, conditions (Figure 13.3; see also "Earth's Changing Climates"). But slowly, unnoticed at first, human activity began to have a global impact, carrying the consequences of cultural abuse of the biosphere far beyond the local scene. The atmosphere, the one part of the biosphere that all the world shares, began to react measurably during the last half of the 20th century to damage that humans had done to it since the beginning of the Industrial Revolution in the 18th century. If those reactions prove permanent

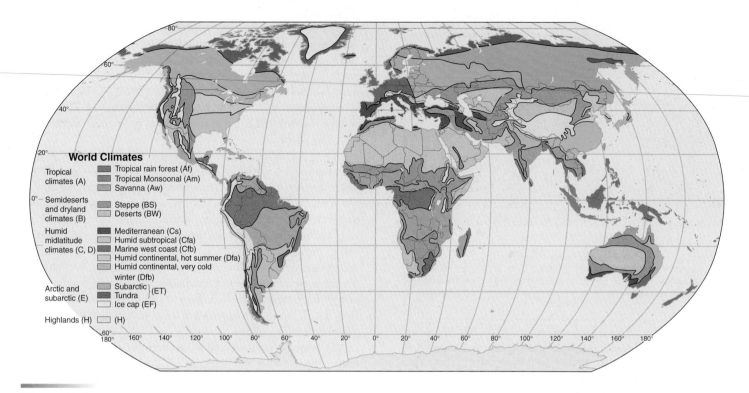

World Climates

Tropical climates (A)
- Tropical rain forest (Af)
- Tropical Monsoonal (Am)
- Savanna (Aw)

Semideserts and dryland climates (B)
- Steppe (BS)
- Deserts (BW)

Humid midlatitude climates (C, D)
- Mediterranean (Cs)
- Humid subtropical (Cfa)
- Marine west coast (Cfb)
- Humid continental, hot summer (Dfa)
- Humid continental, very cold winter (Dfb)

Arctic and subarctic (E)
- Subarctic (ET)
- Tundra (ET)
- Ice cap (EF)

Highlands (H)
- (H)

Figure 13.2 Climates of the world. Complex interrelationships of latitude, land and water contrasts, ocean currents, topography, and wind circulation make the global pattern of climates more intricate than this generalized map reveals.

Earth's Changing Climates

In 1125, William of Malmesbury favorably compared the number and productivity of the vineyards of England with those of France; England has almost no vineyards today. In the 10th century, the Vikings established successful colonies in Greenland; by 1250, that island was practically cut off by extensive drift ice, and by the early 15th century, its colonies were forgotten and dead. The Medieval Warm Period, which evidence indicates lasted from A.D. 800 to 1200, was marked by the warmest climate that had occurred in the Northern Hemisphere for several thousand years. Glaciers retreated and agricultural settlement spread throughout Europe. Those mild conditions were not to last, however. Change and fluctuation in environmental conditions are the rules of nature.

In recent years archaeologists and historians have found evidence that ancient seats of power—such as Sumeria in the Middle East, Mycenae in southern Greece, the Maya civilization in Yucatán, the Peruvian Moche cul-

ture, and Mali in Africa—may have fallen not to barbarians but to unfavorable alterations in the climates under which they came to power. Climatic change certainly altered the established structure of European society when, between 1550 and 1850, a "little ice age" descended on the Northern Hemisphere. Arctic ice expanded, glaciers advanced, Alpine passes were closed to traffic, and crop failures and starvation were common in much of Europe. Systems of agriculture, patterns of trade, designs of buildings, styles of clothing, and rhythms of life responded to climatic conditions vastly less favorable than those of the preceding centuries.

A new pronounced warming trend began about 1890 and lasted to the early 1940s. During that period, the margin of agriculture was extended northward, the pattern of commercial fishing shifted poleward, and the reliability of crop yields increased. But by the 1950s, natural conditions again seemed poised to change. From the late 1940s to the 1970s,

the mean temperature of the globe declined. The growing season in England became 2 weeks shorter; disastrous droughts occurred in Africa and Asia; and unexpected freezes altered crop patterns in Latin America.

This time, humans were aware that changes in the great natural systems were partly traceable to things that they themselves were doing. The problem was, they were doing so many things, with such contrary consequences, that the combined and cumulative impact was unclear. One scenario predicted the planet would slowly cool over the next few centuries and enter a new ice age, helped along that path by the large amount of soot and dust in the atmosphere traceable to human activity that prevents incoming solar energy from reaching and warming the earth. A quite different scenario foretold a planet warming dangerously as different human stresses on the atmosphere overcame a natural cycle of cooling.

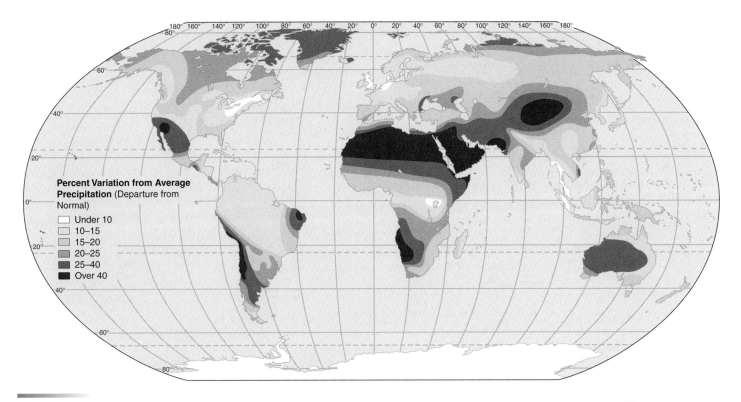

Figure 13.3 **The pattern of precipitation variability.** Note that steppe and desert climate regions have both low total precipitation and high variability. In general, the lower the amount of long-term annual precipitation, the lower is the probability that the "average" will be recorded in any single year. Short-run variability and long-term progressive change in climatic conditions are the rule of nature and occur independent of any human influence.

and cumulative, then established patterns of climates and the biomes based on them are destined to be altered in fundamental ways.

At first it appeared the danger was from overcooling, an onset of a new glacial stage. Part of incoming solar energy is intercepted by clouds and by solid and liquid particles—*aerosols*—and reradiated back to space. An increase in reflectors decreases energy receipt at the earth's surface, and a cooling effect, the **icebox effect,** is inevitable. Aerosols are naturally injected into the atmosphere from such sources as dust storms, forest fires, or volcanos. Indeed, volcanic eruptions trigger cooling cycles. The famous "year without a summer," 1816, when snow fell in June in New England and frost occurred in July, was probably the climatic reflection of the 1815 eruption of the Indonesian volcano, Tambora. That explosion ejected an estimated 200 million tons of gaseous aerosols—water vapor, sulfur dioxide, hydrogen chloride, and others—and upward of 50 cubic kilometers (30 cubic miles) of dust and ash into the atmosphere. The reflective cooling effect lasted for years. (A similar, but less extreme, Northern Hemisphere summer temperature drop in the early 1990s was attributed to the eruption of Mount Pinatubo in the Philippines in 1991.)

Aerosols in solid and gaseous form are products of human activities as well. Ever-increasing amounts of them are ejected from the smokestacks of factories, power plants, and city buildings and from the tailpipes of vehicles and exhaust plumes of jet aircraft. The global cooling that became noticeable by the late 1940s seemed to presage a new ice age, partly the product of natural conditions but hastened and deepened by human pressures upon the atmosphere.

The fears those pressures generated began to be replaced, in the 1980s, by a three-part package of different concerns: (1) a global climate change caused by an intensified "greenhouse" effect, (2) acid precipitation, and (3) ozone depletion. These are all global atmospheric threats, with some parts of the world more responsible than others for the air emissions and inputs that have caused the changes, and some places on earth more likely to suffer the adverse effects because of their geographic location.

Global Climate Change

That humans have significantly altered the chemical composition of the atmosphere since the advent of the industrial Revolution around the year 1750 is beyond dispute. Human activities have increased the concentrations of three greenhouse gases—carbon dioxide, methane, and nitrous oxide, intensifying the natural **greenhouse effect,** leading to **global climate change.** The greenhouse effect is the result of specific atmospheric gases partially capturing the long-wave heat energy radiated from earth back to space and is a necessary condition to heat the earth to temperatures at which life is possible. Without the greenhouse effect, the earth would be substantially colder and its temperatures would fluctuate wildly. What is of global concern today is that human activities have significantly increased the concentrations of greenhouse gases, intensifying the greenhouse effect and causing anthropogenic (human-caused) climate change (Figure 13.4). Humankind's massive assault on the atmosphere presumably began with the Industrial Revolution. First coal and then increasing amounts of petroleum and natural gas

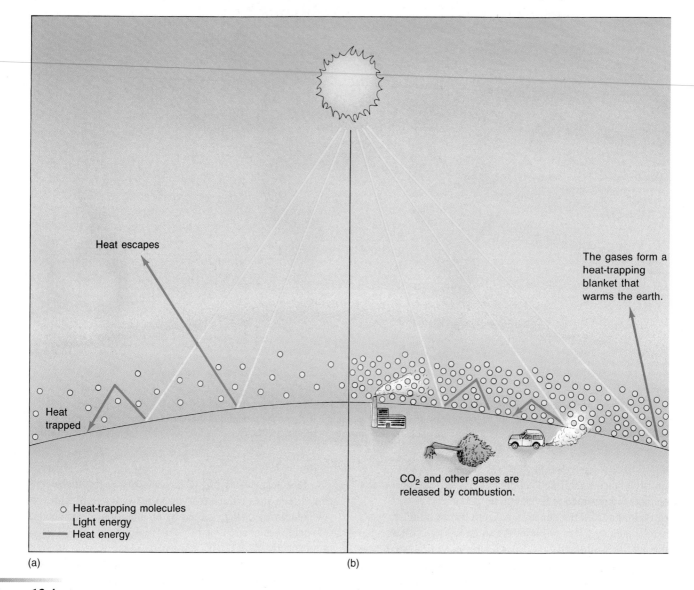

Heat escapes

The gases form a heat-trapping blanket that warms the earth.

Heat trapped

○ Heat-trapping molecules
Light energy
Heat energy

CO₂ and other gases are released by combustion.

(a)   (b)

Figure 13.4 Intensified greenhouse effect. When the level of carbon dioxide (CO$_2$) in the air is low, as in (*a*), incoming solar radiation strikes the earth's surface, heating it up, and the earth radiates the energy back into space as heat. Some of the heat energy is captured by naturally occurring greenhouse gases, thereby heating the atmosphere. The intensified greenhouse effect depicted in (*b*), is the result of the more than 7 billion tons of CO$_2$ that the burning of fossil fuels adds to the atmosphere each year.

have been burned to power industry, heat and cool cities, and drive vehicles. Their burning has turned fuels into carbon dioxide and water vapor. At the same time, the world's forest lands—most recently its tropical rain forests—have been destroyed wholesale by logging and to clear land for agriculture. With more carbon dioxide in the atmosphere and fewer trees to capture the carbon and produce oxygen, carbon dioxide levels have risen steadily.

The role of trees in managing the carbon cycle is simple: Probably more than half the carbon dioxide put into the atmosphere by burning fossil fuels is absorbed by the earth's oceans, plants, and soil. The rest of the carbon dioxide remains in the atmosphere where it traps earth heat radiation. In theory, atmospheric carbon dioxide could be reduced by expanding plant carbon reservoirs, or "sinks," on land. Under actual circumstances of expanded combustion of fuels and reduction of forest cover, atmospheric

carbon dioxide levels now total well over 200% of their amounts at the start of the Industrial Revolution and continue to rise. Yearly carbon emissions that totaled 1.6 billion tons in 1950 reached more than 7 billion tons in 2006. Carbon dioxide gets most media attention but other greenhouse gas concentrations are also increasing (Figure 13.5). Methane levels have increased largely due to agricultural expansion to feed a growing world population. Methane is formed by decomposition processes and is emitted from the intestinal tracts of livestock and from flooded rice paddies. Nitrous oxide emissions are a byproduct of increased fertilizer use, again a consequence of agricultural expansion and intensification.

Warming of the climate system during the 20th and early 21st centuries was unequivocal. The global average temperature increased 0.76°C from the 1850–1899 period to 2001–2005, with an increased rate of warming occurring in the past 50 years. The

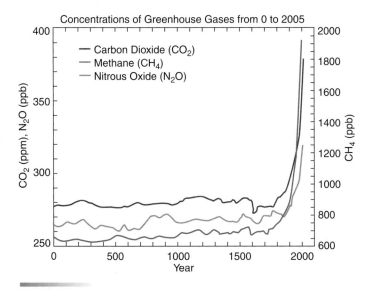

Figure 13.5 Trends in greenhouse gases are upward and due to human activities.

Source: Intergovernmental Panel on Climate Change, Climate Change 2007. The Physical Science Basis, Figure 6-4, 2007.

global mean temperature evidence is supported by shrinking glaciers and ice caps, rising sea levels, rising ocean temperatures, and satellite and weather balloon measurements of temperatures above the earth's surface. The pattern of high and increasing average global temperatures has continued into the 21st century when nearly every year has been pronounced the warmest ever recorded.

Because of the time lag in anthropogenic climate change, temperatures would continue to rise even if carbon dioxide amounts were stabilized at today's levels. If temperatures rise by the "best estimate" made in 2007 by the United Nations' Intergovernmental Panel on Climate Change (IPCC) of 1.8 to 4°C (3.2 to 7.2°F) over the 21st century, the effects on world climates would be profound. The panel, a United Nations and World Meteorological Organization group of more than 2000 scientists from around the world, was established in 1988 to assess the science of climate change, determine the impact of any changes on the environment and society, and formulate strategies to respond.

Past IPPC assessments and predictions were received with skepticism by some who disputed the role of humans in global warming. Those doubters noted that nearly half the observed atmospheric warming occurred before 1940 even though almost all the increased production of carbon dioxide and other greenhouse gases came after that date. Skeptics further argued that every millennium since the end of the last Ice Age has had one or two centuries in which temperatures rose by at least as much as they have in the last 100 years. Those arguments appear now to have been effectively refuted by the IPPC's 2007 assertion in its Fourth Assessment Report that it was at least 90% certain that human emissions of greenhouse gases rather than natural variations are responsible for warming Earth's surface. A 2006 review of available evidence by the federal Climate Change Science Program reached the same conclusion: that there is "clear evidence" of climate change caused by human activities and that trends over the last 50 years "cannot be explained by natural processes alone." Pinpointing the blame, the IPCC reported it was 99% sure that

humankind's reliance on fossil fuels—coal, fuel oil, and natural gas—was the culprit in global warming.

Whatever the causes of global heating and to whatever sources these are attributed, climatologists agree on certain of its general consequences in addition to—and the result of—increasing temperatures:

- Arctic summer sea ice is likely to disappear in the second half of the century.
- Sea levels will rise by 28 to 43 cm (11 to 17 in.) by 2100, with an additional 10 to 20 cm (4 to 8 in.) possible if recent accelerated melting of polar ice continues.
- Islands and coastal areas—including densely settled river deltas—will be inundated, affecting the livelihoods and existence of millions.
- There will be spreading droughts in southern Europe, the Middle East, sub-Saharan Africa, the American Southwest, and Mexico.
- Many world regions facing the greatest risk or certainty of adverse environmental change are among the world's poorest; damage and misery will not be evenly shared.
- Many parts of the world will see an increase in the number of heat waves and an increase in the intensity of tropical storms.
- If climate change proceeds as the IPPC projects, there will be mass extinctions of perhaps one-fourth of the world's species within 100 years.

The onset of these and other human-induced environmental changes is clearly evident. For example, between 1978 and 2005, the coverage of Arctic sea ice in winter decreased by more than 1.2 million square kilometers (almost a half million square miles)—equivalent to an area twice the size of Texas. Further, the average thickness of Arctic ice over the same period declined by 42%, from 3.1 to 1.8 meters (10.2 to 5.9 ft), and open water in August has been observed at the North Pole since 2000. Melting sea ice itself would have no effect on sea levels; however, the already significant melting of the Greenland ice sheet and accelerating retreat of mountain glaciers throughout the world is adding to ocean volumes. Already, sea levels that rose between 15 and 20 cm (6–9 in.) in the 20th century are causing serious coastal erosion and inundation, and even a conceivable 1-meter (3-foot) rise would be enough to cover the Maldives and other low-lying island countries. The homes of between 50 and 100 million people would be inundated, a fifth of Egypt's arable land in the Nile Delta would be flooded, and the impact on the people of the Bangladesh chars would be catastrophic.

Other trends now also seem clear. The prolonged crippling early 21st century droughts in Australia and the American Southwest emphasize the likelihood of the predicted desert advances. In all drought-prone areas of the world, aridity has become more intense and enduring since the 1970s. Earlier IPCC assessments warned that much of the continental interiors of middle latitudes would receive less precipitation than they do now and suffer at least periodic drought if not absolute aridity. More frequent droughts are likely in the U.S. corn and wheat belts, drastically reducing agricultural productivity, bringing to near ruin the rural economy, and altering world patterns of food supply and trade. Higher temperatures and less snowpack would translate into significantly reduced flows of such western rivers as the Colorado, cutting back the water supply of major southwestern cities and irrigated farming districts. In other world areas, the torrential rains and consequent destructive floods of the early 21st century are predicted to increase in severity and frequency. And in many regions, winters no longer get cold enough to kill off a variety of insect pests and diseases formerly kept at lower latitudes and elevations.

Not all the projected impacts of climate change are negative. The IPPC also observed that climate shifts could benefit some regions, though benefits will inevitably be balanced by penalties. It projected more rainfall and longer growing seasons in high latitudes, for example; Canada, Scandinavia, and Siberia will have improved agricultural prospects, even as precipitation is declining in already arid regions of lower latitudes. By 2005, the growing season north of 45°N was already more than 12 days longer than it had been in the mid-20th century, and summer temperatures in Siberia were their warmest in 1000 years. In North America, crop patterns could shift northward, making the northern Great Lakes states and Canada the favored agricultural heartland climatically, though without the rich soil base supporting the present patterns and volumes of production. On average, some climatologists conclude, established middle and upper middle latitude farm districts would be net beneficiaries of global warming through longer growing seasons and faster crop growth resulting from extra atmospheric carbon. Skeptics, however, remind us that a scientific rule of thumb is that a one degree centigrade (1.8°F) rise in temperature above the optimum reduces grain yields by 10%. Long-term studies clearly document the temperature rise/ and yield decline ratio for rice, the staple food for most of the world's expanding population. Greater summer warmth, that is, might reduce, not increase farm productivity.

Because of the effects of decreasing snow and ice cover, higher latitudes will be relatively more heated than equatorial regions. In recent decades, average temperatures in the Arctic have increased almost twice as fast as they have in the rest of the world. Among the consequences of that northward shift of warmth is an already observed 80 to 100 kilometer (50 to 60 mile) poleward shift of the ranges of many animal and bird species. Similar latitudinal shifts in plant associations can be assumed, though they will be slower to materialize. Shifts in structure and distribution of ecosystems and biomes will be inevitable. One 2005 study, for example, foresees the eventual disappearance of the Arctic tundra biome, the loss of Alaska's evergreen boreal forest, and the conversion of that state into a largely temperate zone. Arctic seaways will become more open, finally realizing the long-sought and economical Northwest Passage through the northern seas, though the economy and culture of the Inuit will at the same time be irreversibly altered or destroyed.

Global climate change would impact most severely, of course, on developing countries highly dependent on natural, unmanaged environments for their economic support. Agriculture, hunting and gathering, forestry, and coastal fishing have that dependency, but even in those economic sectors the impact of greenhouse warming is not certain. Studies suggest that warming would reduce yields in many crops, but also that the associated fertilization effect of higher carbon dioxide content would probably offset the negative impact of warming, at least for the next century. Indeed, the

UN's Food and Agriculture Organization observes that global crop productivity could increase by up to 30% if the concentration of carbon dioxide doubles as they foresee over the next 50 years. But certainly, small and poor countries with great dependence on agriculture are potentially most at risk from projected climatic changes. The lower-latitude states would be most vulnerable as increased heat and higher evaporation rates would greatly stress wheat, maize, rice, and soybean crops. Most economic activities in industrialized countries do not have a close dependency on natural ecosystems. The consensus is that the impacts of climate change on diversified developed countries are likely to be small, at least over the next half-century.

Nevertheless, on the world scene, any significant continuing deviation from the present norm would at the very least disrupt existing patterns of economy, productivity, and population-supporting potential. Certainly, the patterns of climates and biomes developed since the last glaciation (Figure 13.2) would be drastically altered. At the worst, severe and pervasive changes could result in a total restructuring of the landscapes of culture and the balances of human–environmental relationships presently established. Nothing, from population distributions to the relative strength of countries, would ever be quite the same again. Such grim predictions were the background for major international conferences and treaty proposals of the 1990s seeking to address and limit the dangers prophesied.

Those conferences culminated in the Kyoto Protocol of 1997 that set variable requirements for national reductions of greenhouse gas emissions below 1990 levels by 2012: the European Union goal was set at an 8% reduction, the United States at 7%, Japan at 5%, for example. To avoid inhibiting their industrial and economic growth, no goals were set for developing countries. The Protocol became a binding part of international law after Russia, the last of the required total of 55 countries, ratified the agreement in February 2005. The United States stood out among industrialized nations when in 2001 President George W. Bush. withdrew from the Kyoto Protocol, refusing to ratify the treaty. However, as of early 2009, the United States indicated interest in working on a new treaty that would fix some of the flaws of the Kyoto Protocol. In the meantime, there is much that can be done to reduce greenhouse gas emissions and much is being done where the right information and incentives are in place. Energy conservation and a switch to renewable energy sources are the most important steps since most greenhouse gases are the result of fossil fuel combustion. Germany, Denmark, and the United Kingdom are just some of the many countries that have shown that energy efficiency and a switch to renewable energy sources can allow economic growth while reducing greenhouse gas emissions (Figure 13.6).

Air Pollution and Acid Precipitation

Every day thousands of tons of pollutants are discharged into the air by natural events and human actions. Air is polluted when it contains substances in sufficient amounts and concentrations to have a harmful effect on living things and human-made objects. Truly clean air has never existed, for atmospheric pollution can and does result in nature from ash from volcanic eruptions, marsh

Figure 13.6 **Technologies for reducing greenhouse gas emissions** are part of the solution as suggested by the IPAT equation. Denmark is a world leader in wind energy, generating about 20% of its electricity in 2007 with renewable wind power, mostly in offshore turbine installations. The Beddington Zero Energy Development (BedZed) is one of many examples of an eco-community. At BedZed in South London, passive solar heating, solar panels to generate electricity, a car-sharing club, and rooftop gardens allow residents to significantly reduce or even eliminate their emissions of greenhouse gases.

gases, smoke from naturally occurring forest fires, and wind-blown dust. Normally these pollutants are of low volume, are widely dispersed in the atmosphere, and have no significant long-term effect on air quality.

Far more damaging are the substances discharged into the atmosphere by human actions. These pollutants come primarily from burning fossil fuels—coal, oil, and gas—in power plants, factories, furnaces, and vehicles, and from fires deliberately set to clear forests and grasslands for agricultural expansion or swidden garden plot clearing and renewal. Air pollution is a global problem; areas far from the polluting activity may be adversely impacted as atmospheric circulation moves pollutants freely without regard to political or other earth-based boundaries.

For example, current full-color satellite cameras regularly reveal a nearly continuous, 2-mile-thick blanket of soot, organic compounds, dust, ash, and other air debris stretching across much of India, Bangladesh, and Southeast Asia, reaching northward to the industrial heart of China. The pollution shroud in and around India, researchers find, reduces sunlight there by 10%, enough to cut rice yields by 3% to 10% across much of the country. The World Health Organization (WHO) reports that of India's 23 cities of more than 1 million people, not one meets the organization's air pollution standards. In southern China and Southeast Asia, as many as 1.4 million people die annually from respiratory ills caused by human-induced pollution that drifts across the Pacific to the Western Hemisphere and beyond.

In addition to the very serious human health consequences of air pollution, the interaction of pollutants with each other or with natural atmospheric constituents such as water vapor may create derivative pollutants highly damaging to vegetation, surface and groundwater, and structures. Among these secondary agents is the acid precipitation that is the second of the recent trio of environmental concerns.

Unexpectedly, acid precipitation is a condition in part traceable to actions taken in developed countries in past decades to alleviate the smoke and soot that poured into the skies from the chimneys of their power plants, mills, and factories. The

Figure 13.7 Before concern with acid rain became widespread, the U.S. Clean Air Act of 1970 set standards for ground-level air quality that could be met most easily by building smokestacks high enough to discharge pollutants into the upper atmosphere. Stacks 300 meters (1000 feet) and more high became a common sight at utility plants and factories, far exceeding the earlier norm of 60–90 meters (200–300 feet). What helped cleanse one area of pollution greatly increased damage elsewhere. The farther and higher the noxious emissions go, the longer they have to combine with other atmospheric components and moisture to form acids. Thus, the taller stacks directly aggravated the acid precipitation problem. Recognizing this, the Environmental Protection Agency in 1985 issued rules discouraging the use of tall smokestacks to disperse emissions. The Clean Air Act Amendments of 1990 required that sulfur dioxide and nitrogen oxide emissions from smokestacks be cut in half.

urban smoke abatement and clean air programs demanded by environmentalists usually incorporated prohibitions against the discharge of atmospheric pollutants damaging to areas near the discharge point. The response was to raise smokestacks to such a height that smoke, soot, and gases were carried far from their origin points by higher elevation winds (Figure 13.7).

But when power plants, smelters, and factories were fitted with tall smokestacks to free local areas from pollution, the sulfur dioxide and nitrogen oxides in the smoke were pumped high into the atmosphere instead of being deposited locally. There they mixed with water and other chemicals and turned into sulfuric and nitric acid that was carried to distant areas. They were joined in their impact by other sources of acid gases. Motor vehicles are particularly prolific producers of nitrogen oxides in their exhausts.

Once the pollutants are airborne, winds can carry them hundreds of kilometers, depositing them far from their source. In North America, most of the prevailing winds are westerlies, meaning that much of the acid precipitation that falls on the eastern seaboard and eastern Canada originated in the central and upper Midwest. Similarly, airborne pollutants from the United Kingdom, France, and Germany cause acidification problems in Scandinavia (Figure 13.8).

When acids from all sources are washed out of the air by rain, snow, or fog the result is **acid precipitation.** Acidity levels are described by the *pH factor,* the measure of acidity/alkalinity on a scale of 0 to 14. The average pH of normal rainfall is 5.6, slightly acidic, but acid rainfalls with a pH of 2.4—approximately the acidity of vinegar and lemon juice—have been recorded. Primarily occurring in industrialized nations, acid precipitation has become a serious problem in many parts of Europe, North America, and Japan. It expresses itself in several forms, though the most visible are its corrosive effects on marble and limestone sculptures and buildings and on metals such as iron and bronze (Figure 13.9) and in the destruction of forests. Trees at higher elevations are particularly susceptible, with widespread forest loss clearly apparent on the hillsides and mountain tops of New England, Scandinavia, and Germany, where acid precipitation had apparently degraded much of that country's famous forests by the early 1990s.

Damage to lakes, fish, and soils is less immediately evident, but more widespread and equally serious. Acid precipitation has been linked to the disappearance of fish in thousands of streams and lakes in New England, Canada, and Scandinavia, and to a decline in fish populations elsewhere. It leaches toxic constituents such as aluminum salts from the soil and kills soil microorganisms that break down organic matter and recycle nutrients through the ecosystem. Acid deposition can harm and decrease yields of many food crops and increase the content of poisonous heavy metals in drinking water supplies.

The Trouble with Ozone

The forest damage usually blamed exclusively on acid rain has, on closer investigation, proved to be at least partially the product of ozone poisoning. **Ozone** is a molecule consisting of three oxygen atoms rather than the two of normal oxygen. Sunlight produces it from standard oxygen, and a continuous but thin layer of ozone accumulates at upper levels in the atmosphere. There it is beneficial because it blocks the cancer-causing ultraviolet (UV) light that damages DNA, the molecule of heredity and cell control. That upper atmospheric shield now appears in danger of destruction by chemicals released into the air by humans (see "Depleting the Ozone Layer").

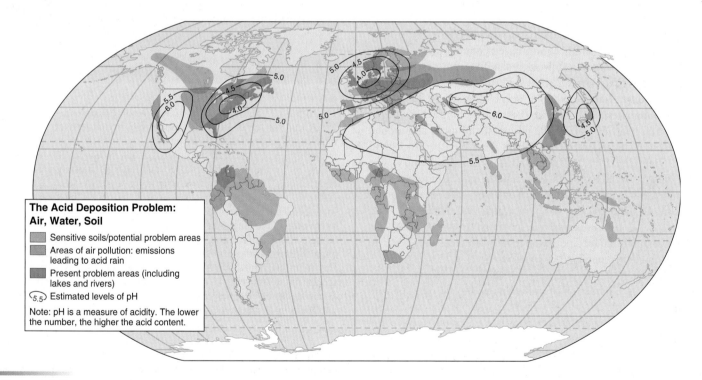

The Acid Deposition Problem:
Air, Water, Soil

- Sensitive soils/potential problem areas
- Areas of air pollution: emissions leading to acid rain
- Present problem areas (including lakes and rivers)
- (5.5) Estimated levels of pH

Note: pH is a measure of acidity. The lower the number, the higher the acid content.

Figure 13.8 Acid precipitation: areas of origin and of current problems. Prevailing winds can deposit acid precipitation far from its area of origin and across international boundaries. The acids in the precipitation harm or destroy soils, vegetation, aquatic life, and buildings. Compare this map with the centers of industrial production in Figure 9.17.

Source: Student Atlas of World Geography, *4th ed. John Allen, Map 55, p. 70. McGraw-Hill/Dushkin, 2005.*

(a)

(b)

Figure 13.9 **The formation and effects of acid precipitation.**
(*a*) Sulfur dioxide and nitrogen oxides produced by the combustion of
fossil fuels are transformed into sulfate and nitrate particles; when the
particles react with water vapor, they form sulfuric and nitric acids,
which then fall to earth. (*b*) The destructive effect of acid rain is evident
on this limestone statuary at the cathedral in Reims, France.

At lower levels, however, the problem is accumulation, not
depletion, of ozone. Relatively harmless to humans, ozone is inju-
rious to plants. Exposed to too much of it, their growth may be
stunted, their yields reduced (by as much as 30% for wheat), or
they may even die. That, apparently, is an important contributor
to forest damage and destruction commonly attributed to acid

precipitation. In the lower atmosphere, ozone is produced in *photochemical smogs* by sunlight and pollution, with the main pol-
lutant being motor vehicle exhaust fumes (Figure 13.10). Their
nitrogen oxides and hydrocarbons are particularly good at converting oxygen to ozone. The resulting smog, unlike the ozone
alone, has serious adverse consequences for human respiratory

In the summer of 1986, scientists for the first time verified that a "hole" had formed in the ozone layer over Antarctica. In fact, the ozone was not entirely absent, but it had been reduced from earlier recorded levels by some 40%. As a result, Antarctic life—particularly the microscopic ocean plants (phytoplankton) at the base of the food chain—that had lived more or less in ultraviolet (UV) darkness was suddenly getting a trillionfold (1 followed by 12 zeros) increase above the natural rate of UV receipt.

The ozone hole typically occurs over Antarctica during late August through early October and breaks up in mid-November. From 1987 when the ozone loss was 60% to 2000 when more than 85% of ozone in the lower stratosphere was destroyed, the hole grew larger, lasted longer, and spread farther outward each year toward South America and Australia. The NASA satellite image shows the pattern of ozone depletion during September, 2003, when the gap at its largest extent measured 29 million square kilometers (11.2 million sq mi), an area almost as large as Africa (30.3 million sq km; 11.3 million sq mi). The color scale below the image shows the total ozone levels; the dark blues and purples indicate the areas of greatest ozone depletion.

Most observers attribute the ozone decline to pollution from human-made chemicals, particularly *chlorofluorocarbons* (CFCs) used as coolants, cleansing agents, propellants for aerosols, and in insulating foams. In a chain reaction of oxygen destruction, each of the chlorine atoms released can over time destroy upwards of 10,000 ozone molecules. Ozone reduction is a continuing and spreading atmospheric problem. A similar ozone hole about the size of Greenland opens in the Arctic, too, and the ozone shield over the midlatitudes has dropped significantly since 1978.

Why should the hole in the ozone layer have appeared first so prominently over Antarctica? In most parts of the world, horizontal winds tend to keep chemicals in the air well mixed. But circulation patterns are such that the freezing whirlpool of air over the south polar continent in winter is not penetrated by air currents from warmer earth regions. In the absence of sunlight and atmospheric mixing, the CFCs work to destroy the ozone. During the Southern Hemisphere summer, sunlight works to replenish it. In either Hemisphere,

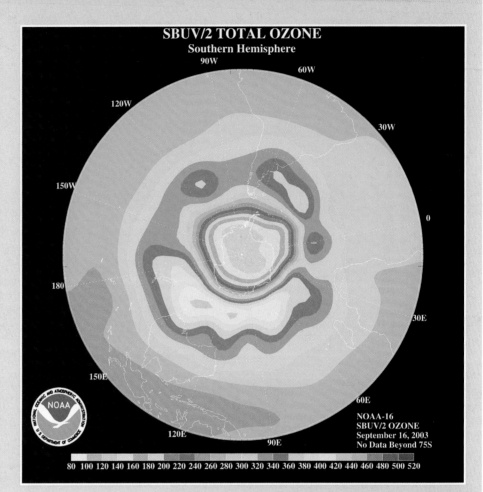

SBUV/2 TOTAL OZONE
Southern Hemisphere

NOAA-16
SBUV/2 OZONE
September 16, 2003
No Data Beyond 75S

80 100 120 140 160 180 200 220 240 260 280 300 320 340 360 380 400 420 440 460 480 500 520

ozone depletion has identical adverse effects. Among other things, increased exposure to UV radiation increases the incidence of skin cancer and, by suppressing bodily defense mechanisms, increases risk from a variety of infectious diseases. Many crop plants are sensitive to UV radiation, and the very existence of the microscopic plankton at the base of the marine food chain is threatened by it.

Some scientists dispute both the existence and the cause of ozone layer depletion and claim "there is no observational evidence that man-made chemicals like CFCs are dangerously thinning the ozone layer. . . ." Nevertheless, production and use of CFCs is being phased out under the Montreal Protocol, a 1987 international agreement made effective in 1992, that requires production of CFCs be ended. The developing countries were given a grace period before they began their phase-out schedule for ending use

of CFCs. Industries involved in the production or use of CFCs initially resisted the agreement but have since responded by finding substitute chemicals. The Montreal Protocol is an encouraging example of the ability of international agreements to successfully address a global environmental problem. Because of those restrictions, ozone depletion is being slowed and even reversed.

Recent oscillations in the extent of the ozone hole suggest its peak may have been reached by 2003 to 2006 although that expectation has been tempered by evidence that ozone-depleting chemicals are still, despite the Montreal Protocol, leaking into the atmosphere from old appliance discharges in the United States and Canada. As a result, the earlier predicted date by which the hole should be mended has been postponed from 2050 to perhaps 2075.

(b)

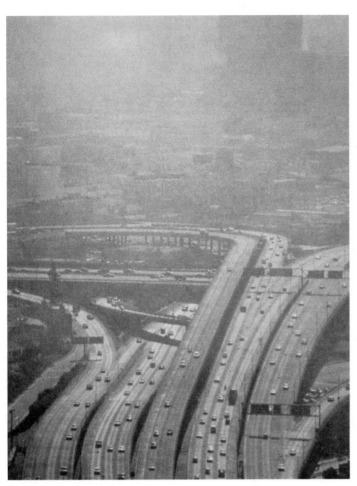

(a)

Figure 13.10 (*a*) Photochemical smog in sunny California during the late 1970s. When air remains stagnant over Los Angeles, it can accumulate increasing amounts of automobile and industrial exhausts, reducing afternoon sunlight to a dull haze and sharply lifting ozone levels. Such occurrences are increasingly rare in Los Angeles—where peak levels of ozone have dropped to a quarter of their 1955 levels—and in other major American cities with past serious smog and ozone dangers. Mandates of the Clean Air Act and, particularly, more stringent restrictions on automobile emissions promise continued improvements in metropolitan air quality. (*b*) The Germans call it *Waldsterben*—forest death—a term now used more widely to summarize the destruction of trees by a combination of ozone, heavy metals, and acidity in clouds, rain, snow, and dust. It first strikes at higher elevations where natural stresses are greatest and acidic clouds most prevalent, but it slowly moves downslope until entire forests are gone. Here at Mount Mitchell in North Carolina, *Waldsterben* is thought to result from pollution traveling eastward from the Ohio and Tennessee valleys. Forests throughout eastern Anglo America from Georgia northward into Canada display evidence of similar pollution-related damage as do forests in the Front Range of Colorado and the San Gabriel Mountains near Los Angeles. Similar impacts are increasingly seen in Europe.

health. The increasing use of automobiles in Europe, not acid precipitation, has done the harm to that continent's forests, a fact that explains the rise of forest destruction during the same years that sulfur dioxide emissions from power plants were being significantly reduced.

There is an element of presumed irreversibility in both global climate change and ozone depletion. Once the processes creating them are launched, they tend to become cumulative and continuous. Even if carbon dioxide levels stayed as they are now, temperatures would continue to climb. Even if all CFCs were immediately banned and no more were released into the atmosphere, it would take more than a century to replenish the ozone already lost. Since population growth, industrial development, and chemical pollution will continue—though perhaps under tighter control—assaults upon the atmosphere will also continue rather than cease. The same disquieting irreversibility seems to characterize three other processes of environmental degradation: *tropical deforestation; desertification* of cropland, grazing areas, and deforested lands; and air, land, and water *pollution*. Each stands alone as an identified problem of global concern, and each is a component part of cumulative human pressures upon the biosphere greater than its recuperative powers can handle.

Land Use and Land Cover

Since the beginning of the 19th century, vast portions of the earth's surface have been modified, whole ecosystems destroyed, and global biomes altered or eliminated. North American and European native forests have largely vanished; the grasslands of interior United States, Canada, and Ukraine have been converted into farmland. Marshes and wetlands have been drained, dams built, and major water impoundments created. Steppe lands have become deserts; deserts have blossomed under irrigation.

Tropical Deforestation

Forests, we saw in Chapter 8, still cover some 30% of the earth's land surface (see Figure 8.30), though the forest biomes have suffered mightily as human pressures on them have increased. Forest clearing accompanied the development of agriculture and spread of people throughout Europe, Central Asia, the Middle East, and India. European colonization had much the same impact on the temperate forests of eastern North America and Australasia. In most midlatitude developed countries, although original forest cover is largely gone, replanting and reversion of cropland to timber has tended to replenish woodlands at about their rate of cutting.

Now it is the tropical rain forest biome that is feeling the pressure of growing population numbers, the need for more agricultural land, particularly for soy bean cultivation, expanded demand for fuel and commercial wood, and a midlatitude market for beef that can be satisfied profitably by replacing tropical forest with cleared grazing land. These disappearing forests—covering no more than 6% of the planet's land surface—extend across parts of Asia, Africa, and Latin America, and are the world's most diverse and least understood biome. About 45% of their original expanse has already been cleared or degraded. Africa has lost more than half of its original rain forest; nearly half of Asia's is gone; 70% of the moist forests of Central America and some 40% of those of South America have disappeared. Every year, the International Tropical Timber Organization reported in 2006, 12 million hectares (46,000 sq. mi) are cleared for agriculture and other purposes. Tropical forest removal raises three principal global concerns and a host of local ones.

First, on a worldwide basis, all forests play a major role in maintaining the oxygen and carbon balance of the earth. This is particularly true of tropical forests because of their total area and volume. Humans and their industries consume oxygen; vegetation replenishes it through photosynthesis and the release of oxygen back into the atmosphere as a by-product. At the same time, plants extract the carbon from atmospheric carbon dioxide, acting as natural retaining sponges for the gas so important in the greenhouse effect. Each year, each hectare (2.47 acres) of Amazon rain forest absorbs a ton of carbon dioxide. When the tropical rain forest is cleared, not only is its role as a carbon sink lost but the act of destruction itself through decomposition or burning releases as carbon dioxide the vast quantities of carbon the forest had stored.

A second global concern is also climate related. Forest destruction changes surface and air temperatures, moisture content, and reflectivity. Conversion of forest to grassland, for example, increases surface temperature, raises air temperatures above the treeless ground, and therefore increases the water-holding capacity of the warmer air. As winds move the hotter, drier air, it tends to exert a drying effect on adjacent forest and agricultural lands. Trees and crops outside the denuded area experience heat and aridity stresses not normal to their geographical locations. It is calculated that cutting the forests of South America on a wide scale should raise regional temperatures from 3°C to 5°C (5.5–9°F), which in turn would extend the dry season and greatly disrupt not only regional but global climates. Demonstrated North American effects of the wholesale forest clearing in the Amazon include severely reduced rainfall in the Gulf of Mexico, Texas, and northern Mexico during the spring and summer growing seasons. Similarly, deforesting in central Africa adversely affects precipitation patterns in the North American Midwest.

In some ways, the most serious long-term global consequence of the eradication of tropical rain forests will be the loss of a major part of the biological diversity of the planet. Of the estimated 5–10 million plant and animal species believed to exist on earth, a minimum of 40% to 50%—and possibly 70% or more—are native to the tropical rain forest biome. Many of the plants have become important world staple food crops: rice, millet, cassava, yam, taro, banana, coconut, pineapple, and sugarcane to name but a very few well-known ones. Unknown additional potential food species

remain as yet unexploited. Reports from Indonesia suggest that in that country's forests alone, some 4000 plant species have proved useful to native peoples as foodstuffs of one sort or another, though less than one-tenth have come into wide use. The rain forests are, in addition, the world's main storehouse of drug-yielding plants and insects, including thousands with proven or prospective anticancer properties and many widely used as sources of antibiotics, antivirals, analgesics, tranquilizers, diuretics, and laxatives, among a host of other items. The loss of the zoological and botanical storehouse that the rain forests represent would deprive humans of untold potential benefits that might never be realized.

On a more local basis, tropical forests play for their inhabitants and neighbors the same role taken by forests everywhere. They protect watersheds and regulate water flow. After forest cutting, unregulated flow accentuates the problems of high and low water variations, increases the severity of valley flooding, and makes more serious and prolonged the impact of low water flow on irrigation agriculture, navigation, and urban and rural water supply. Accelerated **soil erosion**—the process of removal of soil particles from the ecosystem, usually by wind or running water—quickly removes the always thin, infertile tropical forest soils from deforested areas. Lands cleared for agriculture almost immediately become unsuitable for that use partially because of soil loss. The surface material removed is transported and deposited downstream, changing valley contours, extending the area subject to flooding, and filling irrigation and drainage channels. Or it may be deposited in the reservoirs behind the increasing number of major dams on rivers within the tropical rain forests or rising there (see "Dam Trouble in the Tropics").

Desertification

The tropical rain forests can succumb to deliberate massive human assaults and be irretrievably lost. With much less effort, and with no intent to destroy or alter the environment, humans are assumed to be similarly affecting the arid and semiarid regions of the world. The process is called **desertification,** the expansion or intensification of areas of degraded or destroyed soil and vegetation cover. While the Earth Summit of 1992 defined desertification broadly as "land degradation in arid, semiarid and dry subhumid areas, resulting from climatic variations and human activities," the process is often charged to increasing human pressures exerted through overgrazing, deforestation for fuel wood, clearing of original vegetation for cultivation, and burning, and implies a continuum of ecological alteration from slight to extreme (Figure 13.11).

Both satellite measurements and paleoclimatological studies, however, are forcing a reassessment of what is really happening to arid and semiarid drylands along the perimeter of the Sahara and other major world deserts. Imagery dating from 1980 indicates that the Sahel drylands region on the southern border of the Sahara, for example, did not move steadily south as usually assumed. Rather, the vegetation line fluctuated back and forth in response to variable rainfall patterns, with year to year shifts ranging between 30 and 150 miles. Indeed, satellite data show that the desert has been slowly retreating all across the region since the late 1980s, giving way to resurgent young forests and increasing crop production.

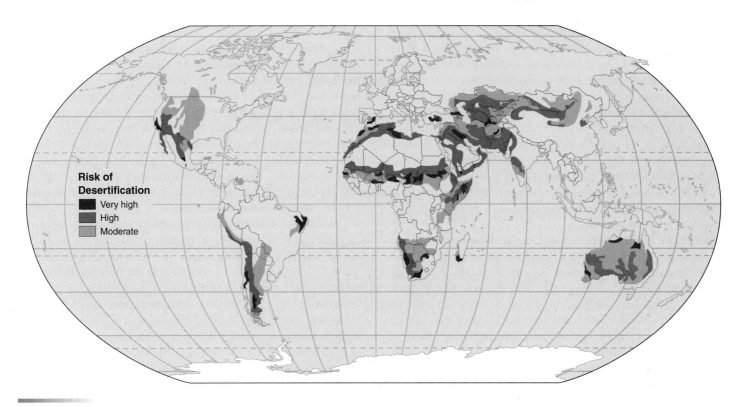

Figure 13.11 Desertification, affecting about 1 billion people in 110 countries, is usually understood to imply the steady advance of the margins of the world's deserts into their bordering drylands, converting through human mistreatment formerly productive or usable pastures and croplands into barren and sterile landscapes. In reality, the process may result from natural climatic fluctuations as much as from human abuse; local and regional variations in those two causal conditions are reflected in the reversal or stabilization of desertification in some areas. Because of different criteria, areas shown as "desert" here are not identical to desert regions of Figure 13.2. See also Figure 13.15.

Sources: Based on H.E. Dregne, Desertification of Arid Lands, *Figure 1.2, 1983 Harwood Academic Publishers; and* A World Map of Desertification, *UNESCO/FAO.*

Dam Trouble in the Tropics

The great tropical river systems have a sizable percentage of the world's undeveloped power potential. The lure of that power and its promise for economic development and national modernization have proved nearly irresistible. But the tropical rain forests have been a particularly difficult environment for dam builders. The dams (and their reservoirs) often carry a heavy ecological price, and the clearing and development of the areas they are meant to serve often assure the destruction of the dam projects themselves.

The creation of Brokopondo in Suriname in 1964 marked the first large reservoir in a rain forest locale. Without being cleared of their potentially valuable timber, 1480 square kilometers (570 sq mi) of dense tropical forest disappeared underwater. As the trees decomposed, producing hydrogen sulfide, an intolerable stench polluted the atmosphere for scores of miles downwind. For more than 2 years, employees at the dam wore gas masks

at work. Decomposition of vegetation produced acids that corroded the dam's cooling system, leading to costly continuing repairs and upkeep. Identical problems have occurred at the Tucuruí dam and reservoir in Brazil, started in 1984 and covering 2850 sq. km (1100 sq mi) of uncleared rain forest.

Water hyacinth spreads rapidly in tropical impoundments, its growth hastened by the rich nutrients released by tree decomposition. Within a year of the reservoir's completion, a 130-square-kilometer (50-sq-mi) blanket of the weed was afloat on Lake Brokopondo, and after another year almost half the reservoir was covered. Another 440 square kilometers (170 sq mi) were claimed by a floating fern, *Ceratopteris.* Identical problems plague most rain forest hydropower projects.

The expense, the disruption of the lives of valley residents whose homes are to be flooded, and the environmental damage of dam projects in the rain forest all may be in

vain. Deforestation of river banks and clearing of vegetation for permanent agriculture usually results in accelerated erosion, rapid sedimentation of reservoirs, and drastic reduction of electrical generating capacity. The Ambuklao Reservoir in the Philippines, built with an expected payback period of 60 years, now appears certain to silt up in half that time. The Anchicaya Reservoir in Colombia lost 25% of its storage capacity only 2 years after it was completed and was almost totally filled with silt within 10 years. The Peligre Dam in Haiti was completed in 1956 with a life expectancy of at least 50 years; siltation reduced its usefulness by some 15 years. El Cajon Dam in Honduras, Arenal in Costa Rica, Chixoy in Guatemala and many others—all built to last decades or even centuries—have, because of premature siltation, failed to repay their costs or fulfill their promise. The price of deforestation in wet tropics is high indeed.

Since Africa's drylands climate has shifted back and forth between periods of extended drought and higher rainfall for at least 10,000 years, many scientists now believe climate variation keeps the drylands in a continual state of disequilibrium. That, rather than human abuse of the land, is thought to be the major influence on dryland ecology and the shifting margins of deserts.

Certainly much past periodic desertification of vast areas has been induced by nature rather than by humans. Over the past 10,000 years, for example, several prolonged and severe droughts far more damaging than the "Dust Bowl" period of the 1930s converted vast stretches of the Great Plains from Texas and New Mexico to Nebraska and South Dakota into seas of windblown sand dunes like those of the Sahara. Such conditions were seen most recently in the 18th and 19th centuries, before the region was heavily settled, but after many explorers and travelers noted—as did one in 1796 in present-day Nebraska—"a great desert of drifting sand, without trees, soil, rock, water or animals of any kind." Today, those same areas are covered only thinly by vegetation and could revert to shifting desert—as they almost did in the 1930s— with a prolonged drought of the type that might accompany global warming. The U.S. Bureau of Land Management's warning that almost half of the Great Plains is prone to desertification was underscored by the prolonged drought of the late 1990s and early 21st century that, particularly in the northern plains, was the most severe in more than a century.

Whatever its causes, every year desertification makes 12 million hectares (46,000 sq mi) useless for cultivation. When desertification results from human rather than climatic causes, it begins in the same fashion: the disruption or removal of the native cover of grasses and shrubs through farming or overgrazing (Figure 13.12). If the disruption is severe enough, the original vegetation cannot reestablish itself and the exposed soil is made susceptible to erosion during the brief, heavy rains that dominate precipitation patterns in semiarid regions. Water runs off the land surface instead of seeping in, carrying soil particles with it and leaving behind an *erosion pavement.* When the water is lost through surface flow rather than seepage downward, the water table is lowered. Eventually, even deep-rooted bushes are unable to reach groundwater, and all natural vegetation is lost. The process is accentuated when too many grazing animals pack the earth down with their hooves, blocking the passage of air and water through the soil. When both plant cover and soil moisture are lost, desertification has occurred.

It happens with increasing frequency in many areas of the earth as pressures on the land continue. Worldwide, desertification affects about 1 billion people in 110 countries and impacts about 1.2 billion hectares—about the size of China and India combined. According to the United Nations—which declared 2006 the "International Year of Deserts and Desertification" to address their problems and solutions—between one-quarter and one-third of the planet's land surface now qualifies as degraded semi-desert. Africa is most at risk; the United Nations has estimated that 40% of that continent's nondesert land is in danger of human-induced desertification. But nearly a fifth of Latin America's lands and a third of Asia's are similarly endangered. China's Environmental Protection Agency reports, for example, that the country lost 94,000 square kilometers (36,000 sq mi)—an area the size of Indiana—to desert from the 1950s to early in the 21st century and each year has an additional 3900 square kilometers (1500 sq mi) buried by sand.

In countries where desertification is particularly extensive and severe (Algeria, Ethiopia, Iraq, Jordan, Lebanon, Mali, and

Figure 13.12 The margin of the desert. Intensive grazing pressure destroys vegetation, compacts soil, and leads to soil degradation and desertification, as this desert-margin view from Burkina Faso suggests. Elsewhere, the Argentine government reports a vast area in the southern part of that country has become part of an expanding desert mainly due to human activities that have degraded the lands to the point that "their use to man is practically nil" and the damage is "economically irreversible." Similarly, China reports its vast Gobi Desert is encroaching into northern crop and grazing lands at a rate of 2500 square kilometers (950 sq mi) per year as a result of overgrazing and "excessive gathering of firewood."

Figure 13.13 Windblown dust is engulfing the scrub forest in this drought-stricken area of Mali, near Timbuktu. The district is part of the Sahel region of Africa where desertification has been accelerated by both climate and human pressures on the land. From the late 1930s to 2000, some 650,000 square kilometers (250,000 sq mi) were added to the southern Sahara. It has expanded on its northern and eastern margins as well. On an annual basis, marginal fluctuation rather than steady expansion is the rule, and some scientists prefer to speak of an "ebb and flow" of the Sahara margins and of land degradation rather than of permanent conversion to true desert.

Niger) per capita food production declined by nearly half between 1950 and 2000 while in the Sahel as a whole, population expanded fourfold between 1930 and 2005, with continuing growth predicted. The resulting threat of starvation spurs populations of the affected areas to increase their farming and livestock pressures on the denuded land, further contributing to their desertification. It has been suggested that Mali may be the first country in the world rendered uninhabitable by environmental destruction. Many of its more than 11 million inhabitants begin their day by shoveling their doorways clear of the night's accumulation of sand (Figure 13.13). The United Nations has identified desertification as a major barrier to poverty elimination in arid regions and has established programs to fight desertification (Figure 13.14).

Soil Erosion

Desertification is but one expression of land deterioration leading to accelerated soil erosion, a worldwide problem of biosphere deterioration. Over much of the earth's surface, the thin layer of topsoil upon which life

Figure 13.14 **Fighting desertification in Nigeria** with a nursery support by the United Nations International Fund for Agricultural Development.

depends is only a few inches deep, usually less than 30 centimeters (1 ft). Below it, the lithosphere is as lifeless as the surface of the moon. A **soil** is a complex mixture of rock particles, inorganic mineral matter, organic material, living organisms, air, and water. Under natural conditions, soil is constantly being formed by the physical and chemical decomposition of rock material and by the decay of organic matter. It is simultaneously being eroded, for soil erosion is as natural a process as soil formation and occurs even when land is totally covered by forests or grass. Under most natural conditions, however, the rate of soil formation equals or exceeds the rate of soil erosion, so soil depth and fertility tend to increase with time.

When land is cleared and planted to crops or when the vegetative cover is broken by overgrazing, deforestation, or other disturbances, the process of erosion inevitably accelerates. When its rate exceeds that of soil formation, the life-sustaining veneer of topsoil becomes thinner and eventually disappears, leaving behind only sterile subsoil or barren rock. At that point the renewable soil resource has been converted through human impact into a nonrenewable and dissipated asset. Carried to the extreme of bare rock hillsides or wind-denuded plains, erosion spells the total end of agricultural use of the land. Throughout history, such extreme human-induced destruction has occurred and been observed with dismay.

Any massive destruction of the soil resource could spell the end of the civilization it had supported. For the most part, however, farmers—even those in difficult climatic and topographic circumstances—devised ingenious ways to preserve and even improve the soil resource on which their lives and livelihoods depended. Particularly when farming was carried on outside of fertile, level valley lands, farmers' practices were routinely based on some combination of crop rotation, fallowing, and terracing.

Rotation involves the planting of two or more crops simultaneously or successively on the same area to preserve fertility or to provide a plant cover to protect the soil. **Fallowing** leaves a field idle (uncropped) for 1 or more years to achieve one of two outcomes. In semiarid areas the purpose is to accumulate soil moisture from one year to apply to the next year's crop; in tropical wet regions, as we saw in Chapter 8, the purpose is to renew soil fertility of the swidden plot. **Terracing** (see Figure 4.23) replaces steep slopes with a series of narrow layered, level fields, providing cropland where little or none existed previously. In addition, because water moving rapidly down-slope has great erosive power, breaking the speed of flow by terracing reduces the amount of soil lost. Field trials in Nigeria indicate that cultivation on a 1% slope (a drop of 1 foot in elevation over 100 feet of horizontal distance) results in soil loss at or below the rate of soil formation; farming there on a 15% slope would totally strip a field of its soil cover in only 10 years.

Farming skills have not declined in recent years. Rather, pressures on farmlands have increased with population growth and the intensification of agriculture and clearing of land for the commercial cropping that is increasingly part of the developing countries' economies. Farming has been forced higher up on steeper slopes, more forest land has been converted to cultivation, grazing and crops have been pushed farther and more intensively

into semiarid areas, and existing fields have had to be worked more intensively and less carefully. Many traditional agricultural systems and areas that were ecologically stable and secure as recently as 1950, when world population stood at 2.5 billion and subsistence agriculture was the rule, are disintegrating under the pressures of nearly 7 billion people and a changing global economy.

The evidence of that deterioration is found in all parts of the world (Figure 13.15). The International Food Policy Research Institute reports that each year some 10 million hectares (25 million acres) of cropland worldwide are abandoned because of soil erosion and diminished production caused by erosion. Nearly 40% of the world's agricultural land is seriously degraded, though the percentages differ by region. Almost 75% of cropland in Central America shows serious degradation, as does 11% in Asia. In Africa, some 500 million hectares (1.2 billion acres) have been affected by soil erosion since the mid-1950s, including as much as 65% of agricultural land, a major factor limiting food production in that continent to, at most, an inadequate 2% annual increase.

Soil deterioration expresses itself in two ways: through decreasing yields of cultivated fields themselves and in increased stream sediment loads and downstream deposition of silt. In Guatemala, for example, some 40% of the productive capacity of the land has been lost through erosion, and several areas of the country have been abandoned because agriculture has become economically impracticable; the figure is 50% in El Salvador. In Turkey, a reported 75% of the land is affected, and 54% is severely or very severely eroded. Haiti has no high-value soil left at all. A full one-quarter of India's total land area has been significantly eroded: some 13 million hectares (32 million acres) by wind and nearly 74 million hectares (183 million acres) by water. Between 1960 and 2000, China lost more than 15% of its total arable land to erosion, desertification, or conversion to nonagricultural use; some 700,000 hectares (1.7 million acres) of cultivated land annually are taken by construction. Its Huang River is the most sediment-laden of any waterway on earth; in its middle course it is about 50% silt by weight, just under the point of liquid mud.

Off-farm erosion evidence is provided by siltation loads carried by streams and rivers and by the downstream deposition that results. In the United States, about 3 billion tons of sediment are washed into waterways each year; off-site damage in the form of reduced reservoir capacity, fish kills, dredging costs, and the like, is estimated at over $6 billion annually. The world's rivers deliver about 24 billion tons of sediment to the oceans each year, while additional billions of tons settle along stream valleys or are deposited in reservoirs (see "Dam Trouble in the Tropics").

Agricultural soil depletion through erosion—and through salt accumulation and desertification—has been called "the quiet crisis." It continues inexorably and unfolds gradually, without the abrupt attention attracted by an earthquake or volcanic explosion. Unfortunately, silent or not, productive soil loss is a crisis of growing importance and immediacy, not just in the countries of its occurrence but—because of international markets and relief programs—throughout the world.

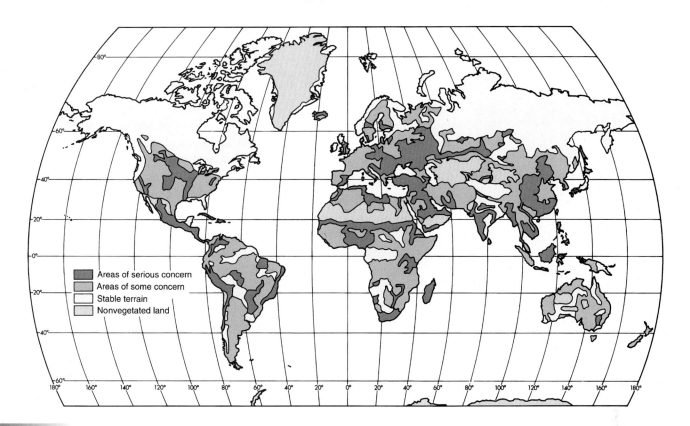

Figure 13.15 **The world pattern of soil degradation concern.** Between 1945 and 2000, nearly 2 billion hectares (almost 5 billion acres) of the world's 8.7 billion hectares (21.5 billion acres) of cropland, pastures, and forests used in agriculture—an area as large as Russia and India combined—were added to the existing total of degraded soils. Globally, about 18% of forest area, 21% of pastures, and 37% of cropland have undergone moderate to severe degradation. Water erosion accounted for 56% of that recorded deterioration, wind erosion for 28%, chemical deterioration (salinization and nutrient loss) for 12%, and physical degradation (e.g., compaction and waterlogging) for 4%.

Sources: World Resources Institute and International Soil Reference and Information Center.

Water Supply and Water Quality

Solar energy and water are the indispensable ingredients of life on earth. The supply of both is essentially constant and beyond the scope of humans to increase or alter although, as we saw with aerosols and atmospheric gases, humans can affect the quality and utility of an otherwise fixed resource. Any threat of reduction in availability or lessening of quality of a material so basic to our very lives as water is certain to arouse strong emotions and deep concerns. In many parts of the world and for many competitors for limited freshwater supplies, those emotions and concerns are already real.

The problem is not with the global amount of water, but with its distribution, its availability, and its quality. The total amount of water on the earth is enormous, though only a small part of the *hydrosphere* (see p. 420) is suitable or available for use by humans, plants, or animals (Figure 13.16). And the total amount remains constant. Water is a renewable resource; the **hydrologic cycle** assures that water, no matter how often used or how much abused, will return over and over to the earth for further exploitation (Figure 13.17). Enough rain and snow fall on the continents each year to cover the earth's total land area with 83 centimeters (33 in.) of water. It has usually been reckoned that the volume of fresh water annually renewed by the hydrologic cycle would

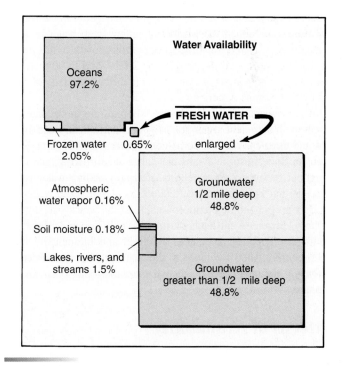

Figure 13.16 Less than 1% of the world's water supply is available for human use in freshwater lakes and rivers and from wells. An additional 2% is effectively locked in glaciers and polar ice caps.

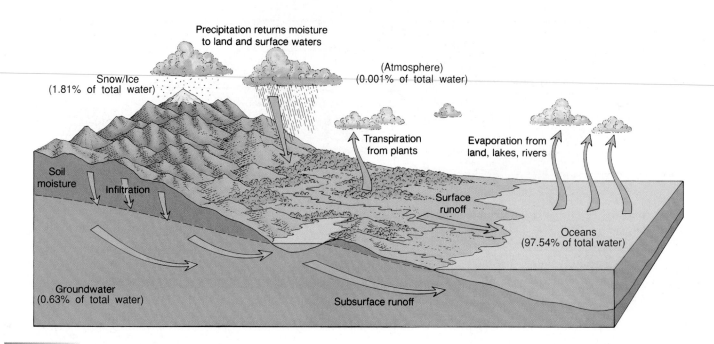

Figure 13.17 **The hydrologic cycle.** Water may change form and composition, but under natural environmental circumstances, it is marvelously purified in the recycling process and is again made available with appropriate properties and purity to the ecosystems of the earth. The sun provides energy for the evaporation of fresh and ocean water. The water is held as vapor until the air becomes supersaturated. Atmospheric moisture is returned to the earth's surface as solid or liquid precipitation to complete the cycle. Precipitation is not uniformly distributed, and moisture is not necessarily returned to areas in the same quantity as it has evaporated from them. The continents receive more water than they lose; the excess returns to the seas as surface water or groundwater. A global water balance, however, is always maintained.

meet the needs of the growing world population. Yet, over the past 75 years, as world population has tripled—with growth particularly rapid in regions of low and variable rainfall—total water demand has increased sixfold. Even now, it is generally agreed, a little more than half of the world's available fresh water is being used each year. Based on current population growth trends alone, that fraction could well rise to 74% by 2025—and to 90% should people everywhere then consume water in the current daily amount used by the average American.

In many parts of the world water supplies are inadequate and dwindling. Insufficient water for irrigation periodically endangers crops and threatens famine; permanent streams have become intermittent in flow; fresh- and saltwater lakes are shrinking; and from throughout the world come reports of rapidly falling water tables and wells that have gone dry. Reduced availability and reliability of supply are echoed in a reduced quality of the world's freshwater inventory. Increased silt loads of streams, pollution of surface and groundwater supplies, and lakes acidified and biologically dead or prematurely filled by siltation and algal growth are evidences of adverse human impact on an indispensable component of the biosphere.

Patterns of Availability

Observations about global supplies and renewal cycles of fresh water ignore the ever-present geographic reality: things are not uniformly distributed over the surface of the earth. There is no necessary relationship between the earth's pattern of

freshwater availability and the distribution of consuming populations and activities. For example, the Middle East and North Africa is home to 6.3% of the world's population but contains only 1.4% of the world's renewable fresh water. Three different world maps help us to understand why. The first, Figure 13.18, shows the spatially variable world pattern of precipitation. The second, Figure 13.3, reminds us that, as a rule, the lower the average amount of precipitation received in an area, the greater is the variability of precipitation from year to year. The recurring droughts and famines of the Sahel region of Africa are witness to the deadly impact of those expected fluctuations in areas of already low rainfall. Finally, Figure 13.19 takes account of the relationship between precipitation receipts and losses through *evapotranspiration,* the return of water from the land to the atmosphere through evaporation from soil and plants and by transpiration through plant leaves. These losses are higher in the tropics than in middle and upper latitudes, where lower rainfall amounts under cooler conditions may be more effective and useful than higher amounts received closer to the equator.

The distribution and vegetative adequacy of precipitation are givens and, except for human impact on climatic conditions, are largely independent of cultural influences. Regional water sufficiency, however, is also a function of the size of the population using the resource, its pattern of water use, and the amount of deterioration in quantity and quality the water supply experiences in the process of its use and return to the system. These are circumstances under human, not natural, control.

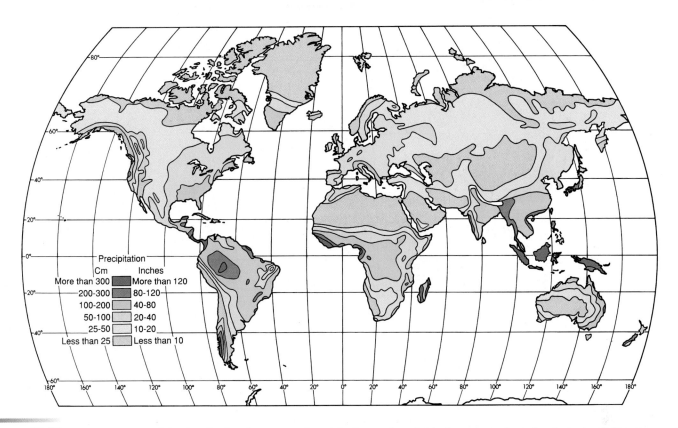

Figure 13.18 **Mean annual precipitation.** Regional contrasts of precipitation receipts clearly demonstrate the truism that natural phenomena are unequally distributed over the surface of the earth. High and very high rainfall amounts are recorded in equatorial and tropical areas of Central and South America, Africa, and South and Southeast Asia. Productive agricultural regions of North America and Europe have lower moisture receipts. The world's desert regions—in North Africa, Inner Asia, the southwestern United States, and interior Australia—are clearly marked by low precipitation totals. But not all areas of low moisture receipt are arid, as Figure 13.19 makes clear.

Water Use and Abuse

For the world as a whole, irrigated agriculture accounts for nearly three-quarters (73%) of freshwater use; in the poorest countries, the proportion is 90%. The irrigation share continues to grow worldwide as irrigation farming expands by between 5 and 6 million additional hectares (12 to 15 million acres) annually. Industry uses about one-fifth (21%) of water consumption, and domestic and recreation needs account for the remainder. World figures conceal considerable regional variation.

Irrigation agriculture produces some 40% of the world's total harvest and 60% of its grain from about 17% of its cropland. Unfortunately, in many instances the crops that are produced are worth less than the water itself; the difference is made up in the huge subsidies that governments everywhere offer to irrigation farming. In areas and economies as different as California's Napa Valley or Egypt's Nile Valley, farmers rarely pay over a fifth of the operating costs of public irrigation projects or any of their capital costs. Unfortunately, the increasing use of diesel and electrically driven pumps since the 1950s has led to extensive overpumping of **aquifers** (porous, water-bearing layers of sand, gravel, and rock). As a result, more than half the world's people live in countries where water tables are falling and wells are going dry, including the three countries that account for half the world grain harvest: China, India, and the United States.

Unfortunately as well, much of the water used for agriculture is lost to the regional supply through evaporation and transpiration; often less than half of the water withdrawn for irrigation is returned to streams or aquifers for further use. Much of that returned water, moreover, is heavily charged with salts removed from irrigated soils, making it unfit for reuse.

On the other hand, most of the water used for manufacturing processes and power production is returned to streams, lakes, or aquifers, but often in a state of pollution that renders it unsuitable for alternate and subsequent uses. Industrial water use rises dramatically with economic development, and in the developing countries, growing industrial demands compete directly with increasing requirements for irrigation and urban water supply.

Although municipal wastewater treatment is increasing in the most developed countries, 90% of raw sewage from urban areas in the developing world is discharged totally untreated into streams and oceans, contaminating surface water supplies, endangering drinking water sources, and destroying aquatic life. Fully 70% of total surface waters in India are polluted, in large part because only 8 of its more than 3000 sizable urban centers have full sewage treatment and no more than 200 have even partial management. Of Taiwan's 22 million people, only 600,000 are served by sewers. Hong Kong each day pours 1 million tons of untreated sewage and industrial waste into the sea. Mainland China's rivers also suffer from increasing pollution loads. More

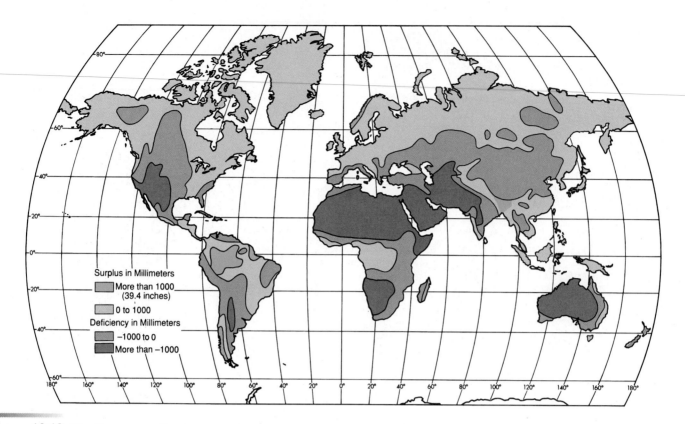

Figure 13.19 **World water supplies.** The pattern of surplus and deficit is seen in relation to the demands of the vegetation cover. Water is in surplus when precipitation is sufficient to satisfy or exceed the demands of the vegetation cover. When precipitation is lower than this potential demand, a water deficit occurs. By this measure, most of Africa (except the tropical rain forest areas of West Africa), much of the Middle East, the southwestern United States, and almost all of Australia are areas of extreme moisture deficit.

A comparison of this map with Figure 13.3 helps demonstrate the **limiting factor principle,** which notes that the single factor that is most deficient in an ecosystem is the one that determines what kind of plant and animal associations will exist there. Moisture surplus or deficit is the limiting factor that dictates whether desert, grassland, or forest will develop under natural, undisturbed conditions.

Source: Redrawn with permission from Malin Falkenmark, "Water and Mankind—A Complex System of Mutual Interaction," Ambio 6 (1977):5.

than 80% of major rivers are polluted to some degree, more than 20% to such an extent that their waters cannot be used for irrigation. Four-fifths of China's urban surface water is contaminated, only six of the country's 27 largest cities have drinking water within the state standards, and the water to be impounded by the massive Three Gorges Dam project, it is predicted, will be seriously contaminated by untreated raw sewage from the dozens of cities along the new reservoir. In Malaysia, more than 40 major rivers are so polluted that they are nearly devoid of fish and aquatic mammals. And even in developed countries of formerly communist Eastern Europe and Russia, sewage and, particularly, industrial waste seriously pollute much of the surface water supply.

When humans introduce wastes into the biosphere in kinds and amounts that the biosphere cannot neutralize or recycle, the result is **environmental pollution.** In the case of water, pollution exists when water composition has been so modified by the presence of one or more substances that either it cannot be used for a specific purpose or it is less suitable for that use than it was in its natural state. In both developed and developing countries, human pressures on freshwater supplies are now serious and pervasive concerns. If current trends of use and water abuse continue,

fresh water will certainly—and soon—become a limiting factor for economic activity, food production, and maintenance of health in many parts of the world (see "A World of Water Woes"). While clean water supplies and sewage treatment are generally taken for granted in developed countries, their absence is a major obstacle to the health, well-being, and economic development of people in the developing world (Figure 13.20). Although a few governments have begun to face the water problem—potentially one every bit as serious as atmospheric pollution, soil erosion, deforestation, and desertification—much remains to be done.

Garbage Heaps and Toxic Wastes

Humans have always managed to leave their mark on the landscapes they occupy. The search for minerals, for example, has altered whole landscapes, beginning with the pockmarks and pits marking Neolithic diggings into chalk cliffs to obtain flints or early Bronze Age excavations for tin and culminating with modern open-pit and strip-mining operations that tear minerals from the earth and create massive new landforms of depressions and rubble (Figure 13.21). Ancient irrigation systems still visible on

A World of Water Woes

Water covers almost three-quarters of the surface of the globe, yet "scarcity" is the word increasingly used to describe water-related concerns in both the developed and developing world. Globally, fresh water is abundant. Each year, an average of over 7000 cubic meters (some 250,000 cubic feet) per person enters rivers and underground reserves. But rainfall does not always occur when or where it is needed. Already, 80 countries with 40% of the world's population have serious water shortages that threaten to cripple agriculture and industry; 22 of them have renewable water resources of less than 1000 cubic meters (35,000 cubic feet) per person—a level generally understood to mean that water scarcity is a severe constraint on the economy and public health. Another 18 countries have less than 2000 cubic meters per capita on average, a dangerously low figure in years of rainfall shortage. Most of the water-short countries are in the Middle East, North Africa, and sub-Saharan Africa, the regions where populations (and consumption demands) are growing fastest. By 2025, two-thirds of the world's population are likely to be living in areas of acute water stress.

In several major crop-producing regions, water use exceeds sustainable levels, threatening future food supplies. America's largest underground water reserve, stretching from west Texas northward into South Dakota, is drying up, partially depleted by more than 150,000 wells pumping water for irrigation, city supply, and industry. In parts of Texas, Oklahoma, and Kansas, the underground water table has dropped by more than 30 meters (100 feet). In some areas, the wells no longer yield enough to permit irrigation, and farmed land is decreasing; in others, water levels have fallen so far that it is uneconomical to pump it to the surface for any use.

In many agricultural districts of northern China, west and south India, and Mexico, water scarcity limits agriculture even though national supplies are adequate. In Uzbekistan and adjacent sections of Central Asia and Kazakhstan, virtually the entire flow of the area's two primary rivers—the Amu Darya and the Syr Darya—is used for often wasteful irrigation, with little left to maintain the Aral Sea or supply growing urban populations. In Poland, the draining of bogs that formerly stored rainfall, combined with unimaginable pollution of streams and groundwater, has created a water shortage as great as that of any Middle Eastern desert country. And salinity now seriously affects productivity—or prohibits farming completely—on nearly 10% of the world's irrigated lands.

Water scarcity is often a region-wide concern. More than 200 river systems draining over half the earth's land surface are shared by two or more countries. Egypt draws on the Nile for 86% of its domestic consumption, but virtually all of that water originates in eight upstream countries. Turkey, Iraq, and Syria have frequently been in dispute over the management of the Tigris and Euphrates rivers, and the downstream states fear the effect on them of Turkish impoundments and diversions. Mexico is angered at American depletion of the Colorado before it reaches the international border.

Many coastal communities face saltwater intrusions into their drinking water supplies as they draw down their underlying freshwater aquifers, while both coastal and inland cities dependent on groundwater may be seriously depleting their underground supplies. In China, 110 mostly large cities face acute water shortages; for at least 50 of them, the problem is groundwater levels dropping on average 1 to 2 meters (3 to 6 ft) each year. In Mexico City, groundwater is pumped at rates 40% faster than natural recharge; the city has responded to those withdrawals by sinking 30 feet during the 20th century. Millions of citizens of major cities throughout the world have had their water rationed as underground and surface supplies are used beyond recharge or storage capacity.

Figure 13.20 This slum in Mumbai, India, sits atop a drainage channel and lacks access to clean water and sanitation. Waterborne diseases, mostly stemming from water supplies contaminated with human wastes, are estimated to cause 1.5 million deaths a year, mostly in young children.

Figure 13.21 About 400 square kilometers (some 150 sq mi) of land surface in the United States are lost each year to the strip-mining of coal and other minerals; far more is chewed up worldwide. On flat or rolling terrain, strip-mining leaves a landscape of parallel ridges and trenches, the result of stripping away the unwanted surface material. That material—*overburden*—taken from one trench to reach the underlying mineral is placed in an adjacent one, leaving the wavelike terrain shown here. Besides altering the topography, strip-mining interrupts surface and subsurface drainage patterns, destroys vegetation, and places sterile and frequently highly acidic subsoil and rock on top of the new ground surface. Current law not always successfully requires stripped areas to be returned to their original contours.

the landscape document both the engineering skills and the environmental alterations of early hydraulic civilizations in the Near East, North Africa, and elsewhere. The raised fields built by the Mayas of Yucatán are still traceable 1000 years after they were abandoned, and aerial photography reveals the sites of villages and patterns of fields of medieval England (Figure 13.22).

Among the most enduring of landscape evidences of human occupance, however, are not the holes deliberately dug or the structures built but the garbage produced and discarded by all societies everywhere. Prehistoric dwelling sites are located and analyzed by their *middens,* the refuse piles containing the kitchen wastes, broken tools, and other debris of human settlement. We have learned much about Roman and medieval European urban life and lifestyles by examination of the refuse mounds that grew as man-made hills in their vicinities. In the Near East, whole cities gradually rose on the mounds of debris accumulating under them (see Figure 11.7).

Modern cultures differ from their predecessors by the volume and character of their wastes, not by their habits of discard. The greater the society's population and material wealth, the greater the amount and variety of its garbage. Developed countries of the late 20th century are increasingly discovering that their material wealth and technological advancements are submerging them in a volume and variety of wastes—solid and liquid, harmless and toxic—that threaten both their environments and their established ways of life. The United States may serve as an example of situations all too common worldwide.

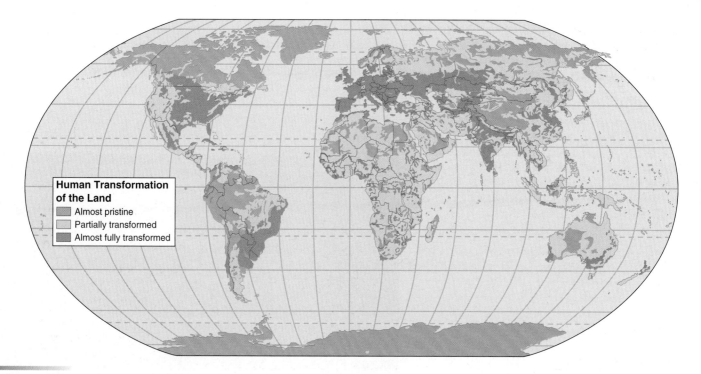

Figure 13.22 Human transformation of the land. Humans have altered much of the earth's surface in some way. The "almost pristine" areas, covered with original vegetation, tend to be too high, dry, cold, or otherwise unsuitable for human habitation in large numbers. They generally have very low population densities. "Partially transformed" describes areas of secondary vegetation, grown after removal of the original cover. Most are used for agriculture or livestock grazing. "Almost fully transformed" areas are those of permanent and intensive agriculture and urban settlement.

Solid Wastes and Rubbish

Americans produce rubbish, garbage, and other municipal waste at a rate of more than 370 million tons per year. About 220 million tons of that—2 kilograms (4.5 pounds) per person per day—is just discarded household rubbish and garbage. As populations grow, incomes rise, and consumption patterns change, the volume of disposable materials continues to expand. Relatively little residue is created in subsistence societies that move food from garden to table, and wastes from table to farm animals or compost heaps. The problem comes with urban folk who purchase packaged foods, favor plastic wrappings and containers for every commodity, and seek (and can afford) an ever-broadening array of manufactured goods, both consumer durables such as refrigerators and automobiles and many designed for single use and quick disposal.

The wastes that communities must somehow dispose of include newspapers and beer cans, toothpaste tubes and empty glass bottles, broken stoves and rusted cars (Figure 13.23). Such ordinary household and municipal trash does not meet the usual designation of *hazardous waste:* discarded material that may pose a substantial threat to human health or the environment when improperly stored or disposed of. Much of it, however, does have a component of danger to health or to the environment. Paints and paint removers, old television sets and computer monitors, used motor oils, pesticides and herbicides, bleaches, many kinds of plastics, and the like pose problems significantly different from apple cores and waste paper.

Landfill Disposal

The supply of open land and a free-enterprise system of waste collection and disposal led most American communities to opt for dumping urban refuse in *landfills*. In earlier periods, most of these were simply open dumps on the land, a menace to public health and an esthetic blot on the landscape. Beginning in the 1960s, more stringent federal controls began to require waste disposal in what was considered a more environmentally sound manner: the *sanitary landfill*. This involves depositing refuse in a natural depression or excavated trench, compacting it, and then covering it each day with soil to seal it (Figure 13.24). Open dumping was outlawed in 1976.

Figure 13.23 Some of the 240 million tires Americans replace each year. Most used tires are dumped, legally or illegally. Some are retreaded, some are exported, and some are burned to generate electricity. But most remain unused and unwanted in growing dumps that remain both fire hazards and breeding grounds for insects and the diseases they carry.

Final
2-foot
earth cover

Daily
1-foot
earth cover

Figure 13.24 **A sanitary landfill.** Each day's deposit of refuse is compacted and isolated in a separate cell by a covering layer of soil or clay. Although far more desirable than open dumps, sanitary landfills pose environmental problems of their own, including potential groundwater contamination and seepage of methane and hydrogen sulfide, gaseous products of decomposition. By federal law, modern landfills must be lined with clay and plastic, equipped with *leachate* (chemically contaminated drainage from the landfill) collection systems to protect the groundwater, and monitored regularly for underground leaks—requirements that have increased significantly the cost of constructing and operating landfills.

Some 71% of the country's municipal waste is disposed of by landfill. In the 1970s and 80s, there was a real fear that the available, affordable, or permitted landfill sites were rapidly disappearing and the cost of solid waste disposal would soon greatly increase. Some two-thirds of all landfills in operation in the late 1970s were filled and closed by 1990, and more than half the cities on the East Coast were without any local landfill sites in the middle 1990s. Because of changes in garbage economics during the 1990s, however, those earlier fears proved unnecessary. First, large waste management companies have built efficient megalandfills, replacing a great many small, local, and inefficient operations, increasing disposal capacity nationwide. Second, widespread adoption of municipal recycling programs—now diverting an estimated 30% of trash away from landfills—has extended the capacity and life span of the remaining landfills. Lack of profitable (or any) market for recyclables, however, caused some cities—New York in 2002 is an example—to suspend or curtail their recycling programs.

Any such recycling program elimination, reduction, or suspension poses serious environmental contamination threats in light of the rapid increase and accumulation of *e-waste*—the refuse from discarded consumer electronic products: computers, cellular phones, televisions, digital cameras, camcorders, iPods, and the like. In addition to their frequently stripped and recycled steel, aluminum, and copper, they contain toxic chemicals and metals more difficult to separate that tend to remain: lead, arsenic, antimony trioxide, selenium, cadmium, mercury, and more. The United States generates more e-waste than any other country, according to the Environmental Protection Agency; more than 2 million tons of it entered U.S. landfills in 2007.

The e-waste pile is growing around the world, with some 20 to 50 million tons produced annually. More and more governments are drafting legislation for the environmentally friendly disposal of this waste; China, for example, instituted regulations in 2004 providing that old electronic devices must be sold to appliance distributors or to enterprises specifically engaged in appliance reclamation. Two European Union directives were issued in 2005 addressing e-waste recycling and toxic content problems; one puts recycling responsibilities on the manufacturers to whom electronic appliances may be returned, the other bans, after mid-2006, six toxic substances, including lead, cadmium, mercury, and chromium-6, present in almost all electronics products. In contrast, the U.S. Environmental Protection Agency had not (2009) issued a clear set of goals and national guidelines to regulate the e-waste that inevitably promises a growing contamination of the land, water, and air, though American manufacturers, to retain access to the European market, will follow EU toxic content directives.

Over the years, of course, many filled dumps have posed problems for the cities that gave rise to them. New York City, for example, for years placed all of its daily 14,000 tons of residential waste into the world's largest dump, Fresh Kills on Staten Island. Opened in 1947 as a 3-year "temporary" 500-acre facility, it became a malodorous 3000 acres of decomposing garbage rising some 15 stories above former ground level. Generating 140,000 cubic meters (5 million cubic feet) of methane gas annually and illegally exuding contaminated water, Fresh Kills—finally closed in 2001 at a cost of more than $1 billion—symbolized the rising tide of refuse engulfing cities and endangering the environment.

Figure 13.25 This waste-to-energy incinerator at Peekskill, New York, is one of the new generation of municipal plants originally but mistakenly expected to convert over one-quarter of the country's municipal waste to energy by A.D. 2000. A Supreme Court ruling that the ash they produce had to be tested for hazardous toxicity and appropriately disposed in protected landfills, growing public rejection and lawsuits, and increasingly stringent controls on the amount and kind of airborne vapors they may emit have in many instances raised the operating costs of present incinerators far higher than landfill costs and altered the economic assessments of new construction. Incineration becomes more cost-effective, however, when cities are unable to dispose of their trash locally and must haul it to distant sites.

Incineration

For cities and regions faced with growing volumes of solid waste, alternatives to local landfill are few, expensive, and strongly resisted. One possibility is *incineration,* a waste-to-energy option of burning refuse to produce steam or electricity that usually also involves sorting, recapturing, and recycling useful rubbish components, such as paper, glass, metals, and the like. Incinerators also produce air pollution, including highly toxic dioxin,[1] so control equipment is required. Acid gases and heavy metals are also released by waste burning. The gases add to atmospheric pollution and acid precipitation, although "scrubbers" and fabric filters on modern incinerators reduce emissions to very low levels; the metals contribute to the toxicity of the ash that is the inevitable product of incineration and that requires landfill disposal.

The likelihood of pollution from one or many incinerator by-products has sparked strong protest to their construction in the United States, though they have been more accepted abroad. A Supreme Court ruling of 1994 that incinerator ash was not

exempt from the nation's hazardous waste law recognized the potential danger and mandated more expensive ash disposal procedures. Nonetheless, the 110 waste-to-energy incinerators operating in the United States at the end of the 1990s continued to burn about one-sixth of the country's municipal garbage (Figure 13.25). The seriousness of the dioxin and toxic ash problem, however, has aroused concern everywhere. In Japan—where about three-quarters of municipal waste is incinerated in more than 1850 municipal and 3300 private industrial incinerators—atmospheric dioxin levels that are triple those of the United States led the Ministry of Health in 1997 to strengthen earlier inadequate dioxin emission guidelines. Some European countries called at least temporary halts to incinerator construction while their safety was reconsidered, and increasingly landfills are refusing to take their residue.

Ocean Dumping

For coastal communities around the world the ocean has long been the preferred sink for not only municipal garbage, but for (frequently untreated) sewage, industrial waste, and all the detritus of an advanced urban society. The practice has been so common and long-standing that by the 1980s, the oceans were added to the list of great environmental concerns of the age. While the carcinogenic

---

[1] Any of several types of hydrocarbon compounds that are extremely toxic, persistent in the environment, and biologically magnified in the food chain. Dioxin is a frequently unavoidable trace contaminant in chemical processes and may also be formed during waste matter incineration or other combustion processes.

effect of ozone reduction had to be assumed from scientific report, the evidence of serious ocean pollution was increasingly apparent to even the most casual observer.

Along the Atlantic coast of North America from Massachusetts to Chesapeake Bay, reports of dead dolphins, raw sewage, tar balls, used syringes, vials of contaminated blood and hospital waste, diapers, plastic products in unimagined amounts and varieties, and other foul refuse kept swimmers from the beach, closed coastal shellfisheries, and elicited health warnings against wading or even breathing salt spray (Figure 13.26). The Gulf of Mexico coast is also tainted and polluted by accumulations of urban garbage, litter from ships and offshore oil rigs, and the toxic effluent of petrochemical plants. Long stretches of Pacific shoreline are in similar condition.

Elsewhere, the Adriatic, Aegean, Baltic, and Irish seas and the Sea of Japan—indeed, all the world's coastal waters—are no better. Environmental surveys of the shores of the Mediterranean Sea show serious damage and pollution. Around Italy, the Mediterranean waters are cloudy with raw sewage and industrial waste, and some of the world's most beautiful beaches are fouled by garbage. The Bay of Guanabara, the grand entryway to Rio de Janeiro, Brazil, has been called a cesspool.

An international treaty to regulate ocean dumping of hazardous trash was drafted in 1972; another, the Ocean Dumping Ban to control marine disposal of wastes, was negotiated in 1988; and a "global program of action" for protection of the marine environment from land-based pollution was devised in 1995, but their effectiveness has yet to be demonstrated. In light of the length of the world's coastline, the number of countries sharing it, and the great growth of urban populations in the vicinity of the sea, serious doubt has been raised whether any international agreement can be fully effective or enforced. Many portents—from beach litter to massive fin- and shellfish kills—suggest that the oceans' troubled waters have reached the limit of the abuse they can absorb.

Whether the solution to solid waste disposal be sought by land, by fire, or by sea, humanity's rising tide of refuse threatens to overwhelm the environments that must deal with it. The problem is present, growing, and increasingly costly to manage.

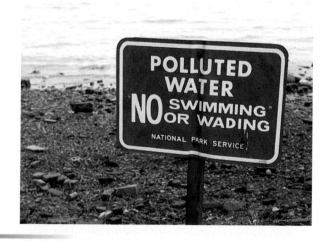

Figure 13.26 Warning signs and beaches littered with sewage, garbage, and medical debris are among the increasingly common and distressing evidences of ocean dumping of wastes.

Solutions are still to be found, a constant reminder for the future of the threatening impact of the environments of culture upon those of nature.

Toxic Wastes

The problems of municipal and household solid-waste management are daunting; those of treatment and disposal of hazardous and toxic wastes seem overwhelming. The definitions of the terms are imprecise, and *hazardous* and *toxic* are frequently used interchangeably, as we shall do here. More strictly defined, **toxic waste** is a relatively limited concept, referring to materials that can cause death or serious injury to humans or animals. **Hazardous waste** is a broader term referring to all wastes, including toxic ones, that pose an immediate or long-term human health risk or that endanger the environment (see definition on p. 420). The Environmental Protection Agency has classified more than 400 substances as hazardous, and currently about 10% of industrial waste materials are so categorized.

Such wastes contaminate the environment in different ways and by different routes. Because most hazardous debris is disposed of by dumping or burial on land, groundwater is most at risk of contamination. In all, some 2% of Anglo America's groundwater supply could have hazardous waste contamination. No comparable world figures exist, but in all industrial countries at least some drinking water contamination from highly toxic solvents, hydrocarbons, pesticides, trace metals, and polychlorinated biphenyls (PCBs) has been detected. Toxic waste impoundments are also a source of air pollutants through the evaporation of volatile organic compounds. Finally, careless or deliberate distribution of toxic materials outside of confinement areas can cause unexpected, but deadly, hazards. Although methods of disposal other than containment techniques have been developed—including incineration, infrared heating, and bacterial decomposition—none is fully satisfactory and none is as yet in wide use.

Radioactive Wastes

Every facility that either uses or produces radioactive materials generates at least *low-level waste,* material whose radioactivity will decay to safe levels in 100 years or less. Nuclear power plants produce about half the total low-level waste in the form of used resins, filter sludges, lubricating oils, and detergent wastes. Industries that manufacture radiopharmaceuticals, smoke alarms, and other consumer goods produce such wastes in the form of machinery parts, plastics, and organic solvents. Research establishments, universities, and hospitals also produce radioactive waste materials.

High-level waste can remain radioactive for 10,000 years and more; plutonium stays dangerously radioactive for 240,000 years. It consists primarily of spent fuel assemblies of nuclear power reactors—termed "civilian waste"—and such "military waste" as the by-products of nuclear weapons manufacture. The volume of civilian waste alone is not only great but increasing rapidly, because approximately one-third of a reactor's rods need to be disposed of every year.

By 2007, 54,000 tons of accumulated nuclear waste (spent fuel) were in storage in the containment pools of America's

103 commercial nuclear power reactors, awaiting more permanent disposition. "Spent fuel" is a misleading term: the assemblies are removed from commercial reactors not because their radiation is spent, but because they have become too radioactive for further use. The assemblies will remain radioactively "hot" for thousands of years.

Unfortunately, no satisfactory method for disposing of any hazardous waste has yet been devised. Although sealing liquids with a radioactive life measured in the thousands of years within steel drums expected to last no more than 40 years seems an unlikely solution to the disposal problem, it is one that has been widely practiced. Some wastes have been sealed in protective tanks and dumped at sea, a practice that has now been banned worldwide. Much low-level radioactive waste has been placed in tanks and buried in the ground at 13 sites operated by the U.S. Department of Energy and three sites run by private firms. Millions of cubic feet of high-level military waste are temporarily stored in underground tanks at four sites: Hanford, Washington; Savannah River, South Carolina; Idaho Falls, Idaho; and West Valley, New York (Figure 13.27). Several of these storage areas have experienced leakages, with seepage of waste into the surrounding soil and groundwater.

Because low-level waste is generated by so many sources, its disposal is particularly difficult to control. Evidence indicates that much of it has been placed in landfills, often the local municipal dump, where the waste chemicals may leach through the soil and into the groundwater. By EPA estimates, the United States contains at least 25,000 legal and illegal dumps with hazardous waste; as many as 2000 are deemed potential ecological disasters.

An even less constructive response, according to increasing complaints, has been the export of radioactive materials—in common with other hazardous wastes—to willing or unwitting recipient countries with less restrictive or costly controls and its illegal and unrecorded dumping at sea—now banned by the legally binding London Convention of 1993.

Exporting Waste

Regulations, community resistance, and steeply rising costs of disposal of hazardous wastes in the developed countries encouraged producers of those unwanted commodities to seek alternate areas for their disposition. Transboundary shipments of dangerous wastes became an increasingly attractive option for producers. In total, such cross-border movement amounted to tens of thousands of shipments annually by the early 1990s, with destinations including debt-ridden Eastern European countries and impoverished developing ones outside of Europe that were willing to trade a hole in the ground for hard currency. It was a trade, however, that increasingly aroused the ire and resistance of destination countries and, ultimately, elicited international agreements among both generating and receiving countries to cease the practice.

The Organization of African Unity in 1988 adopted a resolution condemning the dumping of all foreign wastes on that continent. More broadly and under the sponsorship of the United Nations, 117 countries in March of 1989 adopted a treaty—the Basel Convention on the Control of Transboundary Movements of Hazardous Wastes and Their Disposal—aimed at regulating the international trade in wastes. That regulation was to be achieved by requiring exporters to obtain consent from receiving countries before shipping waste and by requiring both exporter and importer countries to ensure that the waste would be disposed of in an environmentally sound manner. The Basel Convention came into force

Figure 13.27 Storage tanks under construction in Hanford, Washington. Built between 1943 and 1985 to contain high-level radioactive waste, the tanks are shown before they were encased in concrete and buried underground. By the early 1990s, 66 of the 177 underground tanks were already known to be leaking. Of the approximately 55 million gallons of waste the tanks hold, about 1 million gallons of liquids have seeped into the soil, raising the fear that the radioactive waste has already reached underground water supplies and is flowing toward the Columbia River. In mid-2002, construction began on a $4 billion vitrification plant to transform the worst of the radioactive wastes into a stable, granular form of glass, eventually to be buried at Yucca Mountain.

Geography and Public Policy

Environmental Justice

In Houston, a city of some 2 million people, about 25% of the population is African American. Yet, when researchers examined the placement of garbage facilities in the city, they found that 11 of 13 solid waste disposal facilities owned by the city were in mostly black areas and all five of the city's garbage incinerators were in black and Hispanic neighborhoods. Thus, when the city proposed establishing a new dump in a primarily black neighborhood in 1979, near houses and a high school, local residents protested and brought the waste management company to court, charging it with racial discrimination in the selection of the landfill site. The court decided in favor of the company, and the landfill was built.

In 1982, a few states away, in Warren County, North Carolina, the rural, mostly African American residents were shocked to learn that the state was proposing their county as the site of a hazardous waste landfill for disposing of polychlorinated biphenyls (PCBs). Their protests resulted in more than 500 arrests, and the effort to block the landfill failed. The Warren County activists were the first to use the term "environmental racism."

Environmental racism refers to any policy or practice that differentially affects or harms individuals, groups, or communities because of their race or color. The harm may be intentional or unintentional. *Environmental justice* is the fair treatment and meaningful involvement of all people regardless of race, color, national origin, or income with respect to the development, implementation, and enforcement of environmental laws, regulations, and policies. No group of people should bear a disproportionate share of negative environmental consequences. In many cases, environmental racism and injustice result from long-established and unexamined structural inequality: those who have a reduced political voice compared to the dominant groups in society live in the worst environments because authorities and companies have faced little opposition in placing hazardous facilities, such as landfills, in their vicinity.

Legend:
- Facilities releasing toxic wastes

Median Income
- $0–$26,598
- $26,599–$44,459
- $44,460–$56,607
- $56,608–$150,001

Poverty and Environmental Risk The distribution of household income and facilities that release toxic materials in Santa Clara County, California. Black lines represent census tracts. *(Source: Data from M.R. Meusar and A. Szosz "Environmental Inequality in Silicon Valley." www. mapcnjzin .com/EI/index.hmi.)*

---

in 1992, but even by 2007 the United States remained the only developed country that had not yet ratified it.

A still more restrictive convention was reached in March, 1994 when—with the United States dissenting—most Western industrialized countries agreed to ban the export of all poisonous or hazardous industrial wastes and residues to the developing world, the countries of Eastern Europe, and the former Soviet Union. United States' objections concerned the assumed prohibition on export of such materials as scrap metals for recycling within consenting receiving countries. Despite the agreement, a UN committee in 1998 identified the United States, Germany, Australia, Britain, and the Netherlands as continuing major toxic waste exporters, and an estimated 80% of e-waste collected in the United States for recycling is exported to areas such as China, India, and Pakistan, Nigeria, and Mexico. Investigating toxic wastes dumping as a violation of basic human rights, the UN committee reported that Africa still receives masses of developed country toxic waste in spite of its 1988 resolution. The bulk of European waste goes to the Baltic countries and to Eastern and Central Europe. Half of the United States' exports go to Latin America, and those of Britain go largely to Asia.

Prospects and Perspectives

Not surprisingly, the realities of the human impacts upon the environment that we have looked at in this chapter bring us directly back to ideas first presented in Chapter 2, at the start of our examination of the meaning of culture and the development of human geographic patterns on the surface of the earth. Humans, in their increasing numbers and technical sophistication, have been able since the end of the last glaciation to alter for their own needs the physical landscapes they occupy. Humans, it is often observed, are the ecological dominant in the human–environmental equation that is the continuing focus of geographic inquiry.

The problem is not confined to the United States. In most countries, poorer people and minorities tend to live in areas that are disproportionately exposed to polluting industries, waste disposal facilities, toxic soils, and polluted air and water, in Kagiso township, southwest of Johannesburg, South Africa, poor African residents live near a gold mine. In the past, when the gold was extracted from the ore, the waste product was pumped into a waste pile a distance from the residential area. However, the pile was eventually expanded to the extent that it now lies less than 27.4 meters (30 yards) (or less than half the length of a typical city block) from some of the houses. The drying waste produces dust high in alpha quartz particles, or silica, which cause silicosis. The inhalation of silica causes lung disease characterized by shortness of breath, fever, and cyanosis, and leaves its victims susceptible to tuberculosis. The condition is irreversible. The township is dominated by "informal" housing, which has few city services, is overcrowded, and has poor sanitation; it includes areas that were set aside for black Africans during Apartheid.

The United States has taken some steps to rectify the wrongs of environmental injustice. Following the Warren County, North Carolina, protests, President Clinton signed an Executive Order that made environmental justice a national priority and directed all federal agencies to develop policies to reduce environmental inequity, in 1992, the Environmental Protection Agency established an Office of Environmental Equity (now called the Office of Environmental Justice). The agency, however, has had an uneven record since its founding. Organizations outside the government continue to call attention to disturbing conditions often using GIS to identify inequalities.

Consider Louisiana's Chemical Corridor, or Cancer Alley, a 130-Kilometer (80-mi) stretch of the Mississippi River that is home to a chemical plant every half mile and a predominantly poor, African American population. While community groups protested a proposed new polyvinyl chloride (PVC) plant, the state government gave the owners tax exemptions. The EPA delayed the new plant's permit until the state addressed the citizens' environmental justice concerns. In the end, the owners bowed to community opposition and built the new plant 48 kilometers (30 mi) upstream, which may represent a Pyrrhic victory, as the plant will still contaminate air and water nearby.

Environmental injustice has its origins both in neglect and overt discrimination. There are many instances of intentional placing of environmentally hazardous plants and waste sites in areas already home to minorities and the poor. Government attempts to address the issue of environmental injustice has had an uneven track record. A body of case law regarding environmental justice in the United States has not developed yet, and some scholars contend that, because the issue falls between civil rights law and environmental law, development will continue only slowly.

Questions to Consider

1. Environmentally hazardous institutions—landfills, chemical plants, factories—have to be placed somewhere. How should communities and governments make decisions about the relative merits of different sites? Should the activism of local populations affect government decisions?

2. How would you or your college or university react if a company wanted to site a new landfill for toxic wastes nearby?

3. Where are landfills, polluting industries, and other environmental hazards located in your hometown or where you attend school? Are low-income residents and minorities exposed to greater than average amounts of pollution and thus bearing greater health risks than the rest of the population?

Source: Getis and Getis, *Introduction to Geography,* 12e McGraw-Hill, 2008 pp. 326-327.

That dominance reflected itself in the growing divergence of human societies as they separated themselves from common hunting-gathering origins. In creating their differing cultural solutions to common concerns of sustenance and growth, societies altered the environments they occupied. Diverse systems of exploitation of the environment were developed in and diffused from distinctive culture hearths. They were modified by the ever-expanding numbers of people occupying earth areas of differing carrying capacities and available resources. Gradually developing patterns of spatial interaction and exchange did not halt the creation of areally distinctive subsystems of culture or assure common methods of utilization of unequally distributed earth resources or environments. Sharp contrasts in levels of economic development and well-being emerged and persisted even as cultural convergence through shared technology began increasingly to unite societies throughout the world.

Each culture separately placed its imprint on the environment it occupied. In many cases—Chaco Canyon and Easter Island were our earlier examples—that imprint was ultimately destructive of the resources and environments upon which the cultures developed and depended. For human society collectively or single cultures separately, environmental damage or destruction is the unplanned consequence of the ecological dominance of humans. Our perpetual dilemma lies in the reality that what we need and want from the environments we occupy generally exceeds what they are able to yield in an unaltered state. To satisfy their felt needs, humans have learned to manipulate their environment. The greater those needs and the larger the populations with both needs and technical skills to satisfy them, the greater is the manipulation of the natural landscape. For as long as humans have occupied the earth the implicit but seldom addressed question has not been should we exploit and alter the environment, but how can we extract our requirements from the natural endowment without dissipating and destroying the basis of our support?

This final chapter detailing a few of the damaging pressures placed upon the environment by today's economies and cultures is not meant as a litany of despair. Rather it is a reminder of the potentially destructive ecological dominance of humans alongside examples of humans learning to reduce their impacts. Against the background of our now fuller understanding of human geographic patterns and interactions, this chapter is also meant to remind us yet again of the often repeated truism that everything is connected to everything else; we can never do just *one* thing. The ecological crises defined in this chapter and the human geographic patterns of interaction, contrast, and—occasionally—conflict observed in the preceding chapters show clearly and repeatedly how close and complex are the connections within the cultural world and how intimately our created environment is joined to the physical landscape we all share.

There is growing awareness of those connections, of the adverse human impacts upon the natural world, and of the unity of all cultural and physical landscapes. Climatic change, air and water pollution, soil loss and desertification, refuse contamination, and a host of other environmental consequences and problems of intensifying human use of the earth are all matters of contemporary public debate and consideration. Awareness and concern of individuals are increasingly reflected by policies of environmental protection introduced by governments and supported or enforced by international conferences, compacts, and treaties. Acceptance of the interconnectedness and indivisibility of cultural and natural environments—the human creation and the physical endowment—is now more the rule than the exception.

Our understanding of those relationships is advanced by what we have learned of the human side of the human–environmental structure. We have seen that the seemingly infinitely complex diversity of human societies, economies, and interrelations is in fact logical, explicable, and far from random or arbitrary. We now have developed both a mental map of the cultural patterns and content of areas and an appreciation of the dynamics of their creation and operation. We must have that human geographic background—that sense of spatial interaction and unity of cultural, economic, and political patterns—to understand fully the relationship between our cultural world and the physical environment on which it ultimately depends. Only with that degree of human geographic awareness can we individually participate in an informed way in preserving and improving the increasingly difficult and delicate balance between the endowment of nature and our landscapes of culture.

Summary

Cultural landscapes may buffer but cannot isolate societies from the physical environments they occupy. All human activities, from the simplest forms of agriculture to modern industry, have an impact upon the biosphere. Cumulatively, in both developed and developing countries, that impact is now evident in the form of serious and threatening environmental deterioration. The atmosphere unites us all, and its global problems of greenhouse heating, ozone depletion, and particulate pollution endanger us all. Desertification, soil erosion, and tropical deforestation may appear to be local or regional problems, but they have worldwide implications of both environmental degradation and reduced population-supporting capacity. Freshwater supplies are deteriorating in quality and decreasing in sufficiency through contamination and competition. Finally, the inevitable end product of human use of the earth—the garbage and hazardous wastes of civilization—are beginning to overwhelm both sites and technologies of disposal.

We do not end our study of human geography on a note of despondency, however. We end with the conviction that the fuller knowledge we now have of the spatial patterns and structures of human cultural, economic, and political activities will aid in our understanding of the myriad ways in which human societies are bound to the physical landscapes they occupy—and which they have so substantially modified.

 KEY WORDS

acid precipitation 428	fallowing 436	ozone 428
aquifer 439	global climate change 423	rotation 436
biome 421	greenhouse effect 423	soil 436
biosphere (ecosphere) 420	hazardous waste 446	soil erosion 432
desertification 432	hydrologic cycle 437	terracing 436
ecosystem 421	icebox effect 423	toxic waste 446
environment 420	IPAT equation 420	
environmental pollution 440	limiting factor principle 440	

1. What does the term *environment* mean? What is the distinction between the natural and the cultural environments? Can both be part of the physical environment we occupy?

2. What are the components in the IPAT equation? How does the study of human geography inform our understanding of environmental problems?

3. Were there any evidences of human impact upon the natural environment prior to the Industrial Revolution? If so, can you provide examples? If not, can you explain why not?

4. Do we have any evidence of physical environmental change that we cannot attribute to human action? Can we be certain that environmental change we observe today is attributable to human action? How?

5. What lines of reasoning and evidence suggest that human activity is altering global climates? What kind of alteration has occurred or is expected to occur? What do the terms *greenhouse* and *icebox effect* have to do with possible climatic futures?

6. What is *desertification?* What types of areas are particularly susceptible to desertification? What kinds of land uses are associated with it? How easily can its effects be overcome or reversed?

7. What agricultural techniques have been traditionally employed to reduce or halt soil erosion? Since these are known techniques that have been practiced throughout the world, why is there a current problem of soil erosion anywhere?

8. What effects has the increasing use of fossil fuels over the past 200 years had on the environment? What is *acid precipitation,* and where is it a problem? What factors affect the type and degree of air pollution found at a place? What is the relationship of *ozone* to *photochemical smog?*

9. Describe the chief sources of water pollution of which you are aware. How has the supply of fresh water been affected by pollution and human use? When water is used, is it forever lost to the environment? If so, where does it go? If not, why should there be water shortages now in regions of formerly ample supply?

10. What methods do communities use to dispose of solid waste? Can *hazardous wastes* be treated in the same fashion? Since disposition of waste is a technical problem, why should there be any concern with waste disposal in modern advanced economies?

11. Suggest ways in which your study of human geography has increased your understanding of the relationship between the environments of culture and those of nature.

KEY CONCEPTS REVIEW

1. **What are contributing causes and resulting concerns of global warming, acid rainfall, and ozone level changes?** pp. 420–431.
Following the last glaciation, relatively stable world patterns of climates and biomes persisted, broken only by occasional periods of unusual warming or cooling. Great increases in human numbers and their environmental impact over the past century resulted in apparent detectable changes in former earth system stability. Recent global warming has been attributed in significant measure to human-caused increases in greenhouse gases. Increases as well in airborne smoke, soot, and acid gases from factories and cars help produce acid precipitation that corrodes stone and metals, destroys forests, and acidifies to sterility some lakes and soils. Upper-air ozone depletion and lower-level ozone accumulation, both with serious effect on plant and animal life, are also largely atrributed to humans' adverse impact on the environment.

2. **What human actions have contributed to tropical deforestation, desertification, and soil erosion? What are the consequences?** pp. 431–437.
Current rapid destruction of tropical forests reflects human intentions to expand farming and grazing areas and harvest tropical wood. Their depletion endangers or destroys the world's richest, most diversified plant and animal biome and adversely affects local, regional, and world patterns of temperature and rainfall. Their loss also diminishes a vital "carbon sink" needed to absorb excess carbon dioxide. Desertification—the expansion of areas of destroyed soil and plant cover in dry climates—results from both natural climatic fluctuations and human pressures from plowing, woody plant removal, or livestock overgrazing. Those same human actions and pressures can accelerate the normal erosional loss of soil beyond natural soil regeneration potential. Such loss reduces total and per capita area of food production, diminishing the human carrying capacity of the land.

3. **How are emerging water supply and waste disposal problems related to human numbers and impacts?** pp. 437–441.
The hydrologic cycle assures water will be continuously regenerated for further use. But growing demand for irrigation, industrial use, and individual and urban consumption means increasing lack of balance

between natural water supplies and consumption demands. Pollution of those supplies by human actions further reduces water availability and utility.

4. **How are modern societies addressing the problems of solid and toxic waste disposal?** pp. 440–450.
Increasingly, all societies are becoming more dependent on modern manufacturing and packaging of industrial, commercial, and personal consumption items. The easy recycling of waste materials found in subsistence cultures is no longer possible, and humans are presented with increasing needs for sites and facilities to safely dispose of solid wastes. Sanitary landfills and incineration are employed to handle nontoxic wastes. The former demands scarce and expensive land near cities or costly export to distant locations; the latter is often opposed because of unsafe emissions and ash residue. Disposal of toxic and hazardous wastes including nuclear wastes, products of modern societies and technologies, poses problems yet to be satisfactorily and safely solved.

MAP PROJECTIONS

A map projection is simply a system for displaying the curved surface of the earth on a flat sheet of paper. The definition is easy; the process is more difficult. No matter how one tries to "flatten" the earth, it can never be done in such a fashion as to show all earth details in their correct relative sizes, shapes, distances, or directions. Something is always wrong, and the cartographer's—the mapmaker's—task is to select and preserve those earth relationships important for the purpose at hand and to minimize or accept those distortions that are inevitable but unimportant.

Round Globe to Flat Map

The best way to model the earth's surface accurately, of course, would be to show it on a globe. But globes are not as convenient to use as flat maps and do not allow one to see the entire surface of the earth all at once. Nor can they show very much detail. Even a very large globe of, say, 3 feet (nearly 1 meter) in diameter, compresses the physical or cultural information of some 130,000 square kilometers (about 50,000 sq mi) of earth surface into a space 2.5 centimeters (1 in.) on a side.

Geographers make two different demands on the maps they use to represent reality. One requirement is to show at one glance generalized relationships and spatial content of the entire world; the many world maps used in this and other geography textbooks and in atlases have that purpose. The other need is to show the detailed content of only portions of the earth's surface—cities, regions, countries, hemispheres—without reference to areas outside the zone of interest. Although the needs and problems of both kinds of maps differ, each starts with the same requirement: to transform a curved surface into a flat one.

If we look at the globe directly, only the front—the side facing us—is visible; the back is hidden (Figure A.1). To make a world map, we must decide on a way to flatten the globe's curved surface on the hemisphere we can see. Then we have to cut the globe map down the middle of its hidden hemisphere and place the two back quarters on their respective sides of the already visible front half. In simple terms, we have to "peel" the map from the globe and flatten it in the same way we might try to peel an orange and flatten the skin. Inevitably, the peeling and flattening process will produce a resulting map that either shows tears or breaks in the surface (Figure A.2a) or is subject to uneven stretching or shrinking to make it lie flat (Figure A.2b).

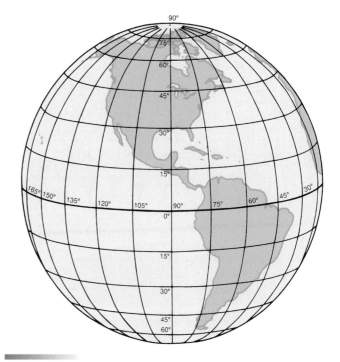

Figure A.1 An orthographic projection gives us a visually realistic view of the globe; its distortion toward the edges suggests the normal perspective appearance of a sphere viewed from a distance. Only a single hemisphere—one half of the globe—can be seen at a time, and only the central portion of that hemisphere avoids serious distortion of shape.

Projections—Geometrical and Mathematical

Of course, mapmakers do not physically engage in cutting, peeling, flattening, or stretching operations. Their task, rather, is to construct or *project* on a flat surface the network of parallels and meridians (the **graticule**) of the globe grid (see p. 18). The idea of projections is perhaps easiest visualized by thinking of a transparent globe with an imagined light source located inside. Lines of latitude and longitude (or of coastlines or any other features) drawn on that globe will cast shadows on any nearby surface. A tracing of that shadow globe grid would represent a geometrical map projection.

In **geometrical** (or **perspective**) **projections,** the graticule is in theory visually transferred from the globe to a geometrical figure, such as a plane, cylinder, or cone, which, in turn, can be

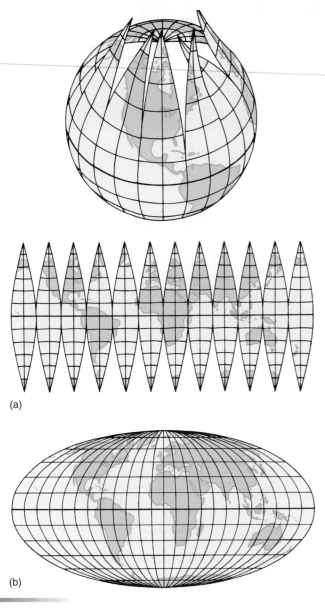

(a)

(b)

Figure A.2 (*a*) A careful "peeling" of the map from the globe yields a set of tapered "gores" which, although individually not showing much stretching or shrinking, do not collectively result in a very useful or understandable world map. (*b*) It is usually considered desirable to avoid or reduce the number of interruptions by depicting the entire global surface as a single flat circular, oval, or rectangular shape. That continuity of area, however, can be achieved only at the cost of considerable alteration of true shapes, distances, directions, or areas. Although the homolographic (Mollweide) projection shows areas correctly, it distorts shapes.

cut and then spread out flat (or *developed*) without any stretching or tearing. The surfaces of cylinders, cones, and planes are said to be **developable surfaces**—cylinders and cones can be cut and laid flat without distortion and planes are flat at the outset (Figure A.3). In actuality, geometrical projections are constructed not by tracing shadows but by the application of geometry and the use of lines, circles, arcs, and angles drawn on paper.

The location of the theoretical light source in relation to the globe surface can cause significant variation in the projection of the graticule on the developable geometric surface. An **orthographic projection** results from placement of the light source at infinity. A **gnomonic projection** is produced when the light source is at the center of the earth. When the light is placed at the *antipode*—the point exactly opposite the point of tangency (point of contact between globe and map)—a **stereographic projection** is produced (Figure A.4).

Although a few useful and common projections are based on these simple geometric means of production, most map designs can only be derived mathematically from tables of angles and dimensions separately developed for specific projections. The objective and need for **mathematical projections** is to preserve and emphasize specific earth relationships that cannot be recorded by the perspective globe and shadow approach. The graticule of each mathematical projection is orderly and "accurate" in the sense of displaying the correct locations of lines of latitude and longitude. Each projection scheme, however, presents a different arrangement of the globe grid to minimize or eliminate some of the distortions inherent in projecting from a curved to a flat surface. Every projection represents a compromise or deviation from reality to achieve a selected purpose, but in the process of adjustment or compromise, each inevitably contains specific, accepted distortions.

Globe Properties and Map Distortions

The true properties of the global grid are detailed on pp. 18–19. Not all of those grid realities can ever be preserved in any single projection; projections invariably distort some or all of them. The result is that all flat maps, whether geometrically or mathematically derived, also distort in different ways and to different degrees some or all of the four main properties of actual earth surface relationships: area, shape, distance, and direction.

Area

Cartographers use **equal-area,** or **equivalent, projections** when it is important for the map to show the *areas* of regions in correct or constant proportion to earth reality—as it is when the map is intended to show the actual areal extent of a phenomenon on the earth's surface. If we wish to compare the amount of land in agriculture in two different parts of the world, for example, it would be very misleading visually to use a map that represented the same amount of surface area at two different scales.[1] To retain the needed size comparability, our chosen projection must assure that a unit area drawn anywhere on it will always represent the same number of square kilometers (or similar units) on the earth's surface.

---

[1]**Scale** is the relationship between the size of a feature or length of a line on the map and that same feature or line on the earth's surface. It may be indicated on a map as a ratio—for example, 1:1,000,000—that tells us the relationship between a unit of measure on the map and that same unit on the earth's surface. In our example, 1 centimeter of map distance equals 1 million centimeters (or 10 kilometers) of actual earth distance. See Figure 1.18.

Figure A.3 The theory of *geometrical projections.* The three common geometric forms used in projections are the plane, the cylinder, and the cone.

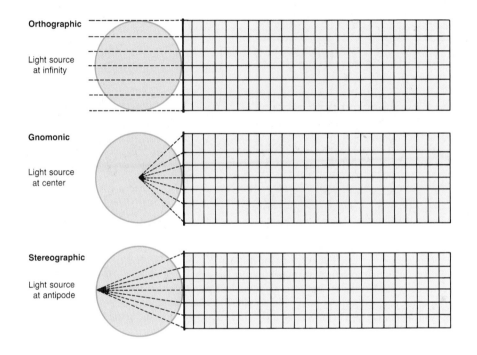

Figure A.4 The effect of light source location on planar surface projections. Note the variations in spacing of the lines of latitude that occur when the light source is moved.

To achieve *equivalence,* any scale change that the projection imposes in one direction must be offset by compensating changes in the opposite direction. As a result, the shape of the portrayed area is inevitably distorted. A square on the earth, for example, may become a rectangle on the map, but that rectangle has the correct area (Figure A.5). *A map that shows correct areal relationships always distorts the shapes of regions,* as Figure A.6a demonstrates.

Shape

Although no projection can reproduce correct shapes for large areas, some do accurately portray the shapes of small areas. These true-shape projections are called **conformal,** and the importance of *conformality* is that regions and features "look right" and have the correct directional relationships. They achieve these properties for small areas by assuring that lines of latitude and longitude cross each other at right angles and that the scale is the same in all directions at any given location. Both these conditions exist on the

Figure A.5 These three figures are all equal in area despite their different dimensions and shapes.

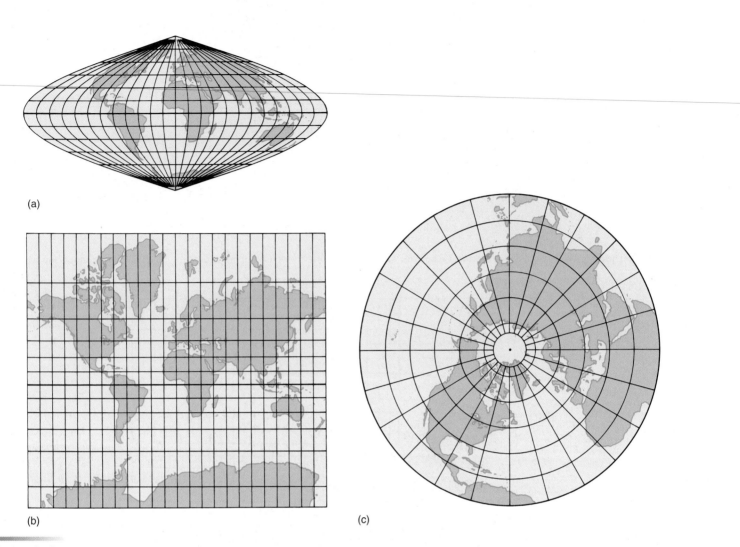

(a)

(b)   (c)

Figure A.6 Sample projections demonstrating specific map properties. (*a*) The equal-area sinusoidal projection retains everywhere the property of *equivalence.* (*b*) The mathematically derived Mercator projection is *conformal,* displaying true shapes of individual features but greatly exaggerating sizes and distorting shapes away from the equator. (*c*) A portion of an azimuthal *equidistant* projection, polar-case. Distances from the center (North Pole) to any other point are true; extension of the grid to the Southern Hemisphere would show the South Pole infinitely stretched to form the circumference of the map.

globe but can be retained for only relatively small areas on maps. Because that is so, the shapes of large regions—continents, for example—are always different from their true earth shapes even on conformal maps. Except for maps for very small areas, *a map cannot be both equivalent and conformal;* these two properties are mutually exclusive, as Figure A.6b suggests.

Distance

Distance relationships are nearly always distorted on a map, but some projections do maintain true distances in one direction or along certain selected lines. True distance relationships simply mean that the length of a straight line between two points on the map correctly represents the *great circle* distance between those points on the earth. (An arc of a great circle is the shortest distance between two points on the earth's curved surface; the equator is a great circle and all meridians of longitude are half great circles.) Projections with this property can be designed, but even on such **equidistant**

maps true distance in all directions is shown only from one or two central points. Distances between all other locations are incorrect and, quite likely, greatly distorted as Figure A.6c clearly shows.

Direction

As is true of distances, directions between all points on a map cannot be shown without distortion. On **azimuthal projections,** however, true directions are shown from one central point to all other points. (An *azimuth* is the angle formed at the beginning point of a straight line, in relation to a meridian.) Directions or azimuths from points other than the central point to other points are not accurate. The azimuthal property of a projection is not exclusive—that is, an azimuthal projection may also be equivalent, conformal, or equidistant. The azimuthal equal-distance ("equidistant") map shown as Figure A.6c is, as well, a true-direction map from the same North Pole origin. Another more specialized example is the gnomonic projection, displayed as Figure A.7.

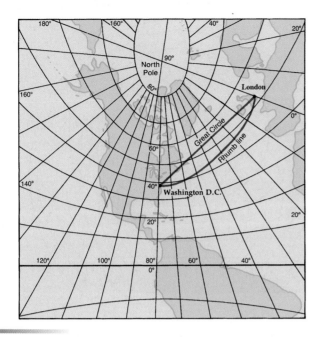

Figure A.7 A gnomonic projection centered on Washington, D.C. In this geometrical projection the light source is at the center of the globe (see Figure A.4), and the capital city marks the "standard point" where the projection plane is in contact with the globe. The rapid outward increase in graticule spacing makes it a projection impractical for more than a portion of a hemisphere. A unique property of the gnomonic projection is that it is the only projection on which all great circles appear as straight lines.

Classes of Projections

Although there are many hundreds of different projections, the great majority of them can be grouped into four primary classes or families based on their origin. Each family has its own distinctive outline, set of similar properties, and pattern of distortions. Three of them are easily seen as derived from the geometric or perspective projection of the globe grid onto the developable surfaces of cylinders, cones, and planes. The fourth class is mathematically derived; its members have a variety of attributes but share a general oval design (Figure A.8).

Cylindrical Projections

Cylindrical projections are developed geometrically or mathematically from a cylinder wrapped around the globe. Usually, the cylinder is tangent at the equator, which thus becomes the **standard line**—that is, transferred from the globe without distortion. The result is a globe grid network with meridians and parallels intersecting at right angles. There is no scale distortion along the standard line of tangency, but distortion increases with increasing distance away from it. The result is a rectangular world map with acceptable low-latitude representation, but with enormous areal exaggeration toward the poles.

The mathematically derived Mercator projection invented in 1569 is a special familiar but commonly misused cylindrical projection (see Figure A.6b). Its sole original purpose was to serve as a navigational chart of the world with the special advantage of showing true compass headings, or *rhumb lines,* as straight lines on the map. Its frequent use in wall or book maps gives grossly exaggerated

Figure A.8 Shape consistencies within families of projections. When the surface of a cone, cylinder, or plane is made *tangent*—that is, comes into contact with the globe—at either a point or along a circle and then "developed," a characteristic family outline results. The tangent lines and point are indicated. A fourth common shape, the oval, may reflect a design in which the long dimension is a great circle comparable to the tangent line of the cylinder.

Redrawn with permission from American Congress on Surveying and Mapping, Choosing a World Map. Special Publication No. 2 of the American Cartographic Association, Bethesda, Md. Copyright 1988. CaGIS. No further use allowed.

impressions of the size of land areas away from the tropics. Equal-area alternatives to the conformal Mercator map are available, and a number of "compromise" cylindrical projections that are neither equal area nor conformal (for example, the Miller projection, Figure A.9a) are frequently used bases for world maps. The Robinson projection (Figure A.9d), used for many of the world maps in this textbook, is also such a compromise. Designed to show the whole world in a visually satisfactory manner, it does not show true distances or directions and is neither equal-area nor conformal. Instead, it permits some exaggeration of size in the high latitudes in order to improve the shapes of landmasses. Size and shape are most accurate in the temperate and tropical zones, where most people live.

Conic Projections

Of the three developable geometric surfaces, the cone is the closest in form to one-half of a globe. **Conic projections,** therefore, are often employed to depict hemispheric or smaller parts of the earth. In the *simple conic* projection, the cone is placed tangent to the globe along a single standard parallel, with the apex of the cone located above the pole. The cone can also be made to intersect the globe along two or more lines, with a *polyconic* projection resulting; the increased number of standard lines reduces the distortion, which otherwise increases away from the standard parallel. The projection of the grid on the cone yields evenly spaced straight-line meridians radiating from the pole and parallels that are arcs of circles. Although conic projections can be adjusted to minimize distortions and become either equivalent or conformal, by their nature they can never show the whole globe. In fact, they are most useful for and generally restricted to maps of midlatitude regions of greater east-west than north-south extent. The Albers equal-area projection often used for U.S. maps is a familiar example (Figure A.9b).

Planar (Azimuthal) Projections

Planar (or **azimuthal**) **projections** are constructed by placing a plane tangent to the globe at a single point. Although the plane may touch the globe anywhere the cartographer wishes, the polar

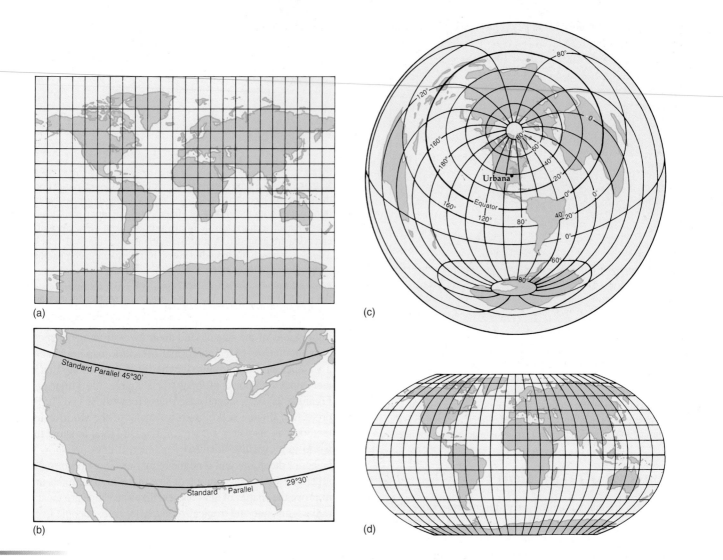

Figure A.9 Some sample members of the principal projection families. (*a*) The Miller cylindrical projection is mathematically derived. (*b*) The Albers equal-area conic projection, used for many official U.S. maps, has two standard parallels: 29 1/2° and 45 1/2° . (*c*) A planar, or azimuthal, equidistant projection centered on Urbana, Illinois. (*d*) The Robinson projection of the oval family; neither conformal nor equivalent, it was designed as a visually satisfactory world map.

case with the plane centered on either the North or the South Pole is easiest to visualize (see Figure A.6c). This equidistant projection is useful because it can be centered anywhere, facilitating the correct measurement of distances from that point to all others. When the plane is tangent at places other than the poles, the meridians and the parallels become curiously curved (Figure A.9c).

Planar maps are commonly used in atlases because they are particularly well suited for showing the arrangement of polar landmasses. Depending on the particular projection used, true shape, equal area, or some compromise between them can be depicted. The special quality of the planar gnomonic projection has already been shown in Figure A.7.

Oval or Elliptical Projections

Oval or elliptical projections have been mathematically developed usually as compromise projections designed to display the entire world in a fashion that is visually acceptable and suggestive of the

curvature of the globe. In most, the equator and a central meridian (usually the prime meridian) are the standard lines. They cross in the middle of the map, which thus becomes the point of no distortion. Parallels are, as a rule, parallel straight lines; meridians, except for the standard meridian, are shown as curved lines. In some instances the oval projection is a modification of one of different original shape. Some of the world maps in this textbook (for example, Figures 8.12 and 13.18) are an oval adjustment of the circular (but not azimuthal) Van der Grinten projection, a compromise projection that achieves acceptable degrees of equivalence and conformality in lower and middle latitudes but becomes increasingly and unacceptably distorted in polar regions.

Other Projections and Manipulations

The geometric projections, we have seen, can all be thought of as developed from the projection of the globe grid onto a cylinder, cone, or plane. Many projections, however, cannot be classified in terms of simple geometric shapes. They are derived from mathematical formulas and usually have been developed to display the world or a portion thereof in a fashion that is visually acceptable or in any shape that is desired: ovals are most common, but hearts, trapezoids, stars, and other—sometimes bizarre—forms have been devised for special purposes. One often-seen projection is the equal-area Goode's homolosine, an "interrupted" projection that is actually a product of fitting together the least distorted portions of two different projections (the sinusoidal projection and the Mollweide, or homolographic, projection) and centering the split map along multiple standard meridians to minimize distortion of either (as desired) land or ocean surfaces (Figure A.10).

The homolosine map clearly shows how projections may be manipulated or adjusted to achieve desired objectives. Since most projections are based on a mathematically consistent rendering of the actual globe grid, possibilities for such manipulation are nearly unlimited. R. Buckminster Fuller, an architect and designer perhaps best known as the inventor of the geodesic dome, produced the Fuller dymaxion projection (Figure A.11). It consists of 20 equilateral triangles, which can be hinged along different boundaries to show interesting earth relationships. The projection minimizes distortion of the sizes and shapes of the world's landmasses.

Map properties to be retained, size and shape of areas to be displayed, and overall map design to be achieved may influence the cartographer's choices in reproducing the globe grid on the flat map. Special effects and properties may also be achieved geometrically by adjusting the aspect of the projection. *Aspect* simply means the positional relationship between the globe and the developable surface on which it is visually projected. Although the fundamental distortion pattern of any given projection system onto any of the developable surfaces will remain constant, shifting of the point or line of tangency will materially alter the appearance of the graticule and of the geographical features shown on the map.

Although an infinite number of aspects are possible for any of the geometric projections, three classes of aspects are most common. Named according to the relation of the axis of the globe to the cylinder, plane, or oval projection surface, the three classes are usually called *equatorial, polar,* and *oblique*. In the equatorial, the axis

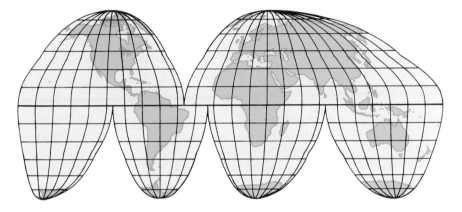

Figure A.10 Goode's interrupted homolosine grafts an upper latitude homolographic (Mollweide) onto a sinusoidal projection at about 40° North and South. To improve shapes, each continent is placed on the middle of a lobe approximately centered on its own central meridian. The projection can also interrupt continents to display the ocean areas intact.

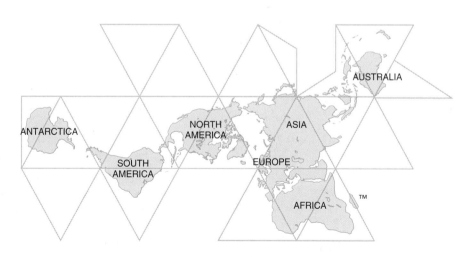

Figure A.11 **The Fuller dymaxion projection.** The equilateral triangles can be folded into a solid approximating the globe.

of the globe parallels the orientation of the plane, cylinder, or cone; a parallel, usually the central equator, is the line of tangency. In the polar aspect, the axis of the globe is perpendicular to the orientation of the developable surface. In the oblique aspect, the axis of the globe makes an oblique angle with the orientation of the developable surface, and a complex arrangement of the graticule results.

A Cautionary Reminder

Mapmakers must be conscious of the properties of the projections they use, selecting the one that best suits their purposes. It is not ever possible to transform the globe into a flat map without distortion. But cartographers have devised hundreds of possible mathematical and geometrical projections in various modifications and aspects to display to their best advantage the variety of earth features and relationships they wish to emphasize. Some projections are highly specialized and properly restricted to a single limited purpose; others achieve a more general acceptability and utility.

If the map shows only a small area, the choice of a projection is not critical—virtually any can be used. The choice becomes more important when the area to be shown extends over a considerable longitude and latitude; then the selection of a projection clearly depends on the purpose of the map. As we have seen, Mercator or gnomonic projections are useful for navigation. Unfortunately, the Mercator projection grossly exaggerates the area of high latitude features, giving a misleading impression when used for books or wall maps. If numerical data are being mapped, the relative sizes of the areas involved should be correct, and equivalence is the sought-after map property. Conformality and equal distance may be required in other instances.

While selection of an appropriate projection is the task of the cartographer, understanding the consequences of that selection and recognizing and allowing for the distortions inevitable in all flat maps are the responsibility of the map reader. When skillfully designed maps are read by knowledgeable users, clear and accurate conveyance of spatial information and earth relationships is made convenient and natural.

 KEY WORDS

Appendix B

2008 WORLD POPULATION DATA

	Population Mid–2008 (millions)	Births Per 1,000 Pop.	Deaths Per 1,000 Pop.	Rate of Natural Increase (%)	Projected Population (millions) mid– 2025	Projected Population (millions) mid– 2050	Projected Pop. Change 2008–2050 (%)	Infant Mortality Rate[a]	Total Fertility Rate[b]	Percent of Population of Age < 15 / 65 +	Life Expectancy at Birth (Years)	Percent Urban	Percent of Pop. 15–49 with HIV/AIDS, 2007	% of Pop. using Improved Drinking Water Sources, 2006	GNI PPP Per Capita 2007 (US $)
WORLD	**6,705**	**21**	**8**	**1.2**	**8,000**	**9,352**	**39**	**49**	**2.6**	**28 / 7**	**68**	**49**	**0.8**	**86**	**$9,600**
MORE DEVELOPED	1,227	12	10	0.2	1,269	1,294	5	6	1.6	17 / 16	77	74	0.5	97	31,200
LESS DEVELOPED	5,479	23	8	1.5	6,731	8,058	47	54	2.8	30 / 6	67	44	1.0	84	4,760
LESS DEVELOPED (excl. China)	4,154	26	9	1.8	5,255	6,621	59	59	3.2	34 / 5	65	44	1.4	82	4,560
LEAST DEVELOPED	797	36	13	2.4	1,139	1,664	109	85	4.7	41 / 3	55	27	3.0	62	1,060
AFRICA	**967**	**37**	**14**	**2.4**	**1,358**	**1,932**	**100**	**82**	**4.9**	**41 / 3**	**54**	**38**	**4.0**	**64**	**2,430**
SUB-SAHARAN AFRICA	**809**	**40**	**15**	**2.5**	**1,161**	**1,698**	**110**	**88**	**5.4**	**43 / 3**	**50**	**35**	**5.0**	**58**	**1,830**
NORTHERN AFRICA	**197**	**26**	**7**	**1.9**	**251**	**307**	**56**	**45**	**3.0**	**33 / 5**	**69**	**50**	**0.3**	**87**	**4,760**
Algeria	34.7	22	4	1.8	43.3	50.1	44	27	2.3	30 / 5	72	63	0.1	85	5,490
Egypt	74.9	27	6	2.0	95.9	117.9	57	33	3.1	33 / 5	72	43	—	98	5,400
Libya	6.3	24	4	2.0	8.1	9.7	54	21	3.0	30 / 4	73	77	—	71	11,500
Morocco	31.2	21	6	1.4	36.6	42.4	36	43	2.4	29 / 6	70	56	0.1	83	3,990
Sudan	39.4	33	12	2.1	54.3	73.0	85	81	4.5	41 / 4	58	38	1.4	70	1,880
Tunisia	10.3	17	6	1.2	12.1	13.2	27	19	2.0	25 / 6	74	65	0.1	94	7,130
Western Sahara	0.5	28	8	2.0	0.8	0.9	89	53	3.0	31 / 2	64	81	—	—	—
WESTERN AFRICA	**291**	**42**	**15**	**2.6**	**419**	**616**	**112**	**96**	**5.7**	**44 / 3**	**51**	**42**	**2.5**	**58**	**1,480**
Benin	9.3	42	12	3.0	14.5	22.5	142	98	5.7	44 / 3	56	41	1.2	65	1,310
Burkina Faso	15.2	45	15	3.0	23.7	37.5	147	89	6.2	46 / 3	51	16	1.6	72	1,120
Cape Verde	0.5	30	5	2.5	0.7	0.9	83	28	3.5	38 / 6	71	59	—	80	2,940
Côte d'Ivoire	20.7	38	14	2.4	26.2	34.7	68	100	4.9	40 / 2	52	48	3.9	81	1,590
Gambia	1.6	38	11	2.7	2.3	3.4	117	93	5.1	42 / 3	58	54	0.9	86	1,140
Ghana	23.9	32	10	2.2	33.7	48.8	104	71	4.3	40 / 4	59	48	1.9	80	1,330
Guinea	10.3	42	14	2.9	15.7	24.5	138	113	5.7	46 / 3	54	30	1.6	70	1,120
Guinea-Bissau	1.7	50	19	3.1	2.9	5.3	205	117	7.1	48 / 3	45	30	1.8	57	470
Liberia	3.9	50	18	3.1	6.8	12.5	216	133	6.8	47 / 2	46	58	1.7	64	290
Mali	12.7	48	15	3.3	20.6	34.2	169	96	6.6	48 / 4	56	31	1.5	60	1,040
Mauritania	3.2	35	9	2.7	4.5	6.4	99	77	4.8	40 / 4	60	40	0.8	60	2,010

	Population Mid–2008 (millions)	Births Per 1,000 Pop.	Deaths Per 1,000 Pop.	Rate of Natural Increase (%)	Projected Population (millions) mid–2025	Projected Population (millions) mid–2050	Projected Pop. Change 2008–2050 (%)	Infant Mortality Rate[a]	Total Fertility Rate[b]	Percent of Population of Age < 15 / 65 +	Life Expectancy at Birth (Years)	Percent Urban	Percent of Pop. 15–49 with HIV/AIDS, 2007	% of Pop. using Improved Drinking Water Sources, 2006	GNI PPP Per Capita 2007 (US $)
WESTERN AFRICA (continued)															
Niger	14.7	46	15	3.1	26.3	53.2	261	81	7.1	49 / 3	57	17	0.8	42	630
Nigeria	148.1	43	18	2.5	205.4	282.2	91	100	5.9	45 / 3	47	47	3.1	47	1,770
Senegal	12.7	39	10	3.0	18.0	25.3	99	61	5.3	44 / 4	62	41	1.0	77	1,640
Sierra Leone	5.5	48	23	2.5	7.6	10.9	99	158	6.1	42 / 4	48	37	1.7	53	660
Togo	6.8	38	10	2.8	9.9	14.1	108	91	5.1	43 / 3	58	40	3.3	59	800
EASTERN AFRICA	**301**	**41**	**15**	**2.5**	**440**	**641**	**113**	**81**	**5.4**	**44 / 3**	**49**	**22**	**5.8**	**54**	**940**
Burundi	8.9	46	16	3.0	15.0	28.3	220	107	6.8	45 / 3	49	10	2.0	71	330
Comoros	0.7	36	8	2.8	1.1	1.8	151	69	4.9	42 / 3	64	28	<0.1	85	1,150
Djibouti	0.8	30	12	1.8	1.1	1.5	75	67	4.2	39 / 3	54	87	3.1	92	2,260
Eritrea	5.0	40	10	3.0	7.7	11.5	129	59	5.3	43 / 2	57	21	1.3	60	400
Ethiopia	79.1	40	15	2.5	110.5	147.6	87	77	5.3	43 / 3	49	16	2.1	42	780
Kenya	38.0	40	12	2.8	51.3	65.2	72	77	4.9	42 / 2	53	19	7.8c	57	1,540
Madagascar	18.9	38	10	2.8	28.0	41.6	120	75	5.0	44 / 3	58	30	0.1	47	920
Malawi	13.6	48	16	3.2	20.4	30.5	124	80	6.3	46 / 3	46	17	11.9	76	750
Mauritius	1.3	14	7	0.7	1.4	1.5	17	15.4	1.7	23 / 7	72	42	1.7	100	11,390
Mayotte	0.2	39	3	3.6	0.3	0.5	174	—	4.5	42 / 2	74	28	—	—	—
Mozambique	20.4	41	20	2.1	27.5	37.2	83	108	5.4	43 / 3	43	29	12.5	42	690
Reunion	0.8	19	5	1.3	1.0	1.1	31	8	2.5	27 / 7	76	92	—	—	—
Rwanda	9.6	43	16	2.7	14.6	21.7	126	86	6.0	44 / 3	47	18	2.8	65	860
Seychelles	0.1	18	7	1.0	0.1	0.1	37	11	2.2	23 / 8	72	53	—	87	8,670
Somalia	9.0	46	19	2.7	14.3	23.8	166	117	6.7	45 / 3	48	37	0.5	29	—
Tanzania	40.2	38	15	2.3	58.2	82.5	105	75	5.3	44 / 3	51	25	6.2	55	1,200
Uganda	29.2	48	16	3.1	56.4	106.0	263	76	6.7	49 / 3	48	13	5.4	64	920
Zambia	12.2	43	22	2.1	15.5	19.3	58	100	5.5	46 / 2	38	37	15.2	58	1,220
Zimbabwe	13.5	31	21	1.1	16.0	19.1	42	60	3.8	40 / 4	40	37	15.3	81	—
MIDDLE AFRICA	**122**	**43**	**14**	**2.8**	**189**	**306**	**151**	**97**	**6.1**	**46 / 3**	**51**	**41**	**2.5**	**52**	**1,550**
Angola	16.8	47	21	2.7	26.2	42.7	155	132	6.8	46 / 2	43	57	2.1	51	4,400
Cameroon	18.5	36	13	2.3	25.5	34.9	89	74	4.7	42 / 4	52	57	5.1	70	2,120
Central African Republic	4.4	38	19	1.9	5.5	6.5	47	102	5.0	43 / 4	43	38	6.3	66	740
Chad	10.1	44	17	2.7	13.9	20.5	102	106	6.3	46 / 3	47	27	3.5	48	1,280
Congo	3.8	37	13	2.5	5.6	8.8	130	75	5.3	42 / 3	53	60	3.5	71	2,750
Congo, Dem. Rep.	66.5	44	13	3.1	109.7	189.3	185	92	6.5	47 / 3	53	33	d	46	290
Equatorial Guinea	0.6	39	10	2.9	0.9	1.4	132	91	5.4	42 / 4	59	39	3.4	43	21,230
Gabon	1.4	27	12	1.5	1.7	2.1	54	58	3.2	36 / 5	57	84	5.9	87	13,080
Sao Tome and Principe	0.2	35	8	2.7	0.2	0.3	85	77	4.1	42 / 4	64	58	—	86	1,630
SOUTHERN AFRICA	**55**	**24**	**16**	**0.8**	**59**	**62**	**12**	**48**	**2.8**	**33 / 4**	**49**	**56**	**18.5**	**92**	**9,140**
Botswana	1.8	24	14	0.9	2.2	2.4	29	44	2.9	38 / 3	49	57	23.9	96	12,420
Lesotho	1.8	27	25	0.2	1.7	1.6	-11	91	3.5	39 / 5	36	24	23.2	78	1,890

	Population Mid–2008 (millions)	Births Per 1,000 Pop.	Deaths Per 1,000 Pop.	Rate of Natural Increase (%)	Projected Population (millions) mid–2025	mid–2050	Projected Pop. Change 2008–2050 (%)	Infant Mortality Rate[a]	Total Fertility Rate[b]	Percent of Population of Age < 15 / 65 +	Life Expectancy at Birth (Years)	Percent Urban	Percent of Pop. 15–49 with HIV/AIDS, 2007	% of Pop. using Improved Drinking Water Sources, 2006	GNI PPP Per Capita 2007 (US $)
SOUTHERN AFRICA															
(continued)															
Namibia	2.1	25	15	1.0	2.3	2.1	3	47	3.6	41 / 3	47	35	15.3	93	5,120
South Africa	48.3	23	15	0.8	51.5	54.8	13	45	2.7	32 / 4	50	59	18.1	93	9,560
Swaziland	1.1	31	31	0.0	1.0	0.8	-33	85	3.8	41 / 4	33	24	26.1	60	4,930
AMERICAS	**915**	**18**	**7**	**1.2**	**1,080**	**1,258**	**37**	**18**	**2.3**	**26 / 9**	**75**	**78**	**0.6**	**94**	**22,260**
NORTHERN AMERICA	**338**	**14**	**8**	**0.6**	**393**	**480**	**42**	**7**	**2.1**	**20 / 13**	**78**	**79**	**0.6**	**99**	**44,790**
Canada	33.3	11	7	0.3	37.6	41.9	26	5.4	1.6	17 / 14	80	81	0.4	100	35,310
United States	304.5	14	8	0.6	355.7	438.2	44	6.6	2.1	20 / 13	78	79	0.6	99	45,850
LATIN AMERICA/															
CARIBBEAN	**577**	**21**	**6**	**1.5**	**687**	**778**	**35**	**23**	**2.5**	**30 / 6**	**73**	**77**	**0.5**	**91**	**9,080**
CENTRAL AMERICA	**150**	**22**	**5**	**1.7**	**180**	**203**	**35**	**22**	**2.5**	**33 / 5**	**74**	**70**	**0.4**	**93**	**10,340**
Belize	0.3	27	4	2.3	0.4	0.5	57	18	3.1	39 / 5	73	50	2.1	91	5,100
Costa Rica	4.5	16	4	1.3	5.6	6.3	40	9.7	1.9	28 / 6	78	59	0.4	98	8,340
El Salvador	7.2	24	6	1.8	9.1	11.2	55	24	2.8	34 / 5	71	60	0.8	84	4,840
Guatemala	13.7	34	6	2.8	20.0	27.9	104	34	4.4	43 / 4	69	47	0.8	96	4,120
Honduras	7.3	27	5	2.2	9.8	12.4	69	23	3.3	38 / 4	72	46	0.7	84	3,160
Mexico	107.7	20	5	1.6	123.8	131.6	22	19	2.3	32 / 6	75	76	0.3	95	12,580
Nicaragua	5.7	26	5	2.1	6.8	7.9	40	29	2.9	38 / 4	71	59	0.2	79	2,080
Panama	3.4	20	4	1.6	4.2	5.0	46	15	2.4	30 / 6	75	64	1.0	92	8,340
CARIBBEAN	**41**	**19**	**8**	**1.1**	**46**	**50**	**24**	**33**	**2.5**	**28 / 8**	**71**	**64**	**1.1**	**84**	**—**
Antigua and Barbuda	0.1	17	7	1.0	0.1	0.1	29	20	2.1	28 / 7	73	31	—	91	12,610
Bahamas	0.3	17	6	1.1	0.4	0.5	34	14	1.9	28 / 6	72	83	3.0	97	—
Barbados	0.3	14	8	0.6	0.3	0.3	-7	14	1.8	22 / 12	76	38	1.2	100	10,880
Cuba	11.2	10	7	0.3	11.2	9.9	-11	5.3	1.4	18 / 12	77	76	0.1	91	—
Dominica	0.1	16	9	0.7	0.1	0.1	-11	16	3.0	29 / 10	75	73	—	97	5,650
Dominican Republic	9.9	24	6	1.8	12.1	14.0	42	32	3.0	33 / 6	72	67	1.1	95	5,050
Grenada	0.1	19	7	1.2	0.1	0.1	-10	17	2.1	29 / 6	68	31	—	94	6,010
Guadeloupe	0.4	15	7	0.8	0.5	0.5	21	8	2.1	24 / 11	79	100	—	98	—
Haiti	9.1	29	11	1.8	11.7	15.1	65	57	4.0	38 / 4	58	43	2.2	58	1,050
Jamaica	2.7	17	6	1.1	3.0	3.4	25	21	2.1	30 / 8	72	52	1.6	93	5,050
Martinique	0.4	13	7	0.7	0.4	0.4	-13	6	1.9	22 / 12	80	98	—	—	—
Netherlands Antilles	0.2	14	7	0.7	0.2	0.2	-4	5	2.0	23 / 10	75	92	—	—	—
Puerto Rico	4.0	12	8	0.5	4.1	3.8	-5	9.2	1.7	21 / 13	78	94	—	—	—
St. Kitts-Nevis	0.05	18	8	1.0	0.1	0.1	31	15	2.3	28 / 8	70	32	—	99	10,430
Saint Lucia	0.2	15	7	0.8	0.2	0.2	30	19.4	1.7	28 / 7	73	28	—	98	7,090
St. Vincent & the Grenadines	0.1	17	8	0.9	0.1	0.1	-13	17.6	2.1	29 / 7	72	40	—	—	5,720
Trinidad and Tobago	1.3	14	8	0.6	1.4	1.3	-1	24	1.6	24 / 7	69	12	1.5	94	14,580
SOUTH AMERICA	**387**	**20**	**6**	**1.4**	**461**	**524**	**36**	**23**	**2.4**	**29 / 6**	**73**	**81**	**0.6**	**91**	**9,290**
Argentina	39.7	19	8	1.1	46.3	52.5	32	13.3	2.4	26 / 10	75	91	0.5	96	12,990

	Population Mid–2008 (millions)	Births Per 1,000 Pop.	Deaths Per 1,000 Pop.	Rate of Natural Increase (%)	Projected Population (millions) mid–2025	Projected Population (millions) mid–2050	Projected Pop. Change 2008–2050 (%)	Infant Mortality Rate[a]	Total Fertility Rate[b]	Percent of Population of Age < 15 / 65 +	Life Expectancy at Birth (Years)	Percent Urban	Percent of Pop. 15–49 with HIV/AIDS, 2007	% of Pop. using Improved Drinking Water Sources, 2006	GNI PPP Per Capita 2007 (US $)
SOUTH AMERICA															
(continued)															
Bolivia	10.0	29	8	2.1	13.3	16.7	67	51	3.7	38 / 4	65	64	0.2	86	4,140
Brazil	195.1	20	6	1.3	228.9	259.8	33	24	2.3	28 / 6	72	83	0.6	91	9,370
Chile	16.8	14	5	0.9	19.1	20.2	20	8.8	2.0	25 / 8	78	87	0.3	95	12,590
Colombia	44.4	20	6	1.4	53.8	59.2	33	19	2.4	30 / 5	72	72	0.6	93	6,640
Ecuador	13.8	26	6	2.0	17.5	20.4	48	25	3.1	33 / 6	75	62	0.3	95	7,040
French Guiana	0.2	32	4	2.8	0.3	0.4	96	10.4	3.9	35 / 4	75	76	—	84	—
Guyana	0.8	21	9	1.2	0.8	0.5	-29	48	2.7	32 / 5	65	28	2.5	93	2,600
Paraguay	6.2	27	6	2.1	8.0	10.1	62	36	3.5	36 / 5	71	57	0.6	77	4,380
Peru	27.9	21	6	1.5	34.0	39.3	41	24	2.6	32 / 6	71	76	0.5	84	7,240
Suriname	0.5	17	7	1.1	0.5	0.5	-8	16	2.5	30 / 7	69	74	2.4	92	6,000
Uruguay	3.3	14	9	0.5	3.5	3.7	11	10.5	2.0	24 / 13	76	94	0.6	100	11,040
Venezuela	27.9	25	4	2.1	34.9	41.1	47	16.5	2.6	31 / 5	73	88	—	—	11,920
ASIA	**4,052**	**19**	**7**	**1.2**	**4,793**	**5,427**	**34**	**45**	**2.4**	**27 / 7**	**69**	**42**	**0.2**	**88**	**$ 5,650**
ASIA (Excl. China)	**2,728**	**23**	**7**	**1.5**	**3,317**	**3,990**	**46**	**51**	**2.8**	**31 / 6**	**68**	**40**	**0.3**	**88**	**5,780**
WESTERN ASIA	**225**	**25**	**6**	**1.9**	**290**	**363**	**61**	**41**	**3.3**	**34 / 5**	**70**	**64**	**—**	**89**	**10,160**
Armenia	3.1	15	9	0.5	3.3	3.3	7	26	1.7	21 / 11	71	64	0.1	98	5,900
Azerbaijan	8.7	18	6	1.2	9.7	11.6	34	12	2.3	24 / 7	72	52	0.2	78	6,370
Bahrain	0.8	20	3	1.7	1.0	1.2	53	8	2.5	27 / 3	75	100	—	—	34,310
Cyprus	1.1	12	7	0.6	1.1	1.1	2	6	1.5	18 / 11	78	62	—	100	26,370
Georgia	4.6	11	10	0.1	4.2	3.3	-28	16	1.4	18 / 15	74	53	0.1	99	4,770
Iraq	29.5	34	10	2.4	43.3	61.9	110	94	4.6	42 /3	58	67	—	77	—
Israel	7.5	21	5	1.6	9.3	11.2	49	3.5	2.9	28 / 10	80	92	0.1	100	25,930
Jordan	5.8	28	4	2.4	7.7	9.7	65	24	3.6	37 / 3	72	83	—	98	5,160
Kuwait	2.7	21	2	1.9	3.6	4.8	80	8	2.6	24 / 2	78	98	—	—	49,970
Lebanon	4.0	19	5	1.4	4.6	5.0	26	19	1.9	27 / 8	72	87	0.1	100	10,050
Oman	2.7	24	3	2.1	3.1	3.9	42	10	3.4	30 / 2	74	71	—	82	19,740
Palestinian Territory	4.2	37	4	3.3	6.2	8.8	113	25	4.6	46 / 3	72	72	—	89	—
Qatar	0.9	17	2	1.5	1.1	1.4	48	7	2.6	23 / 1	75	100	—	100	—
Saudi Arabia	28.1	29	3	2.7	35.7	49.8	77	16	4.0	38 / 2	76	81	—	—	22,910
Syria	19.9	28	4	2.5	26.8	34.0	71	19	3.5	37 / 3	73	50	—	89	4,370
Turkey	74.8	19	6	1.2	87.8	88.7	19	23	2.2	28 / 6	72	62	—	97	12,090
United Arab Emirates	4.5	15	2	1.3	6.2	7.8	75	7	2.0	19 / 1	78	83	—	100	—
Yemen	22.2	41	9	3.2	35.2	55.8	151	77	6.2	45 / 3	61	30	—	66	2,200
SOUTH CENTRAL ASIA	**1,683**	**25**	**8**	**1.7**	**2,089**	**2,605**	**55**	**61**	**3.0**	**33 / 5**	**65**	**30**	**0.3**	**87**	**2,940**
Afghanistan	32.7	47	21	2.6	50.3	81.9	150	163	6.8	45 / 2	43	20	—	22	—
Bangladesh	147.3	24	7	1.7	180.1	215.1	46	52	2.7	34 / 4	63	24	—	80	1,340
Bhutan	0.7	30	7	2.3	0.9	1.0	45	40	3.6	32 / 5	66	31	0.1	81	4,980
India	1,149.3	24	8	1.6	1,407.7	1,755.2	53	57	2.8	32 / 5	65	28	0.3	89	2,740
Iran	72.2	20	5	1.4	88.0	100.2	39	32	2.1	26 / 5	71	67	0.2	94	10,800

	Population Mid–2008 (millions)	Births Per 1,000 Pop.	Deaths Per 1,000 Pop.	Rate of Natural Increase (%)	Projected Population (millions) mid–2025	Projected Population (millions) mid–2050	Projected Pop. Change 2008–2050 (%)	Infant Mortality Rate[a]	Total Fertility Rate[b]	Percent of Population of Age < 15 / 65 +	Life Expectancy at Birth (Years)	Percent Urban	Percent of Pop. 15–49 with HIV/AIDS, 2007	% of Pop. using Improved Drinking Water Sources, 2006	GNI PPP Per Capita 2007 (US $)
SOUTH CENTRAL ASIA															
(continued)															
Kazakhstan	15.7	21	10	1.0	17.1	17.4	11	29	2.5	27 / 8	66	53	0.1	96	9,700
Kyrgyzstan	5.2	24	7	1.6	6.5	8.1	54	50	2.8	32 / 6	66	35	0.1	89	1,950
Maldives	0.3	19	4	1.6	0.4	0.5	73	16	2.2	32 / 5	73	27	—	83	5,040
Nepal	27.0	29	9	2.1	36.5	48.7	81	48	3.1	37 / 4	64	17	0.5	89	1,040
Pakistan	172.8	31	8	2.2	228.9	295.2	71	75	4.1	39 / 4	63	35	0.1	90	2,570
Sri Lanka	20.3	19	7	1.2	23.2	25.4	25	15	2.4	27 / 6	71	15	—	82	4,210
Tajikistan	7.3	27	5	2.2	9.5	11.5	57	65	3.3	38 / 4	67	26	0.3	67	1,710
Turkmenistan	5.2	24	6	1.7	6.5	7.6	47	74	2.9	35 / 4	62	47	<0.1	—	6,640
Uzbekistan	27.2	24	7	1.7	33.3	37.6	38	48	2.7	35 / 5	67	36	0.1	88	1,680
SOUTHEAST ASIA	**586**	**20**	**7**	**1.4**	**709**	**826**	**41**	**31**	**2.5**	**29 / 6**	**70**	**45**	**0.5**	**86**	**4,440**
Brunei	0.4	19	3	1.6	0.5	0.6	67	7	2.0	30 / 3	75	72	—	—	49,900
Cambodia	14.7	26	8	1.8	20.6	30.5	108	67	3.5	36 / 4	62	15	0.8	65	1,690
Indonesia	239.9	21	6	1.5	291.9	343.1	43	34	2.6	29 / 6	70	48	0.2	80	3,580
Laos	5.9	34	10	2.4	8.7	12.3	110	70	4.5	44 / 4	61	27	0.2	60	1,940
Malaysia	27.7	21	5	1.6	34.6	40.4	46	9	2.6	32 / 4	74	68	0.5	99	13,570
Myanmar	49.2	19	10	0.9	55.4	58.7	19	70	2.2	27 / 6	61	31	0.7	80	—
Philippines	90.5	26	5	2.1	120.2	150.1	66	25	3.3	35 / 4	69	63	—	93	3,730
Singapore	4.8	11	5	0.6	5.3	5.3	10	2.4	1.4	19 / 9	81	100	0.2	—	48,520
Thailand	66.1	13	8	0.5	70.2	68.9	4	16	1.6	22 / 7	72	36	1.4	98	7,880
Timor-Leste	1.1	42	11	3.2	1.7	3.0	179	88	6.7	45 / 3	60	22	—	62	3,190
Vietnam	86.2	17	5	1.2	100.1	112.8	31	16	2.1	26 / 7	73	27	0.5	92	2,550
EAST ASIA	**1,558**	**12**	**7**	**0.5**	**1,705**	**1,633**	**5**	**21**	**1.6**	**19 / 9**	**74**	**50**	**0.1**	**89**	**8,380**
China	1,324.7	12	7	0.5	1,476.0	1,437.0	8	23	1.6	19 / 8	73	45	0.1	88	5,370
China, Hong Kong SAR[c]	7.0	10	6	0.5	8.0	8.8	26	1.6	1.0	13 / 13	82	100	—	—	44,050
China, Macao SAR[c]	0.6	9	3	0.6	0.6	0.6	5	2	1.0	13 / 7	79	100	—	—	—
Japan	127.7	9	9	-0.0	119.3	95.2	-25	2.8	1.3	13 / 22	82	79	—	100	34,600
Korea, North	23.5	16	7	0.9	25.8	26.4	12	21	2.0	25 / 8	71	60	—	100	—
Korea, South	48.6	10	5	0.5	49.1	42.3	-13	4	1.3	18 / 10	79	82	<0.1	92	24,750
Mongolia	2.7	21	6	1.5	3.3	3.8	45	41	2.3	29 / 4	64	59	0.1	72	3,160
Taiwan	23.0	9	6	0.3	23.1	18.9	-18	4.6	1.1	18 / 10	78	78	—	—	—
EUROPE	**736**	**11**	**11**	**-0.0**	**726**	**685**	**-7**	**6**	**1.5**	**16 / 16**	**75**	**71**	**0.5**	**99**	**24,320**
NORTHERN EUROPE	**98**	**12**	**10**	**0.3**	**108**	**117**	**19**	**4**	**1.8**	**18 / 16**	**79**	**77**	**0.2**	**100**	**34,490**
Channel Islands	0.2	11	9	0.2	0.2	0.1	-5	3.7	1.4	16 / 15	78	31	—	—	—
Denmark	5.5	12	10	0.2	5.6	5.5	0	4.0	1.8	18 / 16	78	72	0.2	100	36,740
Estonia	1.3	12	13	-0.1	1.2	1.1	-18	4.9	1.7	15 / 17	73	69	1.3	100	19,680
Finland	5.3	11	9	0.2	5.6	5.7	8	2.7	1.8	17 / 17	79	63	0.1	100	35,270
Iceland	0.3	15	6	0.8	0.4	0.4	37	1.3	2.1	21 / 12	81	93	0.2	100	34,060
Ireland	4.5	16	6	0.9	4.9	5.1	13	3.1	2.1	20 / 11	79	60	0.2	—	37,040
Latvia	2.3	10	14	-0.4	2.1	1.9	-16	7.6	1.5	14 / 17	72	68	0.8	99	16,890

	Population Mid–2008 (millions)	Births Per 1,000 Pop.	Deaths Per 1,000 Pop.	Rate of Natural Increase (%)	Projected Population (millions) mid–2025	Projected Population (millions) mid–2050	Projected Pop. Change 2008–2050 (%)	Infant Mortality Rate[a]	Total Fertility Rate[b]	Percent of Population of Age < 15 / 65 +	Life Expectancy at Birth (Years)	Percent Urban	Percent of Pop. 15–49 with HIV/AIDS, 2007	% of Pop. using Improved Drinking Water Sources, 2006	GNI PPP Per Capita 2007 (US $)
NORTHERN EUROPE (continued)															
Lithuania	3.4	10	14	-0.4	3.1	2.9	-14	5.9	1.4	15 / 16	71	67	0.1	—	17,180
Norway	4.8	12	9	0.4	5.6	6.6	38	3.1	1.9	19 / 15	80	79	0.1	100	53,690
Sweden	9.2	12	10	0.2	9.9	10.4	13	2.5	1.9	17 / 18	81	84	0.1	100	35,840
United Kingdom	61.3	13	9	0.3	68.8	76.9	26	4.9	1.9	18 / 16	79	80	0.2	100	34,370
WESTERN EUROPE	**188**	**10**	**9**	**0.1**	**191**	**187**	**-0**	**4**	**1.6**	**16 / 18**	**80**	**75**	**0.2**	**100**	**34,910**
Austria	8.4	9	9	0.0	8.8	9.5	14	3.7	1.4	15 / 17	80	67	0.2	100	38,090
Belgium	10.7	12	10	0.2	10.8	11.0	2	3.7	1.7	17 / 17	80	97	0.2	—	35,110
France	62.0	13	8	0.4	66.1	70.0	13	3.6	2.0	18 / 17	81	77	0.4	100	33,470
Germany	82.2	8	10	-0.2	79.6	71.4	-13	3.9	1.3	14 / 19	79	73	0.1	100	33,820
Liechtenstein	0.04	10	6	0.4	0.04	0.04	17	2.6	1.4	17 / 12	80	15	—	—	—
Luxembourg	0.5	11	8	0.3	0.5	0.6	29	4.4	1.6	18 / 14	80	83	0.2	100	64,400
Monaco	0.03	25	16	0.9	0.04	0.04	9	—	—	13 / 22	—	100	—	—	—
Netherlands	16.4	11	8	0.3	16.9	16.8	2	4.4	1.7	18 / 15	80	66	0.2	100	39,500
Switzerland	7.6	10	8	0.2	8.1	8.1	6	4.0	1.5	15 / 16	82	68	0.6	100	43,080
EASTERN EUROPE	**295**	**11**	**14**	**-0.3**	**272**	**231**	**-22**	**9**	**1.4**	**15 / 14**	**69**	**68**	**0.9**	**97**	**13,210**
Belarus	9.7	11	14	-0.3	9.0	7.7	-20	6	1.4	15 / 15	70	73	0.2	100	10,740
Bulgaria	7.6	10	15	-0.5	6.6	5.0	-35	9.2	1.4	13 / 17	73	71	—	99	11,180
Czech Republic	10.4	11	10	0.1	10.2	9.4	-9	3.1	1.4	14 / 15	77	74	—	100	21,820
Hungary	10.0	10	13	-0.4	9.6	8.9	-11	5.9	1.3	15 / 16	73	66	0.1	100	17,430
Moldova	4.1	11	12	-0.1	3.8	3.2	-23	12	1.3	18 / 10	69	41	0.4	90	2,930
Poland	38.1	10	10	0.0	36.7	31.4	-18	6.0	1.3	16 / 14	75	61	0.1	—	15,590
Romania	21.5	10	12	-0.2	19.7	17.1	-20	12.0	1.3	15 / 15	71	55	0.1	88	10,980
Russia	141.9	12	15	-0.3	129.3	110.1	-22	9	1.4	15 / 14	67	73	1.1	97	14,400
Slovakia	5.4	10	10	0.0	5.2	4.7	-12	6.1	1.2	16 / 12	74	56	<0.1	100	19,330
Ukraine	46.2	10	16	-0.6	41.7	33.4	-28	11	1.3	14 / 16	68	68	1.6	97	6,810
SOUTHERN EUROPE	**155**	**10**	**9**	**0.1**	**156**	**150**	**-3**	**5**	**1.4**	**15 / 18**	**79**	**67**	**0.4**	**—**	**26,230**
Albania	3.2	13	6	0.7	3.5	3.6	11	8	1.6	27 / 8	75	45	—	97	6,580
Andorra	0.1	10	3	0.7	0.1	0.1	-4	2.5	1.2	15 / 12	—	90	—	100	—
Bosnia-Herzegovina	3.8	9	9	0.0	3.7	3.1	-20	8	1.2	18 / 13	74	46	<0.1	99	7,280
Croatia	4.4	9	12	-0.3	4.3	3.8	-14	5.7	1.4	16 / 17	76	56	<0.1	99	15,050
Greece	11.2	10	9	0.1	11.3	10.8	-4	3.7	1.4	14 / 19	79	60	0.2	100	32,520
Italy	59.9	9	10	-0.0	62.0	61.7	3	4.2	1.3	14 / 20	81	68	0.4	—	29,900
Kosovo[d]	2.2	21	7	1.4	2.7	3.2	45	33	2.5	33 / 6	69	—	—	—	—
Macedonia	2.0	11	10	0.2	2.0	1.7	-15	13	1.5	20 / 11	74	65	<0.1	100	8,510
Malta	0.4	10	8	0.2	0.4	0.4	-6	3.6	1.4	17 / 14	79	94	0.1	100	20,990
Montenegro	0.6	12	10	0.3	0.6	0.6	-4	11.0	1.6	20 / 13	73	64	—	98	10,290
Portugal	10.6	10	10	-0.0	10.5	9.3	-12	3.5	1.3	15 / 17	79	55	0.5	99	20,640
San Marino	0.03	10	7	0.3	0.04	0.04	13	3.3	1.2	15 / 16	82	84	—	—	37,080

	Population Mid–2008 (millions)	Births Per 1,000 Pop.	Deaths Per 1,000 Pop.	Rate of Natural Increase (%)	Projected Population (millions) mid–2025	Projected Population (millions) mid–2050	Projected Pop. Change 2008–2050 (%)	Infant Mortality Rate[a]	Total Fertility Rate[b]	Percent of Population of Age < 15 / 65 +	Life Expectancy at Birth (Years)	Percent Urban	Percent of Pop. 15–49 with HIV/AIDS, 2007	% of Pop. using Improved Drinking Water Sources, 2006	GNI PPP Per Capita 2007 (US $)
SOUTHERN EUROPE (continued)															
Serbia	7.4	10	14	-0.4	6.7	5.8	-21	7.4	1.4	16 / 17	73	56	0.1[e]	99[e]	10,220[e]
Slovenia	2.0	10	9	0.1	2.1	1.9	-7	3.1	1.4	14 / 16	78	48	<0.1	—	26,640
Spain	46.5	11	9	0.2	46.2	43.9	-6	3.7	1.4	14 / 17	80	77	0.5	100	30,110
OCEANIA	**35**	**18**	**7**	**1.1**	**42**	**49**	**40**	**25**	**2.4**	**25 / 10**	**76**	**70**	**0.4**	**85**	**23,910**
Australia	21.3	14	7	0.7	24.7	28.1	32	4.7	1.9	19 / 13	81	87	0.2	100	33,340
Federated States of Micronesia	0.1	26	6	2.0	0.1	0.1	21	40	4.1	37 / 4	67	22	—	94	3,710
Fiji	0.9	21	6	1.5	0.9	0.9	8	17	2.6	31 / 5	68	51	0.1	47	4,370
French Polynesia	0.3	18	4	1.3	0.3	0.4	34	6.8	2.2	28 / 5	75	53	—	100	—
Guam	0.2	19	4	1.5	0.2	0.2	38	10.7	2.6	29 / 6	78	93	—	100	—
Kiribati	0.1	27	9	1.8	0.1	0.2	99	52	3.5	36 / 4	61	44	—	65	2,190
Marshall Islands	0.1	38	6	3.2	0.1	0.1	101	23	4.4	41 / 2	66	68	—	88	—
Nauru	0.01	31	10	2.1	0.01	0.02	49	42	3.4	39 / 1	55	100	—	—	—
New Caledonia	0.2	18	5	1.3	0.3	0.4	46	7	2.3	28 / 7	76	58	—	—	—
New Zealand	4.3	15	7	0.8	4.9	5.5	28	5.0	2.2	21 / 13	80	86	0.1	—	26,340
Palau	0.02	13	7	0.6	0.02	0.03	27	20	1.9	24 / 6	71	77	—	89	—
Papua New Guinea	6.5	31	10	2.1	8.6	11.2	73	62	3.9	40 / 2	57	13	1.5	40	1,500
Samoa	0.2	29	6	2.4	0.2	0.2	14	20	4.4	41 / 4	73	22	—	88	3,570
Solomon Islands	0.5	34	8	2.6	0.7	1.0	88	48	4.5	39 / 3	62	17	—	70	1,400
Tonga	0.1	26	6	2.0	0.1	0.1	-27	12	3.7	35 / 6	71	24	—	100	3,430
Tuvalu	0.01	26	10	1.6	0.01	0.02	74	35	3.7	36 / 6	64	47	—	93	—
Vanuatu	0.2	31	6	2.5	0.4	0.5	109	27	4.0	41 / 3	67	21	—	59	2,890

(—) Indicates data unavailable or inapplicable.
[a] Infant deaths per 1,000 live births.
[b] Average number of children born to a woman during her lifetime.
[c] Special Administrative Region
[d] Kosovo declared independence from Serbia on Febuary 17, 2008. Serbia has not recognized Kosovo's independence.
[e] Includes Kosovo

Urban population data are the percentage of the total population living in areas termed urban by that country.
Table modified from the **2008 World Population Data Sheet** of the Population Reference Bureau.

CANADA, MEXICO AND
UNITED STATES REFERENCE MAP

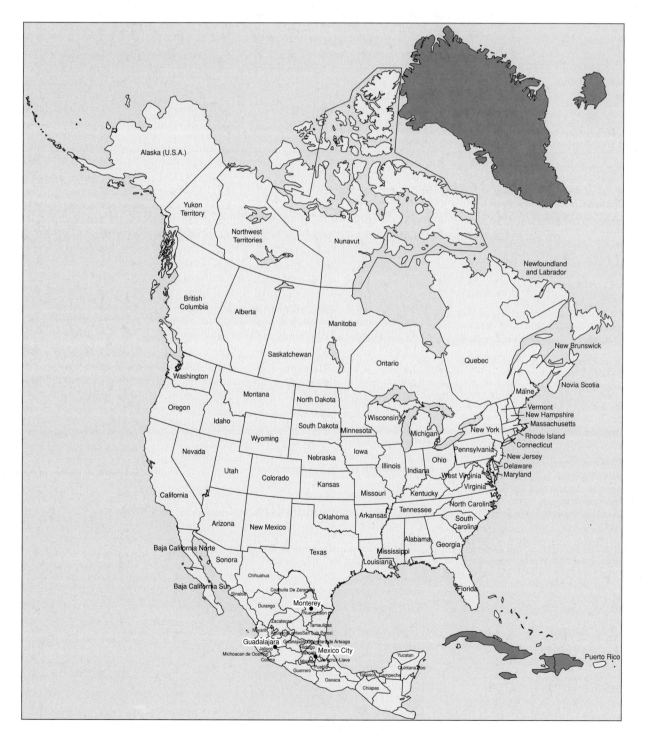

Glossary

Terms in italics identify related glossary items.

A

absolute direction Direction with respect to cardinal east, west, north, and south reference points.

absolute distance (*syn:* geodesic distance) The shortest-path separation between two places measured on a standard unit of length (miles or kilometers, usually); also called real distance.

absolute location (*syn:* mathematical location) The exact position of an object or place stated in spatial coordinates of a grid system designed for locational purposes. In geography, the reference system is the *globe grid* of parallels of *latitude* north or south of the *equator* and of meridians of *longitude* east or west of a *prime meridian.* Absolute globe locations are cited in degrees, minutes, and (for greater precision) seconds of latitude and longitude north or south and east or west of the equatorial and prime meridian base lines.

absorbing barrier A condition that blocks the *diffusion* of an *innovation* or prevents its adoption.

accessibility The relative ease with which a destination may be reached from other locations; the relative opportunity for *spatial interaction.* May be measured in geometric, social, or economic terms.

acculturation Cultural modification or change that results when one *culture* group or individual adopts traits of a dominant or *host society;* cultural development or change through "borrowing."

acid precipitation *Precipitation* that is unusually acidic; created when oxides of sulfur and nitrogen change chemically as they dissolve in water vapor in the *atmosphere* and return to earth as acidic rain, snow, or fog.

activity space The area within which people move freely on their rounds of regular activity.

adaptation (1) Genetic modification making a population more fit for existence under specific environmental conditions; (2) in immigration, the term summarizes how individuals, households, and communities respond and adjust to new experiences and social and cultural surroundings.

agglomeration The spatial grouping of people or activities for mutual benefit; in *economic geography,* the concentration of productive enterprises for collective or cooperative use of *infrastructure* and sharing of labor resources and market access.

agglomeration economies (*syn:* external economies) The savings to an individual enterprise derived from locational association with a cluster of other similar economic activities, such as other factories or retail stores.

agricultural density The number of rural residents per unit of agriculturally productive land; a variant of *physiological density* that excludes urban population.

agriculture The science and practice of farming, including the cultivation of the soil and the rearing of livestock.

amalgamation theory In *ethnic geography,* the concept that multiethnic societies become a merger of the *culture traits* of their member groups.

anecumene See *nonecumene.*

animism A belief that natural objects may be the abode of dead people, spirits, or gods who occasionally give the objects the appearance of life.

antecedent boundary A *boundary* line established before the area in question is well populated.

antipode The point on the earth's surface that is diametrically opposite the observer's location.

aquaculture Production and harvesting of fish and shellfish in land-based ponds.

aquifer A porous, water-bearing layer of rock, sand, or gravel below ground level.

arable land Land that is or can be cultivated.

arithmetic density See *crude density.*

artifacts The material manifestations of *culture,* including tools, housing, systems of land use, clothing, and the like. Elements in the *technological subsystem* of culture.

artificial boundary See *geometric boundary.*

aspect In *map projections,* the positional relationship between the globe and the *developable surface* on which it is visually projected: the polar aspect is tangent at the pole; the equatorial aspect is tangent at the equator; the oblique aspect is tangent anywhere else.

assimilation A two-part *behavioral* and *structural* process by which a minority population reduces or loses completely its identifying cultural characteristics and blends into the *host society.*

atmosphere The air or mixture of gases surrounding the earth.

autonomous nationalism Movement by a dissident minority intent to achieve partial or total independence of territory it occupies from the *state* within which it lies.

awareness space Locations or places about which an individual has knowledge even without visiting all of them; includes *activity space* and additional areas newly encountered or about which one acquires information.

azimuth Direction of a line defined at its starting point by its angle in relation to a *meridian.*

azimuthal projection See *planar projection.*

B

basic sector Those products or services of an *urban* economy that are exported outside the city itself, earning income for the community.

behavioral assimilation (*syn:* cultural assimilation) The process of integration into a common cultural life through acquisition of the sentiments, attitudes, and experiences of other groups.

beneficiation The enrichment of low-grade ores through concentration and other processes to reduce their waste content and increase their *transferability.*

bilingualism Describing a society's use of two *official languages.*

biomass The total dry weight of all living organisms within a unit area; plant and animal matter that can in any way be used as a source of energy.

biome A major ecological community, including plants and animals, occupying an extensive earth area.

biosphere (*syn:* ecosphere) The thin film of air, water, and earth within which we live, including the *atmosphere,* surrounding and subsurface waters, and the upper reaches of the earth's crust.

birth rate The ratio of the number of live births during one year to the total population, usually at the midpoint of the same year, expressed as the number of births per year per 1000 population.

Boserup thesis The view that population growth independently forces a conversion from extensive to intensive *subsistence* agriculture.

boundary A line separating one political unit from another; see *international boundary.*

boundary dispute See *functional dispute.*

Brandt Report Titled *North-South: A Program for Survival,* a report of the Independent Commission on International Development Issues, published in 1980 and named for the commission chairman, Willy Brandt.

break-of-bulk point A location where goods are transferred from one type of carrier to another (e.g., from barge to railroad).

brownfield A former industrial or commercial site that is under-used, vacant, or abandoned where there is the potential for environmental contamination.

Buddhism A *universalizing religion,* primarily of eastern and central Asia, based on teachings of Siddhartha Gautama, the Buddha, that suffering is inherent in all life but can be relieved by mental and moral self-purification.

built environment That part of the *physical landscape* that represents *material culture;* the buildings, roads, bridges, and similar structures large and small of the *cultural landscape.*

C

carrying capacity The maximum population numbers that an area can support on a continuing basis without experiencing unacceptable deterioration; for humans, the numbers supportable by an area's known and used resources—usually agricultural ones.

cartogram A map that has been simplified to present a single idea in a diagrammatic way; the base is not normally true to scale.

caste One of the hereditary social classes in *Hinduism* that determines one's occupation and position in society.

central business district (CBD) The nucleus or "downtown" of a city, where retail stores, offices, and cultural activities are concentrated, mass transit systems converge, and land values and building densities are high.

central city That part of the *metropolitan area* contained within the boundaries of the main city around which suburbs have developed.

central place An *urban* or other settlement node whose primary function is to provide goods and services to the consuming population of its *hinterland, complementary region,* or trade area.

central place theory A deductive theory formulated by Walter *Christaller* (1893–1969) to explain the size and distribution of settlements through reference to competitive supply of goods and services to dispersed rural populations.

centrifugal force 1: In *urban geography,* economic and social forces pushing households and businesses outward from central and inner-city locations. **2:** In *political geography,* forces of disruption and dissolution threatening the unity of a *state.*

centripetal force 1: In *urban geography,* a force attracting establishments or activities to the city center. **2:** In *political geography,* forces tending to bind together the citizens of a state.

chain migration The process by which *migration* movements from a common home area to a specific destination are sustained by links of friendship or kinship between first movers and later followers.

channelized migration The tendency for *migration* to flow between areas that are socially and economically allied by past migration patterns, by economic and trade connections, or by some other affinity.

charter group In plural societies, the early arriving ethnic group that created the *first effective settlement* and established the recognized cultural norms to which other, later groups are expected to conform.

chlorofluorocarbons (CFCs) A family of synthetic chemicals that has significant commercial applications but whose emissions are contributing to the depletion of the *ozone* layer.

choropleth map A *thematic map* presenting spatial data as average values per unit area.

Christaller Walter Christaller (1893–1969), German geographer credited with developing *central place theory* (1933).

Christianity A *monotheistic, universalizing religion* based on the teachings of Jesus Christ and of the Bible as sacred scripture.

circular and cumulative causation A process through which tendencies for economic growth are self-reinforcing; an expression of the *multiplier effect,* it tends to favor major cities and *core* regions over less-advantaged *peripheral* regions.

city A multifunctional nucleated settlement with a *central business district* and both residential and nonresidential land uses.

climate A summary of weather conditions in a place or region over a period of time.

cluster migration A pattern of movement and settlement resulting from the collective action of a distinctive social or *ethnic group.*

cognitive map See *mental map.*

cohort A population group unified by a specific common characteristic, such as age, and subsequently treated as a statistical unit during their lifetimes.

collective farm In the former Soviet *planned economy,* the cooperative operation of an agricultural enterprise under state control of production and market, but without full status or support as a state enterprise.

colony In *ethnic geography,* an urban ethnic area serving as point of entry and temporary *acculturation* zone for a specific immigrant group.

commercial economy A system of production of goods and services for exchange in competitive markets where price and availability are determined by supply and demand forces.

commercial energy Commercially traded fuels, such as coal, oil, or natural gas; excluding wood, vegetable or animal wastes, or other *biomass.*

compact state A *state* whose territory is nearly circular.

comparative advantage The principle that an area produces the items for which it has the greatest ratio of advantage or the least ratio of disadvantage in comparison to other areas, assuming free trade exists.

complementarity The actual or potential relationship of two places or regions that each produce different goods or services for which the other has an effective demand, resulting in an exchange between the locales.

complementary region The area served by a *central place.*

concentration In *spatial distributions,* the clustering of a phenomenon around a central location.

concentric zone model A model describing urban land uses as a series of circular belts or rings

around a core *central business district,* each ring housing a distinct type of land use.

conformality The map property of correct angles and shapes of small areas.

conformal projection A *map projection* that retains correct shapes of small areas; lines of *latitude* and *longitude* cross at right angles and *scale* **(1)** is the same in all directions at any point on the map.

Confucianism A Chinese *value system* and *ethnic religion* emphasizing ethics, social morality, tradition, and ancestor worship.

conic projection A *map projection* employing a cone placed tangent or secant to the globe as the presumed *developable surface.*

connectivity The directness of routes linking pairs of places; an indication of the degree of internal connection in a transport *network.* More generally, all of the tangible and intangible means of connection and communication between places.

consequent boundary *(syn:* ethnographic boundary) A *boundary* line that coincides with some cultural divide, such as religion or language.

conservation The wise use or preservation of natural resources to maintain supplies and qualities at levels sufficient to meet present and future needs.

contagious diffusion A form of *expansion diffusion* that depends on direct contact. The process of dispersion is centrifugal, strongly influenced by distance, and dependent on interaction between actual and potential adopters of the *innovation.* Its name derives from the pattern of spread of contagious diseases.

continental shelf A gently sloping seaward extension of the landmass found off the coasts of many continents; its outer margin is marked by a transition to the ocean depths at about 200 meters (660 feet).

conurbation A continuous, extended *urban* area formed by the growing together of several formerly separate, expanding cities.

Convention on the Law of the Sea See *United Nations Convention on the Law of the Sea.*

core area 1: In *economic geography,* a "core region," the national or world districts of concentrated economic power, wealth, innovation, and advanced technology. **2:** In *political geography,* the heartland or nucleus of a *state,* containing its most developed area, greatest wealth, densest populations, and clearest national identity.

core-periphery model A model of the spatial structure of an economic system in which underdeveloped or declining peripheral areas are defined with respect to their dependence on a dominating developed *core region.*

core region See *core area* **(1).**

counter migration *(syn:* return migration) The return of migrants to the regions from which they earlier emigrated.

country See *state.*

creole A *language* developed from a *pidgin* to become the native tongue of a society.

critical distance The distance beyond which cost, effort, and/or means play a determining role in the willingness of people to travel.

crop rotation The annual alteration of crops that make differential demands on or contributions to soil fertility.

crude birth rate (CBR) See *birth rate.*

crude death rate (CDR) See *death rate.*

crude density (*syn:* arithmetic density) The number of people per unit area of land.

cultural assimilation See *behavioral assimilation.*

cultural convergence The tendency for *cultures* to become more alike as they increasingly share *technology* and organizational structures in a modern world united by improved transportation and communication.

cultural divergence The likelihood or tendency for *cultures* to become increasingly dissimilar with the passage of time.

cultural ecology The study of the interactions between societies and the natural *environments* they occupy.

cultural geography A branch of *systematic geography* that focuses on culturally determined human activities, the impact of *material* and *nonmaterial* human *culture* on the environment, and the human organization of space.

cultural integration The interconnectedness of all aspects of a *culture:* no part can be altered without creating an impact on other components of the culture.

cultural landscape The *natural landscape* as modified by human activities and bearing the imprint of a *culture* group or society; the *built environment.*

culture 1: A society's collective beliefs, symbols, values, forms of behavior, and social organizations, together with its tools, structures, and artifacts created according to the group's conditions of life; transmitted as a heritage to succeeding generations and undergoing adoptions, modifications, and changes in the process. **2:** A collective term for a group displaying uniform cultural characteristics.

culture complex A related set of *culture traits* descriptive of one aspect of a society's behavior or activity. Culture complexes may be as basic as those associated with food preparation, serving, and consumption or as involved as those associated with religious beliefs or business practices.

culture hearth A nuclear area within which an advanced and distinctive set of *culture traits,* ideas, and *technologies* develops and from which there is *diffusion* of those characteristics and the *cultural landscape* features they imply.

culture realm A collective of *culture regions* sharing related culture systems; a major world area having sufficient distinctiveness to be perceived as set apart from other realms in terms of cultural characteristics and complexes.

culture rebound The readoption by later generations of *culture traits* and identities associated with immigrant forebears or ancestral homelands.

culture region A *formal* or *functional region* within which common cultural characteristics prevail. It may be based on single *culture traits,* on *culture complexes,* or on political, social, or economic integration.

culture system A generalization suggesting shared, identifying traits uniting two or more *culture complexes.*

culture trait A single distinguishing feature of regular occurrence within a *culture,* such as the use of chopsticks or the observance of a particular caste system. A single element of learned behavior.

cumulative causation See *circular and cumulative causation.*

custom The body of traditional practices, usages, and conventions that regulate social life.

cylindrical projection A *map projection* employing a cylinder wrapped around the globe as the presumed *developable surface.*

D

Daoism See *Taoism.*

death rate (*syn:* mortality rate) A mortality index usually calculated as the number of deaths per year per 1000 population.

deforestation The clearing of land through total removal of forest cover.

deglomeration The process of deconcentration; the location of industrial or other activities away from established *agglomerations* in response to growing costs of congestion, competition, and regulation.

deindustrialization The cumulative and sustained decline in the contribution of manufacturing to a national economy.

demographic equation A mathematical expression that summarizes the contribution of different demographic processes to the population change of a given area during a specified time period. $P_2 = P_1 + B_{1-2} - D_{1-2} + IM_{1-2} - OM_{1-2}$, where P_2 is population at time 2; P_1 is population at beginning date; B_{1-2} is the number of births between times 1 and 2; D_{1-2} is the number of deaths during that period; IM_{1-2} is the number of in-migrants and OM_{1-2} the number of out-migrants between times 1 and 2.

demographic momentum See *population momentum.*

demographic transition A model of the effect of economic development on population growth. A first stage involves stable numbers with both high *birth rates* and *death rates;* the second displays high birth rates, falling death rates, and population increases. Stage three shows reduction in population growth as birth rates decline to the level of death rates. The fourth and final stage again implies a population stable in size but with larger numbers than at the start of the transition process. An idealized summary of population history of industrializing Europe, its application to newly developing countries is questioned.

demography The scientific study of population, with particular emphasis upon quantitative aspects.

density The quantity of anything (people, buildings, animals, traffic, etc.) per unit area.

dependency ratio The number of dependents, old or young, that each 100 persons in the economically productive years must on average support.

desertification Extension of desert-like landscapes as a result of overgrazing, destruction of the forests, or other human-induced changes, usually in semiarid regions.

developable surface *Projection* surface (such as a plane, cone, or cylinder) that is or can be made flat without distortion.

development The process of growth, expansion, or realization of potential; bringing regional resources into full productive use.

devolution The transfer of certain powers from the *state* central government to separate political subdivisions within the state's territory.

dialect A *language* variant marked by vocabulary, grammar, and pronunciation differences from other variants of the same common language. When those variations are spatial or regional, they are called *geographic dialects;* when they are indicative of socioeconomic or educational levels, they are called *social dialects.*

dialect geography See *linguistic geography.*

dibble Any small hand tool or stick to make a hole for planting.

diffusion The spread or movement of a phenomenon over space or through time. The dispersion of a *culture trait* or characteristic or new ideas and practices from an origin area (e.g., *language,* plant *domestication,* new industrial *technology*). Recognized types include *relocation, expansion, contagious,* and *hierarchical* diffusion.

diffusion barrier Any condition that hinders the flow of information, the movement of people, or the spread of an *innovation.*

direction bias A statement of *movement bias* observing that among all possible directions of movement or flow, one or only a very few are favored and dominant.

dispersion In *spatial distributions,* a statement of the amount of spread of a phenomenon over area or around a central location. Dispersion in this sense represents a continuum from clustered, concentrated, or agglomerated (at one end) to dispersed or scattered (at the other).

distance bias A statement of *movement bias* observing that short journeys or interchanges are favored over more distant ones.

distance decay The declining intensity of any activity, process, or function with increasing distance from its point of origin.

domestication The successful transformation of plant or animal species from a wild state to a condition of dependency on human management, usually with distinct physical change from wild forebears.

doubling time The time period required for any beginning total experiencing a compounding growth to double in size.

E

ecology The scientific study of how living creatures affect each other and what determines their distribution and abundance.

economic base The manufacturing and service activities performed by the *basic sector* of a city's labor force; functions of a city performed to satisfy demands external to the city itself and, in that performance, earning income to support the urban population.

economic geography The branch of *systematic geography* concerned with how people support themselves, with the spatial patterns of production, distribution, and consumption of goods and services, and with the areal variation of economic activities over the surface of the earth.

ecosphere See *biosphere.*

ecosystem A population of organisms existing together in a small, relatively homogeneous area (pond, forest, small island), together with the energy, air, water, soil, and chemicals upon which it depends.

ecumene That part of the earth's surface physically suitable for permanent human settlement; the permanently inhabited areas of the earth.

edge city Distinct sizable nodal concentration of retail and office space of lower than central city densities and situated on the outer fringes of older metropolitan areas; usually localized by or near major highway intersections.

electoral geography The study of the geographical elements of the organization and results of elections.

elongated state A *state* whose territory is long and narrow.

enclave A small bit of foreign territory lying within a *state* but not under its jurisdiction.

environment Surroundings; the totality of things that in any way may affect an organism, including both physical and cultural conditions; a region characterized by a certain set of physical conditions.

environmental determinism The view that the physical *environment,* particularly *climate,* controls human action, molds human behavior, and conditions cultural development.

environmental justice The notion that all people, regardless of race, ethnicity, or income, should live in a safe environment and be equally protected from environmental hazards and pollution.

environmental perception The concept that people of different *cultures* will differently observe and interpret their *environment* and make different decisions about its nature, potentialities, and use.

environmental pollution See *pollution.*

epidemiologic transition The reduction of periodically high mortality rates from epidemic diseases as those diseases become essentially continual within a population that develops partial immunity to them.

equal-area (equivalent) projection A *map projection* designed so that a unit area drawn anywhere on the map always represents the same area on the earth's surface.

equator An imaginary east-west line that encircles the globe halfway between the North and South Poles.

equidistant projection A *map projection* showing true distances in all directions only from the center of the projection; all other distances are incorrect.

equivalence/equivalent projection In *map projections,* the characteristic that a unit area drawn on the map always represents the same area on the earth's surface, regardless of where drawn. See also *equal-area projection.*

erosion The wearing away and removal of rock and soil particles from exposed surfaces by agents such as moving water, wind, or ice.

ethnic enclave A small area occupied by a distinctive minority *culture.*

ethnic geography The study of spatial distributions and interactions of *ethnic groups* and of the cultural characteristics on which they are based.

ethnic group People sharing a distinctive *culture,* frequently based on common national origin, *religion, language,* or *race.*

ethnic island A small rural area settled by a single, distinctive *ethnic group* that placed its imprint on the landscape.

ethnicity Ethnic quality; affiliation with a group whose racial, cultural, religious, or linguistic characteristics or national origins distinguish it from a larger population within which it is found.

ethnic province A large territory, urban and rural, dominated by or closely associated with a single *ethnic group.*

ethnic religion A *religion* identified with a particular *ethnic group* and largely exclusive to it. Such a religion does not seek converts.

ethnic separatism Desired *regional autonomy* expressed by a culturally distinctive group within a larger, politically dominant *culture.*

ethnocentrism Conviction of the evident superiority of one's own *ethnic group.*

ethnographic boundary See *consequent boundary.*

European Union (EU) An economic association established in 1957 by a number of Western European countries to promote free trade among members; often called the Common Market.

evapotranspiration The return of water from the land to the *atmosphere* through evaporation from the soil surface and transpiration from plants.

exclave A portion of a *state* that is separated from the main territory and surrounded by another country.

exclusive economic zone (EEZ) As established in the *United Nations Convention on the Law of the Sea,* a zone of exploitation extending 200 nautical miles (370 km) seaward from a coastal state that has exclusive mineral and fishing rights over it.

expansion diffusion The spread of ideas, behaviors, or articles through a culture area or from one *culture* to neighboring areas through contact and exchange of information; the dispersion leaves the phenomenon intact or intensified in its area of origin.

extensive agriculture A crop or livestock system characterized by low inputs of labor per unit area of land. It may be part of either a *subsistence* or a *commercial* economy.

external economies See *agglomeration economies.*

extractive industries *Primary activities* involving the mining and quarrying of *non-renewable* metallic and nonmetallic mineral resources.

F

fallowing The practice of allowing plowed or cultivated land to remain (rest) uncropped or only partially cropped for one or more growing seasons.

federal state A *state* with a two-tier system of government and a clear distinction between the powers vested in the central government and those residing in the governments of the component regional subdivisions.

fertility rate The average number of live births per 1000 women of childbearing age.

filtering In *urban geography,* a process whereby individuals of a lower-income group replace, in a portion of an urban area, residents who are of a higher-income group.

first effective settlement The influence that the characteristics of an early dominant settlement group exert on the later *social* and *cultural geography* of an area.

fixed cost An activity cost (as of investment in land, plant, and equipment) that must be met without regard to level of output; an input cost that is spatially constant.

folk culture The body of institutions, customs, dress, *artifacts,* collective wisdoms, and traditions of a homogeneous, isolated, largely self-sufficient, and relatively static social group.

folklore Oral traditions of a *folk culture,* including tales, fables, legends, customary observations, and moral teachings.

folkway The learned manner of thinking and feeling and a prescribed mode of conduct common to a traditional social group.

footloose A descriptive term applied to manufacturing activities for which the cost of transporting material or product is not important in determining location of production; an industry or firm showing neither *market* nor *material orientation.*

Fordism The manufacturing economy and system derived from assembly-line mass production and the mass consumption of standardized goods. Named after Henry Ford, who innovated many of its production techniques.

foreign direct investment The purchase or construction of foreign factories and other fixed assets by *transnational corporations;* also the purchase of or merging with foreign companies.

formal region (*syn:* uniform region, homogeneous region, structural region) A *region* distinguished by a uniformity of one or more characteristics that can serve as the basis for areal generalization and of contrast with adjacent areas.

form utility A value-increasing change in the form—and therefore in the "utility"—of a raw material or commodity.

forward-thrust capital A capital city deliberately sited in a *state's* frontier zone.

fossil fuel (*syn:* mineral fuel) Any of the fuels derived from decayed organic material converted by earth processes; especially, coal, petroleum, and natural gas, but also including tar sands and oil shales.

fragmented state A *state* whose territory contains isolated parts, separated and discontinuous.

frame In *urban geography,* that part of the *central business district* characterized by such low-intensity uses as warehouses, wholesaling, and automobile dealers.

freight rate The charge levied by a transporter for the loading, moving, and unloading of goods; includes *line-haul costs* and *terminal costs.*

friction of distance A measure of the retarding or restricting effect of distance on *spatial interaction.* Generally, the greater the distance, the greater the "friction" and the less the interaction or exchange, or the greater the cost of achieving the exchange.

frontier That portion of a country adjacent to its boundaries and fronting another political unit.

frontier zone A belt lying between two *states* or between settled and uninhabited or sparsely settled areas.

functional dispute (*syn:* boundary dispute) In *political geography,* a disagreement between neighboring *states* over policies to be applied to their common border; often induced by differing customs regulations, movement of nomadic groups, or illegal immigration or emigration.

functional region (*syn:* nodal region) A *region* differentiated by what occurs within it rather than by a homogeneity of physical or cultural phenomena; an earth area recognized as an operational unit based upon defined organizational criteria. The concept of unity is based on interaction and interdependence between different points within the area.

G

gated community A restricted access subdivision or neighborhood, often surrounded by a barrier, with entry permitted only for residents and their guests; usually totally planned in land use and design, with "residents only" limitations on public streets and parks.

gathering industries *Primary activities* involving the *subsistence* or *commercial* harvesting of *renewable* natural resources of land or water. Primitive gathering involves local collection of food and other materials of nature, both plant and animal; commercial gathering usually implies forestry and fishing industries.

GDP See *gross domestic product.*

gender In the cultural sense, a reference to socially created—not biologically based—distinctions between femininity and masculinity.

gene flow The transfer of genes of one breeding population into the gene pool of another through interbreeding.

genetic drift A chance modification of gene composition occurring in an isolated population and becoming accentuated through inbreeding.

gentrification The movement into the inner portions of American cities of middle- and upper-income people who replace low-income populations, rehabilitate the structures they occupied, and change the social character of neighborhoods.

geodesic distance See *absolute distance.*

geographic dialect (*syn:* regional dialect) See *dialect.*

geographic information system (GIS) Integrated computer programs for handling, processing, and analyzing data specifically referenced to the surface of the earth.

geometrical projection (*syn:* perspective projection; visual projection) The trace of the *graticule* shadow projected on a *developable surface* from a light source placed relative to a transparent globe.

geometric boundary (*syn:* artificial boundary) A boundary without obvious physical geographic basis; often a section of a *parallel of latitude* or a *meridian of longitude.*

geophagy The practice of eating earthy substances, usually clays.

gerrymander To redraw voting district boundaries in such a way as to give one political party maximum electoral advantage and to reduce that of another party, to fragment voting blocks, or to achieve other nondemocratic objectives.

ghetto A forced or voluntarily segregated residential area housing a racial, ethnic, or religious minority.

GIS See *geographic information system.*

globalization A reference to the increasing interconnection of all parts of the world as the full range of social, cultural, political, and economic processes becomes international in scale and effect.

global climate change Change in the earth's climate system, whether natural or caused by humans.

globe grid (*syn:* graticule) The set of imaginary lines of *latitude* and *longitude* that intersect at right angles to form a coordinate reference system for locating points on the surface of the earth.

glocalization The adaptation of globalized products to local tastes and contexts. The simultaneous presence of both globalizing processes.

GNI See *gross national income.*

gnomonic projection A *geometrical projection* produced with the light source at the center of the earth.

graphic scale A graduate line included in a map legend by means of which distances on the map may be measured in terms of ground distances.

graticule The network of meridians and parallels on the globe; the *globe grid.*

gravity model A mathematical prediction of the interaction between two bodies as a function of their size and of the distance separating them. Based on Newton's *law of universal gravitation,* the model states that attraction (interaction) is proportional to the product of the masses (population sizes) of two bodies (places) and inversely proportional to the square of the distance between them. Thus, the force of attraction, *F,* between two masses *Mi* and *Mj* separated by distance, *d,* is

$$F = g \frac{M_i M_j}{d_{ij}^2}$$

where g is the "gravitational constant."

Henry C. Carey adapted Newton's formulation to demonstrate the theoretical interaction between two cities, noting that expected exchanges *(I)* between two places, *i* and *j,* can be calculated by equating physical mass in the Newton model with population size *(P),* so that

$$I_{ij} = \frac{P_i P_j}{D_{ij}^2}$$

Exchanges (E) between any set of two cities, *A* and *B,* can therefore be quickly estimated:

$$E_{AB} = \frac{\text{Population of A} \times \text{Population of B}}{\text{Distance between A and B}^2}$$

great circle Line formed by the intersection with the earth's surface of a plane passing through the center of the earth; an arc of a great circle is the shortest distance between two points on the earth's surface.

greenhouse effect Heating of the earth's surface as shortwave solar energy passes through the *atmosphere,* which is transparent to it but opaque to reradiated long-wave terrestrial energy; also, increasing the opacity of the atmosphere through addition of increased amounts of carbon dioxide and other gases that trap heat.

Green Revolution A term suggesting the great increases in food production, primarily in subtropical areas, accomplished through the introduction of very high-yielding grain crops, particularly wheat, maize, and rice.

grid system See *globe grid.*

gross domestic product (GDP) The total value of goods and services produced within the borders of a country during a specified time period, usually a calendar year.

gross national income (GNI) The total value of goods and services produced by a country per year plus net income earned abroad by its nationals; formerly called "gross national product."

gross national product (GNP) See *gross national income.*

groundwater Subsurface water that accumulates in the pores and cracks of rock and *soil.*

guest worker A foreign worker, usually male and frequently under contract, who migrates to secure permanent work in a host country without intention to settle permanently in that country; particularly, workers from North Africa and countries of eastern, southern, and southeastern Europe employed in industrialized countries of Western Europe.

H

hazardous waste Discarded solid, liquid, or gaseous material that poses a substantial threat to human health or to the *environment* when improperly disposed of or stored.

hierarchical diffusion A form of *diffusion* in which spread of an *innovation* can proceed either upward or downward through a hierarchy.

hierarchical migration The tendency for individuals to move from small places to larger ones. See also *step migration.*

hierarchy of central places The steplike series of *urban* units in classes differentiated by both size and function.

high-level waste Nuclear waste with a relatively high level of radioactivity.

Hinduism An ancient and now dominant *value system* and *religion* of India, closely identified with Indian *culture* but without central creed, single doctrine, or religious organization. Dharma (customary duty and divine law) and *caste* are uniting elements.

hinterland The market area or region served by an *urban* center.

homeostatic plateau (*syn:* carrying capacity) The application of the concept of homeostasis, or relatively stable state of equilibrium, to the balance between population numbers and areal resources; the equilibrium level of population that available resources can adequately support.

horticultural farming See *truck farming.*

host society The established and dominant society within which immigrant groups seek accommodation.

human geography One of the two major divisions (the other is *physical geography*) of *systematic geography;* the spatial analysis of human populations, their *cultures,* their activities and behaviors, and their relationship with and impact on the physical landscapes they occupy.

hunter-gatherer/hunting-gathering An economic and social system based primarily or exclusively on the hunting of wild animals and the gathering of food, fiber, and other materials from uncultivated plants.

hydrologic cycle The natural system by which water is continuously circulated through the *biosphere* by evaporation, condensation, and *precipitation.*

hydrosphere All water at or near the earth's surface that is not chemically bound in rocks, including the oceans, surface waters, *groundwater,* and water held in the *atmosphere.*

I

icebox effect The tendency for certain kinds of air pollutants to lower temperatures on earth by reflecting incoming sunlight back into space and thus preventing it from reaching (and heating) the earth.

iconography In *political geography,* a term denoting the study of symbols that unite a country.

ideological subsystem The complex of ideas, beliefs, knowledge, and means of their communication that characterize a *culture.*

incinerator A facility designed to burn waste.

independent invention (*syn:* parallel invention) *Innovations* developed in two or more unconnected locations by individuals or groups acting independently. See also *multilinear evolution.*

Industrial Revolution The term applied to the rapid economic and social changes in agriculture and manufacturing that followed the introduction of the factory system to the textile industry of England in the last quarter of the 18th century.

infant mortality rate A refinement of the *death rate* to specify the ratio of deaths of infants age 1 year or less per 1000 live births.

informal economy See *informal sector.*

informal sector That part of a national economy that involves productive labor not subject to formal systems of control or payment; economic activity or individual enterprise operating without official recognition or measured by official statistics.

infrastructure The basic structure of services, installations, and facilities needed to support industrial, agricultural, and other economic development; included are transport and communications, along with water, power, and other public utilities.

innovation Introduction of new ideas, practices, or objects; usually, an alteration of *custom* or *culture* that originates within the social group itself.

insolation The solar radiation received at the earth's surface.

intensive agriculture Any agricultural system involving the application of large amounts of capital and/or labor per unit of cultivated land; this may be part of either a *subsistence* or a *commercial economy.*

interaction model See *gravity model.*

international boundary The outer limit of a *state's* claim to land or water surface, projected downward to the center of the earth and, less certainly, upward to the height the state can effectively control.

International Date Line By international agreement, the designated line where each new day begins, generally following the 180th *meridian.* The line compensates for accumulated 1-hour time changes for each 15 degrees of longitude by adding (from east to west) or subtracting (from west to east) 24 hours for travelers crossing the line.

interrupting barrier A condition that delays the rate of *diffusion* of an *innovation* or that deflects its path.

intervening opportunity The concept that closer opportunities will materially reduce the attractiveness of interaction with more distant—even slightly better—alternatives; a closer alternative source of supply between a demand point and the original source of supply.

in-transit privilege The application of a single-haul *freight rate* from origin to destination even though the shipment is halted for processing en route, after which the journey is completed.

IPAT equation An equation relating the environmental impact of a society to the key factors of population, affluence, and technology.

irredentism The policy of a *state* wishing to incorporate within itself territory inhabited by people who have ethnic or linguistic links with the country but that lies within a neighboring state.

Islam A *monotheistic, universalizing* religion that includes belief in Allah as the sole deity and in Mohammed as his prophet completing the work of earlier prophets of *Judaism* and *Christianity.*

isochrone A line connecting points equidistant in travel time from a common origin.

isogloss A mapped boundary line marking the limits of a particular linguistic feature.

isoline A map line connecting points of equal value.

isotropic plain A hypothetical portion of the earth's surface assumed to be an unbounded, uniformly flat plain with uniform and unvarying distribution of population, purchasing power, transport costs, accessibility, and the like.

J

J-curve A curve shaped like the letter J, depicting exponential or geometric growth (1, 2, 4, 8, 16 . . .).

Judaism A *monotheistic, ethnic religion* first developed among the Hebrew people of the ancient Near East; its determining conditions include descent from Israel (Jacob), the Torah (law and scripture), and tradition.

K

krill A form of marine *plankton* composed of crustaceans and larvae.

L

landlocked Describing a *state* that lacks a sea coast.

land race A genetically diverse, naturally adapted, native food plant.

language The system of words, their pronunciation, and methods of combination used and mutually understood by a community of individuals.

language family A group of *languages* thought to have descended from a single, common ancestral tongue.

Latin American city model A visual description of land uses in Latin American cities. The model combines wedge-shaped sectors and concentric rings emanating from a central business district. The wealthy live along a well-served commercial spine and the poorest residents live in peripheral squatter settlements.

latitude Angular distance north or south of the *equator,* measured in degrees, minutes, and seconds. Grid lines marking latitudes are called *parallels.* The equator is 0°; the North Pole is 90°N; the South Pole is 90°S. Low latitudes are considered to fall within the tropics (23° 30′ N and 23° 30′ S); midlatitudes extend from the tropics to the Arctic and Antarctic circles (66° 30′ N and S); high latitudes occur from those circles to the North and South poles.

law of peripheral neglect The observation that a government's awareness of or concern with regional problems decreases with the square of the distance of an outlying region from the capital city.

law of retail gravitation See *Reilly's law.*

leachate The contaminated liquid discharged from a *sanitary landfill* to either surface or subsurface land or water.

leaching The removal of soluble minerals from the upper soil horizons through the downward movement of water.

least-cost theory (*syn:* Weberian analysis) The view that the optimum location of a manufacturing establishment is at the place where the costs of transport and labor and the advantages of *agglomeration* or *deglomeration* are most favorable.

limiting factor principle The distribution of an organism or the structure of an *ecosystem* can be explained by the control exerted by the single factor (such as temperature, light, water) that is most deficient, that is, that falls below the levels required.

line-haul costs (*syn:* over-the-road costs) The costs involved in the actual physical movement of goods (or passengers); costs of haulage (including equipment and routeway costs), excluding *terminal costs.*

lingua franca Any of various auxiliary *languages* used as common tongues among people of an area where several languages are spoken; literally, "Frankish language."

linguistic geography (*syn:* dialect geography; dialectology) The study of local variations within a speech area by mapping word choices, pronunciations, or grammatical constructions.

link A transportation or communication connection or route within a *network*.

lithosphere The earth's solid crust.

locational interdependence The circumstance under which the locational decision of a particular firm is influenced by the locations chosen by competitors.

locational triangle A simple graphic model in *Weberian analysis* to illustrate the derivation of the least-transport-cost location of an industrial establishment.

longitude Angular distance of a location in degrees, minutes, and seconds measured east or west of a designated *prime meridian* given the value of 0°. By general agreement, the *globe grid* prime meridian passes through the old observatory of Greenwich, England. Distances are measured from 0° to 180° both east and west, with 180°E and W being the same line. For much of its extent, the 180° meridian also serves as the *International Date Line.* Because of the period of the earth's axial rotation, 15 degrees of longitude are equivalent to a difference of 1 hour in local time.

long lot A farm or other property consisting of a long, narrow strip of land extending back from a river or road.

low-level waste Nuclear waste with relatively moderate levels of radioactivity.

M

malnutrition Food intake insufficient in quantity or deficient in quality to sustain life at optimal conditions of health.

Malthus Thomas R. Malthus (1766–1843). English economist, demographer, and cleric who suggested that unless self-control, war, or natural disaster checks population, it will inevitably increase faster than will the food supplies needed to sustain it. This view is known as Malthusianism. See also *neo-Malthusianism.*

map projection A systematic method of transferring the *globe grid* system from the earth's curved surface to the flat surface of a map. Projection automatically incurs error, but an attempt is usually made to preserve one or more (though never all) of the characteristics of the spherical surface: equal area, correct distance, true direction, proper shape.

map scale See *scale.*

marginal cost The additional cost of producing each successive unit of output.

mariculture Production and harvesting of fish and shellfish in fenced confinement areas along coasts and in estuaries.

market economy An economic system in which most goods and services are privately produced and distributed for monetary exchange; an economy characterized by free market exchange with no or only minimum state intervention.

market equilibrium The point of intersection of demand and supply curves of a given commodity; at equilibrium the market is cleared of the commodity.

market gardening See *truck farming.*

market orientation The tendency of an economic activity to locate close to its market; a reflection of large and variable distribution costs.

material culture The tangible, physical items produced and used by members of a specific *culture* group and reflective of their traditions, lifestyles, and technologies.

material orientation The tendency of an economic activity to locate near or at its source of raw material; this is experienced when material costs are highly variable spatially and/or represent a significant share of total costs.

mathematical location See *absolute location.*

mathematical projection The systematic rendering of the *globe grid* on a *developable surface* to achieve *graticule* characteristics not obtainable by visual means of *geometrical projection.*

maximum sustainable yield The maximum rate at which a *renewable resource* can be exploited without impairing its ability to be renewed or replenished.

Mediterranean agriculture An agricultural system based upon the mild, moist winters; hot, sunny summers; and rough terrain of the Mediterranean basin. It involves cereals as winter crops, summer tree and vine crops (olives, figs, dates, citrus and other tree fruits, and grapes), and animals (sheep and goats).

megalopolis 1: A large, sprawled *urban* complex with contained open, nonurban land, created through the spread and joining of separate *metropolitan areas.* **2:** When capitalized, the name applied to the continuous functionally urban area of coastal northeastern United States from Maine to Virginia.

mental map (*syn:* cognitive map) The map-like image of the world, country, region, city, or neighborhood a person carries in mind. The representation is therefore subjective; it includes knowledge of actual locations and spatial relationships and is colored by personal perceptions and preferences related to place.

mentifacts The central, enduring elements of a *culture* expressing its values and beliefs, including *language, religion, folklore,* artistic traditions, and the like. Elements in the *ideological subsystem* of culture.

Mercator projection A true *conformal cylindrical projection* first published in 1569, useful for navigation.

meridian A north-south line of *longitude;* on the *globe grid,* all meridians are of equal length and converge at the poles.

Mesolithic Middle Stone Age. The *culture* stage of the early postglacial period, during which earliest stages of *domestication* of animals and plants occurred, refined and specialized tools were developed, pottery was produced, and semipermanent settlements were established as climate change reduced the game-animal herds earlier followed for food.

metes-and-bounds survey A system of property description using natural features (streams, rocks, trees, etc.) to trace and define the boundaries of individual parcels.

metropolitan area In the United States, a large functionally integrated settlement area comprising one or more whole county units and usually containing several *urbanized areas;* discontinuously built up, it operates as a coherent economic whole.

microdistrict The basic neighborhood planning unit characteristic of new urban residential construction in the planned East European city under communism.

microstate (*syn:* ministate) An imprecise term for a *state* or territory small in both population and area. An informal definition accepted by the United Nations suggests a maximum of 1 million population combined with a territory of less than 700 km² (270 sq mi).

migration The permanent (or relatively permanent) relocation of an individual or group to a new, usually distant, place of residence and employment.

migration field The area from which a given city or place draws the majority of its in-migrants.

mineral A natural inorganic substance that has a definite chemical composition and characteristic crystal structure, hardness, and density.

mineral fuel See *fossil fuel.*

ministate See *microstate.*

model An idealized representation, abstraction, or simulation of reality. It is designed to simplify real-world complexity and eliminate extraneous phenomena in order to isolate for detailed study causal factors and interrelationships of *spatial systems.*

monoculture Agricultural system dominated by a single crop.

monolingualism A society's or country's use of only one *language* of communication for all purposes.

monotheism The belief that there is but a single God.

mortality rate See *death rate.*

movement bias Any aggregate control on or regularity of movement of people, commodities, or communication. Included are *distance bias, direction bias,* and *network bias.*

multilinear evolution A concept of independent but parallel cultural development advanced by the anthropologist Julian Steward (1902–1972) to explain cultural similarities among widely separated peoples existing in similar environments but who could not have benefited from shared experiences, borrowed ideas, or diffused technologies. See *independent invention.*

multilingualism The common use of two or more *languages* in a society or country.

multinational corporation (MNC) A large business organization operating in a number of different national economies; the term implies a more extensive form of *transnational corporation.*

multiple-nuclei model The postulate that large cities develop by peripheral spread not from one *central business district* but from several nodes of growth, each of specialized use. The separately expanding use districts eventually coalesce at their margins.

multiplier effect The direct, indirect, and induced consequences of change in an activity. **1:** In industrial *agglomerations,* the cumulative processes by which a given change (such as a new plant opening) sets in motion a sequence of further industrial employment and *infrastructure* growth. **2:** In *urban geography,* the expected addition of *nonbasic* workers and dependents to a city's total employment and population that accompanies new *basic sector* employment.

N

nation A culturally distinctive group of people occupying a specific territory and bound together by a sense of unity arising from shared *ethnicity,* beliefs, and *customs.*

nationalism A sense of unity binding the people of a *state* together; devotion to the interests of a particular country or *nation,* an identification with the state and an acceptance of national goals.

nation-state A *state* whose territory is identical to that occupied by a particular *ethnic group* or *nation.*

natural boundary (*syn:* physical boundary) A *boundary* line based on recognizable physiographic features, such as mountains or rivers.

natural hazard A process or event in the physical environment that has consequences harmful to humans.

natural increase The growth of a population through excess of births over deaths, excluding the effects of immigration or emigration.

natural landscape The physical *environment* unaffected by human activities. The duration and near totality of human occupation of the earth's surface assure that little or no "natural landscape" so defined remains intact. Opposed to *cultural landscape.*

natural resource A physically occurring item that a population perceives to be necessary and useful to its maintenance and well-being.

natural selection The process resulting in the reproductive success of individuals or groups best adapted to their environment, leading to the perpetuation of their genetic qualities.

natural vegetation The plant life that would exist in an area if humans did not interfere with its development.

neocolonialism A disparaging reference to economic and political policies by which major developed countries are seen to retain or extend influence over the economies of less developed countries and peoples.

Neolithic New Stone Age. The *culture* (succeeding that of the *Mesolithic*) of the middle postglacial period, during which polished stone tools were perfected, the economy was solely or largely based on cultivation of crops and *domestication* of animals, and the arts of spinning, weaving, smelting, and metal working were developed. More formalized societies and *culture complexes* emerged as cities developed and trade routes were established.

neo-Malthusianism The advocacy of population control programs to preserve and improve general national prosperity and well-being.

net migration The difference between in-migration and out-migration of an area.

network The areal pattern of sets of places and the routes (*links*) connecting them, along which movement can take place.

network bias The view that the pattern of *links* in a *network* will affect the likelihood of flows between specific *nodes.*

network cities Two or more nearby cities, potentially or actually complementary in function, that cooperate by developing transportation links and communications infrastructure joining them.

nodal region See *functional region.*

node In *network* theory, an origin, destination, or intersection in a communication network.

nomadic herding Migratory but controlled movement of livestock solely dependent on natural forage.

nonbasic sector (*syn:* service sector) Those economic activities of an urban unit that supply the resident population with goods and services and that have no "export" implication.

nonecumene (*syn:* anecumene). That portion of the earth's surface that is uninhabited or only temporarily or intermittently inhabited. See also *ecumene.*

nonmaterial culture The oral traditions, songs, and stories of a *culture* group along with its beliefs and customary behaviors.

nonrenewable resource A *natural resource* that is not replenished or replaced by natural processes or is used at a rate that exceeds its replacement rate.

North The general term applied in the *Brandt Report* to the developed countries of the Northern Hemisphere plus Australia and New Zealand.

O

official language A governmentally designated *language* of instruction, of government, of the courts, and other official public and private communication.

offshoring The relocation of business processes and services to a lower-cost foreign location; the offshore *outsourcing* of, particularly, white-collar technical, professional, and clerical services.

orthographic projection A *geometrical projection* that results from placing the light source at infinity.

outsourcing 1: Producing abroad parts or products for domestic use or sale; **2:** Subcontracting production or services rather than performing those activities "in house."

overpopulation A value judgment that the resources of an area are insufficient to sustain adequately its present population numbers.

over-the-road costs See *line-haul costs.*

ozone A gas molecule consisting of three atoms of oxygen (O_3) formed when diatomic oxygen (O_2) is exposed to *ultraviolet radiation.* In the upper *atmosphere* it forms a normally continuous, thin layer that blocks ultraviolet light; in the lower atmosphere it constitutes a damaging component of *photochemical smog.*

P

Paleolithic Old Stone Age. An early stage of human *culture* largely coinciding with the *Pleistocene* glacial period. Characterized by *hunting-gathering* economies and the use of fire and simple stone tools, especially those made from flint.

parallel invention See *independent invention.*

parallel of latitude An east-west line of *latitude* indicating distance north or south of the equator.

pattern The design or arrangement of phenomena in earth space.

peak value intersection The most accessible and costly parcel of land in the *central business district* and, therefore, in the entire *urbanized area.*

perception The acquisition of information about a place or thing through sensory means; the subjective organization and interpretation of acquired information in light of cultural attitudes and individual preferences or experiences. See *environmental perception.*

perceptual region A *region* perceived to exist by its inhabitants or the general populace. Also known as a *vernacular region* or popular region, it has reality as an element of *popular culture* or *folk culture* represented in the *mental maps* of average people.

perforated state A *state* whose territory is interrupted ("perforated") by a separate, independent state totally contained within its borders.

periodic market A market operating at a particular location (village, city, neighborhood) on one or more fixed days per week or month.

peripheral model A depiction of the contemporary metropolitan area emphasizing patterns of suburban location and functions.

periphery/peripheral The outer regions or boundaries of an area. See also *core-periphery model.*

permeable barrier An obstacle raised by a culture group or one culture group's reluctance to accept some, but not all, innovations diffused from a related but different *culture.* Acceptance or rejection may be conditioned by religious, political, ethnic, or similar considerations of suitability or compatibility.

personal communication field An area defined by the distribution of an individual's short-range informal communications. The size and shape of the field are defined by work, recreation, school, and other regular contacts and are affected by age, sex, employment, and other personal characteristics.

personal space An invisible, usually irregular area around a person into which he or she does not willingly admit others. The sense (and extent) of personal space is a situational and cultural variable.

perspective projection See *geometrical projection.*

photochemical smog A form of polluted air produced by the interaction of hydrocarbons and oxides of nitrogen in the presence of sunlight.

physical boundary See *natural boundary.*

physical geography One of two major divisions (the other is *human geography*) of *systematic geography;* the study of the structures, processes, distributions, and change through time of the natural phenomena of the earth's surface that are significant to human life.

physical landscape The *natural landscape* plus visible elements of *material culture.*

physiological density The number of persons per unit area of cultivable land.

pidgin An auxiliary *language* derived, with reduced vocabulary and simplified structure, from other languages. Not a native tongue, it is used for limited communication among people with different languages.

place a particular geographic location with its unique biophysical, cultural, and social characteristics.

placelessness The loss of locally distinctive characteristics and identity and replacement by standardized landscapes.

place perception See *perception.*

place utility 1: In human movement and *migration* studies, a measure of an individual's perceived satisfaction or approval of a place in its social, economic, or environmental attributes. **2:** In *economic geography,* the value imparted to goods or services by *tertiary* activities that provide things needed in specific markets.

planar projection (*syn:* azimuthal projection) A *map projection* employing a plane as the presumed *developable surface.*

plankton Microscopic freely floating plant and animal organisms of lakes and oceans.

planned economy A system of production of goods and services, usually consumed or distributed by a governmental agency, in quantities, at prices, and in locations determined by governmental program.

plantation A large agricultural holding, frequently foreign owned, devoted to the production of a single export crop.

Pleistocene The geological epoch dating from 2 million to 11 thousand years ago during which four stages of continental glaciation occurred.

political geography A branch of *human geography* concerned with the spatial analysis of political phenomena.

pollution The introduction into the biosphere of materials that because of their quantity, chemical nature, or temperature have a negative impact on the *ecosystem* or that cannot be readily disposed of by natural recycling processes.

polytheism Belief in or worship of many gods.

popular culture The constantly changing mix of material and nonmaterial elements available through mass production and the mass media to an urbanized, heterogeneous, nontraditional society.

popular region See *vernacular region.*

population density A measurement of the numbers of persons per unit area of land within predetermined limits, usually political or census boundaries. See also *physiological density.*

population geography A division of *human geography* concerned with spatial variations in distribution, composition, growth, and movements of population and the relationship of those concerns with the geographic character of areas.

population momentum (*syn:* demographic momentum) The tendency for population growth to continue despite stringent family planning programs because of a relatively high concentration of people in the childbearing years.

population projection A statement of a population's future size, age, and sex composition based on the application of stated assumptions to current data.

population pyramid A bar graph in pyramid form showing the age and sex composition of a population, usually a national one.

positional dispute (*syn:* boundary dispute) In *political geography,* disagreement about the actual location of a *boundary.*

possibilism The philosophical viewpoint that the physical *environment* offers human beings a set of opportunities from which (within limits) people may choose according to their cultural needs and technological awareness. The emphasis is on a freedom of choice and action not allowed under *environmental determinism.*

postindustrial A stage of economic development in which service activities become relatively more important than goods production; professional and technical employment supersedes employment in agriculture and manufacturing; and level of living is defined by the quality of services and amenities rather than by the quantity of goods available.

potential model A measurement of the total interaction opportunities available under *gravity model* assumptions to a center in a multicenter system.

precipitation All moisture—solid and liquid—that falls to the earth's surface from the *atmosphere.*

predevelopment annexation The inclusion within the *central city* of nonurban peripheral areas for the purpose of securing to the city itself the benefits of their eventual development.

primary activities Those parts of the economy involved in making *natural resources* available for use or further processing; included are mining, *agriculture.* forestry, fishing and hunting, and grazing.

primate city A country's leading city, disproportionately larger and functionally more complex than any other; a city dominating an urban hierarchy composed of a base of small towns and an absence of intermediate-sized cities.

prime meridian An imaginary line passing through the Royal Observatory at Greenwich, England, serving by agreement as the 0° line of *longitude.*

private plot In the planned economies under communism, a small garden plot allotted to collective farmers and urban workers.

projection See *map projection.*

prorupt state A *state* of basically *compact* form but with one or more narrow extensions of territory.

protolanguage An assumed, reconstructed, or recorded ancestral *language.*

proved reserves That portion of a *natural resource* that has been identified and can be extracted profitably with current technology.

psychological distance The way an individual perceives distance.

pull factors Characteristics of a locale that act as attractive forces, drawing migrants from other regions.

purchasing power parity (PPP) A monetary measurement that takes account of what money actually buys in each country.

push factors Unfavorable characteristics of a locale that contribute to the dissatisfaction of its residents and impel their emigration.

Q

quaternary activities Those parts of the economy concerned with research, with the gathering and dissemination of information, and with administration—including administration of the other economic activity levels; often considered only as a specialized subdivision of *tertiary activities.*

quinary activities A sometimes separately recognized subsection of *tertiary activity* management functions involving highest-level decision making in all types of large organizations. Also deemed the most advanced form of the *quaternary* subsector.

R

race A subset of human population whose members share certain distinctive, inherited biological characteristics.

rank-size rule An observed regularity in the city-size distribution of some countries. In a rank-size hierarchy, the population of any given town will be inversely proportional to its rank in the hierarchy; that is, the *n*th-ranked city will be 1/*n* the size of the largest city.

rate The frequency of an event's occurrence during a specified time period.

rate of natural increase *Birth rate* minus the *death rate,* suggesting the annual rate of population growth without considering *net migration.*

reapportionment The process and outcome of a reallocation of electoral seats to defined territories, such as congressional seats to states of the United States.

recycling The reuse of disposed materials after they have passed through some form of treatment (e.g., melting down glass bottles to produce new bottles).

redistricting The drawing of new electoral district boundary lines in response to changing patterns of population or changing legal requirements.

region Any earth area with distinctive and unifying physical or cultural characteristics that set it off and make it substantially different from surrounding areas. A region may be defined on the basis of its homogeneity or its functional integration as a single organizational unit. Regions and their boundaries are devices of areal generalization, intellectual concepts rather than visible landscape entities.

regional autonomy A measure of self-governance afforded a subdivision of a *state.*

regional concept The view that physical and cultural phenomena on the surface of the earth are rationally arranged by complex, diverse, but comprehensible interrelated spatial processes.

regional dialect (*syn:* geographic dialect) See *dialect.*

regional geography The study of geographic *regions;* the study of areal differentiation.

regionalism In *political geography,* group—frequently ethnic group—identification with a particular region of a *state* rather than with the state as a whole.

Reilly's law Also known as the *law of retail gravitation;* the proposition by William J. Reilly that the breaking point or boundary marking the outer edge of either of two cities' trade areas is located by the expression

$$BP = \frac{d_{ij}}{1 + \sqrt{\dfrac{P_2}{P_1}}}$$

where

BP = distance from city 1 to the breaking point (or boundary)

d_{ij} = distance between city 1 and city 2

P_1 = population of city 1

P_2 = population of city 2

relational direction See *relative direction.*

relative direction (*syn:* relational direction) A culturally based locational reference, as the Far West, the Old South, or the Middle East.

relative distance A transformation of *absolute distance* into such relative measures as time or monetary costs. Such measures yield different explanations of human spatial behavior than do linear distances alone. Distances between places are constant by absolute terms, but relative distances may vary with improvements in transportation or communication technology or with different psychological perceptions of space.

relative location The position of a place or activity in relation to other places or activities. Relative location implies spatial relationships and usually suggests the relative advantages or disadvantages of a location with respect to all competing locations.

relic boundary A former *boundary* line that is still discernible and marked by some *cultural landscape* feature.

religion A personal or institutionalized system of worship and of faith in the sacred and divine.

relocation diffusion The transfer of ideas, behaviors, or articles from one place to another through the *migration* of those possessing the feature transported; also, spatial relocation in which a phenomenon leaves an area of origin as it is transported to a new location.

remote sensing Any of several techniques of obtaining images of an area or object without having the sensor in direct physical contact with it, as by aerial photography or satellite sensors.

renewable resource A *natural resource* that is potentially inexhaustible either because it is constantly (as solar radiation) or periodically (as *biomass*) replenished as long as its use does not exceed its *maximum sustainable yield.*

replacement level The number of children per woman that will supply just enough births to replace parents and compensate for early deaths, with no allowance for *migration* effects; usually calculated at between 2.1 and 2.5 children.

representative fraction The *scale* of a map expressed as a ratio of a unit of distance on the map to distance measured in the same unit on the ground, e.g., 1:250,000.

resource See *natural resource.*

resource dispute In *political geography,* disagreement over the control or use of shared resources, such as boundary rivers or jointly claimed fishing grounds.

return migration See *counter migration.*

rhumb line A directional line that crosses each successive *meridian* at a constant angle; a rhumb line shows true direction.

rotation See *crop rotation.*

roundwood Timber as it is harvested, before squaring, sawing, or pulping.

S

Sahel The semiarid zone between the Sahara desert and the grassland areas to the south in West Africa; a district of recurring drought, famine, and environmental degradation and *desertification.*

salinization The process by which *soil* becomes saturated with salt, rendering the land unsuitable for *agriculture.* This occurs when land that has poor drainage is improperly irrigated.

sanitary landfill Disposal of solid wastes by spreading them in layers covered with enough soil to control odors, rodents, and flies; sited to minimize water pollution from runoff and *leachate.*

satisficing location A less-than-ideal best location, but one providing an acceptable level of utility or satisfaction.

scale 1: In cartography, the ratio between the size of area on a map and the actual size of that same area on the earth's surface. **2:** In more general terms, scale refers to the size of the area studied, from local to global.

S-curve The horizontal bending, or leveling, of an exponential or J-*curve.*

secondary activities Those parts of the economy involved in the processing of raw materials derived from *primary activities* and in altering or combining materials to produce commodities of enhanced utility and value; included are manufacturing, construction, and power generation.

sector model A description of urban land uses as wedge-shaped sectors radiating outward from the *central business district* along transportation corridors. The radial access routes attract particular uses to certain sectors, with high-status residential uses occupying the most desirable wedges.

secularism A rejection of or indifference to *religion* and religious practice.

segregation A measure of the degree to which members of a minority group are not uniformly distributed among the total population.

separatism See *ethnic separatism.*

service sector See *nonbasic sector.*

shamanism A form of *tribal religion* based on belief in a hidden world of gods, ancestral spirits, and demons responsive only to a shaman or interceding priest.

shifting cultivation (*syn:* slash-and-burn agriculture; swidden agriculture) Crop production on tropical forest clearings kept in cultivation until their quickly declining fertility is lost. Cleared plots are then abandoned and new sites are prepared.

Shinto The *polytheistic, ethnic religion* of Japan that includes reverence of deities of natural forces and veneration of the emperor as descendent of the sun-goddess.

site The *absolute location* of a place or activity described by local relief, landform, and other physical (or sometimes cultural) characteristics.

situation The *relative location* of a place or activity in relation to the physical and cultural characteristics of the larger regional or *spatial system* of which it is a part. Situation implies spatial interconnection and interdependence.

slash-and-burn cultivation See *shifting cultivation.*

social area An area identified by homogeneity of the social indices (age group, socioeconomic status, *ethnicity*) of its population.

social dialect See *dialect.*

social distance A measure of the perceived degree of social separation between individuals, *ethnic groups,* neighborhoods, or other groupings; the voluntary or enforced *segregation* of two or more distinct social groups for most activities.

social geography The branch of *cultural geography* that studies *social areas* and the social use of space, especially urban space; the study of the *spatial distribution* of social groups and of the processes underlying that distribution.

sociofacts The institutions and links between individuals and groups that unite a *culture,* including family structure and political, educational, and religious institutions. Components of the *sociological subsystem* of culture.

sociological subsystem The totality of expected and accepted patterns of interpersonal relations common to a *culture* or subculture.

soil The complex mixture of loose material including minerals, organic and inorganic compounds, living organisms, air, and water found at the earth's surface and capable of supporting plant life.

soil erosion See *erosion.*

solar energy Radiation from the sun, which is transformed into heat primarily at the earth's surface and secondarily in the *atmosphere.*

South The general term applied in the *Brandt Report* to the poor, developing countries of the world, generally (but not totally) located in the Southern Hemisphere.

space As used by geographers, it does not refer to outer space but to areal extent on the earth's surface.

space-time compression/ convergence Expressions of the extent to which improvements in transportation and communication have reduced distance barriers and permitted, for example, the instantaneous *diffusion* of ideas across space.

space-time prism A diagram of the volume of space and the length of time within which our activities are confined by constraints of our bodily needs (eating, resting) and the means of mobility at our command.

spatial Of or pertaining to space on the earth's surface. Often a synonym for *geographical* and used as an adjective to describe specific geographic concepts or processes, as *spatial interaction* or *diffusion.*

spatial diffusion See *diffusion.*

spatial distribution The arrangement of things on the earth's surface; the descriptive elements of spatial distribution are *density, dispersion,* and *pattern.*

spatial interaction The movement (e.g., of people, goods, information) between different places; an indication of interdependence between different geographic locations or areas.

spatially fixed cost An input cost in manufacturing that remains constant wherever production is located.

spatially variable cost An input cost in manufacturing that changes significantly from place to place in its amount and its relative share of total costs.

spatial margin of profitability The set of points delimiting the area within which a firm's profitable operation is possible.

spatial search The process by which individuals evaluate the alternative locations to which they might move.

spatial system The arrangement and integrated operation of phenomena produced by or responding to spatial processes on the earth's surface.

speech community A group of people having common characteristic patterns of vocabulary, word arrangement, and pronunciation.

spine In *urban geography,* a continuation of the features of the *central business district* outward along the main wide boulevard characteristic of Latin American cities.

spread effect (*syn:* trickle-down effect) The diffusion outward of the benefits of economic growth and prosperity from the power center or *core area* to poorer districts and people.

spring wheat Wheat sown in spring for ripening during the summer or autumn.

standard language A *language* substantially uniform with respect to spelling, grammar, pronunciation, and vocabulary and representing the approved community norm of the tongue.

standard line Line of contact between a projection surface and the globe; transformed from the sphere to the plane surface without distortion.

state (*syn:* country) An independent political unit occupying a defined, permanently populated territory and having full sovereign control over its internal and foreign affairs.

state farm In the former Soviet Union (and other planned economies), a government agricultural enterprise operated with paid employees.

step (stepwise) migration A *migration* in which an eventual long-distance relocation is undertaken in stages as, for example, from farm to village to small town to city. See also *hierarchical migration.*

stereographic projection A *geometrical projection* that results from placing the light source at the *antipode.*

stimulus diffusion A form of *expansion* diffusion in which a fundamental idea, though not the specific trait itself, stimulates imitative behavior within a receptive population.

structural assimilation The distribution of immigrant ethnics among the groups and social

strata of a *host society,* but without their full *behavioral assimilation* into it.

subnationalism The feeling that one owes primary allegiance to a traditional group or nation rather than to the state.

subsequent boundary A *boundary* line that is established after the area in question has been settled and that considers the cultural characteristics of the bounded area.

subsistence agriculture Any of several farm economies in which most crops are grown for food nearly exclusively for local or family consumption.

subsistence economy An economic system of relatively simple technology in which people produce most or all of the goods to satisfy their own and their family's needs; little or no exchange occurs outside of the immediate or extended family.

substitution principle In industry, the tendency to substitute one factor of production for another in order to achieve optimum plant location.

suburb A functionally specialized segment of a large *urban* complex located outside the boundaries of the *central city;* usually, a relatively homogeneous residential community, separately incorporated and administered.

superimposed boundary A *boundary* line placed over and ignoring an existing cultural pattern.

supranationalism Term applied to associations created by three or more states for their mutual benefit and achievement of shared objectives.

sustained yield The practice of balancing harvesting with growth of new stocks to avoid depletion of the *resource* and ensure a perpetual supply.

swidden agriculture See *shifting cultivation.*

syncretism The development of a new form of *culture trait* by the fusion of two or more distinct parental elements.

systematic geography A division of geography that selects a particular aspect of the physical or cultural *environment* for detailed study of its areal differentiation and interrelationships. Branches of systematic geography are labeled according to the topic studied (e.g., recreational geography) or the related science with which the branch is associated (e.g., *economic geography*).

systems analysis An approach to the study of large systems through **(1)** segregation of the entire system into its component parts, **(2)** investigation of the interactions between system elements, and **(3)** study of inputs, outputs, flows, interactions, and boundaries within the system.

T

Taoism (*syn:* Daoism) A Chinese *value system* and *ethnic religion* emphasizing conformity to Tao (Way), the creative reality ordering the universe.

tapering principle A *distance decay* observation of the diminution or tapering of costs of transportation with increasing distance from the point of origin of the shipment because of the averaging of *fixed costs* over a greater number of miles of travel.

technological subsystem The complex of material objects together with the techniques of their

use by means of which people carry out their productive activities.

technology The integrated system of knowledge, skills, tools, and methods developed within or used by a *culture* to successfully carry out purposeful and productive tasks.

technology gap The contrast between the *technology* available in developed *core regions* and that present in *peripheral areas* of *underdevelopment.*

technology transfer The *diffusion* to or acquisition by one *culture* or *region* of the *technology* possessed by another, usually more developed, society.

terminal costs (*syn:* fixed costs of transportation) The costs incurred, and charged, for loading and unloading freight at origin and destination points and for the paperwork involved; costs charged each shipment for terminal facility use and unrelated to distance of movement or *line-haul costs.*

terracing The practice of planting crops on steep slopes that have been converted into a series of horizontal steplike level plots (terraces).

territorial dispute (*syn:* boundary dispute; functional dispute) In *political geography,* disagreement between *states* over the control of surface area.

territoriality An individual or group attempt to identify and establish control over a clearly defined territory considered partially or wholly an exclusive domain; the behavior associated with the defense of the home territory.

territorial production complex A design in former Soviet economic planning for large regional industrial, mining, and agricultural development leading to regional self-sufficiency, diversification, and the creation of specialized production for a larger national market.

terrorism Systematic open and covert action employing fear and terror as a means of political coercion.

tertiary activities Those parts of the economy that fulfill the exchange function, that provide market availability of commodities, and that bring together consumers and providers of services; included are wholesale and retail trade, associated transportational and governmental services, and personal and professional services of all kinds.

thematic map A map depicting a specific *spatial distribution* or statistical variation of abstract objects (e.g., unemployment) in space.

Third World Originally (1950s), designating countries uncommitted to either the "First World" Western capitalist bloc or the Eastern "Second World" communist bloc; subsequently, a term applied to countries considered not yet fully developed or in a state of *underdevelopment* in economic and social terms.

threshold In *economic geography* and *central place theory,* the minimum market needed to support the supply of a product or service.

time-distance decay An influence on the rate of *expansion diffusion* of an idea, observing that the spread or acceptance of an idea is usually delayed as distance from the source of the innovation increases.

tipping point The degree of neighborhood racial or ethnic mixing that induces the former majority group to move out rapidly.

toponym A place name.

toponymy The place names of a region or, especially, the study of place names.

total fertility rate (TFR) The average number of children that would be born to each woman if during her childbearing years she bore children at the current year's rate for women that age.

town A nucleated settlement that contains a *central business district* but that is small and less functionally complex than a *city*.

toxic waste Discarded chemical substances that can cause serious illness or death.

traditional religion See *tribal religion*.

tragedy of the commons The observation that in the absence of collective control over the use of a resource available to all, it is to the advantage of all users to maximize their separate shares even though their collective pressures may diminish total yield or destroy the resource altogether.

transculturation A term describing the relatively equal exchange of cultural outlooks and ways of life between two culture groups; it suggests more extensive cross-cultural influences than does *acculturation*.

transferability Acceptable costs of a spatial exchange; the cost of moving a commodity relative to the ability of the commodity to bear that cost.

transnational corporation (TNC) A large business organization operating in at least two separate national economies; a form of *multinational corporation*.

tribal religion (*syn:* traditional religion) An *ethnic religion* specific to a small, localized, preindustrial culture group.

trickle-down effect See *spread effect*.

tropical rain forest Tree cover composed of tall, high-crowned evergreen deciduous species, associated with the continuously wet tropical lowlands.

truck farming (*syn:* horticultural farming; market gardening) The intensive production of fruits and vegetables for market rather than for processing or canning.

U

ubiquitous industry A *market-oriented* industry whose establishments are distributed in direct proportion to the distribution of population.

ultraviolet (UV) radiation Electromagnetic radiation from the sun with wavelengths shorter than the violet end of visible light and longer than X-rays.

underdevelopment A level of economic and social achievement below what could be reached—given the natural and human resources of an area—were necessary capital and technology available.

underpopulation A value statement reflecting the view that an area has too few people in relation to its resources and population-supporting capacity.

uniform plain See *isotropic plain*.

uniform region See *formal region*.

unitary state A *state* in which the central government dictates the degree of local or *regional autonomy* and the nature of local governmental units; a country with few cultural conflicts and with a strong sense of national identity.

United Nations Convention on the Law of the Sea (UNCLOS) A code of maritime law approved by the United Nations in 1982 that authorizes, among other provisions, territorial waters extending 12 nautical miles (22 km) from shore and 200-nautical-mile-wide (370-km-wide) *exclusive economic zones*.

universalizing religion A *religion* that claims global truth and applicability and seeks the conversion of all humankind.

urban Characteristic of, belonging to, or related to a city or town; the opposite of rural. An agglomerated settlement whose inhabitants are primarily engaged in nonagricultural occupations.

urban geography The geographical study of cities; the branch of *human geography* concerned with the spatial aspects of (**1**) the locations, functional structures, size hierarchies, and intercity relationships of national or regional systems of cities, and (**2**) the *site*, evolution, *economic base*, internal land use, and social geographic patterns of individual cities.

urban hierarchy A ranking of cities based on their size and functional complexity.

urban influence zone An area outside of a *city* that is nevertheless affected by the city.

urbanization Transformation of a population from rural to *urban* status; the process of city formation and expansion.

urbanized area A continuously built-up *urban* landscape defined by building and population densities with no reference to the political boundaries of the city; it may contain a *central city* and many contiguous towns, *suburbs*, and unincorporated areas.

usable reserves Mineral deposits that have been identified and can be recovered at current prices and with current technology.

V

value system *Mentifacts* of the *ideological subsystem* of a *culture* summarizing its common beliefs, understandings, expectations, and controls.

variable cost A cost of enterprise operation that varies either by output level or by location of the activity.

variable costs of transportation See *line-haul costs*.

verbal scale A statement of the relationship between units of measure on a map and distance on the ground, as "one inch represents one mile."

vernacular 1: The nonstandard indigenous *language* or *dialect* of a locality. **2:** Of or related to indigenous arts and architecture, such as a *vernacular house*. **3:** Of or related to the perceptions and understandings of the general population, such as a *vernacular region*.

vernacular house An indigenous style of building constructed of native materials to traditional plan, without formal drawings.

vernacular region A region perceived and defined by its inhabitants, usually with a popularly given or accepted nickname.

von Thünen model Model developed by Johann Heinrich von Thünen (1783–1850), German economist and landowner, to explain the forces that control the prices of agricultural commodities and how those variable prices affect patterns of agricultural land utilization.

von Thünen rings The concentric zonal pattern of agricultural land use around a single market center proposed in the *von Thünen model*.

W

water table The upper limit of the saturated zone and therefore of *groundwater*.

wattle and daub A building technique featuring walls of interwoven twigs, branches, or poles (wattles) plastered (daubed) with clay and mud.

Weberian analysis See *least-cost theory*.

winter wheat Wheat sown in fall for ripening the following spring or summer.

world city One of a small number of interconnected, internationally dominant centers (e.g., New York, London, Tokyo) that together control the global systems of finance and commerce.

Z

zero population growth (ZPG) A term suggesting a population in equilibrium, fully stable in numbers with births (plus immigration) equaling deaths (plus emigration).

zonal model See *concentric zone model*.

zoning Designating by ordinance areas in a municipality for particular types of land use.

Credits

Chapter One

Opener: © Thinkstock/Masterfile; 1.1: © Karl Weatherly/Corbis; 1.10: © Doug Sherman/Geofile; 1.11: © NASA; 1.12a: © Historical Museum of Southern Florida; 1.12b: © South Florida Water Management District; 1.20: © U.S. Geological Survey.

Chapter Two

Opener: © Roger De La Harpe; Gallo Images/Corbis; 2.1a: © Ian Murphy/Getty Images; 2.1b: © Tim McCabe, U.S. Dept. of Agriculture National Resource Conservation Service; 2.2(left): © Walter Gans/The Image Works; 2.2(right): © 1997 IMS Communications/Ltd/Capstone Design. All Rights Reserved; 2.3: © The McGraw-Hill Companies, Inc./Barry Barker, photographer; 2.5: © Getty RF; 2.6: © Corbis RF; Box p.36: © Jon Malinowski/Human Landscape Studio; 2.7: © Wolfgang Kaehler/Corbis; 2.11: © Aubrey Land/Valan Photos; 2.14a: © Galen Rowell/Corbis; 2.14b: © Bojan Brecelj/Corbis; 2.16: © 1998 IMS Communications Ltd./Capstone Design. All Rights Reserved; 2.17a: © The McGraw-Hill Companies, Inc./Barry Barker, photographer; 2.17b: Scott Bauer/USDA Agriculture Research Services; 2.18(top left): © Cary Wolinsky/Stock Boston; 2.18(bottom left): © John Eastcott/Momatiuk/Image Works; 2.18(top right): © Yigol Pardo/Hillstrom Stock Photo; 2.18(bottom right): ©Photodisc/Getty RF; 2.19a: © Vol. 94/Corbis RF; 2.19b: © Getty RF; 2.19c: © Vol. 145/Corbis RF; 2.24: © Geoffrey Hiller/eStock Photography; 2.25(all): Jon C. Malinowski/Human Landscape Studio.

Chapter Three

Opener: © Goodshot/PunchStock; 3.1: Photo by Mark Bjelland; 3.8a: The McGraw-Hill Companies, Inc.; 3.8b: © Hirako Masuike/New York Times/Redux Pictures; 3.20: © Bettmann/Corbis; 3.21: © Jocelyn Augustino/FEMA; 3.22: © Sergio Moraes/Reuters; 3.26: © AP Images/Ron Haviv; 3.28a: © AP Images/Dennis Poroy; 3.33: Courtesy of Arthur Getis.

Chapter Four

Opener: © Goodshoot/Fotosearch; 4.2: © Photodisc/Getty RF; p. 93: © Alasdair Drysdale; 4.17: © Topham/Image Works; 4.18: Lynn Betts, USDA, Natural Resources Conservation Center; 4.23: © Getty RF; 4.24: © U.S. Fish and Wildlife Service, Alaska; 4.28: © The McGraw-Hill Companies, Inc./Barry Barker, photographer; 4.30: © Carl Purcell; 4.32: © Nathan Benn/Corbis.

Chapter Five

Opener: © Jenny Matthews/Panos Pictures; 5.1: Courtesy Susan Reisenweaver; 5.8: © Mark Antman/The Image Works; 5.15: Photo by Mark Bjellend; 5.23: © Corbis RF; 5.25b: © David Brownell; 5.26: © Topham/The Observer/The Image Works; 5.28: © Getty RF; 5.29: © Porterfield/Chickering/Photo Researchers, Inc.; 5.30: © Fred Bruemmer/Valan Photos; 5.32: © Wolfgang Kaehler; 5.33: © Kevin R. Morris/Bohemian Nomad Picturemakers/Corbis; 5.34a: Photo by Mark Bjellend; 5.34b: © Photodisc/Getty RF; 5.35a,b: Photo by Mark Bjellend.

Chapter Six

Opener: © Alamy RF; 6.1: © Philippe Gontier/Image Works; 6.2: © J. Messerschmidt/BCI/Photoshot; 6.3: © Comstock Images RF; 6.7: © Chromosohm Media/The Image Works; 6.14: © Stephanie Maze/Corbis Images; 6.15a: © Creatas/PictureQuest RF; 6.15b: © Harold E. Green/Valan Photos; 6.17: Photo by Mark Bjellend; 6.18: © Rudi Von Briel/PhotoEdit; 6.22: © Martha Cooper/Peter Arnold/Alamy; 6.23: © Tony Freeman/PhotoEdit; 6.24: © Susan Reisenweaver; 6.27: © U.S. Geological Survey Map.

Chapter Seven

Opener: © Corbis RF; 7.1: Library of Congress; 7.2a: © Courtesy of Jean Fellmann; 7.3: © Farrell Grehan/Photo Researchers, Inc.; 7.6a: © Ira Kirschenbaum/Stock Boston; 7.6b: © Pam Hickman/Valan Photos; 7.7a,b: © Courtesy of Professor Colin E. Thorn; 7.7c: © Wolfgang Kaehler; 7.7d: © Steven Rothfeld/Getty Images; 7.7e: © Wolfgang Kaehler; 7.8 a-c: Courtesy of Professor John A. Jakle; 7.9a: © Peter Menzel/Stock Boston; 7.9 b,d: Courtesy of Professor John A. Jakle; 7.9c: © Susan Reisenweaver; 7.10: Jon C. Malinowski/Human Landscape Studio; 7.11a: Courtesy of Professor John A. Jakle; 7.11b: © Susan Reisenweaver; 7.12: © Sharon Wildman; 7.13a: Jerry Fellmann; 7.15: © Susan Reisenweaver; 7.21: © 1997 IMS Communications Ltd/Capstone Design. All Rights Reserved.; 7.22: Jon C. Malinowski/Human Landscape Studio; 7.24: © Michael Dwyer/Stock Boston; 7.25: © Syracuse Newspapers/David Lassman/The Image Works; 7.26: © Joseph Nettis/Stock Boston; 7.27: Image from the Metropolitan Design Center, College of Design, University of Minnesota. © Regents of the University of Minnesota. All rights reserved. Used with permission. (www.dcl.umn.edu); 7.29(all): Photo by Mark Bjellend; 7.32(top left): Courtesy of Indian Wells Brewing Company; 7.32(top right): Courtesy of Uinta Brewing Company; 7.32(bottom left): Courtesy of Ruby Mountain Brewing Company; 7.32(bottom right): Courtesy of Four Peaks Brewing Company; 7.33: Jerry Fellmann.

Chapter Eight

Opener: © Medioimages/Getty RF; 8.1: © Getty RF; 8.3: © Mark Gibson/Gibson Stock Photography; 8.9: © Wolfgang Kaehler; 8.10: © Lindsay Hebberd/Corbis Images; 8.13: © Bill Gillette/Stock Boston; 8.18a: © Larry Lefever/Grant Heilman Photography; 8.18b: © Keith Meyers/New York Times Pictures; 8.19: © Corbis RF; 8.22: © Wolfgang Kaehler; 8.23: Jon C. Malinowski/Human Landscape Studio; 8.24: © Jim Wark/Lonely Planet Images; 8.27: © Cameramann International; 8.29: © Larry Tackett Productions; 8.32: © Cameramann International; 8.33: © Thomas Kitchin/Valan Photos; 8.34: © Medioimages/Superstock RF; 8.35: © United Nations/DPI Photo.

Chapter Nine

Opener: © Sean Sprague/Image Works; 9.1: Photo by Mark Bjelland; 9.6: © Getty RF; 9.14: © Cameramann International; 9.15: © Sharon Stewart; 9.16(top left): © Chris Stowers/Panos Pictures; 9.16(top center): © Steven Harris/Newsmakers/Getty News; 9.16(top right): © Deborah Harse/Image Works; 9.16(bottom left, bottom center): © Mark Henley/Panos Pictures; 9.16(bottom right): © Caroline Penn/Panos Pictures; 9.19: © Peter Pearson; 9.26: © Laurence Fordyce; Eye Ubiquitous/Corbis.

Chapter Ten

Opener: © Sean Sprague/Peter Arnold; 10.1: © Dilip Mehta/Contact Press Images; 10.2a: © Cameramann International; 10.2b: © Jason Clay/Anthro Photo File; 10.4: © Wolfgang Kaehler; 10.5: © Rob Crandall/The Image Works; 10.6: © Bettmann/Corbis; 10.9: © Sean Sprague/Panos Pictures; 10.11: © Betty Press/Woodfin Camp; 10.13: © AP Images; 10.15: © Louise Grubb/The Image Works; 10.17: © David Hiser/Stone/Getty; 10.19: © Liba Taylor/Corbis Images.

Chapter Eleven

Opener: © PhotoLink/Getty RF; 11.1: © Scott Gilchrist/Masterfile; 11.6a: © William E. Ferguson; 11.6b: Courtesy of Colin E. Thorn; 11.6c: © Wolfgang Kaehler; 11.7: © J. Baylor Roberts/National Geographic Image Collection; 11.8, 11.9: © Pixtal/age fotostock RF; 11.17a: © Comstock/Getty RF;

Index

A

aboriginal languages, 127–128, 129
absolute direction, 8–9
absolute distance, 9–10
absolute location, 6, 8, 391
absolute space, 5–6
abstract belief systems, 46
accessibility, 13
acculturation, 52–53, 127, 171–173, 191–192
acid rain, 426–428, 429
activity space, 64
aerial photography, 23
affluence, 105–107, 420
Afghanistan, 54, 154, 174, 400
Africa. *See also* individual
    country name
    agriculture, 238, 241, 243, 244, 246, 248, 255
    carrying capacity, 114
    deforestation, 432
    desertification, 432–435
    early culture hearths, 44
    economic geography, 237, 314, 325
    ethnic geography, 167, 173, 175, 186
    foreign investment, 288
    forestry, 260–261, 261
    garbage and toxic waste, 447
    languages, 138
    political geography, 387, 388
    population issues, 118
    refugee populations, 76
    religion, 154, 157, 159
    trade, 268
    urban systems, 344, 353, 373, 377
    water supply and quality, 438, 441
    women, role of, 334
African Americans, 178, 187, 189–190, 360
Afrikaans, 136
age of mass consumption, 324
agglomeration, high technology, 297
agglomeration costs, 281
agglomeration economies, 283
aging, 119
agricultural density, 112
Agricultural Revolution, 90, 333
agriculture
    commercial, 247–256
    crop production, 244–245
    cultural diffusion, 51
    economic development and, 320–322
    economics of, 238
    ethnic geography and, 179

farm structures, 205
folk culture farming, 212
Green Revolution, 118, 245–247
innovation and, 49
origins and spread, 40–42, 43
population growth and, 105
soil erosion, 435–437
subsistence, 238–244
technology, 46–47
water supply and quality, 439–440
AIDS, 98, 106, 330
air pollution, 426–428
air transport, 279
alcohol, 213
Algeria, 400, 434
alliances, regional, 407–410
amalgamation theory, 172
Amazon basin, 241
American Landsat satellites, 23
Americas, early culture hearths, 44
Amerindians, 130, 175
Amish, 201, 202. *See also* folk culture
Anasazi, 36
anecumene, 111
Anglo America
    acculturation and assimilation, 171–173
    architectural diffusions, 210–211
    Asian populations, 182–183
    black dispersions, 178–180
    building traditions and hearths, 205–210
    charter cultures, 174–176
    cultural transfer, 191–192
    diversity and segregation, 184–191
    drink and music, 225–229
    ethnic geography, 166–168, 173–174, 176–178, 193–197, 212–213
    folk culture, 201–203, 213–215
    French uniformity, 183–184
    hearths, 203–205, 215–217
    Hispanic concentrations, 180–182
    immigration, 168–171, 183
    manufacturing trends, 289, 290–292
    material culture, 221–222
    national uniformity, 218–221
    nonmaterial culture, 211–215
    oral traditions, 215
    regionalism, 196–197, 217–218, 222–229
    urban systems, 342–343
    vernacular regions, 229–230
animal extinction, 36
animism, 145, 158
Antarctica, 385, 430

antecedent boundary, 395
APEC (Asia Pacific Economic Cooperation), 408
Appalachia, 201
aquaculture, 260
aquifers, 439
Arabic language, 133
arable land, 112
architecture, 204, 205–210, 222
area, 454–455
Argentina, 254, 396
    political geography, 408
arithmetic density, 14–15, 112
armed forces, 398
artifacts, 46–47, 191
artificial boundaries, 395
ASEAN (Association of Southeast Asian Nations), 408
Ashkenazim, 148
Asia. *See also* individual country names
    agriculture, 238, 241, 242, 243, 255
    deforestation, 431, 432
    economic geography, 237, 314, 316–317, 321
    ethnic geography, 167
    foreign direct investment, 288
    forestry, 260–261, 261
    high technology and, 296, 297
    manufacturing trends, 289, 294–295
    political geography, 387, 408
    pollution, 427
    religion, 154, 155, 158–159
    urban systems, 345, 375, 377, 379
Asian Americans, 182–183, 187
aspiration level, 78
assimilation, 171–173, 389.
        See also acculturation
asymmetric federalism, 394
atlas maps, 18
atmosphere, 420, 428–431
Australia, 17, 254, 263–264, 266, 431, 448
automobiles, 33, 219, 285, 355–356, 362
autonomous nationalism, 400
autonomy, regional, 401
awareness space, 64
azimuthal projections, 456, 457–458

B

bagpipe, 215
Bahrain, 154
Bali, 155

Balkan states, 174
Bambara, 205
Bangladesh, 242, 255, 321, 427
banjo, 215
banking, 85, 303–304
Bantu, 41, 130, 136
barriers, 54, 70–71
basic sector, economic, 346
Basques, 386, 401
bay head locations, 346
Bazaar Malay, 136
behavioral assimilation, 173
Belgium, 139, 293, 401
beliefs, 46, 215, 385
beverages, 213, 225–229
Bhopal, India, 308
binational state, 386
biogas generators, 320
biomes, 421–423
biosphere, 420
biotechnology, 246–247, 296
birth rates, 89–92, 102–109, 115–116, 171
black dispersions, 178–180
Bolivia, 139, 314, 321
Borlaug, Norman, 245
Borneo, 241
Boserup thesis, 241
Bosnia-Herzegovina, 154, 401
boundaries, 394–397, 405, 410–414
Brandt Report, 310–311, 311–312
Brazil
    agriculture, 254, 255
    economic development, 321
    foreign investment, 288
    manufacturing trends, 289
    mining, 263
    political geography, 394, 408
    urban systems, 341, 375, 376
break-of-bulk points, 280, 346
Bretons, 401
Britain
    ethnic geography, 176, 185, 186
    garbage and toxic waste, 448
    language, 139
    political geography, 394, 401
    religion, 157, 159
    technology, 296
brownfield sites, 365
Buddhism, 144, 146, 156–158, 398
building codes, 362
built environment, 202, 205–210, 222.
        See also urban systems
Burma (Myanmar), 155, 220, 241, 394
Bushmen, 39, 42

483

C

California, 12, 82, 172
Cambodia, 155, 182
Cameroon, 268
Canada
  agriculture, 254
  building traditions and hearths, 207
  communication, control of, 220
  ethnic geography, 176–178, 178
  folk culture, 202–205
  folk music, 215
  forestry, 261
  French Canadians, 54, 177, 178,
    183–184, 207, 400–401
  immigration streams, 170
  language, 139, 141
  manufacturing trends, 290–292
  minerals, 263–264
  multiculturalism, 173
  NAFTA, 285
  political geography, 394, 400–401,
    408, 410–416
  religion, 150, 151, 152
  urban systems, 355, 372
capital, economic, 283
capital city, 393
careers, geography, 7
Carey, Henry C., 61–62
cargo containers, 278, 279
Caribbean countries, 118, 186, 248,
  255, 408
CARICOM (Caribbean Community and
  Common Market), 408
carrying capacity, 39, 113, 117
cartogram, 22
caste systems, 144, 155
Catholics, 92, 118, 150. *See also*
  religion
Caucasian languages, 128
census, 115–116, 411
Central African Federation, 409
Central America, 181, 241, 260–261,
  432. *See also* individual
  country names
central business district, 356
central city, 354, 365–369. *See also*
  urban systems
central-hall house, 210
centralized patterns, 15
central place theory, 349–351
centripetal forces, state cohesion,
  397–399
Chaco Canyon, 36
chain migration, 78, 178, 181, 182,
  185–186
channeled migration, 80–81, 83
Charleston single house, 208, 210
charter cultures, 174–176
charter group, 176
Chechnya, 173–174, 401
Cherokee language, 51
Chile, 396
China
  agriculture, 242, 243, 244, 256
  communication, control, 220
  economic development, 314
  environmental concerns, 427, 434,
    436, 444, 448
  ethnic geography, 173

foreign investment, 288
high technology, 298
manufacturing trends, 289, 294–295
minerals, 263–264, 266
population issues, 91, 93, 118
religion, 157
trade, 269
urban systems, 353, 375, 379
water supply and quality, 439, 441
women, role of, 335
chitemene, 241
choropleth maps, 20–22, 21
Christaller, Walter, 349–351
Christianity, 51, 144, 146, 148–151,
  152, 159–160. *See also* religion
Church of Jesus Christ of Latter-Day
  Saints, 150, 177–178, 192.
    See also religion
circle maps, 21
circular and cumulative causation, 312
circulation, spatial behavior, 63
cities. *See* urban systems
city street maps, 18
civilizations, culture hearths and, 44
Claritas, Inc., 225
Clean Air Act, 427
climate, 110, 421–426, 428–431
climate maps, 18–20
clothing, 47, 48, 217
cluster migration, 177
coal, 265–267, 319–320, 427
coastlines, 405–406
coffee, 225
cohort, defined, 91
colonialism, 311–312, 387
colonies, defined, 385
colonies of immigrants, 188, 189–190
Columbia, 255
commercial agriculture, 247–256
commercial economy, 236–237
commercial fishing, 258–260
commercial forestry, 260–261
commodities, 59
Commonwealth of Nations, 409
communication, 46, 50–51, 68–70, 85,
  172, 219, 399
communism, 158
compact state, 391
comparative advantage, 285–286
competition theory, 173
complementarity, 58–59
complementary regions, 350
computer-assisted cartography, 23–25
concentration, 15
concentric zone model, 357
conflict, 74, 141, 173, 395–397
conformal projections, 455
Confucianism, 144, 146, 158–159.
    See also religion
conic projections, 457
connectivity, 13
consequent boundary, 395
consumption, 116–118, 221–222, 234, 324
contact diffusion, 157
contagious diffusion, 50, 149, 155
contour maps, 20
contraception, 94
contract farming, 249
conurbation, 290, 341
Convention on the Law of the Sea, 407
convergence, cultural, 46

coordinate systems, 6
core area, states, 392
core-periphery models, 312
cornucopians, 118
Costa Rica, 186
costs
  agriculture, 249–251
  least-cost theory, 281
  migration, 80
  spatial behavior and, 60–61, 64, 67
  spatially fixed costs, 275–276
  spatially variable costs, 275–276
  transportation, 279
counter migration, 78, 80
country, defined, 385
Creole language, 135–137
Crete, 44
critical distance, 66
Croatia, 401
crops, 40–42, 244–247. *See also*
  agriculture
crude birth rate (CBR), 91–92
crude death rate (CDR), 96–98
crude density, population, 112
Cuba, 181, 237, 243, 255
cuisine, 212–213
cultural geography
  acculturation, 52–53
  agriculture and, 40–42
  architecture, 210–211
  assimilation, 173, 191–192
  careers in, 7
  changes in, 49–53
  charter cultures, 174–176
  cultural ecology, 34–37
  cultural landscape, 11, 35–37, 151,
    153, 154
  culture convergence, 46, 316
  culture divergence, 39
  culture hearths, 44–46, 316, 386–389
  economic activity and, 234,
    308–309
  fertility and, 95
  globalization and, 85
  integration, 47
  language and, 139–142
  overview, 11, 31–34
  political geography, 401
  regional contacts, 53–55
  roots of, 37–39
  structure of, 46–48
  transfer of, 191–192
cultural lag, 49
culture rebound, 192
cylindrical projections, 457
Czechoslovakia, 141, 401
Czech Republic, 401

D

dams, 433
dance, 212
death, religious practices, 144
death rates, 96–98, 102–109, 115–116
defense, 46–47, 398, 409–410
deglomeration, 283
de la Blache, Paul Vidal, 34
demand, economic, 234, 277.
    See also economic geography

demographic balkanization, 190–191
demographics, 89, 102–109, 115–116,
  118–119
density, 14–15
dependency ratio, 101
dependency theory, 312, 326
desertification, 432–435
desire line map, 14
destiny, geography as, 43
developable surfaces, 454
developing countries, 371–380
development, economic
  agriculture and, 320–322
  assessment of, 322–323
  characteristics of, 317
  complex of development, 317–318
  as cultural variable, 308–309
  definitions, 309–311
  energy consumption, 319–320
  gross national income, 318–319
  measures of, overview, 313–316
  Millennium Development Goals, 313
  model for, 323–326
  noneconomic measures, 326–330
  poverty and nutrition, 322, 323
  technology diffusion, 316–317
  underdevelopment, 311–312
  well-being, measures of, 330–332
  women, role of, 332–336
devolution, 401
Diamond, Jared, 43
diaspora, 147, 149, 178–180
diffusion, culture and, 50–52, 134
diffusion barriers, 53–54
diffusionism, 46
direction, 8–9, 456
direction bias, 62–63, 70–71
discrimination, 100, 186
disease, 98, 104, 105, 106, 117,
  328–330, 377
dispersion, 15, 147, 149, 178–180
distance, 9–10, 53–54, 65–68,
  249–251, 456
distance decay, 60–61, 66, 70–71,
  80–82, 274
diversity, 184–191.
    See also ethnic geography
dogtrot, 211
domestication, plants and animals, 40–42
domestic terrorism, 402
Dominican Republic, 181
dot maps, 20, 21
doubling time, population, 101–102
drinking water, 327–328, 329
drive to maturity, development, 324
drought, 45, 434
dulcimer, 215
Dust Bowl, 434

E

Easter Island, 37
Eastern Christian Church, 149–151
economic alliances, 407–410
economic geography.
    See also spatial interaction
  agglomeration economies, 283
  agriculture, 238–244, 238–245,
    247–256, 320–322